American Musicians II

SEVENTY-TWO PORTRAITS IN JAZZ

WHITNEY BALLIETT

OXFORD UNIVERSITY PRESS
New York   Oxford

For My Berthe Morisot

Oxford University Press

Oxford New York
Athens   Auckland Bangkok   Bogotá   Bombay
Buenos Aires   Calcutta   Cape Town   Dar es Salaam   Delhi
Florence   Hong Kong   Istanbul   Karachi
Kuala Lumpur   Madras   Madrid   Melbourne
Mexico City   Nairobi   Paris   Singapore
Taipei   Tokyo   Toronto   Warsaw

and associated companies in

Berlin   Ibadan

Copyright © 1986, 1996 by Whitney Balliett

First Published by Oxford University Press, Inc., 1986

First issued as an Oxford University Press paperback, 1998

Oxford is a registered trademark of Oxford University Press

Library of Congress Cataloging-in-Publication Data
Balliett, Whitney
American musicians II: seventy-two portraits in jazz/Whitney Balliett—2nd ed.
p. cm.
ISBN 0-19-512116-3 (Pbk.)
A collection of essays originally appearing in the New Yorker.
1. Jazz musicians—United States—Biography. I. Title.
ML395.B36   1996   785.65′092′273—dc20 [B]   96-21232

2 4 6 8 9 7 5 3 1
Printed in the United States of America on acid-free paper

Books by Whitney Balliett

Note

The earliest of the seventy-two biographical portraits in this book was written in 1962 and the most recent in 1991. Fifteen chapters have been added to the original edition, published in 1986, and they deal with Benny Goodman, Mel Powell, Dorothy Donegan, Marie Marcus, Louis Bellson, Charlie Parker, Dizzy Gillespie, Buddy DeFranco, Jimmy Rowles, George Shearing, Ruby Braff, Paul Desmond, Jimmy Knepper, Walter Norris, and Claude Thornhill. The book was not planned; it evolved, and its subjects were generally chosen because they were, for one reason or another, irresistible. Important figures are missing; either there was nothing new to say about them, or they were not interviewable. Hugues Panassié and Charles Delauney are included because of their pioneering and often uncanny proselytizing, and Stéphane Grappelli is included because he and his difficult and brilliant compeer Django Reinhardt were the first true mirrors of what was going on musically in this country in the thirties. The book forms a gapped history, a sort of highly personal encyclopedia, a series of close accounts of how a beautiful music grew, flourished, and (possibly) began the long trek back to its native silence.

January 1996   W. B.
New York City

Contents

American Musicians II

Panassié, Delaunay et Cie

A singular work of musical criticism was published in France in 1934. It was called "Le Jazz Hot," and it was written by a twenty-two-year-old Frenchman named Hugues Panassié. Aside from the erratic "Aux Frontières du Jazz," brought out two years before by the Belgian Robert Goffin, it was the first book of jazz criticism, and it put jazz on the map in Europe and in its own country—an English translation was published here in 1936 as "Hot Jazz"—where the music had been ignored or misunderstood for its forty-year life. (The French are old hands at introducing other cultures to themselves. Edmund Wilson often spoke of how much Taine's "Histoire de la Littérature Anglaise" had influenced him, to say nothing of the English.) "Hot Jazz" is a passionate work. Panassié had found what he believed to be the most beautiful music in the world, and his book rings with superlatives and clarion bursts. He writes of the Chicago clarinettist Frank Teschemacher, who was killed in an auto accident in 1932:

> I can here give you no idea of the power in his execution, that overflowing ardor, that lyric eloquence which gives Teschmacher's solos such expressive force. . . . There is another marvellous thing about Teschemacher: his intonations are so beautiful that they alone move me profoundly.

Of Mary Lou Williams:

> Her style derives from the James P. Johnson and Fats Waller style, but is much more fantastic and ardent. On "Night Life" she has made one of the most beautiful hot piano solo records we have. Her hot, panting righthand phrases, and the swing she gets by the accentuations in the bass by the left hand, must both be admired.

Of Coleman Hawkins:

> Since the end of 1932, Hawkins has devised . . . a style almost entirely free from Armstrong influence. Those violent, villainous phrases, with their steel structures and their tragic import, are gone; instead, there are melodic curves of exquisite charm, full of a sweet sadness, although his intonations have not lost their sombre force.

All first-rate criticism defines *what* we are encountering, and Panassié, revealing an uncommon perspicacity—his book is based almost wholly on phonograph recordings—organizes the music into appropriate schools, grades the performers on each instrument, gives a chapter to Duke Ellington, one to other big bands, and one to big-band arrangers, and attempts to explain the mysteries of improvisation and swinging. He was writing about musicians who as often as not were still neophytes. He marvels at Art Tatum when Tatum had hardly begun recording; at Sidney Catlett, then twenty-three and also hardly recorded; at Duke Ellington, who would not be celebrated in his own country for many years; at Bix Beiderbecke's beautiful (and often maligned) last recordings; and at the pioneer rhythmic excellences of Luis Russell's 1930 band. But Panassié, working three thousand miles from his subject, unavoidably stumbles. He voices his inexplicable (and lifelong) admiration for the abysmal clarinettist Mezz Mezzrow. He scants the great Red Allen. He places the simplistic trumpeter Tommy Ladnier next to Louis Armstrong. He overpraises the Chicago school. (See Teschemacher.) He gets his musical antecedents crossed up. (Jack Teagarden did not come out of Jimmy Harrison; Teagarden was all there when he arrived in New York in 1927.) He gets involved in interminable lists of supposedly promising musicians who remain unknown forty years later. But "Hot Jazz" was a revolutionary celebration, and it turned on the first generation of jazz listeners.

Panassié's next book to be published here, "The Real Jazz," appeared in 1942 and was revised in 1960. (In all, he wrote more than a dozen books—including his six-hundred-page "Summing Up," which came out in France in 1958 and was called "Discographie Critique des Meilleurs Disques de Jazz"—but only five of them have been published in the United States.) It is a reworking of "Hot Jazz," and it demonstrates that Panassié ceased all forward critical motion around 1940, when he was just twenty-eight. (There are exceptions in "The Real Jazz," for he is startlingly correct about the budding Ray Charles, and about Lester Young. "There is something dreamy about Lester," he writes, "a nonchalant accent in the execution which makes his music seem as if it were spoken confidentially to each of his listeners.") He had also come down with Mezzrow fever, a Kafkaesque ailment that causes white men to long to be black, and accordingly he all but dumped the Chicago school, dismissing Beiderbecke and Pee Wee Russell and Joe Venuti and Jess Stacy, and either brushing past or ignoring completely such younger white musicians as Zoot Sims, Eddie Costa, Buddy De Franco, Gerry Mulligan, Tal Farlow, Jimmy Raney, Stan Getz, and Serge Chaloff. Worst of all—in an icy stroke of critical perversity—he declares bebop unconstitutional. It is, he concludes in "Guide to Jazz," which was published here in 1956, a "form of music distinct from jazz because: (1) its players have abandoned the classic instrumental jazz tradition. Instead of making their instruments sing like the human voice with inflections, vibrato, sustained notes and phrases full of contrast [a perfect description of Charlie Parker], the boppers play according to the European instrumental tradition; (2) because the bop rhythm section breaks the continuity of the swing . . . (3) because boppers systematically use chords and intervals adopted from modern European music and destroy the harmonic atmosphere of jazz."

Panassié, riding the momentum of his great originality in "Hot Jazz," inevitably became messianic. He believed he could alter—or at least slow down—the course of jazz, and in 1938 he tried. He came to this country and organized four recording sessions for RCA Victor, which were released on its subsidiary Bluebird label. Three of the sessions presaged the New Orleans revival, which got under way in 1940 and came to a climax in 1947, when Bunk Johnson, hoary and drunken and mythicized, appeared at Stuyvesant Casino in New York. Panassié used, in various combinations, Tommy Ladnier, whom he pried out of retirement, Sidney Bechet, Sidney de Paris, James P. Johnson, and Mezzrow. The records attempted to re-create the classic collective improvisations at the heart of New Orleans jazz, and one reason that they faltered is suggested by Sidney Bechet in his autobiography, "Treat It Gentle":

> The men were supposed to be [at Panassié's record date] pretty early in the morning. But something had got going the night before and when they showed up at the studio they were really out. . . . Tommy [Ladnier] showed up dead drunk. James P. Johnson, he just stretched himself on the piano and passed out. Some of the musicianers didn't know how many fingers they'd got on each hand. But they went ahead and recorded somehow. And after it had all been cut Tommy knew the records weren't what they could have been and he wanted to say something to appease Panassié, who was sitting in the corner holding his head. . . . So he pulled himself up and called out *"Vive la France!,"* and then almost fell flat on his face.

Panassié also organized a somewhat more modern date, which included Frankie Newton, Pete Brown, James P., Al Casey, John Kirby, Cozy Cole, and Mezzrow. Newton is in top form, particularly in his long, crooning, muted solo on "The Blues My Baby Gave to Me," and so is Pete Brown, the mighty three-hundred-pound alto saxophonist whose telegraphic phrases swung so hard. Eddie Condon, who hadn't been invited to participate, issued a mot on Panassié's visit: "I don't see why we need a Frenchman to come over here and tell us how to play American music. I wouldn't think of going to France and telling him how to jump on a grape."

Panassié, who died in 1975, at the age of sixty-two, had an invaluable alter ego during his best days. He is a small, gentle, sad man named Charles Delaunay, and, aside from having been Panassié's sidekick, he has done three inestimable things for jazz: with Panassié he started *Jazz Hot*, now the world's oldest pure jazz magazine; with Panassié he organized the peerless Paris recordings built around Django Reinhardt, Eddie South, Dicky Wells, Rex Stewart, Bill Coleman, and Barney Bigard; and he published, in 1948, "New Hot Discography," the first comprehensive work of its kind. It is a wonder, though, that Delaunay accomplished anything at all, for he was the only child of Sonia and Robert Delaunay—non-stop, teeming geometric painters, who took up a lot of room not only in their own house but in the Paris art world of the teens and twenties and thirties. Gertrude Stein was ambivalent about Robert Delaunay. (Sonia, who was for decades an extremely successful designer, did not make her mark as a painter until the early fifties.) Stein wrote to a friend in 1912, "We have not seen much of the Delaunays lately. There is a feud on. He wanted to wean Apollinaire and me from liking Picasso and there was a great deal of amusing intrigue . . . Now Delauney does conceive himself as a great solitaire and as a matter of fact he is an incessant talker and will tell all about himself and his value at any hour of the day or night." She continued to vacillate in "The Autobiography of Alice B. Toklas":

> Delaunay was a big blond frenchman . . . [who] was fairly able and inordinately ambitious. He was always asking how old Picasso had been when he had painted a certain picture. When he was told he always said, oh I am not as old as that yet I will do as much when I am that age.
>
> As a matter of fact he did progress very rapidly. He used to come a great deal to the rue de Fleurus. Gertrude Stein used to delight in him. He was funny and he painted one rather fine picture, the three graces standing in front of Paris, an enormous picture in which he combined everybody's ideas and added a certain french clarity and freshness of his own. It had a rather remarkable atmosphere and it had a great success. After that his pictures lost all quality, they grew big and empty or small and empty. I remember his bringing one of these small ones to the house, saying, look I am bringing you a small picture, a jewel. It is small, said Gertrude Stein, but is it a jewel.

Delaunay *fils*—gray-haired, with Malraux features—talked one afternoon in 1976 in New York about his life. He had not visited the city for twenty-seven years. He talked slowly, in a low and distant voice, a voice that barely sustained his words. At the end of the afternoon, he inscribed a copy of his discography in gossamer handwriting that echoes his speech: it has become so microscopic that he himself has difficulty reading it.

On How He Came to Love le Jazz Hot: "I first heard jazz when I was fifteen. I happened to be sick, staying six months in bed. My parents had fifty records altogether, and three were jazz—Jelly Roll Morton's 'Black Bottom Stomp,' Duke Ellington's 'East St. Louis Toodle-oo,' and a Frankie Trumbauer with Bix Beiderbecke. The 'Black Bottom' sounded like country dance music, like folklore. I would study what the cornet was playing and then what the clarinet was playing and then what the trombone was playing, and little by little these three came together clearly. Being a jazz lover in Paris in the twenties was like being an early Christian in Rome. I thought I was the only one interested. When I mentioned jazz in school, they'd say, 'Hey! *Alors!* That is nothing—just some Negro music.' But other people listened, and by 1933, when I finished my military service, two students had formed the Hot Club of France. Maybe we had heard three hundred records in Paris, and every time a new one came into a record shop on the Place de l'Opéra the phone was ringing and we'd all get together to listen. Even to have a flyer about an upcoming record— that was precious. We heard our first real jazz musicians at the Ambassadeurs, where Sam Wooding and Noble Sissle played. On summer days, you could hear the music out in the gardens, and you could climb a tree and see the whole band through a window. A musician who helped us was Freddy Johnson, the piano player with Sam Wooding. He was a grand player, but, more important, he was a jazz lover. He taught French musicians, like Alix Combelle, to play, and he taught us how to tell the difference on Fletcher Henderson records between the trumpet players Joe Smith and Tommy Ladnier and Rex Stewart. It was difficult to identify soloists before that. We learned the history of jazz through his words. Then a lot of American jazz musicians started arriving in Paris. Benny Carter came in 1934 or 1935, and most of the English I have now is from him. *Alors*, it was like being in church to meet jazz musicians. We were scared, and it was hard to get a mutual understanding. I met Louis Armstrong in 1934, and I took Django Reinhardt with me. Louis had made some concerts in England, and I think he had some trouble with his lip. So he was like a tourist on vacation in Paris. It was summer, and when we went to see Louis, he was half naked and had a stocking on his head, and he was already getting fat. He was shaving, and after a while I said to him, 'May I ask Django to play?' Well, I knew what Django's dream was, because he told me so many times, 'If Louis would hear me, he would take me to America, where I would be the guest of Clark Gable and play for the Hollywood stars right by their pools.' Django had brought his brother Joseph on rhythm guitar, and they started playing. Louis was still shaving, and every once in a while he would grunt, and when Django and Joseph finished, Louis was washing his face, and he only said, 'Yeh, not bad, man.' And that was all. It was the only time I ever saw Django, who always had a very good opinion of his own playing, looking absolutely blank. Duke Ellington came the first time in 1933, and he gave three concerts at the Salle Pleyel. It was *électrique*. It was the first time we heard a band like that, with all the mutes and the strange rhythms. The hall was packed, even though most of the people did not know what they were hearing. I got to know Ellington in 1939, when he made his second European tour. He was a personality that found everything so pleasant, so interesting. He was full of those small attentions that give you a good feeling. He behaved to everyone like a man who is in love."

On Jazz in Paris During and After the Second World War: "Jazz became popular in France when the Germans came. Suddenly we couldn't have American movies or American records anymore, and it was a shock, like when you stop smoking. French jazz musicians who had no reputation three weeks before became famous. Musicians all became swing cats and wore long coats and thick shoes. Jazz records—the ones that were left— began to sell. Some Germans even liked the music. One night, a German officer, very polite, very *apologétique*, came to the Rue Chaptal, where we published *Jazz Hot*, and asked if we minded if he played our piano. He sat down and played and sang Fats Waller for an hour, and when he finished, he thanked us and said that made him feel much better. The first band to come to Paris after the war belonged to Don Redman. The stores in Paris did not start getting American records again until 1948, and some of the first were by Dizzy Gillespie and Charlie Parker on the Guild label— 'Shaw 'Nuff' and 'Salt Peanuts' and 'Hot House' and 'Groovin' High.' Those records were playing day and night at the Rue Chaptal. Everybody was saying, What is happening? What is that chord? How can he play so fast? What is happening in this music? It created an unbelievable sensation, and when Dizzy Gillespie's big band gave a concert the next year, the same amazement took place. That concert happened in this way: I was informed somehow that Dizzy's big band was stranded in Antwerp without a damn penny. So we got together some money and sent it to Antwerp, and we organized a concert for the band to give in Paris. The band arrived at nine-thirty at night and got onstage at ten-thirty. The band was starving, but something happened on that stage—just like with Duke Ellington in 1933—and the band made such a success it stayed in Paris one month and worked the whole time."

On His Record-Making Days: "I started directing record dates in 1934, when I did Reinhardt's and Stéphane Grapelli's first records together. Then I organized my Swing label and recorded Grappelli and Django and Eddie South and Bill Coleman. When Teddy Hill was in Paris in 1937, I took three of his trumpeters—Coleman and Shad Collins and Bill Dillard—and Dicky Wells and put them with Django plus a rhythm section, and we made 'Bugle Call Rag' and 'Between the Devil and the Deep Blue Sea.' The fourth trumpeter that Hill had, and I did not use, was Dizzy Gillespie, who was just nineteen. What a pity! After the war, I recorded Grappelli and Django again. Their first meeting was in London, where Grappelli had spent the war. They couldn't say anything except *"Mon Frère, mon frère,"* and the first thing they played was 'La Marseillaise.' In 1949, I brought Sidney Bechet over from America and also Charlie Parker and Miles Davis and Max Roach and Tadd Dameron and Kenny Dorham and Hot Lips Page. When Parker heard Bechet, he was astonished. 'Hey, that old man can blow,' he said. 'He's playing things I thought I did first.' I don't know how peasants are in America, but in France they are concrete, solid, no abstractions. They know how things are growing. Bechet was like that. He would talk to anyone on the street. He had that accent that connected with everybody. He played all the time, and he packed all the halls. He became a living legend in France. His records would sell three hundred thousand copies each, and many broke the one-million mark, which is a lot in a country that has only fifty million people."

On Django Reinhardt: "There were two personalities in him. One was primitive. He never went to school and he couldn't stand a normal bed. He had to live in a gypsy caravan near a river, where he could fish and catch trout between the stones with his bare hands, and where he could put laces between the trees and catch rabbits. But Django also had a nobility, even though he could be very mean to the musicians who worked for him. Life for Django was all music. He was full of constant enthusiasm when he played—shouting in the record studio when someone played something he liked, shouting when he played himself. You can hear him on 'Bugle Call Rag.' When he was accompanying in the bass register he sounded like brass, and in the treble like saxophones. He had a constant vision of music—a circle of music—in his head. I think he could see his music. This way, he composed some music for symphony orchestra. He would play it on his guitar, all the parts—for flutes, for strings, for horns—and someone would write it down, and when you heard the piece, it was perfect. There were some waves of Ravel and Debussy, but the rest was Django. Of course, Django had a terrible cicatrix on his left hand. He had been in a fire and two fingers were bent into his palm. So, with him, it was the rapidity of his reactions to the music around him which made him sound so fast. Later, it became a goal for him to play the electric guitar, to dominate the electricity. He died of a stroke after an afternoon of fishing, which was the perfect ending for Django."

On His Beginnings: "I was born January 18, 1911. My father was like an open window. He was Gallic, and he had *la force de la nature*. He was speaking a lot and he was moving a lot. When he was caught by his painting, he would go to his atelier every day from six in the morning until nine at night to catch the last drop of light. And he would be in a very bad humor most of the time. He would be exhausted after only sleeping half the night, worrying about what he was going to paint the next day. He would work and work and work on the same idea, and then suddenly he would stop painting, and not paint again for several months. My father was living in dreams. He would say he was going to build big houses so he could paint big walls. After he went through the Cubist time, his only patience was with colors, with the relations of colors to one another. It became a religion of color to him, an obsession. He was like a chemist: what happens to one color when another color is brought together with it. My mother was more with her feet on the earth. She is much quieter—she is ninety-one and lives in Paris and still paints—and my father found some stability in her. I think they influenced each other as painters. They had some money until the first war; then my mother did very well with her designing. She designed everything—car seats, dresses, scarves, playing cards, rugs, tapestries, stained-glass windows, wigs. After my father died, in 1941, she devoted ten years to making him famous. I think when I was growing up I must have seen fifty per cent of all the well-known people in Paris passing in and out of our apartment—Apollinaire and Kandinski and Stravinsky and Diaghilev and Klee and Mondrian and Breton and Aragon. Of course, in Paris before the war everybody used to meet in the cafés and in their homes. They discussed art. They discussed music. They discussed books. They discussed each other. They discussed all night. Paris was filled with talking before the war. But after the war that all went, and now no one meets anymore. They did not pay attention to me, my parents, even though I was an only child. But things went all right. I did not go to the university, because when the time came I was already drawing ads and making a living at it. I didn't like modern art—what my parents did. I became an Impressionist painter, and my father used to say to me, 'Oh, you're just an old-fashioned guy.' "

On His Great Discography: "The first edition of my discography came about this way. To begin with, I probably had a hundred records in my collection, and, of course, in the twenties and thirties there was almost no information on the label about who was playing or when and where the record was made. Freddy Johnson helped us, and when musicians like Benny Carter started coming to Paris, I took a turntable to their rooms and played records and they helped us with the soloist. I put together a small booklet of personnels, because people were worrying me all the time for information, and I published it in *Jazz Hot*. Then in 1936 we put out the first discography in book form. After the war, I started writing the record companies over here, and then I came over and discovered I could find much information from the union sheets. My discography is still around, but Brian Rust and Jepsen are more complete and up to date—for now, anyway. I am one of more than twenty discographers who are putting together a new discography, starting in 1942 and coming down to the present. It will take about twenty thousand pages. It is incredible. When the volumes come out, they will be already out of date, but you can't do anything about that. Now my record collection has grown to perhaps thirty thousand items, which is nothing when Mr. Bob Altshuler of Columbia Records has a collection of two hundred thousand. But my collection is big enough to force me to move out of Paris—twenty miles north, into a house in a village. I have also practically every *down beat* that has come out since the first one in 1934. And I have pre-Civil War Spanish jazz magazines, and magazines from Japan and Uruguay and Chile. I have record catalogues from France and England and America between 1920 and 1940. I have more than a thousand books on jazz. The earliest, 'Le Jazz,' came out in 1926 and had one hundred and fifty-two pages. The first half was about African musical instruments, and the second half was about Paul Whiteman and George Gershwin. No jazz musician was mentioned in the book."

On Hugues Panassié: "Panassié was born on February 26, 1912. He was from a wealthy family. His father was in industry, but he died early. In his teens, Panassié was crippled by polio in one leg. Because he was crippled and because he was always educated by women, he became very spoiled as a child. I met him in Paris in 1934. He was living in the South of France. He had the gift to communicate his enthusiasm for the music to the people he talked to. That influenced me in a certain way, by helping me to understand things in the music that I didn't understand yet. He discovered more things in jazz than anyone before. He was right in the middle in 'Le Jazz Hot,' and he could see everything accurately. But in 1946, when a friend sent the first Dizzy Gillespie-Charlie Parker records to me in Paris, Panassié was in the South of France. Before he heard the records, I wrote about them in a Swiss magazine and André Hodeir wrote about them in *Hot Revue*, and Panassié, who was used to being the first, to being worshipped, would never accept Gillespie or Parker after that. The trouble is, when you get wrong, as Panassié was, and you want to defend your position, you're getting worse and worse. So since 1946 we never spoke again."

Stéphane Grappelli on Hugues Panassié: "He was very sincere himself. He was a very pure man, very religious, very decent. Not for the gallery. He believed. He did a lot for the jazz music. The only bad thing about Panassié was he was a bit stubborn."

For the Comfort
of the People

The cornettist Joe Oliver was born in or near New Orleans in 1885, or earlier, and was raised by his sister Victoria Davis. Bunk Johnson said that Oliver was a slow musical student, but by the turn of the century he was working in marching bands and in cabarets. He was also a butler in the Garden District. His musical career in New Orleans lasted at least twenty years, and by the time he moved to Chicago, in 1918, he had been nicknamed King by Kid Ory, even though he was probably already past his prime. Except for brief forays to California (1921–22) and New York (1924, 1927), Oliver stayed in Chicago for ten years, leading the Creole Jazz Band and the later and larger Dixie Syncopators. In 1928, he at last committed himself to the exodus to New York, where, the year before, he had made a disastrous decision. Two successful weeks at the Savoy Ballroom had led to an offer to open the new Cotton Club with his group as the house band. But the New Orleans evil, a local affliction made up equally of hubris and perversity, took hold, and Oliver decided he was not being paid enough. He turned down the job, and a newcomer named Duke Ellington took it. But Oliver had been wrongheaded before. He had had lucrative offers from New York for years but had stubbornly stayed in Chicago—so long, indeed, that when he moved to New York he discovered that his music had already been accepted, absorbed, and filed away. During the next three years, Oliver, whose gums and teeth had begun to trouble him, subsisted by making records, writing occasional music, and taking whatever gigs were offered him. Then, in 1931, he put together a good band and went on the road. It was his last mistake. He never got back to New York or Chicago or New Orleans (partly because of the New Orleans evil), and by 1936 he had landed in Savannah, where he spelled out his final days selling fruit and vegetables and sweeping out a pool parlor. He died in Savannah, on April 10, 1938. His body was brought to New York and buried in Woodlawn Cemetery in an unmarked grave.

Within two years, Oliver was enshrined by Frederic Ramsey in the book *Jazzmen*, and by the New Orleans revival movement, which would have put him on Easy Street again. Ramsey made Oliver a tragic, put-upon figure, and quoted several letters that Oliver wrote from Savannah to his niece and sister in New York:

> *Dear Niece,*
> I receive your card, you don't know how much I appreciate your thinking about the old man. . . . I am not making enough money to buy clothes as I can't play any more. I get [a] little money from an agent for the use of my name and after I pay room rent and eat I don't have much left. . . . I've only got one suit and that's the one sent me while I was in Wichita, Kansas. So you know the King must look hot. But I don't feel downhearted. I still feel like I will snap out of the rut some day.
> Well, the old man hasn't got the price of Xmas cards so I will wish you all a Merry Xmas and Happy New Year . . . Love to the entire family including the bird dog and cat.
>
> *Sincerely,*
Uncle

In 1922, Oliver set Louis Armstrong up in business by summoning him from New Orleans to Chicago to play second horn in the Creole Jazz Band. Armstrong borrowed wisely and liberally from Oliver's style, and revered him the rest of his life. He told Richard Meryman, in 1966, what his last visit with Oliver had been like: "So Joe winds up in little cheap rooming houses, landladies holding his trunk for rent. In 1937 my band went to Savannah, Georgia, one day—and there's Joe. He's got so bad off and broke he's got himself a little vegetable stand selling tomatoes and potatoes. He was standing there in his shirtsleeves. No tears. Just glad to see us. Just another day. He had that spirit. I gave him about a hundred and fifty dollars I had in my pocket, and Luis Russell and Red Allen, Pops

Foster, Albert Nicholas, Paul Barbarin—all used to be his boys—they gave him what they had. [If all this is true, Oliver, despite his melancholy protestations that he could not scrape train fare together, could easily have gone North.] And that night we played a dance, and we look over and there's Joe standing in the wings. He was sharp like the old Joe Oliver of 1915. He'd been to the pawn shop and gotten his fronts all back; you know, his suits and all—Stetson hat turned down, high-button shoes, his box-back coat. He looked beautiful."

When Oliver set out from New York, in 1931, everything went well for a time. The bookings were good, and the band travelled in style through the West and Southwest. The trombonist and singer Clyde Bernhardt was in the band, and he has said, "I joined Oliver's band on March 1,1931, and left it in Topeka, Kansas, on November 10th, when I found out he didn't have any intention of coming back to New York again. We played mostly white places—big ballrooms like the Coliseum, in Tulsa—and we didn't have any trouble with whites. In fact, we were treated so nice in Texas and Louisiana that we got scared. These judges and doctors and people like that would ask us to their homes, and we were scared to go and scared not to go. We travelled in a bus that would hold twenty people. The driver, Roy Johnson, was white, and he was our road manager and collected the money and such. Oliver was a Christian-hearted man, but he didn't have no business sense. He couldn't even find himself a place to sleep at night. In those times, we'd stay with families in their houses. The colored hotels was small and very often couldn't put up all fifteen, sixteen of us. I always made a neat appearance, and I'd walk in the colored neighborhood and find this real nice house and I'd talk to them and they'd take me in and Joe Oliver, too. He ate as much as four men, and he always paid double for his food. He'd sit down with me—I was a slow eater, and so was he—and he'd eat a chicken and a whole apple pie. He didn't drink, but he smoked a lot of cigarettes, so I gave him a pack of cigarettes on his birthday, in May, and he was so pleased. 'The rest of them didn't give me a damn thing,' he said, 'but you did, and that feels good to an old man of fifty-four.' So he was older than anybody thought he was—older by eight years, which would have put him in his sixties when he died.

"Those New Orleans musicians were funny. They had strong likes and dislikes. But I was lucky. Oliver knew some of my family in New York, and he treated me as his son. He was very easygoing, and he loved to talk—at least, he liked to talk to me, so much sometimes that he aggravated me. It would go this way:

"OLIVER: Why the hell don't you say something!
"BERNHARDT: I ain't got nothin' to say.
"OLIVER: Well, I'm going to make you sing tonight if you don't open your mouth now.
"BERNHARDT: Who is?

"OLIVER: Who's talkin' to you?

"And on like that. Joe didn't look his age because he was so dark. He was really comical about color. If he spotted someone as dark as he was, he'd say, 'That son is uglier than me. I'm going to make him give me a quarter.' Or he'd light a match and lean forward and whisper, 'Is that something walking out there?' He wouldn't hire very black musicians. I suggested several who were very good players, but he told me, 'I can stand me, but I don't want a whole lot of very dark people in my band. People see 'em and get scared and run out of the place.'

"He had a dental plate by then, and he could play for an hour and a half before his gums would get to aching. Then he'd take down and go off the bandstand and let his other trumpet players go. When his teeth weren't bothering him, he had a strong, piercing tone you could feel right through you."

During 1934 and 1935, the saxophonist Paul Barnes kept a log of the band's ceaseless, swaybacked swings across the South. (In 1932 or 1933, Lester Young, then in his early twenties, joined the band; it was Genesis and Revelation under the same roof.) Here is Barnes' log for the first two weeks of March, 1935. The date is at the left and the money paid each man at the right. (Oliver presumably got double, and there were occasions in his career when his men accused him of shortchanging them.) "N" means a black audience and "W" a white one. "B" means a radio broadcast:

1	Gadsden, Ala.		N	.50
3	Columbus, Ga. (Liberty Theatre)		N	.25
4	Columbus, Ga. (Army camp) B		N	3.00
5	Moultrie, Ga.		N	1.00
6	St. Augustine, Fla.		N	1.50
7	Daytona Beach		N	3.00
8	Lakeland		N	3.00
9	Tampa		N	1.00
11	St. Petersburg		N	2.00
12	Sanford		N	1.50
13	Melbourne		N	1.00
14	Miami		N	3.71
15	West Palm Beach		N	3.00
16	Vero Beach (Firemen's Ball)		W	3.53

Only nine years before, Jess Stacy, just arrived in Chicago from Missouri, had gone to see the famous Oliver in the Plantation Café, at

Thirty-fifth and Calumet. Stacy recalls: "The first time I ever went to hear Oliver he was playing 'Ukelele Lady,' and he was playing the fool out of it, and he took five or six choruses in a row. He played sitting down, and he didn't play loud. He knew his instrument. He wasn't spearing for high notes; he stayed right in the middle register. His chord changes were pretty and his vibrato just right—none of that Italian belly vibrato. You could hear that both Louis and Bix had learned from him. In fact, Bix was nuts about him, and one of the things he liked was that Oliver played open horn a lot. Which reminds me of what Eddie Condon said of those days in Chicago when there was so much music: 'You could take a trumpet out of its case and it would blow by itself.' Oliver's band worked from nine to six—I know, because I was often there—and what with the shows to play for and the dancing, it took an iron lip."

Two or three years earlier, the Creole Jazz Band was still intact and was playing at the Dreamland Café. (Oliver and Armstrong, cornets; Johnny Dodds, clarinet; Honoré Dutrey, trombone; Lil Hardin, piano; Bill Johnson, bass; and Baby Dodds, drums.) Here are three scenes. The first is by Lou Black, the banjoist with the fine white New Orleans Rhythm Kings; the second is from Armstrong-Meryman; and the third was told to Larry Gara by Baby Dodds:

BLACK: "We were at the Friar's Inn for a couple of years, and when we'd finished work, or when there were no more customers to play for, we'd go over to the Dreamland and sit in with Pop Oliver and Louis Armstrong. You know why he was called Pop? When he played, his right eye came almost out of the socket from the force of his blowing. . . . He had enormous lips, too, and his cornet mouthpiece would disappear right inside them. Once in a while he'd stand up there in front of the band, cradle the cornet on its valves in a handkerchief in his left hand, put his right hand in his pocket, and play ten or eleven choruses of 'Tiger Rag' or 'Dippermouth Blues' without ever touching the valves with his right hand and without repeating himself."

ARMSTRONG-MERYMAN: "In those days the bands sat in chairs, and Joe, with his big wad of chewing tobacco in his cheek, would go *pa-choo* into a brass cuspidor, then he'd start beating his foot on top of that cuspidor, setting the tempo, and *blow!* And whatever Mister Joe played, I just put notes to it, trying to make it sound as pretty as I could. I never blew my horn over Joe Oliver at no time unless he said, 'Take it!' Never. Papa Joe was a creator—always some little idea—and he exercised them beautifully. I hear them phrases of his in big arrangements and everything right now. And sitting by him every night, I *had* to pick up a lot of little tactics he made—phrases, first endings, flairs. I'll never run out of ideas. All I have to do is think about Joe and always have something to play off of."

DODDS-GARA: "We had the sort of band that, when we played a number, we all put our hearts in it. Of course that's why we could play so well. And it wasn't work for us, in those days. . . . We took it as play, and we loved it. I used to hate when it was time to knock off. I would drum all night till about three o'clock, and when I went home I would dream all night of drumming. . . . We worked to make music, and we played music to make people like it. The Oliver band played for the comfort of the people. Not so they couldn't hear, or so they had to put their fingers in their ears. . . . Sometimes the band played so softly you could hardly hear it. . . . [It] played so soft that you could hear the people's feet dancing."

Clyde Bernhardt's belief that Oliver was eight years older than people thought explains a good deal—why his teeth and gums and embouchure began to weaken in the mid-twenties, when he was supposedly just forty; why he repeatedly called himself an "old man" in his letters to his niece and sister; why he was so slow to adapt to the new music around him; why his bands played what they did. Oliver—tall, fat, secret, solemn— was old-fashioned and formal, and so was his music, particularly when he had the Creole Jazz Band. It played the sort of contrapuntal ensemble jazz that probably reached perfection in New Orleans around 1915. The musical difference between Louis Armstrong-Earl Hines in 1928 and Oliver just five years before is too great; Oliver must have been mirroring a music at least ten years older. Oliver was summarizing New Orleans jazz with intelligence, wit, honesty, and great cool. The summary, insofar as the Creole Jazz Band is concerned, was not complete, however. Its recordings have few solos, and for good reason: there wasn't time, and tried-and-true ensembles (most were partly written) were safer than improvised solos in the perilous confines of an acoustical recording studio. But Stacy and Lou Black tell us that Oliver soloed often and at great length in the flesh. No matter the tempo, the Creole Jazz Band swung steadily and easily. It beckoned but never shouted, it pointed but never pushed. The ensemble passages were controlled, dense, and full of four-way counterpoint. Each voice was skilled enough to speak comfortably and to blend with the other voices without fault or interference. It was a band completely at ease with itself and its materials. Musicians of greater or lesser skill would have destroyed its fabric. The Creole Jazz Band offered many pleasures: Armstrong, and Oliver's clean, neat unison playing in "High Society"; the great cornet duet breaks in "Sobbin' Blues" (Armstrong-Meryman: "While the rest of the band was playing, Oliver'd lean over to me and move the valves of his cornet in the notes he would play in the next breaks or a riff he'd use. So I'd play second to it"); the steady, enveloping drive, the slowmotion *galloping* of "Dippermouth Blues," "Chattanooga Blues," "Buddy's Habit," "Riverside Blues," and "I Ain't Gonna Tell Nobody"; Armstrong's brilliant-kid solo in "Riverside"; and Oliver's serene three-chorus solo in "Dippermouth," a solo that reverberated throughout jazz for twenty-five years.

Oliver was a classic player. His tone was strong and even, and his vibrato was controlled. He loved the middle and low register, and he was a first-rate melodic embellisher. He liked to play behind the beat, and he never wasted a note. And he had *presence*. Cootie Williams is the third link in the chain begun by Joe Oliver and Bubber Miley, and Oliver at this period sounded the way Williams did in the 1960's—stripped down, primitive, and majestic.

In many ways some of the records Oliver made with his later Dixie Syncopators and in New York are more absorbing. Electronic recording had come in, and one can hear Oliver clearly. Also, he was heroically trying to catch up with what had happened in jazz while he was molting in Chicago. The Dixie Syncopators sides have arrangements and a saxophone section, and they have the sound of pioneer big bands. Much the same is true of the New York recordings Oliver made for Victor between 1928 and 1931, although Oliver plays only occasionally on them. The New York recordings have an eerie quality. They are very much of their time and place, with their soupy saxophones, one-legged rhythm sections, and often halting solos. But Oliver's statements, particularly his muted ones, have a special long-ago sweetness and directness and simplicity. New Orleans musicians were Arcadian no matter where they went. Red Allen, who was Oliver's last protégé, once described his arrival in New York in 1927: "It was my first time away from home. I was an only child and I'd had a lot of care. I wasn't accustomed to taking things to the laundry and making my own bed. I couldn't get used to it. Then I moved in with Oliver and his sister. Oliver and I stayed together like father and son. I used to kid with him all the time and imitate the grand marshal in one of the parades back home, and he'd laugh so hard he'd cry."

Ferdinand La Menthe*

Jelly Roll Morton, though long celebrated by jazz admirers, has yet to find his rightful place. (The Morton jazz industry has been going almost steadily since 1938, when Morton, threadbare and down on his luck, sat at a piano in the Library of Congress with the folklorist Alan Lomax and talked, sang, and played his life into a recording machine. Lomax later culled an autobiography, "Mister Jelly Roll," from the Library of Congress recordings, and selections from them have been issued on L.P.s from time to time.) Morton properly belongs in the nineteenth-century American mythology of Paul Bunyan and Johnny Appleseed and Davy Crockett, of the Yankee Peddlers and tall-tale tellers, of the circuses and minstrel shows. He made hustling his life's work. He was a pool player, a pimp, a bellhop, a tailor, a peddler, a cardsharp, a minstrel, a night-club manager, a fight promoter, and, when he had the time, a musician. He was a nomad, who lived or worked in New Orleans, where he was born, around 1885, and in Meridian, Jacksonville, St. Louis, Kansas City, Chicago, San Francisco, Detroit, Los Angeles, Memphis, Vancouver, Casper, Denver, Las Vegas, Tijuana, South Bend, Seattle, Davenport, Houston, Pittsburgh, Baltimore, Washington, D.C., and New York. He was outsize because of his variety and his ubiquity, and because he was a champion braggart. Morton bragged so much that his bragging took on an autonomous quality. He was already blowing his bugle in 1917, when he worked at the Cadillac Café in Los Angeles with Ada Smith, later known as the cabaret owner Bricktop. "His biggest conversation was always himself," she once said. "He'd run you out of your mind talking about himself. And he wasn't kidding. He meant it. He was always very temperamental, very hard to get along with. But Jelly was a genius before his time." Seven or eight years later, Alberta Hunter sang with him at the Pekin Café in Chicago, and she regarded him somewhat differently: "He was a braggadocio and very good-natured." Morton told Lomax how, in his pre-Los Angeles Days, he would disarm the female population when he landed in a small Southern town:

---

*Long thought to be Jelly Roll Morton's real name. Now, according to recent research by Professor Larry Gushee of the University of Illinois, it seems that Morton was born Ferdinand Lamothe (the name of whites originally from Santo Domingo), and that he changed Lamothe to Mouton, which was finally corrupted to Morton. Gushee has also discovered that Morton was born in 1890, instead of 1885, and that his euphonious god-mother Eulalie Echo was Laura Hécaud. Further, that Anita Gonzalez, his consort on the West Coast, was Bessie Johnson, a sister of the New Orleans musicians Bill, Dink, and Robert Johnson.

I would . . . get a room, slick up, and walk down the street in my conservative stripe. The gals would all notice a new sport was in town, but
I wouldn't so much as nod at anybody. Two hours later, I'd stroll back to
my place, change into a nice tweed and stroll down the same way. The
gals would begin to say, "My, my, who's this new flash-sport drop in
town? He's mighty cute."

About four in the afternoon, I'd come by the same way in an altogether different outfit and some babe would say, "Lawd, mister, how
many suits you got anyway?"

I'd tell her, "Several, darling, several."

"Well, do you change like that every day?

"Listen, baby, I can change like this every day for a month and never
get my regular wardrobe half used up. I'm the suit man from suit land."

The next thing I know, I'd be eating supper in that gal's house and
have a swell spot for meeting the sports, making my come-on with the
piano and taking their money in the pool hall.

Morton claimed that he invented wire brushes, adapted "Tiger Rag"
from a French quadrille and named it, started using the word "jazz,"
originated scat singing, and first used the washboard and the string bass
on a recording. He claimed that "The Pearls" and "The Fingerbreaker,"
which he wrote, were the two most difficult jazz piano pieces of all
time. But he floated his biggest balloon in 1938 when, piqued by a
Robert Ripley "Believe It or Not" radio show in which W. C. Handy
was described as the inventor of jazz and the blues, he sent an immense
letter to the Baltimore *Afro-American* and to the magazine *down beat*.
Here are parts:

It is evidently known, beyond contradiction, that New Orleans is the
cradle of jazz, and I, myself, happened to be the creator in the year 1902.

I decided to travel, and tried Mississippi, Alabama, Florida,
Tennessee, Kentucky, Illinois, and many other states during 1903–04,
and was accepted as sensational.

I may be the only perfect specimen today in jazz that's living.

Speaking of jazz music, anytime it is mentioned musicians usually
hate to give credit but they will say, "I heard Jelly Roll play it first."

Morton should have been genteel and reserved, for he was a Creole—
a black Creole, or "Creole of color." In their great days in the nineteenth
century, Creoles considered themselves the only genuine aristocracy in
America. Morton was born Ferdinand La Menthe, and changed his name
to Morton because, as he told Lomax, he "didn't want to be called
Frenchy." His father, a carpenter and sometime trombonist named F. P.
(Ed) La Menthe, soon vanished, and his mother, a light-skinned Creole
named Louise Monette, died when he was fourteen. He apparently had
little schooling, and he became a musician early. He tried the harmonica,
the Jew's harp, the drums, the violin, the trombone, and the guitar before
he settled on the piano—having cleared his head of the popular New
Orleans belief that only sissies played the piano. He studied classical

piano, and he learned from Tony Jackson, who wrote the song "Pretty Baby" and who appears to have been one of the few musicians whom Morton ungrudgingly admired. Jackson was "the greatest single-handed entertainer in the world," Morton told Lomax. "His memory seemed like something nobody's ever heard of in the music world. He was known as the man of a thousand songs. There was no tune that come up from any opera or any show of any kind or anything that was wrote on paper that Tony couldn't play. He had such a beautiful voice and marvellous range." After Morton's mother died, he was left in the hands of an uncle and a great-grandmother, Mimi Pechet, but he was ostracized at fifteen by his great-grandmother when she discovered he had become a musician. (This snub may be one reason that Morton spent the rest of his life justifying himself, but it never deflected his loyalty to his family. Broke or not, he invariably sent money home.) Morton took off for Biloxi, where his godmother, Eulalie Echo, had a summer place, and he didn't settle down again for any length of time until he landed in Chicago twenty-odd years later. In Biloxi, he played piano in a whorehouse, started carrying a pistol, and had his first taste of whiskey, which didn't agree with him. (Drinking may have gained on him as he grew older, for he pauses now and then on the Library of Congress records to say, "This whiskey is lovely.") Back in New Orleans, he played at Hilma Burt's whorehouse in Storyville. He took off down the Gulf Coast again and, turning up through Mississippi, was mistakenly arrested for having robbed a mail train. He was sentenced to a hundred days on the chain gang but escaped. He told Lomax that "it was some terrible environments that I went through in those days, inhabited by some very tough babies." In 1905, he returned to New Orleans, where he got in a fight in Pete Lala's saloon with Chicken Dick: "I hauled off and hit him with a pool ball and he jumped like he was made of rubber." Morton's sinning always had a testing, adolescent air; beyond a diamond or two, it never did him much good, and he never seems to have harmed anyone. He played more piano in Storyville, and he started writing music. At Tony Jackson's behest, he went to Chicago, where nothing was happening, and he then went down to Houston, where there were "only Jew's harps, harmonicas, mandolins, guitars, and fellows singing the spasmodic blues—sing awhile and pick awhile till they thought of another word to say." He paid his first visit to California, returned to New Orleans for the last time, and took off through the middle South with one Jack the Bear, selling Coca-Cola laced with salt as a cure for tuberculosis. He met W. C. Handy in Memphis in 1908, and three years later passed through New York, where he was heard by James P. Johnson. He joined several minstrel shows, was stranded in Hot Springs and St. Louis, turned up in Chicago again, and in 1917 landed in Los Angeles. He took up with Anita Gonzalez, a clever Creole he had known in New Orleans. They ran hotels and night clubs, and she may have bought him the famous diamond that moved back and forth the rest of his life between pawnshops and one of his front teeth. He turned up in Denver, where he played for the bandleader George Morrison, who was responsible for first bringing Paul Whiteman to New York. Morrison told Gunther Schuller, "He couldn't stay in one band too long, because he was too eccentric and too temperamental, and he was a one-man band himself . . . Oh, but he could stomp the blues out. When he got to pattin' that foot, playing the piano and a cigar in his mouth, man, he was gone—he was gone—he was gone!"

Morton lived in Chicago from 1923 to 1928, and it was the best part of his life. His reputation as a musician must have preceded him, for he made over thirty sides in his first year, including piano solos, duets and trios with King Oliver and with a clarinettist named Voltaire (Volly) de Faut, five numbers with the young white New Orleans Rhythm Kings, and almost a dozen numbers with bands of his own. He also worked his mouth. In the autobiography "Oh, Didn't He Ramble," the New Orleans trumpeter Lee Collins recalls that he and Morton ran around together. Morton "talked to me about making some records with him," Collins writes. "So one day I went over to see him [and] there he was—in bed with two women, one sitting on each side of him . . . Jelly wanted to know was I going to stay in Chicago or run on back home like a lot of other New Orleans musicians did. Then he asked me to come to work with him. 'You know that you will be working with the world's greatest jazz piano player.'. . . I told him I knew he was one of the greatest jazz pianists, but he said 'Not one of the greatest—I am *the* greatest!' " Earl Hines remembers Morton, too. In "The World of Earl Hines," he told Stanley Dance, "The three of them [the pianist Glover Compton, the dancer Lovey Taylor, and Morton] were the loudest fellows I ever heard. When they were standing on the corner, you could hear them for blocks. We used to go to ball games together, and you didn't have to know where they were sitting because you could hear them all over the White Sox park . . . If I came to the game late, I just followed their voices and found them." He also told Dance:

> Jelly Roll Morton . . . was the most popular underworld pianist around. [He] was a fair-complected man and sort of handsome. Nowadays you'd say he was overdressed, but he was the kind of fellow who carried his pearl-handled pistols with him and had plenty of money in his pocket at all times. If anybody tried to put him in a corner . . . he'd say things like, "I've got more suits than you've got handker-chiefs!" or, "I've been further around the world than you've been around a teacup!" He had written any number of tunes and everybody thought a lot of him. Whenever he needed money, he'd write a tune and sell it to one of the downtown publishers like Melrose for fifty or seventy-five dollars. Tunes like "Milenberg Joys" were very popular, and when the bands began to play them he made a lot of money.

Morton may have made some money, but the Melrose brothers made a lot more, having also taken over Morton's "Jelly Roll Blues" (which was famous enough in 1917 to be mentioned in the lyrics of "The Darktown Strutters' Ball"), "The Wolverine Blues," and "King Porter Stomp," an anthem of the big-band era. (When Morton was sounding off years later in a Harlem club, an exasperated listener turned up a radio to drown him out, and "King Porter Stomp" came blasting out.) Late in 1926, the Melroses, intent on ballyhooing Morton's sheet music, got a recording contract for him with Victor, and during the next nine months he set down sixteen classic small-band sides under the name of Jelly Roll Morton and His Red Hot Peppers. He used two bands: George Mitchell on cornet, Omer Simeon or Johnny Dodds on clarinet, Kid Ory or George Bryant on trombone, Stump Evans on alto saxophone (six sides), Johnny St. Cyr or Bud Scott on banjo or guitar, John Lindsay on bass or Quinn Wilson on tuba, and Andrew Hilaire or Baby Dodds on drums. Morton had spent the previous twenty-five years as a hustler who also played the piano and led bands, and it has never been entirely clear where the originality, drive, lyric beauty, and rococo flair of these recordings came from. There is nothing as good anywhere else in Morton's musical life, nor is there anything quite like them anywhere in jazz. Roughness and delicacy, lyricism and straightforwardness, tension and relaxation, simplicity and complexity, campy humor and high seriousness, melody and improvisation, ensemble and solos—all are kept in an easy balance. Morton wrote many of the tunes (most of them a unique combination of ragtime and the blues), arranged them elaborately, and taught his musicians how to play them. Baby Dodds told Larry Gara, in "The Baby Dodds Story," what Morton did in a recording studio:

> At rehearsal Jelly Roll Morton used to work on each and every number until it satisfied him. Everybody had to do just what Jelly wanted him to do . . . We used his original numbers and he always explained what it was all about and played a synopsis of it on the piano. Sometimes we had music and he would mark with a pencil those places which he wanted to stand out in a number. It was different from recording with Louis [Armstrong]. Jelly didn't leave much leeway for the individual musician . . . His own playing was remarkable and kept us in good spirits. He wasn't fussy, but he was positive . . . I never saw him upset and he didn't raise his voice at any time.

Morton's arrangements prefigured Duke Ellington's. He used organ chords behind soloists and counterbalancing fragments of melody and riffs. He used a lot of breaks. He experimented with rhythmic devices and with the makeup of his rhythm section. And he ceaselessly changed his instrumental combinations—a clarinet solo backed only by guitar, and an a-cappella piano solo, a guitar solo backed by organ chords—which gave the effect of a larger, more varied group. He often wrote out the reed solos and the connective ensemble passages, but the main ensembles were jammed and are perhaps the best instances we have of New Orleans polyphonic playing. The sixteen Victor sides range from the stark to the baroque. "Jungle Blues" is deceptively simple. It is based on a blueslike twelve-bar figure, set over a medium-tempo, two-note, rock-rock ostinato bass that persists until the last two choruses. An ad-lib four-bar unison ensemble serves as an introduction, and in the first chorus the cornet plays a melody over the ostinato bass, which is done by the trombone and piano. Morton has Baby Dodds hit a sour-sounding Chinese cymbal every four bars or so through much of the record. The alto saxophone repeats the melody in the second chorus, and a different melody, descending and lyrical, is played by the ensemble for a chorus. Johnny Dodds repeats this melody for a chorus, and there is another ensemble stretch, accented by Baby Dodds' weird cymbal. Morton comes out in a clearing with an unaccompanied piano solo, but he carries on the ostinato bass in his left hand, and near the close of the chorus he exchanges delicate two-bar bits of melody with the guitar. The ostinato bass stops, and the tuba, trombone, trumpet, and reeds play connected ascending two-bar breaks; then there is a fine closing two-chorus ensemble and a four-bar coda that echoes the introduction. Morton establishes a monochromatic, metronomic air in the first chorus and spends the rest of the record slowly breaking it down with affecting melodic breezes, loose, ambling ensembles, and the lyrical, summer-evening exchanges between him and the guitar.

Morton's bands were his sounding boards. There are no stray hairs or ragged cuffs on the 1926–27 sides. Everything fits and flows, and there is never any loss of spontaneity or swing. Each side is multilayered but clear, highly tinted but not gaudy, tailored but not stiff. The records are a distillation of what Morton heard around him in New Orleans during the first decade of the century. They combine with great ease absolute opposites: ragtime, a complex written music that depends on the fluency of its performers and the grace of its melodies for the rather thin emotional responses it provokes; and the blues, a loose harmonic progression, often clothed with notes that don't exist (the so-called blue notes), and mysteriously capable of evoking almost every kind of emotion.

Not long after Morton had recorded the last of the Chicago Red Hot Pepper sides, he moved to New York, which was rapidly becoming the center of the music. One of jazz's lightning shifts in musical emphasis had preceded him, and when he arrived he found he had gone out of fashion. His music was basically an ensemble music, an arranger's music, and jazz had suddenly become a music of soloists—Louis Armstrong, Coleman Hawkins, Jimmy Harrison, Jabbo Smith, Benny Goodman. Nonetheless, Morton made more sides for Victor between 1928 and 1930, when his contract ran out, than he had made in five years in Chicago. Some are minor classics—"Georgia Swing," "Kansas City Stomps," "Boogaboo," "Shoe Shiners Drag," "Shreveport Stomp," "Mournful Serenade," "Deep Creek," "Tank Town Bump," "Smilin' the Blues Away," and "Turtle Twist"—but none quite match the freshness and originality of the Chicago recordings. Morton had an infallible ear for talent, and the young musicians on his New York recordings who became well known include Red Allen, J. C. Higginbotham, Cozy Cole, Russell Procope, Walter Foots Thomas, Sandy Williams, and Tommy Benford. When he wasn't recording, he scrambled. He fronted bands briefly at the Rose Danceland, the Checker Club, and the Lido Ballroom. He put together a revue, "Speeding Along," and worked in Laura Prampin's band in Coney Island. He took pickup groups to country clubs around New York for Saturday-night dances, and he took bands on the road in Pennsylvania and Ohio and New England. He played solo piano at the Red Apple Club, at Seventh Avenue and 135th Street. In photographs of him taken in the thirties in Harlem, he seems always to be talking and gesticulating and smiling. He was a striking-looking man, with a long, aquiline nose, a strong chin, and a high forehead. (Alberta Hunter found him "tall and ugly, with the longest fingers I ever saw.") A number of people who knew him are still around. The first is the guitarist Lawrence Lucie:

> Jelly was a walking encyclopedia, and he was very entertaining. He always smiled after he said something outrageous. He knew exactly what he wanted in his music, and he believed in his style. Some people thought he was old-fashioned, but he was greater than we all thought he was. He'd been ahead of his time for a long time before times caught up to him.

Walter Foots Thomas (reeds):

> Jelly sent for me in Indiana. I was afraid to come to New York. I could read, but I didn't play too much jazz. Jelly influenced my style and my musical thinking, and he inspired me to write. I used to watch him sit down and write a piece off, just like that. He wrote a lot of the clarinet solos in his arrangements, but he didn't write the brass solos. I always felt that his melodies came from New Orleans but that his rhythms came from the Latin countries. When he went on a tour of colleges in Pennsylvania, I drove the band bus. He used to talk all the time about "that good Gulf gas," how he couldn't live without "that good Gulf gas."

Doc Cheatham (trumpet):

> Jelly was a born player, he just naturally stomped. In Chicago, he knew he was the king. He had gold coins in the tips of his shoes, and he wore diamond rings. But he was in bad shape in New York. I think I was one of the few friends he had. He liked me, and when I played he'd say, "Damn! That's the way to play the trumpet. These somebodies don't know *nothing*!"

Bernard Addison (guitar):

Jelly was fine people. He talked aplenty, but I presume he knew what he was talking about. I used to hear him bragging on street corners in Harlem, and he used to hold audiences at the Rhythm Club, where there would be ten or twenty musicians around him. I only made recording dates with him. We rehearsed an hour or so, and then went on wax. Most of what we recorded was by head. I don't think he was in the capacity of Willie the Lion Smith or James P. Johnson. He was more in the honky-tonk style.

Morton was a very different pianist from Smith or Johnson or Fats Waller. He used the stride bass sparingly, and his right hand was less lacy and staccato. He used tenths in his left hand, boogie-woogie bases, off-beat chords, single notes, and silences. His right-hand figures were often more daring than those of the Harlem stride pianists. He liked advanced chords, and he liked to double or triple the time, or slow it down, or use arhythmic figures. Unlike the stride pianists, he was a good blues player. Stanley Dance thinks that Morton had more influence on Earl Hines in the twenties than is generally acknowledged, and he is probably right. Morton is visible in Hines' accompanying, in his arhythmic bursts, and in his over-all legato attack. Mary Lou Williams has long admitted that Morton was her first model.

More voices. The first is the recording executive Ahmet Ertegun:

My brother Nesuhi and I used to drive up to New York from Washington for the Sunday-afternoon jam sessions. It must have been 1939 or 1940. Jelly Roll appeared for a short while in a band led by Sidney Bechet. Big Sid Catlett was there, and Sidney de Paris and Albert Nicholas and Claude Jones, and possibly Omer Simeon. Jelly talked a lot between numbers—about how he invented jazz and that sort of thing. He always looked dapper and had style. If anybody invented jazz, he did, because he predicted so much that was to come. The greatest jazz record of all time is "Shreveport Stomp," with Simeon and Tommy Benford. It was bright and brassy and seven years ahead of the Benny Goodman trio. Obviously, Jelly was the greatest person in jazz—with all due respect to Louis and Duke.

Nesuhi Ertegun (recording executive):

Kid Ory told me about a record session Morton had in Chicago in 1923 on the old Okeh label. Zue Robertson was on trombone, and he refused to play the melody of one of the tunes the way Morton wanted it played. Jelly took a big pistol out of his pocket and put it on the piano, and Robertson played the melody note for note.

John Hammond (recording executive, critic):

I used to see Jelly around New York during the depths of the Depression, around 1934 or 1935, and he was seedy and disillusioned. He sang and played at a place on Seventh Avenue called the Red Apple.

Lester Young used to drop in there after Basie came to town. In 1934, I
did a Wingy Manone date for Vocalion, and Wingy insisted on bringing
Jelly Roll in. He was sloppy that day, and nobody on the date felt good
about him. Somewhere around that time, I read that Duke Ellington was
to appear at a theatre in Queens, and I went out, but who should turn up
but Jelly Roll and a non-union band that included the trombonist Charlie
Irvis. I don't think there were sixty people in the whole place.

Willie the Lion Smith had little tolerance for fools, and in his "Music on
My Mind" he wrote, "Morton was a man with strong spiritual and magnetic forces; when he sat down to play he could hold an audience by the
strength of his strong personality. He was a sharpshooter and had always
travelled in fast company. He was intelligent, had something to offer, and
as far as I could tell, he was always able to back up what he said." When
Alan Lomax was doing his book on Morton, he went to see Mabel
Bertrand, a dancer whom Morton had married just before coming to New
York. She talked of Morton's fastidiousness:

> He was very particular . . . When he'd taken a shirt off, he would miss
> it if I didn't launder it that day . . . He would go through the drawer,
> looking for that particular shirt.
> I'd say to him, "What you looking for?"
> "I'm looking for that pink-striped shirt."
> "It must be in the chiffonier," I'd say, but he'd go straight to the bath-
> room, find it in the clothes basket. "Is it getting too hard for you to do
> the laundry?" Jelly would say.
> "No."
> "May, I'm trying to make it easy on you. Isn't it easier to wash and
> iron one shirt just when I take it off than to wait and let them pile up?"
> "Yes."
> "You don't have a thing in the world to do but keep my laundry
> clean."

Morton got a little crazy in the mid-thirties. He lost money in a business
venture, and he became convinced that a voodoo spell had been put on
him. In 1935, he moved to Washington, D.C., and ended up in a little sec-
ond-floor club in the black district. The photographer William P. Gottlieb
remembers him there: "It had a piano and a few chairs, and Morton
would tend bar and seat people and sometimes play piano. It was a pretty bare place, and I never saw more than a handful of people. Jelly had a
big hole in the front tooth where he'd had his diamond, and his face got
all crinkled when he smiled. He had a routine he used to go through
about how he needed such-and-such a break to reëstablish himself. He
had plenty of bravado, and he exuded optimism. It was a front he never
let down." Lomax recorded Morton in the spring of 1938, and Morton
wrote his famous letter to the papers. People suddenly remembered that
he was alive, and in 1939 he was asked to record eight sides for Bluebird
with such players as Sidney Bechet, Sidney de Paris, Zutty Singleton,

Lawrence Lucie, Claude Jones, and Albert Nicholas. During December, 1939, and January, 1940, he made his last records—a dozen or so piano solos and a dozen band sides. The band sides are dumpy and shrill, but the piano sides, particularly those with Morton vocals, are splendid. He was a beautiful singer, with a gentle baritone voice and marvellous phrasing—one of the best of all jazz singers—and it's a pity he didn't sing more. In the fall of 1940, he heard that Eulalie Echo, his godmother, had died in California, and, fearing that some diamonds she had would be stolen, he decided to head West. He still owned two big old cars, and he hooked them together and set off by himself. On November 9th, he wrote to Mabel Bertrand from Yreka, California, telling her, in fine Morton fashion, that he had hit snowstorms in ten states, that he had slid off the road in Wyoming, that he had had to abandon one car in Montpelier, Idaho, and that he had got stuck on a mountain in Oregon and had to be rescued by the police. The diamonds were gone, but he stayed on. David Stuart, who now owns an art gallery in Los Angeles, got to know Morton:

> I had my Jazz Man Record Shop, and Jelly used to come in, and we became friendly. He loved to talk about the past, and he had a terrific memory. He said that he'd written fourteen hundred songs, that there had been a period in the twenties when he'd write a song a night. One afternoon, a friend and I were driving Jelly around with the thought of stopping to visit the trombonist Zue Robertson. Robertson had a sister in Los Angeles, and he lived in a kind of chicken coop behind her house, and he wanted nothing so much as to get back to New Orleans. Jelly figured out what we had in mind before we got there, and he absolutely refused to go. "No, sir. He hates me, he hates me," he kept saying. Sometimes we'd take him out to hear music in the evening—Kid Ory and Mutt Carey, old New Orleans people like that. The musicians called him "The Roll," and when he appeared they'd all stand up and say, "Here comes the Roll." He got sick before he died, and they put him in a kind of broom closet in the hospital, and they treated him shabbily. I'd go over in the afternoon and sit with him. He'd hold my hand hour after hour, even though I'm sure he had no idea who I was anymore.

Morton died July 10, 1941. The Ellington and Lunceford bands, both in their prime, were playing in Los Angeles, but no one from either group went to the funeral.

Le Grand Bechet

The great New Orleans clarinettist and soprano saxophonist Sidney Bechet was, like Morton, a Creole of color. He was born in 1897, the youngest of seven children. His father, Omar, was a cornettist and a shoemaker, and his mother, Josephine, was an octoroon who loved to dance. When he was six, he was playing the clarinet and taking lessons from the New Orleans master George Baquet, and soon afterward he went to work in his brother Leonard's band. When he was sixteen or seventeen, he and Clarence Williams (the pianist and composer) rode the rods into Texas. Bechet got into a fight with a white man, and fled to Galveston, where another brother lived. At twenty, he joined the Bruce & Bruce Stock Company, and ended up in Chicago. He had played with everyone of consequence in New Orleans (Bunk Johnson, Buddy Petit, King Oliver, Louis Armstrong), and in Chicago he played with Lil Hardin and Roy Palmer, and then with the cornettist Freddie Keppard—another iconoclast, whom he admired enormously. He was heard by the bandleader Will Marion Cook, who had a large, Paul Whiteman-type ensemble, and Cook hired him as a soloist (Bechet could not read music, and never fully learned) and took him to England. It was June of 1919, and Bechet was a sensation. Ernest Ansermet, a thirty-five-year-old Swiss who had conducted the première of Stravinsky's "L'Histoire du Soldat," went repeatedly to hear the band. He also talked with Bechet, and in due course wrote a review in the Swiss *Revue Romande*. Here is part of the last, prescient paragraph:

> There is in the Southern Syncopated Orchestra an extraordinary clarinet virtuoso who is, so it seems, the first of his race to have composed perfectly formed blues on the clarinet. I've heard two of them which he had elaborated at great length [and] they are equally admirable for their richness of invention, force of accent, and daring in novelty and the unexpected. Already, they gave the idea of a style, and their form was gripping, abrupt, harsh, with a brusque and pitiless ending like that of Bach's second "Brandenburg Concerto." I wish to set down the name of this artist of genius; as for myself, I shall never forget it—it is Sidney Bechet.... What a moving thing it is to meet this very black, fat boy with white teeth and that narrow forehead, who is very glad one likes what he does, but who can say nothing of his art, save that he follows his "own way" ... His "own way" is perhaps the highway the whole world will swing along tomorrow.

Cook disbanded, and Bechet stayed on with a drummer named Benny Peyton. Then Bechet got into hot water over an English prostitute and was deported, despite his having bewitched the Royal Family at a command performance at Buckingham Palace. Back in America, he went into a show called "How Come?," with Bessie Smith. Bechet liked Bessie Smith. This is how he described her in "Treat It Gentle," his autobiography: "She could be plenty tough . . . She always drank plenty and she could hold it, but sometimes, after she'd been drinking a while, she'd get like there was no pleasing her. There were times you had to know just how to handle her right." He played with James P. Johnson at the Kentucky Club, and around 1924 joined the fledgling Duke Ellington band. Ellington never got over Bechet's great lyrical bent. He wrote of him in "Music Is My Mistress":

> Often, when Bechet was blowing, he would say, "I'm going to call Goola this time!" Goola was his dog, a big German shepherd. Goola wasn't always there, but he was calling him anyway with a kind of throaty growl.
> *Call* was very important in that kind of music. Today, the music has grown up and become quite scholastic, but this was *au naturel*, close to the primitive, where people send messages in what they play, calling somebody, or making facts and emotions known. Painting a picture, or having a story to go with what you were going to play, was of vital importance in those days. The audience didn't know anything about it, but the cats in the band did.

Bechet slipped away from Ellington, and opened a place of his own, the Club Basha. Then, never still long, he returned to Europe, with Claude Hopkins and Josephine Baker, for a show called "Revue Nègre." Bechet put down his European roots during the twenties. He toured Russia, and roamed Western Europe. But he got into another fracas, in 1928. One morning around eight, he and the American banjoist Little Mike McKendrick had a gun battle outside a Montmartre bar. Bechet grazed McKendrick, hit the pianist Glover Compton in the leg, and wounded a Frenchwoman on her way to work. He went to jail for eleven months. When he got out, he worked at the Wild West Bar in Berlin and then went back to New York. In 1932, he joined Duke Ellington again, and tutored Johnny Hodges on the soprano saxophone, thus indirectly and permanently altering the Ellington band. Bechet put together the first of his New Orleans Feetwarmers bands and took it into the Savoy Ballroom, in Harlem. The group, which included the trumpeter Tommy Ladnier and the pianist Hank Duncan, made six numbers for Victor, which are among the most joyous and swinging of all jazz records. Bechet had met Ladnier in Russia, and the two men spent much time together in the thirties. When the Depression closed in, they quit the music and started a sort of basement store in Harlem, called the Southern Tailor Shop. Willie the Lion Smith remembered it in "Music on My Mind":

> I'd ask Sidney where he was living.
> He would reply, "I'm at 129th Street and St. Nicholas. I'm the

proprietor of the Southern Tailor Shop."

That would gas me. I couldn't figure out what a good jazz clarinet player was doing playing "tailor."

So I said, "How many suits you got in there?"

"Oh," he said, "I've got up to about twenty; but we don't make them, just press 'em."

Then I asked,"Who's we?"

He replied, "Tommy and myself."

Well, I knew Tommy Ladnier from Chicago days. He was a good trumpet player. I found out later that Sidney would press and repair the suits, while Ladnier specialized in shining shoes. . . .

Bechet mentioned they had some good sessions in the back of the shop. So one night I agreed to come around to see what was happening.

But first, I wanted some information. "How much you charge to press a suit ?"

He replied, "Oh, the regular fee."

You see I figured if nothing was going on I could at least get my suit pressed. Then I wanted to know, "What do we sleep on?"

He then said, "I've got a couple of cots in the back. But usually there's a bunch of musicianers playing back there."

"You ain't gonna press any clothes tonight then," I said.

"No, man. I cooked up a batch of red beans and rice to add to a lot of cold fried chicken. We'll have us a party."

When the drummer Zutty Singleton arrived in New York from Chicago in 1937, he moved into the building Bechet and Ladnier shared quarters in. Singleton once said, "They called their place the House of Meditation, and they had a picture of Beethoven on the wall. One day, Ladnier said to Bechet, 'You know something, Bash? You the dead image of Beethoven,' and that pleased Bechet. Bechet and Ladnier would stand in front of this big old mirror they had and watch themselves while they practiced. They listened to classical music, and they talked a lot about their travels—when Bechet wasn't talking about the Rosicrucians. He was a hell of a cat. He could be mean. He could be sweet. He could be in between."

Jazz concerts were beginning to take hold by 1940, and that year Bechet gave one in Washington, D.C. It was organized by Nesuhi Ertegun. "Not long after I came to the United States, I decided to give a jazz concert built around Sidney Bechet," Ertegun has said. "My father was the Turkish Ambassador, and I lived at the Embassy in Washington, so I decided to give it in Washington. I had in mind a concert with a mixed band and a mixed audience, but Washington was still a Southern racist town, and no concert hall would touch such an affair. Finally, the Jewish Community Center, which had a four-hundred-seat auditorium, agreed. In addition to Bechet, I wanted Sidney De Paris on trumpet, Vic Dickenson on trombone, Art Hodes on piano, Wellman Braud on bass, and Manzie Johnson on drums. The alternating group would be Meade Lux Lewis and the blues shouter Joe Turner. I found Bechet at the Mimmo Club, in Harlem. He was backing a slick show, with a chorus line and singers and all that, and the band was in tuxedos. It all looked very prosperous. But the truth was that Bechet, who was already a hero in France, wasn't doing at all well here. The next day, he invited me to his apartment for a drink and something to eat. After we sat down, his wife came in and said to Bechet, 'Who's that? What does he want?' Bechet introduced me and said he'd brought me home for a bite. She said, 'You know there's no food in this house. Now, go on, get out and find your own food!' We went to a bar and had a drink and worked out the details of the concert. When the band arrived in Washington, they came to the Embassy, and we had an elegant lunch. I knew Bechet loved red beans and rice, so we had red beans and rice, and he was astonished. He wanted to know if we had a Creole cook, and I said no, a Turkish cook, and that beans and rice was a common dish in Turkey, too. Bechet couldn't believe it, and he said we must be copying the Creoles, and a very pleasant argument went on for some time about the roots of red beans and rice. The musicians were relaxed and in a good mood, and the concert, which was in the afternoon, was a tremendous success musically.

"From then on, Sidney and I were very friendly. He was deceptive. With his white hair and round face, he looked much older than he was. He also had this genial, sweet Creole politeness and a beautiful, harmonious way of talking. In many ways, he seemed like a typical Uncle Tom. But once you got to know him—once you had broken the mirror and got inside and found the true Bechet—you discovered he wasn't that way at all. He couldn't stand fakery or hypocrisy, and he was a tough and involved human being. He was far more intelligent than people took him for, and he knew what was going on everywhere. I never heard him play badly, even with bad groups. He was an incredibly rich player. Years later, when I was running a John Coltrane record date, Coltrane told me that Bechet had been an important influence on him."

Like most New Orleans clarinettists, Bechet used the Albert-system clarinet, which has a formal, luxurious, Old World tone. New Orleans clarinet playing tended to be rich and florid. Vibratos were wide, glissandi were favored, and emotions were high and unashamed. Bechet, along with Johnny Dodds, Jimmy Noone, and Barney Bigard, belonged to the second generation of New Orleans clarinettists. (The first included Alphonse Picou, Lorenzo Tio, Jr., Big Eye Louis Nelson, and George Baquet.) Noone and Bigard concentrated on legato attacks, fed and enriched their tones, and perfected showy melodic swoops and arcs. They liked being serene and airborne. Bechet and Dodds were rhythm players. They broke up their phrases ingeniously, used a great many blue notes, and had acidic, almost disagreeable timbres. Bechet used growls, strange bubbling sounds, and wide, swaggering notes. He shook his sounds out. When he took up the soprano saxophone, in the early twenties, he transferred his clarinet playing to this odd and difficult instrument. The soprano saxophone defies being played on pitch, and Bechet and his star pupil, Bob Wilber, are practically its only pitch-perfect practitioners. (The deliberate tonal distortions used by many modern soprano saxophonists make it impossible to tell whether they are in tune.) Bechet developed an enormous tone that incorporated qualities of the trumpet, the oboe, and the horn. The sheer strength of his sound, and his rhythmic drive, allowed him to rule every band he played in. Wise trumpet players stood aside or were blown to smithereens. As an improviser, Bechet used the chords of a song but also followed the melody, which kept reappearing, like sunlight on a forest floor. His melodic lines were pronouncements. They were full of shouts and swoops; they gleamed and exploded. The solos left his listeners with the feeling that they had been in on important things. When he played a slow blues, he exhibited a melancholy, an ancient grieving. And when he played a slow ballad he was honeyed and insinuating and melodramatic. Johnny Hodges grew up in both sides of this divided house.

In 1946, Bechet moved to Brooklyn and opened a sort of music school. The jazz critic Richard Hadlock took some lessons from him, and wrote about them in the San Francisco *Examiner*:

> Sidney would run off a complex series of phrases and leave me alone in his room for a couple of hours to wrestle with what he had played. One lesson could easily take up an entire afternoon, and Sidney favored giving a lesson every day.
>
> "Look, when you emphasize a note, you throw your whole body into it," he would say, cutting a wide arc with his horn as he slashed into a phrase.
>
> "I'm going to give you one note today," he once told me. "See how many ways you can play that note—growl it, smear it, flat it, sharp it, do anything you want to it. That's how you express your feelings in this music. It's like talking.
>
> "Always try to complete your phrases and your ideas . . . There are lots of otherwise good musicians who sound terrible because they start a new idea without finishing the last one."

Bob Wilber has described another facet of Bechet:

> One thing he was very interested in was the concept of interpreting a song. You start out with an exposition of the melody in which you want to bring out the beauty of it. And then you start your variations, but at first they are closely related to the melody. Then, as you go on to another chorus, you get further away—you do something a little less based on the melody but more on the harmony. Sidney was much more harmonically oriented than most of the players of his generation . . . Then at the end, you would come back to the melody and there would be some kind of coda which would bring the thing to a conclusion. . . . The idea of the form was very important to him.

Bechet settled in France in 1951. He had filled the forties with gigs in and around New York and in Chicago. The pianist Dick Wellstood worked with him at Jazz Limited, in Chicago, and at the Bandbox, in New York. "He was very autocratic and nineteenth-century," Wellstood once said. "It was like working for Bismarck. There was a right way and a wrong way, and if you did it the wrong way it was mutiny. There was a right tempo and right chords, and that was the way you reached the people. He had a gentlemanly and courtly exterior. He spoke softly, using the New Orleans accent of 'poil' and 'erster' for 'pearl' and 'oyster.' But when he was annoyed he'd lash out, and I think he always carried a knife. Once, at Jimmy Ryan's, in New York, his piano player was late, and Bechet asked me—I just happened to be there—to sit in. When the piano player arrived, Sidney bawled him out publicly, and told him,'I want you to give that boy five dollars.' I think he got increasingly egocentric. At the Bandbox, he sat in a thronelike chair backstage, and people paid court to him. Alfred Lion, of Blue Note records, would bring him champagne and all but kneel at his feet. His sense of humor was strange. One night, in Chicago, he played this game with his trombonist Munn Ware. The horn players were supposed to stand up to solo, but after Sidney had taken his solo and sat down and Munn had stood up Sidney got up again and started playing and Munn sat down. Sidney played several choruses and sat down, and when Munn stood up again to solo Sidney stood up, and on it went. Later, Munn shot him in the back of the head with a water pistol, and I waited for lightning to strike, but Sidney only giggled. The truth is, I was scared to death of him the whole time I worked for him."

Bechet's autobiography, done in France with the help of Joan Reid, Desmond Flower, and John Ciardi, was published the year after his death, in 1959. The first two-thirds of the book is remarkable. It opens with a long, mythlike account of the life and death of his grandfather, a freed slave named Omar. Omar becomes obsessed with a young slave girl on a nearby plantation, and one night he takes her to the edge of the bayou and makes love to her. But the girl's owner, also bewitched by her, follows them. He shoots Omar in the arm and takes the girl home. Then he spreads word that Omar has raped his daughter and search parties scour the bayou, where Omar hides. He sees the girl once more, at great peril, and is murdered by a slave seeking the reward. The girl has a baby, who becomes Bechet's father. It does not matter how much improvisation there is in the story. Bechet's language is dense and mysterious and poetical:

> All those trees there, they was standing like skeletons after the hide of the animal has disappeared. There was moonlight on their tops like blossoming, and there was the darkness under them, the light and the darkness somehow part of one thing that was darker than just plain dark, and all so still.

The book is full of folk wisdom:

> So many people go at themselves like they was some book; they look
> back through themselves, they see this so and so chapter, they remem-
> ber this one thing or another, but they don't go through the pages one
> after the other really finding out what they're about and who they are
> and where they are. They never count their whole story together.

He talks of spirituals and the blues:

> In the spirituals the people clapped their hands—that was their
> rhythm. In the blues it was further down; they didn't need the clapping,
> but they remembered it . . . And both of them, the spirituals and the
> blues, they was a prayer. One was praying to God and the other was
> praying to what's human. It's like one was saying, "Oh, God, let me go,"
> and the other was saying, "Oh, Mister, let me be."

Bechet's life in France appears to have fulfilled him. He married a
German woman he had known in the twenties, and he kept a mistress, by
whom he had a son. He made a lot of money, bought a small estate outside
Paris, and drove a Salmson coupé at high speeds. In 1957, he recorded a
tight, to-the-point collaboration with the modern French pianist Martial
Solal. It is one of his best records. The next year, he played beautifully at the
Brussels World's Fair. The impresario and pianist George Wein was in the
band. "I never encountered the evil side of Bechet," Wein has said. "Two
things that probably caused it were his stomach, which bothered him for
years, and trumpet players who tried to grab the lead in bands he was in.
I think he was kind to musicians who were his inferiors, and hard on musicians who were his equals. I filled in at a Bechet concert at the Academy of
Music, in Philadelphia, in 1948, when James P. Johnson failed to show, and
he *made* me feel like I was playing beautifully, even on 'Summertime,'
which was his big number, and which I'd never played before. He was a
great lyrical force, and he had great personal force. He filled a room when
he came into it. I think he could have been as big as Louis Armstrong if he
hadn't mistrusted all bookers and managers. There was no reason for
Bechet to come back from France after he settled there. He was happy and
was worshipped. But he did come back a few times in the early fifties, and
on one of his visits he played a gig at Storyville, my club in Boston. His
stomach acted up, and we put him in Massachusetts General Hospital.
They told him he had to have an operation, and what did he do? He went
back to France and had the operation there. He trusted the French more
than he did the Americans. Until the very end, that is. I was in France in
1959, and Charles Delaunay told me that Sidney was dying. I called him up
at his house outside Paris and asked him what I could do. 'Come and see
me,' he said. I'm very bad at such visits, but I went, and Sidney told me he
wanted to go home. I told him O.K., we'd try and make arrangements and
such, but before anything could be done he was gone."

The Blues Is a Slow Story

Red Allen's style was fully formed by 1930. Louis Armstrong hovered in its background, but Allen's originality dominated it. It was an elegant, fearless style, and it was perfectly balanced. His full, often declamatory tone was crimped by growls or piercing high notes; his basically legato approach was enlivened by rushes of on-the-beat notes; his seemingly straightforward melodic content was enriched by long, sagacious phrases and by a daring choice of notes. Allen was particularly striking at slow tempos. He would linger over his notes, holding them far longer than any other trumpeter, and he would bend them and press them, coloring them with a distinct and disturbing melancholy. His slow solos were often requiems. But this sadness, which lifted at faster tempos, was invariably toughened and guided by a subtle, leashed power. By 1934, he had become a full-fledged innovator; indeed, in the recordings he made with Fletcher Henderson he is a one-man avant garde. His solos are full of long, roving lines, unexpected off-notes, and free rhythmic turns. It is the sort of crossing-the-bar-lines improvising that was perfected five or six years later by Lester Young and Charlie Christian and that still sounds absolutely fresh. Some of Allen's solos with Henderson had such completeness and authority that they were studied a few years later by Harry James when he was with Benny Goodman, and several were scored for whole sections of the Henderson band. Allen's playing changed in the forties. It became brassy and harsh, and his unevenness, theretofore occasional, became pronounced. He would start a solo with a beautiful, languorous phrase, pause, lose the impetus of it, and wander off into an entirely different mood. But this uncertainty began to lessen in the early fifties, and in 1957 he made a startling recording for Victor. It included several long ballads, and Allen converted each into a massive lullaby. He sounded like Art Farmer and Miles Davis. He flowed around his horn (lower register notes—almost trombone notes—would be planted beside soft, high flutters), and the blues underlay almost every passage. He made equally good recordings after that, and gorgeous patches appeared in every solo he took in night clubs or at concerts, no matter how hard he was blowing.

Allen died in 1967, aged fifty-nine. For the last twenty-seven years of his life, he lived with his wife, Pearlie May, and assorted children and grandchildren on the fifth floor of a yellow-brick walk-up on Prospect Avenue in the east Bronx. Jobs were scarce in the year or two before he died, and he welcomed visits from friends.

Allen was tall and he had gotten portly, but he took the stairs in his apartment house at a fast pace, and he was not winded when he reached his floor. He pushed his doorbell and there was a thumping sound inside. A muffled voice said, "Is that you, Allen?"

"I'm here, Pearlie May. Open up." There were more confused sounds and the word "doing" came through the door. Allen chuckled. "She's putting the dog away. He's a big white German shepherd that we call White Fang after another White Fang we had, and he'll jump all over you, cover you with hair. But he's a fine watchdog. When I come in late, I ring the bell downstairs and Pearlie May lets him out and he runs down to meet me."

A chain rattled and the door opened. Mrs. Allen, who is short and plump and has a round, pretty face, was fastening the top button of a house dress. "Lord, that dog is so *curious*," she said. "Wants to see what everybody looks like comes in the house, and then sits all over them. I put him in the bathroom, where he won't bother anyone."

Mrs. Allen stepped back, and Allen led the way down a short, dark hall and past a small, cheerful kitchen. An impressionistic painting of Allen hung by the kitchen door, and farther along, on the opposite wall, there was a large photograph of a thin, young, smooth-faced Allen dressed in a dapper double-breasted suit and holding an extremely long trumpet. A small room with a day bed and a television set and a couple of chairs was at the end of the hall, and opening out of the hall to the left, behind glass doors, was a larger room. "This is the front room, which is what we call the parlor," Allen said. The room had a small green sofa, several red chairs, and two end tables. A silver tea service and a pair of tall orange china swans were on one of the tables. A dark abstract painting hung on one wall, and another painting of Allen across from it. On the wall near the doors were two plates, one with the message "God Bless This Allen Home." The venetian blinds at the only window were down, but the slats were open. The room was in pleasant half-light.

Allen sat down heavily in one of the chairs, his legs spread wide, his toes pointing in. His face was a study in basset melancholy. He had a high, narrow forehead and thin, dark hair. A single, ironbound furrow ran across the lower part of his forehead, and it seemed to weigh on his eyes, which were heavily lidded and slanted down at their outer corners. Two deep furrows bracketed his generous nose and his mouth, and he had a cleft chin. His cheeks were heavy but firm. His smile was surprising; it easily lifted and lit the mass around it. His speech was full of New Orleans oddities. He was apt to start sentences with "der"—in the manner of the French "*donc*"—or to use it to fill a pause, and he pronounced "rehearsal" and "bird" "rehoisal" and "boid." Allen yawned, tweaked his nose, and rested his thick, square hands on his thighs. "My first visit to New York was when King Oliver called for me to come and meet him," Allen said. "I was leery of leaving New Orleans. I'd heard of too many New Orleans musicians getting stranded up in the North. But I went because Oliver had worked in my dad's brass band. I lived in a boarding

house with Omer Simeon and Barney Bigard and Paul Barbarin, New
Orleans friends and all in Oliver's band, before I moved in with Oliver
and his sister. Oliver's teeth had gone bad by then and he wasn't playing
much, so I'd take most of the solos at the Savoy, where we were appearing, and pretty soon people started calling me King Oliver. Then Oliver
was supposed to go into the Cotton Club, but somebody brainwashed
him about the money, telling him he should get more, so he didn't take
the job. Duke Ellington, who was just starting out, did, and that was the
beginning of *that* story. Oliver's band was booked into a park in
Baltimore, but we had rough luck there with weather, and that job didn't
work out, either. When we got back to New York, I couldn't take it anymore. I made my first record with Clarence Williams—and the next day I
took off for home. I'd saved my fare money—kept it in my shoe—so I
didn't have to send to my father for money. I was only gone two months
and I was happy to get back. Even the coffee was bad in New York. In
New Orleans it was so strong it stained the cup, but I drank so much of
it I got headaches if I didn't drink it. In New York I drank the same
amount, but the headaches just got worse, so I gave it up. And I don't
drink much of it to this day, unless I'm in New Orleans on a visit."

There was a commotion in the hall, and White Fang appeared outside the
glass doors. Mrs. Allen grabbed him by the collar and started pulling him
back toward the kitchen. Allen laughed. "Let him be, Pearlie May!" he
shouted. "Just put that chair against the door so's he can't get in." Mrs.
Allen wedged a chair under the door handle. She shook a finger at the
dog, and said, "You want to come out, you act like a grown boy." The dog
sat down, his nose pressed against the glass. He stared at Allen, and then
he jumped up on the chair and resumed his vigil.

"I joined Fate Marable's band when I got back," Allen said. "Fate
worked the riverboats on the Streckfus line, and during the winter we'd
stay in New Orleans and play one-nighters. Go up the river a little way
and turn around and come back. When it warmed up, we'd head for St.
Louis and stop at towns along the way and dock and play dances on the
boat. We stayed in St. Louis about three months, and though we played
on the boat we lived in the city. You had to go out and find a room—
which was called every tub on its bottom, or being on your own. There
were some rough places in St. Louis. The Chauffeurs' Club was so bad
they built a fence of chicken wire around the bandstand to protect the
musicians when fights broke out. In 1929, I started getting letters and
wires from New York. Luis Russell, who had been with Oliver when I
was and who had the band now, wrote me to join him, and Duke
Ellington wired me. I knew most of the people with Russell. Pops Foster,
who'd been a longshoreman with my father, was on bass. Charlie Holmes
was on alto. And old Paul Barbarin, who had instigated my joining Oliver
in 1927, was on drums. I knew about J. C. Higginbotham, on trombone,
and I'd heard of Bill Coleman and Otis Johnson, who were on trumpets.

So I told Russell yes, and turned down Ellington. Barney Bigard was the only person I knew in his band. I believe he hired Cootie Williams instead. Fate Marable said O.K., I could go. He also said, 'Red'—that was a nickname given me because I was lightskinned and my face got red when I blew—'Red, if you see my man Jelly Roll Morton, tell him hello. He used to work for me, you know.' The first time I ran into Jelly in New York, I gave him the message. Well, Jelly Roll had a lot of posing and hot air in him, always saying things like 'My car is so long I got to go over to Central Park to turn it around,' and he just stood there and looked around and after a while he said, 'Oh, Fate Marable. He had this big old band that wasn't doing *nothing* and so one time I let him use my name to help him out.' " Allen laughed and rubbed his hands together.

"That first week back in New York was scary," Allen went on. "Teddy Hill, who played tenor for Russell, met me at the train and took me straight to the Roseland Ballroom, where the band was playing. I was to learn it was the kind of band that hung out like a family. It had brotherly love going. It was also the most swinging band in New York. It put the audiences in an uproar. One of the reasons was rhythm. Ellington had switched from tuba to bass and from banjo to guitar, and so had Russell. All the New York bass players were taking lessons from Pops Foster, and they even began carrying their basses on their shoulders, like the New Orleans men. Before that, you'd see them in the street carrying that fiddle in front of them in their arms like a baby. Russell did most of the arrangements, and whenever you took a solo there was a lot of fire up and down the band. But it wasn't Russell that made me nervous that first week. It was the after-hours jam sessions. I'd heard a lot about them and about the 'cutting' contests and I didn't know if I'd make it or not. I couldn't look to alcohol or tobacco for support, either. My father had never allowed me to drink or smoke, and I obeyed him. I don't believe I took my first strong drink until the forties, and I still don't smoke. I hadn't been in New York but a day or two when Alphonse Steele, who was a drummer, began taking me to the sessions at the Rhythm Club, on a Hundred and Thirty-second Street. He used to be a Paul Revere, sending around the news of sessions and announcing a new man in town. They would have trumpet nights and trombone nights and saxophone nights at the Rhythm Club. The first sessions I went to, every trumpeter was there—Cootie Williams, Rex Stewart, Ward Pinkett, Freddy Jenkins, Sidney de Paris. I don't believe Joe Smith showed up, but I learned later that when he did you were really in the lion's mouth. Whoever was on piano decided on the key and set the tempo, and then everyone soloed. If you wanted extra choruses, you stomped your foot. The applause decided the winner." Allen laughed. "I guess I did all right, because I'm still in New York. But those sessions were more than just outblowing someone. They were the only way of getting noticed, they were our publicity. If you made a good appearance, stood on your own, the word got around, and that's where the jobs come from. If you lost out too often, you just wouldn't make it. There were challenges all the time. One night, Big Green challenged Higginbotham. It was late, so Big Green went back to the Saratoga Club, where he was working, to get his horn and had to break down the door, which was locked. He came on back and I believe Higgy took care of him. Another time, the St. Louis clarinettist Thornton Blue—'the reputed Blue,' he called himself—took on Prince Robinson and Omer Simeon and Buster Bailey. When Buster got going on 'Tiger Rag,' that sealed it up. I heard Rex Stewart and Bix Beiderbecke battle, but, all due respect for the dead, Rex must have been in better form that night. And of course the bands battled all the time—at the Roseland and the Savoy and the Renaissance. And white musicians came up from downtown to sit in or listen: Jack Teagarden and the Dorseys and Krupa and Red Nichols and Goodman and Bunny Berigan. And there were breakfast dances at Small's Paradise, which began around four or five in the morning and went on half the day. I'd developed a strong embouchure on the riverboats, where the hours were long, so I could stand it."

There was muffled barking, and two little girls in school uniforms appeared outside the doors. "Oh, that's nice," Allen said, and smiled. "Here's the grands, home from school. Their address is with my son and his wife, who are only four blocks away, but they practically live here. They come by every day to do their homework and spend the night. They only go home on Saturdays, but their parents stop in most every day, too. That way we get to see them. The grands call Pearlie May 'Mama' and me 'Papa.' " "The taller girl opened one of the doors and came in and kissed Allen. "This is Alcornette," Allen said. "She's eleven. Pearlie May's maiden name is Alcorn, and of course there had to be some mention of a trumpet or cornet. And this is Juretta. She's named after my mother. She's six. They go to a Catholic school nearby. Go change your clothes and get on that homework. And close the door.

"I stayed with the Russell band until 1933, when I got a telegram from Fletcher Henderson asking me to meet him at a drugstore uptown. Russell Smith, who played trumpet with him, mainly persuaded me to join. I didn't like leaving the Luis Russell band, which was my home. But I guess Henderson offered me more money, and it was *the* band. Most of the arrangements were by Fletcher or Horace, his brother, and they were in difficult keys—D natural and the like. I'd learned all the keys in New Orleans by playing along with records set at every different speed. Each speed would put the music in a new key. I'd try all kinds of things with Fletcher, loafing through the channel of a number like 'Yeah Man,' with the result that Horace liked what I'd done so much he wrote it out for the brass. Horace would just sketch out the chords for new numbers and you could skate on that. I got accustomed to him. Take my thirty-one bars, or whatever, and get out. I was with the band for a year, and during that time Coleman Hawkins left and Lester Young replaced him. He only stayed a couple of weeks. He had a light tone and it just didn't fit with the arrangements, which called for a rich, deep sound. But I was happy for Lester to be in the band, because his father and my father had played together in New Orleans. Ben Webster took his place. I got ninety dollars a week when I joined, and I made something on the side with small-band dates for Brunswick. They paid a hundred dollars a date. I picked the men—mostly from Henderson's band—and we made popular things like 'Red Sails in the Sunset' and 'If I Could Be Twins' and 'Boots and Saddle.' They sold very well in Europe. Fletcher always had money, even when he said he didn't. It seems he had these special pockets—a two-dollar pocket, a five-, a ten-. Because whenever you asked him for a slight advance he'd go to such-and-such a pocket and bring out just the amount. In 1934, things got bad. Henderson couldn't find work. The Mills Blue Rhythm Band, which was fronted by Lucky Millinder, was having trouble, too, but when Lucky sent for Higgy and Buster Bailey and me, we went. Irving Mills made the proposition for making me the leader of the Blue Rhythm Band, but I couldn't see cutting in on Lucky. I was satisfied to be what I was. Every band I'd been in I'd been featured. I got good money and didn't have the headaches. It's not so easy to relax when you're the leader. Imagine, you have fifteen or sixteen minds going you have to control. I joined Louis Armstrong's big band in 1937, which was like coming home again, because it was still the old Russell band, but expanded. Higgy came with me. Louis was very good to me. He gave me little solo parts here and there. In fact, it was just the other month Louis and Lucille Armstrong climbed these five flights to come and see me. They'd heard something had happened to me, but it was only rumor. We had a fine dinner together."

Mrs. Allen put a bowl of ice, Old-Fashioned glasses, and a bottle of Scotch on a table. "You hungry, Allen?" Mrs. Allen asked. "I got something coming up in a few minutes." She leaned into the next room, where Juretta and Alcornette were. "Now hurry up and change those clothes," she said. "And, Alcornette, when you finish, set up that card table in the front room."

"I eat around two o'clock in the evening and after work," Allen said. He poured a little water in his glass and took a sip and coughed. "Even though I got to be a leader, the forties were all right for me. John Hammond arranged for me to see Barney Josephson, the owner of Café Society Downtown. We weren't doing all that much work with Louis, so I formed my own group in 1940, with Higgy and Edmond Hall. We were at Cafe Society a year with people like Pete Johnson and Billie Holiday and Art Tatum and Hazel Scott and Lena Horne, who was in the chorus at the Cotton Club in 1934, when I played there. I took the band to Boston from Café Society for a long gig at the Ken Club. Sidney Bechet played with us. Don Stovall replaced Edmond Hall, and Kenny Clarke came in on drums, and later Paul Barbarin. We had another long stay at the Down Beat Room in Chicago, where we worked with Billie again. She missed a lot of shows and so we'd use a girl named Ruth Jones, who was always hanging around waiting for the chance to sing. I'd announce her—burlesque style—as Dynamite Washington, which later became Dinah when she joined Lionel Hampton. I added Ben Webster to the band. Later, we worked in San Francisco, and in Salt Lake City and at the Onyx and Kelly's Stable on Fifty-second Street, and back to Chicago and to Boston. They were all long engagements. I went into the Metropole in 1954. I had Higgy and Buster Bailey and Cozy Cole, and I took Claude Hopkins out of deep freeze and put him on piano. It was a seven-year gig. The owners of the Metropole were very good to me. *They* didn't make us play loud. It was the people. We'd try a soft number or two, and they'd say, 'Now what's the matter with you, Red? You sick or something?' And we'd go up again. "

Juretta sidled into the room and handed Allen some schoolwork papers. He held them at arm's length, read through them slowly, and handed them back. He smiled, "That's just fine, darlin'. Lovely. You go and finish now." Alcornette brought in a card table, and Allen heaved himself to his feet and helped her set it up. Then he walked around the room, peered through the venetian blind, and went back to his chair.

Mrs. Allen called from the kitchen, "Alcornette, put on that white tablecloth that's in the chest in your room! And set some plates and glasses and napkins, please!"

"You got some peppers, Pearlie May?" Allen called.

"I got them right here, Allen," she replied.

"The most influence Louis Armstrong had on me was on the records he made in the twenties—the 'Savoy Blues,' 'Cornet Chop Suey.' We used to learn those numbers from the recordings in New Orleans. And I'd hear Whiteman recordings that Mr. Streckfus brought back from New York with him. I also listened to people in New Orleans like Buddy Petit and Chris Kelly, who never recorded. And to Kid Rena and Punch Miller. Rena was the first trumpeter I ever heard play high. Those things worked together to make my style, and the rest was me. When you play, so many things work together. You have your brain. You have your fingers. You have your breathing. You have your embouchure. Playing, it's like somebody making your lip speak, making it say things he thinks. I concentrate a couple of bars ahead at all times. You have to have an idea of where you are going. You have more expression of feeling in the blues. And you have more time. The blues is a slow story. The feeling of the beautiful things that happen to you is in the blues. They come out in the horn. You play blues, it's a home language, like two friends talking. It's the language everybody understands. You can inject into people with the instrument, I think. I've had nights when it was better than others, but I've been a little fortunate in my loving to play so much."

Mrs. Allen brought in a platter of fried chicken and a dish of boiled cabbage. She put a jar of pickled hot peppers between them. Allen grunted, pulled his chair up to the table, and helped himself. "Bring some of that

Rheingold, please, Pearlie. We call these hot peppers birds' eyes. My aunt just sent them from New Orleans. It's what they make Tabasco Sauce from. People live on hot peppers and mustard and garlic in New Orleans."

"You eat them with every meal, you get used to them," Mrs. Allen said. She was standing arms akimbo. Juretta stood beside her, staring at the chicken. "All right, a *small* piece," Mrs Allen said. "Otherwise, you'll ruin your supper. And don't chew all over the carpet."

"I visit my mother and my aunt in New Orleans every year," Allen said. "My mother is eighty-two and spry. She still lives in the house where I was born, at 414 Newton Street, in Algiers, which is to New Orleans what the Bronx is to New York. My father passed in 1952. He was seventy-five. He was born in Lockport, Louisiana. Everyone was in his brass band at one time or another—Punch Miller, Papa Celestin, King Oliver, Louis Armstrong, Sidney Bechet. My father played trumpet. His brother Samuel was a bass player, and a younger brother, George, played drums. The band generally had two trombones, three trumpets, a bass horn and a baritone horn, a peck horn, a clarinet, and two drummers. The trombones marched in front, so they wouldn't hit anybody in the back. The bass and the baritone came next, then the clarinet and the peck horn, the trumpets, and then the drummers—bass drum to the left and snare drum to the right. The bass drummer played his drum and a cymbal attached to it, and the other drummer played snares. The two of them got a sound like a regular set of drums. The horn players needed strong embouchures. The roads were rough, and if you stepped into a hole you had to hold on to that horn to not break your notes. Maybe that was the reason King Oliver never marched with the band but always next to it, on the sidewalk, where it was smoother. There were generally parades on Sundays, and of course when there was a decease and for special occasions, like housebuildings and the regular outings of the social clubs. I don't know how many social clubs there were—the Money Wasters, the Square Deals, the Bulls, the West Side Friends of Honor. You paid dues and when you passed, your club paid for a band and for putting you away. The big men belonged to four or five clubs and they'd have four or five bands. My father had six when he passed. If you wasn't a member of any club, they put a saucer on your chest while you lay in the front room, and pretty soon there'd be enough for the proper arrangements. Each club had its own colors and its own banner. In parades, the two men who carried the banner got twenty-five cents apiece, and the man who carried the American flag got fifty cents. And each club had its own button—black on one side and its colors on the other. You'd wear the colors for regular parades and the black for funerals. The men who played in the bands were stonemasons or slaters or plasterers and such, and their jobs would let them off for a funeral. These funerals went according to the Bible—sadness at birth and rejoicing at death. If the deceased belonged to several clubs, he'd generally stay on view in the front room for three or four days to give all his brothers time to pay their respects. If you were very sacred, you'd stay with the deceased some while, then you'd go through to the kitchen, where they'd have a bousin [pronounced "boozeanne"], which is a Creole term for a party. There would be gumbo and ham salad and burgundy and sangaree, a kind of punch." Allen helped himself to another piece of chicken and more cabbage.

"On funeral days, the club and the band assembled at the deceased's house and then they'd march to the church," he said. "The band played very slow, very slow. The snare was taken off the snare drum, giving a kettle effect. When the deceased went by, everyone in the street would stop talking and moving and take off their hats and put them over their hearts, and then go back to what they were doing. While everyone was in the church, the musicians sometimes went to a saloon nearby, and it was my job when I was little to run from the church to the saloon when the service was over and get the musicians together. We'd march to the cemetery, and the band would stand in the road and wait until the moans and cries went up, which meant that the preacher was saying, 'Ashes to ashes, dust to dust' and throwing the dirt on the coffin. Then the drums rolled like thunder and the band would break into a fast 'Oh, Didn't He Ramble' and march back. On a wide avenue, when there was more than one band, the first band would split in half, one half lining up on one side of the avenue and the other on the other side, and the band right behind would march between these lines. The bands would be playing different tunes. Then the second band would split open and the first one would form up again and march through *them*. You could tell by the applause of the onlookers who was best, and the winner would go a roundabout way to the house of the deceased and play there up on the gallery, really swinging, for ten or fifteen minutes, and then go inside and enjoy the bousin. Pearlie May, let me have one more beer!" After shouting to the kitchen, Allen pushed himself back from the table and took a bite of a red pepper the size of his finger.

"Of course, we played at dances, too," he said. "The men in the band would get three dollars apiece and the leader four, and there was a dollar allowed for phone calls and such. And there were building parties. When a man decided to build himself a house, it was like pioneering days. The members of his club and his neighbors would all gather on a weekend on his plot—wives and children, too. The men would put down the foundation and get the frame up. There would be a few kegs of beer or some home brew—Sweet Lucy or Son Kick Your Mammy—and a band to play. They'd build and eat and build and drink and build and laugh and have a fine bousin. The man whose house was being put up would turn around the next time a house had to be built and help with that. At Mardi Gras, musicians got scarce in New Orleans, and a week or so before, my father would hitch up a sulky and travel maybe a hundred miles into the country to round up musicians he'd heard or heard about. He took me when I got big enough. The roads were poor, and we never went too fast for fear the horse's legs might get stoved up or swollen. We'd stop and visit every few miles and spend the night with relatives or friends."

Mrs. Allen cleared the table and brought more beer. Then she went to the window and looked out, her hands clasped behind her. The room was darker and Allen switched on a lamp.

"I started on the violin. My mother preferred it because most of the boys who took up the trumpet got balls in their cheeks and necks from all that blowing. But I'd practice on my father's trumpet, and he'd keep telling me to tell my mother it would be all right, I wouldn't get those balls in my cheeks, and finally she said yes. From the age of eight I played the upright alto—the peck horn—in my father's band. He'd carry me in parades some of the way and then put me down on a corner and I'd play and a little crowd would gather and he'd tell everybody 'Sonny's got it, Sonny's got it.' My first teacher on trumpet was Manuel Manetta, but my father taught me to read. I did pretty nice in school. I had to—my father signed the report cards. He was a serious man, a strict man. I had to obey the New Orleans curfew, which was nine o'clock. It was sounded by a calliope on one of the riverboats. Come nine every evening, you'd see nothing in the streets but children running, this way, that way, like mice. I also indulged in track in high school, and I set up a few records in the cross-country. My father was never rich, but he tried to give me everything I'd think of. At one time, I even had a couple of horses—a pacer, which puts down two feet at a time, and a racker, which puts down one foot at a time. We were building a neighbor's house once, and I was sent over the canal into the woods to drag back a cross-stile, which was made of six-by-twelve beams, and when my horse got on the bridge over the canal he balked. He wouldn't move. I blew a whistle and rang this bell I had, and all of a sudden that horse moved. He moved right into the canal, cross-stile and all, everything mired down in mud. Sometimes I'd go to auctions where they were selling horses and watch the pep man. He stood kind of backstage, and before the horse—it was usually an old nag— came out of the chute to where the people was, the pep man would take a rag soaked in turpentine and whap the horse right across his rump end and that horse would come shooting out of the chute, head up, prancing and looking like a colt, and then, after somebody had bid and bought, he'd sag and his head would go down and he'd look like the used-up horse he was. Some afternoons after school, when my father was still at work, I'd take my horse and ride over to the pool-room—Louis Kohlman's poolroom—and tie him up outside. The horse got so used to the route that once when my father asked me to ride him over to the ferry to New Orleans, the horse got to the corner near the poolroom, and instead of going straight to the ferry he turned the corner, with me pulling and straining at him, and headed right for the poolroom and stopped dead in front of it. My father looked at me and I didn't say anything. He said, 'Sonny, I thought you didn't hang around here.' Then he smiled, and I knew I was off the hook. My father wanted me to be a musician and nothing else, so I was already working in brass bands and in cabarets when I was in my teens. You weren't allowed to wear long pants until you were eighteen; just short pants—knickers they were. Leonard Bocage would bring me home at night, or my father would come and get me. He got so set in the habit that when I visited him not long before he passed and went out somewhere and didn't get home until three or four in the morning, I found him in the front room waiting up for me—and me not a junior anymore but a grown man."

Mrs. Allen was sitting in a chair, her head resting on one hand, watching Allen. "You used to try and get him to stop playing when he got old, Allen."

Allen smiled. "That's right, but you said I was wrong. 'Let him play,' you said. 'It's good for him. He'd suffer without it.' He played right up to the end."

"My father died when I was but fourteen," Mrs. Allen said, "and my mother when I was two. I was born a Creole—the last of three children. My father was a slater. New Orleans was famous for its slate steeples, and most of the roofs were slate, too. I went to public schools and then to New Orleans University. My parents were gone, but I had thirteen people on each side of the family, and they contributed to put me through. I took a general course, and then I went to Guillaume College for a business course for two years, and then went to work teaching in Utica, Mississippi, for a year. I was working for an insurance company in New Orleans when I met Allen. He was playing at the Pelican, a ballroom, and I sold tickets there at night. We were married in New York in 1930, and my son Henry—he's our only child—was born in 1931."

"He's been with the New York police for eight or nine years," Allen said. "Before that, he was an M.P. in the Marines in Korea. He plays trumpet, too, and he's good. Pearlie May and I have never been apart much. If I was on the road more than a week, she'd come and stay. If I was away and had a couple of days off, I'd come home for a quick visit. We're rare ones. Most of the others have been divorced and married three or four times. Pearlie May knows how to carry things on. She's very good brainwise. All my flexible brains are musicwise. She pays the bills and does the taxes. I get the loot."

"If I can close myself up in my room, really get my brain to it, the taxes don't take too long," she said.

"We have relations in Chicago and Michigan and New Orleans, and we have a tremendous phone bill," Allen said.

"A letter's something you keep putting off," Mrs. Allen said. "'I'm gonna write, I'm gonna write, I'm gonna write, and then you never do."

"If you do, then you call up the person on the phone and say, 'Oh, here's something I forgot to say in my letter.'"

"We have plans to move out of this neighborhood someday. We've been in this apartment since 1940. Before that, we lived at St. Nicholas Place, around a Hundred and Forty-eighth Street."

"One day, my boy got tagged up there with a brick," Allen said. "Kids in the street called him out and then dropped a brick on his head from the roof. We lived on the ground and we were robbed a couple of times."

"That's why we live on the fifth floor. I like it here. I know everyone in the neighborhood and they know me. People'll carry your groceries up for you and things like that. Allen can leave his car unlocked, and if he's parked on the wrong side of the street someone calls up and tells him he better move, the policeman's coming."

"I love to play; that horn is good for me. So when I pass is when I'll retire. When I'm not working, I sit in front of the television when there is a decent musical show and play along with it. Or I go and sit in at Jimmy Ryan's. A couple of weeks ago, I played with Tony Scott at the Dom on St. Marks Place. I think those young cats were a little surprised."

"When Allen's on television, the children and I watch. Even that dog sits and watches, turning his head from side to side. When he finishes, we applaud."

"Jobs are scarce now," Allen said. "But this isn't the first time."

"In 1934, Allen told me, 'Let's pull in the belts and tighten up a little.' " Mrs. Allen laughed, showing perfect teeth. "You get a few nickels together in the good times and you survive the bad ones."

"Nineteen-thirty-four was with Fletcher," Allen said. "We'd been booked to go to Europe and before that we were supposed to go into Connie's Inn. We never made either scene. In fact, I didn't get to Europe until 1959." He took a sip of his beer. "They ask me what I've done, I don't have any regrets. Pearlie May is happy. She has her grands. I've raised my family, even if I don't have a mansion. If I was anyway fixed financially, I would still want to play the music on my way out, all the way. The only thing gets to me once in a while is the dropouts, the guys that are gone. Just yesterday I was listening to a record I made with Lionel Hampton in 1939—'Haven't Named It Yet.' It shook me some when I looked at the label. Sid Catlett gone, Artie Bernstein gone, Charlie Christian gone, Earl Bostic gone, Clyde Hart gone. Just Higgy and Hampton and me left. But I guess we carry on for them. Least, that's the way I like to look at it."

New York Drummers

For a long time, drummers held jazz together. They kept the beat, colored and shaded ensembles, lifted soloists, added timbres and textures, hypnotized audiences, and determined the very sound and character of a band. Drummers reigned during the twenties and thirties and forties and into the fifties, when their function began slowly and subtly to change. Instead of keeping time—in much of the avant-garde, there is no longer any time to keep—they now assemble a surrealistic flow of cymbal, snare-drum, and tom-tom sounds, and they are frequently noted for their "melodic" attacks. The drummer's position has been seized by the bassist, who, armed with electricity and with guitar and sitar techniques, has become the rhythmic governor. In their great days, drummers congregated in New York, where they could sit in and show their wares, and where they could engage in "cutting" contests with other drummers. Some of those New York drummers are almost unknown, and some are world famous. Some spent decades in New York, and some only short periods: Tony Sbarbaro, Kaiser Marshall, Freddie Moore, George Stafford, Old Man Brooks, Tommy Benford, Baby Dodds, Zutty Singleton, Bill Beason, Sonny Greer, Keg Purnell, Slick Jones, Art Trappier, Cuba Austin, Manzie Johnson, Chick Webb, Walter Johnson, Arthur Herbert, Alphonse Steele, Ben Pollack, Sam Weiss, Joe Grauso, Chauncey Morehouse, Stan King, Vic Berton, Razz Mitchell, Alvin Burroughs, Yank Porter, Harry Dial, Cozy Cole, Paul Barbarin, Sid Catlett, Gene Krupa, Dave Tough, Jo Jones, Lionel Hampton, O'Neil Spencer, Jimmy Crawford, Cliff Leeman, Moe Purtill, Danny Alvin, George Wettling, Ray Bauduc, Ray McKinley, Nick Fatool, Buddy Rich, Louis Bellson, Lee Young, Specs Powell, Shelly Manne, J. C. Heard, Eddie Dougherty, Gus Johnson, Panama Francis, Kansas Fields, Jack the Bear Parker, Morey Feld, Kenny Clarke, Art Blakey, Denzil Best, Max Roach, Hal West, Osie Johnson, Shadow Wilson, Tiny Kahn, Roy Haynes, Art Taylor, Specs Wright, Philly Joe Jones, Sam Woodyard, Joe Morello, Charlie Persip, Ed Thigpen, Sonny Igoe, Mousie Alexander, Don Lamond, Ed Shaughnessy, Connie Kay, Jimmy Madison, Mel Lewis, Jake Hanna, and Elvin Jones.

Jazz drumming grew out of military drumming. The pioneer jazz drummers picked up syncopation from ragtime and translated it into afterbeats and offbeats and press rolls, most of them carried out on the snare drum and tomtoms. By the thirties, the center of jazz drumming had shifted to the cymbals and the snare-drum rims, although the snare and tomtoms were still heavily used in solos. The bebop drummers moved the center again. They transferred timekeeping from the bass drum to a "ride" cymbal, using the bass drum only for offbeats, or "bombs." In the twenties, drum sets, or traps (which were invented when drummers began to play sitting down), consisted of a tall, fat bass drum, often decorated with a painting of a bucolic scene and lit from within by an electric bulb, which also kept dampness at bay; a wooden-sided snare drum that resembled a parade drum; an Indian tomtom, its skins fastened on with brass studs; and a cymbal attached upside down to the wooden top of the bass drum. By the late twenties, the snare drum had become sensitive enough to be used with wire brushes—sprays of steel wire fastened to metal or wooden handles. There were several tomtoms and several cymbals, which were hung over the bass drum on goose-necked or straight rods. Two more cymbals, called a high-hat, appeared at the drummer's left elbow on a three-foot metal stand, and were opened and closed by a foot pedal to produce a marvellous variety of whispers, shushes, splashes, and whaps. Drummers had begun to pay attention to the sound of their instrument; they tuned their snare drums and tomtoms and bass drums, and they spent long reverberating hours selecting their cymbals at the Zildjian factory, in Quincy, Massachusetts. The bebop drummers did disturbing things to the drum set in the forties. Their snare drums grew thinner and thinner, and emitted a high nervous chatter; the bass drums shrank, and their sound grew sharp and elbowy; and the cymbals became larger and larger, and gave out a heavy, high hum. The drum sets now used by many rock and "fusion" drummers are works of fantasy. The drums, which are frequently made of translucent plastic, seem to multiply before one's eyes, and may include a couple of bass drums and snare drums, and at least four tomtoms. A dozen giant, steeply canted cymbals form a reflecting shield around this assemblage, which is lit from below, so that it produces an aurora-borealis effect, with the drummer at its brilliant, frenzied center.

The older drummers have not vanished. Many are constantly busy, among them Buddy Rich and Freddie Moore and Art Blakey and Shelly Manne and Tommy Benford and Lionel Hampton and Roy Haynes and Sonny Greer. Three of them—by virtue of their tenure, their distinguished style, and their undiminished skill— should be celebrated. All three are in their seventies. They are Benford, Moore, and Greer.

Tommy Benford was born in Charleston, West Virginia, on what he likes to call "the nineteenth day of the fourth month of oh-five." He is short, neat, and forthright, and has a gruff voice, flat gray hair, and a square bespectacled face. There is a metallic cast to him; if he were struck with one of his mallets, he would ring. He has never been famous, but he was one of the first modern drummers. He taught Chick Webb when Webb arrived in New York, in 1924, at the age of sixteen, and he and Sid Catlett traded inventions in the early thirties. Catlett went on to become the supreme jazz drummer, and Benford became his indefatigable image. His accompanying recalls Catlett's. He uses similar cymbal and bass-drum breaks, and some of the same intricate snare-drum figures—holding one stick on the drumhead and hitting it with the other, then letting the stationary stick bounce once on the head, to produce a quick, echoing eighth note. His rare solos are short, and are an even mixture of rolls and rimshots and cymbals. His wire-brush work is tricky and adroit. Benford sits very straight when he plays, and his time is prim and exact. Benford's memory hovers around him, and when he needs an address or a name from fifty or more years ago it is handed to him forthwith. He talks easily, and he often surrounds his sentences with buffering silences, which give his speech a beneficent, upholstered air. He is a proud man, and he walks with his head slightly raised and his arms stiff as drumsticks at his sides. This is what he said:

"I went to Europe the first time in 1932 with Sy Devereaux, who had a seven-piece band. We opened at the Chez Florence, in Paris, and—oh, my God!—Europe was really Europe then. We couldn't do wrong. The pianos were *always* in tune and everything was always clean, and every club, no matter how small, had a room for the musicians to go to between sets—not like it is here, where you have to walk up and down the sidewalk when you're not playing. I worked with Freddie Taylor, who had his own club, the Chez Harlem, and then with Eddie South, who was billed as the 'dark angel' of the violin. I worked in Holland a lot, and at the Paris Exposition in 1937. I recorded with Coleman Hawkins—a prince!—and with Django Reinhardt and Stéphane Grappelli. And I got married for the first time. My wife was Sophia Mezzero, and she was a dancer and singer and pianist from Vienna. She died in Paris, in 1939, giving birth to my oldest son, Tommy. I was married again, in 1952, to Dorothy Morgan, and we had three children—Lisa, Cynthia, and Charles. He was killed in the South Bronx when he was twenty, and for three days we didn't know he was dead. After Charles' death, we moved from the Bronx out to Mount Vernon. We live in a two-family house. Anyway, I was with Willie Lewis when the war broke out in Europe in 1939, and we made our way to Switzerland and into Spain and then Portugal, working all the time. I took Tommy, who was twenty-one months, to a bullfight in Madrid, and when the matador killed the bull Tommy applauded with everyone and sat down and then stood by himself and applauded again and the whole audience stood with him and clapped, too. We came back on the Exeter in October of 1941, and a German bomber flew right over us and everybody fell down on their knees and prayed. I moved in with one of my sisters in New York. I'd been away nine and a half years.

"I had come to New York in 1920. My first job was at a dance hall, the Garden of Joy, which was built on 'the rock,' at Seventh Avenue and a Hundred and Thirty-ninth Street. A saxophonist, name of Bob Fuller, had the band, and we followed Mamie Smith and Her Jazz Hounds. Coleman Hawkins was still with the Jazz Hounds, and that's when I met him. Harlem was full of piano players—Willie Gant and James P. Johnson and Willie the Lion Smith and Luckey Roberts and Fats Waller. The best of them was Fats. He played so clear and clean I never heard him hit a bad note. Then I went into a dime-a-dance place, the Rose Danceland, on a Hundred and Twenty-fifth Street. I believe Freddie Moore played there later. I shifted over to Marie Lucas at Goldgraben's, at a Hundred and Thirty-third and Lenox Avenue. She was Will Marion Cook's niece, and she played piano and trombone, and arranged and conducted. We jumped out of New York with her and into Washington, D.C. We had seven pieces and she added three, and one of them was Juan Tizol, who was with Duke Ellington later. After a couple of months, we went to the Smile-a-While Inn in Asbury Park and then to the Tent in Atlantic City. Jean Goldkette used to come in and conduct the band. Those were summer jobs, and in the fall we were hired into the Everglades Club, at Forty-eighth and Broadway. Ethel Waters was there, and Adelaide Hall, who lives in England, was her understudy. Edith Wilson sang, too, and—what!—she's still beautiful and can sing. Red Fletcher took over the band, and we went on the road to places like Binghamton and ended at the Metropolitan Burlesque, on Fourteenth Street. I jumped back to Marie Lucas—this was about 1925 or 1926—at the Hoofer's Club, which was under the Lafayette Theatre, at Seventh Avenue between a Hundred and Thirty-first and a Hundred and Thirty-second. Willie the Lion Smith came over from Newark, and he replaced Marie Lucas. He was a know-it-all who'd give people who didn't know him a fit. Chick Webb was in New York, and his uncle, George Young, had introduced us and asked me would I mind teaching him what I could. I let him sit in at the Hoofer's Club, and it used to drive Willie the Lion crazy, because Chick still didn't have it together. The best drummers in New York then were Walter Johnson and Kaiser Marshall and George Stafford and Old Man Brooks, who was in the pit band at the Lafeyette. Sid Catlett came in 1930, and he was my main man. We used to swap ideas, and if he got two jobs he'd give me one, and I'd do the same. When we walked down the street together, I'd say to him, 'Sid, you're too big. I don't want anyone to see me lookin' so short next to you, so I'm going to walk in front.' Later, we used to get on him all the time because he never went to bed. We'd say, 'Why don't you go home and get a good night's rest?' He was a terrific gambler, and he'd say, 'Oh, man, I feel like I can make some money tonight,' and he'd play cards into the next day and then go to work. He just wore himself out is what killed him.

"I joined Charles Skeete at the Strand Ballroom, a dime-a-dance in Brooklyn. I was there two or three years, then I jumped to my brother Bill's band at a place on a Hundred and Twenty-fifth. Jelly Roll Morton started coming in, and he'd ask my brother if he could sit in and sing. He took a liking to us and he'd bring his music and we'd run it down right there. We had heard of him, but we didn't know how good he was until he asked us to record with him for RCA Victor. I guess we made about a dozen records between 1928 and 1930—titles like 'Fussy Mabel' and 'Pontchartrain' and 'Boogaboo' and 'Mournful Serenade' and 'Little Lawrence.' Jelly Roll had brought Omer Simeon from Chicago, and he was on some of them. So was Geechy Fields, and Ward Pinkett, and Bubber Miley, who was with Duke Ellington. Ellington couldn't stand Morton's music, but Claude Hopkins couldn't stand Ellington's, so it equalled out. Jelly Roll still had that diamond in his front tooth. He bragged a lot, but I liked him. Anyway, we didn't have any trouble with him. His music sounded old-fashioned at first, but after a time you realized it was just a different kick. You play his music now, of course, it sounds beautiful. I worked a while for Wilbur de Paris during the fifties at Jimmy Ryan's. I wouldn't have done it but for his brother Sidney, who was a great trumpet player. People would give us tips and Wilbur would always take them. One night, I got twenty dollars and I waved it in front of him and then put it in my pocket so he could see me doing it, and he didn't say a word. He fired me, because he wanted Zutty Singleton, and when Zutty only lasted three months Wilbur told me he wanted me back, but I was finished working with him. Zutty was a press-roll drummer, and all that rolling would tire his wrists and the tempo would slip some.

"After my brother's band, I went into the Alhambra Theatre with Edgar Hayes, and then I started rehearsing with Eddie South. We opened Ben Marden's Riviera, across the George Washington Bridge—which was brand-new. Paul Whiteman played opposite us, and he had Jack Teagarden and George Wettling. Milt Hinton came in with us on bass, and Everett Barksdale on guitar. Bing Crosby and Martha Raye worked there, too. I'd seen her sit in up in Harlem, and she was a very good singer and a hell of a dancer—what! Fats Waller needed a drummer, so I went on the road with him. He'd buy us drinks, but he always told us first, 'You get drunk on the bandstand, that'll mean your job.' He had Hank Duncan on piano, because he liked to get up and direct the band and clown around, and sometimes the two of them would play duets. Fats would order two or three meals at one sitting in a restaurant, and drinks to match, but I never saw him stagger one day in my life.

"I started out an orphan. I was the youngest of two boys and two girls. I never knew my mother, and my father died when I was five. He was a carpenter, and he played tuba and drums, which is odd, because that's what my brother Bill and I play. My father was William and my mother was Ann, and I've been told she played organ. When I was a baby, I was taken to an aunt, Lillian Campbell, in Charleston, South Carolina. Her husband was a tailor. Bill and I went there, and our sisters went with our father's sister. I believe we stayed at my aunt's two or three years, and when I was five and my brother eight were put in the Jenkins Orphanage, in the same city. It was a big brick building at No. 20 Franklin Street. The Reverend Dr. Jenkins was a wonderful person, and we were treated very well. They had three different bands, with twenty-five or so members in each. I started on the alto and baritone horns and the trombone, but it wasn't long before I went over to the drums. The bands played blues and overtures and marches, and they travelled all over the country giving concerts. We went to England in 1913, and played for the king and queen.

When we got back, we were sent to rest at a farm upstate that the Reverend Jenkins had. Musically, they started you right at the bottom at the orphanage and worked you up through the rudiments until you knew your instrument backward and forward. Some first-rate musicians came out of the orphanage—my brother Bill, Gus Aiken, who played trumpet with Sidney Bechet, Cat Anderson, who was with Duke Ellington so long, and Jabbo Smith, who recorded with Ellington and had Chicago on its head in 1929 with his trumpet playing. People say he was the first Dizzy Gillespie, and they're right. When I was sixteen, I ran away from the orphanage. We knew about the money that musicians were making on the outside, and we wanted some. Bill and I ran away, and we got ourselves to Virginia, where we joined a minstrel show called Green River. Then we went with a doctor show, where the man sold patent medicines. We'd play two or three tunes, the man would talk about his medicines, and we'd play another selection while the people paid up. He had his own bus, and we travelled in that. The orphanage caught up with us in Georgia. We stayed two or three months, and ran away again. I got a job in a hotel in Charleston as a bellhop, and we joined a circus and stayed six months, until it reached Cincinnati. We played in the band. Bill went to New York, and I got a job in the pit band at the Lincoln Theatre. The blues singers all came through, and one of them was Jackie Mabley, who became Moms Mabley. I stayed three or four months, then went on to Chicago for a couple of years. I was in a band at the Columbia Tavern, at Thirty-first and State, led by a violinist named Brownie. Happy Caldwell, the tenor saxophonist, was in that band. We heard King Oliver's Creole Jazz Band, and it was beautiful. It was a loud band, and Johnny Dodds was the main soloist. Those New Orleans musicians played a lot of slow blues and medium tunes, and when they went to New York they were amazed because New York musicians played so fast. The New Orleans drummers used press rolls all the time, and sometimes they sounded like they were just going to slow down and stop. I heard Freddie Keppard, and I didn't care for him too much, but Sammy Stewart, who brought Sid Catlett to New York, had a very good band. And Earl Hines was knocking everybody out. Then I jumped out of Chicago with a show that played Indianapolis and Pittsburgh and ended in New York, where I moved in with my brother and his wife. I already knew it didn't matter where I was. When I'm behind my drums, I'm home."

Freddie Moore looks like Erich von Stroheim. He is bald and short, and has powerful brown eyes. His skin is tight and smooth, and he has an invincible voice. Many of the older drummers grew up in vaudeville, and they come in two parts—the showman and the musician. Like Benford, Moore learned much of what he knows as a minstrel-band drummer around the time of the First World War. There were no microphones, and the performers worked more in shadow than in light. Exaggeration got their acts across: singers were loud, comedians were hammy, and musicians were exhibitionistic. Moore still uses the showoff stuff he picked up sixty years ago. He pops his eye on the final beat of a tune, and makes them roll when he sings, which he does in a hopsack, over-the-mountain voice. Before his vocal on "Ugly Chile," he puts on a horrendous orange wig and dark glasses with white frames, and on "Tiger Rag," in the strain where the trombone makes tiger-roar noises, he turns his snare drum over and blows like a demon on the wire snares, producing a wild wind-tunnel sound. He also takes a drum solo in which he uses five sticks. He begins with a stick held pirate fashion in his teeth, one under each arm, and one in each hand. As he plays, he rapidly revolves them—the stick in his mouth moves under his right arm, the one under his right arm goes into his right hand, the one in his right hand is switched to his left, the one in his left goes under his left arm, and the one under his left arm is clamped in his teeth—without losing a beat. All the while, he flashes his eyes and shakes his lips, and the whole is phantasmagoric. ("When you get tired of drummin'," he says, "you start clownin'.") Moore is also a solid, driving drummer of a kind almost gone. He favors press rolls and a single, heavy cymbal beat, and his rimshots splinter and crack. There is no subtlety in his playing, nor is there any hesitation or confusion. You could build a house on his beat. He lives in a development in the Bronx with his wife, Lucille, whom he married in 1941. He is a serious, steadfast talker, and his rare smiles are startling. After he had set up his drums for a gig at One Fifth Avenue one Friday, he talked:

"Fred Moore was born August 20, 1900, in Little Washington, North Carolina. I had three sisters and three brothers, and I was the baby. I don't know much about my father outside of his name, Giles Moore, because he died when I was nine weeks old. My mother was Hattie Moore. She was short, and part Cherokee. When I was little, she moved us all to New Bern, North Carolina, which was about forty miles south. Later, I got my limp by trying to snag a caboose to go visit Little Washington and getting my foot caught between the ties and tearing my knee. I did about four years in school. As long as I can remember, I wanted to be a drummer. There was a place called the Frog Pond, where they had dances and a piano player and a drummer. The piano player's name was Hootie Green, and he played stride and boogie-woogie. I don't recall the drummer's name, but I paid him a dime when I had the money to let me sit in on his drums, and I'd get up there and hit anything and not make any sense at all. I practiced on boxes and chairs and table legs around the house, but my mother didn't care for that, so when I was fourteen I ran away. I went with the A. G. Allen minstrel show. It travelled by train, and they kept the tent for the show in the parson's belly under a car. The show had an eight-piece band, and an old-time comedian who blacked his face and put white on his lips, a soubrette, and six chorus girls. We ate beef stew and potatoes, collard greens, ribs, neck bones, and beans and rice. When we got to a new town and they were unpacking and setting up the tent, the band would get into its clothes, which were long red coats, fezzes, and dickeys with wing collars. The band would march around the town to announce the show, and sometimes it would cover three or four miles. I was called 'the walking gent.' I'd walk right alongside the drummer, watching him, and when the march was finished and the band all in a sweat it was my job to spread their coats out on bushes and on the grass so they'd be dry for the first show. During the shows, I'd sit and watch the drummer, and that way I learned. When I'd been with the show three months, the drummer took sick and they asked me could I play. I didn't know if I could or not, but I was young and wil', young and fly, so I played the show. I'd been getting three dollars a week, and by the time I quit the show, four months later, I was making twenty dollars.

"I got a job in Birmingham, Alabama, playing with an organist for the silent pictures. When new pictures came, I'd go down in the morning and rehearse, so that I'd know where the thunder and lightning was and the gunshots and the stampedes. I stayed in Birmingham about seven years, and besides the moving pictures I played for attractions who came through—Ida Cox, and Bessie Smith, who was shorter than you expected and not too fat, and Sara Martin, and Ma Rainey. Ma Rainey was some ugly. She had a diamond in a lower front tooth and a twenty-dollar gold piece hanging down her front and a ten-dollar gold piece on each ear. She sang songs you never heard other singers do, and I'd say she was between a blues singer and a folk singer. She used her hands a lot. Mamie Smith came through, too, and she had the trumpeter Johnny Dunn, who was the first I ever heard use the plunger mute. I left Birmingham with the William Benbow show, and we worked Macon, Georgia, and Havana, Cuba, and we ended up at the Savoy Theatre in Detroit, Michigan. It had six balconies and sat three thousand people. After a while, I put together my own seven-piece band—Buddy Moore and His Carolina Stompers. They had got to calling me Buddy with A. G. Allen, and I hadn't changed to my real name yet. We played what we called 'swing' music—not 'Dixieland,' which was a term we had never heard. In 1928, I came to New York. I had saved my money, and I had a few dollars. The first night, I spent about fifty dollars buying drinks, paying my way in. I heard Chick Webb at the Rose Danceland, and I'm telling you that shut me up a little. The next night, I heard Cozy Cole, who was a tame drummer, at the Primrose Dance Land, and a couple of nights later I heard Tommy Benford. He was smooth, and made the band feel good and happy. I worked at the Lafayette Theatre with Wilbur Sweatman, and then I went into the pit band of Eubie Blake's 'Shuffle Along,' at fifty-five dollars a week. I recorded with King Oliver in 1930, and went on the road with him in 1931. He was a sweet man. I think people wanted him to blow up a storm, but his gums were bad and he couldn't make those arrangements, and, maybe because of that, we didn't do so good. He was offered the chance to open at the Grand Terrace in Chicago, but he wanted too much money, and Earl Hines went in instead and stayed off and on for about ten years. We called Oliver Google-Eye behind his back, because one eye was almost shut from some accident. He didn't drink, but he'd sit down and eat a loaf of light bread and a whole fried chicken, and drink two quarts of milk and a pitcher of ice water with plenty of sugar in it.

"'When I saw that the tour wasn't going anywhere and Oliver had no notion of returning to New York right away, I left and came back and got me a little band at the Victoria Café, at a Hundred and Forty-first and Seventh Avenue. I had Pete Brown on alto saxophone and Don Frye on piano. All the white musicians from downtown—Tommy Dorsey and Gene Krupa and Jack Teagarden—would sit in after work, and they'd still be there at ten in the morning. Then we went into the One-Hundred-One Ranch Club, at a Hundred and Thirty-ninth and Lenox Avenue, and from there into the Brittwood club, where John Kirby took over the band. He brought along Buster Bailey and Chu Berry and Frankie Newton. It was too much of a clique, and I didn't want that. They didn't want me, either. Kirby fired me, and then he fired Pete Brown, and then Frye, and we ended up back at the Victoria. I was with Edgar Hayes a while, and I spent three or four years at the Circle Ballroom, at Fifty-eighth and Eighth. It was a taxi-dance place. Every time I hit the wood block, the customer would have to give the girl another ticket, and sometimes one ticket only lasted two choruses. I went into the Village Vanguard with Max Kaminsky and Art Hodes in 1939, and we stayed a few years. I played the Sunday-afternoon jam sessions at the old Jimmy Ryan's in the forties, and in the fifties I was house drummer at the Stuyvesant Casino, on Second Avenue. I also worked for a spell with Wilbur de Paris. I consider myself very fortunate. I've worked all my life. A lot of people have asked me to get my own band, but I don't want the headaches. Same time, I can't ever stop playing. If I did, I'd fall dead."

Sonny Greer is an elegant pipestem, with a narrow, handsome face and flat black hair. His eyes are lustrous, and his fingers are long and spidery. He was with Duke Ellington for almost thirty years, and sat godlike above and behind the band, surrounded by a huge, white, blazing set of drums. He played with vigor and snap. He switched his head from side to side to accent beats and, his trunk a post, windmilled his arms. His cymbals dipped and reflected his sudden smiles. His playing was homemade and unique, and he isn't sure himself where it came from. He used timpani and tomtoms a lot, filling cracks and cheering the soloists. He used deceptive, easy arrays of afterbeat rimshots that drove the band while remaining signals of cool. He flicked cowbells to launch a soloist, and he showered everyone with cymbals. He sparkled and exploded, but his taste never faltered. He and Ellington set the streamlined, dicty tone of the band; after Greer left, the band never fully recovered. Ellington didn't care for drum solos, but Greer takes a lot of two-bar breaks on "Jumpin' Punkins," and during a soundie (a three-minute film made to be shown on a jukebox equipped with a small screen) Greer takes a crackling, expert double-timing twelve-bar solo on "C Jam Blues" which matches his idol, Sid Catlett. Greer lives in a new building on Central Park West with his wife, Millicent, who was a Cotton Club dancer when he married her in the late twenties. They have one daughter, and a granddaughter who is a vice-president of a bank in Omaha. Greer's life has been distilled in his mind into a collection of tales that are elastic, embroidered, interchangeable. He likes to tell them in the same way he plays the drums—with poppings of his eyes and quick, geometric gestures. His voice is low and hoarse, his speech legato. He often sits at his dining-room table and talks, his back to a window, his face alternately smiling and straight. He remembers his own dictum "When you're getting ready to lie, don't smile." He talked one afternoon:

"I first met Duke Ellington and Toby Hardwicke on a corner in front of a restaurant near the Howard Theatre in Washington, D.C., and they asked me what New York was like, and I painted a beautiful picture for them. I liked Duke and Toby right away, and we were inseparable the next thirty years. I first took them to New York on March 10, 1921—Toby, Duke, Artie Whetsol, and Elmer Snowden—and when we got there the booker said he wanted names, so the job collapsed. I introduced them around—to James P. Johnson and Luckey Roberts and so forth—and if I didn't know somebody I introduced them anyway. New York amazed them—all the music you could desire, and much more. We got jobs playing house-rent parties—one dollar plus eats. We ran into Bricktop on Seventh Avenue. She was the chanteuse at Barron Wilkins', and she helped us out. We played a lot of pool. We survived. We ended up back in Washington, but when we returned to New York, in 1923, we went into the Kentucky Club, at Forty-ninth and Broadway, and we were there three or four years. It was a basement club, and if a revenue agent came around the doorman stepped on a foot buzzer and the place turned into a church. Johnny Hudgins, who did pantomime, was in the show, and so was the trumpeter Joe Smith, who made talking sounds on his horn with his hands. Fats Waller was in the show, along with singers and dancers. People like Texas Guinan and Polly Adler came in. Duke and I played a party for Polly Adler once. Fats would sit at a little piano in the middle of the floor, and I'd sing risky songs with him. When Leo Bernstein, who was one of the owners, got plastered, he'd ask me for 'My Buddy.' I'd sing a long version, and he'd start crying and tell me he wanted to give me the joint and everything else he had. We went from there into the Cotton Club, where Duke and the band began to be world famous.

"I made a deal back then with the Leedy drum people, in Elkhart, Indiana. In return for my posing for publicity shots and giving testimonials, they gave me a drum set that was the most beautiful in the world. Drummers would come up to me and say, 'Sonny, where did you get those drums? You must be rich, man,' and I'd nod. I had two timpani, chimes, three tomtoms, a bass drum, a snare—the initials S.G. painted on every drum—five or six cymbals, temple blocks, a cowbell, wood blocks, gongs of several sizes, and a vibraphone. The cymbals were from the Zildjian factory. I'd go out to Quincy when we were working in the Boston area, and one of the Zildjians would take me around. He'd tell me to choose cymbals with flat cups—that's the raised portion at the center —and instead of hitting a cymbal to show me how it sounded he'd pinch the edge with his fingers, and you could tell just by the ring. I learned how to keep my drums crisp, to tune them so they had an even, clear sound. I knew about showmanship, about how audiences eat it up—that it ain't what you do but how you do it. Things like hitting three rimshots and opening and closing one side of my jacket in time. I always strove for delicacy. I always tried to shade and make everything sound beautiful. It was my job to keep the band in level time, to keep slow tempos from going down and fast tempos from going up. Those things meant more to me than solos, which I rarely took.

"My parents taught me that way of caring. I was born December 13, 1902, in Long Branch, New Jersey, which is just this side of Asbury Park. My mother was a modiste. She copied original gowns for wealthy white people. She was tall and had a charming personality. My father was about the same height and he was a master electrician with the Pennsylvania Railroad, and his greatest ambition was for me to follow in his footsteps. There were four children—Saretta, who was the oldest, then me, and Madeline, and my brother Eddie. I was named after my father—William Alexander Greer, Jr. I was interested in the affection our parents showed us, but beyond that our life was an everyday occasion, except that we never went hungry a day. I always had an ambition to make an honest dollar, to make money and not have money make me, and that's the way it's been. When I was twelve, I'd take my homemade wagon and load up at the fish place after school for fifty cents—cod, blowfish, blues, bass. My customers would wait for me on corners, and some of those fish were so big you had to bake them. I also had a paper route, and I delivered groceries. My first love was playing pool, ten cents a game. I practiced pool like other kids practice violin or piano. I'd practice two hours a day. I'd hide a pair of long pants, and after school put them on and go to the poolroom. I had a natural knack for it. Nobody in my family was musically inclined, including me, so my becoming a drummer was an accident—a hidden talent. We had Keith vaudeville in Long Branch, and when J. Rosamond Johnson brought his company through he had a drummer named Peggy Holland—Eugene Holland. He was tall and thin and immaculate—the picture of sartorial splendor. He could sing and dance and play, and he had great delicacy. He fascinated me. The company was in town two weeks, and every time he came into the poolroom I'd beat him. I told him I admired his playing, and he said, 'Kid, teach me to play pool like you play, and I'll do the same for you.' I bought him a box of cigars just to put an edge on it, and he gave me six or seven lessons, and some of the things he showed me I still use. I went to the Chattle High School, where they had a twenty-five piece band. Mme. Briskie was in charge of it. She also taught languages, at which I was very good. I didn't think the drummer was too hot, so I told Mme. Briskie, 'I can beat that guy playing.' I gave her a light taste, then I poured a march on her, and all the kids watching were prancing. I got the job. I could sing, too—like a mockingbird. We put together a small band, and it had six white boys, two white girl singers, and me, the Indian. Jersey was like Georgia then, it was so prejudiced, and I was learning how to look trouble in the face. Along with my other money-making enterprises, I was a first-class caddie, and for a year I'd been the personal caddie to one of the daughters of Krueger Beer. One day, she sliced a ball into a water hazard, and when I got there I laid the bag of clubs down and started into the water. Then I saw that a snake had that ball in his mouth, and I said, 'Oh, no.' She got mad and I quit and walked away and left her there, bag and all. Later that summer, our little band played a dance at the country club where she played golf, and she was sitting at ringside. She kept looking at me—she could hardly help it, because I was the sore thumb—and asking who I was. Finally, she asked me, 'Don't I know you? Didn't you used to caddie for me?' I told her, 'No'm. Not me. That was my twin brother.' She didn't find out the truth until I met her backstage years later at Carnegie Hall after an Ellington concert.

"I left high school the year before graduation, and that broke my parents' hearts. But my soul was set on the music. Sundays, I used to go up to New York for rehearsals at the Clef Club with Will Marion Cook, who had a lot of Lester Lanin-type bands. My mother asked me what we were rehearsing for, and I said, 'A trip to Russia.' She said, 'A trip to what? That's it! No more rehearsing!' When I was around nineteen, I played in the Plaza Hotel on the boardwalk at Asbury Park. Fats Waller was on piano and Shrimp Jones on violin. A string ensemble called the Conaway Brothers worked there, too, and I became friendly with them. They were from Washington, D.C., and they invited me down for three days, and I stayed several years. Marie Lucas had a band at the Howard Theatre, and one morning the manager came into the poolroom next door and said Marie Lucas needed a drummer, since hers had run off to Canada with the alimony agents after him. That was my first Washington engagement. The bootleggers had the habit of stacking money on a table for the entertainers who worked at the Dreamland Café, around the corner from the Howard. Soon I was doubling there with Claude Hopkins and Harry White from midnight until six in the morning, and after we collected our money from that table we had so much in our pockets it was a sin.

"Duke Ellington was like my brother, and I was like his. He was once-in-a-lifetime, and I wish I had a third of his personality. It overshadowed everybody else. He was sharp as a Gillette blade. His mother and father drilled that into him—Uncle Ed and Aunt Daisy, we used to call them. His father was a fine-looking man, and *polished*. Duke learned his way of talking from Uncle Ed. Fact, his father taught him everything he knew. Duke would never let a guy associated with the band down, no matter what hour of the day or night the trouble might be. He couldn't tolerate dissension in the band, or trouble from a new guy. He could sense right away when a guy wasn't right. But he never had a mean streak in his life. Duke was sort of a dreamer. Even when he'd play cards with us on the train, he'd have a song or a piece of music going through his head. That was his life. Every tick of the clock, somebody in the world is playing an Ellington tune.

"We first went to Europe in 1933—right from the Cotton Club. We went directly to London, where we played the Palladium. After, we did a party for Lord Beaverbrook—champagne and brandy in front of every one of us. I poured a glass of each to get my nerves together. Anna May Wong was a guest, and Jeannette MacDonald, and the future King George. He sat in on piano, and he and Duke played duets. Then I noticed this skinny little guy squatting near the drums and watching me, and pretty soon he asks can we play 'The Charleston.' We did, and he danced like crazy. Then he asked me could he sit in on drums, and I said, 'Of course, my man.' Somebody told me who he was: the Prince of Wales. I christened him the Whale, and it stuck. After I'd left the Duke, in the fifties, he came across the street from El Morocco to the Embers, where I was working, and I called him the Whale, and we sat and talked and told a few lies.

"By the early forties, the band was a bunch of admired stars, each with a different style. Johnny Hodges was very even-mannered. He was a thoroughbred. Whenever you'd wake Toby Hardwicke up, he was ready to go. But Ben Webster was the *king* of the playboys. We called him Frog, or the Brute, even though he was most congenial. Cootie Williams liked to gamble, but he didn't drink much. Lawrence Brown didn't drink, either, but he loved the ladies. Tricky Sam Nanton—he and Ben Webster and Toby were all in the same category: curiosity always got the better of them. Jimmy Blanton was a lovely boy, and he was crazy about his instrument. He'd stay up with us all night just to hear other people play. Ben was his umbrella and watched out for him. Ray Nance was a cocky kid and we called him the Captain. He was always ready when asked— 'Just a minute, I'll be right with you.' Barney Bigard was the best, and here is how he got his nickname—Creole. Once, when we were down South and in a bus on our way back to our Pullman car after a job, we stopped at a greasy spoon to get something to eat. Duke sent Bigard and Wellman Braud in, because they looked practically white. They were in there a long time before the door banged open and Barney came out shouting, 'I'm Creole! I'm Creole!' The owner of the place was right behind him, waving and shouting back, 'I don't care how old you are, you can't eat in here!' We travelled by Pullman before the war—one car to sleep and eat in, and one car for our instruments and baggage. That way, we didn't have to face the enmity of looking for a place to stay. No other band travelled as well or looked as well. If we did six shows a day in a theatre, we changed our clothes six times.

"I feel good, and I can still play. Lazy people retire. As long as you feel active, be active. Retired people lie under a tree and play checkers, and first thing you know they're gone. Last time I saw Duke in the hospital, he said, 'I want you to go out and play again, Nasty.' He called me that because I had always defended him against all comers through the years. I guess the Man isn't ready for me yet. The only regret I have is that my parents and my sisters never saw me play with the Duke Ellington band. My brother Eddie did, but somehow they didn't, and I'm still sorry about that."

Starting at the Top

Jabbo Smith was born in 1908, and he has been a legend half his life. Or, to put it another way, he was only in his mid-thirties when he began to slide into obscurity. At seventeen, he joined Charlie Johnson's excellent band, and within a year he had the New York brass establishment on its ear. Just short of nineteen, he recorded two spectacular takes of "Black and Tan Fantasy" with Duke Ellington and was asked by Ellington to join his band. Full of oats, Smith turned Ellington down. Four months later, he joined James P. Johnson and Fats Waller in the "Keep Shufflin' " band, and recorded four classic Victor sides with Johnson, Waller, and the reedman Garvin Bushell. The show closed in Chicago late in 1928, and Smith stayed put. He gave Louis Armstrong an ecstatic run for his money by recording nineteen small-band sides for the Brunswick label, which are still startling. His career, just five years old, began to slow down, and after a two-year stint with Claude Hopkins (1936–38) and a spell at the New York World's Fair (1939) he vanished. By the mid-forties, he had settled in Milwaukee, and by the mid-fifties he was out of music. His legend had formed. In 1953, the English *Jazz Journal* began a search for Smith. Two years later, the bassist Milt Hinton was quoted by Nat Hentoff and Nat Shapiro in their oral history "Hear Me Talkin' to Ya": "Jabbo was as good as Louis [in 1930]. He was the Dizzy Gillespie of that era. He played rapid-fire passages while Louis was melodic and beautiful . . . He could play soft and he could play fast but he never made it. He got hung up in Newark . . . He had delusions of grandeur and he'd always get mixed up with women . . . If he made enough for drinks and chicks in any small town like Des Moines or Milwaukee, that would suffice." A painter named Phil Stein heard Smith when we was hung up in Newark. "I was a member of the Newark Hot Club," Stein has said, "and we used to go into the black section all the time looking for rare recordings. We also went into the black bars that had music, and we went enough so that we became accepted. One night in 1941, we stopped at the Alcazar, and there

was a blues group, playing very easy. It had an interesting trumpet player, rather muffled and subdued, but it was so dark we couldn't tell who
it was. When we learned it was Jabbo Smith, we couldn't believe it. We
knew all his Brunswicks and his four Deccas. We spoke to him immediately, and discovered that he was kind of down and out. He was sickly
and his lip was bad, and he had a miserable room in a boarding house.
We visited him there, and he had all these pencil portraits of himself. He
said he wanted to be an artist. He seemed to me a very introverted person, very frail, a poetic kind of person. We were concerned with trying to
pull him up, so we organized a little concert for him to raise some money,
but it wasn't a success. He did go back with Claude Hopkins for a while,
and we went to see him in his apartment after he moved to Harlem, but
then the war came along, and the next I knew the *Jazz Journal* was looking for him."

In 1961, Roy Eldridge, Sammy Price, and Jo Jones had this conversation:

"I saw [Jabbo Smith] two years ago in Newark," Eldridge said to
Price. "And he was playing trombone, too!"
"Jabbo Smith?" Price exclaimed. "Why, he's dead, man! Here, I'll bet
you a hundred dollars."
"Dead? He lives in Milwaukee,"Jones said . . . "I've got his address
right in my book."
"Put up your money, " Price said to Eldridge.

In 1968, Gunther Schuller gave five admiring pages to Smith in "Early
Jazz," pointing out along the way that Smith was indeed living in
Milwaukee, where he worked for a car-rental company. Three years later,
the trumpeter made the first of several visits to Europe, and he was heard
by the Swedish clarinettist Orange Kellin, who urged him to move to
New Orleans, where Kellin said he could get him work. Smith eventually went. He played briefly at Preservation Hall, and then joined the band
in the musical "One Mo' Time."

Jazz categorists have long declared Jabbo Smith a second-rate Louis
Armstrong, which is like calling Scott Fitzgerald a second-rate
Hemingway. Armstrong was guided by rhythmic and melodic consider-
ations, but Smith was directed largely by technique. Armstrong was
lyrical and poetic: he tacked along in the sun behind the beat, and he created arching, supernal melodies. He was able to say beautifully everything he had in his mind. When he made occasional nonsense forays into
his highest register, it destroyed the serene balance of his style. Smith's
style was never completely balanced. He kept poking at his technical
boundaries, playing high notes and wild intervals and sixteenth-note
runs that had never been played before. This was particularly true after
he arrived in Chicago and challenged Armstrong, whom he had known
only from recordings. Before that, in New York, Smith's playing was sly
and sinuous and lyrical. There was little straining for effect, and the sur-

prises were quiet and steady. He preferred the silver forests around high C, and his high notes, almost all of them quick and glancing, gave his playing a subtle urgency. He played with smoothness and aplomb, and there are passages in "'Sippi" and "Thou Swell," recorded with Fats Waller, Garvin Bushell, and James P. Johnson, where he displays the dancing ease of Charlie Shavers. In Chicago, the shadow of Louis Armstrong seems to have unnerved him. He grew agitated on the Brunswick recordings, and his once creamy melodic lines jump and zigzag. He misses notes, and he blares. He goes after intervals and arpeggios that Armstrong couldn't have managed either. He shows off. The Brunswick records were designed to compete with Armstrong's successful Hot Fives and Hot Sevens. The instrumentation of trumpet, clarinet, piano, banjo, and bass is similar, and there are many passages where Smith sounds as if he were consciously imitating Armstrong. ("Croonin' the Blues" is a rough copy of "West End Blues.") But the New York Jabbo keeps breaking through, and is there on "Sweet and Low Blues," "Tanguay Blues," "Decatur St. Tutti," and "Boston Skuffle." His dynamics are superb (two muted choruses on "Tanguay Blues"), he is leaping and mercurial, he is full of sorrowing blue notes, and he delivers several scat-sung vocals that surpass Armstrong. There are many intimations: Roy Eldridge breaks; legato passages that suggest the Henry Allen of 1933; fast muted runs ("Sweet and Low Blues") that resemble Dizzy Gillespie.

Jabbo Smith is of medium height, and has the flat, rectangular look of thin older men. He is very dark, and this tends to minimize his features, which are strong—a square chin, high cheekbones, widely spaced eyes, and a broad forehead. His fingers are thick and strong. His speech rises and falls rapidly, and some of his sentences are opaque: the words move by without pause, and meaning goes under. He has a rapid, jouncing laugh. The cocksure twenty-year-old trumpet player who set out to dethrone Louis Armstrong is no longer visible, but now and then he peers out from behind the blinds. Smith talked one day:

"To me, all this is beautiful. My chops are getting better and better working every night, and within a month or so my playing should make pretty good sense. Of course, if I hadn't laid off twenty years I'd probably be burned out now. I've always had lip trouble. We were taught to use a lot of pressure when I started out—pressing the mouthpiece against your upper lip real hard—which cut off the circulation and made all kinds of problems. They don't teach that anymore, and that's probably why trumpet players can go so high now—high enough so you don't even know what notes they're playing. The ability to improvise has never left me. I keep the melody in my mind, and I don't think about the chords, which you're supposed to know anyway. You never have too much time to think, but things always come to you—little melodic things that sound good and add decoration. What I like to do is paint the melody. My aspiration is also to be a songwriter. I've written about two hundred songs, and I'm betting on those. The two songs I sing in 'One Mo' Time'—'Love' And 'Yes, Yes'—are mine.

"The show is supposed to be set in the twenties, and it's not that different from 'Keep Shufflin',' which I joined in 1928. James P. Johnson had the band, and Fats Waller was in it. Fats was a beautiful personality, just like he was on the stand. James P. was more calm. But they were night-and-day buddies. After the show closed, I became the house trumpeter at the Sunset Café, and, of course, I met Louis Armstrong. Louis was with Carroll Dickerson, and he was playing things like 'West End Blues.' I sat in with him, and I don't think anybody won. We played different styles. He was more melodic, and I played running horn, with a lot of notes. He and Zutty Singleton were fabulous people. We'd meet here and there, and one time Louis talked about him and me teaming up together, but nothing came of it. Early in January, 1929, I recorded with the banjo player Ikey Robinson, and Mayor Williams, who was booking the race talent for the Brunswick label, heard me and asked me to make some records under my own name. I used Ikey and Omer Simeon, who had worked with King Oliver and Jelly Roll Morton. I also had a piano and bass, and we did almost twenty sides that year, and they didn't go anywhere. They've been reissued, though, and people tell me they're doing a lot better now than when they first came out. I worked with everybody in Chicago—Erskine Tate and Dave Peyton and Charles Elgar, and with Tiny Parham and Jimmy Bell and Burns Campbell. I didn't meet Oliver until I was passing through Savannah in 1937, a year before he died. I was standing in the street talking to someone, and he came by. All I recall is that he was quiet and looked like an old man. Around 1930, I began moving back and forth between Milwaukee and Chicago, with side trips to Detroit. You get in a little trouble in Chicago, you run to Milwaukee; you get in a little trouble in Milwaukee, you run to Chicago. I had my own eight-piece band off and on for six years at the Wisconsin Roof in Milwaukee. I worked with Jesse Stone—Jesse Stone's Cyclones—and he had a lot of violins and people playing bottles with spoons. In 1936, I was at the Norwood Hotel in Detroit, and Pete Jacobs, the drummer, came running out of a restaurant shouting my name. He was with Claude Hopkins' big band, and they were inside eating and had seen me go by. Claude asked me to join him, and I did, in New York. It was a very good band. Jerry Blake was in it, and the trombonist Fred Norman and the singer Orlando Robeson. We spent a lot of time at the Roseland Ballroom, so we didn't have all that bouncing from town to town. But we made up for it when we did go on the road. We'd go from Waltham, Massachusetts, to Detroit to Chicago and back to Waltham in four days, and once, when we were booked into Charleston, West Virginia, Claude had a run-in with the gent who hired us. Claude was pretty haughty, and he said no to the man after he asked us to ride around in a truck playing and ballyhooing our performance. The man gave us fifteen minutes to get out of town. I left

Claude in St. Louis, and went back to New York and took a little band
into the Midway Inn at the World's Fair. Then I was at the Alcazar in
Newark, first with my own band, and later with Larry Ringold's. We
played for shows and dancing. I moved to Milwaukee for good in the forties, and worked on and off until the fifties, when I quit music and went
to work for Avis. I have a house, and I'm married to a girl from South
Dakota named Willie Mae, and I have two grown daughters in California.
I don't know why I missed the big time, except you get tied up with those
girls and things and you stay where you're most comfortable. Also, it
doesn't help to start at the top, which was where I was by the time I was
eighteen or nineteen.

"I was born the day before Christmas, in Pembroke, Georgia. I had a
cousin born the same time, and her mother named her Gladys. On
account of that, and since my mother was a schoolteacher and intellectual, she named me Cladys. Jabbo was hung on me later by a friend named
James Reddick. He had been given the name after an ugly Indian in a
William S. Hart movie, and he passed it on to me. My father was a barber, but I don't have any recollection of him. My mother took me to
Savannah when I was four, which was about when my memory started
working. My mother was a nice-looking person, about my height, with
an Indian cast to her face. She played the organ in church, and before she
was a teacher she worked cleaning Pullman cars. She couldn't take care
of me, too, and I was all over Savannah, which was why she decided to
put me in the Jenkins Orphanage, in Charleston, South Carolina. That
was in 1914. She took me up on a Pullman, because they rode her free,
and I cried for three months after I got there. The orphanage was famous
all over that part of the South. Mothers used it as a weapon: 'You watch
out, now, or I'll send you to Jenkins!' It had been started by the Reverend
D. J. Jenkins, and it had already turned out about three thousand kids.
Kids used to come to his house begging for food, and he found out they
were living in boxcars and suchlike, so he'd take them in, and the word
spread about his kindliness, and pretty soon he had quite a few children
on his hands. The city of Charleston gave him the old Marine Hospital,
and he started the orphanage. Eventually, the state gave him two hundred dollars a year to help out. He was a stately man with a beard, and
he looked seventy or eighty to me, but I don't think he could have been
that old. There were four hundred kids at Jenkin, and we did pretty well.
We had a two-hundred-and-ninety acre farm upstate,where we grew all
our food, and we'd get day-old bread that had been saved in barrels at
stores, and we'd get leftover fish down at the docks. We'd have molasses
and bread at supper. Jenkins was strict. At six o'clock in the morning,
there would be a prayer meeting, and after that the roll would be read,
and if you did anything bad the day before you'd be called up and tied
to a post and whipped with a rope or a piece of rein. To raise money for
the orphanage, the Reverend Jenkins organized bands of maybe twelve

kids each, eight to twelve in age, and we'd play on the street corners and pass the hat. We played on street corners all over Charleston, and we'd get sent to New York and Jacksonville and Savannah and suchlike to do the same. We also gave concerts at the churches in those places, at eight o'clock in the evening. On the street corners, it was every tub on its own bottom, every kid doing his own thing. All you needed to know was the melody, and then you'd take off from there. They've been saying all these years that jazz started in New Orleans, and all that, but what were we doing? Of course, when we performed in the churches it was overtures and marches. We stayed three months in New York once, and we went out and played on street corners all over New Jersey and Pennsylvania. We lived the whole time in two rooms in a rooming house at a Hundred and Thirty-third Street and Fifth Avenue, and the people that ran the place must have had a bellyful of us.

"At Jenkins, they started you in playing when you were about eight years old. The orphanage took children from the cradle, and the little ones stayed in the yard and were called yard boys. When the time came to learn an instrument, the teacher would come out in the yard and call, 'You! Come here! *You*! Come here!' They taught everybody in the same room. They started me on the trumpet, but I learned to manage all the brass instruments. And they taught you to read right off. Musicians were always amazed later that I could read anything at sight. The trumpet player Gus Aiken, who was older, had run away to New York and played there, and when he was brought back I picked up things from him, too. I started running away when I was fourteen, and I must have run away six or seven times. When they put you in the orphanage, they signed you up until you were twenty-one, so running away was the only method to get out earlier. The first time I took off was in Jacksonville. When we travelled to New York or Jacksonville, we went by boat, and this time, marching back to the boat in line double-breasted, like we marched everywhere, James Reddick and I took off around a corner. We stayed with a boy in Jacksonville we knew, and we lived on money we had knocked down. 'Knocking down' was keeping a little of what we collected in the hat when we played in the street. I was already a wild kid, and I got a job with Eagle Eye Shields' band. I was pretty good, and people thought maybe I was going to be somebody. Shields had twelve in the band, and it was the first large band I'd played in. When you ran away, Jenkins notified the police, and they caught us after three months. They called me the ringleader, and I got three days in a cell, but it wasn't long before I ran away again.

"When I was sixteen, I got in real trouble. Some of my buddies— Reddick and Timothy and Mike and two brothers we called Perry No. 1 and Perry No. 2—had gone over to South Carolina State College, in Orangeburg, and I wanted to play in their band. I hadn't been there long before I accidentally shot myself in the leg with a pistol I'd picked up— just fooling around, and not knowing there was still a bullet in the cham-

ber. They fixed me up and sent me back to the orphanage, and the
Reverend Jenkins took me up on the veranda and said he'd done all he
could for me—that they couldn't keep me any longer, because I was too
wild. He gave me nine dollars in an envelope to go to Savannah, where
my mother still lived. But I wanted to go North. I had run away to
Philadelphia before, and my older half sister lived there, so I got on a
train with my crutches and went to stay with her. I auditioned at the
Waltz Dream Ballroom for Harry Marsh's band, and I was with him three
months. Then I went to Atlantic City and ran into Gus Aiken, who was
with the Drake and Walker Show, and I joined them for a month. I went
back to Atlantic City, and met Charlie Johnson, and he said he wanted
me. It was 1925, and Charlie Johnson had the best band in New York. It
had Sidney de Paris, who was my idol. I liked the way he blew his horn
and the way he used mutes. I never acquired his style, but he influenced
me. Johnson also had Benny Carter and Edgar Sampson and Charlie Irvis
and the great drummer George Stafford. I had a pretty good notion of
myself and what I wanted to be paid, so I told Charlie I had to have a
hundred dollars a week, which was practically unheard of then. He
offered me sixty-five and tips, but I said no, so he said all right, a hundred, and he'd keep the tips. People threw a lot of money out on the floor
after a show, and when we played for Ethel Waters and suchlike they'd
come off with a bosomful of it. Charlie Johnson had a location band—
Smalls' Paradise in Harlem in the winter and a similar place in Atlantic
City in the summer. We had a lot of contests with visiting bands. We
always won. I was doing all right with Charlie, but this is how I left: Ed
Smalls, who owned the Paradise, adopted me. He was from Charleston,
and all eighteen of his waiters were from Charleston. I was undepend-
able, and I was late a lot for the show, which hit at nine o'clock. And it
was two bits in the pot for the Christmas party every time you were late.
So Ed Smalls told me to just get there by midnight and everything would
be fine. The musicians didn't like anyone getting such special treatment,
particularly a kid. Charlie called a meeting and said, 'You, Jabbo, bring
yourself in at nine, or that's it.' The composer Con Conrad had been after
me to join the band of 'Keep Shufflin',' which he was producing. So I quit
Charlie Johnson. Late in 1927, I had made a recording of 'Black and Tan
Fantasy' with Duke Ellington, and Duke had asked me to go into the
Cotton Club with him. He'd offered me ninety dollars, but by that time
everybody claimed I was the best in New York and I was getting a hundred and fifty a week. I said no, and he hired Freddy Jenkins. The night
before I recorded with Duke, somebody stole my horn. I had to go to a
music store and get a replacement, and the mouthpiece was way too big.
I had a hell of a time hitting that opening high C in my solo, but I made
the session."

Light Everywhere

Richard Sudhalter, the cornettist and biographer of Bix Beiderbecke, once mused over the trumpeter Adolphus (Doc) Cheatham: "The trumpet is an almost athletic instrument, and most trumpet players, through sheer fatigue, start to go off the rail in their sixties. So to hear a trumpeter that old play well is rare, but to hear Doc Cheatham, who's well into his seventies, play without any quaver or cutting back of tone or loss of clarity is truly exceptional. Of course, he rations himself. He takes short solos, and he never overblows, so when he has to he delivers. I used to see him at Mahogany Hall, in Boston, when I was a kid, and I remember the way he stood, just so: the arms out, the horn up, everything strong and right on the button—and, my Lord, that was in the early fifties. I think Joe Smith was the great light in his life as a trumpeter, and that's heartening—to see a man go not the way of Louis Armstrong but another way and succeed so beautifully for so long." Sudhalter was lucky to catch sight of Cheatham at all. Cheatham had begun the twenty or so years he spent as a lead trumpeter with Latin-American bands, and his occasional jazz appearances were generally limited to gigs with Wilbur De Paris's band, in which he played second trumpet to Sidney De Paris. In 1957, when he was chosen to appear on the CBS "Sound of Jazz" program with such trumpeters as Red Allen, Rex Stewart, Joe Wilder, Emmett Berry, Roy Eldridge, and Joe Newman, he refused to take any solos, agreeing only to play obbligatos behind Billie Holiday on her blues "Fine and Mellow." Before the fifties, Cheatham had been a lead trumpet with Sam Wooding and with Cab Calloway. He had also been part of Eddie Heywood's band, a small ensemble group built around its leader's Earl Hines piano. He was more audible in the sixties. He made a beautiful recording on the Prestige label with Shorty Baker, and he played no fewer than four solos on a Victor recording built around the New Orleans alto saxophonist Cap'n John Handy. He also worked with Benny Goodman. Since the late seventies, he has become almost commonplace in New York. This exposure has strengthened him. Cheatham plays with more confidence and beauty now than he did when Sudhalter first heard him.

He belongs with those choice lyrical trumpeters who first came forward in the thirties and forties—Bill Coleman, Frankie Newton, Benny Carter, Joe Thomas, Buck Clayton, Shorty Baker, Emmett Berry, Harry Edison, Bobby Hackett, Charlie Shavers, Joe Wilder. Their idols were Louis Armstrong and Joe Smith and Roy Eldridge, and they have been distinguished by their originality and melodic grace, by their humor and poetic intensity. They like the middle register, their tones are handsome and range from Berry's rough querulousness to Hackett's and Wilder's luminosity, and they are almost all legato players. With the exception of Shavers and Coleman, who are baroque players of the first order, these trumpeters favor spareness. Some are epigrammatic. Having grown up in the big bands (Lucky Millinder, Count Basie, Andy Kirk, McKinney's Cotton Pickers, Benny Carter, Duke Ellington), most of them prefer the roominess and acoustic ease of small groups. Their ranks have thinned and only Edison and Cheatham—one in the West and the other in the East—keep the lamp of lyricism burning.

Cheatham lives in a four-room apartment in a small housing development on upper Lexington Avenue. The parlor is banked by a couple of blue settees and a small sideboard. It opens into a polished white kitchen, which contains a round table, with four chairs, and a big electric wall clock. The kitchen has a northeast window that slams like a cannon when the wind blows. A short hall leads to Cheatham's bedroom, where the pictures on the walls and the orderly clutter betoken the room of a kid who has just gone off to school, or of a bachelor, which Cheatham is most of the time. He is thin and snappy and patrician. He wears a trenchcoat and a cap, and sometimes he affects aviator glasses. His face is smooth and aquiline, and he has a tall, clear forehead. His frequent laugh is jumpy, and he speaks quickly, often repeating the final sentence of each paragraph. He sat in his kitchen and talked:

"My wife, Amanda, works for a family that lived on Park Avenue and moved to East Hampton. They wouldn't let her leave them, so she moved out there, and she comes in weekends. She's an Argentine, and I met her in the fifties when I was on tour with Perez Prado. I didn't think I'd get married again, but we have two children—a daughter and a son. I've always been a loner, and never much of a ladies' man. I married first in the thirties' when I got back from playing in Europe with Sam Wooding. It didn't last long. My second wife was a dancer at the Cotton Club. We were married seven years. I was with Cab Calloway then, and when I got sick and wasn't strong enough to play she'd harp on me: 'Why don't you get a job? Why don't you get a job?' I can't stand that. I'd rather be alone. She finally went home to Texas and married somebody else. I like being alone. I shop, I cook, I iron, I clean the house. I was taught how to do those things as a kid. That was in Nashville, where I was born in 1905. It was a pleasant place to grow up. My mother was named Alice Anthony, and she was from Atlanta. She taught school there and in Nashville, and later on she was a laboratory assistant. She was the kind of mother who's always in your corner. My older brother, Marshall, became a dentist. He was named after my father, who was from Cheatham County, Tennessee. I never knew much about his family. I do know that he was partly descended from the Choctaws and Cherokees who settled Cheatham County, and that he had a lot of brothers and sisters, one of them a teacher at Tuskegee Institute. His mother might have been white, perhaps English. My father was a barber, and he had travelled a lot, particularly on the Mississippi riverboats. He was a proud man who stood straight as an arrow. He had his own barbershop, right in the heart of the business district. In fact, he owned the whole building. That came about this way: he had helped a Mr. Mooney, an immigrant, start a candy concern, and Mooney had made a lot of money, so he bought a building for my father. The building had three stories. The barbershop, which had four chairs, was on the ground floor, and there was a tailor on the top floor, and baths on the second floor, so that when a gentlman came in he could have a shave and shine and cut, take a bath while his suit was pressed, and come out looking and feeling like a million dollars. My father worked seven days a week—on Sundays he shaved the sick, who couldn't get out. We had our own house, in a good neighborhood. It cost seven thousand dollars, and my father bought it through his friends. He also had a car, and sometimes I'd drive him to work, but he would never let me leave him off in front of the shop, because he thought it would look like he was putting on airs. He loved to walk, and we walked forever. And he loved to go to ballgames. Our team, in the old Negro leagues, was the Nashville Elite Giants."

"I started playing music when I was about fifteen. There was a little beatup church in our neighborhood called the Phillip's Chapel, and the deacon was an intelligent, stubby man named Meredith. He organized a band for kids, the Bright Future Stars. I started on drums, and he switched me to cornet. I practically taught myself. The only lessons I had were from two brothers, Professor N. C. Davis and Professor C. M. Davis. They came once a week and gave lessons for a quarter each. They'd been circus trumpeters, and they drank a lot. When one was too drunk, the other one came. You'd smell the whiskey on their breath. I don't remember hearing much of anything musically in Nashville in 1920. Radio was just coming in, and there wasn't much yet in the way of jazz recordings. But Paul Whiteman and Ted Lewis came through, and so did the blues singers. By 1923 or 1924, I was working in the pit band at the Bijou Theatre. A New Orleans trumpet player, George Jefferson, was in the band, and he was a lot of help. The rough element went to the Bijou, but I'd see the principal of the high school there, his face covered with a newspaper. I worked behind all the great blues singers—Mamie Smith and Bessie Smith and Clara Smith. Clara Smith was twice as powerful as Bessie. She shook the rafters. And she was rough. You better not make one mistake when she came off the train tired and mean and evil. Ethel Waters also came through. She brought Fletcher Henderson on piano and Joe Smith on cornet. Joe Smith wore white bell-bottoms, and when he played he'd stand with one foot on a hassock. He looked beautiful, and he sounded beautiful."

"I left Nashville the first time in 1925, and by 1926 I was in Chicago. I left with Marion Hardy's band, and when I got to Chicago I was with John Williams' Synco Jazzers. He married Mary Lou Williams around that time. My parents didn't care for my becoming a musician at all. I think they hoped I'd somehow study to be a doctor, because I used to

play in a little band over at the Meharry Medical College—which is how
I got my nickname. My father had seen enough drunken circus musicians, and he didn't want me to end up that way. So it hurt him very
bad when I left home and went on the road. I spent a year in Chicago.
I didn't have much luck, and I lost a lot of weight. The New Orleans
musicians had everything wrapped up. But landladies were very sympathetic in those days, and six of us got a room together, and we managed
to make it, with God's help. There was a little restaurant nearby called
Poor Me, and I'd go get the food and we'd divide it up. I met Lil
Armstrong, and I had some gigs with her, and Albert Wynn, the trombonist, put me in his band as a saxophonist. I'd taken up the saxophone
about the same time as the cornet, and I played it just about as well. Once,
Louis Armstrong asked Albert Wynn could I sit in for him with Erskine
Tate at the Vendome Theatre. Louis had a feature number, 'Poor Little
Rich Girl,' which I played with Wynn. Louis was a sensation, and the
Vendome was packed every night. I'll never forget how that audience
screamed when I came onstage and how, when the spotlight caught me
and the audience realized I wasn't Louis, they got quieter and quieter. I
had memorized Louis's solo, and I played it note for note. I got nice
applause, but the musicians in the band, they wouldn't talk to me—not
one word. Later, Louis and I became very good friends."

"I heard a lot of music in Chicago. King Oliver had a soft band. The
New Orleans style was very different. It was a sweet type of jazz—a
melodic type of jazz. Oliver himself was very different from Joe Smith
and Johnny Dunn, who were the best horn players I'd heard. He had a
nice, quiet tone, and he knew what he was doing every minute. He used
a lot of mutes—I picked up my mute technique from him—and he'd
growl a little. Freddie Keppard reminded me of a military trumpeter
playing jazz. He was very loud, and he didn't have any of Oliver's polish. One night, he blew a mute right out of his horn and across the dance
floor, and it became the talk of Chicago. After that, everybody piled in
night after night to see him do it again, but he never did. It was true about
his fear of other musician's stealing his stuff. I saw him put a handkerchief over his valves when he was playing, so that nobody could follow
his fingering."

Listening to Doc Cheatham play is like looking at a Winslow Homer:
there is light everywhere. Some of the light is reflected. Here is a Louis
Armstrong connective phrase, a Buck Clayton vibrato, a Joe Smith sustained note, a Joe Thomas epigram. But Cheatham is a courteous, generous man, and perhaps these reflections are more in the nature of salutes—
of nods thrown in the direction of people he admires. The elegance and
lyricism of his playing are his own, as is his sense of structure. His solos
are flawlessly designed. Each phrase follows the last freshly and without
hesitation. There is none of the disconnected brittleness or brassy striving
that afflicts many jazz trumpeters. Presented to the listener in their glis-

tening perfection, Cheatham's solos give the impression that they have been written, edited, and tested—when, of course, they have been instantly spun out of his head. The light in his improvisations brings up pure, soft colors, and the planes his solos are built of—planes that turn ceaselessly this way and that—are alizarin and taupe and ultramarine and viridian. There is no silver or gold, no black or white. Cheatham's tone is complete and jubilant. At first, his rhythmic sense seems old-fashioned. He has a staccato, elbowing attack. Each note clears away the silence before it. Each note is an announcement. But he is also a legato player, whose rests allow beats to slip by, and though he is invariably on time at the end of each solo, he is cool about how he has done it. He likes big intervals and sudden off-course phrases. When he uses a plunger mute he can growl and muse and flutter and whisper with all the sly bravado of Cootie Williams. A long time ago, one of Cheatham's aunts told him, "Stand up straight when you play, throw out your chest, hold your arms horizontal, and keep your head back." And there he is: his arms winglike, his back concave, his trumpet pointed to the sky. It is a heraldic stance.

"I gave up on Chicago in 1927," Cheatham said, "and joined Bobby Lee's band at the Silver Slipper in Philadelphia. We played the Sea Girt Inn, in New Jersey, that summer, and in the fall I went back to Philly with Wilbur De Paris. He was a tight man. I lived at his house, and he charged me for rent and food—he kept a file on all the extra biscuits I ate. The later part of 1928, I went to New York, where I heard Jabbo Smith, who was faster than Louis and seemed even greater to me. I was with Chick Webb for a bit, and Sam Wooding grabbed me and I travelled around Europe three years in his band. I could read like a top by then, and I played lead trumpet while Tommy Ladnier handled the jazz solos. Ladnier was a moody man, a moody player, but he could go when he wanted to. We played nothing but first-class places, and it was very exciting to me. I rejoined Marion Hardy when I got back, then went to McKinney's Cotton Pickers. Joe Smith and Rex Stewart were in the band, and it was like a college of jazz. But one of the teachers wasn't in the band, and that was Bix Beiderbecke. All trumpet players had been playing alike when Bix came along a year or two before and opened the gate. He was doing things we had never heard. He was a lyrical player, but he was also staccato and bright. He had a speaking, *trumpet* way of playing. Anyway, the Cotton Pickers ran out of money, so somebody stole the band book and wouldn't give it back until everything was settled up. The Depression was beginning to hit the regional bands hard, and they were falling by the road. It wasn't until Benny Goodman made it in 1935 that people started going out again to hear the bands, and Benny did it in a *national* way for the first time. I had an offer to go with Cab Calloway at the Cotton Club in 1931, and I took it. I was with Cab eight years, and he was the greatest leader I ever worked for. He ran around with us, and he could be playful, and even rowdy, but you had to be at work on the dot and you had to play it right. Cab had learned to read and he had a good ear. That band made tables of money. They made so much some nights they'd pack it in the drum case. I got a hundred dollars a week every Friday like clockwork, and once I got paid twice and was told to keep it.

"I've never been strong, and in 1939 I fell sick. I was rundown and anemic, and they hospitalized me for nine weeks. I guess it was being on the road so much and not eating and resting properly. It certainly wasn't drink, because I have never been a drinker. I discovered a long time ago that you can't drink and play jazz well. You have to stay sober to think fluently. Drunks tend to be cliché players. Of course, you're not too popular when you don't drink. You're considered a sissy. They never did figure out what was wrong with me, and I didn't regain my full strength, so that I could play the way I really wanted to, until the sixties. It took that long, and at one point a doctor told me, `Doc, I don't know. Maybe you better just lay down the rest of your life.' When I got out of the hospital, I went to Europe for a few months to rest. Then I joined Teddy Wilson's big band and after that Benny Carter's, but I wasn't up to par. I quit playing and took a job in the post office. In 1943, I tried it again, in Eddie Heywood's little group—which wasn't too hard, because Eddie wrote everything out and took long piano solos. It was around this time that I ran into my friend Juan Tizol, who was with Duke Ellington, and he said, 'You should be in the Ellington band. Come over to the theatre in Brooklyn where we're working and I'll introduce you to Duke.' Well, I have never asked anyone for a job. I couldn't do it—on pride, and because it puts you in their power. But I went. I went to Duke's dressing room and I sat there all day like a fool. Duke would change and do a show and change again and do another show and change again, and the whole time he never said a thing to me beyond 'How you been?' and like that. And, of course, there were a lot of people around. Duke always had his entourage. So finally I said, 'Nice seeing you, Duke. So long.' And we shook hands. That was it until the early seventies, when his sister called me and asked me to join the band. But I'd had an operation, and I couldn't make it."

"I live with my horn. I practice every day—sometimes until ten o'clock at night. I listen to records of all my favorite players—Charlie Shavers and Sidney De Paris and Shorty Baker and Joe Thomas and Louis. Taking a solo is like an electric shock. First, I have no idea what I will play, but then something in my brain leads me to build very rapidly, and I start thinking real fast from note to note. I don't worry about chords, because I can hear the harmonic structure in the back of my mind. I have been through all that so many years it is second nature to me. I also have what I think of as a photograph of the melody running in my head. I realize quickly that there is no one way to go in a solo. It's like travelling from here to the Bronx—there are several ways, and you must choose the right way immediately. So I do, and at the same time I never forget to tell a story in my solo. I have always listened for that in other horn players, and it's the only way I know how to play. I'm not a high-note player generally, but sometimes the things I'm playing run me up there, and it frightens me a little. But I get down all right. I keep in shape by walking. Like my father. I'll walk down to Forty-second Street, go over to the musician's union, on West Fifty-second Street, and walk home. I don't like getting back from work at three or four in the morning anymore. I like getting back early, so I can take my sitz bath and go to bed and be up at seven or eight. I love the morning, the morning air—the country air, which is what city air is like in the morning if you catch it quick enough. And I love a big breakfast, which doesn't taste the same later in the day. I'll make myself juice and oatmeal. Or I'll cook fried oysters that I get from a friend out in Jamaica. Or I'll have grits and some fish. Sometimes I'll have chicken or turkey, or sliced tomatoes and pancakes. I guess I'm kind of retired now. I get the Social Security, and I only work three or four nights a week— unless I get a month in Europe or a couple of weeks in Toronto. I got a standing ovation in Toronto a while ago, and that felt very good. It doesn't happen often in a lifetime, and it makes all the rough times worth it. I'm almost the last of the line. I've talked to kids who come to hear us who don't even know who Louis Armstrong is. But they listen. 'How do you do that?' they'll ask. 'That's beautiful' they'll say. When I'm gone, it'll be just about over, my kind of playing. It will be as if it hadn't existed at all, as if all of us hadn't worked so long and hard."

Fats

Fats Waller got going early. He was born Thomas Wright Waller, in New York, on May 21, 1904. He was the seventh of eleven children, only five of whom survived. His parents, Edward Waller and Adeline Lockett, had moved from Virginia in 1888, when they were sixteen. Edward Waller was a successful carter, and, a self-cured stammerer, he became a preacher for the Abyssinian Baptist Church. Young Waller started at the harmonium and piano at six, and at fifteen he was playing the piano and organ at the Lincoln Theatre in Harlem, for twenty-three dollars a week. It was not a career his father favored. He was also hanging out with the pianists Willie the Lion Smith and James P. Johnson. Smith summed Waller up neatly in "Music on My Mind." "When we met, he wasn't born yet," Smith wrote. "He was wished on me. From that time on he followed the Lion and The Brute [Johnson] around. We both tutored him and I was the one who first told him to sing and make faces to draw attention. He was always mimicking West Indian talk; I could see where he was a natural as a showman. He had that magnetic personality with big brown eyes . . .

He was shy at first and I would loosen him up with sauterne. Later he drank ABD's [anybody's drink] and started travelling so fast through life . . . he just never took the time to set himself in the right direction. When he jumped from the basement to five thousand dollars a week, I told him to slow down. 'Lion,' he would say, 'one never knows, do one!' "

In 1920, Waller's mother, whom he doted on, died, and he moved into a schoolmate's home. The next year, he married Edith Hatchett, and they had a son, Thomas, Jr. But Waller was either on the town or on the road, and they separated. (Waller was not designed for the diurnal life; during the next decade, Edith Waller had him sent to jail twice for failure to pay alimony.) By the time he was in his early twenties, he had met Count Basie and given him pointers on the organ, made his first records (piano solos: "Muscle Shoals Blues" and "Birmingham Blues"), written his first songs, and begun studying with Leopold Godowsky, the pianist and composer. Waller married Anita Rutherford in 1926, and they had two sons, Maurice and Ronald. In 1928, after working in Chicago with Louis Armstrong and Earl Hines, he wrote half the music for "Keep Shufflin'." He and James P. Johnson played double piano in the pit, and they made four numbers for Victor with Jabbo Smith on trumpet and Garvin Bushell on reeds. Waller was on pipe organ and Johnson on piano, and the music was a unique combination of the roaring and the delicate and the mercurial. Waller also wrote a revue called "Hot Chocolate" with Andy Razaf the next year, and, as was becoming his scandalous wont, sold the rights—to Irving Mills, for five hundred dollars. ("Ain't Misbehavin' " and "Black and Blue" were among the songs.) Waller first heard Art Tatum in 1931, was duly thunderstruck, and took off for Paris, where he played the "Godbox" in Notre Dame. He weathered the early Depression with radio jobs (WLW in Cincinnati and WABC in New York), and in 1934 he made the first of four hundred or so small-band sides for Victor. The recordings put him squarely before the jazz public, and by 1938 Waller was probably as well known as Louis Armstrong. The two men were recorded that year on a radio show but, rather surprisingly, did not mix well. Waller's staccato high-register accompaniment gets in Armstrong's way, and Armstrong's longer melodic lines make Waller sound chunky. Armstrong loved Waller's esprit, but he never hired a stride pianist.

Waller's small-band records were hobbled by a fixed instrumentation (trumpet, tenor saxophone or clarinet, piano, guitar, bass, drums), second-class musicians (Herman Autrey, Bugs Hamilton, Eugene Sedric, Al Casey, Cedric Wallace, Slick Jones), the three-minute time limit, and often abysmal materials ("Florida Flo," "The Love Bug'll Bite You," "Us on a Bus"), but they were remarkably flexible and springy. The order of solos and vocals, who was to accompany whom, whether to use mutes or not— all were ceaselessly fiddled with. The success of the records depended on Waller, for he was never inaudible, and when he was on course (most of the time), they swung very hard. Waller's famous ad-libs seemed to spill right out of his records, and were addressed to his musicians or to the listener or to the subject of the song. These side-of-the-mouth utterances gave his records a kind of universality. He starts "Serenade for a Wealthy Widow" by saying, "Woman, they tell me you're flooded with currency. Well, come on—give, give, give!" On "How Can You Face Me," he urges a trombone soloist on with "Ah, you're a dirty dog, get out in the street, get out, get out! How can you face me now," which is followed by "No, I didn't go there last night. No, you know I wasn't there, either. I went to the other place." At the close of "Do Me a Favor," he talks very fast: "Listen, honey, have you got a dollar-ninety, cuz I got the dime? You might as well go out there and find the parson." And at the close of "Your Feet's Too Big" he says, "Your pedal extremities are really obnoxious." Perhaps his classic ad-lib came in the middle of a slow, lyrical version of "Sometimes I Feel Like a Motherless Child," done as an organ solo a few months before he died. Midway, Waller, who has been still, says, "I wonder what the poor people are doin' tonight. I'd love to be doin' it with 'em." At first, the remark seems to shatter the mood; then it seems both funny and wrenching.

Waller took his band all over the country between recording sessions, and in the late thirties or early forties Eudora Welty heard him and wrote a strange and indelible short story called "Powerhouse." The surface is expressionistic and slightly ominous. Powerhouse is playing a white dance in a small town in Mississippi, and just before intermission at midnight he tells his musicians that he has received a mysterious telegram from a Uranus Knockwood, saying "YOUR WIFE IS DEAD." Powerhouse talked to his wife on the telephone the night before, and she threatened to jump out the window. The rest of the story is taken up by Powerhouse's self-pitying and angry embellishments on the notion that his wife has done what she said. At first, the band members believe him, then they understand and go along with the fantasy: imagine the worst and you keep at bay the devil and all the "no-good pussyfooted crooning creepers" that hang around musicians. You also keep your ego intact. Being on the road in the black Southern night tries the soul, and humor is its balm. Eudora Welty's observations of Powerhouse/Waller are marvelous. Romanticism is a form of astonishment, and here is how she introduces him:

> There's no one in the world like him. You can't tell what he is. "Nigger man"?—he looks more Asiatic, monkey, Jewish, Babylonian, Peruvian, fanatic, devil. He has pale grey eyes, heavy lids, maybe horny like a lizard's, but big glowing eyes when they're open. He has African feet of the greatest size [Waller wore a fifteen shoe], stomping, both together, on each side of the pedals. He's not coal black—beverage colored—looks like a preacher when his mouth is shut, but then it opens—vast and obscene . . . He's in a trance; he's a person of joy. . . He listens as much as he performs, a look of hideous, powerful rapture on his face. Big arched eyebrows that never stop travelling . . . There he is with his great head, fat stomach, and little round piston legs, and long yellow-sectioned strong big fingers.

Powerhouse starts a tune:

> His hands over the keys, he says sternly, "You-all ready? You-all ready
> to do some serious walking?"—waits—then, STAMP Quiet. STAMP, for
> the second time . . . Then a set of rhythmic kicks against the floor to com-
> municate the tempo. . . . O Lord! . . . hello and good-by, and . . . they are
> all down the first note like a waterfall.

Powerhouse sings:

> On the sweet pieces such a leer for everybody! He looks down so
> benevolently upon all our faces and whispers the lyrics to us. . . . He's
> going up the keyboard with a few fingers in some very derogatory
> triplet-routine, he gets higher and higher, and then he looks over the end
> of the piano, as if over a cliff.

The band goes to a black beer joint during intermission, and the
exchanges with the waitress are perfect. Powerhouse says, "Come here,
living statue, and get all this big order of beer we fixing to give."

> The waitress, setting the tray of beer down on a back table, comes up
> taut and apprehensive as a hen. "Says in the kitchen . . . that you is Mr.
> Powerhouse. . . . "
> "They seeing right tonight, that is him," says Little Brother.
> "You him?"
> "That is him in the flesh," says Scoot.
> "Does you wish to touch him?" asks Valentine. "Because he don't bite."

Duke Ellington knew that the only constant on the road is motion, and
he often asked Harry Carney where they were going next. Powerhouse
says to one of his musicians,

> "What you tell me the name of this place?"
> "White dance, week night, raining, Alligator, Mississippi, long ways
> from home."
> "Uh-huh."

The musicians return to the stand after intermission:

> He didn't strike the piano keys for pitch—he simply opened his
> mouth and gave falsetto howls—in A, D and so on . . . Then he took hold
> of the piano, as if he saw it for the first time in his life, and tested it for
> strength, hit it down in the bass, played an octave with his elbow . . . He
> sat down and played it for a few minutes with outrageous force, and got
> it under his power—a bass deep and coarse as a sea net—then produced
> something glimmering and fragile, and smiled. And who could ever
> remember any of the things he says? They are just inspired remarks that
> roll out of his mouth like smoke.

Waller's life was far less phantasmagoric. He had never cared for the road
and its discomforts, physical and racial, and he frequently expressed

amazement at how white audiences would cheer their heads off when he was on the stand and then send him across the tracks to spend the night. More and more, he quit engagements before they were over, or simply didn't turn up, pleading homesickness for Harlem, where he could be found a day or two later, cooling it at home or sitting in at the nearest club. Waller had become an alcoholic, and it was eroding his life. He was a master illusionist, who fooled everyone, including himself. He made a perpetual joke of his drinking, and it became part of the furniture of his huge, comic, boisterous self: the ever-present bottle on or under the piano at recording dates and on the bandstand; the "liquid ham-and-eggs" he had for breakfast the moment he awoke; the multitude of drinks he had backstage at his Carnegie Hall concert, in 1942, which was a disaster. But Waller had a cavernous capacity, and his drinking rarely got in the way of his music. On his records, his playing and diction are invariably clean and clear. There is no evidence of uncertain time or of anything out of control.

Waller's comic spirit was ungovernable. He offered the rare gift of comic catharisis, and apparently it never failed him, onstage or off. He was always on, whether he was meeting for the first time a precocious piano player and singer named Bobby Short ("He marched right over, picked me up in his arms, and hugged me. 'You could be my son,' he said. 'You even look like me a little bit . . . Say, who's your mother?' ") or sixteen-year-old Mary Lou Williams ("I played for him and he picked me up and threw me in the air"). One can do the Freudian two-step with Waller, but it isn't much help. Did he poke fun at everything because he was trying to offset the melancholy caused by his mother's death and his father's obtuseness? Did he make people laugh to conceal his deep shyness? Did he laugh (and drink) out of sheer terror at life? Joel Vance offers this gloomy paragraph in "Fats Waller: His Life and Times":

> His attention span was that of a small boy: he wrote tunes as toys, forgetting them as quickly as they ceased to please him or to bring him quick money. He was constantly in search of adventures, but the adventures had to take place in comfortable and convivial surroundings—the company of his musical peers in Harlem, a backstage bash with cast and chorus girls, or a gargantuan eating session. Waller's high living was a succession of self-induced birthday parties. He never completed the emotional transition from childhood to maturity. At the price of preserving his childhood in alcohol, he managed to let his creative powers flow to the fullest . . .

Whichever or whatever, Waller was a funny man, even when he played the piano and kept his mouth shut. He was the last of the great stride pianists, and he perfected the style. Stride piano had grown out of the oompah bass and filigreed right hand of ragtime. Its main concerns were rhythmic and melodic: keep that rocking two-beat motion going, no matter how slow, and keep the melody uppermost, no matter how strong the urge to embellish. It was a chordal way of piano playing, both in the left hand, where tenths alternated with seesawing chord-and-single-note figures (Waller's huge hands spanned more than a tenth), and in the right, where chords, often played staccato or against the beat, were spelled by pearly, Lisztian runs. When Waller reached his prime, in the early thirties, stride piano had been made to seem old-fashioned by the brilliant inventions of Earl Hines, who had put jazz piano playing on a four-four basis, straightened out and added muscle to its arpeggios, substituted single-note melodic lines for the squat right-hand chords, and added various punctuations to the left hand. Hines notwithstanding, two great—and antithetical—pianists came out of Waller: Count Basie and Art Tatum. Basie turned Waller's style into ingenious musical telegraphy; he used two notes for every twenty of Waller's and got even stronger results. Tatum was probably influenced by Waller harmonically and pianistically, but the only time he openly bowed in his direction was at breakneck tempos, when he used an unbelievably fast oompah bass that was both affectionate and needling. (In 1938, when Tatum dropped in to hear Waller at a club on Fifty-second Street, Waller introduced him by saying, "I just play the piano, but God is in the house tonight.") Waller's pianistic humor was both sheer exuberance and an inability to let foolishness be. He would use right-hand trills and tremolos and high, bouncing offbeat figures (pianistic falsetto) and, in his left hand, booms, and even an occasional boogie-woogie bass—a form he said he despised. When the material he had to record was particularly maudlin (it is not clear whether Victor's A. & R. men thought it would make hits or were slyly feeding it to Waller to see how fine he would grind it), he gave it the rhapsody treatment, using lots of loud pedal and low, theatrical single notes that summoned up Eddy Duchin. Waller was a superb pianist. His touch was firm and clear, he rarely missed notes, and he had a nice sense of dynamics. His time was metronomic yet had the infinitesimal looseness that is part of swinging. Waller loved the organ. It gave him room for subtleties not possible on the piano and for his histrionic tendencies. (Vance quotes Eugene Sedric as saying that Waller often told him that "someday he might become a preacher and go out and give sermons with a big band behind him.") He could moon and whisper and make bird and wind and wave sounds; he could disport himself without saying a word. But there was a weakness in Waller's instrumental attack: he had little feeling for the blues. His rare blues excursions are glancing and breezy, and there isn't much emotion. This peculiar lack afflicted all the stride pianists as well as such Eastern pianists as Hines, Tatum, and Erroll Garner.

Waller's endless vocal effects—mock-English and West Indian accents, Bronx cheers, heavy aeolian sighs, parlando, rubbery staccato diction—have been duly celebrated, but it should be said that he was a first-rate singer. He had an excellent light baritone, faultless diction (when he chose), and perfect intonation. Once in a while, he would sing a song almost straight, and the slightly delayed rhythmic attack and occasional embellishments revealed his respect for Louis Armstrong, part of whose vocal on a 1932 "When It's Sleepy Time Down South" Waller copies or parodies on the final bridge of "Breakin' the Ice." Waller the songwriter was a third and inseparable self. He wrote his songs quickly, and they are notable on several counts: their very melodies swing, they often resemble ragtime, and they are extremely catchy. But the catchiness of "Ain't Misbehavin' " and "Jitterbug Waltz" is dangerous, for, as Alec Wilder has pointed out, the "Beer Barrel Polka" is similarly attractive. Wilder continued, "I don't think Waller had great melodic sensibility. I don't think he knew how to write long melodic lines. Jerome Kern would have told him how, but I doubt that Waller knew such an area of popular music. His melodic lines are all made up of little pieces, of imitations. Each phrase is sustained by an imitation, or partial imitation, of the previous phrase. In a sense, he wrote like a barroom piano player. His songs are often like the little glistening phrases that good barroom piano players come up with. He was the opposite of a pianist like Cy Walter. Walter didn't like to improvise, and he didn't like jazz. But when he wrote a song, it had a long and often complex melodic line. Waller was a Tin Pan Alley writer. He wrote for fun. His songs fell right in. They were written for the counter, for immediate sale. Give them to the band, give them to the singer. His songs were very different from, say, 'You Go to My Head,' a complicated and beautiful song that astonishingly became a hit, or from 'Star Dust' which is even harder to sing than 'The Star-Spangled Banner.' The intensity and brilliance squeezed into such songs escaped Waller completely. But his songs make you think of him, of his playing, of his joy of living, and there's certainly nothing wrong with that."

By the early forties Waller was making very good money. But he was still casting about. Was he a comedian, a bandleader, a songwriter, or a jazz musician? He recorded on organ and celeste behind Lee Wiley (he was a superb accompanist on both piano and organ), and he gave his depressing Carnegie Hall concert. He wrote the music for "Early to Bed," which had a decent run on Broadway and was the first non-black musical written by a black. He filmed "Stormy Weather," with Bill Robinson and Lena Horne, and he appeared on the radio with Edgar Bergen and Charlie McCarthy. He was on the verge of going national. He went on the soft-drink wagon for a year, then switched to sauterne. But his massive appetite had weakened, and so had his resistance. Late in 1943, he worked the Zanzibar Room in Los Angeles and caught a bad cold. He took ten days off and couldn't completely shake it, but finished the job. He entrained for New York, telling his manager Ed Kirkeby that he was exhausted. He slept an entire day and night, and died in his sleep of bronchial pneumonia just as the train pulled into Kansas City.

Deathbed utterances are immutable, but misinterpretations aren't. Kirkeby reported in his "Ain't Misbehavin' ":

> About two [the morning of Waller's death] I opened the door to the sleeper and was hit by a blast of cold air.
> "Jesus, it's cold in here!" I said, as I saw Fats was awake.
> "Yeah, Hawkins is sure blowin' out there tonight," Fats replied.
> The train was roaring through the Kansas plains in a howling blizzard, which reminded Fats of the blustery sax playing of his friend Coleman Hawkins.

Both Vance and Maurice Waller repeat Kirkeby's poetic allusion, but that is surely not what Waller meant. A "hawkins" in the old black argot is snow or ice or a cold wind.

In The Wilderness

The number of jazz musicians in this country who piece out their lives in the shadows and shoals of show business has always been surprising. They play in roadhouses and motel lounges. They play in country inns and small hotels. They appear in seafood restaurants in ocean resorts and in steak houses in suburban shopping centers. They play in band shells on yellow summer evenings. They sit in, gloriously, with famous bands on one-night stands when the third trumpeter fails to show. They play wedding receptions and country-club dances and bar mitzvahs, and they turn up at intense Saturday-night parties given by small-town businessmen who clap them on the back and request "Ain't She Sweet," and then sing along. Occasionally, they venture into the big cities and appear for a week in obscure nightclubs. But more often they take almost permanent gigs in South Orange and Rochester and Albany. There is a spate of reasons for their perennial ghostliness: The spirit may be willing but the flesh weak; their talents, though sure, are small; they may be bound by domineering spouses or ailing mothers; they may abhor traveling; they may be among those rare performers who are sated by the enthusiasms of a small house in a Syracuse bar on a February night. Whatever the reasons, these musicians form a heroic legion. They work long hours in seedy and/or pretentious places for minimum money. They make sporadic recordings on unknown labels. They play for benefits but are refused loans at the bank. They pass their lives pumping up their egos. Some of them sink into sadness and bitterness and dissolution, but by and large they remain a hardy, ingenious group who subsist by charitably keeping the music alive in Danville and Worcester and Ish Peming.

One of the most steadfast of these common-grass musicians is Marie Marcus, a Boston-born pianist who has spent most of her forty-year career on Cape Cod and in Miami Beach. She is a household name on the Cape, where she lives. Short, round, talkative, and accessible, she plays very good Fats Waller piano, and keeps her ego alongside her sugar and tea bags. She lives in a tiny gray cottage with blue shutters in a part of Harwich where the houses shoulder one another and where a Stop & Shop and a Howard Johnson's are around the corner. The house, compact and spotless, has a living room, a kitchen, a bedroom, and a bathroom. The living room looks as if it could be packed up and moved in minutes. It contains a sofa and an armchair, a stereo, a television, a sewing machine, a piano, and a corner wardrobe. The walls are bare except for photographs of her grandchildren and an autographed picture of Oscar Peterson. One afternoon, the front door and both windows were open, and a smart Cape Cod breeze was funneling through. Marie Marcus was on the phone. She was wearing a voluminous housedress, and her blond hair was piled on top of her head. She hung up and perched like a pigeon at one end of the sofa. "That was my mother," she said. Her voice is high, and the edges of her Boston accent have been rubbed smooth. "She's worried because I killed a spider in here last night that looked after I'd sprayed it like it might be a black widow. It probably wasn't, because you don't hear much about black widows on the Cape, but she's all bothered about it. She hates the Cape anyway, and she and my stepfather, Lou Martin, are moving back to Boston next week. He's a fine man, and he plays ragtime. They just celebrated their twenty-fifth, but they're young in action. Then, my mother has always been young-minded. She married my father, whose name was Dougherty, when she was sixteen or seventeen, and she was a live wire, full of pep and energy. She sang in the church choir, and she played piano by ear. And she and my father were great ballroom dancers. They were on the dance floor two or three nights a week at the Totem Pole or Nutting's-on-the-Charles or Loew's State Ballroom. She taught my son Bill, who's a jazz piano player, how to ballroom dance, and he was amazed. He'd never heard of dancing like that. The house where I grew up, in Roxbury—the ghetto is there now—was always full of music, and it was always full of people, too. My mother and father lived in an attic apartment in the house, which was big and old and was owned by my grandmother. She was a fantastic woman who lived to be ninety-three, a woman of the old-fashioned Irish stock, and she ran the roost, which also numbered my uncle and my four aunts. They weren't that much older than I was, and after my grandfather died —I was just three—she raised them all. I was an only child, and for seventeen years I was an only grandchild and an only niece, so in one way I was spoiled. But it was a very religious Catholic household, and those were still the seen-and-not-heard days. So I never seemed to get the kind of affection that my four children give me now. My father was a plumber, and a good one, and he worked at the Charlestown Navy Yard. He was considerate to me and saw to it that I had all the piano lessons and education I needed. But he had a drinking problem that finally drove him and my mother apart. He couldn't help himself, and, of course, there was no AA then. On top of that, drinking was considered a sin, and not a sickness. The poor man died when I was in my late twenties. He was coming home from work on payday, and three men jumped him, and that was it. They never found out who did it. But the music in the house is what's stayed with me. One of my aunts, Mrs. Parnell, would have been a great jazz piano player, but she gave it up when she married. My mother had a player piano and all those rolls by Fats Waller and James P. Johnson, and there were always musicians from Boston in the house. People like Joe Sullivan—not the Chicago jazz pianist Joe Sullivan—who was good in the ragtime style, and Billy Paine, who was a fine singer. It was all an influence on me, and when I was about four I got up on the piano stool and played a whole number. I started lessons, when I was eight or nine, with Miss Teitelbaum, who was a wonderful musician and teacher. We used to kid her about being a nice Jewish lady from Ireland, which she was. I studied with her four years, and when I was thirteen I gave a recital at Judson Hall, in Boston. I continued my music at the New England Conservatory and attended Roxbury Memorial High at the same time. But my career began elsewhere. When I was fourteen or fifteen, I got a job playing piano once a week on a children's radio show, 'Bill Toomey's Stars of Tomorrow.' I accompanied the other kids, and I also had my own solo spot. Then I was hired by Big Brother Bob Emery, who had the most famous children's radio program in New England. He was a strict, smart man and a radio pioneer who'd been on the first Boston station, WGI. I had become a pretty fair tap dancer, and for a while I didn't know whether I wanted to dance or play piano. When I played and danced for a week one summer at a Chinese restaurant in Boston called the Mahjong, I asked the orchestra leader, Jimmy Gallagher, whether he thought I should be a dancer or a pianist, and he told me I had something special on the piano and that there were girl dancers under every stone, and that made up my mind. When I graduated from high school, Bob Emery got a call to do a radio show in New York, and he asked me to go with him. It was nineteen thirty-two, and I was just eighteen. We were supposed to stay at the Royalton, on West Forty-fourth Street, but somehow I got turned around and ended up at the Claridge, which wasn't far away. Emery was in a state of shock when he found me. He told me my mother would have his head, which she would have. So I moved to the Royalton, and I met Robert Benchley, who lived there. He was a friend of Emery's, and he was a delightful man. I had lunch with him several times, and I was fascinated with his witty sayings. I started with Emery at WEAF for Humphrey's Remedies. The show was sort of philosophical, with poetry readings, and I played background music. Then we went over to WNEW, which we helped open, and finally we ended with a children's program on WOR. My mother and father came up from Boston not long after I was in New York, and we took an apartment at the Hildona, over on Forty-fifth Street, between Eighth and Ninth Avenues. I loved the movies, and I went to every show in New York, but I was bored with all the spare time I had. A friend of Emery's owned a bar and grill on Amsterdam Avenue that had a Hawaiian trio, and he hired me as the intermission pianist. After a while, the boss and some of the waiters asked me to go to Tillie's Chicken Shack, in Harlem. It was a fried-chicken place, and Bob Howard, who sounded just like Fats Waller, was on piano. We went up there quite often, and one night Fats himself came in. I remember the whole room lighted up. He played, and then Howard persuaded me to play, even though I was scared to death. Fats listened, and when I'd finished he pointed to his heart and said, 'For a white gal, you sure got it there.' I was amazed, but I guess he was, too, since practically the only women who were playing jazz then were Mary Lou Williams and Lil Armstrong, and they were still working mainly out West. We got to talking, and I told him that I would like to further my education in jazz and did he know a good teacher? He looked at me and said, 'How about me?' I thought he was putting me on, but he wasn't. He had a small office, with two pianos, in the Brill Building, at 1619 Broadway, and during the next year or so, when he wasn't on the road or making records, he'd call me up and say, 'Come on down and let's play some piano.' You couldn't exactly call them lessons. We'd play duets, and then he'd play and have me listen carefully to the things he did. He'd tell me, 'When you're playing jazz, remember the rhythm, remember the rhythm. Make the number of notes count. Tell a story, and get that feeling across to the people. Please the people by making it come from here.' He was very serious when we were working together, and I was grateful for every minute. And I could never get over his reach on the keyboard. He had stubby hands, but he could span way over a tenth, which gave him that great left hand."

Marie Marcus got up and went into the kitchen to get a glass of water. She sat down again and laughed. She is a pretty woman with a prominent nose, a high forehead, and a long face. It is a cheerful New England face, and it is also a child's birthday-party face. "I never make excuses about my weight," she said. "I love to eat, and that's it. I've been fighting the battle of the bulge for ten years. I have a sign on my icebox door: 'Marie Marcus is a big fat slob,' and one of these days I'm going to pay attention to it. I did try Weight Watchers a while ago. You have to be weighed every time you go, in front of a whole bunch of women, and you get embarrassed. But a couple of jobs came up, and I couldn't fit it in anymore. Now I've started the water diet. Eight glasses a day and just meat and fish. The trouble is I can't stand water. I did take off forty-five pounds a couple of years ago, but I put it right back on. So I know my health is in jeopardy, and that's a constant elbow in my side. You tend to let yourself go, living alone. My second husband, Bill Marcus, died seven years ago. He had perfect health, but he had a heart attack and died right on the bandstand. He was a trumpet player, a society-band trumpet player, who worked for

Meyer Davis and the Lanins and Ruby Newman. We had just bought the big house next door, and this place—I wouldn't even say what my mother calls it—was the garage. He was a lawyer, graduated from BU, and he had hung out a sign and was starting to practice again, and he had fixed this up as his office, which accounts for the linoleum floor and the paneling. After he passed, I moved in here, and now my three aunts and my uncle live next door. So I use this place for sleeping and eating, and it's all I need." She took a sip of water and made a face.

"My next job was at a speakeasy on Eighth Avenue owned by Dutch Schulz. I worked from ten-thirty till seven in the morning, and then did my radio show late in the afternoon. I was in a little room next to the saloon-type bar, and I was treated beautifully. I built up a following of fans who would come in and scat-sing new phrases they'd heard uptown, where they'd take me on my day off. We'd go to the Savoy Ballroom to hear Chick Webb and Ella Fitzgerald, and it was one of the experiences of my life. Another was being at Benny Goodman's famous opening at the Paramount. I'd heard an early Goodman band in Boston, and something about it told me that this was the coming music. I was at the Paramount for the first show—the ten-o'clock morning show—and I couldn't believe what happened. That music just carried everybody away, and people started dancing in the aisles and on their seats. Somebody grabbed me, and there I was, dancing away like crazy. The quartet in particular knocked me out, and although I wouldn't wait for St. Peter today, I stayed through three or four shows that morning. From Dutch Schulz's place I moved over to the Venetian Palace, which I think was owned by Frank Costello. It was scary there. Kids were naïve in those days, and I was the most naïve of all. I didn't drink or smoke, and I'd been taught all my life that sex was a dirty word. One night the bosses sent me and this little red-headed singer to play at a private party in a hotel, and when I got there I couldn't find any piano, and I began to realize I was in a strange situation. So I up and said to the hoods who were there, 'If you force me to do anything, it'll be like your kid sister.' They took one look at my Boston Irish face and sent me back to the club. But I never saw the singer again. The Venetian didn't last long, and after a couple of jobs in between I finally made it to Fifty-second Street, to the Swing Club. It was paradise. Stuff Smith and Jonah Jones were working next door, and Art Tatum was across the street, and Billie Holiday was two doors away. I learned and I learned, not so much from piano players as from horn players and singers. It was a fantastic time in New York; there was so much good music.

"In 1937, I got married the first time. I married a native New York boy named Jack Brown. He was a singer and an m.c., and he ran shows at a couple of Chinese restaurants on Broadway in the Forties. We got a job together at Barkley's, in Brooklyn, and we moved out there. In 1938, my son Jackie was born, and I had to go back to work two weeks later, because my husband had had a nervous breakdown. He was in a hospital in Brooklyn and then in a sanitarium, where he was for quite a while. Things were never quite the same after that, and eventually we drifted apart and separated, and he died several years later. I raised Jackie, with help from my mother and my aunts, from the time he was fifteen months. I stayed on at Barkley's, and I also worked at the Embassy Club, where I had my own band, and where there were big plans to make a star out of me. But my agent decided I was bushed and that first I should go up to the Coonamessett Club, in Falmouth, on the Cape, where the work would be light and I'd get a rest. It was 1942, and the war had just started. I came by train and I got off at Falmouth, and a hostess from the club met me. It was the dead of winter, and I looked around and thought, My God, I'm in the wilderness. But within a week my love affair with the Cape began, and I never did get back to New York. The Coonamessett, which is gone now, was a huge place, with a bowling alley and ballrooms and restaurants, and the work was anything but light. The day after I arrived was St. Patrick's, and the whole of Camp Edwards came over. I was at the Coonamessett or over at Camp Edwards, where I became a sort of mother confessor to the wounded boys, during most of the war. I was working at the Panama Club, in Hyannis, on V-J Day. It was a high-class steak pub and the number one club on the Cape. It's gone now, too. In fact, I seem to turn most of the places I've worked in up here into parking fields. It was at the Panama Club that I met Bill Marcus, and we were married just after the war. We started going to Florida for the winter, and my two girls, Mary and Barbara, were born there. We worked every winter in Miami Beach and every summer on the Cape until 1961. After that, we stayed up here all year. It was in Miami that I really got deeply into Dixieland for the first time. I joined Preacher Rollo and the Five Saints—Preacher was a drummer named Rollo Layan—and I was with them five or six years, and we were a big hit. We worked every hotel in Miami Beach and had a national radio hookup five days a week and a recording contract with M-G-M. We were on Steve Allen's 'Tonight Show' and the 'Dave Garroway Show' and Arthur Godfrey's program. But it was very hard work. I didn't finish until three or four in the morning, and I had to take several different buses going home and then be up at seven to get the kids off to school. My Dixie experience has continued ever since. In the fifties, I toured the Midwest with Wild Bill Davison, and I worked for George Wein in Boston. I got $108 and I worked seven nights a week, and when I asked him for a day off he said, 'Fine, but I'll have to dock your pay.' So I quit."

Marie Marcus took a sip of water and made another face. She looked at her hands and flexed them slowly. "I have arthritis. I can't even bend this finger. A doctor fan told me to keep playing and to keep squeezing two little rubber balls he gave me." The telephone rang, and she talked briefly. "That was my friend Mildred. She calls me every day. She lives near here, with her husband, in a great big house that looks over the water and has an Olympic-size indoor swimming pool. I love to swim, and I always have the whole pool to myself. Up and down, up and down, and nobody to bother me. I love golf, too. I was a very good woman golfer. I played in the low eighties when I was at the Coonamessett, and they used to talk to me about going in tournaments. But I've been too busy running all over the Cape and working in every place imaginable. I play full-time summers and maybe two or three nights a week during the off season, when I sometimes do a little teaching to fill in the chinks. Since I've settled here, I've worked the Nauset Inn, in Orleans, which is now the Olde Inn. I played duets there with a wonderful piano player, Leo Grimes, who's at the Ritz in Boston now. He's self-taught, and he told me once that he can't help himself, that he thinks about music twenty-four hours a day—on the street, when he eats, when he dreams, when he gets up in the morning, all the time figuring out new things to play. In 1963, after the Nauset Inn, I formed a partnership with Carl German—he pronounces it 'Germane'—which is still going on. He's a bass player and a singer, and we sing duets. I have a little Bonnie Baker voice, and I sing only with him, because I get very nervous by myself. Carl commutes from Mattapoisett, where he lives, and it's an hour and a half each way. We worked the winter of 1963 at Mildred's Chowder House, in Hyannis, and the summer in Mashpee, at Ellie's Drift Inn, which is now called On the Rocks. It was the same two places in 1964 and 1965, and then we went into the Windjammer Lounge, in Hyannis, where we built up a terrific following. We worked the Windjammer the next four years, with a side job at the Orleans Inn. In 1970, we were at the Gateway Yacht Club, in West Yarmouth, and at La Coquille, in Dennis, and we did the Lighthouse Inn, the Sandbar, and Deacon's Perch. The winter of 1971, I was with Bobby Hackett at the Gateway, which was a ball, and during the summer Carl and I were at the Hereford House, in Dennisport. And this summer it's the Charcoal Pit, in Chatham."

Marie Marcus looked at her watch. "I'm going over to Mildred's and take a swim, and then I have to get dressed for our Sunday afternoon concert at the Olde Inn. It's with my Dixieland band, which was formed seven years ago. We work eight or nine months of the year, at least once a week, at clubs and private parties and at outdoor concerts. The last outdoor concert we gave it rained, and the electric piano I was playing got wet and I had to stop. Every time I touched the keys I got a shock. Everybody in the band has day jobs, except for Alan Pratt, our drummer, and me. Jim Blackmore, our cornetist, designs heating systems for houses and such all over the Cape, and Paul Nossiter, who plays clarinet and sings and is our m.c., is a teacher at the Sea Pines School, in Brewster. Our trombonist, Charlie Tourjée, teaches at the Dennis-Yarmouth Regional High School, and Jimmy Cullum, the bassist, runs a music store, Musictronics, in Orleans. We hit at four and play until seven-thirty, when I have to get to my regular job."

● ● ●

It was a little after four, and the band was deep in a medium-tempo version of "Pee Wee's Blues." It was set up in a big bay window at one end of a high, raftered room. A dance floor in front of the bandstand was surrounded by tables with redchecked tablecloths. Half the tables were already full. The band finished the blues, moved easily through Louis Armstrong's "Swing That Music," and started the rarely heard verse of "After You've Gone." The band sounded trim and compact and unhurried. Its ensembles revolved slowly and surely, and its solos were brief and to the point. It had a nice sense of dynamics and kept its volume at the conversation level. Blackmore is a gentle, sweet cornet player, cast in the mold of his friend Bobby Hackett, and Tourjée, who is free of the harrumphing approach that afflicts most white Dixieland trombonists, suggests Jack Jenney and even Benny Morton. Nossiter is a fluent clarinetist who favors the chalumeau register. Marie Marcus looked very different now. She was wearing a smart blue overblouse and a long black skirt, and she had vanished into her music. Her mouth moved continually while she played, as if she were spelling out difficult words to herself, and her head went through an endless series of dips, nods, and snaps. Her shoulders rolled, and her feet swung back and forth, back and forth—a little girl sitting on a porch railing and eating a cone. At first, her style seems a simple mélange of chunky chords and brief connective runs, but on closer examination it is a repository of the jazz piano playing of the thirties and forties. In her left hand, she uses Waller oompahs and Teddy Wilson tenths and quick, stabbing Nat Cole punctuations, and her right hand works through short Tatum runs and dense Bob Zurke chords and spacious Jess Stacy intervals. Her melodic lines are short and often affecting, and they duck and bob and weave through complicated chordal patterns that are occasionally lightened by single-note figures. She is a driving pianist, but she never hurries, and her solos have a serene, homey texture, as if she were crocheting them. Her solos meet the listener exactly halfway. She does not bother with dynamics, and she rarely pauses between phrases. The "Satanic Blues" followed "After You've Gone," gave way to Jelly Roll Morton's "Doctor Jazz," and it was intermission time.

Marie Marcus sat down, dabbed her brow, and ordered a diet Coke. A swarm of admirers appeared, and she was alternately patted, squeezed, kissed, and poked. They included Roland Sears, a sometime drummer, photographer, painter, electronics expert, and disk jockey, who runs a funny weekly jazz program for the Orleans station, WVLC; Heinie Greer, a retired New York lawyer and banjoist, who lives in Dennis and spends most of his evenings faithfully touring the jazz spots on the Cape; Bobby Hackett, who lives in Chatham, and who told Marie Marcus it was high time they made a record together; and Alec Wilder, who had just flown over from Nantucket for a few days' visit. "That felt pretty good," Marie Marcus said. "And I'm in a good mood. The mood I'm in and what I'm thinking about directly affect my music. It's gotten to the point where if I play something in a certain way, people can tell right off what's in my mind. When I do a ballad, I try and interpret the story that the composer gets across in the lyrics. And I'm more melody-conscious than chord-conscious. The melody runs along the back of my mind, and I listen and try to fit pretty chords to it. There are certain tunes I associate with certain people, and when I play them I see their faces before me. They might be old fans who always request that particular tune, or musicians like Bobby Hackett. I'll play 'Memories of You' alone at night in my house and I'll see Bobby in my mind. Playing is always a question of trying to project the right feeling, the feeling of the heart. Sometimes, when you get warmed up, it's a carried-away feeling, and you come up with things that surprise even you—phrases that you *know* you've never played before. This will happen mostly with a good audience—generally a concert audience and not a noisy nightclub crowd. A good audience is like food to me. It sparkles my imagination, and I can run twice as fast. And playing with my band does that, too. I don't like to play alone, the way I am now down at the Charcoal Pit. I don't even have Carl German; the boss let him go, because he said there wasn't enough business. Anyway, the room is big and cold, and I don't feel like anyone when I'm working in there."

Paul Nossiter made an announcement to the effect that Bobby Hackett and the clarinetist Joe Muranyi would sit in for the next set, and the band went back to work. There were now a cornet and a trumpet, and Nossiter switched to soprano saxophone. The first tune was a medium version of "Struttin' with Some Barbecue." The dance floor filled up rapidly, and Marie Marcus was lost from sight for a moment. When the dancers parted, she looked radiant. Her face was shining and her mouth was going.

Sunshine Always Opens Out

Late in the winter of 1964, Earl "Fatha" Hines gave a concert at the Little Theatre, on West Forty-fourth Street, that is still mentioned with awe by those fortunate enough to have been there. The obstacles Hines faced that night were formidable. He was fifty-nine, an age when most jazz musicians have become slow-gaited; he had, except for a brief night-club appearance, been absent from New York for ten years, and the occasional recordings that had floated east from Oakland, where he had settled, had done little to provoke demands for his return; and he had never before attempted a full-length solo recital—a feat that few jazz pianists, of whatever bent, have carried off. He met these hindrances by first announcing, when he walked on stage, that he was not giving a concert but was simply playing in his living room for friends, and by then performing with a brilliance that touched at least a part of each of his thirty-odd numbers. Not only was his celebrated style intact, but it had taken on a subtlety and unpredictability that continually pleased and startled the audience. Even Hines' face, which has the nobility often imparted by a wide mouth, a strong nose, and high cheekbones, was hypnotic. His steady smile kept turning to the glassy grimace presaging tears. His eyes—when they were open—were bright and pained, and his lower lip, pushed by a steady flow of grunts and hums, surged heavily back and forth. He made quick feints to the right and left with his shoulders, or rocked easily back and forth, his legs wide and supporting him like out-riggers. Between numbers, that smile—one of the renowned lamps of show business—made his face look transparent. It was exemplary show-manship—not wrappings and tinsel but the gift itself, freely offered.

Not long after, Hines took a small band into Birdland for a week, and he stayed at the Taft Hotel. The Birdland gig had upset him: "Man, that's a hard job at Birdland," he said quickly and clearly. "It's ten to four, which I'm not used to anymore, and it wears me out. I got to bed at seven yesterday, but I had to be up and downtown for my cabaret card, then to a booking agency, then to a rehearsal for the Johnny Carson show. I didn't get to bed until six-thirty this morning, and then some damn fool called me at nine and said [his voice went falsetto], 'Is this Earl Hines, and did you write "Rosetta"?' I won't say what I said. So I'm a little stupid. I'm *breathing*, but I don't feel like jumping rope."

Hines was stretched out on his bed in his hotel room watching an old Edward G. Robinson movie on television. He had on white pajamas, a silver bathrobe, and brown slippers. A silk stocking hid the top of his head. The room was small and hot and cluttered with suitcases, and its single window faced a black air shaft. Hines' eyes were half shut and there were deep circles under them. "I haven't eaten yet, so I just ordered up some chicken-gumbo soup and a Western omelette and plenty of coffee and cream. It'll probably come by suppertime, the way room service goes here. Yesterday, I asked for ham and eggs for breakfast and they sent a ham steak and candied sweets and string beans and rolls, and when I called down, the man said he was two blocks from the kitchen and how could he help what the chef did?" Hines laughed—or, rather, barked—and rubbed a hand slowly back and forth across his brow. "I mean, I don't know what has caused New York to tighten up so. All the hotels—including this one—want musicians to pay in advance. My goodness, it's almost dog-eat-dog. Pittsburgh, where I'm from, is a country town compared to New York, where it takes every bit of energy to keep that front up. The streets are all littered up, and last night I go in the back door at Birdland and three guys are laying there, sick all over theirselves. Next time, I go in the front door, and two guys want a dime, a quarter. I've been all over this country and Canada and Europe, and how clean and nice they are. I'd be ashamed to tell people I was from New York. Maybe I been away from home too long. It's three months now. I finish this recording date I have with Victor tomorrow and the next day and—boom!—I'm off. Stanley Dance set up the Victor date. He's coming by around now with tapes of some records I made with my big band in the late thirties that Victor is bringing out again. He wants me to identify a couple of the soloists. My man Stanley."

There was a knock, and a portly, mustached man walked briskly in. He was carrying a small tape recorder. "Hey, Stanley," Hines said, and sat up straight.

"Did you get a good sleep?" Dance asked, in a pleasant Essex accent.

"Oh, people start calling at eight or nine again, but I'll sleep later, I'll rest later. I'm not doing *nothing* for a month when I get home."

"If it's all right, I'll play the tapes now, Earl." Dance put the machine on a luggage stand and plugged it in.

Hines stood up, stretched, and pummelled his stomach, which was flat and hard. "I haven't been sick since I was twelve years old. In the thirties, when we were on tour in the East, I'd work out with Joe Louis at Pompton Lakes. We'd sit on a fence a while and talk, and then we'd throw that medicine ball back and forth. That's why my stomach is so hard today." He sat down next to the tape recorder, crossed his ankles, clasped his hands in his lap, and stared at the machine. Dance started the tape. The first number, "Piano Man," was fast and was built around Hines' piano.

Hines listened attentively, his head cocked. "I haven't heard that in I don't know *how* long," he said. "That was a big production number in the show at the Grand Terrace, in Chicago, where I had my band from 1928 to 1940. I played it on a white grand piano and all the lights would go down, except for a spot on me and on each of the chorus girls, who were at tiny white baby grands all around me on the dance floor. When I played, they played with me—selected notes I taught them. Just now at the end I could picture the girls going off. Gene Krupa came in a lot, and he used that number for *his* show number—'Drummin' Man.' He just changed the piano parts to drum parts. I told him he was a Tom Mix without a gun." Hines laughed. "What's that?" he asked when the next number began.

"'Father Steps In,'" Dance said.

Hines hummed the melody with the band. A trumpet soloed. "That's Walter Fuller. He was my work horse." An alto saxophone came in. "That's Budd Johnson, my Budd. He'll be down at Victor tomorrow. He usually played tenor." Hines scat-sang Johnson's solo note for note. "He sounds like Benny Carter there."

"G. T. Stomp," "Ridin' and Jivin'," and "'Gator Swing" went by. "The only trouble with this record, Earl, is there are so many fast tempos," Dance said.

"It was a very hot band. That's why the people were all so happy in those days. Nobody slept at the Grand Terrace. When we went on the road, the only band we had trouble with in all the cutting contests there used to be was the Savoy Sultans, the house group at the Savoy Ballroom, in Harlem. They only had eight pieces, but they could swing you into bad health. They'd sit there and listen and watch, and when you finished they'd pick up right where you'd left off and play it back twice as hard. We had a chance, we ducked them. *Everybody* did."

A waiter rolled in a table and placed it beside the bed. "Am I glad to see you, even if it is almost suppertime!" Hines barked, and he sat down on the bed. "Stanley, could we finish that after I've had something to eat? I only eat twice a day, and never between meals, and I get hungry. Take some coffee. Did they bring enough sugar? I like a lot of sugar and cream." He opened a suitcase beside the night table and took out a two pound box of sugar. "I never travel without my sugar bag. I learned that long ago." Hines filled a soup bowl from a tureen and buried the soup under croutons. Dance sipped a cup of coffee and watched Hines. "Earl, you were talking a bit the other day about what it was like to be the leader of a big band."

Hines looked up from his soup and put his spoon down. He wiped his mouth with a napkin. Then he picked up his spoon again. "An organization is no bigger than its leader, Stanley. You have to set an example—let them know you know what you're doing. An animal will fear you if you're leading, but you let down and he'll get you. Same thing with handling a big band. For that reason, I used to stay a little apart from the band, so there wouldn't be too much familiarity. But I had to be an understanding guy, a psychologist. I had to study each man, I had to know each man's ability. I'd be serious with one, joke with another, maybe take another out for a game of pool. Once in a while I'd give a little dinner for the band. But I was very strict about one thing. The band had to be on time, particularly on the road. There was a twenty-five-dollar fine if you missed the curtain in a theatre, and a dollar a minute after that. It cost five dollars if you were late for the bus, and a dollar a minute after that. We even fined the bus driver if he was late. The fines worked so well, after a while I could take them off. As I said before, I've always stayed physically in condition. The band knew I'd fight at the drop of a hat, even though I had an even disposition. I believe the only time I lost my temper was on the road when a trombonist I had was bugging me and I picked him up and had him over my head and would have thrown him off the bus if the boys hadn't stopped me.

"The Grand Terrace was very beautifully done—a big ballroom with a bar in the back and mirrors on the walls, with blue lights fixed here and there on the glass. Those mirrors were like looking at the sky with stars in it. The bandstand was raised and had stairs coming down around both sides for the chorus girls and the show. The dance floor was also elevated. The Grand Terrace was the Cotton Club of Chicago, and we were a show band as much as a dance band and a jazz band. We worked seven days a week, and how we did it I don't know. There were three shows a night during the week and four on Saturday. The hours were nine-thirty to three-thirty, except on Saturday, when we worked ten to five. The chorus girls—we had fourteen or sixteen of them—were very important.

They were ponies—middle-sized girls who were not overweight and could dance. Or they were parade girls, who were taller and more for just show. The chorus line, coming down the stairways, opened the show. Then there was a vocalist, he or she. A soft-shoe dancer or ballroom team came next. Then maybe a picture number, with fake African huts and a big fire and such. The highlight of the show was a special act, like the four Step Brothers or Ethel Waters or Bojangles, and then everyone on for the finale. Sometimes a comedian like Billy Mitchell took the dancers' spot. He had a trick of turning one foot all the way around, so that that foot pointed one way and the other the other way, and he'd walk along like it was nothing and bring down the house. It was always a good hot show, with everything jumping. The girls were its heart, and they really danced. They'd come off the floor wringing wet. They spent a lot of money on their costumes, and we always had two women backstage to put on buttons and fasten snaps and adjust new costumes that sometimes didn't arrive until half an hour before show time. I was a stickler for the boys in the band dressing, too, and we had a costume fund. One cause of my feeling for clothes was George Raft. I'd visit him in his hotel room when he was in town and he'd have three trunks of clothes. He'd tell me not to buy expensive suits—just suits that looked good—and to have plenty of them and change them all the time and that way they'd last. I had shoes made to fit my suits from the Chicago Theatrical Shoe store. They were dancers' shoes—sharp-looking, with round toes, and soft, so that they fitted like a glove. Wherever I went, they'd send a new pair if I needed them, because they had my measurements. A valet took care of my clothes, and there was another valet—a band valet—for the boys."

Hines emptied the tureen into his soup bowl. "The Grand Terrace was always in an orderly place. The audiences were mixed. Segregation never crossed anyone's mind. Friday nights we had college kids and we had to learn the college songs. Saturdays we got the office and shop people. Sunday was 75 per cent colored, and Mondays were tourists. On Wednesdays we got elderly people and played waltzes. The racketeers owned 25 per cent of the Grand Terrace, and they always had four or five men there—floating men. They never bothered us. 'We're here for your protection, boys,' they'd say. If they were going to run some beer from Detroit to Chicago, they'd figure the job out right in the kitchen. I'd be sitting there, but it was hear nothing, see nothing, say nothing if the cops came around. There was pistol play every night during prohibition. No shooting; just waving guns around. I was heading for the kitchen one night and this guy went pounding past and another guy came up behind me and told me to stand still and rested a pistol on my shoulder and aimed at the first guy and would have fired if the kitchen door hadn't swung shut in time. Some of the waiters even had pistols. The racketeers weren't any credit to Chicago, but they kept the money flowing. My girl vocalist might make fifteen hundred a week in tips for requests, and she'd split it with the boys, and they'd put it in the costume fund. The racketeers owned me, too, and so did the man who controlled the other 75 per cent of the Grand Terrace. This was something I didn't fully realize until late in the thirties. We were always paid in cash—one hundred and fifty a week for me and ninety apiece for the boys in the band. I couldn't complain. The Grand Terrace was our seat nine months of every year, and we had a nightly coast-to-coast radio hookup, which gave us solid bookings for the two or three months we were on the road. I couldn't afford to hire stars for the band, so I had to *make* my stars. In this way, I brought along Ivie Anderson, the singer, and Ray Nance, the trumpet player. Duke Ellington took both of them from me. And I developed other singers, like Ida James and Herb Jeffries and Billy Eckstine and Sarah Vaughan, and I had musicians like Trummy Young and Budd Johnson and Dizzy Gillespie and Charlie Parker."

Hines exchanged his soup bowl for the Western omelette and poured more coffee. He chewed carefully. "We had a doctor at home, Dr. Martin, and he always said all your sickness derives from your stomach. I've never forgotten that. I was a wild kid in the twenties and thirties and I drank a lot, but what saved me was I always ate when I was drinking. The music publishers had something to do with my drinking. After we had our radio hookup, they'd come around every night, trying to get me to play this tune or that." Hines shifted into falsetto again: "'I got a little tune here, Earl, and I wish you'd play it and blah blah blah'" and then he'd buy me a drink and another publisher would buy me a couple of more drinks and I'd end up drinking all night and then I'd have to drink some more, if we had a record session early the next day, to keep going. I'd forget where I left my car, and I got so tired sometimes I'd put on shades and play whole shows asleep, with George Dixon, my sax man, nudging me when I was supposed to come in. I never considered myself a piano soloist anyway, so I was happy to just take my little eight bars and get off. It's the public that's pushed me out and made me a soloist. Then one night the owner of the Grand Terrace said, 'Earl, you're drinking yourself to death.' I thought about that and I decided he was right. When we went on the road soon after, I quit. I was all skin and bones. I bought a camera and took a picture of every pretty girl I saw to pass the time, and when I came back to Chicago I weighed one hundred and eighty-five. I only drink now after I'm finished work. But people *still* are after me to buy me drinks, and you hate to keep saying no. It almost agitates you."

Hines pushed his plate away and lit a big cigar. He arranged a couple of pillows against the headboard, leaned back, and swung his feet onto the bed. He puffed quietly, his eyes shut. "The excitement of the Grand Terrace days was something you couldn't realize unless you were there," he said, in a low voice. "It was a thrill when that curtain went up and us in white suits and playing and you knew you'd caught your audience. I bought my way out of the Grand Terrace in 1940 after I finally learned about all the money I was making and wasn't seeing. I kept the band together until 1948. By then it had twenty-four musicians and strings. But things were changing, with the entertainment tax and higher prices and fewer and fewer bookings in theatres and ballrooms. I saw the handwriting on the wall, and I disbanded and went with Louis Armstrong's All Stars. I didn't care for being a sideman again after all the years I'd spent building my reputation. Play some more of that tape, Stanley. Let me hear that band again."

Midway in the fourth or fifth number, Dance looked over at Hines. His cigar was in an ashtray on the night table, his eyes were shut, and his mouth was open. He was asleep.

Hines' view of himself as reluctant soloist was surprising, for although he has spent a good part of his career as a leader of big and small bands, he is valued chiefly as a pianist. When he came to the fore in Louis Armstrong's celebrated 1928 recordings, the effect he created was stunning. No one had ever played the piano like that. Most jazz pianists were either blues performers, whose techniques were shaped by their materials, or stride pianists, whose oompah basses and florid right hands reflected the hothouse luxury of ragtime. Hines filled the space between these approaches with an almost hornlike style. He fashioned complex, irregular single-note patterns in the right hand, octave chords with brief tremolos that suggested a vibrato, stark single notes, and big flatted chords. His left hand, ignoring the stride pianists' catapult action, cushioned his right hand. He used floating tenths and offsetting, offbeat single notes, and he sometimes played counter-melodies. Now and then he slipped into urgent arhythmic passages full of broken melodic lines and heavy offbeat chords. Hines and Louis Armstrong became the first jazz soloists to sustain the tension that is the secret of improvisation. Each of Hines' solos—particularly any that lasted several choruses—had a unity that was heightened by his pioneering use of dynamics. He italicized his most felicitous phrases by quickly increasing his volume and then as quickly letting it fall away. At the same time, he retained the emotional substance of the blues pianists and the head-on rhythms of the stride men. His earliest recordings still sound modern, and they must have been as shocking then as the atonal musings of Ornette Coleman first were.

That night at Birdland, Hines sat down at the piano ten minutes before the first set. The bandstand was dark and Hines unreeled a progression of soft, Debussy chords. He finished, and a couple of spotlights went on, but the illumination seemed to come from Hines himself. He was immaculate; his smile was permanently in place for the evening, and he was wearing a dark suit and a white shirt and dark shoes. His jet-black hair was flat and combed straight back, and he appeared as limber as a long-distance swimmer. Stanley Dance had pointed out that the group Hines happened to have at the moment was the sort of ingenuous, good-time, doubling-in-brass outfit that used to be a part of the stage show at the Apollo Theatre. It was, Dance had said, a surprising group—for Hines and for Birdland. It had a drummer and an organist, a male vocal trio, and a female alto saxophonist who sounded like Charlie Parker and who also sang. The next forty-five minutes were totally unpredictable, and Hines' assemblage soon seemed twice its actual size. The vocal trio sang together and separately; the organist soloed and sang a couple of numbers; the lady saxophonist not only emulated Charlie Parker but sang by herself or with the trio; the drummer took over for a long spell; and Hines, after eight-bar sips here and there, played a fifteen-minute solo medley. All this was executed with the precision of a Grand Terrace show, and when it was over, Hines was soaking wet. "I'm trying something nobody else is," he said, mopping himself. "'I've had this group six months and I want to reach young and old. You play Dixieland, you get the old and drive away the young. You play modern, you get the young and keep away the old. A girl asked me last night, 'Are you Earl Hines' son? My mother used to listen to your dad at the Grand Terrace in 1930.' The young don't believe I'm me and the old are too tired to come and see. But I want both, and the manager has told me he's seen types of people in here all week he's never seen before. People have also said I'm crazy to have such a group, that the public wants to hear my piano, and that's why I put that medley in every show. This band is a kind of variation of what I was trying to do in my own club in Oakland, which opened last December. It had an international tinge. I had Irish and Chinese dancers and Italian and Japanese vocalists. I had Negro and Chinese and white waiters. I had Jewish musicians. I had Mexican and Chinese comedians. Then I found out one of my partners wasn't international and that the other didn't know much about show business, and I got out."

Hines ordered coffee, and lit a cigar. He was quiet for a while, then he said: "I don't *think* I think when I play. I have a photographic memory for chords, and when I'm playing, the right chords appear in my mind like photographs long before I get to them. This gives me a little time to alter them, to get a little clash or make coloring or get in harmony chords. It may flash on me that I can change an F chord to a D-flat ninth. But I might find the altering isn't working the way it should, so I stop and clarify myself with an off-beat passage, a broken-rhythm thing. I always challenge myself. I get out in deep water and I always try to get back. But I get hung up. The audience never knows, but that's when I smile the most, when I show the most ivory. I've even had to tell my bass player I'm going into the last eight bars of a tune because he wouldn't know where the hell I was. I play however I feel. If I'm working a pretty melody, I'll just slip into waltz time or cut the tempo in half. My mind is going a mile a minute, and it goes even better when I have a good piano and the audience doesn't distract me. I'm like a race horse. I've been taught by the old masters—put everything out of your mind except what you have to do. I've been through every sort of disturbance before I go on the stand, but I never get so upset that it makes the audience uneasy. If one of my musicians is late, I may tell the audience when he arrives that I *kept* him off the stand because he needed a little rest. I always use the assistance of the

Man Upstairs before I go on. I ask for that and it gives me courage and strength and personality. It causes me to blank everything else out, and the mood comes right down on me no matter how I feel. I don't go to church regularly, because I'm generally too tired from the hours I have to keep. I'd only fall asleep, and I don't believe in going just to say, yes, I go to church every Sunday. One Easter Sunday, I played in the Reverend Cobbs' church in Chicago—a standing-room-only church, he's so popular with his parishioners. I played 'Roses of Picardy.' They had three hundred voices in the choir. I played the first chorus; the choir hummed the second behind me and sang the lyrics on the third. Good God, it shook me up, the sound of those voices. I was nothing but goose pimples, and I stood right up off the piano stool. It was almost angelic."

Hines looked fresh and eager the next day. He was smoking a pipe and watching television, and he was wearing a black silk suit, a striped tan sports shirt, and pointed shoes trimmed with alligator leather. He had on a dark porkpie hat and dark glasses. Stanley Dance was telephoning. "He's checking Budd Johnson to make sure he's left for the studio," Hines said. He pointed to his glasses. "I wear these to shut out those photographers who turn up at every record session and seem like they're popping pictures of you from right inside the piano."

"Budd's on his way," Dance said. "And Jimmy Crawford and Aaron Bell are definite for drums and bass."

"Fine, fine. Stanley, bring that fake book, please, in case they ask me to play something I recorded forty years ago. Everybody but me remembers those tunes."

Hines leaned back in the cab and tilted his hat over his eyes. It was drizzling and the traffic was heavy. "Coming down in that elevator puts me in mind of Jack Hylton, the English bandleader, and the time he came to Chicago in the thirties. He was staying at the Blackstone and asked me if I'd come and see him. When I got there, the elevator man told me to take the freight elevator around back. Like a delivery boy. That upset me and I refused and pretty soon the assistant manager and the manager and Hylton's secretary and Hylton himself were all there and it ended in my going up in the front elevator. I don't say much about race, but it's always in the back of my head. I've tried to handle it by thinking things out up front and avoiding trouble if it can be avoided—like when I bought my house in Oakland four or five years ago. It has four bedrooms, a maid's room, family room, kitchen, parlor, and a fifty-foot patio in back. It's almost too much house. It was a white neighborhood before my wife and I and our two girls came, and I knew there might be trouble. The house belonged to a guy down on his luck and it was a mess inside and out. It's in an area where people keep their lawns nice, so before we moved in I painted the outside and installed a watering system and hired a Japanese gardener. I painted the inside and put in wall-to-wall carpets and drapes. When it was the best-looking place around, we moved in. We haven't had

any trouble. But I've learned those precautions the long, hard way, beginning when we were the first big Negro band to travel extensively through
the South. I think you could call us the first Freedom Riders. We stayed
mostly with the Negro population and only came in contact with the
Caucasian race if we needed something in a drug or dry-goods way. On
our first tour, in 1931, we had a booker named Harry D. Squires. He
booked us out of his hat, calling the next town from the one we'd just
played and generally using his wits, like once when we got stopped for
speeding. Squires told us before the cop came up, 'Now, we'll just tell him
we're a young group and haven't had any work. So get out all your
change and put it in a hat to show him what we're worth. And that's just
what we did. The cop got on the bus and we all sat there, looking forlorn
and half starved and he looked in the hat, which had ten or twelve dollars in it, and he let us go. That was our first acting duty. Going South was
an invasion for us. We weren't accustomed to the system, being from the
North, and it put a damper on us. Things happened all the time. They
made us walk in the street off the sidewalk in Fort Lauderdale, and at a
white dance in Valdosta, Georgia, some hecklers in the crowd turned off
the lights and exploded a bomb under the bandstand. We didn't none of
us get hurt, but we didn't play so well after that, either. Sometimes when
we came into a town that had a bad reputation, the driver would tell us—
and here we were in our own chartered bus—to move to the back of the
bus just to make it look all right and not get anyone riled up. We pulled
into a gas station early one morning and a trombonist named Stevens got
out to stretch his legs. He asked the gas-station attendant was it O.K., and
he said, "Go ahead, but I just killed one nigger. He's layin' over there in
the weeds. You don't believe me, take a look for yourself.' Stevens got
back on the bus quick, and the next day we read about the killing in the
papers. They had a diner at another gas station, and my guitarist, who
was new and very, very light-skinned, ducked off the bus and went right
into the diner. He didn't know any better and we didn't see him go in.
When we'd gassed up, I asked our road manager, a Jewish fellow who
was swarthy and very dark, to get us some sandwiches. The counterman
took one look at him and wouldn't serve him, and my road manager
glanced up and there was my guitarist at the counter, stuffing down ham
and eggs. We never let that manager forget. It was a happening we kept
him in line with the rest of the trip."

Hines laughed quietly and looked out of the window. It was raining
heavily and the cab was crawling through Twenty-eighth Street. "We
played a colored dance somewhere in Alabama and it worked out there
was a gang of white people sitting back of us on the stage because there
wasn't any more room on the floor. They'd been invited by the Negro
who was giving the dance, since he worked for one of the whites. We'd
only been playing fifteen minutes when along came this old captain, this
sheriff man, and told me, 'You can't have those white people up there.
You get them off that stage.' I said I didn't know anything about it. Fifteen

minutes more and that cap'n was back.'You and these niggers get out of
here and out of this town. You have half an hour.' He escorted us per-
sonally to the town line. I found out later he knew all those white people,
but they were the cream in the town and he was afraid to say anything to
them, except to tell them after we'd gone that one of my boys had been
looking at a white woman and that was why he drove us out. But I had
me a victory in Tennessee. I went into a dry-goods store to buy some
shirts. The clerk said, 'You want something, boy?' I told him. He took me
to the cheapest section. I told him I wanted to see the best shirts he had.
'Where you from, boy, to ask for things like that?' I pointed at some ten-
dollar silk shirts. 'Give me five of those,' I said.'You want five of *those*?'
He started to laugh and I showed him a fifty-dollar bill. After that, that
man couldn't get enough of me. Money changed his whole attitude.
Money shamed him. I spent close to eighty-five dollars, and when I came
out all these local colored boys were looking in the front windows, noses
on the glass. They said, 'You go in *there*? Don't *no one* go in there!' Well,
those were the days when if you were a Negro and wanted to buy a hat
and tried it on it was *your* hat whether it fitted or not.

"But there were good times, too. We were always seeing new territory,
new beauty. In those days the country was a lot more open and sometimes we'd run into another band and just park the buses by the road and
get out and play baseball in a field. We travelled by train, also, but buses
were only twenty-eight cents a mile and you kept the same bus and driver throughout a whole tour. There was always a little tonk game on the
bus at night. The boys put something for a table across the aisle and sat
on Coke boxes and hung a flashlight from the luggage rack on a coat
hanger. I generally sat on the right side about four seats back of the driver, where I kept an eye on things. They played most of the night, and it
was amusing and something to keep you interested if you couldn't sleep.
Our radio broadcasts made us well known after a while and sometimes
we felt like a Presidential party. People would gather around the bus and
say, 'Where's Fatha Hines? Where's Fatha Hines?' Fatha was a nickname
given to me by a radio announcer we had at the Grand Terrace, and one
I'd just as soon be shut of now. I had a kiddish face then and they expected an *old* man from my nickname, so I'd just slip into the hotel and maybe
go into the coffee shop, but when these people found out who and where
I was they'd come in and stand around and stare at me. Just stand and
stare and not say anything, and if I looked up they'd pretend to be looking away in the distance."

Hines is greeted at the R.C.A. Victor recording studio, which is on East Twenty-
fourth Street, by Brad McCuen, an A. and R. man of Sydney Greenstreet pro-
portions. Hines goes immediately into the studio, which is bright and chilly and
thicketed with microphones. Jimmy Crawford is setting up his drums and Aaron
Bell is putting rosin on his bow.

HINES *(in a loud, happy voice):* O solo mio, o solo mio. Hey, Craw, man. And Aaron. A *long* time, a *long* time. *(All shake hands warmly.)* We're going to do something today. But just leave all the doors open so we can git out when everything goes wrong.

CRAWFORD: You look wonderful, Earl. Just wonderful.

HINES: I feel like a million dollars. *(He takes off his coat and sits down at a grand piano and rubs his hands together and blows on them. McCuen leaves a list of prospective tunes and a large gold ashtray beside Hines, who lights a cigar. McCuen is followed into the control room by Dance, still carrying the fake book. A round, genial man enters the studio. He is dressed all in brown and has an Oriental face.)* My Budd. Budd Johnson. *(The two men embrace and laugh and pound one another. Hines returns to the piano and plays ad-lib chords, which gradually crystallize into a slow "It Had to Be You." Crawford and Bell join in. Hines has already vanished into what he is doing. His mouth is open slightly and his lower lip moves in and out. His face, disguised by his hat and glasses, looks closed and secret. A photographer comes out of the control room, lies down on the floor near Hines, and starts shooting pictures. Hines finishes two choruses and stops.)* Hey, Mr. Camera Man, would you mind waiting on that? You're getting me all nervous. *(The photographer retreats into the control room.)* You ready, Budd? Tenor would be nice for this. Rich and slow and warm. *Pretty* tenor. I'll take the first two choruses and you come in for one. I'll come back and you come in again for the last sixteen bars.

MCCUEN *(in a booming voice over the control-room microphone):* Ready to roll one, Earl?

HINES: Let's do one right away. *(After the last note dies away, Hines jumps up, laughs, snaps his fingers, and spins around.)* Ooooo-wee. Budd, how'd you like that ad-lib ending? I couldn't do that again to save my life. I didn't know if I was going to get out alive or not. Shoo, man.

MCCUEN: We'll play it back.

HINES: No, let's do another real quick. I feel it. Here we go. *(The second take is faster and the ending more precise.)* All right, let's hear *that.* *(The music comes crashing out of two enormous loudspeakers. Hines gets up and moves over beside the nearest wall. His hands hang loose at his sides. He throws back his head, opens his mouth, and listens. He is even more concentrated than when he plays. He doesn't move until the number ends. Then he does a little dance and laughs.)* I'll buy it. I'll buy it. Beautiful, Budd. Just beautiful. You can shut those doors now. *(During the next couple of hours, the group does "I've Got the World on a String," "A Cottage for Sale," "Linger Awhile," and a fast original by Hines. Two or three takes suffice for each tune. Hines wastes no time, and after each play back he starts playing again.)*

HINES: "Wrap Your Troubles in Dreams." Budd, you rest on this one. We'll do about four choruses. *(The first take is indifferent, but on the*

*second one Hines suddenly catches fire, moving with extraordinary inten-
sity into the upper register in the third chorus and shaping the fourth chorus into a perfect climax.)*

MCCUEN: Let's try another, Earl. That opening wasn't quite right. *(Hines
looks surprised, but immediately makes another take. After the playback, he
shakes his head.)*

HINES: I don't know. Let's go again. *(In all, twelve takes, including false
starts, are made. Each is slightly faster, and each time Hines appears less
satisfied. The last take is replayed. Hines is leaning on an upright piano in
the center of the studio, Bell and Johnson flanking him.)* You know, I
don't *feel* it, I'm not *inside* that tune. I'm not bringing it *out.*

BELL: Earl, you know it's getting faster and faster?

HINES: Yeh? I didn't notice.

JOHNSON: Earl, you were *cookin'*, man, way back there on that second
take, and they never did play it back for you.

HINES *(looking puzzled)*: That right? Hey, Brad, can you play that second
take for me. You never did, and I can't recall it. *(It is played, and slowly Hines' face relaxes. Johnson snaps his fingers and Bell nods his head.)*
Budd, you got it, man. You were right. *That's* it, and we wasting all
that time when the *good* one is just sitting there waiting to be heard.
Man, I feel *young* again.

   *(It is now almost six o'clock, and McCuen suggests that they meet
again the next day. He thanks the musicians. Hines moves to the center of
the studio, lights a fresh cigar, and stretches his arms wide. Crawford and
Bell and Johnson fall into a loose semicircle before him.)*

HINES: Thank you, Craw, and Aaron. Just fine, man. Just fine. Budd, I
haven't heard that baritone of yours in I don't know how long. You
take Harry Carney's job away he doesn't look out. *(Johnson beams.)*
The piano they got here makes it feel good, too. You play on a bad
instrument and you want to take just eight bars and get out. So
many clubs now have cheap pianos. It's the last thing the owners
think of. They wouldn't put a well behind their bars and dip water
out of it, instead of having faucets, so why do they have pianos that
are cheap and out of tune?

JOHNSON: That's right, Earl.

BELL: Yeah, Earl.

HINES: In the forties, we played a place in Texas and they had a miserable
piano. It was even full of water from a leak in the roof first night we
were there. When the job was finished, Billy Eckstine and some of
the boys decided to take that piano apart. Man, they clipped the
strings and loosened the hammers and pulled off the keyboard and
left it laying all over the floor. *(All laugh.)* I just finished four weeks
in Canada, and the owner of that club must have had a hundred-
dollar piano, it was so bad. And he had this fancy bandstand with a
great big Buddha sitting on each side of it and they must of cost a
thousand dollars apiece. I asked him, "Man, why do you spend all

that money on Buddhas and decorations and not on a piano?", and he answered blah blah blah, and got mad. Now, that's crazy.

CRAWFORD: Well, you told him, Earl.

HINES: It's the same thing nowadays with dressing rooms. No place to put on your makeup or rest and change your clothes between sets. *(Hines voice has slowly grown louder and he is almost chanting. His listeners intensify their responses.)* They got one room down at Birdland, one small room, man, and we can't use it when Vi Redd—she's my saxophonist—goes in there, and when she's finished there's no time left anyway. I have to go back to the hotel between every set and change clothes. It's only a couple of blocks and I don't mind, but what if it snowing or raining and I catch my death?

JOHNSON: Earl, I was down to the Copa a while ago and it's the same there. You got to go out and walk the sidewalk.

HINES: That's what I mean. That's what I mean. You remember the old days all the theatres had good dressing rooms and places to sit down? Of course, these young musicians don't dress anyway, so maybe it doesn't matter. The band opposite me at Birdland, led by that young trumpet player—what's his name?

BELL: Byrd? Donald Byrd?

HINES: Yeh. Well, the first night they all dressed in different clothes and have scuffy shoes and no neckties. We come on, all spruced and neat— ties, of course—and you watch, the next night they got on ties and suits and their hair combed and they look *human*. And those young musicians don't know how to handle themselves before an audience. Never look at the audience or tell it what they're playing or smile or bow or be at all gracious. Just toot-toot-a-toot and look dead while the other guy is playing and get off. No wonder everybody having such a hard time all over. No one—not even Duke or Basie—raising any hell anymore. They just scuffling to keep the payroll going. That's why I have this different group, to reach the young people and teach them the old ways, the right ways, not the rock-and-roll ways. I've always helped the young people along, developed them, showed them how to dress and act and carry themselves properly. I've been at it so long I couldn't stop. Well, man, all we can do is be examples. A man can't do no more than that.

JOHNSON: Amen, Earl. Amen.

The rain had stopped, and Hines found a cab on Third Avenue. He was still wound up from his oration and the recording session, and he sat on the edge of his seat, puffing at his cigar. "'Why didn't somebody tell me I still had these dark glasses on? I wondered why I couldn't see anything when I came out of that building. The reason I've always looked out for the young people, I guess, is because my dad always looked out for me. I don't think there was anyone else in the world who brought up their children better than my mother and dad. We lived in Duquesne, where I was born, and my mother was a housewife. My dad started on a hoisting machine—or histing machine, as they called it—on the coal docks and worked his way up to foreman. He was a loosely type fellow. He never chastised me for the medium things, and I didn't have over four solid whippings from him. I never was brought in at night at the time the average kid in my neighborhood was, and it looked like I was let run helter-skelter and my dad was criticized for that, but he defended himself by saying if you don't chastise your child continually he will confide in you. When I was twelve, he sat down with me one night at evening table after my mother had gone out and told me I was too old to whip anymore and how to conduct myself. 'I'm not a wealthy men,' he told me. 'So I can't get you out of serious trouble.' He told me *everything* that night—about all the different kinds of women and men I'd come up against, and how to tell the good from the bad, about thinking you're outsmarting someone else when he's probably outsmarting *you*, about staying on lighted streets at night, and such as that. It gave me the confidence that's always guided me. A lot of the children of strict parents where I grew up ended in jail. The exceptions were far and few.

"My family was very musical. My mother was an organist and my dad played cornet. My uncle knew all the brass instruments and my auntie was in light opera. My dad was also the leader of the Eureka Brass Band, which played for picnics and dances and outings. I was nine or ten when I was taken on my first outing. We travelled from McKeesport about twelve miles in four open trolleys, which were chartered. The band rode the first trolley and played as we went. After the picnic there was dancing in a hall and the children who were allowed to stay were sent up to a balcony, where they had a matron to watch us. Some of the kids rough-housed, but I just leaned over the rail and listened and watched. It was such a pretty thing to see all those people dancing and flowing in one direction. The men seemed so pleasant to the women and the women back to the men. My mother started teaching me the piano when I was very young. I also tried the cornet, after my dad, but it hurt me behind the ears to blow, so l gave it up. I had my first outside piano lessons when I was nine, from a teacher named Emma D. Young, of McKeesport. My next teacher, Von Holz, was German and pretty well advanced. I was studying to be a classical artist. I loved the piano and I was always three or four lessons ahead in my book. My auntie lived in Pittsburgh, and when I went to Schenley High School, where I majored in music, I lived with her. I was interested in conducting and watched the directors of pit orchestras every chance I got. And I memorized all the music I heard, some of it even before the sheet music came out. When I was about thirteen, my life changed. I had a cousin and an uncle who were play-time boys and they used to take me downtown to the tenderloin section with them. I was tall and they fitted me out in long trousers. The first time they took me to the Leader House, which had dancing upstairs and a restaurant downstairs, I heard this strange music and I heard the feet and the beat and so much laughter and happiness I asked my uncle and cousin could I go upstairs and listen. They put a Coca-Cola in my hand and I did. Pittsburgh was a wide-open town and there wasn't such a ban then on children going into clubs. A hunchback fellow named Toadlo was playing the piano. He was playing 'Squeeze Me', and singing. His playing turned me around completely. It put rhythm in my mind, and I went home and told my auntie that that was the way I wanted to play. In the meantime, I was shining shoes and had learned barbering and for the first time I had enough money to get around. I formed a little trio, with a violinist and a drummer, and then Lois B. Deppe, who was a well-known Pittsburgh singer and bandleader, hired me and my drummer for his band at the Leader House. It was summer and I talked to my dad and he said it was all right and I went to work. Fifteen dollars a week and two meals a day. Toadlo still worked there, and so did a pianist named Johnny Watters. He was dynamic. He was more advanced than Toadlo. He could stretch fourteen notes with his right hand and play a melody at the same time with his middle fingers. He liked Camels and gin and in the afternoons I'd buy him a pack of cigarettes and a double shot of gin and we'd go upstairs at the Leader House, and he would show me. Then, at a party, I heard a piano player named Jim Fellman playing tenths with his left hand, instead of the old oompah bass. It was so easy and rhythmic. *He* liked beer and chewed Mail Pouch, so I got him upstairs at the Leader House, too, and he showed me those tenths. I got my rhythmic training from a banjoist named Verchet. He was a musical fanatic. He tried to make his banjo sound like a harp, and he had all these nuts and bolts for tightening and loosening the strings, only the damn thing always fell apart when he played. His instrument case was full of tools and he sounded like a plumber when he picked it up. But he was a heck of a critic of tempo. He'd sit there, strumming like lightning and rocking back and forth in half time, and if I got away from the beat, he'd say,'Watch-it-boy, watch-it-boy.' So I began to form my little style. I still had the idea of the cornet in my head and I would try things that I might have played on the cornet—single-note figures and runs that were not ordinary then on the piano. And I hit on using octaves in the right hand, when I was with a band, to cut through the music and be heard."

The cab stopped in front of the hotel. Upstairs, Hines ordered a bottle of Scotch and ice and glasses. Then he took off his hat for the first time that afternoon and flopped down on the bed. He looked tired but pleased. "That Budd Johnson is something, isn't he, Stanley? He was a playing fool today. He was in my big band almost ten years. But I've always been lucky in my musicians. I formed my first band in 1924 and Benny Carter played baritone in it and his cousin Cuban Bennett was on trumpet. He was a *great* trumpet player, but nobody remembers him. We went into the Grape Arbor, in Pittsburgh, and stayed there several months. Eubie Blake used to come through town once in a while, and the first time I met him he told me, 'Son, you have no business here. You got to leave Pittsburgh.' He came through again while we were at the Grape Arbor, and when he saw me, he said, 'You *still* here? I'm going to take this cane'—he always carried a cane and wore a raccoon coat and a brown derby—'and wear it out all over your head if you're not gone when I come back.' I was. That same year, I went to Chicago to the Elite No. 2 Club, an after-hours place. Teddy Weatherford, the pianist, was *it* in Chicago then, and soon people began telling him, 'There's a tall, skinny kid from Pittsburgh plays piano. You better hear him.' Teddy and I became friends, and we'd go around together and both play and people began to notice me. They even began to lean toward me over Teddy. Louis Armstrong and I first worked together in the Carroll Dickerson orchestra at the Sunset. Louis was the first trumpet player I heard who played what *I* had wanted to play on cornet. I'd steal ideas from him and he'd steal them from me. He'd bend over after a solo and say way down deep in that rumble, 'Thank you, man.' Louis was wild and I was wild, and we were inseparable. He was the most happy-go-lucky guy I ever met. Then Louis and I and Zutty Singleton, who was also with Dickerson, formed our own group. We were full of jokes and were always kidding each other. We drove around in this old, broken-down automobile we had, and when we got home after work we'd leave it parked in the middle of the street or in front of someone else's house. But there wasn't *that* much work and we like to starve to death, making a dollar or a dollar and a half apiece a night. So we drifted apart, and I worked for Jimmie Noone for a year, and then I went to New York to make some QRS piano rolls. I had a little band rehearsing at the same time, and it was then I got a call to come and open up the Grand Terrace."

The whiskey and ice and glasses arrived. Dance gave Hines a brandy from a bottle on the dresser and poured himself a Scotch-and-water. Hines lifted his glass in the air. "This is for Stanley. If it hadn't been for him, I'd probably be out of this business now. I was ready to quit about a year ago. In fact, my wife and I were talking about opening a little shop out on the Coast. But Stanley kept after me on that long-distance phone, and persuaded me to come here last winter, and then he set up the record session. I was down low again when I got here last week. But something *good* happened today, and it's going to happen tomorrow. I try never to worry. The greatest thing to draw wrinkles in a man's face is worry. And why should I be unhappy and pull down my face and drag my feet and make everybody around me feel that way too? By being what you are, something always comes up. Sunshine always opens out. I'll leave for the Coast day after tomorrow in my car, and I'll stop and see my mother in Duquesne. My sister, Nancy, and my brother, Boots, still live with her. I'll see my mother-in-law in Philadelphia and she'll give me a whole mess of fried chicken. I'll put that on the seat beside me, along with those cigars and my pipe and pipe tobacco and a map and a gallon jug of water. I'll open the window wide and keep my eye on the road. Stanley, let me have a little more of that brandy, please."

Out Here Again

Mary Lou Williams at the Hickory House, after a long period of semiretirement: Dressed in a black sleeveless gown, cut low in the back, she looked extremely pretty. Her black hair was arranged in a loose helmet, and on her right arm she had a watch with a wide gold strap. She sat straight, her body motionless and her elbows brushing her sides, as if she were pouring tea. Her head and her face, however, were in steady, graceful motion. Sometimes she shut her eyes and tilted her chin up, so that the light from a spot bounced off her high, prominent cheekbones. Sometimes, her eyes still shut, she moved her head counterclockwise in an intense, halting manner, punctuated with rhythmic downward jabs. When she was pleased by something her bassist or her drummer did, she rocked gently back and forth, partly opened her eyes, and smiled. She never looked at her long, thin fingers, which lay almost flat on the keys.

The triumph of Mary Lou Williams' style is that she has no style. She is not an eclectic or an anthologist or a copyist; she is a gifted and delicate appreciator who distills what affects her in the work of other pianists into cool, highly individual synopses. The grapes are others', the wine is her own. In the late twenties and early thirties, echoes of Jelly Roll Morton and Fats Waller and Earl Hines hurried through her work. The mountainous shadow of Art Tatum passed over around 1940, and by 1945 she had become an expert bebop pianist. Since jazz piano—the otherworldly convolutions of Cecil Taylor aside—has not moved very far since then, she is now a post-bebop performer, her chords and single-note melodic lines applauding such juniors as Bill Evans and Red Garland. But while discreetly judging her peers she often scoops them. In the forties, she advanced certain dissonant chords that became part of Thelonious Monk's permanent furniture. She also outlined the sort of Debussy impressionism that no modern pianist confronted by a number like "Polka Dots and Moonbeams" would be caught without. In the thirties, she perfected an airy, slightly joshing form of boogie-woogie that pointed a way out of the mechanized morass that that singular music had sunk into. Mary Lou Williams' present work is an instructive history of jazz piano—a kind of one-woman retrospective of an entire movement. Fragments of boogie-woogie basses—in six-eight, rather than four-four or four-eight, time—frequently appear in her introductions. These are relieved by muted left-hand figures and right-hand chords that abstract the melody. Spare single-note lines surface in the right hand; their arpeggios are mere serifs, and they include generous rests. These melodic lines, strung between the chords of the tune like telephone wire, soon thicken, and she moves on to intense chords, often in double time or placed off the beat. Things begin to rock insistently and lightly, and after a few cloud-like melodic statements she returns to the six-eight introduction. Along the way, a Waller stride bass or an Ellington dissonance drifts by; a Basie aphorism is struck; big-interval Hines chords leap up and down the keyboard; a serpentine Bud Powell figure is carefully unspooled. But uppermost are a delicacy and wit and lofty invention that imply absolute knowledge. Rarely conscious of tempo, one is simply carried along at speeds that suggest wings and plenty of space.

The music stopped. Mary Lou Williams, having announced the intermission pianist, got down from the stand, and, after speaking a few words to a group of well-wishers, retired to a booth at the rear of the room. A waiter brought her a cup of coffee.

"I never could drink," she said. "When I was with the Andy Kirk band, back in the thirties, the boys had what they called the Hot Corn Club—named for the corn liquor they bought—and they were always trying to get me to drink. Backstage during a tonk game, somebody would make me a drink and I'd take one sip, and when I wasn't looking they would refill the glass, so I always thought I hadn't had but a taste. Once I was back at the piano, it would go right to my head, and I'd almost faint, and sit there woozy, saying 'Oh, my heart! Oh, my heart!,' and that broke the boys up." Miss Williams laughed—a low, tumbling, girlish chuckle in the quick flow of her talk—and lit a cigarette. The smoke closed her eyes, which are brown and slanted and heavy-lidded.

"I was off yesterday and I'm as stiff as a board," she said. "My fingers get stuck in the cracks. And that bass player of mine—if he'd only play jazz! He plays the bass like a guitar, with all those slurs, and he runs high notes when I'm trying to play funk. He's not with me, and it makes me mad. I'm going to call him tomorrow and nail his foot right to the floor and tell him he should go with the symphony." She shook her head, and laughed again.

"The madder I am, the more I smile," she went on. "And when I stomp my foot on the beat, it means nothing is happening. I'm dry. When I stop, it's like Erroll Garner said—'When Mary keeps her leg still, look out. Something is starting to *build*.' But all I've been doing tonight is bang my foot. Sometimes you get cold, you freeze up, but you just play until the inspiration comes. You play what you know, and play it as well as you can, and then the feeling starts. A bad audience or a waiter dropping a tray can take your inspiration. If you have a dead rhythm section, you shut it out of your mind, and you learn this the hard way. If you make a mistake, you work something good out of that mistake. We were doing 'How High the Moon' a while ago, and I hit a wrong note in a chord, and what I did was go off immediately on a different tack and work that wrong note into a pattern that fitted. It sounded way out, but it was all right. You have to be on your tiptoes every minute. No one can put a style on me. I've learned from many people. I change all the time. I experiment to keep up with what is going on, to hear what everybody else is doing.

I even keep a little ahead of them, like a mirror that shows what will happen next. One reason I came out here again is the sounds I hear in modern jazz. They're disturbed and crazy. They're neurotic, as if the Negro was pulling away from his heritage in music. You have to love when you play. Lord, I've talked talked talked music to young musicians, but they don't listen. So I've decided to show them, make them *hear* the soul." Mary Lou Williams ground out her cigarette and took a sip of coffee. "Young musicians—and old ones, too—are coming in every night, and they're listening," she said. "Too many young musicians learn from records, and copy wrong chords and wrong notes and don't know it. I can hear them, because I have perfect pitch. I'm going to stay out here and teach them."

She looked at her watch and rose.

"I've got to talk to my stepbrother," she said. "He's due in now. Tomorrow morning I'm going up to Elmsford to my dressmaker. She moved up there recently from New York. I've grown fat since I last played, and I have to have all my dresses let out. Joe Wells—he owns Wells' Restaurant, up on Seventh Avenue—is going to drive me. At ten o'clock."

Several sets later, the bassist was running high notes, Mary Lou Williams was smiling, and it was obvious from the posting motions of her skirt that she was banging her foot.

Mary Lou Williams lives alone in a two-and-a-half-room apartment on the second floor of a yellow brick building on Sugar Hill, near 144th Street and St. Nicholas Avenue. A small, cheerful kitchen faces the front door. To its left is a living room, crowded with an upright piano, a sofa, a couple of cabinets, a portable phonograph, an aluminum worktable, and a glass-topped coffee table. The top of the piano is covered with religious statues. There are three bright windows. Mary Lou Williams appeared, carrying a shopping bag filled with clothes. She had on a brown nutria coat, a brown woollen dress, and tan leather boots. Her hair was in mild disarray, and her eyes were puffy with sleep.

"Mornin'," she said.

"My, my. You ready?" Wells asked. He is short, solid, and nattily dressed, and he was wearing horn-rimmed glasses and smoking a cigar.

She replied by opening the front door. Wells trooped downstairs after her. "We used to have a doorman years ago," she said in the foyer. "But he wouldn't let *anybody* in, so we got rid of him."

It was raining outside, and Wells' car, a new tan Buick, was pebbled with water. "You get in back," Wells ordered Mary Lou Williams. "No sense jamming the front. Now, where's this Elmisford, Mary?"

"Elmsford," Miss Williams said. "Elmsford, New York." She pulled a slip of paper from her pocket. "Get on the Major Deegan and the Thruway, and get off at Exit 8. Then I'll tell you where."

Wells crossed the 149th Street bridge and worked his way onto the Deegan through the Bronx Terminal Market.

"How far is this Elmsford?" he asked.

"She said about twenty-five miles. A half hour."

"Lord! I've got a twelve-o'clock appointment—with a lady. And I make it a rule never to keep a lady waiting."

"You kept me waiting plenty of times. Get over in the middle lane, Mr. Wells."

"Cool and easy. I've never had an accident in my life."

"Well, I've had two. It's the people who have had the accidents are the good drivers. It gives them mother wit on the road."

Rain, wiping at the car from all sides, erased conversation, and no one spoke for several minutes.

"I've been driving since I was twelve," Miss Williams said eventually. "When I was eighteen, I was driving one of the cars the Kirk band travelled in. My first husband, John Williams, who played alto and baritone, had been with Kirk about six months—the band was still led by T. Holder then—and I'd been jobbing around Memphis waiting for him to send for me. I wasn't playing regularly with the band yet. I'd wait outside ballrooms in the car, and if things went bad and people weren't dancing, they would send somebody to get me and I'd go in and play 'Froggy Bottom,' or some other boogie-woogie number, and things would jump. The regular pianist, Marion Jackson, was a wanderer, and I replaced him around 1930. My, what a band that was! It was a happy band, a good-looking band, an educated band. We had love for each other. There was a lot of love among musicians in the thirties—not like it is now, with everyone out for himself. We had the type of boys that even if a woman they met didn't respect herself, they did. I was never allowed to go around by myself. My husband or two or three of the boys were always with me. I was well sheltered. But we had a hard, hard time at first. We were stranded all over—in Buffalo and Chicago and Cincinnati and Greeley, Colorado. When Kirk came backstage after a job with his head down, we'd know he hadn't been paid, and one of the trumpet players would take out his horn and play the 'Worried Blues,' and we'd all laugh. I made a little extra by manicuring the boys' nails. They paid me a nickel, and I'd take it out of the money they made from cards, which I held for them. In Greeley, we stayed next to a cornfield, and I ate corn right up to the farmer's back door. The boys played a little semi-professional baseball there. It was hot summertime, and I carried water for them. Stumpy Brady, the trombonist, nearly got himself killed chasing balls he couldn't see. It seems you've got to starve a little before you can get on. Else you get that swelled head. My husband never let me get one. He trained me. Once, I developed an introduction I liked so much that I played it and played it until he finally knocked me right off the piano stool: 'You don't play the piano that way. Just because you did that "Twinklin"—that was another of my numbers—'you think you're something.' He said unbelievable things to me, but they worked. I was learning to arrange all this time. Don Redman was my model. I could hear my chords in my head but didn't know how to write them. Kirk helped me—he was a good musician—and I learned. I was very high-strung and sensitive. When the boys fooled around at rehearsals with what I wrote, I got mad and snatched the music off their stands and began to cry and went home to bed. I'd discovered I had perfect pitch, and I couldn't stand hearing wrong notes, any more than I can now. But I could expand with that band, and try all sorts of things. We played everything—ballads, jump tunes, novelties, slow blues—and they were all different. We even extracted things from Lombardo records to play at ofay college dances. Exit 4, Mr. Wells."

"I see it, Mary."

"When we weren't on the road, we spent most of our time around Kansas City, and there were after-hours sessions every night. They were something else. A good one went right through the next day. Style didn't matter. What mattered was to keep the thing going. I'd stop in at a session after work, and they would be doing 'Sweet Georgia Brown.' I'd go home and take a bath and change my dress, and when I got back—an hour or more later—they'd still be on 'Georgia Brown.' Ben Webster came and threw some gravel on the window screen one night and woke me and my husband up and asked my husband if I could come to a session, because they were out of piano players. I went down, and Coleman Hawkins was there—Fletcher Henderson was in town—and he was having a bad time. He was down to his undershirt, and sweating and battling for his life against Lester Young and Herschel Evans and Ben, too. But they weren't cutting sessions. I recall Chu Berry sitting out front at a session and listening and not moving. When he got on the stand, he repeated note for note the last chorus the man before him had played—just to show how much he admired it—and then he went into his own bag. Whenever we were in Cleveland, I stayed close to Art Tatum, who worked there—he came from Toledo—when he wasn't in New York. When I had a day or two off, we played pinball in the afternoons, and at night we went to Val's, a little after-hours place, where we sometimes stayed until eleven in the morning. Tatum played, and they gave him fifty dollars. Then I played—usually some boogie—and they gave me five dollars. Tatum taught me how to hit my notes, how to control them without using pedals. And he showed me how to keep my fingers flat on the keys to get that clean tone. Of course, he didn't *show* me anything. He just said, 'Mary, you listen.' But once I showed *him* something. Buck Washington—of Buck and Bubbles—had given me a little run in Pittsburgh, which I used one night at Val's. Tatum said, 'What's that run, Mary? Where'd you get that? Play it for me again, please.' I did, and he developed that run—it covered just about the whole keyboard—and used it until the end of his life. Around 1940, something went wrong between me and the Kirk band. I don't think it was jealousy—or I don't

like to think it was, anyway. He had hired several new people, and maybe
I wasn't getting as much attention as I used to, and little things upset me
—untuned pianos, pianos with nine or ten keys that didn't work. I began
to feel my time was up, and one night, in Washington, D.C., I just left.
God must have got the ball rolling to move me somewhere else. Exit 6,
Mr. Wells."

The rain was heavier, and it had got chilly. Dark escarpments on both
sides of the road turned the air gray. Miss Williams shivered, and
hunched down in her coat.

"'You have a little heat, Mr. Wells? I'm cold. I was so upset when I left
Kirk I decided to leave music, and I went home to my mother's, in
Pittsburgh. But Art Blakey kept coming over to the house and pestering
me to form a group. So I finally did. We worked a park in Cleveland, and
then went into Kelly's Stable, on Fifty-second Street. Shorty Baker—he
was my second husband—had left Kirk by this time and he came with us.
Then John Hammond persuaded me to go to Café Society. We were kind
of a family there, and Barney Josephson thought of us that way. Josh
White was around a lot, and I loved to hear him laugh. He had one of
those laughs that come right from the stomach. I was feeling low after
work one night, and I didn't want any more of the teasing that was
always going around. So I flounced out with some dresses I had to get
cleaned. Josh said, 'Where you going, Pussycat?'—which is what they
called me. 'We'll take you home.' I said, 'I'm going home by myself. I'm
tired of all this mess,' and went and got a cab. About halfway up the West
Side Drive, we had a flat tire. It was near zero and blowing hard, and after
a while I stepped out and saw another cab coming. It slowed down, and
it looked like Josh and some of the others in it. I hollered with all my
might, and it must have sounded like '*josSSHHhh*' as they went by. The
cab stopped, and somebody got out and walked back. It was Josh. 'Is that
you, Pussycat?' he said. He started laughing, and he laughed so hard he
fell down on the road and lay there, hawing and holding himself. I used
to be very quiet in those days—a zombie. When people talked to me, I
looked at them and nodded, but in my mind I was writing an arrangement or going over a new tune or thinking about something I had played
the last set. And I never smiled while I was playing, so Josh would stick
his head out of the curtain backstage and make a face, and that would
break me up, and I'd smile. I came closest to getting a swelled head at this
time. People would tell me, 'Mary, you're the greatest girl pianist in the
world,' and 'Mary, you're the greatest pianist in the world,' and for a
while I believed it. But I remembered what John Williams used to tell me.
So I discarded those compliments, and it's never happened since. After I
left Café Society Downtown, I worked on Fifty-second Street with
Mildred Bailey. She was a wonderful, big, salty person. She always had
dachshunds, and she'd walk from her living room to her kitchen to get a
drink, rock, rock, rock"—Miss Williams swung stiffly from side to side
and tramped with her boots in time—"with these little dogs all around

her, and back into the living room, rock, rock, rock, the dogs still there. She joked all the time. People said you couldn't get along with Mildred, but I got along with her fine. All during this time, my house was kind of a headquarters for young musicians. I'd even leave the door open for them if I was out. Tadd Dameron would come to write when he was out of inspiration, and Monk did several of his pieces there. Bud Powell's brother, Richie, who also played piano, learned how to improvise at my house. And everybody came or called for advice. Charlie Parker would ask what did I think about him putting a group with strings together, or Miles Davis would ask about his group with the tuba—the one that had John Lewis and Gerry Mulligan and Max Roach and J. J. Johnson in it. It was still like the thirties—musicians helped each other, and didn't just think of themselves. Exit 8, Mr. Wells."

Mary Lou Williams fished her instructions from her pocket. "First light, turn left, go past Robert Hall. Turn left on Payne Street. It's the yellow house at the top of the hill."

Robert Hall swung by, and Payne Street appeared, on our right.

"Payne Street, Mary," Wells said.

"She said it was on the left. Maybe that's it down the road by that garage."

Wells obligingly drove down a narrow, winding road through a rubbish-filled field.

"Now, isn't this disappointing?" Miss William said. "I was expecting a nice house with a view. That's how she described it."

The road ended in a mountain of old tires, and Wells turned around. "Let's go back and try the other Payne, dollin," he said. "Somebody's mixed up."

The other Payne went up a steep hill, and near the top was a small yellow house. A tall woman in a sweatshirt and blue jeans opened the door. Two miniature white poodles were dancing around her feet.

Miss Williams apologized for being late.

"That's all right, honey," the dressmaker said. "There's nobody here at the moment. You come in and we'll get right to work. Mr. Wells, make yourself comfortable in the living room. We won't be too long. "

Wells sat down on a wrought-iron love seat. A dining alcove with more wrought-iron furniture was at one end of the room and a giant picture window at the other. The walls and ceiling were soft violet. A clump of plastic lilies and a stand containing brass fire irons flanked a raised fireplace. A photograph of a handsome young woman, done in the peekaboo mode of décolleté eighteenth-century portraits, hung over the mantel. A Pollock-type abstraction, full of racing reds and blacks, faced it.

Wells crossed his legs and lit a fresh cigar, and looked out at the rain. "Eleven-fifteen," he said. "I'll never make my twelve-o'clock. And I have an appointment at one, and another at two-twenty. I get very upset when I miss appointments. It tightens my stomach. But I'll do anything for Mary. I've known her since the early forties, and we've had little deals off and on through the years. Right now I'm pushing that record she just made—'St. Martin de Porres,' about the Negro saint. It has a chorus of voices, and she plays. Very lovely. She's the most brilliant woman I know. A little nervous, maybe, but brilliant."

A steady hum of talk came from the next room, and Wells, occasionally jumping up to flick ashes into the fireplace, delivered a discourse on the restaurant business, which, he said, was very good. Then it was noon, and Miss Williams appeared. She looked wide-awake and pleased, as if she were already in one of her altered dresses.

Wells drove back to the Thruway hunched over, the minutes ticking away in his head.

Miss Williams began chanting in time to the windshield wipers: "Watch out. Watch out. Watch out. Da de-da, da de-da," and hummed a little tune, using the same rhythm. "This weather reminds me of the time I got stranded about fifteen miles outside of Pittsburgh. I wasn't more than twelve, and I'd played a job with a union band, and when it was over they wouldn't pay us. We walked all the way home. We moved to Pittsburgh from Atlanta, where I was born, when I was five or six. I've had a lot of names. I was born Mary Elfrieda Scruggs, and later I was Mary Lou Winn and Mary Lou Burley, after stepfathers. I don't know where the Lou came from, but I got the Williams when I was married. I don't remember seeing my father until twelve years ago, when I went to Atlanta. I said to him, 'I bet you don't know who I am,' and all he could say was 'What have you brought me?' I said, 'You have the nerve, after all these years of doing nothing for your children!' But my mother was a good person. She worked most of the time, and my sister, Mamie, and my stepbrother, Willie, took care of me. My mother told my sister she'd kill her if anything happened to me. Of course, things did. I swallowed a pin once, and another time a Great Dane who was rabid bit me and they took me to the hospital for those shots. We had a cousin who could dance, and he and my sister dared me to jump over a box with a lighted candle on top. I did, and I tripped and broke my arm. I was so scared of what my mother would think that I crawled under my bed, with that broken arm, and stayed there for over an hour, until I finally came out crying. People shouldn't say things like 'I'll kill you' to their children. I used to stutter— I still do when I get upset—but I cured myself of the habit. My mother's almost eighty now, and has a heart condition. She played the organ, and she used to hold me on her lap when I was three, and I'd play. She wouldn't allow for a music teacher to come into the house, but she invited different musicians, and I'd listen. By the time I was six or seven, I was playing the piano in neighbors' houses all afternoon and evening—my cousin or sister taking me—and sometimes I came home with twenty or thirty dollars wrapped in a handkerchief. All I bought was shoes. My mother was a size two and a half, and I was already a five. Up to then, I used to wear her shoes to school, and they hurt so much I had to walk home barefooted. I got to be known all over our part of Pittsburgh. Miss Milholland, the principal of the Lincoln School, took me to afternoon teas at Carnegie Tech, where I played light-classical things. She also took me to the opera, but I guess I was too young, because I still don't like it. I played a home-talent show in an old theatre out in East Liberty, and did all this clowning with my elbows on the keys. One time, the Mellon family sent their chauffeur in a big car into our district looking for a Negro pianist for one of their parties. Somebody told him about me, and that night he drove me and a friend to this mansion, and I played the party. They gave me a check for a hundred dollars. My mother was very upset, and called to see if there was a mistake, but there wasn't. The first pianist who made an impression on me was Jack Howard. He played boogie so heavy he splintered the keys. I also heard a woman pianist in a theatre I went to with my brother-in-law. I can't recall her name. She sat sidewise at the keyboard with her legs crossed and a cigarette in her mouth, and she was wonderful. Earl Hines was a Pittsburgh boy, and, of course, I listened to him every chance I got."

A truck slammed past us, throwing up a curtain of water that landed with a thump on the windshield. Some of it flew in at Wells' window and sprayed Mary Lou Williams.

"That went right on me," she said, and dabbed at her face with a sleeve."Close your window, please, Mr. Wells, and I'll open mine a crack."

"You open yours a crack and you'll give me a crick," Wells replied.

She laughed. "That's what an old man gets for driving around on a day like this," she said.

"'Listen, dollin'. I'm just thinking about getting myself engaged. Old man!" said Wells.

Mary Lou Williams laughed again. The rain was letting up, and there was blue sky over a hump of woods. "My first real professional job was with the union band I got stranded with," she said. "My next was with a vaudeville group, The Hottentots. They had a pianist who was an addict, which in those days was about as familiar as going to the moon. He disappeared, and they sent someone to find me. I was playing hopscotch in the yard. When this man saw me, he said, 'Oh, man! Why did they send me all the way out here? This a *baby*!' We went inside, and he hummed a couple of tunes, and I played them back perfectly. I joined the show for the summer. I was about twelve or thirteen, and a friend came with me. We toured carnivals and such, and it was an animal life. The worst kinds of people. I was a good student, but I quit high school in my first year and went with another vaudeville group, Seymour and Jeannette. I was in the band, and so was John Williams. They had a trombonist who worked his slide with his foot, or danced the Charleston when he played. After Seymour died, we came to New York, and I sat in for a week with Ellington's Washingtonians in a theatre pit. I remember Sonny Greer and Tricky Sam Nanton. Tricky Sam drank whiskey out of a big jug held over one shoulder. I met Fats Waller at that time—that was about 1926—and I played for him, and he picked me up and threw me in the air. I didn't weigh more than eighty or ninety pounds. He played organ for the movies at Lincoln Theatre, and people screamed, he was so good. Then John Williams formed a group, and we gigged around the Midwest until he joined T. Holder. I took over the band after he left. One of the people I hired was Jimmie Lunceford. I had some rough times with gangsters, and the like, and in a roadhouse I worked near Memphis without the band, this white farmer from Mississippi came in every night and sat out front and stared at me. It shook me. Then the cook told me the farmer said he'd give him fifty dollars if he helped him take me to his farm in Mississippi. When I heard that, I never went back."

The car was rolling along beside the Harlem River, and the sun had come out.

"You want to go back to your house, Mary?" Wells asked.

"Take me down to my thrift shop, please, Mr. Wells. I got to pay the rent. It's on Twenty-ninth Street, right near Bellevue."

Wells shook his head. "I'm going to miss my one-o'clock, too."

"I started this thrift shop to help get my Bel Canto Foundation going," Mary Lou Williams said. "The idea for the Bel Canto came to me in 1957. It's a plan to help jazz musicians in trouble with drugs or alcohol. If I ever raise the money, I'll buy a house in the country. I'll only take a small number of patients, and I'll have doctors and nurses and soundproof rooms where the musicians can meditate and play. But they'll work, too—hard physical work. I'm not an organizer, but I *know* musicians. I've worked with them all through the years. Almost everybody has come to me at one time or another. I put the worst cases in a room down the hall from my place I rent cheap from a neighbor. They stay a couple of weeks, and I talk to them and pray with them and help them get a job. But I can be very hard in my charity, and sometimes I tell them, 'You've got to be a man. Stand up and go downtown and get a job. No use lying around Harlem and feeling sorry for yourself.' Sometimes they come back in worse shape and ask for money, and sometimes they get on their feet. One boy I've been helping has a job at Gimbels, and he's doing just fine. I've also sent musicians to the Graymoor Monastery, near Garrison. Brother Mario there has been a lot of help to me. I gave a benefit concert at Carnegie Hall to get the Bel Canto started, but it used up more money than it made. Then I tramped all over downtown until I found this place for a thrift shop. I fixed it up, and people in and out of music sent thousand-dollar coats and expensive dresses. I worked twelve hours a day collecting stuff and running the shop. In the evening, I went over to Bellevue to visit with musicians who were there. I raised money, but it went to rent and musicians I was helping. I was living mostly on royalty checks from records and arrangements, and then in 1960 I ran out of money and had to go to work at the Embers. I couldn't find anybody I could trust to run the shop. It's been closed off and on almost a year now, but I'm still working on money for the foundation. Some club ladies in Pittsburgh are very interested."

Wells turned into Twenty-ninth Street and pulled up in front of a modest store.

"I won't be long, Mr. Wells."

Wells turned around, his eyes wide, and said, "Mary dollin,' I've already missed two appointments. You take a cab home, please."

"O.K., and thank you," Mary Lou Williams said.

The car roared away. Mary Lou Williams unlocked the shop door. On the floor were a couple of Con Edison bills and a letter addressed to her. The walls were covered with paintings by amateurs, whose enthusiasm ranged from Grandma Moses to Picasso. Two handsome evening dresses hung in the windows, and around the shop were odd pieces of china, a sewing machine, a butcher's mallet, a rack of clothes covered with a plastic sheet, a cue stick encased in a fancy scabbard, serving trays, a tin lunchbox, rows and rows of shoes, assorted lamps, vases, and pitchers, and a cut-glass bowl. In the back, behind a partition, were piles of books and records, and two automobile tires in good condition. Everything was peppered with New York grit.

"Lord, this place is dirty," Mary Lou Williams said. "I've got to come down next Monday and clean. Those new-looking moccasins are from Duke Ellington—and this alpine hat, too. Here's a drawerful of shirts from Louis Armstrong, and those dresses are from Lorraine Gillespie, Dizzy's wife."

She opened her letter. "It's from a convict upstate—I don't know him," she said. "He says he's about to get out, and wants to know if I can help him get a job. He saw a piece in the *Christian Science Monitor* about Bel Canto. I'll write him and tell him to pray and call me when he gets here. I receive letters like this all the time."

Mary Lou Williams put her Con Edison bills in her bag, and sighed.

"You know, I'm tired," she said."1 only slept four or five hours last night. There's a kosher butcher around the corner who has the best ground beef in New York. I'll cook a hamburger at home."

Miss Williams bought the meat and, at a fish market across the street, picked up a filet of sole for supper. She hailed a cab. It was after two-thirty when she reached her apartment.

"I'm not used to running around like this," Mary Lou Williams said in her living room after lunch. "If I didn't have my prayers, they'd have to put me in a straitjacket." She laughed, and lit a cigarette. "My life turned when I was in Europe. I played in England for eleven months, and spent money as fast as I made it. But I was distracted and depressed. At a party given by Gerald Lascelles—he's an English jazz writer and a member of royalty—I met this G.I. He noticed something was wrong, and he said, 'You should read the Ninety-first Psalm.' I went home and I read all the Psalms. They cooled me and made feel protected. Then I went to France, and played theatres and clubs, but I still didn't feel right. Dave Pochonet, a French musician, asked me to his grandmother's place in the country to rest. I stayed there six months, and I just slept and ate and read the Psalms and prayed."

The living room had settled into twilight. Mary Lou Williams' face was indistinct. She stood up and stretched. Then she knelt on the sofa and, cupping her chin in her hand, looked out the window at St. Nicholas Avenue. It was a little girl's position. "When I came back from Europe, I decided not to play anymore," she said."I was raised Protestant, but I lost my religion when I was about twelve. I joined Adam Powell's church. I went there on Sunday, and during the week I sat in Our Lady of Lourdes, a Catholic church over on a Hundred and Forty-second Street. I just sat there and meditated. All kinds of people came in—needy ones and cripples—and I brought them here and gave them food and talked to them and gave them money. Music had left my head, and I hardly remembered playing. Then Father Anthony Woods—he's a Jesuit—gave Lorraine Gillespie and me instruction, and we were taken into the Church in May of 1957. I became a kind of fanatic for a while. I'd live on apples and water for nine days at a time. I stopped smoking. I shut myself up here like a monk. Father Woods got worried, and he told me, 'Mary, you're an artist. You belong at the piano and writing music. It's *my* business to help people through the Church and your business to help people through music.' He got me playing again. The night before I opened at the Hickory House, I had a dream, and it was filled with dead musicians, all friends of mine. Oscar Pettiford was in it, and Pha Terrell and Dick Wilson from Kirk's band. They were all rejoicing on this kind of stage, and there was a line of showgirls dancing and singing. Oscar was very happy because I was coming out again. It was a good sign."

Coleman Hawkins

Coleman Hawkins and Lester Young—the emperors of the tenor saxophone and the inventors of so much regal, original music—were opposites. Hawkins was a vertical improviser, who ran the chord changes and kept the melody in his rearview mirror. Young was a horizontal improviser, who kept the melody beside him and cooled the chord changes. Hawkins had a voluminous, enveloping tone. Young had an oblique, flyaway sound. Hawkins played so many notes in each chorus that he blotted out the sun. Young handpicked his notes, letting the light and air burnish them. Hawkins played with a ferocious, on-the-beat intensity. Young seemed to be towed by the beat. Hawkins was handsome, sturdy, and businesslike. Young was slender, fey, and oracular. Hawkins had a heavy voice, and he spoke rapidly and articulately. Young had a light voice and talked elliptically, in a funny, poetic language of his own. Hawkins appeared to grow bigger and denser when you looked at him. Young verged on transparency. But the two were not totally dissimilar. Hawkins eventually destroyed himself with alcohol, and so did Young, although he did the job quicker. (Hawkins died at the age of sixty-four, in 1969, and Young at the age of forty-nine in 1959.) Both were assiduous dressers, with Hawkins being something of a fashion plate. Both were consumed by their music, and have countless musical descendants.

Hawkins invented the tenor saxophone in the way that Richardson invented the novel: he took an often misunderstood instrument and made it work right for the first time. The saxophone, like the tuba, had been used for comic effects and in marching bands, and it was regarded—half brass, half reed—as a hybrid. It took Hawkins ten years to figure out completely what the instrument was capable of. He hit upon using an unusually wide mouthpiece and a hard reed, and by 1933 he had developed a tone that had never before been heard on a saxophone. (There were saxophone virtuosos before Hawkins, but they had a facile tone, and concentrated on creamy glissandos and dazzling arpeggios.) His tone had the edgelessness of cellos and contraltos. It filled the mind with images of firelit mahogany, of august spaces, of great elms. Hawkins talked (when he talked—he was taciturn) the way he played: crowding his words together, and steadily gaining momentum. Here he is on an autobiographical recording made in the fifties for Riverside. He is discussing his style: "It changed automatically through different things that I heard. It always shows in your music. I mean it just comes spontaneously. I mean you don't have to practice it. I never practiced anything like that, you know. I never practiced any particular thing to learn a style or anything like that. I never did in my life. I find myself playing a lot of things, changing them around and playing them completely different than what I would perhaps have played them a year before. But that just came through, I mean, different things I've heard. You know, I've heard it and I remembered it, you know what I mean. The next night, I perhaps didn't remember it, but maybe six months later it would show up in the music. . . . That's what used to happen. That's why the style used to change all the time. And I tell you something else I used to do. I was the only one—there wasn't anybody else doing this. I used to go out on these road trips with Fletcher [Henderson]. Every time we came in after a road trip, I always had me some new things. And you know where I used to find them? In these little clubs and places, in all these little towns we used to go in and play. . . . I've never stopped, you know; I'm still doing the same thing today. I hear every musical organization of any interest that there is." And here he is, on the Riverside record, talking about the effect of New York on newly arrived country-mouse musicians: "This place makes all musicians sound funny when they come around. When they first come here—I don't care what they were in their home towns—when they first come here, they get cut. They get cut every time. They have to come here and learn all over again, practically. Then when they come back they're all right, or if they stay here they'll develop to be all right."

Hawkins walked quickly, in an erect, the-meeting-will-now-come-to-order fashion. He did not smile much; he was a reserved man, surrounded by lawns of reticence. But reserved people often conceal hellions. Hawkins loved to play jokes on his friends, and he loved to drive fast. The trombonist Sandy Williams told Stanley Dance, in "The World of Swing," "I remember coming with him and Walter Johnson from Philly once, and he had just got a new Imperial. He decided to open it up on a long stretch, and he had it up to a hundred and three miles an hour. That was the first time I ever did over a hundred an hour, but Hawk was a good driver. 'Hell, I don't want to kill myself,' he'd tell you right quick. 'What are you worried about?'" Hawkins had no showmanship, and when he played he closed his eyes and held his horn to the right of him, almost at port arms.

Hawkins was born in 1904, or perhaps earlier, in St. Joseph, Missouri. He was the second child of Cordelia Coleman and Wil Hawkins. (Their only other child, a girl, died in infancy.) He liked to tell interviewers that he was born at sea while his parents were returning from a European vacation—he was a great leg-puller and a good mythologist. His father was an electrical worker who was killed accidentally in the twenties, and his mother was a schoolteacher who lived to be ninety-five. (A grandmother reached a hundred and four.) He took up the piano when he was five, studied cello for several years, and was given a tenor saxophone when he was nine. By the time he was thirteen, he was full-grown, and his parents had sent him to Chicago, where he lived with friends and went to high school. He also heard King Oliver and Louis Armstrong and Jimmie Noone. He is supposed to have attended Washburn College, in Topeka, but there is no proof he did. In 1921, he was working at the Twelfth Street Theatre in Kansas City, where he was heard by the blues singer Mamie Smith, whose accompanists included the Ellington trumpeter Bubber Miley and the reedman Garvin Bushell. Bushell told Nat Hentoff, in *The Jazz Review*, "We played the Twelfth Street Theatre and that's where I first met Coleman Hawkins. They had added a saxophone to play the show with us in the pit. He was ahead of everything I ever heard on that instrument. It might have been a C melody he was playing then. Anyway, he was about fifteen years old—I remember that because one night we went to his mother's house in St. Joseph and asked her to let him go with us, and she said, 'No, he's only a baby; he's only fifteen.' He was really advanced. He read everything without missing a note. I haven't heard him miss a note yet in thirty-seven years. And he didn't— as was the custom then—play the saxophone like a trumpet or clarinet. He was also running changes then, because he'd studied the piano as a youngster."

Hawkins joined Mamie Smith's Jazz Hounds in 1922, and Fletcher Henderson's first band in 1923. He stayed eleven years. The Henderson band—powerful, erratic, undisciplined—was the first big swing band and the model for almost every big band of the thirties. It was also an academy for such first-rate jazz musicians as Louis Armstrong, Rex Stewart, Red Allen, Roy Eldridge, Joe Thomas, Jimmy Harrison, Sandy Williams, Benny Morton, J. C. Higginbotham, Dicky Wells, Keg Johnson, Benny Carter, Ben Webster, Lester Young, Chu Berry, John Kirby, Walter Johnson, and Sidney Catlett. Rex Stewart, in his "Jazz Masters of the Thirties," recalls Hawkins in the early thirties: "As usual, on hitting a town, we all went to look the burg over, and it so happened that I found myself with Coleman in a department store. He went to the cosmetic counter and bought several bars of a very expensive soap. Hawk's remark that this was the year's supply and a great bargain made me wonder how he could figure that six bars of soap would last him a whole year. But the next morning in the hotel, I found out. First, out came a pair of ornate washcloths, then the special soap, then some ordinary soap. One cloth was for the special soap, the other for the ordinary, and never the twain should meet. The fancy soap was daintily applied to a corner of washcloth number one. That was for his face and around his eyes only. Then, the ordinary soap, applied to the other cloth, was used on his body." Stewart went on to say, "Another facet of Mr. Saxophone's character is his frugality . . . This is not to imply that Hawk is cheap; it's just that he is cautious. Before he got over his mistrust of banks, it was common for him to walk around with $2,000 or $3,000 in his pockets! One time, he carried with him his salary from an entire season of summer touring, about $9,000. When we became stranded, for some reason or other, Hawk laughed while showing his roll. But he wouldn't give a quarter to see the Statue of Liberty do the twist on the Brooklyn Bridge at high noon."

In 1934, Hawkins, tired of Henderson's lackadaisical ways as a leader and a businessman, and curious about the high-class things he had heard about Europe, wired the British bandleader Jack Hylton, was offered a job, and took a six-month leave of absence. He remained abroad five years, and it may have been the happiest time of his life. He was one of the first great jazz soloists, and he was treated like royalty wherever he went. He played in England and Wales, then settled on the Continent, where he worked in Belgium, Holland, Switzerland, Denmark, and France. He recorded with English and Dutch and French and Belgian musicians, among them Django Reinhardt and Stéphane Grappelli, and with such Americans as Benny Carter, Tommy Benford, and Arthur Briggs. According to Chris Goddard, in "Jazz Away Home," Briggs once gave this picture of Hawkins in Paris: "He was such a wonderful person. I couldn't believe that anyone could drink so much alcohol and that it would have so little effect on him. When we were working together in Belgium . . . he would drink a bottle of brandy a day . . . He would be featured at the tea dance. He did three numbers so most of the time he was free in the baccarat room. He didn't gamble. He'd just be at the bar. And when I sent someone to fetch him to play he'd come on as straight as ever. I never knew him to practice. . . . He didn't talk much. But he had wonderful taste. I remember him paying twenty dollars for a pair of socks. He was crazy about beautiful shirts in silk and things like that. He would dress like a prince. I think Europe was a rest cure for him."

Hawkins returned from Europe in July of 1939. In October, he recorded (as an afterthought) his celebrated "Body and Soul" for Victor, and early in 1940 he put together a big band. Hawkins' playing passed through four phases in his life, and he was about to enter his third and best period. His neophyte period had lasted until the late twenties. During that time, he had a hard sound, and his rhythmic attack was aggressive and staccato and congested. He even used slap-tonguing, a device that had originated in New Orleans and that resembled the sound of a ratchet. He entered his second phase in the early thirties. His tone filled out, he abandoned much of his staccato attack, and he developed a rich vibrato. He began playing slow ballads like "It's the Talk of the Town," "Out of Nowhere," and "Star Dust." Jazz had been a rough-and-ready, shouting, realistic music; Hawkins proved it could be romantic, and changed it forever. When he came home, his always imperious confidence intact, he went out on the town and was paid court to at every place he stopped. But he must have felt some nervousness, and the uncanny popular success of the Victor "Body and Soul," which consists of two unvarnished, uninterrupted choruses of improvisation, certainly cheered him. He did not record between 1940 and 1943 (a musicians'-union recording ban was part of the reason), but from 1943 to 1947 he recorded over a hundred numbers, some of them as brilliant as any jazz recording. Bob Wilber remembers him on Fifty-second Street in the early forties: "We'd go to Kelly's Stable to hear Coleman Hawkins and he'd come out in a gray pinstriped suit and I guess we were expecting the extraordinary but all that happened was his piano player said, 'What you want to play, Hawk?' and Hawkins said, 'Body,' meaning 'Body and Soul', which was his big thing then. After that, he'd do one of his riff tunes based on the chords of 'I Got Rhythm' or something like that, and you wouldn't see him again for a couple of hours." His playing had reached its peak. His slow numbers were distinguished by his great welcoming tone, his almost discursive vibrato, and the seignorial new melodies he imposed on whatever he improvised on. His up-tempo numbers were headlong. He poured through the chords, restructuring them as he went. He never paused to breathe, and he built a rampaging momentum, transposing to his horn with great speed everything he heard in his head. His rare missed notes immediately vanished in the surrounding perfection. His improvisations at this time were rivalled in density, daring, and sheer strength only by Art Tatum's. (Hawkins had first heard Tatum in the early thirties, and Tatum had made a strong impression.) Hawkins began working Norman Granz's Jazz at the Philharmonic tours in the late forties, and when he settled down again in the fifties something had happened to his style. He had entered his final period. At times, he was exceptional, but there were increasing signs of unsteadiness. His vibrato fell away or became quavery. His tone hardened, recalling the sound he had in the late twenties. He began using alarming shrieks and cries—Lear sounds. The bursting melodic invention withered, the great rhythms faltered.

Hawkins' big band was not a success and lasted less than a year. For a time, he played and lived in Chicago, where he met a white woman named Delores Sheridan. They were married in 1943 in New York, and they had three children—Colette, Rene, and Mimi. The rest of his career was spent with Jazz at the Philharmonic or with small groups generally made up of him and a rhythm section. He suffered some neglect in the early fifties but came to the fore again in the mid-fifties and remained more or less in view until the last year or two of his life. He had for a long time been a renowned eater, but his drinking slowly supplanted food. He eventually drank steadily and ate almost nothing. He became thin and careworn, and he grew a patriarchal beard, perhaps as a sort of disguise. He sometimes sat down on a chair when he played. Not long after his death, his old friend Roy Eldridge talked about him: "Coleman was a first-class cat all the way down the line. He was the old school. He never travelled economy, and, of course, he was like a genius on his horn. I guess I knew him as well as anybody. I got my first job—for twelve dollars a week, in 1927— through him, by copying his solo, note for note, off Fletcher Henderson's record of 'Stampede.' And I was the first person near him after he came back from five years in Europe in 1939. I had a Lincoln and he had a Cadillac, and we followed each other to gigs—double things like that. He was a person people were afraid to talk to. If anything went wrong on a job, they wouldn't go to him, they'd always come to me. He was proud, but he wasn't cold, and he had a sense of humor. He just stayed away from cats he didn't like. People said he didn't like Lester Young, who was supposed to be his great rival. Man, I remember Coleman and I sat up all one night with Lester in the fifties, when we were with Jazz at the Philharmonic, trying to find out why Lester was up so tight. We never did. The last five years, Coleman was sick, and he just about quit eating. All he had eyes for, when he ate at all, was Chinese food, like Lester. But I'd call him in the evening and tell him what I was cooking. I'd tell him such-and-such, and he'd say, 'That sounds pretty good. I'll have to come out and get me some.' The next day, I'd call again, and he'd forgotten everything. Coleman always had money, and he always spent it the right way. He'd have a Leica and a Steinway and three-hundred-dollar suits, but before anything else he always laid out six hundred dollars a month to take care of his rent and his wife and children. I often wondered if he had a little income of his own, but I never knew, because money was one thing we didn't discuss. Just a while ago, I went out with Coleman when he wanted to look at a Rolls-Royce to buy, and I said to him,'You'd look ridiculous riding around in that.' So he bought a Chrysler Imperial. Eight thousand in cash. I don't think he got to put more than a thousand miles on it."

In the fifties and sixties, Hawkins often worked with younger musicians, like the drummer Eddie Locke, the pianist Tommy Flanagan, and the bassist Major Holley. They recently spoke of Hawkins. Flanagan said, "He was a very humorous man. He'd tell stories at great length in that bass voice of his. It was always bigger than anyone else's voice. It reminded me of his horn. He was at home with every kind of music. A master musician."

Locke: "He opened my ears to classical music. I believe that he incorporated that in his music. That separated him from other saxophone players. He played jazz, but it was classical-jazz. He loved the piano, and he always had piano players visiting him—guys like Joe Zawinul and Monk. Monk loved Coleman. He was a different person around him. Nothing weird or strange, just straight conversation."

Major Holley: "He was a very knowledgeable man. He'd amaze you with the things he would tell you that didn't pertain to music. He knew about the assembly of automobiles—I could tell, I had worked in a factory. He knew about art. He knew about flowers. He had impeccable taste in clothes. He was a connoisseur of wine. He was a culinary expert. When he did a stew, it was like European cooking—a whole potato, a whole carrot. If he invited you over to eat, he would be put out if you didn't come. He played the piano, and he could do things that full-time players were hard-pressed to do. He had learned circular breathing, which was why he could play those very long lines. And I once saw him pick up a cello and play it very well after not touching one for forty years. He was a master at setting up comedy, a master jokesman. He would ask a whole bunch of us to his apartment on Central Park West—maybe Tommy Flanagan and Roland Hanna and Lew Tabackin and Zoot Sims. He'd play classical records by the hour, and maybe get into Chopin, and then suggest that Roland Hanna play one of the Chopin études we had just heard, and, of course, by this time Hanna had consumed a fair amount of brandy—and, well . . . Sometimes Hawkins would call me and I'd answer the telephone and all I would hear would be him shaking a glass of ice in it, and laughing in the background, and he'd hang up. He was very private and very shy. He had great concern for people, and he did a lot of stuff he never talked about. When he went out on the road, he would visit some musician he knew in prison, whether he knew him well or not. Or he would go to see his mother in St. Joe. He had rules, he had morals. He had the sort of courtesy that has to be taught you when you're a kid. He was always interested in young people and in getting his ideas across to them. He had a great ambition to play for younger people. We worked together for two or three years. He was my friend. But I would like to have known him better. I didn't really get to understand him We didn't have enough time."

A Good One-Two

On March 16th, 1977, Marian McPartland gave her old friend and former husband Jimmy McPartland a surprise seventieth-birthday party at the Café Carlyle. McPartland put the gathering in focus when he and Marian cut his birthday cake and he said, "I suggest that all married people get divorced and begin treating each other like human beings," which is exactly what the McPartlands did seven years before. He lives on the south shore of Long Island in a salt-box full of cats, and she lives a few miles away, in a red brick house. They talk on the telephone every day and see each other a couple of times a week. They discuss problems neither would discuss with anyone else. McPartland does errands for Marian, and she sometimes borrows his car. They go to the beach, and they play gigs together. "Unfortunately, these tributes are almost always paid posthumously," Marian said before the party. "So why not do it properly this time—when the old man is alive and can enjoy it?"

The old man is not only alive but jumping. He has shed a lot of weight, and his eyes are clear and quick. His voice, always of hog-calling dimensions, is strong, and he still enters rooms at about sixty miles an hour. When he talks, he rocks from side to side, like a boxer, which he was, and he frequently punctuates what he says by biffing the air with a good one-two. He likes to stir things up, whatever way. His Scottish face, with its long nose and broad forehead, is handsome and firm, and his gray hair has its scottish curl. The party was scheduled for eight, and McPartland drove Marian in from the Island an hour before. He was wearing his uniform: a blue blazer, a blue-and-white striped shirt, a four-in-hand foulard tie, and trousers of a dark-green-and-red tartan. Marian had told him only that they would be playing a private party in the Café. When they arrived, she deposited him in the cubicle that the Carlyle had offered her as a dressing room, and told him to wait there until she called. He had his horn and two thermoses, one of hot tea and one of hot coffee. He carries them in a black bag everywhere he goes. They are his comfort and his crutch, for after struggling with alcohol much of his life he stopped drinking in the late sixties. He has discovered that he plays better, feels better, thinks better, and looks better. "The drinking was just kidding myself," he said in Marian's dressing room. "It didn't help a thing, it only aggravated it. I started going to A.A. in 1947, and I've slipped six times, the last nine years ago. I've learned to be completely honest with myself." McPartland was sitting in a corner of the room, which was furnished with a clothespress, a bureau, two chairs, and a telephone. A thermos top of tea was by his right foot, and he had his cornet in his right hand. He likes to talk, and between conversational bursts he worked on his embouchure.

Five years ago, when a front tooth began mysteriously receding, he started moving his embouchure slightly to his right, and he is still getting
used to the change. He placed the mouthpiece slowly and precisely, as if
he were affixing a stamp to a document, and blew: *"pew pew pew."* He
took a breath, recemented the horn, and blew again. "You have to work
on your embouchure every day," he said. "You blow five or ten minutes,
and have a cup of tea, then you blow five or ten minutes more, and have
another cup of tea. Keeping your chops in shape is an athletic business.
It's like being a ballet dancer. You lay off one day, it's bad. Two days, it's
worse. Three days, forget it. These muscles"—he pointed to the muscles
on either side of his mouth—"give out, and everything goes blah. It's dis-
tressing. But when my chops are in shape and I'm playing with four, five,
six musicians who have empathy, it's like a fine conversation. We're listening to each other, and we're talking in between, and it's no place for a
loner. This perfection doesn't happen often, but it's a lovely and gratifying experience. Whatever emotions you have that day go right to the
edge, and then come out. You forget about yourself, because you're too
busy treating the other musicians like gentlemen and artists, which they
are. Before I improvise, I just listen, and that triggers me. I don't see anything, and nothing goes through my mind except the melody, which I
keep at the back."

McPartland has been improvising professionally since 1923, the year
before he replaced Bix Beiderbecke in the Wolverines. Alec Wilder once
said: "There is a treasure there behind the banner of age and the assump-
tion he is too old to do anything different from what he did with the
Wolverines. All kinds of lovely sounds come out when he is relaxed and
playing with non-Dixieland musicians. I don't see any relationship to Bix.
It is simply the sound of excellent music." McPartland at his best plays
with a no-gloves lyricism, a singing, pursuing quality, as if jazz were a
race instead of a form of meditation. His playing rounds its shoulders
and runs. It suggests an admiration for the Louis Armstrong of the early
thirties, and it suggests Beiderbecke's tone and bemused legato attack.
When McPartland met Beiderbecke, who was his idol, Beiderbecke produced a nicely shaded mot, which McPartland has probably repeated a
thousand times. "I like you, kid," Beiderbecke said. "You sound like me,
but you don't copy me." Beiderbecke, his feet already on Olympus, was
twenty-one and McPartland seventeen. The school of playing that
Beiderbecke unwittingly founded—Bobby Hackett, Red Nichols, Rex
Stewart, and McPartland are its best-known graduates—has unswerving
characteristics: a beautiful tone, a fondness for big intervals and small,
curling connective runs, a straightforward rhythmic attack, a holding up
of handsome melodic mirrors. It is an attractive way of playing the cornet, but it has been dismissed as a minor strain of jazz brass playing.
Armstrong has long been regarded as king, but the truth is that
Armstrong and Beiderbecke each thought the other a nonpareil in their
day and they played together every chance they got.

McPartland made several *"pew"*s, and poured himself another cup of tea. Marian called to say that it would be half an hour before they were ready. They had to move the piano, she said. "Move the piano, my eye," McPartland boomed. "I think she has something in mind down there, but I don't want to ruin her fun. Anyway, it takes me a while to get my chops ready. It's not like the old days, when you just picked up your horn and—bam!—you were ready to blow, which is what we were crazy to do. When I was thirteen or fourteen, we moved to Austin, on the west side of Chicago, and after I graduated from the John Hay grammar school, I went to Austin High, where I met Bud Freeman and Frank Teschemacher and Jim Lanigan. We all played the violin, the way kids play the guitar now, and we hung out after school in the Spoon and Straw, where there was a table covered with records that you could play on a windup. There were Paul Whitemans and Rudy Wiedoefts, but one day a new record, by the New Orleans Rhythm Kings, appeared, and we went nuts. Lanigan took up the bass and Teschemacher the clarinet and Freeman the C-melody saxophone and me, the loudmouth, the cornet, and we also had my brother Rich on guitar, Dave North on piano, and a kid from Oak Park High named Dave Tough on drums. We'd get together and play the New Orleans Rhythm Kings' records and the Creole Jazz Band and Bix and the Wolverines, and we'd play them two bars at a time and try to memorize them. Not their solos—no, sir. Everybody had to do his own solos. When we got good enough, we played anywhere for anybody, and we got to be known as the Austin High gang. I was apt and got better faster, I guess. When I was sixteen and in my second year of high, I worked for a boxer named Eddie Tancil, who had a saloon near Hawthorne, the race track. It was six nights a week, and fifty-five dollars. The trombone player Joe Quartell told the leader he'd heard a kid clarinet player who was sensational. I had just gone into bell-bottoms, but when this kid showed up he was still in shorts. He prayed 'Rose of the Rio Grande,' and I was flabbergasted at the way he got around the instrument. His name was Benny Goodman, and we started running together. That New Year's Eve, Vic Moore, who'd just left the Wolverines, heard me and said, 'Christ, you sound just like Bix.' Then Dick Voynow, of the Wolverines, sent a wire asking me to join the band at the Cinderella Ballroom, in New York. Bix had been hired by Jean Goldkette, and they wanted me. The telegram offered eighty-seven-fifty a week, but I thought it was all a gag. I wired back for transportation money, to see what would happen, and they sent thirty-five dollars. Everybody saw me off at the La Salle Street station in Chicago. It took me three days to get to New York, via Buffalo, because I'd taken some sort of milk train. I met Bix after my first rehearsal. He'd been sitting there the whole time and I hadn't recognized him. Voynow put me in a double room at the Somerset with Bix, and we stayed together eight days while he showed me the fine points.

"The bouncer at the Cinderella was Frankie Fleming, and I got to know him by knocking a guy cold who pulled a knife on him. Fleming found out I was a boxer—my father had taught me—and he took me to Philadelphia Jack O'Brien's gym and had me work out, and he was all ready to book me. I asked Voynow what he thought, and he told me that I must be crazy even to think about it, that I'd have to be one or the other—a cornet player needs all his teeth and a boxer doesn't. When the Wolverines got back to Chicago, we went to work at Barone's. I brought Jim Lanigan and Freeman and Tesch into the band, along with my brother Rich and Dave Tough, who became one of the great drummers. He would get a beat going that pushed you so hard you couldn't help yourself—you could ask anybody, including Sid Catlett. Husk O'Hare took over promotion and the band became Husk O'Hare's Wolverines under the direction of Jimmy McPartland. I was nineteen, and making good money and behaving myself. I had quit high school after two years, so every chance I got at college gigs I sat in on classes and was given books and pointers and every sort of kindness. We worked the White City Ballroom, on the South Side of Chicago, and Louis would come by all the time. He wouldn't play. He'd just sit at the back of the bandstand and listen. After hours we'd go to the Nest, where Jimmie Noone was, or to the basement of the Three Deuces, and sit in with Louis and Bix and Pee Wee Russell and Frankie Trumbauer. Which reminds me of when I ran into Louis in Philadelphia in the fifties, and he said, his voice down in the coal cellar"—McPartland makes an excellent Louis Armstrong voice—"Hey, McPartland! I been listening to that album you made, that "Shades of Bix." Man, you blow the hell out of that horn!' That set me up for about a decade. One morning, back in Chicago, Bix and I left the Nest, and three tough guys were standing in front of a barbershop, and one of them tried to grab my horn. I set it down and—bang!—he was gone. And then— bang!—the second guy was gone. Bix took care of the third. He could really hit. He was a hell of a tennis player and a good ballplayer, but you never would have known, because he didn't talk about it. In fact, he didn't talk much at all unless he was around musicians."

McPartland stood up and stretched. "Where's Marian?" he said. "They must be moving that piano around the block." He sat down and picked up his horn and released three heavy *"pew"*s. "Everybody worked for the mob in Chicago. Al Capone used to come into one place where I was, and he always asked for 'My Gal Sal.' Then he'd send one of his torpedoes over with a fifty or a hundred. One night, one of 'em shot a hole in Jim Lanigan's bass and then asked me how much a new one would cost. I knew Lanigan had paid two hundred, so I said eight hundred and fifty. He gave it to me on the spot, and I passed Lanigan three hundred and fifty and kept the rest. I left the Wolverines before they broke up, and went with Art Kassel and then with Ben Pollack, who got a gig at the Little Club, in New York. Bix was in town with Paul Whiteman, and we lived together for a while at the Forty-fourth Street Hotel. Bix had reached the point where he had to take a slug of Gordon's gin before he answered the phone in the morning. Later, when the Little Club job blew up, I didn't eat for three days. I ran into Bix at a Park Avenue party where they had plenty to drink but no food, and asked him for a loan. All I needed was ten or twenty dollars, but he gave me five fifties. 'Take it, kid'—which is what he always called me, never my name—'and pay me back when you're working.' Pollack landed a job at the Park Central Hotel, where Arnold Rothstein was killed, and we doubled for a while in Lew Fields's 'Hello Daddy,' and made records every other day. Benny Goodman and Jack Teagarden and Glenn Miller were in the band, and after work we went uptown and sat in with Fletcher Henderson and Duke Ellington and Willie the Lion. But we took care of ourselves, or at least Benny and I did. Benny was very athletic, and he and I sometimes played handball before work, which was fine until Pollack got tired of me coming to the bandstand with dirty shoes and fired me. When that happened, Goodman told Pollack he'd quit, too, and he did. About this time, I married Dorothy Williams, of the Williams sisters, and Roger Wolfe Kahn, who had a fine band, married Hannah, her sister. Neither marriage lasted very long, but Dorothy and I had a daughter, and on nice afternoons Jimmy Dorsey and I wheeled our babies down through Central Park to Plunketts, a speak at Fifty-third and Seventh where musicians hung out. Plunketts was the last place I saw Bix. It was the summer of 1931, and he had a terrible cold. I had long since paid him back, and he asked me if I could help him out. I gave him what I had—about a hundred and fifty dollars. He died three days later, of pneumonia, out in Queens, and everybody at Plunketts cried. I was with Russ Columbo and Smith Ballew and Horace Heidt after Pollack, and I spent most of the thirties in Chicago with my brother's group and with my own bands. In 1939, I worked at Nick's with Pee Wee Russell and Georg Brunis, and then I joined Jack Teagarden's big band and stayed until the war."

The phone rang, and Marian told McPartland to come down in ten minutes. He leaned his chair against the wall and fired off half a dozen well-spaced *"pew"*s, each delivered as if he were pushing a pig across a pen. "Some musicians tried to duck the war, but I was a patriotic drunk and enlisted in the Army, and ended up in automatic weapons. I had my cornet, and on the troopship to Scotland I formed a band. But I was still a corporal down in the hold. Then the third mate, who'd heard me at Nick's, wangled it so that I could move into his cabin for the rest of the trip. That cabin was full of whiskey, and I stayed drunk until we went over the side and into the tender in the harbor at Greenock. I was standing on the deck, and suddenly I remembered 'The Blue Bell of Scotland,' so I took out my horn and played it. It was early morning and as still as church and you could hear for miles. The townspeople and the bagpipers were lined up on the dock, and I played it real pretty, jazzed it up in the middle, and went back to the melody. When we got ashore, the mayor ran around shouting 'Where is the mon that played the trompet? Where is the mon that played the trompet?' and when he found out there was a lot of hugging and celebrating. We practiced for the invasion off the coast of

Wales, and I went in on D Day-plus-4. I was in a Jeep fitted out with a
fifty-calibre machine gun. I was scared. Very scared. All I could do, seeing everybody getting hit around me, was apply for help Upstairs, and I
got the word: Go ahead, you're trained, you're strong. I relaxed and was
all right. I went through Saint-Lô and the Bulge and got five battle stars
and was never hit, and I've never been scared of death since. But, man, I
got tired of thinking about it, and finally they transferred me to Special
Services. I met Marian playing in a tent in the Ardennes. She rushed the
tempo, this English girl playing jazz piano, but her harmonies killed me.
She tried to talk and act G.I., but I knew she was a lady. I courted her for
weeks, and we got married in February of 1945 in Aachen. We played at
our own wedding."

McPartland put his horn in its case, hunched into his blazer, and took
the elevator down to the Carlyle lobby. When he got to the door of the
Café, which is glass, he peered through into the darkness, hesitated a second, and opened the door. "Happy Birthday," played by Marian, Bob
Wilber, and Vic Dickenson, hit him, his face went blank, then regrouped,
and he charged over to the piano and gave Marian a kiss. McPartland
made a short speech; greeted his guests (Willis Conover, Bob and Jean
Bach, Gene Shalit, George Shearing, John Lewis, Teddi King, Mabel
Mercer); read some telegrams, one of them from Benny Goodman, which
prompted him to recall that he had taken Goodman to Marshall Field in
Chicago when they were kids to help him buy some knickers, and to suggest that Goodman was probably still wearing them; and played several
numbers with Lewis, Wilber, and Dickenson. Then he sat down at a table
in a corner and ordered some tea. "My mother taught me 'The Blue Bell
of Scotland,' " he said. "Her name was Jeannie Munn, and she came from
Paisley, near Glasgow. She had sharp features and was very pretty. She
always wanted me to be a little gentleman. She had been a schoolteacher,
and had seven sisters, one of whom, Aunt Bell, is still alive and is a peach.
Her father's name was Dugald, which accounts for my name—James
Dugald McPartland. Old Dugald was a tool-and-die maker and an inventor. I remember a patent-infringement case he won. He also was a thirty-
second-degree Mason. Every Sunday, he would read the Bible to me, and
his burr was so thick I couldn't understand a word. But he paid me fifteen cents, and afterward I'd shoot craps under the 'L' at Lake and
Paulina, which was a tough neighborhood. My father was born in
Burlington, Iowa, and he met my mother in Chicago, where they were
married. He was big and husky and looked like me. He could do anything, including drink, which he didn't start doing until he was twenty-
one and didn't stop doing until he was dead. He was a boxer and a baseball player and a musician. He played third base with Anson's Colts, who
became the Chicago Cubs. He started me on violin when I was six and
boxing a year or so later—by the time I was twelve or thirteen, I was in
the club fights, which were like the Golden Gloves now, and I never lost.
But when I was seven, my mother and father separated, and my brother

Rich and I were put in an orphanage—the Maywood Baptist Orphanage. Ruth and Ethel, my two sisters, and both older, went with an aunt. Rich got sick and went to stay with my mother, and I got in an argument with Roy McGilvey's son and knocked him through a glass door. It was snowing, but they gave me my little bundle and three cents carfare and told me to get the hell out. My mother and father were back together, so I lived with them and went to the William H. Brown grammar school, on Warren and Hermitage. It wasn't long before Rich and I were in the Hermitage gang, which had pulled a half-million-dollar train robbery. I was the leader of the younger kids. We'd draw chalk circles in the street and stand in 'em and challenge anybody and everybody to knock us out. I knew how to hit and move, and the only fight I didn't win was a draw. Then we took a forty-five automatic from the side pocket of a touring car parked outside of Jimmy Murphy's Bucket of Blood, and started stealing chickens. We'd go out to isolated houses around Cicero, a lot of them with their own chicken coops, and twist the chickens' necks enough to keep them quiet, then sell them to restaurants, no questions asked. Pretty soon, I had ninety-one dollars in the bank. But one night somebody fired a shotgun at us and we fired back, and there was a headline in the local paper 'chicken thieves armed.' Then Baldy, who was in the gang, got caught in a coop, and the police found the gun, and Rich and I were up for reform school. All that kept us out was my mother. She used to make extra money translating in court, mainly for immigrants, so she knew the judge we came up before. He told my mother he wouldn't send us away if she moved to a decent neighborhood. He put us on probation for a year, and we moved to Austin, and after that things began to straighten out. My Uncle Fred Harris was a big help. He was married to one of my father's sisters, and was a well-to-do lawyer. During the summers, he took Rich and me fishing in Indiana and Michigan, and even to Rifle, Colorado. He taught us how to swim, and he taught us just about everything about fishing and fish—about habitats, where fish spawn, when they are at the bottom, how they feed along the shore in the evening. He made us learn the Latin names—*Esox masquinongy* for the muskie, *Oncorhynchus kisutch* for the coho salmon, *Esox niger* for the chain pickerel. I even got good enough to work one summer as a guide at Ed Gabe's Lost Lake Resort, in Sayner, Wisconsin. Uncle Fred was a fine gent."

Davy Tough

Dave Tough was born in Oak Park, Illinois, the youngest child of James and Hannah Fullerton Tough, both of whom were born in Aberdeen, Scotland. He had two brothers, George and James, and a sister, Agnes. His father was a bank teller, who dabbled in real estate and the commodities market. His mother died, of apoplexy, in 1916, when he was nine, and in 1921 his father married a sister of his mother's. Tough continued to call her "aunt," even though she was now his stepmother, and this gave rise to the half truth that he lived with his aunt and uncle. He went to Oak Park High School, but he never graduated. By the time he was fifteen or sixteen, he was playing drums and hanging out with the Austin High School Gang. Tough was already, as Art Hodes puts it, a "runner-around." He was also two people—the hard-drinking drummer and the bohemian, who read voraciously, did some painting and drawing, took language and literature courses at the Lewis Institute, and hung out at a night club called the Green Mask, where he accompanied poetry readings by such as Max Bodenheim, Langston Hughes, and Kenneth Rexroth. His old friend Bud Freeman says in his book "You Don't Look Like a Musician" that Tough took him to a Cézanne show at the Chicago Art Institute. Mezz Mezzrow, the clarinettist, hustler, and embroiderer of tales, recalls in his "Really the Blues" how Tough talked:

> Dave Tough, who tipped delicately over his words like they were thin ice, always used to lecture me on how important it was to keep your speech pure, pointing out that the French and people like that formed their vowels lovingly, shaping their lips just right when they spoke, while Americans spoke tough out of the corners of their mouths . . . I thought Dave's careful way of talking was too precise and effeminate. He thought I was kind of illiterate, even though he admired my musical taste and knowledge. He was always making me conscious of the way I talked because he kept on parodying the slurs and colloquial kicks in my speech, saying that I was just trying to ape the colored man.

Tough's profession and drinking had already estranged him from his family. In 1927, barely twenty, he married and went to Europe with his wife and the clarinettist Danny Polo. He worked with various bands in Paris, Ostend, Berlin, and Nice. The Prince of Wales, who seemed to do little else at this period, sat in on his drums, and Tough drank a great deal. Bud Freeman says that Tough wrote limericks with Scott Fitzgerald, and that Tough was shocked when he discovered that Freeman, over on a short visit, hadn't read "The Sun Also Rises." Tough returned to America in 1929, worked for a time with Red Nichols, and went back to Chicago, where he entered what his biographer, Harold S. Kaye, calls his "dark period." He seems, for the next four or five years, to have been a derelict. Jess Stacy was in Chicago in the early thirties, and he remembers Tough. "He'd always had trouble with drinking," he said recently. "I used to see him all the time before I joined Benny Goodman, in 1935, and he was in terrible shape. He looked like a bum and he hung out with bums. He'd go along Randolph Street and panhandle, then he'd buy canned heat and strain off the alcohol and drink it—this being during Prohibition. I played with him in Goodman's band in 1938, right after Krupa left and Goodman was running through drummers a mile a minute. Goodman said to Tough one day just before show time, 'Hey, Davy, I want you to send me,' and Tough replied, 'Where do you want to be sent?' He was a brilliant little guy, and I always wondered if he wasn't torn between being a writer and being a drummer." Tough moved on to New York in 1935, but he still wasn't well enough to work regularly. Joe Bushkin has said, "I was with Bunny Berigan at the old Famous Door, on Fifty-second Street, in 1935, and Davy'd come by with his drums and set up and sit in. It was the fashion then to take the Benzedrine strip out of an inhaler and put it in a Coke, and he'd do that for courage. When he drank too much, he was gone. He was totally out of body. Sometimes, when I was still batching it, I'd take him home with me. He weighed less than I did. I've always been around a hundred and twenty-eight, but he must have been close to a hundred pounds. He was so much of an artist that having a bank account would have been appalling to him. He was a natural musician who did things effortlessly, and that always made you comfortable."

Half of Tough's career was over, and he didn't seem to have much to show for it. But this was deceptive. He certainly had helped inspire the great rhythmic drive of the Chicago players, and he must have helped shape whatever subtlety they had. He had worked his way through the styles of the New Orleans drummers Baby Dodds and Zutty Singleton, and, by ceaselessly experimenting, had become a first-rate, original drummer. He knew books and art, and this added stature and class to the popular image of the jazz musician as an uncouth primitive. His great gifts were far more visible during the last half of his career. Tommy Dorsey, starting his own band, hired Tough in 1936, and appears to have helped him back to some sort of normality. (Tough and his wife were divorced the same year.) He stayed with Dorsey for more than two years, lifting his soloists and giving what was basically a big Dixieland band a fresh and buoyant feeling. He also took on an advice-to-drummers column for the monthly music magazine *Metronome*. Much of what he wrote tends to be facetious, but it knocked out his peers and gave him the reputation of being a writer. He considers drummers and chewing gum:

> After considerable spade work on my research into the effects of chewing gum on swing-drumming, I have turned up a few hitherto unpublished secrets of world-shattering importance: George Wettling

and Maurice Purtill chew nothing but Juicy Fruit. James Crawford, the gent who beats out all that gyve with Lunceford—solid man!—prefers Spearmint. The two Rays, McKinley and Bauduc, are Black Jack men down to the ground.

Once in a while he would get down to business:

> This discussion reminds me of Ed Straight, the old Chicago drum teacher, to whom stick grips were a phobia. He was a kind, likable old chap who was usually very calm and patient in his methods. That is, was calm and courteous until you tightened the first two fingers of your left hand around the stick in an attempt to close up your roll. Then he'd raise hell. You'd be rolling along trying to smooth it out nice and even, and suddenly he'd knock the stick out of your left hand. If it flicked out easily, he'd smile; if it didn't, you were in the dog-house. His rule was: at all times during the roll, the left stick should be held so loosely—with the wrist, the thumb and third finger doing all the work—that it can be easily dislodged with just a light flick.

Or even do a one-sentence Hemingway parody:

> But I can say this, sir, that Chick Webb is much better than whom and who and he's good and he's very, very good and he does everything there is to be done to a drum and he does it beautifully and sometimes he plays with such stupefying technique that he leaves you in a punch drunk stupor and ecstatically bewildered as this sentence has wound up to be.

Tough left Dorsey early in 1938, and during the rest of the year moved erratically from Bunny Berigan back to Dorsey to Benny Goodman to Bud Freeman, establishing behavior patterns that would become more and more unpredictable. He passed through Jack Teagarden's big band in 1939 and was with Joe Marsala's jumping small band on Fifty-second Street in 1940. He rejoined Goodman in 1941, was with Marsala again, had a good stint with Artie Shaw, and was briefly with Woody Herman. He was in Charlie Spivak's band in 1942, and then he became part of Artie Shaw's Navy band. Shaw has said, "I first knew Davy in the thirties when he was with Tommy Dorsey, and we'd go up to Harlem to listen to music. He was a sweet man, a gentle man, and not easy to get to. He was shy and reclusive. He had great respect for the English language. He read a lot and I read a lot, so we had that in common. During the Second World War, he was in my Navy band, and we'd manage to get together once in a while and talk. He was an alcoholic, and, like all alcoholics, he always found things to drink. I'd assign a man to him if we had an important concert coming up—say, for the crew of an aircraft carrier—and that man would keep an eye on him all day. This was so he wouldn't get drunk and fall off the bandstand, which he had done a couple of times. I think he was the most underrated big-band drummer in jazz, and he got a beautiful sound out of his instrument. He tuned his drums, he tried to achieve on them what he heard in his head, as we all do, and I think he came as close as you can get. He refused to take solos. Whenever I pointed to him for twelve or eight or four bars, he'd smile and shake his head and go on playing rhythm drums."

The Shaw band spent the year of 1943 in the South Pacific, and Tough, worn out, was discharged in 1944. When he recovered, he married Casey Majors, a black woman he had met in Philadelphia, and he rejoined Woody Herman, who had a wild new, young band. Tough, showing verve and brilliance, became the foundation of the First Herman Herd, which lasted until 1946 and was one of the hardest-swinging of all big jazz bands. He suddenly began winning music-magazine polls, and became a star.

Tough's style had evolved steadily. By the time he rejoined Tommy Dorsey, it had pretty well set, although there were still traces in it of New Orleans drumming—press rolls, ricky-tick on the drum rims. His cymbal playing as well as his bass-drum work grew increasingly dominant. Bob Wilber has said, "His cymbal playing was completely legato—that is, each cymbal ring melted into the next one. He fashioned a kind of cymbal shimmer behind whatever band he played with. It was a lateral flow. He kept his bass-drum heads very loose, so that he got a dull thud instead of a boom-boom-boom. And he used a great many bass-drum off beats, in the manner of the early bebop drummers. He also developed a habit on slow tempos of implying double time, thus giving the tempo a lift and a double edge. It's a device every modern drummer uses."

The drummer Ed Shaughnessy, long in the "Tonight Show" band, hung around Tough when he was fifteen or sixteen and Tough was with Woody Herman. He once said of him, "No drummer could match his intensity. He used a heavy stick with a round tip. He had the widest tempo, the broadest time sense, and in that way he was like Elvin Jones. He was always at the center of the beat, even though he gave the impression he was laid back. He played loosely, with not much tension on the stick, and he tuned his drums loosely. He kept a glass of water and a cloth on the bandstand, and before each set he would dampen the cloth and wipe the foot-pedal head of his bass drum with a circular motion. That drumhead was so loose it almost had wrinkles in it. He told me he did this because he didn't want the bass drum to be in the same range as the bass fiddle. He didn't want the two to compete. And he tuned his snare and tomtoms the same way, so that they were almost flabby. He was a master cymbal player—maybe the greatest of all time. He had a couple of fifteen-inchers on his bass drum, plus a Chinese cymbal and what we call a fast cymbal—a small cymbal you use for short, quick strokes. And he had thirteen-inch high-hat cymbals. He'd use his high hat, either half open or open-and-shut behind ensembles, and when things roared he would shift to the big, furry sound of the Chinese cymbal. He had a very loose high-hat technique, and he was always dropping in offbeats on it with his left hand. He often used cymbals for punctuation where other drummers used rimshots or tomtom beats. He told me he didn't want to interrupt the rhythmic wave. When he played, he looked sort of like a bird, his arms moving in birdlike arcs. But they moved as if he were playing under the water—not very heavy water. He was a surprisingly strong brush player, and he could easily carry a big-band number with brushes. He hated soloing. I remember in 1946, when he'd won the *down beat* poll and he was with Joe Marsala at Loew's State Theatre, and Marsala announced, 'We will now have a drum solo from Dave Tough, winner of the *down beat* poll,' Davy looked like he was having his wisdom teeth pulled. He was always putting himself down, by saying things like 'I can't even roll on the goddam snare,' or, talking about bebop drumming, 'I can't change gears now and play the way you guys do.' He always liked everything that was new, though. He listened to all the young drummers, and he thought Max Roach was terrific."

The bassist Chubby Jackson worked beside Tough in the Herman band, and he spoke of him: "He was a champion of my life. We'd sit together on the bus between gigs and endlessly talk rhythm. In those days, there was great motivation between the drummer and the bass player, and the relationship could be like a happy marriage. He taught me to play non-metronomic time—that is, to play organized time. He said that human beings weren't metronomes, and drummers shouldn't be, either. Sometimes he would slow the beat down slightly so that the band would have a bigger sound, and sometimes he would speed up half a peg if things were getting sluggish. Or he'd hit five quarter notes in a row as a signal to the boys to pep up. He was the little general of that First Herman Herd. He did strange things to his cymbals. He'd remove all the sizzles except one or two from his Chinese cymbal, and he'd cut a wedge out of a ride cymbal to get a broader sound. He played differently behind each soloist. He'd say Bill Harris plays on the top of the beat, and Flip Phillips plays in the center of the beat—and he'd do specific things for each of them. But during the final ensembles he and I went our way, and some of those ensembles lifted off the roof. I don't think there has ever been a big band with more feeling and excitement. It was Woody's idea to hire Davy, and we all thought he was nuts. We were in our twenties and here was this old guy who had been around forever. Because he *was* the oldest guy in the band, he lived in fear of being thought old. So he thought young, and he was always doing things in his drumming to make it sound modern. And he was always looking for approval. We'd finish a set, and he'd say, 'Hey, Snuggy'—which is what he called me—'how was that? How'd you like that?' He never talked like a musician—no lingo or cutie-pie-Hey-man-what's-happenin' sort of thing. He talked more like a writer or lecturer."

The sound of Tough's cymbals changed constantly in the background. The splashing opening high hat gave way to the shining ride cymbal (behind a clarinet), which gave way to a roaring Chinese cymbal (behind a trombone), which gave way to a tightfisted closed high hat, with clicking afterbeats struck on the high-hat post with one stick (behind a piano), which gave way to pouring half-open high-hat figures (behind a trumpet), and, finally, to the open high hat or Chinese cymbal (behind the closing ensemble). He used occasional, often indistinct accents on his snare drum and a steady panoply of jarring bass-drum accents. He created a ringing jubilance with his cymbals. They were also the canvas for the soloists to paint on. It was never clear whether his dislike of drum soloing—in a time when drum solos were the height of jazz fashion—was because he wasn't good at it (his solos, always short, generally consisted of rolling, with accents on the rims, and concluding cymbal splashes) or because he simply disapproved of the custom. Jimmy McPartland has said that Tough's beat was "relentless," and it was. There was no place for laggards or fakes in his musical world, and he would either change them or demolish them.

Tough's drinking, quite controlled with Herman, finally drove him out of the band in September of 1945. He went back to Joe Marsala, and in 1946 he helped Eddie Condon open his new night club in Greenwich Village. (This was when William Gottlieb took his famous gaminlike photograph of Tough in Condon's cellar—his eyes sad and bleared, a cigarette in his mouth, his sticks poised over a rubber practice pad.) He worked on Fifty-second Street with Charlie Ventura and Bill Harris, the former Woody Herman trombonist. In 1947, he went to Chicago with his old friend Muggsy Spanier. He was deteriorating physically, and he was worried by bebop, whose rhythmic intricacies he was certain (wrongly) he could never absorb. He was losing his saturnine good looks. He had a long, wandering, bony face, a high, domed forehead, and black hair with a widow's peak—it was a face, perched on his tiny shoulders, of a bigger man. He spent most of his last four months of his life in the Veterans Administration Hospital in Lyons, New Jersey. Late in the afternoon of December 8, 1948, when he was apparently on his way to the apartment he and his wife had in Newark, he slipped on the street, hit his head on a curb, and fractured his skull. It was dark and he was drunk. He died in a hospital the next morning. He had no identification, and his wife did not find him for three days.

Even His Feet Look Sad

The clarinettist Pee Wee Russell was born in St. Louis, Missouri, in March of 1906, and died just short of his sixty-third birthday in Arlington, Virginia. He was unique—in his looks, in his inward-straining shyness, in his furtive, circumambulatory speech, and in his extraordinary style. His life was higgledy-piggledy. He once accidentally shot and killed a man when all he was trying to do was keep an eye on a friend's girl. He spent most of his career linked—in fact and fiction—to the wrong musicians. People laughed at him—he *looked* like a clown perfectly at ease in a clown's body—when, hearing him, they should have wept. He drank so much for so long that he almost died, and when he miraculously recovered, he began drinking again. In the last seven or eight years of his life, he came into focus: his originality began to be appreciated, and he worked and recorded with the sort of musicians he should have been working and recording with all his life. He even took up painting, producing a series of seemingly abstract canvases that were actually accurate chartings of his inner workings. But then, true to form, the bottom fell out. His wife Mary died unexpectedly, and he was soon dead himself. Mary had been his guidon, his ballast, his right hand, his helpmeet. She was a funny, sharp, nervous woman, and she knew she deserved better than Pee Wee. She had no illusions, but she was devoted to him. She laughed when she said this: "Do you know Pee Wee? I mean what do you *think* of him? Oh, not those funny sounds that come out of his clarinet. Do you *know* him? You think he's kind and sensitive and sweet. Well, he's intelligent and he doesn't use dope and he is sensitive, but Pee Wee can also be *mean*. In fact, Pee Wee is the most egocentric son of a bitch I know."

No jazz musician has ever played with the same daring and nakedness and intuition. His solos didn't always arrive at their original destination. He took wild improvisational chances, and when he found himself above the abyss, he simply turned in another direction, invariably hitting firm ground. His singular tone was never at rest. He had a rich chalumeau register, a piping upper register, and a whining middle register, and when he couldn't think of anything else to do, he growled. Above all, he sounded cranky and querulous, but that was camouflage, for he was the most plaintive and lyrical of players. He was particularly affecting in a medium or slow-tempo blues. He'd start in the chalumeau range with a delicate rush of notes that were intensely multiplied into a single, unbroken phrase that might last the entire chorus. Thus he'd begin with a pattern of winged double-time staccato notes that, moving steadily downward, were abruptly pierced by falsetto jumps. When he had nearly sunk out of hearing, he reversed this pattern, keeping his myriad notes back to back, and then swung into an easy uphill-downdale movement, topping each rise with an oddly placed vibrato. By this time, his first chorus was over, and one had the impression of having passed through a crowd of jostling, whispering people. Russell then took what appeared to be his first breath, and, momentarily breaking the tension he had established, opened the next chorus with a languorous, questioning phrase made up of three or four notes, at least one of them a spiny dissonance of the sort favored by Thelonious Monk. A closely linked variation would follow, and Russell would fill out the chorus by reaching behind him and producing an ironed paraphrase of the chalumeau first chorus. In his final chorus, he'd move snakily up toward the middle register with tissue-paper notes and placid rests, taking on a legato I've-made-it attack that allowed the listener to move back from the edge of his seat.

Here is Russell in his apartment on King Street, in Greenwich Village, in the early sixties, when he was on the verge of his greatest period. It wasn't a comeback he was about to begin, though, for he'd never been where he was going. Russell lived then on the third floor of a peeling brownstone. He was standing in his door, a pepper-and-salt schnauzer barking and dancing about behind him. "Shut up, Winkie, for God's sake!" Russell said, and made a loose, whirlpool gesture at the dog. A tall, close-packed, slightly bent man, Russell had a wry, wandering face, dominated by a generous nose. The general arrangement of his eyes and eyebrows was mansard, and he had a brush mustache and a full chin. A heavy trellis of wrinkles held his features in place. His gray-black hair was combed absolutely flat. Russell smiled, without showing any teeth, and went down a short, bright hall, through a Pullman kitchen, and into a dark living room, brownish in color, with two day beds and two easy chairs, a bureau, a television, and several small tables. The corners of the room were stuffed with suitcases and fat manila envelopes. Under one table were two clarinet cases. The shades on the three windows were drawn, and only one lamp was lit. The room was suffocatingly hot. Russell, who was dressed in a tan, short-sleeved sports shirt, navy-blue trousers, black socks, black square-toed shoes, and dark glasses, sat down in a huge red leather chair. "We've lived in this cave six years too long. Mary's no housekeeper, but she tries. Every time a new cleaning gadget comes out, she buys it and stuffs it in a closet with all the other ones. I bought an apartment three years ago in a development on Eighth Avenue in the Chelsea district, and we're moving in. It has a balcony and a living room and a bedroom and a full kitchen. We'll have to get a cleaning woman to keep it respectable." Russell laughed—a sighing sound that seemed to travel down his nose. "Mary got me up at seven this morning before she went to work, but I haven't had any breakfast, which is my own fault. I've been on the road four weeks—two at the Theatrical Café, in Cleveland, with George Wein, and two in Pittsburgh with Jimmy McPartland. I shouldn't have gone to Pittsburgh. I celebrated my birthday there, and I'm still paying for it, physically and mentally. And the music. I can't go near 'Muskrat Ramble' any more without freezing up. Last fall, I did a television show with McPartland and Eddie Condon and Bud Freeman and Gene Krupa and Joe Sullivan—all the Chicago boys. We made a record just before it. They sent me a copy the other day and I listened halfway through and turned it off and gave it to the super. Mary was here, and she said, 'Pee Wee, you sound like you did when I first knew you in 1942.' I'd gone back twenty years in three hours. There's no room left in that music. It tells *you* how to solo. You're as good as the company you keep. You go with fast musicians, housebroken musicians, and you improve."

Russell spoke in a low, nasal voice. Sometimes he stuttered, and sometimes whole sentences came out in a sluice-like manner, and trailed off into mumbles and down-the-nose laughs. His face was never still. When he was surprised, he opened his mouth slightly and popped his eyes, rolling them up to the right. When he was thoughtful, he glanced quickly about, tugged his nose, and cocked his head. When he was amused, everything turned down instead of up—the edges of his eyes, his eyebrows, and the corners of his mouth. Russell got up and walked with short, crabwise steps into the kitchen. "Talking dries me up," he said. "I'm going to have an ale."

There were four framed photographs on the walls. Two of them showed what was already unmistakably Russell, in a dress and long, curly hair. In one, he was sucking his thumb. In the other, an arm was draped about a cocker spaniel. The third showed him at about fifteen, in military uniform, standing beneath a tree, and in the fourth he was wearing a dinner jacket and a wing collar and holding an alto saxophone. Russell came back, a bottle of ale in one hand and a pink plastic cup in the other. "Isn't that something? A wing collar. I was sixteen, and my father bought me that saxophone for three hundred and seventy-five dollars." Russell filled his cup and put the bottle on the floor. "My father was a steward at the Planter's Hotel, in St. Louis, when I was born, and I was named after him—Charles Ellsworth. I was a late child and the only one. My mother was forty. She was a very intelligent person. She'd been a newspaperwoman in Chicago, and she used to read a lot. Being a late child, I was excess baggage. I was like a toy. My parents, who were pretty well off, would say, You want this or that, it's yours. But I never really knew them. Not that they were cold, but they just didn't divulge anything. Someone discovered a few years ago that my father had a lot of brothers. I never knew he had any. When I was little, we moved to Muskogee, where my father and a friend hit a couple of gas wells. I took up piano and drums and violin, roughly in that order. One day, after I'd played in a school recital, I put my violin in the back seat of our car and my mother got in and sat on it. That was the end of my violin career. 'Thank God that's over,' I said to myself. I tried the clarinet when I was about twelve or thirteen. I studied with Charlie Merrill, who was in the pit band in the only theatre in Muskogee. Oklahoma was a dry state and he sneaked corn liquor during the lessons. My first job was playing at a resort lake. I played for about twelve hours and made three dollars. Once in a while, my father'd take me into the Elks' Club, where I heard Yellow Nunez, the New Orleans clarinet player. He had a trombone and piano and drums with him, and he played the lead in the ensembles. On my next job, I played the lead, using the violin part. Of course, I'd already heard the Original Dixieland Jazz Band on records. I was anxious in school—anxious to finish it. I'd drive my father to work in his car and, instead of going on to school, pick up a friend and drive around all day. I wanted to study music at the University of Oklahoma, but my aunt— she was living with us—said I was bad and wicked and persuaded my parents to take me out of high school and send me to Western Military Academy, in Alton, Illinois. My aunt is still alive. Mary keeps in touch with her, but I won't speak to her. I majored in wigwams at the military school, and I lasted just a year. Charlie Smith, the jazz historian, wrote the school not long ago and they told him Thomas Hart Benton and I are their two most distinguished nongraduates." Russell laughed and poured out more ale.

"We moved back to St. Louis and I began working in Herbert Berger's hotel band. It was Berger who gave me my nickname. Then I went with a tent show to Moulton, Iowa. Berger had gone to Juárez, Mexico, and he sent me a telegram asking me to join him. That was around the time my father gave me the saxophone. I was a punk kid, but my parents—can you imagine?—said, Go ahead, good riddance. When I got to Juárez, Berger told me, to my surprise, I wouldn't be working with him but across the street with piano and drums in the Big Kid's Palace, which had a bar about a block long. There weren't any microphones and you had to blow. I must have used a board for a reed. Three days later there were union troubles and I got fired and joined Berger. This wasn't long after Pancho Villa, and all the Mexicans wore guns. There'd be shooting in the streets day and night, but nobody paid any attention. You'd just duck into a saloon and wait till it was over. The day Berger hired me, he gave me a ten-dollar advance. That was a lot of money and I went crazy on it. It was the custom in Juarez to hire a kind of cop at night for a dollar, and if you got in a scrape he'd clop the other guy with his billy. So I hired one and got drunk and we went to see a bulldog-badger fight, which is the most vicious thing you can imagine. I kept on drinking and finally told the cop to beat it, that I knew the way back to the hotel in El Paso, across the river. Or I thought I did, because I got lost and had an argument over a tab and the next thing I was in jail. What a place, Mister! A big room with bars all the way around and bars for a ceiling and a floor like a cesspool, and full of the worst cutthroats you ever saw. I was there three days on bread and water before Berger found me and paid ten dollars to get me out." Russell's voice trailed off. He squinted at the bottle, which was empty, and stood up. "I need some lunch."

The light outside was blinding, and Russell headed west on King Street, turned up Varick Street and into West Houston. He pointed at a small restaurant with a pine-panelled front, called the Lodge. "Mary and I eat here sometimes evenings. The food's all right." He found a table in the back room, which was decorated with more panelling and a small pair of antlers. A waiter came up. "Where you been, Pee Wee? You look fifteen years younger." Russell mumbled a denial and something about his birthday and Pittsburgh and ordered a Scotch-on-the-rocks and ravioli. He sipped his drink for a while in silence, studying the tablecloth. Then he looked up and said, "For ten years I couldn't eat *any*thing. All during the forties. I'd be hungry and take a couple of bites of delicious steak, say, and have to put the fork down—finished. My food wouldn't go from my upper stomach to my lower stomach. I lived on brandy milkshakes and scrambled-egg sandwiches. And on whiskey. The doctors couldn't find a thing. No tumors, no ulcers. I got as thin as a lamppost and so weak I had to drink half a pint of whiskey in the morning before I could get out of bed. It began to affect my mind, and sometime in 1948 I left Mary and went to Chicago. Everything there is a blank, except what people have told me since. They say I did things that were unheard of, they were so wild. Early in 1950, I went on to San Francisco. By this time my stomach was bloated and I was so feeble I remember someone pushing me up Bush Street and me stopping to put my arms around each telegraph pole to rest. I guess I was dying. Some friends finally got me into the Franklin Hospital and they discovered I had pancreatitis and multiple cysts on my liver. The pancreatitis was why I couldn't eat for so many years. They operated, and I was in that hospital for nine months. People gave benefits around the country to pay the bills. I was still crazy. I told them Mary was after me for money. Hell, she was back in New York, minding her own business. When they sent me back here, they put me in St. Clare's Hospital under an assumed name—McGrath, I think it was— so Mary couldn't find me. After they let me out, I stayed with Eddie Condon. Mary heard where I was and came over and we went out and sat in Washington Square park. Then she took me home. After three years."

Russell picked up a spoon and twiddled the ends of his long, beautifully tapered fingers on it, as if it were a clarinet. "You take each solo like it was the last one you were going to play in your life. What notes to hit, and when to hit them—that's the secret. You can *make* a particular phrase with just one note. Maybe at the end, maybe at the beginning. It's like a little pattern. What will lead in quietly and not be too emphatic. Sometimes I jump the right chord and use what seems wrong to the next guy but I know is right for me. I usually think about four bars ahead what I am going to play. Sometimes things go wrong, and I have to scramble. If I can make it to the bridge of the tune, I know everything will be all right. I suppose it's not that obnoxious the average musician would notice. When I play the blues, mood, frame of mind, enters into it. One day your choice of notes would be melancholy, a blue trend, a drift of blue notes. The next day your choice of notes would be more cheerful. Standard tunes are different. Some of them require a legato treatment, and others have sparks of rhythm you have to bring out. In lots of cases, your solo depends on who you're following. The guy played a great chorus, you say to yourself. How am I going to follow *that*? I applaud him inwardly, and it becomes a matter of silent pride. Not jealousy, mind you. A kind of competition. So I make myself a guinea pig—what the hell, I'll try something new. All this goes through your mind in a split second. You start and if it sounds good to you you keep it up and write a little tune of your own. I get in bad habits and I'm trying to break myself of a couple right now. A little triplet thing, for one. Fast tempos are good to display your technique, but that's all. You prove you know the chords, but you don't have the time to insert those new little chords you could at slower tempos. Or if you do, they go unnoticed. I haven't been able to play the way I want to until recently. Coming out of that illness has given me courage, a little moral courage in my playing. When I was sick, I lived night by night. It was bang! straight ahead with the whiskey. As a result, my playing was a series of desperations. Now I have a freedom. For the past five or so months, Marshall Brown, the trombonist, and I have been rehearsing a quartet in his studio—just Brown, on the bass cornet, which is like a valve trombone; me, a bass, and drums. We get together a couple of days a week and we *work*. I didn't realize what we had until I listened to the tapes we've made. We sound like seven or eight men. Something's always going. There's a lot of bottom in the group. And we can do anything we want— soft, crescendo, decrescendo, textures, voicings. What musical knowledge we have, we use it. A little while ago, an a. & r. man from one of the New York jazz labels approached me and suggested a record date—on his terms. Instead, I took him to Brown's studio to hear the tapes. He was cool at first, but by the third number he looked different. I scared him with a stiff price, so we'll see what happens. A record with the quartet would feel just right. And no 'Muskrat Ramble' and no 'Royal Garden Blues.'"

Outside the Lodge, the sunlight seemed to accelerate Russell, and he got back to King Street quickly. He unlocked the door, and Winkie barked. "Cut that out, Winkie!" Russell shouted. "Mary'll be here soon and take you out." He removed his jacket, folded it carefully on one of the day beds, and sat down in the red chair with a grunt.

"I wish Mary was here. She knows more about me than I'll ever know. Well, after Juárez I went with Berger to the Coast and back to St. Louis where I made my first record, in 1923 or 1924. 'Fuzzy Wuzzy Bird,' by Herbert Berger and his Coronado Hotel Orchestra. The bad notes in the reed passages are me. I also worked on the big riverboats—the J. S., the St. Paul—during the day and then stayed at night to listen to the good bands, the Negro bands like Fate Marable's and Charlie Creath's. Then Sonny Lee, the trombonist, asked me did I want to go to Houston and play in Peck Kelley's group. Peck Kelley's Bad Boys. At this time, spats and a derby were the vogue, and that's what I was wearing when I got there. Kelley looked at me in the station and didn't say a word. We got in a cab and I could feel him still looking at me, so I rolled down the window and threw the derby out. Kelley laughed and thanked me. He took me straight to Goggan's music store and sat down at a piano and started to play. He was marvellous, a kind of stride pianist, and I got panicky. About ten minutes later, a guy walked in, took a trombone off the wall, and started to play. It was Jack Teagarden. I went over to Peck when they finished and said, 'Peck, I'm in over my head. Let me work a week and make my fare home.' But I got over it and I was with Kelley several months." Russell went into the kitchen to get another bottle of ale. "Not long after I got back to St. Louis, Sonny Lee brought Bix Beiderbecke around to my house, and bang! we hit it right off. We were never apart for a couple of years—day, night, good, bad, sick, well, broke, drunk. Then Bix left to join Jean Goldkette's band and Red Nichols sent for me to come to New York. That was 1927. I went straight to the old Manger Hotel and found a note in my box: Come to a speakeasy under the Roseland Ballroom. I went over and there was Red Nichols and Eddie Lang and Miff Mole and Vic Berton. I got panicky again. They told me there'd be a recording date at Brunswick the next morning at nine, and don't be late. I got there at eight-fifteen. The place was empty, except for a handyman. Mole arrived first. He said, 'You look peaked, kid,' and opened his trombone case and took out a quart. Everybody had quarts. We made 'Ida,' and it wasn't any trouble at all. In the late twenties and early thirties I worked in a lot of bands and made God knows how many records in New York. Cass Hagen, Bert Lown, Paul Specht, Ray Levy, the Scranton Sirens, Red Nichols. We lived uptown at night. We heard Elmer Snowden and Luis Russell and Ellington. Once I went to a ballroom where Fletcher Henderson was. Coleman Hawkins had a bad cold and I sat in for him one set. My God, those scores! They were written in six flats, eight flats, I don't know how many flats. I never saw anything like it. Buster Bailey was in the section next to me, and after a couple of numbers I told him, 'Man, I came up here to have a good time, not to work. I've had enough. Where's Hawkins?'

"I joined Louis Prima around 1935. We were at the Famous Door, on Fifty-second Street, and a couple of hoodlums loaded with knives cornered Prima and me and said they wanted protection money every week—fifty bucks from Prima and twenty-five from me. Well, I didn't want any of that. I'd played a couple of private parties for Lucky Luciano, so I called him. He sent Pretty Amberg over in a big car with a bodyguard as chauffeur. Prima sat in the back with Amberg and I sat in front with the bodyguard. Nobody said much, just 'Hello' and 'Goodbye,' and for a week they drove Prima and me from our hotels to a midday radio broadcast, back to our hotels, picked us up for work at night, and took us home after. We never saw the protection-money boys again. Red McKenzie, the singer, got me into Nick's in 1938, and I worked there and at Condon's place for most of the next ten years. I have a sorrow about that time. Those guys made a joke of me, a clown, and I let myself be treated that way because I was afraid. I didn't know where else to go, where to take refuge. I'm not sure how all of us feel about each other now, though we're 'Hello, Pee Wee,' 'Hello, Eddie,' and all that. Since my sickness, Mary's given me confidence, and so has George Wein. I've worked for him with a lot of fast musicians in Boston, in New York, at Newport, on the road, and in Europe last year. I'll head a kind of house band if he opens a club here. A quiet little group. But Nick's did one thing. That's where I first met Mary."

At that moment, a key turned in the lock, and Mary Russell walked quickly down the hall and into the living room. A trim, pretty, black-haired woman in her forties, she was wearing a green silk dress and black harlequin glasses.

"How's Winkie been?" she asked Russell, plumping herself down and taking off her shoes. "She's the kind of dog that's always barking except at burglars. Pee Wee, you forgot to say, Did you have a hard day at the office, dear? And where's my tea?"

Russell got up and shuffled into the kitchen.

"I work in the statistics and advertising part of Robert Hall clothes," she said. "I've got a quick mind for figures. I like the job and the place. It's full of respectable ladies. Pee Wee, did I get any mail?"

"Next to you, on the table. A letter," he said from the kitchen.

"It's from my brother Al," she said. "I always look for a check in letters. My God, there is a check! Now why do you suppose he did that? And there's a P.S.: Please excuse the pencil. I like that. It makes me feel good."

"How much did he send you?" Russell asked, handing Mrs. Russell her tea.

"You're not going to get a cent," she said. "You know what I found the other day, Pee Wee? Old letters from you. Love letters. Every one says the same thing: I love you, I miss you. Just the dates are different." Mary Russell, who spoke in a quick, decisive way, laughed. "Pee Wee and I had an awful wedding. It was at City Hall. Danny Alvin, the drummer, stood up for us. He and Pee Wee wept. I didn't, but *they* did. After the ceremony, Danny tried to borrow money from me. Pee Wee didn't buy me any flowers and a friend lent us the wedding ring. Pee Wee has never given me a wedding ring. The one I'm wearing a nephew gave me a year ago. Just to make it proper, he said. That's not the way a woman wants to get married. Pee Wee, we ought to do it all over again. I have a rage in me to be proper. I don't play bridge and go to beauty parlors and I don't have women friends like other women. But one thing Pee Wee and I have that no one else has: we never stop talking when we're with each other. Pee Wee, you know why I love you? You're like Papa. Every time Mama got up to tidy something, he'd say, 'Clara, sit down' and she would. That's what you do. I loved my parents. They were Russian Jews from Odessa. Chaloff was their name. I was born on the lower East Side. I was a charity case and the doctor gave me my name, and signed the birth certificate—Dr. E. Condon. Isn't that weird? I was one of nine kids and six are left. I've got twenty nephews and nieces." Mary Russell paused and sipped her tea.

"Pee Wee worships those inchbrows. Lucky Luciano was his dream man."

"He was an acquaintance," Russell snorted.

"I'll never know you completely, Pee Wee," Mrs. Russell said. She took another sip of tea, holding the cup with both hands. "Sometimes Pee Wee can't sleep. He sits in the kitchen and plays solitaire, and I go to bed in here and sing to him. Awful songs like 'Belgian Rose' and 'Carolina Mammy.' I have a terrible voice."

"Oh, God!" Russell muttered. "The worst thing is she knows all the lyrics."

"I not only sing, I write," she said, laughing. "I wrote a three-act play. My hero's name is Tiny Ballard. An Italian clarinet player. It has wonderful dialogue."

"Mary's no saloon girl, coming where I work," he said. "She outgrew that long ago. She reads about ten books a week. You could have been a writer, Mary."

"I don't know why I wrote about a clarinet player. I hate the clarinet. Pee Wee's playing embarrasses me. But I like trombones: Miff Mole and Brad Gowans. And I like Duke Ellington. Last New Year's Eve, Pee Wee and I were at a party and Duke kissed me at midnight."

"Where was I?" he asked.

"You had a clarinet stuck in your mouth," she said. "The story of your life, or part of your life. Once when Pee Wee had left me and was in Chicago, he came back to New York for a couple of days. He denies it. He doesn't remember it. He went to the night club where I was working as a hat-check girl and asked to see me. I said no. The boss's wife went out and took one look at him and came back and said, 'At least go out and talk to him. He's pathetic. Even his feet look sad.' "

Russell made an apologetic face. "That was twelve years ago, Mary. I have no claim to being an angel."

She sat up very straight. "Pee Wee, this room is hot. Let's go out and have dinner on my brother Al."

"I'll put on a tie," he said.

More Ingredients

Bobby Hackett is a maze of paradoxes. His mood-music recordings, made in the fifties with Jackie Gleason, can be heard daily as piped-in music in supermarkets across the land, but very few people know what they are hearing. He is possibly the most respected trumpet player in the business, but recently he has taken jobs where he could find them—playing with a tuba-and-banjo band, with a trio led by a society pianist, and in a club owned by a cousin, to say nothing of intermittent and wearying field trips to Japan, Canada, Italy, and Australia. He is a tiny man (five feet four and a half, a hundred and twenty-five pounds; an admirer recently said he looks like the groom on a wedding cake) who achieves a baronial, walk-in sound. He has been celebrated for years by his adherents as a successor to Bix Beiderbecke, but his passion is Louis Armstrong. Hackett was a rhythm guitarist for two years in Glenn Miller's band, but the most famous solo ever played on a Miller recording is his exquisite twelve-bar statement on cornet in "String of Pearls." His flat hair and narrowed eyes and miniature hawk features give him a furtive twenties appearance, but he is the gentlest and most vulnerable of men. He has been playing for over forty-five years, but he has one of the smallest recorded oeuvres in jazz. He is the most assured and relaxed-sounding of trumpeters, but he practices a couple of hours every day. And he is a born-and-bred city slicker who lives in the woods on Cape Cod. His style is equally deceptive. He is a lyrical, even emotional performer, yet his solos have an almost mathematical logic. His friend Alec Wilder has said of him: "Hackett is a master of distillation and understatement. For his comment, whatever it may be, is made with the least number of (in his case) notes and each one is essential. He has never fallen into the 'etude' fashion, chasing his tail with neurotic arpeggiations. Nor has he felt the need to flex his musical muscles by means of hysterical high notes. He is both a poet and an essayist. He is never aggressive or noisy; rather he is tender and witty. I have never heard him play a phrase I would prefer otherwise." Hackett plays with sharp rhythmic agility, but he invariably sounds as if he were loafing. His tone is sweet and generous. He is not a great blues player, even though the coloring and feel of the blues are in every solo. When he plays the melody, it sounds verbatim, but close examination of the placement and choice of notes reveals improvisation of the most subtle order. He sounds best when he is playing with stylistic opposites, and some of the most affecting music he has set down has been in the company of Pee Wee Russell and Vic Dickenson and Dizzy Gillespie.

A recent visitor to Chatham found that Hackett looked very different from the last time he had seen him, almost three years before, in 1969. That was at the annual jazz party given in Colorado by Dick Gibson, the Denver businessman. Hackett had had a couple of drinks at a gathering in Denver the night before the party began. He is a reformed alcoholic and a diabetic, and with the compounding effect of the altitude he fell asleep immediately on the bus to Aspen the next morning, and by the time the bus reached Loveland Pass, which is twelve thousand feet up, his life appeared in danger. He looked like a fish out of water. His mouth was open, his breathing was heavy, and his face was shrunken and gray. Vic Dickenson, who was on the bus and is his great friend, got some food into him when the bus stopped for lunch, and before Aspen was reached he had revived. On the Cape, he looked marvelous. He had a discreet tan, his eyes were bright, and he was full of pep. "You know, this place is something" he said as he went down the stairs to his basement music room. "The air and the quiet and the privacy get to you. I'm up at nine, ten every morning, instead of at one or two in the afternoon, and I feel alive again. I fell in love with the Cape when I first played here, thirty-eight years ago, and I've been aiming at living here ever since. Two years ago, I had a gig all winter in Hyannis, and we did a tremendous business, and that decided it. Hell, when I lived in Queens I spent most of my time trying to make enough money to keep up the mortgage payments, so why not do the same thing in a place like this, where it's beautiful and cheap? So I sold the house down there. Everybody on the Cape is so great. Even in the bank I use. It's run by a lot of ex-show-biz types who give you apples and candy and coffee every time you go in, and then lend you money. Find a bank like that in New York."

A small, dark-haired boy came in and said, "Pop, can you drive me somewhere ?"

"Where?"

"Fishing. I want to go fishing."

"Yeh, I'll take you later. Now go find your grandma."

Hackett talks in a deep, soft monotone fretted by a Providence drawl which falls somewhere between a Brooklyn accent and a South Boston one. "That's my daughter's kid, Bobby. He and his sister, Michelle, spend the summer with Edna, my wife, and me. Their mother works in New York, but my son lives with us. He's a drummer and he gigs around on the Cape. They said it would never last with Edna and me. We met in Providence, where we were both born, when we were ten—at a Halloween party. I even left my ukulele at her house to give me an excuse to go back and see her. Edna's mother was French, and it's funny, I've always had a French thing. I love their music—Ravel, Debussy, Edith Piaf—and I love everything else about them. Edna and I were married in the late thirties. I had just gone to New York and I was working with the Lanins. Lester was taking a group to Nantucket for the summer, and he said I could come if I played slide guitar. I said fine, and borrowed one and learned it. I went to all the trouble because I wanted to get married so bad, and going to Nantucket made it possible. It also made a nice honeymoon."

Hackett put down a trumpet he had been oiling and turned on his stereo system. There were four speakers in the room, and Louis Armstrong's "Jubilee" came booming out. It was followed by "S.O.L. Blues" and "Jeepers Creepers." He turned the volume down. "That's part of a nine-hour tape I put together of Pops' stuff. It has recordings from the twenties to the sixties, and it's all mixed together. I play it all day when I'm here. I can't really feel that bad about his death. I mean, he isn't dead, because we're listening to him right now. And he had a good life. He did everything he wanted and he was worth maybe a couple of mill when he went. I worshiped him. I heard my first Armstrong record in a Providence department store when I was a kid, and it turned me around. The sound has never left me. Later, I got to know him real well, and he was a saint. He was the softest touch in the world. Whenever I went into his dressing room at Basin Street, or someplace like that, it would be full of broken-down musicians and show-biz types looking for a buck. It finally got so that Joe Glaser, who managed Pops most of his life, put a twenty-dollar lid on each handout. Even so, I think he helped support hundreds of people. It was one of his greatest pleasures. He always made you feel relaxed, made you feel at home. Probably because his philosophy about life was, Man, it's all in fun. In fact, he told me once—that voice way down there in his shoes—'It's good thing Joe Glaser don't know it, but I'd do all this for nothing.' I'd visit him in Queens whenever we were both in town. Once, he was playing at Freedomland, and I met him there when he was finished. We went to his house and he got into his Bermuda shorts. Then we went to some nightclub nearby, and walking in with Pops was like walking in with God. We went to a Mrs. Davenport's house in Astoria after and we ate. She had a Hammond organ, and Pops sat down and played for a good half hour, just ad-libbing and composing little things to himself. I think it was the musical highlight of my life. We went back to his house and we wound up in his bedroom, with him on the bed in his underwear and me sitting in a chair, and we talked about trumpet players. He always said good, nice things about other horn players, like 'Sweets Edison should take that mute out,' but you had to read him close sometimes, because he'd get names and words all mixed up. Al Hirt always came out 'Milt Hoit,' after the organist Milt Herth, and he always called George Wein 'Ted Weems.' What tickled me was when somebody pressed him real hard once about saying who was better— Billy Butterfield or me—he thought a while and finally said, 'Bobby. He got more ingredients.'"

Hackett is a chain smoker, and he paused and lit another cigarette. "I'm going to get some coffee." He turned the Armstrong tape up again, and "Bye and Bye" came on. The room was cool and dark and comfortable.

The shades were drawn—an occupational badge in musicians' houses. Hackett's stereo equipment was laid out on floor-to-ceiling shelves against one wall, and there was a piano against another wall. On the two other walls were an abstract oil, done in 1961 by Pee Wee Russell; an affecting photograph of Hackett seated outdoors and looking down at a trumpet he is holding between his knees; and two photographs of Armstrong. In one, he is standing in a room in his house beside a row of Eskys—Oscar-like statuettes awarded each year in the forties to poll-winning musicians by Esquire. The picture is signed "'Best Wishes to 'Bobby.' They Don't Come Any Finer—Louis Satchmo." In the other, Armstrong stands beside Hackett and has an arm draped around his shoulders. Hackett is dressed in a rakish trenchcoat and is smiling brilliantly. The "West End Blues'" started, and Hackett reappeared with his coffee. He dragged the piano bench over and put the cup on it. Then he turned down the music again and lit another cigarette.

"Pops taught me so much. Once, on one of those Timex television shows, I was supposed to play a solo between his vocal and Jack Teagarden's. It was a slow, slow number, and the first time I tried it I just stumbled. He leaned over to me and said, 'Play whole notes, Bobby, play whole notes.' And, of course, he was right. And the reason I've finally switched from cornet to trumpet is that he was after me to do it for years. He kept saying that if the cornet was all that good everybody would play it. Right again. He also taught me by his example that the key to music, the key to life, is concentration. When I solo, I listen to the piano and the other instruments, and I try to play against what they're doing. But the ideal way to play would be to concentrate to such an extent that all you could hear was yourself, which is something I have been trying to do all my life, to make my music absolutely pure. You either hit home runs or you strike out in this business. Anything in between, you're second-rate. The tune itself has a good deal to do with the way I play. If it's a good tune, I don't change the composer's lines. Any player who edits Ellington or Gershwin or Fats Waller implies that he knows more. The challenge in an Ellington tune is to see what you can do to embellish it. But to tamper with the harmony is like altering a great architect's work. I respect harmonic law and I live within that law. The best way to think when you solo—I learned this from Vic Dickenson—is in subdivisions of four, like four bars at a time. And, of course, all good players play rubato. Your tempo has to be firm, but you are flexible within that. You rob notes here and put them there, and you rob notes there and put them here. The hardest thing of all is to play straight melody and make it sound like you. It's stripping the medium down to its bare parts. I try and practice two or three hours a day, and when I do I feel right when I play that night. And I've studied—with Ernest Williams, a great trumpet teacher in Brooklyn, and with Benny Baker, who's worked with ninety per cent of the trumpet players in New York. You've got to learn the underneath before you can do the top, just as you can't start school in the ninth grade. One of the most important things I learned, though, was from Glenn Miller. He showed me that most jazz musicians have everything backward. They tend to play two beats to the bar at slow tempos when they should play four beats, which would close up all those holes, and they play four beats at fast tempos when they should play two, which would make things sound less cluttered."

Hackett crumpled up an empty cigarette pack and wedged it into the ashtray, which was a midget version of the standing ashtrays that used to populate hotel lobbies. He opened a new pack and took out a cigarette and lit it. "Miller hired me as a rhythm guitarist in nineteen forty-one. He made me get an electric guitar, which very few people played then, and I carried that amplifier all over the United States, but I never plugged it in. He was a brilliant man, an honorable man. He was a great leader, with a fantastic sense of programming. When a band sounds the same all the time, it's like wearing white on white. And he was a genius for editing arrangements. He'd listen to a new one and he'd suggest a slightly different voicing or a different tempo or a different background behind a solo, and the whole thing would suddenly fall into place. Like 'Chattanooga Choo-Choo,' which was a million-seller. I was with the band when the picture *Orchestra Wives* was made. Ernie Caceres, who played baritone saxophone and clarinet with the band, was my buddy, and we'd be out until five or six every morning, and we'd be a wreck when we got to the studio at eight. So we persuaded Lucien Ballard, who was the head cameraman, to let us sit at either end of the band, where we'd be out of camera range and could doze. He did, and the only time you can see me in the picture is in a quick pan shot that if you blinked during it you'd miss me completely. Miller's death was a tragedy. The band, of course, goes on and on, and so does the estate, which must be worth millions. It's weird. I was a luxury to him, because he certainly didn't need a guitarist. I think the reason he hired me was that often at the end of shows, late at night, he'd call me down front and we would play duets. He'd play the melody on trombone and I'd work around it on cornet. I think he loved that."

Hackett stood up and stretched. "You wouldn't know it in here, but it's a beautiful day outside. Let's go up and sit on the balcony, maybe get a little sun tan." Hackett went up the stairs and through the living room. A television set was on, and the draperies were drawn. He opened the draperies and stepped out through a sliding door and onto a sun deck that ran around two sides of the house. There were a couple of beach chairs and a small table on it. Hackett sat down with his back to the sun. He looked almost transparent in the light.

"After Miller went in the service, I went with NBC for a year, and then with Glen Gray's Casa Loma band for two years. I took Red Nichols' place. While I was with the band, I finally quit drinking. Muggsy Spanier had put me on to AA, and that helped. I went to Spike, which was Glen Gray's nickname, and told him I'd be a wreck for a couple of weeks, that

I probably wouldn't even be able to find my mouth with my horn. AA saved my life. I would have been gone by now. And one thing that has helped me toe the mark is my diabetes, which was discovered ten or twelve years ago. I take a shot every day, and every day it tells me to behave myself. Being an alky hurts in other ways. I was seriously considered for the sound track of *Young Man with a Horn*, with Kirk Douglas, but somebody at the studio heard I was an alky—even though I hadn't touched a drop in years—and Harry James got the job. And he was paid seventy-five grand. I went to ABC from the Casa Loma band, and I was with them fifteen years. In nineteen fifty-one, I made the first of the mood-music albums with Jackie Gleason. I'd met him on the set of *Orchestra Wives*. He was playing the part of the bass player in the band and working at Slapsie Maxie's, and nobody had ever heard of him. We had a lot of laughs together on the set, and it was the damnedest thing, because the last words he said to me were 'We've got to make some records with you and a lot of strings.' That was in nineteen forty-two. The first album "Music for Lovers Only" cost Gleason seven or eight thousand dollars, and he had a hell of a time getting a record company interested. He had a whole floor at the Park Sheraton at the time, and he was living like King Farouk. He gave a big party there for all the record-company boys, and all those geniuses told him he was crazy. Mitch Miller was with Columbia then, and he said to Jackie, 'Look, I've got all these Harry James things on the shelf and I can't sell them, so how can I sell Bobby Hackett?' Finally, a kid who was with Capitol persuaded them to invest a thousand dollars in the record, and the rest is history. We made six albums, and all in all I made about thirty or forty thousand. Gleason has probably cleared a couple of million. I guess Cozy Cole summed it all up when he said, 'The big ones keep eating the little ones.'"

Edna Hackett, who is a trim, shy woman with dark hair, appeared with a tray. On it were a plate of toasted peanut-butter-and-bacon sandwiches and coffee. She told Hackett she had to do some shopping, and he peeled a twenty off a roll of bills.

"Edna and I have been together one way or another for forty-seven years. She lived just down the street from me in Providence. I had six sisters and two brothers. There were about five of them older than me. We were very, very poor. We moved from house to house. My father was a blacksmith. He worked for the railroad; he shoed horses. He was an uneducated guy, a wonderful guy, but he couldn't catch up with everything. My mother was a little Irishwoman, and she never went out of the house. She was always there. When I got my first cornet, around twelve, she'd hide it all the time. She couldn't stand the noise. By then I was already playing ukulele and banjo and violin. The first group I played with was a Hawaiian one led by a man named Joe Peterotti. We'd go to his house one night a week to play. And my first regular job was in a six-piece group that played in a Chinese restaurant called the Port Arthur. We played three sessions a day seven days a week, and I made twelve dollars a week. But the spirit was good, and we were on the radio all the time. I quit high school after my first year to take the job, and I must have been fourteen. Joe Lilley played piano in that band, and later he was a choir director for Kate Smith and a musical director at Paramount. The best places to work in Providence in those days were the two ballrooms, the Arcadia and the Rhodes, so I shuffled back and forth between them as a guitarist. I made my first money as a cornetist at the Rhodes. Cab Calloway was playing a one-nighter, and I'd gone down to hear him. He was missing a trumpet player, so they pushed me up on the bandstand. I couldn't read or anything, and, boy, the notes went flying by. Claude Jones, the trombonist, was sitting beside me, and he had a pint of gin, which we swigged, and that kept my morale going. At the end of the evening, Cab gave me twenty-five dollars. That was a week's pay then. I put the money on the kitchen table when I got home, and my mother said, 'You got to bring that back to where you stole it.' She couldn't get it in her head that anybody could make that much money in one day. The first gig I had outside of Providence was with a New England band led by Herbie Marsh. It was a winter gig at the Hotel Onondaga, in Syracuse, and two things about it stand out. My ears were puffed up from the cold all winter, and one night after I'd been stumbling all over on the cornet Marsh told me that the hotel manager had told him that if I played one more solo on the cornet the whole band would be fired. Payson Ré, the pianist and society bandleader I played with all last summer, was in the band, and that summer I worked my first job on the Cape with him, at the Megansett Tea Room, in North Falmouth. He encouraged me on the cornet, and gradually I got better. Pee Wee Russell was also in the band, and we did a lot of arranging. He'd sing things to me and I'd write them down, and one of the things we worked out—a 'Muskrat Ramble'—later became a staple in the Jimmy Dorsey book. In the fall, I went to Boston and got my speakeasy training. Pee Wee got me a job at the Crescent Club, which was an upstairs speak. Teddy Roy was on the piano. I used to sit right on the piano and play—guitar and cornet. Some Helen Morgan! I met most of the bad boys in town. I remember one in particular. He was feared. He had six or seven killings under his belt. He took a liking to me, and he'd say "Hey, kid. Take care of my girl,' while he went out for an hour and bumped somebody off. Years later, I met him at a hotel in New York where I was playing. He came in with a big group, and one of them was in a monsignor's garb. Near the end of the evening, they all suddenly disappeared. Vanished, the 'monsignor' included. They'd jumped the check, which was seventy or eighty bucks, and I got stuck with it because I was dumb enough to sit down with them. Then I went into the Theatrical Club, in Boston, which was a high-class speak run by Al Taxier. He was sharp and looked like a movie star, and was way ahead of everybody else. We opened the place, and the first week we played regular sets to an absolutely empty house. The sound of the music would leak out to the street, and when somebody would try and come in he'd be told the place was all booked up. The word got around about this fantastically popular new place, and the next week they started letting people in. They grossed a million dollars the first year. I guess we had the first real jazz band in Boston. I had Teddy Roy, and Brad Gowans, the valve trombonist, and two sax men, Pat Barbara and Billy Wilds, and the drummer Russ Isaacs. Everybody passing through town sat in—Bunny Berigan, Benny Goodman, Gene Krupa, Murray McEachern, Fats Waller —and the place was always full of Roosevelts and people like that. Fats was a bundle of joy. Wherever he was, everybody was happy. He'd walk into a room and shout, 'The joint is officially jumping!' and that was the truth. He drank a lot of Scotch-and-water, which he always called liquid ham and eggs."

The telephone rang, and Hackett went in to answer it. The sun had moved down behind the trees, and the backyard was full of shadows. It was empty, save for a clothesline, and it dropped off into a deep gully. There were pine trees everywhere, and no other house was visible. Children's voices rang in the woods, and a dog barked twice. A pair of gulls drifted sidewise over the trees, and way up, sunlight winked on a soundless jet. Hackett came back, grinning from ear to ear.

"That was Vic—Vic Dickenson. I didn't know he was back in New York. He's still with the World's Greatest Jazzband. He and I had been working together for a year or so when Dick Gibson, who put the World's Greatest together, asked me if he could hire Vic. He was very nice about it, and I knew it would be a great chance for Vic, and better money. So he went, even though he was dead set against it. He didn't want to have to wear his glasses and read music. Benny Morton took Vic's place with me, and when we went to hear Vic, just after he'd joined the band, Benny said "He won't have any problems. After three nights, he'll have everything memorized. Vic has ears like a vacuum cleaner.' What I'd like, if I can swing it, is to go into either Dunfey's or the Sheraton-Regal, in Hyannis, this fall with my own group. I'd like to have my son, Ernie, on drums, and Dave McKenna, who lives on the Cape and is the best piano player alive. And a local bass player named Tony DeFazio, who's great. He was a child prodigy, and he tunes pianos now. And do you know what else I'd like to do? One night a week would be open time for people to come and sit in. The Cape is full of people who have been frustrated musicians all their lives—people like Heinie Greer, who plays good banjo, and Monk Morley, who plays alto like Frankie Trumbauer. Music is supposed to be fun, and that's what it would be. No seriousness, no self-consciousness. Just blowing, and to hell with the musicology. And I've got another ace up my sleeve—my own record company. It's called Hyannisport, and it'll be mainly mail-order. Our first release will be stuff we recorded live last winter, with Dave McKenna and my son, Ernie, and me.

"Well, when I was still at the Theatrical, Pee Wee Russell called me from New York and told me to come down. I'd never been to New York, and I was scared from the moment I got off the train at Grand Central with my guitar and cornet. When I went to the Famous Door, where Pee Wee was playing with Louis Prima, who comes on like a hurricane on the stand, I got so scared I got drunk, and I went back to Boston the next day. But I came back again, and when I did I met Eddie Condon, who was on guitar with Joe Marsala at the Hickory House, and met the singer Red McKenzie. I replaced Condon with Marsala and then I went down to Nick's, where I had my first gig as a leader in New York. I think I had Georg Brunis on trombone and Dave Bowman on piano and a New Orleans clarinet player named Bourgeois. Sharkey Bonano had the other band. Nick Rongetti was terrific to work for. People sat in all the time and after someone Nick had never heard played he'd ask me if the guy was any good. If I said yes, he'd tell me to hire him. At one time, I had twelve guys in the band. Eventually, it worked out that there were four trumpet players there—Chelsea Quealey, Muggsy Spanier, Maxie Kaminsky, and me. Nick would pit us against each other. Whichever one of us was sober, he led the band while the other three were off drunk somewhere. But one night all of us ended up in Julius's bar, across the street, and all we could do was sit there and look owl-eyes at each other and say "Well, we finally put one over on the old guy.' It was around nineteen forty by this time, and everybody had a big band. Muggsy Spanier had a big band, Fats Waller had a big band, everybody had a big band. So I put one together, too, and it lasted six months, and it was a disaster. I got myself several grand in the hole, and the guy who got me out, by hiring me as a third cornet, was Horace Heidt—Horace Heidt and his Musical Knights. It was a musical circus, and I just kept laughing. I was the only guy in the band allowed to wear a mustache, which I guess was a mark of respect."

Hackett stood up and flicked his cigarette into the backyard. "I have to change my clothes. I got a benefit concert tonight up on the Orleans baseball field with the World's Greatest Jazzband. I think Jim Blackmore will drive me up, since the only place I know how to get to on the Cape in a car is my bank in Hyannis. Jim plays cornet when he's not being a plumber. In fact, he plays one of my cornets. He's a great friend. He says that when he and his wife, Chloë, first moved to the Cape they went to sleep every night listening to the Jackie Gleason records. They've been married twenty-six years, and they celebrated their twenty-fifth anniversary by going to the church with their nine kids and getting married again." Hackett laughed. "So scuffling's the name of the game. But getting in and out of trouble is where your laughs come from. So far, I've been able to blow my way out of any situation. But as you get older you have to get better. I don't believe in time or age. I feel better now than I did ten years ago. If you do things right, you defy time. You become fadproof. The word 'retire' scares me. Once you get as close to a horn as I have, it's a lifetime proposition. It's a permanent marriage."

Hodes' Blues

The blues pianist Art Hodes left New York for good in 1950. He had lived there twelve years, and he left as the leader of a New Orleans-Chicago all-star band to play an indefinite engagement at the Blue Note, in Chicago. But the band and the gig fell apart after eleven weeks, because there were sometimes almost as many bottles on the stand as musicians. (Hodes had quit drinking a year or two before.) He had first come to Chicago with his parents and two sisters when he was six years old. "I'm not completely correct on when I was born," he has said. "It was in Nikolayev, Russia, somewhere between 1904 and 1906. We left hurriedly, and we had no papers." He had been raised in Chicago, and he and his wife, the late Thelma Johnson, decided they might as well settle back in. Hodes began appearing again in New York for brief periods in the early eighties.

Hodes is a fragile, primitive pianist, who grew up between Earl Hines and such blues pianists as Pine Top Smith and Cow Cow Davenport. He has a light, nervous touch, and he is most comfortable at slow tempos; his fast numbers, which tend to be spidery and jumpy, seem to spend their energy on getting finished. His style is chordal, and he rarely indulges in arpeggios or in complex single-note melodic lines. His playing is filled with the blues. Fragmentary boogie-woogie basses keep appearing in the left hand, and he uses a lot of tremolos and trills and blue notes in the right hand. He makes rags and "The Sunny Side of the Street" and "The Battle Hymn of the Republic" and "Ain't She Sweet?" sound like blues. His slow blues are full of evening light, of keening winds, of a sense of endings and departures. They have no self-pity, and they seem to encompass every emotion. In their intensity and depth, they match those of any other blues pianist.

The blues are the simplest of all jazz materials, yet they are the most difficult to play well—slow blues in particular. Their freight is emotion, and sustaining the mood and atmosphere that must be established in the first four or five bars demands great steadiness and invention. A blues solo can be destroyed by a whisper or a cough. It can be destroyed by the slightest flagging of intensity, by a poor chord change, by an uncertain rhythmic turn. Great blues solos—Pee Wee Russell's on "Mariooch," Red Allen's on "Jimmie's Blues," Benny Carter's (trumpet) on "Feather Bed Lament"—are seizures: they possess both the player and the listener. When Hodes goes "down" into a slow blues, he takes you with him and you don't get out until the last bar. He often stays in the three lowest registers of his instrument, and he will start with a descending right-hand tremolo pitted against irregular left-hand tenths. If he is in the key of C, he takes his tremelo into F and back to C, then passes through G and F and back into C with a short, wobbly right-hand run. In his next chorus, he fashions a brief ascending five-note figure in his right hand and repeats it with slight variations throughout the chorus. He settles into thunderous left-hand chords at the start of his third chorus, allows them to blow smartly away, and finishes with quick right-hand glissandos. His fourth chorus goes immediately into a clump of single notes struck above middle C, which have a falsetto effect, and he sinks back to the lowest register, where he rumbles up and down for most of the next chorus. He eases the pressure in his final chorus with a series of repeated right-hand figures and with snatches of a Jimmy Yancey bass. Hodes is as affecting to watch as he is to listen to. His head is shaped like a long egg. The top is mostly bare, and the bottom sharpens into a long chin. His frequent new-moon smiles slide from the right to the left. He has small hands. When he plays, he shuts his eyes, his mouth tightens, and his head moves in two or three directions at once—from side to side, up and down, and back and forth. At the end of a set, he springs to his feet, nods his head, and—still vibrating— bobs up and down half a dozen times.

Hodes worked almost constantly once he was established in New York in the late thirties, but he also took on the role of teacher and prophet. For a year in the early forties, he had a radio program on WNYC. He played the New Orleans-Chicago small-band jazz he loved, and once or twice during every show he played the piano. Hodes said recently, "Gene Williams and Ralph Gleason, who ran a little magazine for jazz-record collectors called *Jazz Information*, suggested I try out for a radio show on WNYC that Ralph Berton was leaving. I did, and I got it, and they wrote some scripts for me. When I strayed from what they had written, they left me on my own. I didn't have many records, so I had to borrow things to play, which led me to get interested in collecting. I got really involved, and I haunted the record shops and junk shops and rummage sales. The program was on six days a week in the early afternoon, and generally it lasted a half hour on weekdays and an hour on Saturday, when I'd ask guests in to play. I was playing the recordings I grew up with. It was beautiful jazz music going out into the air, and all I had to do, except for saying a few words, was sit there and listen. Everything was fine until the day Mayor LaGuardia broadcast right after me. While he was waiting to go on the air, he heard me announce what label each tune was on, and the label number. I guess it was the first time he'd ever heard the show, and he told the station manager to get rid of me—that I was giving commercials on a noncommercial station. Of course, what I was doing was giving my listeners the information they needed to get the records I had played. Otherwise, they would write to me by the dozen, and I'd have to write them all back myself."

A couple of months before his radio program ended, Hodes started a monthly magazine, *The Jazz Record*, with a printer and writer named Dale Curran. The magazine became the first preserver of jazz's oral history, and it was something of a racial pioneer: the cover photographs were strictly alternated between black and white musicians. "The existing jazz magazines were for record collectors," Hodes said recently. "There was nothing that gave the musician a voice, a chance to talk for himself. We'd invite musicians to the office, which was in a basement on Tenth Street near Seventh Avenue, and we'd give them a bottle and ask them questions. After a drink or two, they relaxed and didn't talk too fast, and Dale would take down every word on his typewriter. We got down Cow Cow Davenport and Omer Simeon and Zutty Singleton. John Hammond wrote for us, and the television writer Robert Alan Aurthur, and Carl Van Vechten, and Allan Morrison. We put out about sixty issues between 1943 and 1947. Our circulation never got above eleven hundred, and we never made any money, but I think we did a lot of good."

In 1977, the University of California Press published a collection of pieces from *The Jazz Record* called "Selections from the Gutter," which is the title of one of Hodes' blues. Here is Cow Cow Davenport on the first sixteen or seventeen years of his life:

> When I was a boy down in Alabama [around 1900], the people who played music played only guitars. The guitars were carried swung on the neck with a long string, and people called them easy riders. My father didn't like that idea of his son being an easy rider so he wouldn't let me learn music. In those days the musicians had all the girls, and daddy despised it; so he didn't allow me to play in his house. He had purchased a piano, though. My mother was pianist for a church they organized. My mother admired me because I could play, and my daddy hated me because I could play. He was going to make out of me what he wanted me to be, that was a preacher. He sent me to Selma University, a Baptist college in Alabama.

The magazine had a great variety of textures. The novelist, critic, and photographer Carl Van Vechten describes in his slow, orotund style what it was like to see Bessie Smith in 1925 at the Orpheum Theatre in Newark:

> She was at this time the size of Fay Templeton in her Weber and Fields days, which means very large, and she wore a crimson satin robe, sweeping up from her trim ankles, and embroidered in multicolored sequins in designs. Her face was beautiful with the rich ripe beauty of southern darkness, a deep bronze brown, matching the bronze of her bare arms, walking slowly to the footlights, to the accompaniment of the wailing, muted brasses, the monotonous African pounding of the drum, the dromedary glide of the pianist's fingers over the responsive keys, she began her strange, rhythmic rites in a voice full of shouting and moaning and praying and suffering, a wild, rough Ethiopian voice, harsh and volcanic, but seductive and sensuous too, released between rouged lips and the whitest of teeth, the singer swaying slightly to the beat, as is the Negro custom . . .

Hodes contributes autobiographical pieces, and he has an elliptical, easy-as-you-go style:

> And so I got a bit calloused. I watched people get drunk. I saw a lot of night life. I got better acquainted with the piano. Singers began to like my playing. I got a bit relaxed, I began to look around, visited other joints, met the help.

He meets the one-armed New Orleans trumpet player Wingy Manone:

> And so started a most important period in my life. In a short time we were roommates—then buddies—the best and closest of friends. We lived every minute of each day—and each day was a complete life in itself. . . .
>
> Wingy had a big bear coat that we both took turns wearing. Louis [Armstrong] used to greet us with: "Who's the bear tonight?" . . . Louis and the boys in the band kept a flat especially for themselves, to be able to drop in at all hours and relax. You know the conversation that takes place on the record by Armstrong called "Monday Date" where Louis says to Earl Hines: "I bet if you had a half pint of Mrs. Circha's gin" . . . well, that was the name of the woman who kept the flat for the boys. For a half-buck you got a cream pitcher full of gin which was passed around as far as it would go. In those days that was what the boys drank.

Hodes talks more formally than he writes. He talks slowly and softly, and when he listens he closes his eyes, as if he were playing what he is hearing. He talked about himself one night:

"My parents settled in Chicago about a mile from the Loop, in the Twentieth Ward—the Bloody Twentieth, people called it. It was an Italian neighborhood, with a sprinkling of Russian Jews. My sisters were named Sema and Zena. One lives in New Mexico and the other in Chicago. My father's name was William, and he was a tinsmith. He was a hard-working homebody, a free soul who liked solitude and quiet. He didn't play cards, but he shared some conviviality with our relatives. He was kindly inclined and the smile was there quite often. He loved music—Chaliapin, Caruso. He had studied singing in Russia but had been told by his teacher that he was not good enough to be a professional. This somehow gave my father the idea that music was not a profession that a young man should follow. He dreamed that I would be a civil engineer. My mother, Dorothy, dreamed that I'd be a concert pianist. My father was medium-sized, but my mother was shorter and had a little more weight. She had dark hair and very expressive eyes, and her face came down to a point instead of fattening out. She was artistically inclined without being artistic, and she was affectionate and helpful to the neighbors. I didn't have any trouble in grammar school, but then my father exercised his reasoning and got me to go to a trade high school. A gap of understanding opened between us. I didn't fit in the school, I was out of step. I started skipping classes. I discovered vaudeville, and I'd sit next to the pit orchestra. I saw Jimmy Durante, and I was fascinated, and my fascination lasted a month before my father found out what I was doing. When he got over his anger, he told me it was either go to school or get a job. I went to a regular high school and finished very well. My father had bought a piano on time when I was six, but he lost his job and the piano was taken back. When it reappeared, I started to study. I enrolled at Jane Addams' Hull House with the Smith sisters. One taught voice and the other piano, but you had to take one to take the other. So I learned to sing soprano, alto, tenor, and bass, and it developed my harmonic sense, and I studied classical piano. I also started playing for dances and discovered I was a natural swinger—that is, that it was very easy for me to play in time. I hadn't heard any jazz yet, but I listened to the Coon-Sanders Nighthawks and to Paul Whiteman on my crystal set. When I got out of high school, I took all sorts of jobs. I was a messenger, I copied letters, I delivered mail, I worked in a can factory. I never lasted too long. Meanwhile, I had started playing at Italian weddings and at dime-a-dance halls. A drummer named Freddy Janis asked me would I like to audition for the Dago— Dago Lawrence Mangano. He owned a place on Madison Street called the Rainbow Gardens. One flight up, twenty-five steps, and you were in a room that held about seventy-five people. When I went for the audition, the Dago took out a banjo, which he had tuned like a ukulele, and sang all these dirty songs. I played along behind him, and he said, 'You're hired.' He paid me thirty-five a week, which I don't know if my father got that much. On top of that, I made a lot in tips, and pretty soon I had myself a little car. The Dago had a couple of girl singers who alternated going from table to table singing, and I played for them and by myself. There were no intermissions, and whenever things got quiet the Dago would say, 'There's a lull in the joint. *Do* something.' All of us entertainers were supposed to divide the tips, and one night I caught one of the girls putting a big bill down the front of her dress. I accused her and slapped her and walked out. I stayed away one day, and when I came back the Dago lectured me: 'It's always better to listen than talk because you never know who you're talking to.' It turned out the girl I had hit was a gangster's moll. I had walked into the Rainbow Gardens knowing nothing, but I got a liberal education. I learned my trade in the midst of gangster kingdom. The Rainbow was managed by the Dago's girl, Lucy Labriola. One night, she had a hurry-up call that the Genna brothers and a big party were coming. They had reputedly killed her husband, and they thought it was funny to have her wait on them. She was in tears the whole evening. They also thought it was funny to buy me drinks and make me drink them. Eighteen in all, and it nearly killed me. Another night, a couple of wiseacres posing as federal agents went around the room sampling customers' drinks. One got away, but the Dago and his boys beat the other up and threw him down the stairs. I have never seen a person get hurt that badly or since, and I never want to see it again. I was also getting a musical education. I had to play songs like

'Melancholy Baby' and 'I Wonder What's Become of Sally' and 'My Man', and I was learning different keys and how to accompany singers.

"I quit the Rainbow after a year and a half, and I spent the summer in a band at the Delavan Gardens, on Delavan Lake, Wisconsin. I went with Earl Murphy, a banjo player, and he had a windup Victrola and a lot of records by Bessie Smith and Louis Armstrong and Bix Beiderbecke, and those records turned me on. I listened day and night. Back in Chicago, I met Wingy Manone and moved in with him. I learned to play the blues from a pianist named Jackson and from Walter Davis and Pine Top Smith. Jackson really reached me. One day, he disappeared, and when he came back a couple of weeks later he was all spiffed up and he wasn't playing the blues anymore. I asked him how come, and he said, 'Man, I don't *have* the blues. I stood around at the Savoy Ballroom with King Oliver and Louis and Manone. Louis told the jokes, he was the star, and we warmed ourselves at the fire. I watched his fans carry him across the ballroom to the bandstand, he was that popular. I listened to Earl Hines and he made me feel like taking my hands and throwing them in the river. I played rent parties, and I heard a lot of blues piano players at a black barbecue place where you could get fried fish and apple turnover and ribs. I heard Bessie Smith at the Michigan Theatre. She was wearing a white gown and she hardly moved when she sang. She sang staring at the floor, and she sang to herself. I walked the streets of the South Side, and there was music everywhere—jukeboxes, Victrolas, people whistling at each other. I sat in with Bix Beiderbecke once, and it was interesting. I think his records made him seem more powerful than he was. They must have stationed him right by the recording horn. He didn't play at all loud in the flesh—not much louder than Bobby Hackett. Armstrong was far more powerful, and they must have positioned him at the back of the recording studio.

"By the late twenties, most of the people I had worked with in Chicago had moved on to New York, but I stayed, because there were so many blues players. My friend Jess Stacy was also there, and I had enough work with my own groups and with bands led by Frank Snyder and Floyd Towne." (Stacy has said, "Hodes was a good cat, and we were good friends. Any time I'd finish a job, I'd recommend him, and he'd do the same for me. It wasn't dog eat dog—and we were all starving to death. Hodes stuck to his guns. He liked to play the blues, and he played them. We used to go to a little barbecue place to hear blues piano players. There was always an old drummer there named Papa Couch. He had a beat-up set of drums, with one of those old leather pedals, and he'd shake his head and say, 'I sure will be glad when this radio craze dies out.'") "By 1938, Chicago had become a ghost town. Accordions had come in, and strolling singers. I had begun to read about what was happening in New York. I had married my wife, Thelma—she was from Montana—and we packed our car with all our belongings and headed for New York. We found a place in the East Nineties and then the West Nineties; then we moved to the Village.

"The blues is twelve bars of music. Each bar has four beats, so there are forty-eight beats in a chorus. It's what you do with those forty-eight beats. The blues is an emotion that is happening inside you, and you're expressing it. Now, you can play the blues and just go through the changes and not feel it. That has happened to me for periods of time, and I can fool anybody but me. Right now I'm in a blues period. The blues heal you. Playing the blues becomes like talking trouble out. You work the blues out of you. When I play, I ignore the audience. I bring all my attention to bear on what I'm playing, bring all my feelings to the front. I bring my body to bear on the tune. If it's a fast tune—a rag—I have to make my hands be where they should be. I make sure they're following dictation. I'm from the old school—work, work, work. People say to me, 'Why don't you look at the crowd and smile when you play?' I can't do that. I'm trying to get lost in what I'm doing, and sometimes I do, and it comes out beautiful.

"Five of my six children are alive. One lives near New York and one in Virginia, and the rest are within a few miles of me in Chicago. I even have two great-grandchildren. Why should I retire from something that gives me so much joy and seems to give joy to others, too? I'll quit when I'm not doing justice to what I'm playing. Because my personal needs are so in hand, I don't have the pressure to work all the time. I'll never let them do to me what they did to Joe Venuti in his last years—run, run, run. I'm going to stay out of that trap. I'm going to talk to myself about that. If I work three or four times a week, that's enough."

Benny

Benny Goodman was born to parents of Russian-Jewish extraction in Chicago in 1909, the eighth of eleven children, and he became a proficient clarinettist in his early teens. When he was sixteen, he was hired by Ben Pollack, who brought him to New York in 1928. He quit Pollack a year later, and for the next four years he was a busy New York radio, pit-band, and recording musician, who appeared with André Kostelanetz, Bessie Smith, Paul Whiteman, Enric Madriguera, Sam Lanin, Red Nichols, Ruth Etting, Hoagy Carmichael, Ted Lewis, and Bix Beiderbecke. He put together his first band in 1932 (for Russ Columbo, at the Woodmansten Inn, on the Pelham Parkway), and another in 1934, which became a weekly fixture on the three-hour Saturday-night "Let's Dance" radio show. ("If anyone were to ask what was the biggest thing that has ever happened to me," Goodman once said, "landing a place on that show was it.") In the middle of 1935, Goodman and the band set out on a cross-country tour, and for a long time it was disastrous. The band bombed in Michigan and then in Denver, where it competed with and lost to Kay Kyser (who later traveled as Kay Kyser and His Kollege of Musical Knowledge). Jess Stacy had just joined the band, and he described Goodman's reaction: "Goodman began saying he was going to quit this nonsense and go back into radio in New York. I said, 'Benny, get over the mountains first and see what happens.' I didn't tell him 'I told you so,' but when we got to Sweet's Ballroom in Oakland they were standing in lines a block long, and when we got down to the Palomar Ballroom in Los Angeles everybody went crazy. And on our way back it was that way in Chicago, at the Congress Hotel, and then in New York, at the Pennsylvania Hotel and the Paramount Theatre." Goodman was on radio almost nightly after his success on the Coast, and the near-riot that attended the band's Paramount Theatre appearance was the first instance in this country of the frightening power of electronics. He kept a band together for ten years, finally disbanding after having graduated from his Swing Academy the likes of Bunny Berigan, Bud Freeman, Harry James, Ziggy Elman, Gene Krupa, Jess Stacy, Charlie Christian, Teddy Wilson, Lionel Hampton, Mel Powell, Billy Butterfield, Lou McGarity, Stan Getz, Zoot Sims, and Jimmy Rowles. After that, a man of means, he worked as he saw fit, with jazz and classical groups of all sizes and in every imaginable place.

Most eccentrics are private people, and Goodman was no exception. As a result, he has long been surrounded by legends, some true and some not. One is the legend of the Jack Benny skinflint who delighted in paying his musicians low wages and then cadged their cigarettes. Zoot Sims, who first played with Goodman in 1943, once brought an apple with him to a recording session and put it on his music stand. When Sims took his first solo, Goodman picked up the apple and started eating it. After Sims's first chorus, Goodman had him take another and then another. Sims was only seventeen and never said a word, but it is the longest solo Goodman ever gave him. Another legendary Goodman was a Simon Legree at rehearsals and on the stand. Goodman was a perfectionist about his own playing, and he expected no less than perfection of his musicians. When he was displeased by a sideman, he'd fix him with a stony look that came to be known as "the ray." Still another legendary Goodman was the befuddled, inarticulate maestro. Instances abound of elaborate anecdotes left hanging, of sentences delivered in low gargles. When he was questioned about having fired the great drummer Sidney Catlett in 1941, he replied, "It's always been one of my enigmas—drummers." But there was never any confusion about Goodman the musician. He was one of the first jazz virtuosos, and the first jazz musician to cross the barrier between jazz and classical music and become an adept and respected classical soloist. (It is not a move he was ever settled about; he felt his jazz playing may have suffered because of his adventurousness, and he knew he was not the best of all classical clarinettists.) Though it was once a pervasive jazz instrument, the clarinet has had little influence outside its own intense and difficult discipline. So it is not clear how much effect Goodman's playing has had on jazz improvisers. He helped iron out the rhythmic chunkiness that had afflicted jazz phrasing since the twenties. He made jazz musicians more conscious of tone, which had been wholly intuitive. He was the first serious improviser to champion melodic playing. Entire solos followed the melody closely or were ingenious and subtle paraphrases. And when he broke loose, his improvisations, no matter what their speed, were a flow of new melodies that continually intimated their originals: the flicker's sharp undulations constantly suggesting pure arcs. Goodman was also a *hot* player, of which there have been surprisingly few. He used a "dirty" tone and intense on-the-beat and staccato phrasing, and he frequently sank into the chalumeau register, which endows the clarinet with great intimacy and lyricism. He favored fast tempos—the high winds of jazz playing, which invariably give the effect, even when the musicians are being blown galley-west, that everyone is swinging like crazy. But, above all, there was a rare ease about his playing. Bix Beiderbecke and Frankie Trumbauer had it, and both Goodman and Lester Young learned from them.

By 1938, Goodman was almost as famous as Franklin Roosevelt, and when it was announced that he was going to give the first jazz concert ever held in Carnegie Hall, the tickets went so fast he had difficulty getting his family in. The concert consisted of twelve numbers by the big band (chief soloists: Goodman, Harry James, Jess Stacy, Vernon Brown, Gene Krupa), two numbers by the trio (Goodman, Teddy Wilson, Krupa), five numbers by the quartet (the trio plus Lionel Hampton), re-creations of the Original Dixieland Jazz Band, Ted Lewis, and Louis Armstrong, and three numbers by a group of ringers (Bobby Hackett, Count Basie, Freddie Green, Walter Page, Buck Clayton, Lester Young, Cootie Williams, Johnny Hodges, Harry Carney). Irving Kolodin had suggested that the evening include a brief history of the previous twenty years in jazz, and John Hammond had suggested that some Basie and Ellington sidemen might add texture and color to the proceedings. Hackett played a Beiderbecke solo, and the Ellington musicians did "Blue Reverie." The Ellingtons and Basies, together with Goodman, Krupa, James, and Brown, played a long "Honeysuckle Rose" that was designed as a jam session. The recording of the concert brought out twelve years later by Columbia—it is one of the biggest-selling jazz albums of all time—reveals a curious evening. The band sounds aggressive, and Krupa, who was inadvertently overrecorded on the single microphone, is loud and uneven. The trio and quartet numbers are too long, and three are taken at dismaying killer-diller tempos. The jam session is stiff (Basie, Young, and Clayton were used to Jo Jones's bicycling drumming, not Krupa's piston attack), and so is "Sing, Sing, Sing," the band's piece de resistance—except, of course, for what has come to be recognized as the single classic stroke of the concert: Jess Stacy's unscheduled two-minute solo, an airy, calm, circular improvisation that rose heedless into the noisy air. The late Bob Bach, a longtime jazz fan, was there. "I went with a friend and his mother," he once said. "She was an elegant Park Avenue lady who attended the opera and the Philharmonic. Her presence created a certain amount of tension, because everybody knew how much the older people looked down on the concert. Of course, we had our own nervousness, too. The atmosphere was like having someone in your family bar mitzvahed or doing the valedictory at commencement. We were deeply immersed in the Goodman band. We hung out in the Madhattan Room at the Pennsylvania Hotel, and we knew Gene Krupa and Harry James. We'd been to Central Park to the softball games between the Goodman band and the Basie band. Harry James pitched for the Goodmans, and Gene Krupa and Harry Goodman and Babe Russin and Chris Griffin were the infield. Lester Young pitched for the Basies, and Herschel Evans played first and Earle Warren caught. Basie and Jimmy Rushing would come out in their fedoras, and so would the song pluggers and the flotsam and jetsam of the music business, but you never caught Benny there. We knew what we'd hear at Carnegie—the trumpet riffs in 'Sing, Sing, Sing' and the ride-outs in the last chorus of the hot numbers and Gene Krupa wrapping everything up with a solo, but we didn't know what would get the biggest applause, what would blow the roof off. Truthfully, nothing really did. The jam session didn't catch fire, and Martha Tilton's singing was pretty dull. But there was a real jam-session moment—a moment of unexpected greatness—and that was when Jess Stacy suddenly took off near the end of 'Sing, Sing, Sing.' It made all the excitement we'd suffered for weeks worthwhile." Another longtime jazz enthusiast, William Shawn, remembers the concert somewhat differently: "Two things have stayed in my mind about the evening. The first was 'Don't Be That Way,' which the band started off with. The atmosphere was very highly charged in the hall. In fact, I can't remember any other musical event quite like it, unless it was a particular Toscanini concert or Oistrakh's first appearance here. So when 'Don't Be That Way' came rolling out, it was as if a hundred-piece band were blasting at you. It was even brassier and louder and more hard-driving than we had dreamed. The other thing that has stayed with me was Jess Stacy's solo. For some reason, I was standing in the back of the hall when it started, and a magical stillness came down immediately over the audience. I recall thinking, This is certainly the finest thing that has happened tonight. One has to remember that Goodman's band was simply a *dance* band. Wherever it played, people danced to it. Jazz concerts hadn't begun yet—or, rather, they began that night—and the sitting-and-listening places, like the clubs on Fifty-second Street, were just getting started. Hearing the Goodman band in Carnegie Hall wasn't just startling. It somehow gave jazz an aesthetic stature it hadn't had before."

The concert was held on a cold Sunday night. The *Times* sent its first-string music critic, Olin Downes, who wrote at considerable length for the Monday editions. It took him several paragraphs to warm up, after which he announced:

> Jazz has given way to "swing." "Swing" is that subtle creative some-
> thing, the je ne sais quoi in popular music, which has superseded the
> older product and gained a greater power of popular appeal . . . than
> jazz ever exerted.

Having unwittingly put his thumb in jazz's terminological soup,
Downes continued:

> It may therefore be imagined with what a thumping of the heart the
> present scribe got into his seat, in good time before the concert began, to
> hear the very first notes of Goodman's orchestra. It may be said imme-
> diately that he was enormously impressed, though not in the precise
> way he expected. When Mr. Goodman entered he received a real
> Toscanini send-off from the excited throng. It took some minutes to
> establish quiet. There was quivering excitement in the air, an almost
> electrical effect, and much laughter. The audience broke out before the
> music stopped, in crashing applause and special salvos as one or anoth-
> er of the heroes of the orchestra rose in his place to give his special and
> ornate contribution to the occasion.

He then bore down on the music:

> This form of sound is a curious reduction, almost disintegration of
> music into its component elements. There is hardly an attempt at beau-
> ty of tone, and certainly none at construction of melody. A few fragments
> of well-known popular tunes suffice for a sort of rough material, subject
> to variation by the players. They do such feats of rhythm and dexterity
> as occur to them on the tune's basis. The tone of the brass instruments,
> almost continually overblown, is hard, shrill and noisy. The other instru-
> ments add what they can to swell the racket. . . . The playing last night,
> if noise, speed and syncopation, all old devices, are heat, was "hot"
> as it could be, but nothing came of it all, and in the long run it was
> decidedly monotonous.

Goodman, Wilson, Hampton, and Stacy played up to and over their
heads at the concert, and so did the Ellingtons and Basies in their brief
stints, but Downes, as Lester Young used to say, had no ears for what he
was hearing. He boomed on:

> Nor is Mr. Goodman, when he plays his clarinet, anything like as
> original as other players of the same instrument and the same sort of
> thing that we have heard. Nor did we hear a single player, in the course
> of a solid hour of music, invent one original or interesting musical
> phrase, over the persistent basic rhythm. Not that they lacked technical
> accomplishment and amazing mastery of their medium. Musically, they
> let us down.

Near the close of his review, Downes looked into the future. " 'Swing'
of this kind," he predicted, "will quickly be a thing of the past."
The *Herald Tribune* sent its second-string music critic, Francis D.

Perkins, and he was a lot lighter on his feet than Downes. He even managed, after vivid pictures of Krupa and Goodman, some pioneering and quite accurate jazz criticism:

> The foremost contributor to [the visual aspect of the concert] was Mr. Gene Krupa, the group's super-expert percussionist, whose gestures and facial expressions proved unusually engrossing for those near enough to note them in detail, and suggested that he has talents as an actor as well as an instrumentalist. In the usual symphony concert the conductor has the major share of the gesturing, but here Mr. Goodman was the calmest in mien, even when he did incredible work on his clarinet, and he presided over the sessions of the trio and the quartet with an air of paternal benevolence.
>
> To an incompletely initiated listener, last night's swing had not altogether departed from certain fundamental features of the jazz set forth by Mr. Whiteman fourteen years ago [the Aeolian Hall concert at which Whiteman introduced George Gershwin's "Rhapsody in Blue" but played just two jazzlike numbers], except that it suggested a turning away from the trend toward politer music and more sophisticated forms represented in more recent programs of Messrs. Whiteman and Grofé. The fundamental rhythmic one-two beat pervaded the program throughout, as in the jazz of yore, although the variations of rhythm over this basic beat have become freer, more changing and higher-flying before returning home; the individual soli are more elaborate, more venturesome and considerably more brilliant and effective. As before, there is a notable range of instrumental sonorities and colors, from proclamative, ear-filling plangence and rousing brilliance to mellow smoothness, and another prominent feature was the expert dynamic control of the orchestra, especially in long gradual crescendi which aroused the audience to roars of applause.

Goodman talked about his music one afternoon in 1978, eight years before his death. He looked much as he had forty years before at Carnegie Hall. But his face was bigger, and whereas he once had a grocery-clerk look, his expression had become owlish and quizzical. His patent-leather hair was tousled and somewhat thinner, and his rimless spectacles had given way to horn-rimmed ones. His once tight-lipped mouth bore permanent clarinet scars; that is, it sloped toward his right, forming a kind of sluice, out of which his words came. Goodman talked in clumps, which lasted two or three minutes before ending suddenly in reverberating silences. He laughed a lot, but it was not the kind of laugh you laugh along with, because it demanded a great deal of breath. It went on and on metronomically on the same note, and it called to mind a stone being skipped across the water.

"It's remarkable after forty years that I'm still here," he said. "Particularly when you think of all the musicians at the 1938 concert who are gone—Carney and Hodges and Lester Young and Hackett and Gene Krupa. I suppose the concert changed the nature of the business. It wasn't very long afterward that everybody was playing concerts. I wish

I could say that the whole thing was my idea, but it wasn't. In fact, a press agent named Wynn Nathanson came to me and asked, 'You want to play Carnegie Hall?' I remember saying, 'Are you out of your mind? What the hell would we do there?' I acquiesced, but there was a certain reluctance, an apprehensiveness. I went to see Bea Lillie after I'd accepted, to talk her into doing a skit. I was a great fan of hers, and I thought it would relieve the monotony, and anyway the stage shows we played in theatres always included comics. She was smart enough to say no. Sol Hurok's name was on the evening, but he had nothing to do with it outside of sending me a wire reminding me to tell the musicians they would be playing in Carnegie Hall and to be on their best behavior. That was an interesting band. It didn't get uptight about anything. It had its good and bad nights, but that particular night it was on. We'd rehearsed for the concert a couple of days in Carnegie to get used to the acoustics, which is what you might call bringing the musicians in to hear the hall. We'd been playing in the Madhattan Room, where the sound was stuffy and dense, and to go into a place where it was so lively was very upsetting at first. Big bands were always difficult to handle acoustically anyway, because of their unorthodox instrumentation."

Then Goodman talked about clarinet playing. "Jimmie Noone was one of my favorite players, and Leon Roppolo was another," he said. "Noone had a clarinet clarinet sound, but Buster Bailey had an academic sound. Bailey and I shared the same teacher in Chicago, and we used to do duets together. Frank Teschemacher was talented, and I liked Volley De Faut, whose name was Voltaire De Faut, and Larry Shields, who was with the Original Dixieland Jazz Band. I think Pee Wee Russell was kind of an anachronism. I first heard him in St. Louis. I don't think he knew much about the clarinet. In fact, I think his clarinet was leaking air half the time. Artie Shaw was a hell of a clarinet player. My time was always more legato than his, but his sound was more open. It carried a lot farther. And, of course, Bob Wilber is a superb clarinettist.

"Hindemith wrote a clarinet concerto for me in 1947, and I played it with the Philadelphia. I listened to it recently—the version by Louis Cahuzac, the great French clarinettist. It takes some doing, that piece. You always have to have chops if you play classical music. I studied with Reginald Kell, and he was the sort of teacher who analyzed every inch of what you were playing. He was terrific in that sense. He wanted to know what you were *doing*. The pressures are quite violent in classical music. You reach your art on the far side of technical matters, yet every once in a while you have to go back to the basics. People have often said to me, 'You're so relaxed when you play.' Relaxed, my elbow. It's practice. You do the same thing over and over so many times that it comes to sound relaxed and easy. But, to turn it around, I've never been able to play one of my own transcribed jazz solos. Louis Armstrong and Lester Young and Bix Beiderbecke and Earl Hines didn't learn to improvise out of a book. They learned the tradition of it first. When Mel Powell joined me on piano,

Dixieland was about finished, but he knew all the old pieces, like 'That's a Plenty' and 'Riverboat Shuffle.' It was the same with Charlie Parker. His blues were older than time. When you improvise, you're thinking partly about the chords and partly about the melody. You think about a scale you might have been working on, or a motif that's been in your head. Improvisation also depends on the tune you're playing. Fletcher Henderson tried to arrange songs that swung to begin with. Good improvising has to be done with complete authority, and with taste and grace. And I always have to know the lyrics first. I sing them to myself, and that helps to get the tempo right. The quality of a lyric—the way the words fit the melody—can affect the way you play. You don't always put the greatest things down. You have moods about music, just the way you have about sunshine or darkness. Jazz is very romantic. I've frequently thought of Brahms as one of the great jazz composers. The last movement of his first clarinet sonata sounds like Bix Beiderbecke." Goodman hummed a melody rapidly, in falsetto. "The *sound* of instruments doesn't seem to matter the way it used to. Bix and Louis and Chu Berry all got big, fat sounds. Sometimes I think about the jam sessions we used to have. The whole damned thing was quite beautiful. You were sent—to use an old expression. I've occasionally thought about my position in music, then discarded the thought. It's terribly hard for one who has made history to talk about it, to be objective. As a musician, I see myself in others' reactions, and that stretches all the way from Glenn Miller to Dennis Brain. I don't think I'll ever stop playing. The clarinet is difficult to play as you get older—just as difficult as a brass instrument. There's a good deal of physical wear, I've noticed, and you have to pace yourself. I'd miss all the problems if I quit. But I'm very lucky. I can pick and choose the problems I want."

Back from Valhalla

Even during its most celebrated phase, between the years 1935 and 1945, the career of Jess Stacy had a suspended quality. It seemed recollected while it was happening. One reason was that Stacy spent most of these years as a big-band pianist with Benny Goodman and Bob Crosby and Horace Heidt, and his main job was to supply an endless flow of accompanying chords and fill-ins behind the sections and the soloists. (Stacy was cast even farther into the shadows of the Goodman band by the presence of a second and equally superb pianist, Teddy Wilson, who became the hero of the Goodman trios and quartets.) Another reason for Stacy's shadowiness had to do with his style. He *was* often audible within a band, but his marvellous background countermelodies had a way of—to use his word—"melting" into the whole. And the rare solos he was given didn't free him of the scrim he seemed trapped behind, for they had an exclusive, hurrying quality. The sparkling bell chords drifted away like smoke, the quiet, flashing runs disappeared almost before they registered, and the silken tone verged on transparency. But in spite of himself, Stacy did take a famous solo. It came about accidentally, during Goodman's bellwether 1938 Carnegie Hall concert. The band was nearing the closing ensemble of its elephantine showpiece, "Sing, Sing, Sing," when, after a Goodman-Gene Krupa duet, there was a treading-water pause, and Stacy, suddenly given the nod by Goodman, took off. The solo lasted over two minutes, which was remarkable at a time when most solos were measured in seconds. One wonders how many people understood what they were hearing that night, for no one had ever played a piano solo like it. From the opening measures, it had an exalted, almost ecstatic quality as if it were playing Stacy. It didn't, with its Debussy glints and ghosts, seem of its time and place. It was also revolutionary in that it was more of a cadenza than a series of improvised choruses. There were no divisions or seams, and it had a spiralling structure, an organic structure, in which each phrase evolved from its predecessor. Seesawing middle-register chords gave way to double-time runs, which gave way to dreaming rests, which gave way to singsong chords, which gave way to oblique runs. A climax would be reached only to recede before a still stronger one. Piling grace upon grace, the solo moved gradually but inexorably up the keyboard, at last ending in a superbly restrained cluster of upper-register single notes. There was an instant of stunned silence before Krupa came thundering back, and those who realized that they had just heard something magnificent believed that what they had heard was already in that Valhalla where all great unrecorded jazz solos go. Stacy, it seemed, had pulled off his finest vanishing act. But Goodman has always worked in mysterious ways. Twelve years later, long after Stacy had left the scene to settle in California and piece out a living as a soloist in desolate piano bars, and long after his triumph at Carnegie Hall had come to seem a twist of the imagination, Goodman announced that his sister-in-law Rachel had discovered some old records in a closet of his recently vacated New York apartment. They were recordings of the 1938 concert. The concert, it turned out, had been relayed to a recording studio on West Forty-sixth Street. The recording was made at the behest of a well-to-do entrepreneur named Albert Marx, who presented one of the two copies to his wife, Helen Ward, a Goodman vocalist, and the other to Goodman, who put the records in the closet and forgot them. A two-L.P. set was released by Columbia, and hundreds of thousands of copies were sold. The records reveal that memory does not always exaggerate.

A man of consummate modesty, Stacy was evasive and belittling when he was asked about the solo. The night before, he had ended a fourteen-year retirement by playing in Carnegie Hall at the 1974 Newport Jazz Festival-New York and now he was in a cab headed for the studios of Chiaroscuro

Records, on Christopher Street, where he was to record his first solo album in fifteen years. He appeared as relaxed as he had the previous night, when, entering the hall for the first time since the Goodman concert, he sat down without ado, reeled off three near-perfect ballads, and received a roaring ovation. "Well, that 1938 solo was a funny thing," he said, in his soft Southern voice. "Benny generally hogged the solo space, and why he let me go on that way I still don't know. But I've thought about it, and there are two things that might explain it. I think he liked what I'd been doing behind him during his solo, and I think he was mad at Teddy Wilson and Gene Krupa and Lionel Hampton, because they had all told him they were leaving to form their own bands. When I started to play, I figured, Good Lord, what with all the circus-band trumpet playing we've heard tonight and all the Krupa banging, I might as well change the mood and come on real quiet. So I took the A-minor chord 'Sing, Sing, Sing' is built around and turned it this way and that. I'd been listening to Edward MacDowell and Debussy, and I think some of their things got in there, too. I didn't know what else to do, and I guess it worked out pretty well. It ended up, of course, that I left Goodman myself later that year in San Francisco and went with the Bob Crosby band.

"Benny wasn't easy to work for. He had this way of looking right at you and not seeing you. Once, at the Congress Hotel, in Chicago, I was fooling around with a little blues before a set started, and he came over and stood next to me and listened awhile, and then said, 'That's the blues?' I hadn't been with him very long, and I was crushed. I joined him in 1935, just before the band hit it big. I was working in a group in Chicago led by Maury Stein, Jule Styne's brother, and I got a call one night from New York from somebody who said he was Benny Goodman. I thought it was a put-on, but it was Benny. He told me that John Hammond had heard me in a joint called the Subway Café and had recommended me and that he wanted to hire me. He said the band was about to leave for the West Coast and that he'd pay me sixty-five dollars a week." Stacy's eyes twinkled and he laughed. "And, you know, I worked him all the way up to a hundred and seventy before I left! Well, I was nothing in that band at first. I felt like a little outcast sitting there with people like Goodman and Gene Krupa and Bunny Berigan. But Benny had the Fletcher Henderson book, and I loved to listen to those arrangements. It's history that the band laid an egg all the way across the country. We played some tacky ballroom in Michigan and thirty people— most of them musicians—turned up, and when we did the Elitch Gardens, in Denver, everybody was across town listening to Kay Kyser. Goodman couldn't see very well at night, so I'd drive him home after work, and he began saying he was going to go back to New York. But when we got to Sweet's Ballroom, in Oakland, you couldn't hardly get in, and down at the Palomar, in Los Angeles, it was pandemonium. The big star after Benny, of course, was Krupa. I mean, you can't ask all drummers to keep good time, but he was our salesman, our showman, and he worked hard. You could wring water right out of his sleeves when he finished a set."

Hank O'Neal, the owner of Chiaroscuro Records, greeted Stacy at the studio and asked him if he'd like a drink. "No, thanks," he said, "but I'll take a Coke. I don't know what it is, but when I take liquor these days it goes right to my fingertips. So I try and stay away from it, just like cigarettes, which I gave up in 1951. I guess I just got tired of burning holes in pianos and dropping ashes all over myself. Let me just sample that piano." Stacy took off his jacket, which was royal blue, and hung it on the back of a chair. The rest of his ensemble lit up the studio—bright-red pants, a red-and-white checked shirt, and blue sneakers. He has taken on a front porch, but he looks much the way he did when he was a fixture around New York in the mid-forties. His handsome, aquiline Irish face is compact and smooth, and his hair is still dark and combed flat. His ready smile is shy and pursed, and his eyebrows, which shoot up a lot, are imperious. Stacy sat down, worked his way through several choruses of the blues, and got up. He played twin arpeggios in the air with his fingers, then kneaded each hand. "That piano's loose as a goose. I like 'em to fight back a little. And the upper registers sound a little flat. But I don't suppose it matters. I've got the check Hank O'Neal sent me for the session right in my pocket, and if the session don't work out I'll just hand it right back to him." O'Neal reappeared, with Stacy's Coca-Cola, and told him a tuner was overdue and to make himself comfortable meanwhile. Just then the tuner walked into the studio, nodded at O'Neal, and went to work on the piano.

Stacy sat down on a sofa and sipped his Coke. "I surprised myself last night, because I wasn't a bit nervous when I went on that stage. The only problem was the air-conditioning backstage: it turned your hands to ice. Teddy Wilson was back there, and we talked about the Goodman concert—how it was so crowded in the hall they'd seated people right on the stage, making it so your arms were practically pinned to your sides when you played. Last night was easy compared to what I had to do to get ready for it. It was like training for a fight. I'd let myself go something terrible when Marie St. Louis, from the Newport Festival office, called to ask if I'd like to come East and play in the Festival. Fact, when I got to the phone from out in the back yard, where I was watering, I was puffing like a buffalo. I was really out of kilter. But I told her yes, I'd do it, because I figured it might be my last picture show. Then, after I'd signed the contract, I got so nervous I started throwing up. I'm a natural worrier and I began asking my wife, Pat, What if no one comes to the concert? And I told her if they didn't to please clap long enough so that I could get seated at the piano. The only playing I'd done since I quit, in 1960, was some Bach preludes, which I struggled through. So I started practicing, doing double thirds and double sixths and scales and octaves. Right away, to my chagrin, I found my back was weak, and I couldn't sit at the keyboard more than twenty minutes at a time. I began doing sit-ups, going for two at first and finally getting up to thirty. And Pat and I took four- and five mile walks every day, and I went on a diet. Pretty soon I was practicing three and four hours a day, and it all began to come back to me.

"I hadn't been sorry at all to leave the music business. After the Bob Crosby band broke up, in 1942, I rejoined Goodman, at the New Yorker Hotel, and stayed with him about a year. It really makes me laugh now, because he fired Jimmy *Rowles* to hire me. After that came a low point in my life. I joined Horace Heidt when Frankie Carle left him to form his own band. He paid me three hundred a week and tried to make a show-man out of me, which was ridiculous. I married Lee Wiley in 1943, and that lasted two and a half years. She had million-dollar tastes and I didn't have any money. She got me to form a big band and she wanted equal billing and it was a disaster what with the bum wartime bookings and so many good musicians being in the service. So in the late forties I went to California to live and started playing in piano bars. It was all new to me. I'd always been a band pianist, and I hardly knew any tunes. I did have five or six years that were all right. The people in the bars would ask for 'On Moonlight Bay' or 'Clair de Lune,' which I always thought of as 'Clear the Room.' But they'd pretty much leave me alone, and sometimes they'd even clap or some guy would lay a tip on me. But around 1955 TV began keeping the nicer people home, and I came to feel those piano bars were snake pits. I had to walk around the block six or seven times every night to get up enough courage to go in. While I was playing, somebody would put a nickel in the jukebox or some fellow would ask me if I'd play real quiet so he could watch the fights on the bar TV. Or else they'd all get drunk and sing along. My last job was in a snake pit in La Crescenta on Friday and Saturday nights, and I stayed friendly as long as I could, but it was so bad I finally got the message and jumped ship. I took a job in the mail room at Max Factor. It was a lowly job, and I guess you'd call it beneath my station. I walked ten miles a day delivering mail, but at least I enjoyed the first vacations with pay I'd ever had. I worked there six years, and when I hit sixty-five they retired me."

The piano ready, Stacy warmed up with "How Long Has This Been Going On," and then made an excellent take. His style has long been said to be a direct offshoot of Earl Hines', but the resemblances—the little tremolo-vibratos at the end of key phrases, the easy tenth chords in the left hand, and the busy, packed right-hand chords—are balanced by Stacy's originality. His playing muses. Each number has a quiet, firm inner voice that never varies, no matter the tempo. It suggests many things: a maiden aunt summoning up her childhood, moonlight blowing through green trees, a lemon slice sliding over hot tea. But this lyrical Stacy is deceptive, for every now and then—in a singing, two-handed tremolo, in a deftly placed blue note in a complex, intense run—deep emotion suddenly appears. Then cheerful octave chords and short arpeggios brightly surface, and the solo moves quickly back into the sunlight.

Stacy allowed his melancholy strain to appear briefly in two long, ruminative takes of "Gee, Baby Ain't I Good To You" and in an otherwise sturdy, straightforward "Lover Man." Then he shook his fingers out and
declared he needed a rest. He sat down on the sofa and took a sip of Coke.

"When I play, it's mostly coming off the top of my head. Nothing is
contrived or ahead of time. I don't know what I'm doing and I can't
explain it to anybody. But I wish I could, because I'd give it to them for
nothing. It's a kind of cybernetics. I can hear what I'm going to do a couple of bars ahead, and when I get near the end of those bars a couple more
open up. I often think of my playing as a crap game—sometimes I get real
lucky. I can't remember lyrics, but I think of the melody all the time and
execute around it. Maybe the guy who wrote the tune would hate me for
saying it, but in my mind I think I'm improving the melody. I don't look
for every note to be a pearl. Sometimes they turn out to be meatballs.
Which was mostly what I played until I finally made it to Chicago, in
1925. I'd been born an only child in nineteen-and-four in Bird Point, a
train layover in southeast Missouri, where we lived in a boxcar. It was
right on the Mississippi—was, because it's since been washed away. My
dad, Fred Stacy, was from De Soto, Illinois, which is close to Little Egypt.
He was a railroad engineer. He took the first high-speed express train
from Centralia, Illinois, to New Orleans, in 1898. It had a speedometer in
the observation car, and I believe it registered as high as eighty-five miles
an hour. Five years before that, when he was carrying gold from Centralia
to the Chicago World's Fair, his train was robbed. The gold was in the
baggage car, right behind the coal tender, and the robbers unhooked the
rest of the train and told my dad to drive what was left of it to a cross-
roads where a truck was waiting. One of the robbers had a pistol trained
on my dad, and suddenly, while they were highballing along, my dad
turned and cold-cocked him. The robber fell out of the cab and lost both
legs. The railroad gave my dad a medal and some shares of stock, which
must have been et, because I never saw any of them. When he was in his
fifties, his eyesight began to fail, and after he couldn't drive a locomotive
anymore he spent most of his time hunting. He had a big heart and was
carefree and he never worried, which was the exact opposite of my mother. She was born Vada Alexander, in Union City, Tennessee, and all her
folks fought on the Confederate side in the Civil War. My mother was a
seamstress, and she supported us when my dad's eyes went bad. We
were poor as Job's turkeys. I helped out by being a Western Union boy
and sweeping out the town drugstore in the mornings and jerking sodas
in the afternoons. If you made fifty cents a day, it was darn good money.
By then, we'd moved to Malden—about seventy-five miles from
Bird Point.

"Neither of my parents was musical, so the first music I heard was
played by an old music teacher, from across the street, who knew things
like 'Memphis Blues' and 'In the Blue Ridge Mountains of Virginia.'
When I was twelve, my mother took in an orphan girl—actually, her

mother had died and her father had run off—named Jeannette McCombs. She had a piano, which was moved in, and she took lessons. I'd listen to her practicing and then sit down and play what I'd heard by ear. When my mother caught me doing that, she said I should have lessons. The teacher was Florina Morris, and she'd get you in and out pretty fast and give you a piece of pie along the way to keep you from playing too much. In 1918, we moved to Cape Girardeau, Missouri, which is right on the Mississippi. It had a population of about ten thousand souls, and every one of 'em was as square as a bear. But it was where I first heard the music I wanted to play. Word had come from Cairo, about fifty miles downriver, that there was a fantastic band on the Streckfus boat the S.S. Capitol. It was led by Fate Marable, and I heard it when the boat stopped in Cape Girardeau for a moonlight excursion. That band had Louis Armstrong and Johnny Dodds and Baby Dodds, and they played big hits like 'Whispering' as well as the Dixieland numbers. Marable was a tremendous band pianist, and I marvelled at the way he held everything together. I took lessons in Cape Girardeau from Professor Clyde Brandt, and he had me playing Beethoven sonatas and Mozart and Bach partitas, and I think it was then I realized that Bach was the first swing pianist. I'm sorry now I didn't practice more, but all I wanted was to play in a dance band and get the hell out of Cape Girardeau. I'd played at country clubs and at fraternity dances in a school group called the Agony Four, and after I graduated from high school, in June of 1920, I got my first chance. The steamer Majestic stopped in town, and the band on board, which was led by a fiddle player named Berry, needed a piano player, because theirs had drowned up in Alton. I was with that group a month and a half, and then I joined Tony Catalano on the Capitol. He was a New Orleans trumpet player, and we had to play a lot of Dixieland or else they would have pulled the boat over in the bulrushes and thrown us off. We travelled from Paducah, Kentucky, to Red Wing, Minnesota, and part of my job was to play the calliope, for which I got five dollars extra a week. It was up on the top deck, and it had one hundred and fifty pounds of steam pressure and a piano keyboard of two octaves. The keys were made of copper, and you had to practically stand on 'em to make 'em move. They got so hot I had to keep my fingers taped, and I had to wear a raincoat and a hat, so that the steam and cinders didn't make me unpresentable when I went back downstairs to join the band. I'd play the calliope to announce all-day excursions or moonlight excursions. It could be heard thirty miles away, and we called it the Whooper.

"'When we got to Davenport, Iowa, Bix Beiderbecke came aboard and sat in with Catalano. He'd already made his first records, with the Wolverines, and so we knew who he was. But the first thing he did was sit down at the piano and play 'Baby Blue Eyes' and 'Clarinet Marmalade,' and I couldn't believe it. He played what I'd been hearing in my head but couldn't do yet. When he took up his cornet, there was no effort; his cheeks never even puffed out. And his fingering was just as unorthodox as it was on the piano. He was a shy person, and I genuinely believe he didn't know how good he was. I was a jitterbug over Bix. Later, in Chicago, I'd see him walk into the Sunset Café when Louis was playing there, and Louis would turn almost white. But I think they were scared of each other. I left Catalano in Davenport, in August of 1924, and joined Joe Kayser, who had a territory band. In those days, every town of three hundred people had its own dance hall, so we played all over Wisconsin and Iowa and Illinois. The band made it to Chicago, and we were at the Arcadia ballroom for six months, and then we had a summer job in Duluth before the band broke up and I found myself back in Chicago, stranded and on my own. It was the beginning of a ten-year scuffle. I worked for every imaginable kind of group. I was with Floyd Town, who had Muggsy Spanier and Frank Teschemacher, and I remember Benny Goodman coming in when he was still a kid and standing behind a pillar to listen to Tesch, who was *the* clarinet player then. I worked for Earl Burtnett, who had fiddles and a harp and needed an Eddy Duchin piano player instead of me. I was in Art Kassel's band, and I worked in the Canton Tea Garden with Louis Panico, who didn't tell me how to play. Most of the time, I was in Chicago, but one summer I played on the Million Dollar Pier, in Atlantic City, with Al Katz and His Kittens. We wore funny hats and all that, and we had a radio wire, and when we went on the air Katz would say, 'Are you ready, kittens?' And we'd shout 'Meow!' and he'd say 'All right. Let's go.' Joe Venuti and Eddie Lang were at the Silver Slipper, and I'd bought all their records in Chicago. In those days, you got in trouble if they found booze on you, but pot was still legal—in fact, it was better for you than most of that rotgut bathtub gin— and when Eddie Lang found I'd brought two Prince Albert tins of it with me he stayed so close it got stuffy.

"I lived on the North Side of Chicago, on Wilson Avenue, which was a bad neighborhood even then. When the Depression hit, people like Eddie Condon and Gene Krupa and Dave Tough went on to New York, but I'd gotten married to my first wife and had a kid, and it was all I could do to keep my family alive where I was. There was no choice but to work for the gangsters. They didn't pay much, but they didn't bother us, either. We'd play forty-five minute sets, starting at ten and ending at six in the morning. If you played the North Side, you worked for Bugs Moran, and if you worked on the South Side, it was for Al Capone. At one point I told Bud Freeman, who was still in Chicago, that it might be better to get into the delicatessen business or something, but he said all our musician friends would come and eat on the cuff and put the store out of business. The best days in Chicago were the early ones, when Louis Armstrong and Earl Hines were in a band at the Sunset Café led by Carroll Dickerson. I'd go there with people like Muggsy Spanier, and we'd stay until five or six in the morning, even though it would take us hours to get home. I was sitting there one night digging Hines, who had an influence on me, when Jelly Roll Morton, who was making his Hot Pepper records, tapped me on the shoulder and looked over at Hines and said, 'That boy can't play piano.' Cab Calloway used to go around and sing at the tables, and we'd chase him away when he tried to drink our gin."

Stacy sat down at the piano, and within an hour he had made good takes of "Riverboat Shuffle," "Memphis in June," "I Would Do Anything for You," "Doll Face," and a blues for Eddie Condon. He finished the session with two of his own tunes—"Lookout Mountain Squirrels" and "Miss Peck Accepts." The latter is a medium-tempo blues and the former a complex, up-tempo number built around a tricky ascending-descending figure. Stacy made three takes before he felt he had it right. Then he put on his jacket and told O'Neal he would see him the next day for a session with a Bud Freeman trio. He found a cab on Christopher Street and headed uptown to his hotel. "Those last two numbers were inspired by my present wife, who was Miss Peck, and by all the squirrels we have on our little place, which is on Lookout Mountain Avenue, up in the Hollywood Hills. Pat and I married in 1950, even though I'd told her I was just a band pianist and that I had a miserable past. I couldn't ask for a better wife. She was a botany major, and she's eighteen years younger than I am. When we got married, we bought the five-room house we have now. We own it, and the taxes are less than seven hundred a year. It's eleven hundred feet above sea level, and it's on a lot that's a hundred and twenty-five feet deep. We have seven holly bushes, one plum tree, two peach trees, two apricots, and three apples. And we have grapefruit and lemons and limes. When we get up there, it's quiet, it's like the wilderness, even though you're only five minutes from Sunset Boulevard. There are deer running around, and all those squirrels the song is about, and sometimes you can hear the gophers munching on the irises in the front yard. And coyotes bay at night. There's a big forest right behind us, and because of the fire danger I keep it very wet back there. My job is to water and cut the grass and do the weeding, and I also do the housework and the vacuuming, since Pat has a part-time job in a small business-management company. We're stay-at-homes and lazy, and we've learned to live on practically nothing. I may even give lessons on how to do it."

Stacy appeared once more during the Festival, in an Eddie Condon memorial concert, and right after that he flew back to the Coast. A month later, a letter arrived: "A few evenings ago, Pat and I took a walk a way up the mountain, and all of a sudden this big police dog appeared and bit me in the rear—right through my pants and all. Well, I'm scared of dogs anyway, and I began worrying about rabies and such. I had a tetanus shot and we found out that the dog was O.K. But I think that that dog was trying to tell me something, trying to say, 'You may be a big shot when you're in New York, making records and playing in Carnegie Hall, and all that, but around here you're nothing.' "

Whatever Happened
to Mel Powell?

There are two Mel Powells. One played brilliant piano and wrote brilliant arrangements for the Benny Goodman band of 1941 and 1942—and then, after several years of backing and filling, gave up jazz altogether. The other is the quietly famous composer (school of Milton Babbitt, Elliott Carter, Pierre Boulez, Luciano Berio) and professor of composition at the California Institute of the Arts. The two communicate easily—unlike the older and younger selves of the same person who meet in Max Beerbohm's drawings—and last fall they met again briefly. This occurred when Powell accepted an invitation to play on a two-week jazz cruise, and, after six months of heavy, restorative practicing, performed beautifully in seven concerts with the likes of Dizzy Gillespie, Ruby Braff, Dick Hyman, Tal Farlow, Bob Wilber, and Buddy Rich. Powell talked about the cruise not long ago when he was in town for the New York première of his Woodwind Quintet. He was staying with Madelin Gilpatric, an old friend, on Park Avenue. She supplies him with comfortable quarters and a housekeeper who appears at the appointed hour with breakfast or lunch or tea. "I agreed to go on a jazz cruise six months before it took place," he said. "I had not played much jazz for a long time, and my fingers had turned to spaghetti. I forced myself to go to the piano every day, and by the time of the cruise I was ready. In fact, I probably played with more exuberance than anyone else because I hadn't been playing. What surprised me was that I could play fast tempos, and what didn't surprise me was that I didn't have the endurance I used to have. Playing for ten straight hours was nothing in the Goodman days. Now, of course, my fingers are spaghetti again, but they're not so bad that I can't get off a little Bach or Beethoven in my classes."

Why Powell quit jazz for the world of formal music is not as puzzling as it once appeared. He was eighteen when he joined Goodman, but he had already had a dozen years of serious classical training on the piano, had studied theory with a Juilliard professor, and had written chamber music. One morning, he had this to say about his crossing-over: "I have decided that when I retire I will think through my decision to leave jazz with the help of Freud and Jung. At the moment, I suspect it was this: I had done what I felt I had to do in jazz. I had decided it did not hold the deepest interest for me musically. And I had decided that it was a young man's music, even a black music. Also, the endless repetition of material in the Goodman band—playing the same tunes day after day and night after night—got to me. That repetition tended to kill spontaneity, which is the heart of jazz and which can give a lifetime's nourishment."

Like many consummate teachers, Powell is a marvellous talker. He has a Paul Robeson voice—big stones roll around in it. He speaks in a careful, orotund, mock-facetious way, surrounding himself with the sonority and the small jokes that are the academic's defense against philistinism. Powell is over six feet, and has narrow shoulders—a tall building seen from the sidewalk. He has large blue eyes, a large, soft, settled face, and a wide smile. He still wears his hair, now largely white, in a pompadour; the effect, above his high forehead, is of a thunderhead coming over a mountain. He has difficulty getting in and out of chairs, and he walks slowly, with a cane. "I have muscular dystrophy," he said. "It hit about five year ago when I was on my way to play tennis. I had stopped to buy a paper and suddenly I found myself flat on my back. There are forty varieties of the disease, and mine affects my quadriceps, which are the lifting muscles in the front of the thighs. There is no pain, and I do what I do only a little more pensively. I have to plot things. Self-pity comes because I can no longer play tennis. I had, of course, long since given up baseball. I grew up in a building on 161st Street in the Bronx that overlooked right field at Yankee Stadium. I used to go up on our roof and sell peanuts to the spectators during the games. In fact, so many people went up there to watch games that Jacob Ruppert raised the rightfield wall and blocked us out. But we had the satisfaction of having players like Lefty Gomez and Tony Lazzeri live in our building. I became friendly with Bill Dickey, the great Yankee catcher, and he coached me. I played first base for a dollar a game for a team sponsored by Garcia Grande cigars. We played in the sandlot across from the stadium. Then, one day, the shortstop rifled a ball at me and I caught it on my right thumb—I was a lefty— and the thumb got beaten up. There was a family conference about whether I would play baseball or play the piano. The piano won.

"I was born Melvin Epstein, in 1923—February 12th, which meant I never had to go to school on my birthday. The name Melvin was impossible and I didn't find Epstein a beautiful sonic structure. I changed my name to Mel Powell just before I joined Benny Goodman. The Powell was borrowed from a Polish uncle on my father's side who had written some songs and changed his name from Poljanowsky. My mother's maiden name was Mildred Mark, and my father was Milton Epstein. They were both from Russia, and I always like to think of my mother as having come from Minsk and my father from Pinsk, although they probably didn't. My mother was deeply devoted to her father, who lived with us. He was from Prussia, a man of God, a Talmudic scholar, a true patriarch. Reaching for the butter before he did was out of the question. My mother, in her way, was a matriarch. She was dour and severely Orthodox. She was said to have been a great beauty in the Lillian Russell mode, and as such she met the Jewish ideal of female beauty. She was almost completely nonintegrated into American life. But my father took to this country as though it had been custom-designed for him. He had been a professional boxer who used the name Kid Dougherty, but he was knocked out too often and gave it up. He went into the jewelry business and was very successful until 1929. Then he became a traveling salesman, and one of the reigning professional bridge players. He was always off to bridge clubs in Tulsa or Houston. He had embraced the world of credit and frivolity, and once, when I was with Benny Goodman, he called me and said he needed $500. I was delighted to help him, and he arrived in a Cadillac with a liveried chauffeur. I asked why, if he was so broke, he didn't use the subway. He said 'Where is this, the subway?' He also said that when he owed his chauffeur enough money he drove and the chauffeur sat in the back. He and my mother eventually got a divorce, and he married someone younger than I was and had two children, whom I have never met. He died nine or ten years ago. I have an older sister, Elinor Lenz, who lives in Westwood, in Los Angeles, and is retired from U.C.L.A. I tend to be cavalier about sociology and politics, but they are her life. I also had a brilliant brother, Lloyd, who died when he was twenty-one. To this day, we feel pain when we speak of him.

"In 1934 or 1935, my family moved downtown to 865 West End Avenue, at 102nd Street. Lloyd was a jazz aficionado, and it was around this time that he got me interested in the music. I remember our sitting in our beds, blankets up to our necks, listening to remote broadcasts of the big bands. I went to De Witt Clinton High School and on to City College when getting into City College was an achievement—when Bertrand Russell was teaching there, and giving lectures on free love. He immediately got my philosophical support. I majored in French literature, for reasons I no longer understand. I had studied piano for years with a severe German lady named Sara Barg. My grandfather, in one of his dazzling Turkish-bazaar arrangements, taught her nephews Hebrew in exchange. She was not above slapping your hands with a ruler—not so much for poor fingering as for poor preparation. I won third prize in a citywide competition for young pianists, and it was bruited about in the family that the judges must have been anti-Semitic because I had not won first prize. Walter Damrosch, who commanded limitless musical vistas in New York at the time, recommended that I go to Germany and study. But other currents were flowing through me.

"The first jazz group I ever saw was the Benny Goodman band at the Paramount Theatre on Broadway. I was thirteen. Lloyd and I sat in the first row, and the movie with the show was *Maid of Salem*. We saw it five times. I had never heard anything so ecstatic as this music, and yet so gleaming and crystalline in its precision. Teddy Wilson's pianism in particular astonished me. And when Lionel Hampton lost one of his mallets and it flew off the stage and landed in my lap it was almost too much. At the time, I was preparing Beethoven's first Sonata in F Minor for Miss Barg, and at my next lesson I took the liberty of varying a passage, and

Miss Barg said, 'Melvin, what are you doing?' I said, 'I'm improvising,' and she slapped me with the ruler.

"There were a bunch of kids in my neighborhood who played stickball and had a little band. Their piano player came down with a cold once, and I was asked to fill in. The band had a job at a Polish wedding, and it paid three dollars. The first tune was 'Goody Goody,' and I did what I could, which meant reading it off, ticktock, ticktock. They didn't use me again. But in that group was a man who became a kind of mentor to me. He played cornet and a little piano. His name was Heggie, and he was in his twenties and he was tiny. He made me listen to Art Hodes and Jess Stacy and Bix Beiderbecke's 'I'm Coming Virginia,' and then to Earl Hines and Fats Waller. Heggie was a purist. He didn't tolerate Benny Goodman; Pee Wee Russell was his clarinettist. He'd cart me around to places like Nick's, where we heard Sidney Bechet and Zutty Singleton and Bobby Hackett. I started playing jazz piano, and I thought I was pretty good. I stayed up later and later, I began peeling off from C.C.N.Y., and I never graduated. Anyway, I asked to sit in one night at Nick's. Heggie was at the bar, and there was a black man sitting about fourteen inches from my left elbow. When I finished, he leaned over and said, 'You're going to be a real one.' Well, it was Art Tatum, and after he had spoken to me he sat down and played. I was never nervous about performing after that. Nick hired me to work with Brad Gowans and Pee Wee and Eddie Condon. At the urging of George Simon, the jazz writer, I auditioned for Benny Goodman one afternoon, then sat in with the band the same night at Madison Square Garden. I guess Benny was impressed, because he hired me. I followed the pianist Johnny Guarnieri in the band, and Benny paid me $500 a week, which was very good money then. My contribution to my family suddenly became significant, because the Depression had hit them seriously. I liked to think that I behaved like a Harriman or a Rockefeller when Benny and I negotiated, and that he had the impression I came from an affluent family. Actually, part of the reason he paid me so well was that I handled both the big- and the small-band work, and I began contributing arrangements. I was ecstatic for the first eight or nine months with the band. Imagine working at age eighteen with the likes of Sidney Catlett and Cootie Williams and Billy Butterfield and Benny, and imagine what it felt like to be on that stage at the Paramount when it rose into view at the start of each show! Catlett was a particular delight. He had delicacy as powerful as a bomb. The comfort his support gave you!

"Benny was always a little paternal with me, even the last time I saw him four or five years ago. I live in Los Angeles, and he called early one morning from the Ambassador Hotel and invited me for breakfast. He always stayed there, even though it had seen better days. I had a lecture to give, but I postponed it, because I hadn't seen him in a long time. I arrived with my walking stick, and he was very solicitous and told me I should swim every day. I told him that when I first worked for him he had been about thirty and I had thought of him as an old man, but that now we were just about the same age. He said, 'Wait a minute, sonny' — which is what he always called me—'I've discovered there's a big difference between seventy-two and seventy-two and a half.' You were never sure where Benny's mind was. Backstage at the Paramount in the early days of bebop, George Simon asked Benny what he thought of Dizzy, meaning Dizzy Gillespie, and Benny said, 'What's Dizzy?' I adored traveling with the band, but I began to tire musically after a year or so. So I quit late in the summer of 1942 and came back to New York. I prepared myself to spend what looked like the rest of my life in the service. I went for my physical with Charlie Christian, who had t.b. and God knows what else. When he was deferred, he said, 'Mel, you know why I'm 4-F? It's because I wear glasses.'

"I was drafted and sent to Fort Dix and went through basic. Then I got word from Glenn Miller that he wanted me for his Army Air Forces band. It was enormous, and had a string section and some fine players—Ray McKinley on drums, Carmen Mastren on guitar, Peanuts Hucko on clarinet, Bernie Privin and Zeke Zarchy on trumpets, and the singer Johnny Desmond. Miller was a Midwesterner like Benny, but he was from a very different background. He was a lot more austere, and he was fussy about both musical articulation and personal things. Sometimes we'd rehearse nine hours a day. But he was like a fan with his jazz players. About this time, my musical schizophrenia was taking hold. I began to write some string trios and brass-quintet pieces. It was a marvellous opportunity, because there were straight players in the band, and when I would write a new piece they'd get together and play it. The band was on its way by ship to the Pacific theatre when they dropped the bomb on Japan. We were in mid-ocean, and they turned the boat around. Ray McKinley had taken over after Glenn disappeared on that flight from England to Paris. He flew in a seven-seater, a C-45, I think, and Ray, Johnny Desmond, and I were supposed to go, too. But Glenn, who hated flying, said that since the weather was bad wouldn't it be better to keep the plane light and maneuverable? So he took off with the pilot and we followed later in a C-47, which is the old DC-3. What happened to Glenn's plane was a complete mystery until a year or two ago when a retired R.A.F. bombardier said he remembered seeing a plane like Glenn's go down over the Channel at about the time Glenn disappeared. The R.A.F. plane was on its way back from an aborted bombing run and it jettisoned the bombs it had over the Channel. The R.A.F. bombardier guessed that the smaller plane, which was low over the water, was hit by one of the bombs, and that somehow mention of the incident had got left out of the flight log."

No jazz musician of comparable stature has had as short a career as Powell. It lasted about five years, and the amount of time Powell actually spent improvising can probably be counted in hours. His playing therefore never had a chance to go stale, to fall into mannerisms and preconceived patterns. His style drew on Teddy Wilson, Art Tatum, Jess

Stacy, and Billy Kyle, all descendants of Earl Hines. Powell was never a copyist; he celebrated his idols with little exuberances—a Jess Stacy tremolo, a tumbling, on-the-beat single-note Kyle passage, a nifty, complex, zigzag ascending Wilson run—then went his inimitable way. His touch was oblique and dancing. Powell's fast solos steamed. His single-note lines, decorated with little tremolos, flashed. His chords jumped three steps at a time. His accented notes, sounding every three or four measures, pressed the momentum. His slow solos were delicate and exploratory. He would examine every facet of the original melody in a leisurely, behind-the-beat Billie Holiday manner, turning it this way and that, holding it to the light, testing its beauty and strength. Then he would draw new melodies from it, embellish them once or twice if he liked them enough, and move on. He had a superb sense of dynamics. His climactic chords were delivered in shouts, his runs in whispers, his single-note figures as conversation.

It was one o'clock, and Madelin Gilpatric's housekeeper, a small blond woman with tightly swept-back hair, appeared with a tray of soup and sandwiches and coffee. Powell gave a deep "aaah," laughed, and thanked her, saying that if home were like this he would never leave it. Then he pushed himself up from his armchair, seized his cane, and moved slowly across the room to a window. Bent slightly to one side, he moved like a sailing ship just under way. He lit a cigarette and apologized, and, returning to his chair, turned his back to it and fell, his arms braking his descent.

"I was fairly well committed to composition after the war," Powell said. "But first I got a call from M-G-M on the Coast asking if I'd be interested in a staff job. It seemed silly to me—writing backup stuff for Mario Lanza, and such. But Lenny Hayton and André Previn were out there, and they told me, 'Come on out. We'll have a ball.' I went for a year, and it was awful. Writing a glissando when the mouse ran up the clock. I had married the actress Martha Scott in 1946. We had met on a bond-selling tour before I went into the service. She's from Missouri, near Kansas City. She was Emily in *Our Town* on the stage and in the film, which got her an Oscar nomination. During the past ten years, she's become an accomplished producer, although she still acts in movies. She and Henry Fonda and Bob Ryan founded a repertory theatre called the Plumstead Playhouse. We have two daughters. Mary, who's the older, is a musician. She's a singer and songwriter who is probably too refined to be successful. Kati is a struggling actress. Martha has a son from a previous marriage—Carleton Scott Alsop. He's a very successful stage manager. There isn't a straight man among us.

"From Hollywood, I went directly to Yale. I had submitted a composition to Paul Hindemith, who was in residence there, and he accepted me. My notoriety was good for my ego when I was standing in those long lines waiting to register. I'd hear whispers: 'Do you know who that is? Mel Powell. He played with Benny Goodman.' None of this impressed

Hindemith. He found out quickly that I was a glib writer, and he didn't let me get away with it. He'd give me an exercise in which I had to write two-part counterpoint using whole notes against whole notes. I was reminded of Miss Barg. She paid less attention to finger dexterity than to musical content. She'd say to me: 'No, you must not *show* the subdominant, Melvin. You must *express* it.' Hindemith had the greatest pedagogical mind I've ever been in contact with. My style of teaching derives from him. He wouldn't tolerate cafeteria talk. Our work was as serious as if we were surgeons in a lab. Once, a student brought in a piece of work, and Hindemith, in his German accent, said, 'Vot is dis?'—pointing to a passage. The student said, 'I felt that—' Hindemith interrupted him, and said, 'I didn't ask how you feel. Dot is for your doctor.' He didn't try to charm you when he taught, and he didn't admire mere beauty of sound. He'd say that Ravel had a little French dressing, that Stravinsky had a little Russian dressing. When he heard my 'Filigree Setting,' a string quartet written in 1959, he said, 'I see you haf gone over to der enemy.' I said, 'No, I learned that from you.' He replied, 'I do not teach interesting noises.' When Stravinsky gave the Norton lectures at Harvard, he spoke in French. When Hindemith gave them, he spoke in English, as difficult as it was for him. He was short, and he may well have had some of that brusque Napoleonic temperament. Pierre Boulez, who is a foot shorter than I am, reminded me the other day that all good contemporary composers have been short—Schoenberg, Stravinsky, Bartók, Babbitt. I said there was at least one exception.

"During the early fifties, I still had one leg in the jazz world. I did occasional gigs with Benny Goodman, and I made recordings for John Hammond. But most of that had petered out by the time I taught my first course at Yale, in 1957 or 1958. It was called 'Late Renaissance Polyphony,' and I knew enough to stay about a week ahead of my students. Eventually, I taught myself to lecture without a syllabus or notes. The amount of preparation it took was unbelievable—sometimes I spent five days on one lecture. But this kind of showoff stuff has its advantages. It keeps you flexible and allows you to constantly rethink things. I loved Yale, partly because of the intellectual life and partly because it was the sort of place where the great literary scholar W. K. Wimsatt and I could lunch together off and on for a year at George and Harry's and not know each other's name. I was Hindemith's assistant for three or four years, and when he left I became chairman of the Composition Department. I also became a full professor.

"Then, in the mid-sixties, Aaron Copland recommended me to Herbert Blau and Robert Corrigan, who were in the process of founding the California Institute of the Arts. They wanted to start a place where artists of every sort would be integrated, where playwrights and dancers and actors and poets and painters would all lunch together. They wanted me to start the music school. I wasn't sure I could do it. I had never administered anything, and it would be a severe change, quite uprooting.

Kingman Brewster was the head of Yale, and when I told him what I was thinking of doing he looked at me as if I were mad. 'All they have out there is carnivals,' he said. But this gathering of artists was very attractive to me, and I accepted. There were the inevitable growing pains: terrific conflicts between the faculty and the trustees, mostly left-right things, and before I knew it I had been appointed provost of the institute, a job that I held from 1972 to 1976. Then I rebelled. I said I hadn't moved out there to worry about faculty-student ratios. I resigned and appointed myself to the faculty and forbade myself ever to attend another committee meeting. We have between 700 and 800 students, and a hundred and thirty of them are in the school of music. We are the least academic of academic institutions. I teach a course called 'The Musics of Modernism,' and I have five or six graduate students in composition. I think it is crucial for composers to be taught by a composer. I also think it is crucial for a professor to cease teaching when it becomes a drudgery. I don't see it happening to me. Here I am at sixty-four, delighted to be working every day with bright young people of twenty, watching them experience the pleasures of discovery.

"I'm supposed to belong to the highly intellectual group of American composers which includes Babbitt and Carter. I like being thought of not as atonal but as nontonal. My music tends not to be long, and I tend to avoid the feverish expressivity of those of my colleagues who are even more influenced by the Europeans than I am. I like to think I have thinned out the self-pity—the whining quality I hear in their music. I try to keep the surface of my music dry. I am a slow worker—two pieces a year is very good for me. There is always the preposterous disproportion between the physicality of doing notation and the actual reality of the music. It's a kind of temporal dislocation. You are slowly writing down notes that will be played off in seconds. Before I put down the first of the many drafts I do of a piece, I try to do what Mozart is supposed to have been able to do—see an entire composition in a flash. I learned from Hindemith to have a godlike view of what you are about to do. Obviously, this view will not be greatly detailed. It will not include every C-sharp. Here is the first sketch of my 1982 String Quartet. It was the sketch I pinned to my lampshade as I went ahead with the work." Powell picked up a pencil from the coffee table in front of him, and rapidly drew this:

"What this means is that the piece begins with a great degree of complexity that is gradually resolved, like a haircut. You have to think through your whole structure. I would not dare to attempt writing a piece, small or large, without the knowledge of where it is going to end. I once heard a story about Charlie Chaplin asking Stravinsky at a gathering on the Coast, 'How do you know when to end a composition?,' to which Stravinsky said, 'Before I begin.'

"Composing is like the experiment with the ape. A banana is put outside his cage just beyond his reach. But a stick has been left in the cage, and eventually the ape sees the stick and uses it to reach the banana. You have to find the stick. When I worked under Hindemith, we were never allowed to touch a piano when we composed. Any instrumentalist who composes will perforce hear that instrument in his inner ear before he writes. Listen to the triad at the beginning of Stravinsky's 'Symphony of Psalms.' Nobody but a pianist sitting at his piano would write something like that. What has been particularly exciting for me recently in my music is working out the implications of what Schoenberg introduced in 1908 when he created nontonality. Not the problem of pitch but the problem of time. Up until now, Schoenberg's discoveries have largely been superimposed on a Brahmsian rhythmic structure. What we should be looking for is the analogy in time. We need a nontonal music that is also a nonperiodic music. There is a hierarchy in tonality—C major is boss. But in nontonality all pitches are equal, in principle. In the same way, tonality belongs to a two by two, singsong world. Rhythmic pulsing is its heart. This is inappropriate for nontonal music, which should be non-pulse. Finding out how to make it so is exciting. When I improvise, on the other hand, I live dangerously. I absolutely focus on the instant. I often find that I'm not thinking, beyond falling into certain patterns which may be dictated by finger convenience. Sometimes, when I play an Art Tatum run or a Mel Powell run, it is a signal that Powell is out of ideas, but he'll be back. He's flowing, but getting ready to fly. I used to hear this in Chopin. These are just breathing spells, and we're damn glad, we pianists, that they are there."

Powell laughed. "Who knows? Maybe I'll give up music and become a painter. In the late seventies, I was asked to give a lecture on modern music to some painters at CalArts, and I drew a graphic analogue to the structure of a Schoenberg piece I was going to discuss. I enjoyed doing it so much that in time I started doing watercolors. I found that I loved ordering color. I also found that it gave me instant gratification. I could put a beautiful red on the paper and see it winking at me, while I might have to wait five years to hear the notes I had just written down. We began to hang these watercolors in the house, and one day Keith Holzman, who used to be the head of Nonesuch Records, was visiting and looked at one and said, 'This would make a lovely cover for your new album.' He asked me if I happened to know the artist, and I said I knew him very well."

Big T

Jack Teagarden was obsessed by music and by machines. In New York in the late twenties, when he was with Ben Pollack's band, he would sometimes play around the clock. He would start at 6 P.M. with Pollack at the Park Central Hotel and would finish somewhere in Harlem, where he had gone to jam, the afternoon of the next day. In the autobiographical fragment he recorded for Riverside Records, Coleman Hawkins described those nights: "They [Teagarden and the trombonist Jimmy Harrison] used to come up to my house practically every night. Oh, I don't know how we'd make that, because we'd sit up there and fool around until two and three and four o'clock in the afternoon. No sleep. We were working [downtown] every night, and we'd just sit there and drink all night and eat these cold cuts and cheese and crackers and play— Jimmy and Jack both jivin' each other, one of them trying to figure out what he lacked that he could get from the other, and the other one doing the same thing." Or Teagarden would end up in an apartment shared by Harrison and the drummer Kaiser Marshall. Marshall said, in Nat Hentoff and Nat Shapiro's "Hear Me Talkin' to Ya," "[Harrison] liked Jack Teagarden, who used to come to our house often, sometimes staying all night, and we would have a slight jam session . . . Jack would play the piano, Jimmy trombone, Hawkins tenor, and myself on my rubber pad I kept at home. Then Hawkins would play piano, Jack and Jimmy trombone. My, what fun we had!" Teagarden's love of machines was an extension of his love of his instrument. He thought of his trombone as a kind of machine, and he spent his life mastering its deceptive, resistant techniques, and redesigning mouthpieces, water valves, and mutes. His father, an engineer who took care of Texas cotton gins, taught him mechanics. When Teagarden was thirteen, he replaced the pipes in his grandmother's house, and a year later he became a full-fledged automobile mechanic. As an adult, he rebuilt and drove two Stanley Steamers. He was a flamboyant inventor. When he had a big band, in the forties, he designed an immense fan that cooled his musicians but blew their music away. Then he built a portable band box. It was supposed to hold the band's music, and it had outlets for electric shavers and such, but it was so heavy that it was unmanageable. Sometimes he built machines simply for the sake of building them. He constructed one that filled a room, and when he was asked what it did he replied, "Why, it's runnin', ain't it?"

His trombone and his machines were the interchangeable lyrical centers of his life, and they helped hold it together. It was, in many ways, a desperate life. Women flummoxed him. He was married four times, and none of the relationships worked very well. (He had two children by his first wife, and one by his last.) He had no head for money, and he was a gargantuan drinker—almost in the same class as his friends Fats Waller and Bunny Berigan. He was careless about his health: he had lost all his teeth by the time he was forty, and he had several bouts of pneumonia. He had little sense about his career. In 1933, he signed a five-year contract with Paul Whiteman's huge, démodé orchestra, thus removing himself from the jazz marketplace—from a starring job with any of the big swing bands. (A year or so before Teagarden's Whiteman tenure expired, Otis Ferguson, writing in *The New Republic* said of him, "Though still a fine musician, he seems tired and cynical, his creation a bit shopworn.") After he left Whiteman, he put together his big band. It was never a commercial success, and before he gave it up, in 1946, he was fifty thousand dollars in debt. A year later, he joined Louis Armstrong's All-Stars (Barney Bigard, Earl Hines, Sidney Catlett), a group of superstars who after Catlett's departure, in 1949, hardened into disgruntled vaudevillians. Teagarden stayed until 1951. He spent the last thirteen years of his life— he died in New Orleans in 1964—in a comparatively agreeable way: recording, leading a variety of small bands, and making a four-and-a-half-month State Department tour of the Far East. That trip exhilarated him, and he talked about it in 1959: "We played a kind of fair in Laos before about two thousand people, and they just stood there for two hours, with their arms folded, the women with babies on their backs. They didn't clap, they didn't say anything. But they didn't *move*, either. They stayed till the last note. The King of Thailand is a good jazz clarinet player and a fine songwriter. We had a six-hour jam session with him in his palace, and his wife—well, she's a beautiful girl who would make the traffic stop here, like Marilyn Monroe—gave Addie [Teagarden's wife] a ring and bracelet that had been in her family for a hundred and fifty years. The King said he wanted to come over and listen to all the musicians he's been hearing on records all his life. I told him when he does I'll get them together in a big hall for him and let them go. He also said,'You tell your friend Eisenhower that you're the finest thing he's ever sent us.' "

Teagarden's demeanor and appearance always belied his travails. He was tall and handsome, solid through the chest and shoulders. He had a square, open face and widely spaced eyes, which he kept narrowed, not letting too much of the world in at a time. His black hair was combed flat, its part just to the left of center. He was sometimes confused with Jack Dempsey. He liked practical jokes, and he had an easy, Southern sense of humor, the kind that feeds on colloquialisms. (Asked once why he slept so much, he said that, like all Southerners, he was a slow sleeper.) Early jazz chroniclers used to say that he was of Indian extraction, but the Teagardens had come from Germany sometime before the Revolutionary War, and his mother's parents, Henry Geingar and Tillie Foulk, were German and Dutch. Charles Teagarden, his father, and Helen Geingar were married in 1903; she was thirteen and he was twenty-four. Teagarden was born August 20, 1905, in Vernon, Texas, a supply depot on the old Western Trail. At the suggestion of a novel-reading aunt, he was called Weldon Leo, but that was replaced by plain Jack soon after he became a professional musician. His sister, Norma, was born in 1911; Charles, Jr., in 1913; and Clois (known as Cub) in 1915. Norma became (and still is) a pianist, Charles became a trumpeter (he is now retired), and Cub became a drummer (he died in 1969). All three worked with their brother at various times, and Jack and Charlie eventually became known as Big T and Little T.

Norma Teagarden Friedlander (she married John Friedlander in 1955) lives in San Francisco, and she once said about her childhood: "My mother was short and a little dumpy, and she lived to be ninety-two. She loved children, and had all the patience and sweetness you could want. She was a widow with four children by the time she was twenty-eight—my father was taken by the influenza epidemic of 1918—so we all made our way early in life. We grew up in a little house—a real common house, without electricity or running water. We didn't have any money, but we were never hungry. My mother would have been a wonderful musician if she had had the time and the money to practice. She could sing well and play anything—piano, guitar, horn. She taught us all to read music. I don't remember much about my father. He worked on cotton gins and such, and he was away most of the time. But I do remember he was very strict." Charles Teagarden, who played weak but industrious cornet in the town band, did not believe in letting his children socialize, so he put a fence around his property and discouraged visits to and from neighboring children. Jack Teagarden turned to music early. He first took up the piano and the peck horn, and he was given a trombone when he was eight. He was proficient on it by the time he was ten or eleven. Charlie Teagarden, who lives in Las Vegas, has added this, "Jack never thought of his trombone as a slide instrument. He had played the peck horn, which has valves, and that stuck with him. He never moved his slide more than a foot, a foot and a half." After the father's death, the family moved to Chappell, Nebraska, where Helen Teagarden taught music and played for silent movies (sometimes accompanied by Jack, who also helped run the projector), and then to Oklahoma City, where Helen and her mother ran a small restaurant. By the time Teagarden was fifteen, he was on the road, and during the next seven years or so he roamed the Southwest with such groups as Cotton Bailey, Peck Kelley and His Bad Boys, Doc Ross and His Jazz Bandits, the Original Southern Trumpeters, Willard Robison's Deep River Orchestra, the Youngberg-Marin Peacocks, and the New Orleans Rhythm Masters. He spent two years with the legendary pianist Peck Kelley. Kelley was "the biggest musical pickup for Jack," Charlie Teagarden said. "Kelley was very advanced, more like Art Tatum than a stride pianist." Kelley, who died not long ago, became a legend simply by refusing to leave Texas and by refusing to record. (He finally did in 1957.) In 1927, Teagarden got himself to New York. He struggled at first but was found by Pee Wee Russell, who had worked with him in Kelley's band.

The story of how Teagarden was discovered by the white New York jazz community early in 1928 has been told often, and the particulars vary. Jimmy McPartland has recounted it this way: "I first heard Jack Teagarden play in a speakeasy over a cigar store on West Fifty-first Street in 1928. Pee Wee Russell called Bud Freeman and me one day at our hotel at one or two in the afternoon and said we'd better come and hear this trombone player he'd told us about named Jack Teagarden. We went over to the speakeasy, and Teagarden and Russell and some other people were sitting there drinking beer. Teagarden had a cap on, and his trombone was in some kind of sack. Somebody suggested he get his horn out, and he did. He played 'Diane,' slow, and a cappella, as they call it. We were knocked out—the tone, the phrasing were fabulous. That night, we had a jam session in somebody's hotel room, and Jack and every other white musician in town played. Freeman and I were in Ben Pollack's band at the Park Central Hotel, along with Glenn Miller and Benny Goodman, and when Pollack heard Teagarden he had to have him." The black New York jazz community probably first heard Teagarden at Roseland, where he was playing with Billy Lustig's Scranton Sirens. Coleman Hawkins, who was in Fletcher Henderson's band opposite Lustig, remembered it this way:

> The first time we ever heard Jack Teagarden was in Roseland. . . . I went downstairs to get Jimmy Harrison, and started kidding him about it. I says, "Ump. There's a boy upstairs that's playing an awful lot of trombone."
> "Yeh, who's that, Hawk?"
> "The boy's from New Orleans or Texas or something. What do they call him? Jack Teagarden or something. Jimmy, you know him?"
> "I don't know anybody. If he's a trombone player, he play like the rest of the trombones, that's all. . . . Trombone is a brass instrument. It should have that sound just like a trumpet. I don't want to hear no trombone sounds like trombones."
> I said, "But, Jimmy, he don't sound like those trombones. He plays up high, and he's makin' these—he sounds a whole lot like trumpets to me.
> "Oh, man. I can't pay that no mind."

Teagarden worked with Pollack three or four years, passed through Mal Hallett's band, and signed on with Paul Whiteman. His famous style had set, and it changed little. It was very much of the Southwest, which has produced many of the most lyrical and affecting of all jazz musicians. Their music is imbued with the blues, they wear their emotions on their sleeve, they swing effortlessly, their sounds are rich and spacious. In his early days, Teagarden sought out black musicians and black church music, probably as antidotes to the sentimental popular music played in the Teagarden household and to the martial and light-classical music he played with his father in the Vernon town band. Teagarden had several different tones: a light, nasal one; a gruff, heavy one; and a weary, hoarse one—a twilight tone he used for slow blues, and for ballads that moved him. He had a nearly faultless technique, yet it never called attention to itself. Opposites were compressed shrewdly in his style. Long notes were balanced by triplets, double-time spurts by laconic legato musings, busyness by silence, legitimate notes by blue notes, moans by roars. Teagarden developed a set of master solos for his bread-and-butter tunes—the tunes that his listeners expected and that he must have played thousands of times: "Basin Street Blues," "A Hundred Years from Today," "Beale St. Blues," "Stars Fell on Alabama," "St. James Infirmary," "I Gotta Right to Sing the Blues," "After You've Gone." Each time, though, he would make generous and surprising changes—adding a decorative triplet, a dying blue note, a soaring glissando—and his listeners would be buoyed again. Sometimes he sank into his low register at the start of a slow blues solo and rose into his high register at its end. Like his friend and admirer Bobby Hackett, he stayed in the bourgeois register of his horn, cultivating his lyricism, his tones, his sense of order and logic. Teagarden was a good jazz singer. His singing, a distillation of his playing, formed a kind of aureole around it. He had a light baritone, which moved easily behind the beat. The rare consonants he used sounded like vowels, and his vowels were all puréed. His vocals were lullabies—lay-me-down-to-sleep patches of sound.

Teagarden gathered friends wherever he went. His playing stunned them when they first heard it, and it still stuns them. Jess Stacy:

"I thought he was the best trombonist who ever lived. When I made those Commodore sides with him in 1938—'Diane' and 'Serenade to a Shylock'—he just walked in, warmed up, and hit out, and he played like an angel. He was an ace musician who could talk harmony like a college professor. He'd sit at the piano after a take and say, 'Try this chord on the bridge, this C with a flatted ninth,' and he'd be right. Of course, he was a wizard with tools, too. He always carried a tuning fork. He had perfect pitch, and he couldn't stand out-of-tune pianos. So he'd work at a bad piano between sets until he got it where it didn't drive him crazy anymore. They couldn't make them any nicer than Jack—never any conceit, never got on anybody's nerves."

Norma Teagarden Friedlander:

"When Jack and Charlie were out playing for Ben Pollack and Paul Whiteman, they weren't always good about sending money home. I guess they were young and careless and drinking a lot. I don't mean Jack wasn't generous. It was just that whoever was closest to him—was right *there*—got what he had: a new overcoat, a hat, a twenty-dollar bill."

The trumpeter, pianist, composer, and bandleader Dick Cary:

"I first heard him in the flesh with his big band in Providence in 1940. He had Danny Polo, and his brother Charlie, and Ernie Caceres. The band sounded somewhat like the Bob Crosby band—only looser, not so tight.

But I didn't meet him until 1946 or 1947, not long before I went with the early version of Louis Armstrong's All-Stars. There was not a harsh word among us, and we never knew what we were going to do musically. The band hadn't become a vaudeville show yet. We hung out all the time. Sid Catlett took us to a big ballroom in Minneapolis, and Jack and I were the only whites there. We sat in, and when they turned the lights way down, the music got very soft and you could hear this enormous sound of dancing. Sid and Jack were wary of each other at first, but one night they got drunk, and after that they were buddies. Louis and Jack really got on together. When we were on the bus out in the midlands, Louis used to play practical jokes on us, and once, to get back, Jack built this little engine—it didn't *do* anything, just ran. Louis was admiring it, and Jack told him to cross two little wires and suddenly the engine started, and Louis almost jumped out of his skin.

"I don't think many people knew how bitter Jack was about a lot of things. He was always in debt, and people took advantage of him, because he was a simple man who never moved fast. I know he was only being paid five hundred dollars a week with the All-Stars, and a lot of that was withheld. I remember he said to me, 'Gate, if I don't have enough money to buy a pint of Four Roses every day, I'm quitting music.'

"Jack was a very soft player. He used the microphone. He had that certain stance—his right foot forward and pointing to the right, his head tilted to the left, his eyes shut, a placid expression on his face. He didn't move his arm much, because he used a lot of false positions on his slide and could get what he wanted with little flips of the wrist and with his marvellous lip control. This lip control came from his embouchure, which was unusual—a sort of big rectangular space around his mouth. He seldom made a mistake. It always seemed to me that he would choke off a note if it was coming out wrong. There's no way to know, but that's how it sounded if you listened real close."

The trumpeter Don Goldie:
"I played for Jack from 1959 to 1963, but I had known him from the time I was five years old, when my father, Harry Goldfield, and Jack were with Paul Whiteman. Jack's lip facility was extraordinary. He could play any kind of long run, obbligato, triplet. He generally only used three positions on his slide, and his fingers rarely moved below the bell of the horn. And he didn't hold his slide between his thumb and index fingers as most trombonists do, but held it between his index and middle fingers. He was always using his mechanical knowledge to improve his playing and your playing. He invented a mouthpiece that enabled me to play a whole octave higher. He invented a new water valve, a kind of petcock, that gave his horn a better seal. He invented a musical slide rule that showed you, for instance, exactly what chords the notes in the C scale could be used in. He started every trombonist in the country using Pond's Cold Cream on his slide, and later he switched to Pam, the cook-

ing lubricant. His ear was as extraordinary as his lip. When we flew, he'd tell me exactly how many r.p.m.s the engine was making, and what key it was in.

"Jack was a giver, not a taker. He was a country-type boy—in some ways an unsophisticated man, a very personal man. He always opened the evening in a club or at a concert by saying 'Good evening, folks.' He was a shy man who found small talk difficult and who hated the telephone. He was gentle and kind. If he couldn't say something nice about someone, he didn't say anything."

The cornettist Ruby Braff:
"He wasn't disciplined into the kind of hustling that makes a performer a top-drawer attraction. But he was a big-timer who was serious about his position as a musician, who guarded that position. He was not one who got into bar talk. He had his own thoughts. The few times I worked with him, I always talked to him and he always had wonderful things to say. I told him one night at the Metropole that his band was playing so loud I could barely hear him. He said, 'They're doing it of their own accord. I don't pay them to play loud. Anyway, they're not going to bruise me.' Another time, I said to him, 'You're always consistent, no matter where you play. If I play in a room with a lot of rugs and drapes—as opposed to a nice, empty wooden room—it ruins me, and I might as well go home.' He said, 'That's because you bring a certain sound to work with you. Forget that sound and just bring your horn and trust the fact that your sound will just naturally drop in on you, no matter how closed up the room is. Just play nice notes and don't worry and it will happen to you.' He was always cool. Once, we were standing on the grass at the Newport Jazz Festival, listening to an avant-garde saxophonist make animal noises, and Jack turned to me and said, 'What's going on up there? I had a Stanley Steamer that had a horn that sounded fifty times better than that.' "

Jimmy McPartland:
"I left the Pollack band in late 1928, and I didn't work with Jack again until 1939, when I joined his big band. Jack's brother Charlie was on first trumpet, and I took most of the hot solos and did a little singing—duets with Jack, that sort of thing. When Jack was ill—that is, when he'd had too much to drink—I fronted the band and took his solos and did all the singing. The band wasn't making any money, so Charlie and I took turns driving the van that carried the instruments. Jack often drove the band bus, and he did the repairs when it broke down. He was a great musician. He was equally fluent in all the tough keys—from B-natural to A-concert, from E-natural to F-sharp. Style is being able to express what you want in the way you want to express it, and that's what he did. He had great depths of feeling, and he had great tenderness, and he showed them both on his horn. He was always a natural delight to be with. We never had a

bad word for each other in all the time we were together. He called me Jimson and I called him Jackson. I saw him not long before he died. He had a group at the Metropole, and he looked bad—all puffy and white. And he played sitting down. I'd heard he had started drinking again after being on the wagon a long time. I told him that I had joined A.A., and that anyway we couldn't drink at our age the way we used to in the twenties and get away with it. He just looked at me and said, 'Ah, Jimson,' and patted the back of my neck and turned away."

Three Tones

Early one morning in the summer of 1967, when Duke Ellington had finished work at the Rainbow Grill and was having a steak at Jilly's with a group of friends, he was asked why he had never hired Vic Dickenson. It was evidently not a question he wished to answer directly, so he repeated the trombonist's name twice and added his own question: "Does he still have his three tones?" Ellington rarely put down exceptional musicians who hadn't passed through his academy, and what he probably meant was: Does Vic Dickenson still play as simply and beautifully as ever? The answer then was yes, and the answer now is still yes.

Since the forties, when Dickenson quit travelling with big bands, he has been almost constantly on view in New York, and he has invariably worked and recorded with the champions. Dickenson's presence brightens every band he plays with. He is tall and thin, and he has a long, wry, Lincoln face. His eyes are generously lidded. He has a medium-sized, middle-register voice of a kind that winds between other voices in a gathering. He is a slow, laconic talker, and his laugh is concentrated and nasal. He is a calm, cool, funny man who wishes no offense to life and hopes life will return his sentiments. In recent years, he has preferred to sit down with his legs crossed when he plays; he leans slightly to his left and balances himself by pointing his trombone to the right. When he heads his own group, he pauses a long time between numbers and shuffles through a pile of plastic-covered three-by-five cards on which are typed the names of some three hundred songs. Then, the next number decided upon, he puts the cards back in a pocket, picks up his trombone, and bangs off the time on the piano. He plays with his eyes open, but sometimes after he has offered an epigrammatic reading of the melody and is about to improvise he will close his eyes and disappear. He has the air of an Edwardian bachelor, but he was married in 1932 to Otealia Foye, whom he first met in Cincinnati in 1928. They live in Parkchester, in the East Bronx, and they have never had children.

Dickenson talked about his life this way:

"I was born in Xenia, Ohio, on August 6, 1906. It's about fifteen miles from Dayton, and it had a population of about nine thousand. My father, Robert Clarke Dickenson, had his own plastering business. He was tall, and if anybody thinks I'm handsome—well, I look like him. He used to play little ditties on the violin. He died in 1929. My mother was thin and beautiful, like an angel. They tell me she played the organ, but I don't remember it. I used to think when I was little that I wanted to die if my mother died, even though my father used to let her do the strictness. I believe she came from Ironton, Ohio, and I believe my father came from Virginia or West Virginia. There were nine of us children, and I was the seventh. Arthur, Ernest, Anna, Edward, Carlos, Walter, Nettie, Edith, and me, Victor. I'm the only one left. Carlos was a good saxophone player who ended in the mail service. He was also a thirty-third-degree Mason. I was proud of that. Another brother fought in the First World War and worked for International Harvester, although he was always ailing after the war. One sister died when she was just about to graduate from college, and another was a schoolteacher. Edith, Ernest, and Walter didn't survive childhood. We lived in a house on the outskirts of town, and we had about twelve acres. We tried to raise corn and such, but the ground was poor. Across the street from our house was a wood, and the Ku Klux Klan used to meet there. They'd stand in a circle in their robes in that wood and burn their crosses, and that upset me all during my childhood. I was sickly, too. I had pleurisy, and at one time they thought I was on the verge of t.b., and they had me go to the t.b. hospital, which put me behind in my schooling. When I went back to school, they didn't back-teach me, so I didn't get a chance to learn the things I could have.

"When I was sixteen or seventeen, I had an accident that changed my life. I was trying to learn my father's business. I was carrying a hod full of mortar up a ladder, pulling myself up the rungs with one hand and balancing the hod, which weighed maybe seventy pounds, with the other. A rung broke and, with all that weight, I pitched backward, and gave my back a terrible wrench. I couldn't pick anything up. In fact, I still can't pick much up beyond my trombone. That accident caused me to decide to become a musician full time. I had already started playing trombone in the school band. I tried to play it like a saxophone or trumpet. I pretended I could read, but what I did was read the notes the way you read them when you're singing—just getting the drift of the melody. I played my first job when I was fifteen, with the Elite Serenaders at an Elks' dance in Lebanon, Ohio. After that, a bunch of us tried to put a band together. The center of it was my brother Carlos and a cousin, Herb Waide, who played piano—but only in the key of F-sharp. We also had a trumpet player and an alto saxophonist and a drummer. We had moved to Columbus, and Carlos and I roomed together. We were on starvation row. We'd get a gig playing the Saturday matinée in the movie house and a dance at the Elks' that night, and that might be it for the week, at three or four dollars a throw. That wasn't enough to fill a tooth with. We also played occasional gigs with Watkins' Syncopators. Watkins was a cousin of the bandleader Lloyd Scott and his brother Cecil Scott. In between jobs with Watkins, I'd work with Tom Howard, who had the distinction of having his whole band beaten up by whites in Florida after a dance. I played with Earl Hood, and travelled around the state, and in 1926 Don Phillips hired me and I joined him at the Broadway Gardens, in Madison, Wisconsin. His bass player sold me a trombone, which I needed, for sixty dollars. I was getting thirty-five a week, and I had to give him fifteen, so that left me twenty for room and board and everything. At the end of a month, when I'd finished paying off the bassist, I was fired, and I didn't have enough money to get back to Columbus. A local drummer I'd met asked me if I knew a piano player he could use that night, and I said I could play piano in the key of C, so I made enough to get home. I'd been fired because I couldn't read music, so I vowed after that to learn to read and write music, and I did. Self-taught—which I am on the trombone, too. I worked with Bill Broadhus in Lexington, Kentucky. Then Helvey's Troubadors motored down from Cincinnati. J. C. Higginbotham was in the band, and when he left to go to Buffalo I took his place. Around this time in Columbus, Lloyd Scott came through, and he had Dicky Wells, who made a big impression. I also heard Coleman Hawkins and Buster Bailey and Joe Smith and Louis Armstrong. Jimmy Harrison played a lot like Louis, and I liked Benny Morton, who played like Harrison. Of course, when we were kids we listened to Bessie Smith and Mamie Smith and Ma Rainey and Jelly Roll Morton—all on records. When the spring broke in the Victrola, we'd push the turntable around with our fingers and the music sounded like a sick cow.

"In 1929, I went with Speed Webb, and that was a daggone good band. Roy Eldridge and Teddy Wilson were in it, and Reunald Jones, who was later with Duke Ellington. We got as far east as Boston. My aunt was living in Brooklyn, and my mother happened to be staying with her, so I ducked down to New York. New York fascinated me. I joined Zack Whyte after Webb, and then went with Thamon Hayes and his Kansas City Rockets. Harlan Leonard took over that band after I left. When we were in Memphis in 1933, I got a telegram from Blanche Calloway, and I was with her three years, before going with Claude Hopkins. I was with Hopkins until 1939. Jabbo Smith was in Hopkins' band for a while, and he was something special. He still played sensationally. I was with Benny Carter's big band after that. Benny let just about everybody solo, but that didn't happen in a lot of big bands. You'd sit there week in and week out, playing those notes, and never get a solo, or maybe get just eight bars on a bridge, and silence for another couple of weeks. I was with Count Basie for a year after Carter, and sometimes Basie only gave me one solo a week, and that was disappointing. Everybody liked each other in the Basie band. It was like brothers. We were on the road *all* the time, and in those days you stayed in people's houses, because the hotels wouldn't let you in, so Lester Young and I always tried to find a place together. He spoke his own language. If he agreed with you, it was 'You rang the bell—ding ding.' I still say 'Ding ding' before I take a drink."

Dickenson's style is wasteless and lyrical and funny. He listened to Louis Armstrong in the twenties, as every jazz musician did, and he was much taken by Dicky Wells, whose work he distantly echoes. High jinks are always around the corner in his playing. He growls a lot, particularly in ensembles, and the growls add a lazy, bibulous texture to the counterpoint. He likes to poke fun at fulsome ballads, and in 1946 he made a classic recording of "You Made Me Love You," with faultless smears and growls and whispered asides. Even when he plays the melody of a good song straight, he seems to be laughing up his sleeve. He decorates it with bunched triplets and questioning vibratoless bursts, and he lets the melody run on in the silences in between, like a movie with the soundtrack off. Dickenson doesn't sound like a trombonist. His tone is gentle and downy, and his playing is a direct extension of the way he talks and sings. It has none of the nasal, brassbound sound that affects most trombonists. But when his musical environment gets heated, he plays with great passion. Then he uses staccato phrases, adroit repetitions, emery growls, Dicky Wells shouts, and tumbling curving runs, and he will end his solo with a resounding hammerlike note. He invariably swings, and it makes no difference whether he is neighing at a poor ballad or going at top speed. Like all great lyrical workers, he sometimes slides into a slough in which he depends on patterns—his triplets and growls and smears—that he has long since perfected. But even these predigested solos are graceful and funny. Dickenson's playing has diminished little. He may rely on his patterns more than he once did—they started out, after all, as his inventions—but he also manages to surprise you in almost every solo with an oblique cry, a slyly placed silence, a short humming blue note. He likes mutes and he often puts his left hand inside the bell of his horn, making it sound as if he were playing in the next room. He also hangs a beret over his bell, which gives him a soft, ruffling sound— a bird landing. His dynamics are superb. Every solo is a mixture of muted sounds, growls, warning roars, and soft, sliding connective phrases. Many jazz soloists are disconcertingly egocentric. They exude self-pity, or querulousness, or disdain, but Dickenson appears bent on lifting his listeners with humor and warmth and beauty, all the while making it clear that he won't hold us up any longer than is absolutely necessary.

"I play in an unorthodox way," Dickenson said. "I don't lip correctly. You're supposed to put the mouthpiece over your face skin, but I put it on my lip skin, over the inside part of my lip. That's the way I learned, and because of it my chops sometimes wear out, and I can't play the high notes Dicky Wells and Trummy Young do. I do a growl two different ways: I make a strong humming sound in my throat or I do it with special tonguing. There are two sets of positions on the slide that you can get the same notes with—the outer position and the inner position. I get a better sound with the inner position, and I don't have all that weight you have when you use the outer position and the slide pulls the mouthpiece loose. I think about improvising as if I'm singing. It's what I'd do if I were humming. When you improvise, you see your feelings in your mind, and you form certain feelings for numbers that you play over and over. You keep the melody in your mind, too. If you lose it, you can get into an outer-space situation. Sometimes you think a bar ahead, sometimes four bars. If I hit a wrong chord or a wrong note, I try and have a follow-up bar in reserve in my mind to take care of it. Most of that thinking ahead is in rhythmic patterns. A lot of times, you have a framework set up in your head of what you're going to start a solo with and the guy soloing before you doesn't stop when he's supposed to, he dribbles over into your first measure, and that fouls you up and you tell him mentally, Oh, well, hell, go ahead and play another chorus, only stop when you're supposed to. I think maybe I know ten thousand songs. I keep about two or three hundred typed on index cards, which I carry to almost every job as reminders of what to play. They're my repertory cards. If I typed up all the tunes I know, I couldn't carry them with me; they'd be too heavy. I write my own tunes, too, and not one of them has been a hit or has brought in any residuals—'Constantly,' 'I'll Try,' 'Mistletoe,' 'What Have You Done with the Key to Your Heart?' Some I have written down but haven't exposed yet.

"Of all the wonderful musicians I've worked with, my happiest days of playing were with Bobby Hackett. We first worked together at the old Child's Paramount in the fifties. We worked together in the fifties and sixties and seventies. Bobby could never manage business things right. He put too much dependence on people, and they took him for what they could. He always trusted the wrong people. He loved to give you things. He'd give you an expensive gift, just like that. I miss him all the time—him and his beautiful, perfect playing.

"If I had it to do over, I'd have a good manager. I'm like Bobby in that respect: I'm a poor businessman. But I know I wouldn't have been a good doctor, and I wouldn't have been a good cook. I know I wouldn't have been a good janitor, and I don't have the patience to be a good teacher. I'd slap them on the finger all the time, and the last thing I ever want to do is mess up my cool. Sometimes I feel like retiring. My ankles swell up after an evening of playing, and my teeth aren't as strong as they used to be. My health is crumbling a little, and I don't like to travel much anymore. I wish I could play when I feel like it and not play when I don't feel like it. In other words, be semi-retired. I would like to have played with Duke Ellington at one time, but he already had such a good trombone player—Lawrence Brown—that I wouldn't have been an addition. I first heard Lawrence Brown play over the air, and he dedicated a number to his mother. I liked that."

Little Jazz

Slowed by various ailments and by the deep fatigue that sooner or later afflicts all brass players, the trumpeter Roy Eldridge, now seventy-four, gave up playing in public in 1979, thereby diminishing American musical life. For the last ten years of his career, he had been on almost constant view at Jimmy Ryan's, on West Fifty-fourth Street, leading a small swing band and proving, night after night, that his great engines still worked very well. Joe Muranyi, his longtime clarinettist at Ryan's, has said of him, "Roy is complex, but he's very much in touch with his feelings, and out they'd all come in his music. They came out when he wasn't playing, too. He liked to act out the same dramas every day. He fought his battles with race, with his playing, with managers over and over. And he and I would have terrible arguments. He'd make me mad as hell by telling me that I didn't sound like a Hungarian clarinet player, that I must be Polish. And when I'd make him mad it was Mt. Vesuvius to the fifth power. A few years ago, he had a heart attack. We had done a gig up in Connecticut not long before that, and after we had set up and were going out for food Roy just sat there on the stand and said to bring him a cheeseburger. Then he said, 'I'm sick and tired of this. What do I need it for?' But even toward the end there was no notable loss in his playing. He could still be fiery. He would start slowly every evening, pacing himself until he got it all together."

Eldridge had a restless career. He played in every size and kind of band from jam groups to Boyd Raeburn's forward-looking big band. He played for the best black bands (McKinney's Cotton Pickers, Fletcher Henderson, Count Basie) and for the best white bands (Gene Krupa, Artie Shaw, Benny Goodman). He led his first band, Roy Elliott and his Palais Royal Orchestra, in Pittsburgh, where he was born, before he was twenty. Then he joined Horace Henderson's Dixie Stompers, and in 1929 and 1930 he was with the Nighthawks, Zach Whyte, and Speed Webb. He also worked in Milwaukee with Johnny Neal's Midnite Ramblers. He moved to New York in 1930, and he went from Cecil Scott to a famous Elmer Snowden band that included Dicky Wells, Al Sears, Otto Hardwicke, and Sidney Catlett and that made a highjinks short film, "Smash Your Baggage." Hollywood still disguised the few blacks it showed, and everyone in the band was dressed as a Pullman porter. He passed through Charlie Johnson, Teddy Hill, and McKinney's Cotton Pickers, and in 1936 joined Fletcher Henderson. He formed his own band the same year and held forth for a long spell at the Three Deuces, in Chicago. Angry over racism, he quit music in 1938 and studied radio engineering. By 1939, though, he had put together a new band, which played mostly mild dance music at the Arcadia Ballroom, on Broadway. In 1941, after stints at the Apollo Theatre, Kelly's Stable, and the Capital Lounge, in Chicago, he went with Gene Krupa, forcing that mundane band to play with joy and fervor. Krupa broke up the band in 1943, and Eldridge gigged around New York, and joined Artie Shaw in 1944.

Shaw once talked about him this way: "He was a cute little stocky, chunky guy, a feisty guy, in many ways a tragic guy. It was very tough for him racially in my band, just as it had been for Billie Holiday when she was with me in the thirties. With Hot Lips Page, who was in the band in 1941, it was different, because he had the attitude of 'I can't change it, so I'll put up with it'—maybe because he came from the South. When I hired Roy, I told him he would be treated like everyone else in the band, and that he would be paid very well, because he was the best. I told him that I could handle racial matters when we were on the stand, but that there was very little I could do when we were off. Droves of people would ask him for his autograph at the end of the night, but later, on the bus, he wouldn't be able to get off and buy a hamburger with the guys in the band. He used to carry a gun, and I'd try and discourage him, and he'd tell me that he'd rather take his chances with the police than run up against some crazy unarmed. He saw himself as travelling through a hostile land, and he was right. Things came to a head at the San Francisco Auditorium when he arrived late and they wouldn't let him in the main entrance. He was a bitch of a player, and everybody in the band loved him."

Eldridge stayed with Shaw a year, had another band of his own, rejoined Krupa for a short time, and, in 1950, went to Europe with Benny Goodman. He stayed on in Paris after Goodman had gone home, returning to New York in 1951 to make a sensational appearance at the Old Stuyvesant Casino, down on Second Avenue. He spent much of the fifties in Norman Granz's Jazz at the Philharmonic. Then he accompanied Ella Fitzgerald for two years. He was with Count Basie in 1966, and he led his own groups and appeared at festivals until he moved into Jimmy Ryan's. He was on the CBS television show "The Sound of Jazz" in 1957. Not long before he became ill, he played at the miniature jazz festival that President Jimmy Carter held on the south lawn of the White House—a gracious affair that included many of Eldridge's peers and descendants.

Eldridge's style was incandescent, lyrical, melancholy, indelible, and erratic. He learned the hard way, as he told John Chilton for the liner notes of a Columbia album called "Roy Eldridge—The Early Years": "When I was young I used to go out and look for every jam session going. I used to stand out on the sidewalk smoking, listening to the band inside, summing up the opposition. Eventually I'd walk in and try to cut them. All my life, I've loved to battle. And if they didn't like the look of me and wouldn't invite me up on the bandstand, I'd get my trumpet out by the side of the stand and blow at them from there." He also told Chilton, "The cats in New York were a hard bunch, guys were coming in from all over the country trying to prove themselves, and those who had got there first elected themselves as the judges. The rule seemed to be that you told newcomers the things you didn't like about their playing, and not the things you liked. So, Hot Lips Page heard me, and said, 'Why are you playing like an ofay?' Well, he knew his stuff, so I took note of that. And Chick Webb, who was guaranteed to speak his mind, said, 'Yeah, you're fast, but you're not telling me any story,' and those words sunk right into me. At that time I had this thing about playing as fast as I could all the time. I double-timed every ballad I did, and never held a long note. I was able to run the changes on any song, and do nice turn-arounds at the end of each eight bars, but I wasn't developing my solos." His phrasing and way of building a climax resembled Louis Armstrong's, and he has said that he learned from Rex Stewart and the white cornettist Red Nichols. He has said, too, that he learned much from saxophonists like Coleman Hawkins and Benny Carter, which helps explain the flow and momentum of his playing. He spent time with the flashing, mercurial Jabbo Smith in the late twenties, and Smith's speed and quirkiness must have affected him. And he heard the strange notes and dark sound and laid-back attack that Red Allen used with Fletcher Henderson in 1933 and 1934. All this coalesced into a stunning and original style, which in due course brought forth Dizzy Gillespie. Eldridge's style comes in two parts. The most celebrated is his up-tempo, upper-register attack, as heard on Gene Krupa's 1941 recording of "After You've Gone." Following some introductory clowning (cheers from the band and quotes by Eldridge from a Sousa march and from "Yankee Doodle"), Eldridge hurtles through three choruses of the song. He does the first more or less straight, and he improvises the next two. Along the way, he plays five exhilarating four-bar breaks. In the first, he falls through three registers, his fingers and lips releasing notes the way a dog shakes off water; he rockets up and down his horn in the second and third, producing avalanches of notes somewhere between arpeggios and glissandos; in the fourth, he mixes giant intervals and teeming arpeggios; and in the fifth he connects descending steplike notes with racing staccato passages. The record is dazzling showing off; it moves on the rim of chaos. Eldridge settles to earth in his slow and medium-tempo ballads and blues. His gruff, dense tone expands, his improvisational skills blossom, his delicate vibrato comes into view, and the emotion always present in his playing pours out. There is a strong melancholy strain in Eldridge, and it imbues all his ballads and blues. His blues are monumental, and so are some of his ballads (consider the 1953 Verve recording of "The Man I Love" and his Krupa "Rockin' Chair"). But sometimes his emotions engulfed him. His sporadic stagefright would cause this, and so would situations—a roomful of listening peers, say—that he could not control. At such times, he would work so hard and grow so excited that he would end up caroming around his highest register and sounding almost mad. But even then he was majestic. Eldridge is a fine, scampish jazz singer, with a light, hoarse voice and a highly rhythmic attack. He sings the blues much in the manner of Hot Lips Page, and his nonsense vocals ("Saturday Night Fish Fry," "Knock Me a Kiss") rock. Although he doesn't play anymore, he still takes an occasional gig as a singer.

Eldridge lives with his wife, Vi, and his only child, Carole, in a small two-story house in Hollis, at the back of Queens, not far from Belmont Park and Nassau County. His house is in a sea of small houses, each afloat on its patch of green, each moored to several trees. Eldridge is not much over five feet. Compact, bristling, cheerful, beamy, he still fits the nickname — Little Jazz—given him long ago by Otto Hardwicke. His hair is graying, he wears Harry Truman glasses, and his teeth remain the most beautiful in the business. Eldridge's living room has a thick greenish rug, a fireplace with a mirror over it, a television set, a sofa, two wide-shouldered leather chairs, a picture window that looks out on the street, and a stairway to the second floor. A kitchen is visible beyond the stairway, and to its left is a dining room. In a small alcove-den between the dining room and the front door are some of Eldridge's trophies—a *down beat* award for placing first in the 1946 trumpet poll, an Esky statuette from *Esquire* in 1945, a certificate of appreciation from Mayor John Lindsay, a letter of appreciation from President Carter for playing at the White House. On a table covered with family photographs is a card that Vi gave him. Headed "How to Know You're Growing Older," it lists these hints:

> You get winded playing chess.
> You join a health club and don't go.
> You look forward to a dull evening.
> Your back goes out more than you do

One afternoon, Eldridge sat on a low stool in front of his picture window and talked about the present and the past. He does not particularly relish being interviewed, partly because, like most of the surviving musicians of his generation, he is interviewed-out, and partly because he is a proud man who does not like giving away things of value unless he is sure they will be treated the right way. He looked steadily out the window as he talked, registering each car and truck and human being that passed, and occasionally commenting ("Man, look at that old cat all bent over! At least I can walk standing up straight"). He speaks the way he sings, and he laughs a lot. There were long pauses between some of the things he said, and he jumped all around the landscape of his life.

"New York is mean," he said, "but I wouldn't live anywhere else. When I was on the road I searched Europe and South America for the perfect place to live. No place had the right feel—not even Copenhagen, which is my favorite European city. Of course, Europe has changed. They met you with flowers in Scandinavia in the fifties. Now it's like going to Newark. Vi and I have been married since 1936. Her maiden name was Viola Lee. Her father was Chinese. She was a hostess at the Savoy

Ballroom. I carried both Vi and Carole, who's a legal secretary, over to Europe one year on tour, and were they glad to get back! Doing one-nighters, you see the airport, the road to the hotel, the place where the concert is, the place you eat at after the concert, the hotel, and, the next morning, the road back to the airport. Near the end, I'd hear them saying in the next room, 'Only four days to Christmas,' then 'Only two days to Christmas'—Christmas being the day we were scheduled to fly home. We've been in this house twenty-seven years. It was nicer around here when we first moved out from New York. There was a butcher, a drug-store, a theatre. I've had two or three heart attacks in the past six years, and I've quit playing. I've also got some kind of emphysema. I don't miss the music anymore. I've had enough fun and praise and ovations to keep me. I played fifty years, and that was long enough. Anyway, I found out the main doors were always locked. The color thing. I also found out I'd never get rich. At first, after I got sick, I'd play along with the television commercials all evening, but I don't do that anymore. I used to play piano and drums, but I gave my piano away, because it got wet down in the cellar, and I still haven't gotten around to putting the drums Gene Krupa gave me back in shape. When I stopped playing, I fell into anoth-er slot. I didn't have to wear a watch, I didn't have to break my back. There's so much to do around here I don't have the time to do it.

"Playing was my life. Before I went onstage, I would sit in my dressing room and run over in my mind what I was going to do. But when I got out there I didn't try and make the B-flat or whatever I was thinking of, because I'd go right into a void where there was no memory—nothing but me. I knew the chords and I knew the melody, and I never thought about them. I'd just be in this blank place, and out the music would come. It wasn't always easy. Riding up on that stage at the Paramount Theatre with the Krupa band scared me to death. When the stage stopped and we started to play, I'd fall to pieces. The first three or four bars of my first solo, I'd shake like a leaf, and you could hear it. Then this light would surround me, and it would seem as if there wasn't any band there, and I'd go right through and be all right. It was something I never understood.

"I'd go all over from the late twenties to the forties looking for people to challenge on trumpet. One occasion broke my heart. It happened in 1930. I already knew Rex Stewart, and he came into Small's Paradise, where I was with Elmer Snowden's band, and said he'd meet me later at Greasy's, an after-hours place. Gus Aiken and Red Allen showed up, and a lot of guys from the Henderson band. They were great agitators at cut-ting sessions. At these sessions, we used to stomp. That means that eight bars before your solo started you'd stomp your foot to let the cat who was finishing his solo know that you were going to come in. Rex and I got to battling and exchanging choruses at Greasy's, and after he finished a cho-rus I stomped him and screamed a G. At the end of my chorus, he stomped me back and screamed a B-flat. I'd never heard the note he hit, and he had played something I couldn't play. I brooded all the next day. He had hit that note, but he hadn't played up to it or come down from it. I found the note and worked on it until I could play up to it and down from it, and the next time we met I showed it to him. A couple of years before that, I had a run-in with Jabbo Smith in Milwaukee. We met at a place called Rails, and Jabbo used my horn. We played fast and slow. I could play fast all over, but when the tempo got down it wasn't my stick. The crowd thought I had cut Jabbo, and he didn't talk to me for two weeks, but I didn't fool myself. I knew he had cut me. A session I enjoyed a lot more around the same time took place in Detroit. When I went into this club to sit in, the band was off and the stand was empty except for a girl sitting there. I asked her where the trumpet player was, and she said, 'I'm the trumpet player.' Her name was Doll Jones. The next set, she started out and my mouth gapped. I couldn't believe it. We jammed together until three o'clock in the afternoon.

"Coleman Hawkins and I were very tight and very good together. I dug him, and he dug me. He told me that he first heard me on records when he was in Europe in the late thirties, and that he'd never heard anyone play the trumpet like that. He was used to the best of everything. If a new camera came out, he had to have it. The same with binoculars or a watch. Coleman had class.

"I first met Lester Young in Baltimore in the mid-thirties when he was with Fletcher Henderson. I met him jamming. I used to pick him and Jo Jones up in Chicago when they were with Basie and had finished work. Lester loved to jam, and that was where we hit it.

"I loved Big Sid Catlett. He was so smooth. He had that weight without being noisy. But Chick Webb was the best drum soloist I ever heard.

"When Ben Webster was sober, he was the nicest cat you ever met, but when he was drinking he'd turn rough. Sometimes he'd slap me or something like that, and I'd end up chasing him down the street, big as he was."

Eldridge stopped talking, reared back, and shouted at the ceiling, "Vi! Hey, Vi! You want the heat up? It's cold in here." He lowered his voice. "I have to watch the cold now, with this emphysema. I listen to all the medical shows in the morning, and they say don't eat chicken, don't eat veal, don't eat this, don't eat that. They say look at the dinosaurs—they ate nothing but greens. And I say, 'Where are they now?' "

Vi Eldridge came down the stairs. She is pretty and medium-sized. Eldridge asked her again if she wanted more heat, and she said, "How can you tell?" She turned up the heat and asked Eldridge if he wanted anything to eat or drink. He said no, and she went upstairs.

Eldridge looked sharp left out his window. "I wonder if those cats are stripping that car or fixing it," he said. "They've stripped the tires off of my station wagon, nothing else. You have to have a car out here, or you're smothered. Sometimes I drive over into Nassau, but I don't go into New

York much anymore. It's expensive going places now, and they don't always know who you are. Anyway, all my old clothes are too big.

"I grew up on the north side of Pittsburgh. My brother Joe was two and a half years older. My mother played some piano, and had the kind of ear where after she came home from the movies she could repeat exactly what she'd heard the pianist in the pit do. And I'd accompany her on my little drum, which I took up at six. She was a nice-looking woman. She was from somewhere around Winston-Salem. My father was from Petersburg, Virginia. He was my height, but heavier built, and darker. He had a lot of brothers. He was a contractor, and he was good with horses. He didn't drink or smoke. He was religious. I'd fight at the drop of a hat, and somebody was always coming to the house and telling him, 'Your son hit my boy aside the head with a rock.' After the man had gone, my father would say, 'What's the matter with you, boy? You act like a savage.' We lived near the Pennsylvania Railroad, and he made the top of our house into a dormitory where the railroad men could pay and stay. He also set up a shoeshine stand for my brother and me. And he had a restaurant downstairs that my mother and a cousin from North Carolina ran. My father was a good businessman. Then we moved up to Irwin Avenue. The house was on a hill, and you could look over the north side. My father ended up leaving me about six houses, but I was always travelling, and, what with bad tenants and the like, I lost them. After grammar school, I went to David B. Oliver High. Pittsburgh was a funny place. We had to sit in the peanut gallery at the movies, but the schools weren't segregated. I played drums in the local drum-and-bugle corps. The day of a parade, I'd be up at six waiting for the sun to come up and give me enough heat so I could get my snare head tuned right. I started on trumpet because one day when we were out at the cemetery they handed me a bugle and told me to play 'Taps.' I was shaking like this. My brother got my parents to give me a trumpet. I had a good ear, and anything I heard I could play. My brother taught me to read in 1928, when I was with Horace Henderson, and by the time I was with Fletcher Henderson in 1936, I was able to handle all those difficult keys Fletcher wrote his arrangements in. My mother died when I was about eleven. I got kicked out of the ninth grade. I wasn't interested in schoolwork, and I refused to play in the band. I'd tap out drum riffs all day on my desk. I was supposed to go back to school the next fall, but I got a gig with a touring company and took off. I didn't know hardly anything—how to work the spit valve, how to care for the horn. I didn't tell my father I got the job, and I didn't take any clothes. I just went."

Big Sid

Sidney Catlett, the magisterial drummer who died in 1951, has yet to be matched. He has outstripped two batches of pursuers—the drummers of his own generation or persuasion and the modernist drummers. And he has remained the Master despite those periods since his death when almost none of his recordings were available in any form—when, in truth, he was in oblivion.

Here are the bones of his life: He was born January 17, 1910, in Evansville, Indiana, and was raised on the South Side of Chicago. There he attended Tilden Technical High School. Between 1929 and 1944, he worked for Sammy Stewart, Elmer Snowden, Benny Carter, Rex Stewart, the Jeter-Pillars band, Fletcher Henderson, Don Redman, Louis Armstrong, Benny Goodman, and Teddy Wilson. He led his own groups from 1944 to 1946, and then joined the Louis Armstrong All-Stars. A heart attack in 1949 forced him to leave the All-Stars. During the last two years of his life, he shuttled back and forth between Chicago, where he was the house drummer at Jazz Ltd., and New York, where he might turn up at Central Plaza or Jimmy Ryan's. He died backstage at the Civic Opera House in Chicago, of a heart attack, on Easter Sunday. He had gone there not to play but to visit with his friends, who were legion, and some of whom will be heard here.

The first is the singer Helen Humes:

"There was a whole bunch of us standing around backstage at the Opera House, where a concert was going on. Sid had come over to say hello from Jazz Ltd. He was standing behind me and had his arms clasped around my waist, and he was telling one of his stories. It came near time for me to be onstage, so I said, 'Sid, let me go put some powder on. I'll see you after.' I walked away, and right off I heard this funny sound a kind of *whumnpp*. I turned around and there was Sid lying on the floor, and that was all there was to it. He died right away."

ARVELL SHAW (bass): He had his first heart attack at Billy Berg's club, in Los Angeles, in 1949. He complained of pains in his chest one night after work. He left the All-Stars at the Blue Note, in Chicago, not too long after, and Red Saunders took over until Cozy Cole arrived.

JOHN SIMMONS (bass): It's a wonder he lasted as long as he did. After his first heart attack, Joe Glaser sent him to the mountains for a rest, but he didn't stay long enough. But way before that I'd say to him, "Sid, one of these days you're going to crumble up in small pieces. "The reason was that he never went to bed. After work, he'd go to after-hours places, and when he'd finished playing in them he'd go out and play the numbers all day.

JOHNNY WILLIAMS (bass): He'd go home after work and take a shower and change his clothes. Then maybe he'd stop in at the Apollo and sit around backstage and gab and play cards. Then it was over to an after-hours place on the Hill, where they served whiskey in coffee cups. Then he'd go home again in the morning and take a shower and change his clothes and go back out and be on the streets all day, until it was time to shower and change again and go to work.

SIMMONS: He'd get home an hour and a half before work and sleep some. By the last set at work that night, his eyes would be at half-mast, but later he'd pep up and start the same old routine again.

SHAW: He loved life. He loved to play cards. He loved to gamble. He loved women. He liked to be around the guys. He didn't like to waste his time sleeping.

JOHN HAMMOND: I don t know how many hundreds of dollars he was in to me over the years. I never knew anyone so crazy about gambling.

RUBY BRAFF (cornet): He was not a well person in the last couple of years of his life, and it showed. If you asked him how he was, he'd say, "What do you care?"

GLADYS CATLETT (his widow): He had rheumatic fever as a child and that gave him an enlarged heart. And he had dropsy at the end, too. He didn't rest enough after his attack. He wasn't supposed to be going up and down stairs and climbing all those hills around a Hundred and Fifty-sixth Street, where we lived. And he had no business being out there in Chicago working.

Catlett was nobly constructed. He was six feet three or four inches tall, and everything was in proportion: the massive shoulders, the long arms and giant, tapering fingers, the cannon-ball fists, the barn-door chest and the tidy waist, his big feet, and the columnar neck. His head was equally imposing. He had high, flaring cheekbones, large, wide-set eyes, and a full, governing nose. His forehead was high, and he wore his hair flat, as was the custom. Majestic expressions flowed across his face when he played. He would stare into the middle distance and look huge and mournful, or he would send out heavy, admiring glances to the pretty women in the room. Big men are often more graceful than small men, and Catlett was no exception. He could swim, play football and basketball, and dance beautifully. But he never learned to drive a car.

SIMMONS: He was a good athlete. His mother didn't want him to play football, but he did, and one day he came home wearing his football uniform. When she opened the door and saw him standing there in all those shoulder pads and such, she said, "What have they done to my son?" Oh, my, he'd laugh so hard when he told that story. He was a great storyteller and a great comedian. When we were in Louis Armstrong's big band, Louis and Sid would sit up on the bus or train and tell each other jokes, from town to town, all night. Louis would type some of them up, and I think he even had a little collection called "The Big Sid Joke Anthology." Louis always typed up jokes that way, and instead of writing people letters he'd mail them a joke. Anyway, Sid could have become a comedian or a dancer or a singer. He was a good singer, and he even wrote songs, which were good, too. He was a marvellous dancer. He learned by watching and listening to dancers like Teddy Hale and Baby Laurence. He'd back them up, and then play exactly what they had danced on his drums.

GLADYS CATLETT: His parents were very unselfish, loving people. He was an only child, and they thought there was no one good enough on the earth for him. His father chauffeured and his mother was a good cook, who worked for wealthy people. I believe his Aunt Minnie worked for those same people. It was through them that he took some drum lessons from an old German teacher. Sidney was the only colored student he had. His mother wanted him to be a lawyer, but the teacher told her, "You let this boy play the drums and he'll be the greatest drummer in the world."

MILT HINTON (bass): I knew Sid at the Wendell Phillips High School, at Thirty-ninth and Calumet. He went to Tilden, but it seems he must have hung out a lot with us. You hear about the Austin High School in Chicago, but not much about Wendell Phillips. Ray Nance went there, and Nat Cole and Lionel Hampton and Hayes Alvis and Razz Mitchell and myself. The bandmaster was Major N. Clark Smith. He was a Negro, and he was a stickler for dignity and discipline who wasn't above throwing a drumstick at your head and knocking you down if you didn't behave. Zutty Singleton was the drummer in Chicago, and Sid learned from him, pestering Zutty to let him sit in. Sid also learned from Jimmy Bertrand, who was with Erskine Tate at the Vendome Theatre. Bertrand could read music. He could play the xylophone, and he had a solo he played on tuned tympani. And there was a drummer around Chicago named Jimmy McHendricks. He was dark and short and had a lisp, but he had flash, throwing his sticks in the air and carrying on like that. Hampton and Sid would watch him all the time.

EARL HINES: Sid left Chicago for New York in 1930, in Sammy Stewart's band. It was a hotel-type orchestra, a hicky-dicky group. Stewart only hired light-complected guys, so he took Sid but he wouldn't have anything to do with Louis Armstrong and myself.

TOMMY BENFORD (drums): I believe he picked up a lot around New York when he first came from Chicago. He listened to Kaiser Marshall and George Stafford and Walter Johnson and old man Brooks. And he learned a little from me, too.

HAMMOND: I'd grown up thinking Gene Krupa was a great drummer. I had heard him on the McKenzie-Condon records in 1928, and I heard him in the pit band at Gershwin's "Girl Crazy." He was always George Gershwin's favorite drummer. In 1931, I was at Yale and playing violin in a string quartet, and every chance I got I went up to Small's Paradise, in Harlem. Elmer Snowden had the band, and in it were Sid and Roy Eldridge, who both had just come in from the Midwest, and Dicky Wells and Don Kirkpatrick and a sax section of Wayman Carver and Otto Hardwicke and Al Sears. I would go night after night with Artie Bernstein, the cellist in my quartet, and what did I hear? This huge, powerful drummer, this huge, powerful ensemble musician who made that whole band go, and I realized: *here* was a great drummer.

DICKY WELLS (trombone): When you came into Snowden's band, Sid asked you what you wanted him to play behind you. If you told him brushes, he'd play brushes. If you told him sticks, he'd play sticks. If you told him the Chinese cymbal, he'd play the Chinese cymbal. And he'd do whatever it was until you told him to change it. He was a dear, a beautiful person, the prettiest person in the world.

ROY ELDRIDGE (trumpet): Sid was a big cat, a fun-loving cat, and very nice. I can't recall any time he'd get so upset he'd want to go to war. What was so amazing about him, for all his size, was he was so smooth. He was smooth as greased lightning. Me and him and Chu Berry would hang out together in New York. We'd make sessions after work, and sometimes we didn't get home until two or three in the afternoon. That was where you did your practicing, at those sessions. We all drank in those days, but Sid was always clean on the job.

HINES: He was a great soloist and a great accompanist. He never overshadowed whoever was performing around him. He had a feeling for embellishment, for what you were doing in your solo, that made it seem like he knew what you were going to play before you did yourself.

BOB WILBER (clarinet): Hearing Sidney de Paris and Catlett together was something. DeParis had a unique rhythmic sense. He'd place his notes anywhere but where you expected him to, and Sid would go right along with him, anticipating his weird placements with accents and playing this complex hide-and-seek with him.

BRAFF: He arranged his drums so tightly around him they looked like little balls hanging off him. Watching him take a solo was a thrill. He hypnotized you. His sticks went so fast they were blurred. But they also looked like they were moving in slow motion. Each solo had a beautiful sense of composition. Most drummers can't even count, but if he took a twelve-bar solo he played exactly twelve bars and if he took a thirty-two-bar solo he played exactly thirty-two bars. And each solo sang its own song.

Catlett's accompanying had an unfailing freshness and authority. He made eveything that went on in front of him sound new. "Why, man, I never heard you play *that* before," he seemed to say to each instrumentalist. His wire brushes achieved a graceful, padding effect at slower tempos and a hurrying, relentless effect at faster tempos. When he switched to drumsticks in mid-performance, as he often did, it was dramatic and lifting. His library of accompanying techniques was endless. He used different cymbals behind different instruments—a heavy ride cymbal behind a trumpet; the high hat, its cymbals half closed, behind a trombone; a Chinese cymbal, with its sizzling sound, behind a clarinet. All the while, his left hand worked out an extraordinary series of accents on the snare drum. They never fell where you expected them to, and they were produced in a variety of ways. He would hit the snare directly, or hit the snarehead and the rim (a rim shot), or rest one stick on the snarehead and hit it with the other, or tick the snare rim. His bass-drum accents were loose and booting, and were scattered ingeniously through these punctuations. Catlett was supremely subtle. He implied more than he stated in his background work, yet he controlled every performance. He told Ruby Braff he could swing seventeen men with a single wire brush and a telephone book to play it on, and he was right. He reined in the obstreperous, pushed the laggardly, and celebrated the inspired. His taste was faultless, his time was perfect (most drummers, no matter how proficient, play a split second behind the beat, but Catlett was *purposely* a split second ahead), and the sound he got on his drums was handsome, careful, and rich.

Most drum solos exist for themselves, but Catlett's heightened the mood and texture around him, and they were free of clichés. His solos on alternate takes of his recordings are invariably different, and so were the solos he played during a night's work and from night to night. They were rhythmically irresistible. There is a section of his long and empyrean solo in "Steak Face" on the Decca "Satchmo at Symphony Hall" album in which he plays a repeated figure with a loose, and then increasingly complex, arrangement of rim shots, and it is astonishing. It makes you want to dance and jig and shake. Its timing and taste and impetus are such that the passage stands at the very heart of rhythm. One of his simpler solos might start with unbroken, surging, snare-drum rolls, whose volume rose and fell sharply, and whose wavelike patterns became more and more intense before suddenly exploding into rim shots. Then a stunning silence—followed by lightning shots delivered all around his set, by another silence and several choked-cymbal beats, and the solo was over. His solos grew more complex at faster tempos. They also had an urgent, buttonholing quality. He'd start with a fusillade of rim shots, sink into a sashaying figure that strode back and forth between his tomtoms, go back to his snare for more crackling rim shots, this time unbelievably laced with double-time strokes, drop into a silence, wade heavily and joyously through his cymbals, start roaring around his set, and finish with a sequence of funny and limber half-time bass-drum beats. His solos had an uncluttered order and logic, a natural progression of textures and rhythms and timing that made them seem predesigned. One was transfixed by the easy motion of his arms, the postlike rigidity of his body, and the soaring of his huge hands, which reduced his drumsticks to pencils. He was also a sensational show drummer. He'd spin a stick in the air, light a cigarette, and catch the stick. Or he'd bounce his sticks off the floor and catch them. Or he'd get up and dance around the set. But it wasn't disruptive clowning; it was cheerful and enhancing and breathtaking.

HINES: I loved Sid very much. He was a very jovial fellow. In fact, the only harm he ever did in his life was to himself. He never knew how to say no, and he never raised an arm in anger. I saw him stand up and cry in front of Louis. Louis would say things once in a while to Sid that weren't tasty, that weren't nice, and Sid would bite his lip and cry. Yet Sid was always Louis's favorite drummer.

ZOOT SIMS (tenor saxophone): Sid was beautiful and easy to work with, but he didn't care for ethnic crossups. One night in New York, Sid said, Let's go uptown. He flagged an empty cab and the cab went right by but stopped a block away at a light. Sid ran up the street and— you know how big he was—pulled the driver out of the cab and held him in the air and dropped him back in his seat, and we got in and went uptown.

TEDDY WILSON (piano): He was a great big nonviolent man, and yet he was very emotional. His feelings were easily hurt. And he could shed a tear when that happened. He was also quick to laugh, and in between shows at Café Society Uptown he'd entertain us backstage for forty-five minutes at a time with his jokes.

He also entertained everybody out front. One night, he filled in, at Teddy Wilson's behest, for a member of the floor show who was late. He started on his cymbals with his wire brushes, a whispering of breezes, and ended ten minutes later with his sticks, having reached a density and momentum that were volcanic.

BARNEY BIGARD (clarinet): He was like a big baby, real gentle, real fine. There's nothing bad anyone could say about Sid.

SHAW: When I first joined the Louis Armstrong All-Stars, I was real green, Sid took me under his wing. He taught me about show business, about how to be on the road, about the music. He said the drums and bass should be a single pulse, and he taught me how to produce my part of the pulse. He'd say to me, "If you're not going to do the best you can when you go onstage, why go on at all?"

HARVEY PHILLIPS (tuba): The drummer in the Ringling Brothers' Circus band was Red Floyd. He had a lined, pruny face, and looked like Old Man Time. I think he had played in New Orleans. He had a crippled left arm, but he was an extraordinary musician. He played all the mallet instruments, and he did a beautiful snare-drum roll with one hand by holding two sticks parallel in that hand like extra fingers and seesawing them so fast they became a blur. When we played New York, Sidney Catlett would spend all afternoon at the Garden watching Red, and then ask him to autograph a pair of his sticks.

BRAFF: He took me everywhere with him when I first came to New York from Boston. He'd arrive at a job and tell the manager, "I brought the other person."
"What other person?"
"Ruby Braff."
"I didn't hire him."
"If you hired me, you hired him."
And I'd be hired.

SIMMONS: Sid loved children. They called him Uncle Sid, and he always gave them silver dollars from the roll he carried with him.

Three scenes from a life spent travelling:

SHAW: He and Earl Hines were deathly afraid of flying, and when the All-Stars went to the Nice Jazz Festival, in 1948, he and Hines walked from New York to Paris on that plane. Up and down, up and down. Every bump, Sid's eyes would get as big as pizzas. He was a nervous wreck when we landed.

BRAFF: I'd drive him around in the Chevy coupe I had, and he always sat in the front seat. In fact, he was a famous front-seat driver, and I don't know how many front seats he ruined, pushing his knees into the dashboard and leaning back in the seat until it nearly broke. When he got into my coupe to come to New York, the right side of the car went down until it about touched ground. I thought Sid had broken the springs. So I said, "Sid, get out a minute, and let's see if the car comes back up again." Well, it did, so he got in again and off we went, the right side down low and the back of the car piled with suitcases full of his clothes, which he had so many of it was unbelievable.

WILLIAMS: When we'd cross the country on the train in the early forties with Louis Armstrong's big band, Sid and I would go back to that little platform outside the observation car. We'd sit there and get all smutty, get soot in our noses and mouths, and we'd listen to the humming of the wheels on the tracks, to the different rhythms the train made when it went over a crossing, to the changes in the rhythms when the train slowed or speeded up. Sidney would tap out the rhythms with his hands on the railing around the platform, and later I'd hear those rhythms in one of his solos.

Catlett's adaptability was endless. Some of the musicians he recorded with between the end of 1943 and the end of 1945 were Eddie Condon, Lester Young, Louis Armstrong, Art Tatum, Albert Ammons, Ben Webster, Billie Holiday, Harry the Hipster Gibson, Earl Hines, Teddy Wilson, Sidney De Paris, James P. Johnson, Charlie Parker, Dizzy Gillespie, Sidney Bechet, Don Byas, and Duke Ellington.

Musicians revered Catlett, but his name never got before the public in the way that Gene Krupa's and Buddy Rich's did. The closest he came to celebrity was during the short, disastrous time he spent with Benny Goodman in 1941. Catlett was with Goodman four months, and then Goodman fired him. The episode has long been a puzzle:

HAMMOND: The rhythm section that Benny put together in 1941 terrified him, and he had no control over it. Charlie Christian was on guitar, John Simmons on bass, Mel Powell on piano, and Big Sid on drums. When I heard that Sid had nearly caused a riot with his solo during Benny's concert at Soldier Field in Chicago, I thought, Oh Jesus. Sidney's cooked.

SIMMONS: We played a concert at Soldier Field, and Sid took a solo in "Don't Be That Way." Well, he started playing and then he threw a stick in the air—and dropped it. On purpose, of course. He got up and walked around in front of his drums and picked up the stick and sat down and started playing again. Then he threw the stick in the air and dropped it again—and so forth. They were rolling in the aisles, and when he finally stopped horsing around and got down to business, that place nearly blew up. I remember watching Benny's face. It wasn't a cheerful sight. Benny didn't like anyone taking away the spotlight. When we got back to New York, we had a little layoff, and the night Sid reported for work at the hotel where Benny was, he found another drummer sitting up on the bandstand in his place. Benny gave Sid two weeks' notice and told him to report every night at nine until his time was up—just in case he needed him.

HINES: He loved to play just for the sake of playing, and he loved to play the way he wanted to play. Which is one of the reasons he and Benny Goodman couldn't get on. In the old days in Chicago, when all the young musicians would come in to where Louis and Zutty and myself were playing they'd ask to sit in, and of course we'd say yes. But Benny wanted to be *asked*, and Louis would never do it. So there Benny'd stay, standing over behind a pillar.

MEL POWELL: I always thought that this giant of a man had no peer as a percussionist. After all, he was playing on nothing but a set of traps—a snare drum, a couple of tomtoms, a bass drum, and some cymbals. Yet he invariably sounded like he was playing delicately tuned drums. Where he hit his snare with his stick, how hard he hit it, where and how he hit his cymbals and tomtoms—all these things transformed ordinary sounds into pitches that matched and enhanced what he heard around him. His sensitivity and delicacy of ear were extraordinary. So was his time. He'd fasten the Goodman band into the tempo with such power *and* gentleness that one night I was absolutely transported by what he was doing. Watching him lift and carry us, I took my hands off the keyboard and missed the beginning of a solo. I don't think I have ever been more awed by a musical performance. Sid's personality reflected his playing. He was lovable and loving. He was gentle. He was compassionate and concerned. He was also vulnerable. I saw tears in his eyes the night he was told just after he'd joined the band that his uniform wasn't ready yet, that he'd have to play in his street clothes, and so—to him—look unfinished. He had a wonderful sense of humor, and, among other things, he liked to take off black stereotypes. He had never flown—in fact he had carefully avoided flying. But the only way to get to a gig we had in Canada was by plane. Sid asked to sit next to me, and when they were starting to rev the engines, one of the boys in the band called out, 'Hey! What's that weird noise in the engine?' Sid turned to me and rolled his eyes and said, 'Oh, merciful God!' It was flawless Stepin Fetchit—and it almost hid his fear. I have never been able to figure out why Benny fired Sid. All that comes to mind is that Benny was not a follower and neither was Sid. But Benny was the boss.

Big Sid used to go over to Jimmy Ryan's on Monday nights around 1949 or 1950 and sit in. Tommy Benford remembers: "I have a pair of Sid's drumsticks, and this is why. I was at Ryan's with Jimmy Archey's band, and one Monday, after Sid had sat in, he left his sticks behind on the stand. I called to him as he was leaving. 'Sid, you left your sticks,' and he said, 'That's all right, man, I'll be back next week.' But he never did come back."

The Music Is More Important

"Please don't call it a vibraphone," Red Norvo said. "I play the vibra*harp*, a name coined by the Deagan Company, which invented the instrument in 1927 and still supplies me with mine. Of course, I started on the xylophone and marimba in the mid-twenties, and up until then they were vaudeville instruments, clown instruments. They differ from one another chiefly in range, like tenor and alto saxophones. The xylophone is higher than the marimba, but both have piano-like keyboards, with three registers. The bars, or what would be the keys of a piano, are made of rosewood. The vibraharp has the same keyboard, but it is lower in range than the marimba. It's an electronic instrument, and its bars are made of aluminum. It's electronic because the resonator tubes that hang down underneath the bars, like an upside-down organ, have little paddle-shaped fans in them called pulsators that are driven by a small electric motor. When they're in motion, they enable the performer to get that rolling, mushing-out vibrato you hear from most vibes players. Vibraharps also have loud, or damper, pedals, similar to the piano's, which lift the bars off felt pads, and when you use the damper pedal *and* the pulsators you get that *uh-uh-uh-uh-uh* sound. On the vibraharp—pardon my saying it—you can cheat by using the pulsators and the damper pedal. It's been done and is done. I've never used a motor, but what I do have now is an amplifier, which Jack Deagan designed for me around 1960. It helps acoustically in bad rooms. Before, if you had just one microphone and you set it near the center of the keyboard, the upper and lower registers would be cold. Deagan put little crystal mikes in each resonator tube, but at first I couldn't get even amplification, and once when I flew into Las Vegas for a gig they left the instrument out in hundred-and-twenty-degree heat at the airport and all the mikes melted. The mallets you use affect the sound of the instrument. I have hard-rubber ones for the xylophone, and on the marimba rubber ones with a twine cover, which I use on vibraharp, too. Dixie Rollini, Adrian's widow, still wraps them for me. She doesn't do it for anyone else now. It's a nice gesture and I appreciate it. I also use slap mallets, which I invented in 1928. They're rectangular and flattish and the size of a big kitchen spoon, and they're made of cork covered with felt and buckskin, and they cause a dead, tramping effect. The vibraharp is a peculiar instrument because it tends to take on the characteristics of the people who play it. Sometimes the instrument becomes the personality. And it's peculiar because vibra-harpists are a pretty warm fraternity. Guitarists are also like that. Certain people choose certain instruments, and vibraharpists in general are gen-tle, quiet people. Trumpet players and drummers, on the other hand, can be pretty argumentative. But the main thing is to play the *right* instru-ment. So many musicians go through their lives on the wrong instrument. You hear guitarists who should be tenor players and pianists who should be trumpeters and drummers who should maybe be out of music altogether."

Norvo was sitting in his living room in Santa Monica. The room is big and blue and white, with a fireplace at one end and a Pennsylvania Dutch dining table, surrounded by Windsor chairs, at the other. A sofa and sev-eral more chairs, one of them a handsome eighteenth-century corner chair, ring the fireplace, and over the mantel is a painting of Norvo play-ing his vibraharp. An apothecary's chest is against one wall, and near it, in a bay window, stands a marimba. The dining area is weighed down by a pine cupboard filled with Staffordshire china and a Shaker dry sink filled with spongeware. Opposite the marimba, a pair of open glass doors lead out into a small patio.

Norvo poured himself a cup of coffee from a small espresso pot. "Ralph Watkins, who used to run the Embers in New York, gave me this pot. You can't buy them here, or at least I've never been able to find one. You have to go to New York or San Francisco, and it's the same with the coffee. I used to drink it straight all day, but now I water it down some." He jumped up and opened a couple of windows behind the marimba. "It's hot in here, and I don't see why I have to keep all the windows shut. This is Santa-Ana-wind weather. The wind blows straight from the desert and across the mountains to the ocean. I was up early last Sunday and we went up to the Angeles National Forest to do a little varmint hunting. There were a lot of deer hunters down in the gullies and we were up on the high rocks, and so were the deer. We could see the brush fires starting and the wind was blowing like hell. It's usually very cold up there, but when we got out of the car it was *hot*, in the nineties. It was a shock. I hunt every chance I get. In Vegas you can practically lean out and touch the mountains from downtown, which makes hunting there a cinch."

In profile, Norvo, who is medium-sized, is S-shaped. He holds his head forward and his shoulders are bent from more than forty years of stoop-ing over his instruments. He has a comfortable front porch and his legs

bow out behind, like a retired hurdler's. Head on, he suggests a mischie-
vous Scottish laird. His blue eyes laugh, and they are set off by V-shaped
laugh lines. His nose is generous but subtly beaked, and he has a beard.
The beard is orange-red, and so is his receding hair, which is long and
thick in back. When he laughs, his eyes nearly close, and his teeth, in the
surrounding foliage, shine like the sun in a fall maple. His voice is even
and rich, and it anchors him.

A short, pretty woman with dark hair in a feather cut and a Rubens figure came into the room. It was Norvo's wife, Eve. She was dressed in a
nurse's white uniform, with white stockings and shoes, and she had a
wide, dimpled smile and serene eyes. She stood in front of Norvo with
her hands crossed and said, "Can I get you some more coffee?" He said
no. "Where are you playing tonight, Red?"

Norvo consulted a pad. "In a motel in Huntington Beach called the
Sheraton Beach Inn. We start around nine and I don't know where it
is, so I better leave at seven. That'll give me time for getting lost and
setting up."

Norvo waited until she had left; then he got up and waved his arms
around and laughed. "Eve took the job she has at St. John's Hospital,
which is near here, a couple of years ago, when I was playing a long gig
in Las Vegas. I was home one weekend and she said she was getting tired
of sitting around, so I said, 'Go out and get a gig.' Well, she did, but when
the job in Vegas was over I told her she might as well quit. 'Quit?
What do you mean, quit?' She got real insulted. When she got her first
paycheck she came home real cool and laid twenty dollars on me, she
was that proud. I laughed and told her, 'Some big spender.'

"Eve and I were married in 1946, a year before we moved out here from
New York. She's always called me Red, but my first wife, Mildred Bailey,
called me Kenneth, and so did John Hammond and my mother. They
were the only people who always called me Kenneth. Norvo isn't my real
name. I was born Kenneth Norville, in Beardstown, Illinois, in three thirty-one oh-eight. My daughter, Portia, who lives with us, is twenty-two,
and she even has a little towhead kid. I got the name Norvo from Paul
Ash, in vaudeville. He could never remember my name when he
announced me. It would come out Norvin or Norvox or Norvick, and one
night it was Norvo. *Variety* picked it up and it stuck, so I kept it. Norville
is Scottish, and my family came from around Roseville, which is a little
town near Galesburg. I had two brothers and a sister—Howard, Glen,
and Portia. They're all gone. My father was a railroader, a dispatcher for
the C. B. & Q.—the Chicago, Burlington & Quincy. He worked for the
railroad all his life, and we moved around a lot before I arrived. I believe
Portia was born in Hillsdale and Howard in Macomb and Glen in East
Alton. My mother was eighty when she died out here, and we buried her
in Roseville. My father was tall and dark and bald. He was stern but
quiet-tempered. He liked to say things like 'It takes you all your life to
learn to live, and when you have, you don't have time left to live.' He

didn't drink, but he'd smoke a cigar and he was religious. He died a thirty-second-degree Mason. He built the new Masonic Temple in Beardstown and they gave him the door knocker from the old one. I still have it around the house. He played piano—you know, mainly chords— and he'd sing in a big voice. He died before I was twenty. My mother was blond, always very thin and very proud. And she was astute about people—she never missed. Her name was Estelle, and we called her Stell. She was always very strong on getting us out of small-town life. Of my parents, she had the edge where humor was concerned. Beardstown had a population of about seven thousand, and we lived on the edge of town. My brother Glen had a pony, Prince, and when he went away to college he kind of passed it down to me, but I never felt it was mine, so once when he was home on vacation I said,'You should give me that pony. I don't feel it's mine.' 'All right,' he said. 'Jump off this porch and onto that pony and open up and get around the block in a minute flat and I'll give it to you.' My mother was in the back of the house, and she looked out the window and saw me streaking by and she came running out and yelled, 'The pony's running away with Kenneth, the pony's running away with Kenneth,' and when I came tearing around the corner of the house she could see—she'd known horses all her life—that I was in control, and we all laughed. I used to go into town on Prince to get groceries, and they'd load me up with a bag under each arm and I'd ride home using just my knees. Prince would stop right by the front door when I had groceries, but if I didn't have any he'd lickety-split it right into his stall and I'd grab an iron bar over the door and let him go and drop to the ground. Every Saturday we rode out into the country, and in the fall I got up real early and went up in the hills to get walnuts and pecans. We were on the Illinois River, and I got to know all the riverboats. The Capitol tied up at Beardstown around six o'clock in the warm weather and everyone piled on and she cruised until eleven. She always had a dance band, and one whole floor, one whole deck, would be a ballroom. There were all-day excursions that started at eight in the morning. Some stores gave out tickets like supermarkets give out trading stamps and the boat would go to a picnic ground and come back around six. Showboats came, too, twice a summer. They were like floating theatres, and they gave all the old clichés—'The Drunkard' or a minstrel show or 'Little Eva.' I remember one night excursion I heard Bix Beiderbecke and Frank Trumbauer. I couldn't have been more than ten or eleven. I was fascinated with Trumbauer. I spent the whole evening sitting and watching. I was thrilled, it sounded so good. And of course it was on the riverboats that I first heard Louis Armstrong."

Norvo's son Kevin, who's around sixteen or seventeen, sauntered in. He was dressed in a T-shirt and blue jeans, and he is a miniature Red Norvo. He has an undeveloped S-figure, red hair, pale skin, and freckles. "I've got an orthodontist's appointment at four," he said.

"O.K.," Norvo replied. "But will you pick up my shirts at the cleaners'?

I don't have any to wear tonight. The ticket's out on the harvest table by the front door. I'll feed you when you get back."

"Money?" Kevin asked.

"Money! I gave you some money the other day."

Kevin smiled and backed out of the room.

"Isn't he something? The other night some people were here and he told them I was the oldest beatnik in California. Where was I? Oh, the river. Every spring the river rose, and sometimes the levees held and sometimes they didn't. The water rose as high inside houses as that apothecary's chest, and I can remember fishing off our front porch. Once it rained and rained, and the principal of our school called us into assembly one morning and said, 'Grab your stuff and get home as fast as you can. The levee's broken.' The water was above my knees when I got home. I put Prince on the front porch and got his feed bag and straw and bedded him down. The cellar flooded and the heat and lights went out. It was cold. That lasted a couple of days, and my father decided to send my mother and my sister and me down to Rolla, Missouri, where my brother was in college at the Missouri School of Mines. We got through very slowly on the train, and I guess we stayed down there six weeks or so, and that's where it all began. When I was six or seven, I'd taken piano lessons and I'd had a dozen before my teacher discovered I couldn't read a note of music. I was doing it all by ear. One of my brothers or my sister would play what I was supposed to practice and I'd learn it by ear. My teacher rapped my hands with a ruler when she found out—she didn't mean anything by it—and I got frightened and never went back. But in Rolla I heard a man named Wentworth playing marimba in the pit of the theatre. I got fascinated and watched him every night. I was about fourteen. Then it turned out that Wentworth was in the same fraternity as my brother, and he told me I could go over to his room any time and fool around with the marimba he had there. I did, and when I got back to Beardstown it started eating on me and I thought about that marimba and thought about it. A friend of my father's who played wonderful blues piano got me a Deagan catalogue and I saw what I wanted. So I sold Prince for a hundred dollars and worked all summer on a pickup gang in the railroad yards, loading ties and jacking up the cars so that the wheels could be repaired or ground. The reason I sold my pony and went to work was that my father told me, 'You want this marimba bad enough, you get it.' I guess he was tired of paying for lessons and instruments when nothing came of it—like when one of my brothers came home from college, where he had taken up football, and put his violin away for good because it was considered sissy for a football player to play violin. My father was right. It was the best thing in the world for me because it made me serious about it. When I'd saved enough I bought a table-model xylophone for a hundred and thirty-seven dollars and fifty cents. I never took any lessons. I taught myself to read as I went along and I learned harmony later, when I was on the road."

Norvo went into the kitchen and got a 7-Up. "I haven't had any beer in
the house since 1952, when I gave up drinking. And I gave up smoking
in 1961. Once when I came home from a gig in Vegas I was smoked out
and I decided that's that. What I did was fast for a whole week. All I took
was a little grapefruit juice and hot water or a little grapefruit, and I was
so busy thinking about how hungry I was that I forgot all about smoking.
When I started eating again, the desire was gone.

"The training the marimba and xylophone gave me taught me about
evenness of tone. The notes die very quickly on wooden bars and you
have to hit each one just right to get the time value you want. If you need
a legato passage you really have to *play* legato and not depend on the
damper pedal or pulsators, and staccato or fast things have to be clean
and hard. If I want a vibrato effect, I add a little roll or tremolo to the end
of the phrase, which has to be perfect and is one of the hardest things to
do on the instrument. I can never play anything the same twice. Years
ago, when I worked in vaudeville, I used to think I had to play things
people could latch onto, things they would associate with me. So I
worked out about a dozen figures, and every time I tried one it came out
differently. Improvisation is like somebody running. Your reactions are
fast and you're listening all the time. One ear's on what you're playing
and the other's on what's being played behind you. You develop so you
listen at a distance, you listen about twelve feet around you. I use the bass
line—the melodic flow the bassist is getting—and I improvise against
that. The bass line compensates for the way you are going to roll.
Improvising is never dull. Each night is like a new happening to you.
Tempos, moods, atmosphere, they vary all the time. One night you might
play 'I Surrender, Dear' real legato and another night you might find
yourself doubling and even tripling the tempo. I work with the construction of a tune, too. I consider its harmonies and linear design and its
bridge. What is characteristic notewise in the tune you're working on can
be the key to what you do."

Norvo yawned and shook his head. "Nap time. I'm up early every
morning, but I need a couple of hours in the afternoon to get me through
the evening. And I have no idea what this Huntington Beach gig will be
like." He got up and went into the kitchen, a spacious, bright room with
a gas stove, a wall oven, and a charcoal grill he had encased in brick. "At
one point we had so much Colonial furniture and stuff I had to rent a
garage near here to keep the overflow in. I started collecting when I was
with Mildred, and it has become a kind of madness with me. I drop into
junk shops and antique shops wherever I am in the country, and I've
picked up a lot of things out here. People from the East bring beautiful
furniture and china out with them, and then they die and their kids don't
want anything *old* in their houses, so they sell it." Norvo had passed
through the kitchen into a formal dining room. "Those candlesticks and
goblets on the shelves in front of the window are Sandwich glass. That
one's a sapphire blue and that's vaseline and that's canary. Those are

green and purple, and we call the milky color clam broth, and that blue is cobalt. Most of the lamps in the house are also Sandwich glass. I generally convert them myself. The corner cupboard is cherry and it's from Ohio. The china inside is Eve's. It's Canton. The old clipper-ship captains brought it over as a kind of ballast and then sold it when they got here. The other corner cupboard is Connecticut, and you can see how much more delicate it is than the Ohio one. The dining chairs are Queen Anne side chairs with block-and-turn legs and Spanish feet. You wouldn't believe it, but I got them from a *museum*. Museums get overstocked, and I picked them up that way." Norvo went into a big front hall. "The grandfather clock in the corner is extremely rare. It's from Lebanon, Pennsylvania, and is by a clockmaker named Miety. The wood is maple, and the horizontal stripes in it gave somebody the bright idea of calling it tiger maple. The harvest table is tiger maple, too. That's a tilt-top candlestand, and the graceful little feet are snake feet, and the sofa by the clock is—oh, hell, what is it?—O.K., a camelback Chippendale. And that's a Queen Anne wing chair across from it." Norvo went through the front room into the bedroom, which was filled with a canopy bed and two highboys—one with a delicate fluted top and one with a heavy, sedate bonnet top. "This is my little room in here," Norvo said. "Eve never touches it, and as a result it's filthy. I keep my Bennington ware in this cabinet. It was made about a hundred years ago and I've got everything—a footwarmer, which I found covered with dirt in a junk shop in New York, and mugs, pitchers, coachman jugs, picture frames, doorknobs. You name it, I've got it. I'm told it's much sought after now. And I keep my gun collection in this closet." It was a walk-in closet. Part of one wall was hung with rifles, and a long row of pistols, each in a leather case, were lined up on a shelf. Big glass jars held bullets of every size and shape, and on a small workbench were two pistols in repair. "Maybe I love guns the most. There's nothing more beautiful than a beautiful gun used in the right way."

Norvo is the father of his instrument, and, like many originators, he is a visionary. In 1933, he made a startling avant-garde recording on xylophone that had Benny Goodman on bass clarinet, Dick McDonough on guitar, and Artie Bernstein on bass. One side was Bix Beiderbecke's "In a Mist," and the other was Norvo's "Dance of the Octopus." Both numbers are full of odd harmonies and notes and arhythmic collective passages that suggest free jazz. A couple of years later, he formed a small band that tidily mirrored a big band, using arrangements and riffs and the like. It was, as Norvo has pointed out, the first non-Dixieland small band. His professional liaison with Mildred Bailey marked the first time a jazz vocalist had a first-rate jazz band built around her. In 1945, he headed a brilliant, groundbreaking recording date that brought together bebop (Dizzy Gillespie, Charlie Parker) and swing (Teddy Wilson, Flip Phillips, Slam Stewart, Specs Powell), and not long after that he played with

Benny Goodman and Wilson and Stewart in Billy Rose's famous revue, "The Seven Lively Arts." Then he joined Woody Herman, and made small-band recordings that echoed his own band of a decade before. He assembled a trio in the late forties, with Tal Farlow on guitar and Charlie Mingus on bass, that remains one of the most celebrated in jazz. It lasted nearly a decade, with varying personnel, and in the late fifties Norvo went into the recording studios again, to make four timeless sides for Victor with Harry Edison on trumpet, Ben Webster on tenor saxophone, and Jimmy Rowles on piano. Since then he has had a steadily changing succession of small groups, each challenging and original, each light on its feet and light on the ear.

Norvo's style owes very little to anyone else. There are suggestions in his minute tremolos and in his admixture of sudden runs and lagging single notes of Earl Hines, whom he listened to in the late twenties, and his compactness and fleetness sometimes recall Teddy Wilson. He is always improvising. In the first chorus of a number, he will lead the ensemble with a refined, airy version of the melody, generally played somewhat behind the beat. He picks out the best notes, suspending them briefly before the listener like a jeweller holding good stones up to the light. When he goes into his solo, everything doubles in intensity. He chooses single notes in the upper register with his right mallet, occasionally offsetting them with contrapuntal left-hand notes, inserts a two-handed ascending rush that is topped by octave chords, returns to right-hand single notes (the last of them played flatfooted, with the mallet held on the bar after the note is struck to deaden the sound), plays a two-handed run that covers all three registers in both directions, and finishes his first chorus with a legato statement of the melody. Norvo's flow of notes is startling; a pianist has the equivalent of ten mallets, but Norvo only has four. His rhythms shift constantly, and his choice of notes and harmonies is daring. His solos are extrovert: a slow blues, though ruminative, will be clean and gentle and free of self-pity. A first-rate Norvo solo is like a piece of Eve Norvo's Canton china; its color and weight and glaze and design are in fluid balance.

Fred Seligo, a professional photographer and an admirer of Norvo, was seated in a dark circular room on the main floor of the motel in Huntington Beach where Norvo was to play. The floor was carpeted and the walls were carved wood. There were hanging plants, and a circular dance floor, set in a well, was surrounded by tables and a trellis wall. Seligo looked around him. "Early phony Polynesian," he said. "And I'll bet that bar in there is called the Lanai Lounge. I guess Red plays at a lot of places like this all over the West—motels and hotels and the lounges in the casinos at Vegas. Red told me once that the owner of a place in Vegas where he had a gig called him into his office one afternoon and said he had to shave his beard off. In half an hour, Red and the band were packed and headed back to the Coast. Not only that. Nobody listens to you in those places. The whole scene is sad when you think of it, but it doesn't seem to bother him. And I think he plays better now than he ever has." Norvo had set up about fifteen feet from the outside of the trellis in the entrance of what Seligo called "the piano bar." He had bass and drums with him, and he went into "Blue Moon," in cha-cha time.

"Blue Moon" was followed by a brisk "Sunday" and an exceptional "I Surrender, Dear," which started at a slow tempo, slipped into double time, with Norvo dodging back and forth between the original tempo and the new one, and ended in a triple time closed by a free-fall return to the first speed. "Undecided" came next, and the set ended with a fast blues. Norvo talked to his musicians for a minute and then sat down at the table and ordered a coffee.

"Boy, what a set! Nothing went right. I couldn't hear the piano and the drums sounded like they were underwater, and the piano and drums couldn't hear me. And the lighting is crazy. Whenever I lift the bars with the loud pedal, the light catches the aluminum and it makes me feel seasick, a little dizzy. My musicians are all down in the mouth, so I just told them, 'All right, the set was bum, but it's over, and there's nothing you can do about it now. You're all good musicians, professionals, and you *know* what the trouble is, so you can fix it in the next set.' If you're a leader, you can't show your feelings about depression and the like. You can't excuse yourself that way, any more than you can let drunks and such get to you. If they do, it's your fault.

"The main thing is that jazz should be fun. After all, the music is more important than any of us musicians. I'm beginning to think it's not that way anymore, which is too bad. We've come into an age of geniuses, of big musicians swaggering down the sidewalk, and nobody has any fun anymore. I've never done anything musically unless I liked to do it. Of course, experience is the most important factor in being a musician. Gradually, through the years, you build a higher and higher level of consistency, and no matter how bad the conditions are—in an impersonal place like this you almost always feel like you're in left field—you never drop below that level. but if things *do* go wrong, you just accept it, and I've found at my time of life that that's the hardest thing of all. Like with my hearing, which I've had trouble with since I was a kid and had mastoids and the doctor lanced my ears. Then I got a fungus condition in Florida in the thirties, and that took a long time to clear up. Then early this year, in Palm Springs, there were times when I couldn't hear the piano, and one night I discovered that the E-flat I thought I was hearing in my head was coming in my ear a D. It scared me. I came home and my whole left ear—my right one has only had sixty-per-cent hearing since I was a kid—collapsed. It was frightening. I got so I couldn't hear a dial tone, and I watched TV with the sound off. I stopped playing, and in June I was operated on, and when I was back in my hospital room my hearing was perfect. Since then it has been off and on. Sometimes I have trouble hearing the top and bottom of the keyboard, but the bones in the ear have begun to vibrate again, and that's a good sign. So now I just try to stop second-guessing myself when I play, to stop being so damned critical and just move straight ahead."

The next set began with "Our Love Is Here to Stay." The drummer had tightened his drumheads and he sounded crisp and clear, and the lid of the piano had been propped open. Norvo himself seemed to open up, and his solos took on urgency. Even his motions became more exuberant. He stooped over his vibraharp like a chef sniffing sauces. His head was jutted forward, chin up, and it swivelled from side to side, giving the impression that he was searching the audience for a friend. At the same time, he rocked on his feet, his cocked, outrigger elbows keeping him upright. Occasionally he looked down at his hands, following closely a complex run as if he were an entomologist tracking an ant, but then the head came up again, the beard pointing and the eyes scanning. A bossa nova and a slow ballad followed and Norvo picked up his slap mallets and played a funny stoptime chorus. In the next number, he sat down beside his vibraharp and played bongo drums, laughing and rocking back and forth. The group caught his spirit, and the final number, "Perdido," with Norvo back in the pilot's seat, was a beauty.

The Norvos' house, which is on Alta Avenue in Santa Monica, is gray and hugged by shrubs and—because it is clapboard—it is an oddity in southern California. The street is wide and pleasant. Towering palms and short magnolia trees line it, and the lawns are manicured. The ocean is only a block or two away. A light fog was ballooning up the street as Eve Norvo pulled up in front of the house the next morning. "I don't see Red's car," she said, taking off her glasses. "I guess he must have gone out for a few minutes. I'm a transplanted Easterner, too. I guess I don't miss the seasons anymore. If we want snow we can go up in the mountains, and of course we have the ocean. Sometimes I walk over and take a path that runs for three miles beside it. It's never the same. One day it will be peaceful and blue and the next it will be black and angry. And as Red says, New York had an atmosphere it doesn't have anymore. He used to feel that if he left town and just went to Chicago that he was camping out. And everyone in New York goes like a locomotive. Here the pace is sensible. I was born in Great Barrington, Massachusetts, and I grew up in Lee, which isn't far from there. My father was a tailor and my mother worked with him. Six months before I graduated from high school they moved to New York, and I stayed in Lee with friends until I was finished. I met Red backstage at the Paramount, where he was with Benny Goodman. Five days later he called me—he already knew my brother, Shorty Rogers, the trumpet player and asked me to have dinner with him. I had been married before, and I have a son, Mark. I think Red's greatest asset is his humility. He is a humble, kind, generous man, and— oh, there he is."

Norvo was standing in the front door of the house.

"I thought you were out," she said.

"They took the car to put new plugs in it."

Eve Norvo went into the kitchen to make some espresso.

"We're getting straightened around down there at the motel. We moved the vibes a little forward and opened the piano up all the way and we began to hear each other by the last set. A couple of guys came in late, and one of them asked me if I was the same Red Norvo who played the Commodore Hotel in New York with Mildred Bailey in 1938, and I said I was, and the guy with him told me, 'He jackknived so fast to get in here when he saw the sign "Red Norvo" out on the road that the car nearly turned over.' Tonight they're coming back with their wives and families. The same thing happened to me a while ago at the Rainbow Grill. People came up and said, 'Do you remember me? You played a dance in Pottstown, Pennsylvania, in 1936, and that was the night I met my wife.' Well, you can't remember those things, but it gives you pleasure that other people do. The thirties were a bad time for a lot of people, but Mildred and I—we were married in 1930—made it pretty well. I spent the last part of the twenties in vaudeville. I tried college twice—once at the University of Illinois and once at the University of Detroit. But it never took, and by Thanksgiving both times I was back on the road with the Collegians or the Flaming Youth Revue in some vaudeville troupe. I sang and played piano or xylophone, and I worked out a routine where I traded breaks with myself, playing xylophone and dancing. But I was never really happy in vaudeville. I had a Victrola I took everywhere, and I drove everybody backstage crazy playing jazz records on it. Then I worked my way up to being a single, and finally to leading house bands in Milwaukee and Kansas City and Detroit and Minneapolis, and when I went up to Chicago in 1929 I got a staff job with N.B.C., and we played radio broadcasts with Paul Whiteman and backed Mildred, who was with him then. I was already playing vibraharp and even a little timpani. I had my first band in New York with Charlie Barnet, and after that was the summer known as the Maine Panic. We got a gig to play Bar Harbor, and I got together Chris Griffin on trumpet and Eddie Sauter, who were both with Goodman later, and Toots Camaratta, and I think we had Herbie Haymer on sax and Pete Peterson on bass and Dave Barbour on guitar. I was the director of the band, and I'd got arrangements by Fletcher Henderson and Teddy Hill, but the people up there were used to Meyer Davis. They'd never heard wild music like ours, and we didn't get paid because no one came back to hear us, and the only way we kept alive was with little gigs around Maine. We came back from one of them in a pickup truck, and when we got home we looked in the back and all the instruments were gone. We'd bounced them out, so the next day we retraced the road and we'd find a saxophone in a ditch and a trumpet in a cornfield and a snare drum in the bushes. We survived on apple pies made from stolen apples, flounders, and clambakes on the beach, with butter bummed from a farmer. Finally it got so bad, though, that Mildred had to come up and get me. But it was the most enjoyable panic of my life. Not long after, I put together my first real group. It had trumpet and tenor and clarinet and bass and guitar and xylophone. No drums and no piano. We opened at the Famous Door. I had the group a couple of years and we worked the Hickory House and Jack Dempsey's, on Broadway, and the Commodore, where I enlarged into a thirteen-piece group. Mildred joined us at the Blackhawk, in Chicago, in 1936. We were there all winter and came to be known as Mr. and Mrs. Swing, compliments of George Simon, the jazz writer. I had the group until 1940, but I had to give it up when Mildred developed diabetes and had to quit travelling."

Eve Norvo brought in the espresso and poured Norvo a mugful. "I got the idea for my trio, which I put together in 1949, after I'd moved out here. I figured a group with just vibes and guitar and bass could go into almost any place on the Coast, which would mean I could spend more time at home. Naturally, what happened was that our first booking was into Philly. We were playing opposite Slim Gaillard, who was swinging hard and making a lot of noise, and I felt naked. I wanted to know, what do you *do* behind a guitar solo with a vibraharp? Use two mallets, four mallets? What? It was awful. But by the last couple of days it began to unfold for me a little. Then we went to New York, and one night I stopped in to eat at Billy Reed's Little Club, where they had this sissy group. The guitarist, who I didn't know, played sixteen bars of something that spun my head. Mundell Lowe was on guitar with me, and he wanted to stay in New York, but he said he knew a guitarist who would be just right and I told him I'd heard one who would be just right, too. I insisted Mundell hear my man and Mundell insisted I hear his man, and you know what happened—they turned out to be the same guy, Tal Farlow. I took the trio to Hawaii, and when we got back to the Haig, here in Los Angeles, my bass player wanted to leave, and one night Jimmy Rowles came in and asked me if I remembered the bass player I had used when we backed Billie Holiday in Frisco a while back. I said I did—Charlie Mingus. We called all around Frisco and no one knew where he was, and finally we found him right down here—carrying mail. He wasn't playing at all and he was big. I'd watch him sit down and eat a quart of ice cream and I'd say, 'Hey, what are you doing?,' and he'd say, 'Man, I can eat *three* of these at one sitting.' But he went down in weight with us, and by the time we opened at the Embers he was fine. He could play those jet tempos that most drummers can't touch and he was a beautiful soloist. We stayed at the Embers a year or so, and Mingus was with us a couple of years."

Eve Norvo appeared with her daughter, Portia, who was carrying her son, Christopher. Norvo kissed Portia, who in figure and coloring is another chip off the old block, and took Christopher and held him at arm's length. "Well, how is it today?" he asked Christopher. "Have they been feeding you right?" Christopher blinked and looked at Norvo's beard. "You're sort of pensive this morning." Norvo put Christopher on his feet by the coffee table.

Eve Norvo and Portia sat down, and Christopher sidled over to his mother.

"He's a swinger, when he has a mind for it," Norvo said. He picked up a pair of bongo drums and put them between his knees and began an easy rock-and-roll beat. Christopher smiled and edged his way around the coffee table, stopped, looked at Norvo and then up at the painting over the fireplace. He pointed at it and pointed at his grandfather. Then he giggled, sat down abruptly, and got up again. Norvo continued playing. "Come on, what's the matter with you? Don't you want to swing this morning?" Suddenly Christopher let go of the coffee table and started a tentative dance. He swung from side to side, arms crooked, and Norvo laughed. "Now we're going, now we're going." Christopher danced some more, lost his balance, and tipped over, and his mother picked him up. Both women laughed, then Eve Norvo got up. "We have to go out and do some shopping, and then I have to get ready for work, so I'll see you later. How did it go last night? How long did it take to get there?"

"It was a drag for a while, but it picked up. It's an hour or so down there, but I didn't have any trouble finding it. It looks like at least a two-week gig."

The women left with Christopher, and Norvo settled back in his chair, holding his coffee cup on his stomach. "My years with Mildred are a hard thing for me to put together now. They were wonderful years in my life, but it's been so long ago it's almost like I read it all in a book. When I met her in Chicago, in 1929, she gassed me as a singer. I really dug her, and we started having a bite together now and then. The first thing we were going together, and after we were married and came to New York with Whiteman we lived in an apartment in Jackson Heights and then we bought a house in Forest Hills, on Pilgrim Circle. It was a great house. It was open in back all the way to Queens Boulevard, and when it snowed —there was a little hill down to the garage—we'd get snowed in. There wasn't much jazz in New York then, outside of a few theatres and the Savoy and some Harlem clubs, so we had a lot of musicians and music in the house. The Benny Goodman trio came into being there. One night Teddy Wilson and Benny were there and they started jamming. Carl Bellinger was on drums. He was at Yale at the time, and on weekends he flew down from New Haven to Roosevelt Field in a little Waco he had and sat in on drums, which he left out on our sun porch. Teddy and Benny hit it off, and they brought in Gene Krupa, and that was that. Bessie Smith and her husband came to the house, too. Bessie was crazy about Mildred. She and Mildred used to laugh at each other and do this routine. They were both big women, and when they saw each other one of them would say, 'Look, I've got this brand-new dress, but it's got too big for me, so why don't you take it?' and they'd both break up. And Fats Waller came out. We loved to go to his place, too, and eat. His wife and mother-in-law did the cooking. Fats was always a boisterous man. It was no put-on. And Jess Stacy came out, and Hugues Panassié and Spike Hughes and Lee Wiley and Bunny Berigan and Alec Wilder. Red Nichols lived right across the street. Sometimes, in those days, people came up to me and said, 'When did you start playing vibes? You had the Five Pennies, didn't you?' That would get me and I'd introduce myself as Red Nichols, and Red told me that the same thing happened to him, and he'd introduce himself as Red Norvo. Mildred was a great natural cook, and she loved to eat. After she knew about her diabetes and was supposed to be on a diet, she'd say, 'Now I've ate the diet, so bring on the food.' She was an amazing person—very warm, very talented. She had a childlike singing voice, a microphone voice, but what singer hasn't? I think her diction got me almost more than anything. It was perfect. When she sang 'More Than You Know' I understood the words for the first time. She made you feel that she was not singing a song because she wanted you to hear how she could sing but to make you hear and value that song. And she had an emotional thing with audiences. I heard it once at the old Blue Angel when there was an ugly hoopla crowd, a messy crowd, and Ellis Larkins, her pianist, played the intro and she started, and before two bars were over—silence. Mildred loved to laugh and she was very inventive in language. She nicknamed Whiteman Pops. People's opinions of her were very different. They used to say she was temperamental. Sometimes when people don't do or think exactly what they're told they're called temperamental. Either that or they're called geniuses. Mildred got the temperamental bit. She was just astute. She *knew* what was right and she stayed by that knowledge. The first time she heard Billie Holiday, who was just a kid, she said, 'She has it.' Then later she spotted another kid, Frank Sinatra, the same way. She had imaginative ears. We had some pretty strong brawls. Some of them were funny when you look back on it. Once, in the thirties, Benny Goodman and I went fishing out on Long Island, and every time we stopped at what looked like a good place Benny said, 'Come on, Red. I know a better place further on.' Pretty soon we were near Montauk. We stayed a couple of days—Montauk was a sleeper jump then—and when I got home I could tell that Mildred was hacked. Things were cool, but I didn't say anything, and a night or two after, when we were sitting in front of the fire—I was on a love seat on one side and she was on one on the other side—Mildred suddenly got up and took this brand-new hat she had bought me at Cavanaugh's and threw it in the fire. I got up and threw a white fox stole of hers in the fire, and she got a Burberry I'd got in Canada and threw that in. By this time she was screaming at me and I was yelling at her, so finally I picked up a cushion from one of the love seats and in it went. The fire was really burning. In fact, it was licking right out the front and up the mantle, and that was the end of the fight because we had to call the Fire Department to come and put it out."

Norvo laughed, and went to the window. The fog was thicker and the light in the room was gray. "But we were compatible most of the time. I don't know what happened eventually. It developed into a thing where there were no children. She wanted children very badly, and it got to the point where we were talking about adopting a child. We lived on Thirty-first Street by then, and I looked around me and it was a madhouse—the maid running around, dachshunds running around, the telephone ringing—and I thought, This is no place to bring kids up in. But it was a slow thing. The car skids a little before it stops, the carburetor skips a little before it quits. I'd move out and we would go back together and I'd move out again. It lasted twelve years before we were divorced. But I always had cordial relations with Mildred. After Eve and I were married, we would take the kids up to Mildred's farm, in Stormville, New York. She loved the children and she gave each of them a dappled dachshund. We still have one of the descendants out in the patio. Mildred died on December 12, 1951. I was at the Embers with the trio, and when I arrived for work I got a message to call home immediately. Mildred had wanted me to do something for her in New York, and I had talked to her earlier that evening on the phone. She was in the hospital in Poughkeepsie for a checkup—she had had pneumonia the year before—and when I reached Eve she told me that the hospital had called and that Mildred had died peacefully in her sleep. It was her heart. She was just forty-four."

Art Tatum

Art Tatum died in Los Angeles on November 5, 1956. He was forty-seven, and had been born in Toledo, Ohio. John Lewis, the leader of the Modern Jazz Quartet, has said that Tatum was "the greatest player that jazz has produced," that "maybe he was the greatest of all pianists." Such praise was prevalent during Tatum's lifetime, and continues to be heard among musicians who saw him. The pianist Gene Rodgers once said, "I met Art Tatum in the late thirties in Cleveland. I had started as a jazz pianist, but at that time I was part of a vaudeville act called Radcliffe and Rodgers. I believe we were on the same level as Buck and Bubbles. Anyway, we had just come back from England, and some people I met on the boat had told me about Art Tatum. We were booked into a theatre in Cleveland, and Art was working an upstairs room in a night club. A mutual friend introduced us. We had a beer or two—Art loved beer—and then I said, 'Hey, man, I'd like to hear you play,' and Tatum said, 'You play first.' Well, I was young and eager, so I did. When I finished, he said, 'Hey, I like your style very much,' which made me feel good. I said, 'Your turn,' and Art asked me what I wanted to hear, and I said something like 'Tea for Two.' Art was blind in his left eye, but he could see a little in his right eye, and he had these two guys escort him to the piano—that looked dramatic and got everyone's attention. The piano was an upright, and as he sat down he started playing with his left hand while he put his beer down. Then he dropped his right hand on the keyboard, and I couldn't believe what I heard. I'm about six foot four, and I was leaning against the piano and my legs just went to water. By the time he got through three more numbers, I couldn't take it anymore. I went back to my hotel, and I was in tears. I had never heard anything like that in my life."

Great talent often has a divine air: it's there, but no one knows where it comes from. Tatum's gifts were no exception; his background was plain and strict. His younger brother, Karl, who is a social worker for New York City, has said of their parents, "My father was Arthur Tatum, Sr., and he came from Statesville, North Carolina. He was a workingman, a chipper in a steel mill. He was tall and brown-skinned, and there wasn't any foolishness about him. He played some piano at home—mostly church songs and things like that. My mother was Mildred Hoskins Tatum, and she came from Martinsville, Virginia. I believe they moved North sometime just after the turn of the century. She was a housewife, a family person. She was short and medium weight, and she was brown-skinned, too." Karl Tatum's older sister, Arline Taylor, lives in the house Tatum grew up in, in Toledo, and she has said of their parents, "My mother and father were lovely people. My dad was tall and imposing. Everybody used to think he was a doctor, because of his personal blessings. He played piano and he loved the harp—the Jew's harp. My mother played piano, too, and a little violin, and sometimes they'd have a session together. Church music. My father was athletic and loved sports, as Art did. Don't let a football game get on the radio or the TV Art bought us when they first came out, and they'd sit in the front room yellin' and carryin' on, and my mother would say, 'There they go!' She was short and a very good cook. She passed after Art, but my father passed before him, in 1951. The first child they had died, then there was Art, and seven years later me, then Karl, who's two years younger.

"Art was born with sight, but he had diphtheria as a baby, and that congested his eyes some way. He was operated on when he was eight or ten, and he told Mama that whatever color he saw first he'd buy her a dress of the same color. He saw lavender, and he bought her a lavender dress from some money he'd saved. When he was in his teens and was walking home early one morning, he was mugged. He got hit in his left eye, and lost the sight in it forever, and he would never agree to another operation. He could see enough in his right eye to play shooters and, later, cards. After he was mugged, I was up under him and close to him all the time I was so afraid something else would happen to him. I cooked for him and washed and ironed his shirts and took his suits to the cleaners. He was playing the piano to my remembrance ever since I was old enough to realize he was my brother. It was a gift. He could listen to anything on the radio, and in two shakes he'd have it exactly on the piano. He'd kick up under the keyboard when he was too little for his feet to touch the floor, and my mother never would let anyone touch those marks. He studied with a Mr. Overton Ramey at the Jefferson School, and he read music by Braille and by sight. After the Jefferson School, he went to a school for the blind in Columbus, and pretty soon after that he met the singer Adelaide Hall, and she took him to New York. Art was the kind of person that when he became famous nothing excited him so much he didn't know his own family. He always came home two or three times a year, and he'd go round and see his friends and play pinochle. He was married twice—first, to Ruby, and then, at the end of his life, to Geraldine, who lives out on the Coast."

Tatum left Toledo with Adelaide Hall in 1931. He was one of her two piano accompanists. The other was the stride pianist Joe Turner. Before that, he had his own group, and worked in Speed Webb's band. He had broadcast over WSPD, in Toledo, and had appeared, sometimes for money, sometimes free, at rent parties, at the Chateau La France, at Chicken Charlie's, and at the Secor Hotel. He joined Milt Senior's band in 1930, and when he left he was replaced by Teddy Wilson. In New York, he played at the Onyx Club, on Fifty-second Street, and made his first solo recordings for Brunswick. Between 1933 and 1935, while his fame seeped through the jazz world, he shuttled from New York to Cleveland to Chicago to Detroit. He went to California for the first time in 1936, and to England for the only time in 1938.

Tatum was always kind to young musicians. Jimmy Rowles has told of meeting him in the early forties in Los Angeles: "I was playing solo piano in a little place at Eighth and Vermont. One night, when I was on the stand and the place was practically empty, the front door opened and closed and somebody came in and sat at the bar. It was very dark. I got this funny feeling—shivers, really funny vibrations. I finished what I was playing and got off real quick. Tiny, the owner, said, 'I want you to meet somebody,' and it was Art Tatum. He said he had enjoyed what he had heard, and asked me if I'd like to walk him back to where he was playing, because his intermission was about over. He was the kindest and most gentlemanly of people, and he became a marvellous friend. He loved piano players, and he listened to everybody. He'd show me things all the time. In fact, he showed me so much I could barely absorb it. I used to listen to him all the time at an after-hours place called Alex Lovejoy's. I heard him play 'In the Still of the Night' there for almost three hours. Non-stop. At a fast tempo. And all the while he'd drink his shots of whiskey and his beer chasers with one hand and keep playing with the other. To make things interesting, he kept changing keys, until he had run through them all. Two pianists he mentioned who influenced him were Fats Waller and Lee Sims. Of course, Tatum knew how good he was, and when he had to wipe out another pianist he'd lower the boom and let 'im go. Anybody who thought—or who thinks—he can replace Art Tatum is out of his mind."

• • •

From the late thirties on, Tatum moved ceaselessly between the two coasts, with side trips to Chicago, Cleveland, and Toledo. He played in night clubs, which often depressed him, because they were so noisy. Jazz pianists rarely gave concerts in concert halls, and jazz festivals hadn't been invented. By the mid-forties, his style—if, indeed, he had a style— had formed. The pianist and teacher Felicity Howlett says this about Tatum's style in her pioneering dissertation, done in 1983 for Cornell:

> He did not pilot a single style as much as he piloted his musical genius through the available styles—refining some areas that he touched and setting flares to illuminate other areas for further exploration as he moved along.

Tatum did not fit comfortably in jazz, for his playing, which was largely orchestral, both encompassed it and overflowed it. He occupied his own country. His playing was shaped primarily by his technique, which was prodigious, even virtuosic. Tatum had an angelic touch: no pianist has got a better sound out of the instrument. He was completely ambidextrous. And he could move his hands at bewildering speeds, whether through gargantuan arpeggios, oompah stride basses, on-the-beat tenths, or single-note melodic lines. No matter how fast he played or how intense and complex his harmonic inventions became, his attack kept its commanding clarity. The Duke Ellington cornettist Rex Stewart, who turned into something of a writer in his later years, said of Tatum in his "Jazz Masters of the Thirties":

> Tatum achieved much of [his dexterity] through constant practice. . . . He did not run through variations of songs or work on new inventions to dazzle his audiences. Rather, he ran scales and ordinary practice exercises.
>
> Another form of practice was unique with Tatum. He constantly manipulated a filbert nut through his fingers, so quickly that if you tried to watch him, the vision blurred. He worked with one nut until it became sleek and shiny from handling. When it came time to replace it, he would go to the market and feel nut after nut—a whole bin full, until he found one just the right size and shape for his exercises.
>
> Art's hands were of unusual formation. . . . When he wanted to, he somehow could make his fingers span a twelfth on the keyboard. . . . Perhaps the spread developed from that seeming complete relaxation of the fingers—they never rose far above the keyboard and looked almost double-jointed as he ran phenomenally rapid, complex runs.

Tatum was a restless, compulsive player who abhorred silence. He used the piano's orchestral possibilities to the fullest, simultaneously maintaining a melodic voice, a harmonic voice, a variety of decorative voices, and a kind of whimsical voice, a laughing, look-Ma-no-hands voice. The effect was both confounding and exhilarating.

Tatum had two main modes—the flashy, kaleidoscopic style he used on the job, and the straight-ahead jazz style, which emerges in fragments from his few after-hours recordings and from some of the recordings made with his various trios (piano, guitar, and bass), which seemed to galvanize him. (Tatum did not have an easy time playing with other instruments; he tended to compete with them, then overrun them.) He offered the first style to the public, which accepted it with awe, and he used the second to delight himself and his peers. One of his famous public numbers would go like this: He would play a four- or eight-bar introduction, made up of an oblique variation of the melody. (Most of Tatum's materials were popular songs; he wrote very little music.) Then he would go into eight bars of ad-lib melody, using single notes in his left hand and loose chords in his right, break this with a two-bar descending arpeggio, return to the melody for four more bars, insert a two-bar dissonance, and pick up the melody again. The eight-bar bridge would consist of a see-sawing left-hand figure overlaid with a winding, ascending arpeggio, which, when it reached its top, would pause, then fall down the other side of the mountain, landing in a flush of single notes and a two-bar double-time coda. In the last eight bars of the chorus, he would ease into a medium tempo, and would gently shower us with Fats Waller chords. He might approach the second and final chorus by continuing in tempo, then interrupting himself with one of the arhythmic swirls he borrowed from Earl Hines and loved so much; by releasing a series of arpeggios, the ropes that held his music together; by rebuilding the song's harmony with altered chords; or by doubling the tempo, using left-hand oompah chords and an interpolation of, say, "Rhapsody in Blue." During the last five or six years of his life, his public style grew increasingly congested. He seemed to need to change his attack every two or three measures. Tatum like to dazzle his peers, but sometimes he would set aside his grandstanding and swing unbelievably hard to do it. This would take the form of long, complicated, leaping single-note melodic lines in his right hand that suggested a fast car on a bumpy road.

In addition to Fats Waller and Lee Sims, Tatum certainly listened to James P. Johnson. He also admired Earl Hines. And he could play Chopin and possibly Bach. When he was little, he listened to a good deal of player piano and could apparently emulate what he heard note for note—and piano rolls were sometimes cut by two pianists or by machines. The influence that Tatum had on other musicians is still being uncovered. He shocked Coleman Hawkins in the early thirties, and he did the same thing to Charlie Parker in the late thirties. He probably had more to do with introducing the rococo strain that still flows so strongly through jazz than anyone else.

Musicians love to talk about Tatum. Gene Rodgers:

"When I met Art again in Los Angeles in the early forties, we'd go around to the little after-hours rooms when we had finished work, and we became good friends. Whenever he called me on the telephone, he'd say, 'Mr. Art Tatum would like to know when he can have the pleasure of

Mr. Gene Rodgers' company.' One of those times, I discovered what a memory he had. We were standing at a bar talking, and this man came up and said,'Hey, Mr. Great Art Tatum, I bet you don't know who I am.' Art said,'I'm with friends. Don't bother me now,' and this guy went on, 'I'll bet the great Mr. Art Tatum fifty dollars he don't know who I am.' I could tell Art was getting annoyed, but all he said was 'I know who you are, so why don't you go away and leave us alone?' I said I'd take half the bet, and another man standing with us took the rest, and Art said, 'Your name is Such-and-Such and the last time I met you was on such-and-such a day in such-and-such a year at the Three Deuces on Fifty-second Street in New York City, and you were just as rude then as you are now.' We each won our twenty-five dollars."

MARGARET WHITING: "I heard Art Tatum every opportunity I got—on Vine Street in Hollywood, in Chicago, in New York. He'd always play some of my father's songs and things like 'Willow Weep for Me.' I had never heard such harmony before, and I haven't heard it since. Once, in New York, I went to dinner with some relatives of my singing teacher Lillian Goodman, and Art was the other guest. After dinner, he said, 'Let's go to the piano,' which was in the next room. I sang 'It Had to Be You,' and he played for me, and we went on like that for two solid hours. It was the most memorable music of my life."

JIMMY MCPARTLAND: "I had a group at the Three Deuces in Chicago in the late thirties, and Art was the intermission pianist. We talked a lot, and I told him about a book I'd read on this German sea captain named von Luckner. He'd cruised all over the world during the First World War on an armed ship that was disguised as a neutral tramp steamer, and he'd sunk millions of dollars of Allied shipping. I think Lowell Thomas wrote the book. Anyway, Art was fascinated, so I started going to his hotel in the afternoon and reading it to him. We'd drink beer, and I'd read, and it was most delightful. He was a great listener. Sometimes when I'd get off the stand after a set, he'd sing phrases back to me that I'd played and that he particularly liked."

JOE BUSHKIN: "Art Tatum and I opened the Embers in 1951. We were there sixteen weeks. I had a small group, and he was by himself. Fats Waller had introduced him to me at the Three Deuces in Chicago in the late thirties, when I was with Muggsy Spanier's Dixieland band. They loved each other, and there were always these hugs. Art wasn't near as big as Fats, but he was heavy, broad. He had a gravelly, low voice, almost a basso profundo. He punctuated everything with a laugh, and he had a set way of being. I never saw him in anything but a white shirt and a dark suit and a simple tie. He was prone to catching colds. He'd call me when he had one and ask if I minded doing the first set, and, of course, I didn't. When he wasn't playing, he'd stand at the bar. He drank boilermakers all evening—V.O. and beer chasers. He'd go back to the bar after his last set and he'd always ask me to play 'Squeeze Me'—a Waller tune he never played and never recorded. He would get a little raucous after a whole evening of drinking, and he'd kind of shout, 'Play "Squeeze Me," Joey.' The Embers was a very noisy place, and when Art was cooking he'd sail right through it—if you're born with a great talent like his, you have a superior inspiration that carries you most times. But when the noise got to him he'd stop dead and wait until it quieted down. Then he would go into something soft like 'Willow Weep for Me,' and take his time getting through the rest of the set. He liked a little humor in his music, and he'd stick four bars of a march or 'America' into the middle of a solo. Leonard Lyons brought Horowitz in one night, and he heard Art fooling around like that, and he got a great kick out of it. I consider Horowitz as hip as you can get—one of the cats, the way he changes things a little here, a little there. Tatum knocked him out, and Horowitz told him so. Tatum was a complicated man. He saw with his hands and his mind. The temptation for someone like Art is to get too romantic, but he kept the romantic overhead low. When one of his slow ballads began to get a little thick—they reminded me of French Impressionists—he'd stick in a fantastic run and break the mood. He told me one of the best ways to practice is to take a tune and play it in every key you can, even if you don't know some of them too well. Keep at it, he said, and suddenly all these ideas will come to you that you never imagined. Tatum couldn't stand bores or drunks. He'd just turn his back and walk away."

MARIAN MCPARTLAND: "The first inkling I had of Art Tatum was his recording of Dvořák's 'Humoresque,' which I heard when I was still in England. I couldn't believe it. Then I saw some of his piano transcriptions, and they were even more unbelievable. I think I met him at the Embers in New York in the early fifties, and I spent some time with him at the Sky Bar in Cleveland, where he heard me play. I don't know how I had the courage, but he was very nice afterward. Once, at Olivia's Patio, in Washington, he came to hear me unannounced. I had Joe Morello and Bill Crow with me, and they didn't notice him, but I did, and I was so shook up I barely finished. The last time I heard him was at the Club Tijuana, in Baltimore. It was sort of a dump, and I remember thinking, What's this great musician doing here, playing for people who aren't listening and barely know who he is?"

Tatum, like all the musicians of his generation, had gone out of fashion by the early fifties. Bebop was entrenched, and hard bop, its dull child, was around the corner. Tatum died of uremic poisoning, leaving an estate of barely six thousand dollars. His sister, Arline Taylor, talked with him the night of his death: "My husband and I were living in Milwaukee then, and the phone rang and it was my mother, calling from Toledo. She said, 'You're going to have to go to Los Angeles on the airplane. Art's sick and he wants you.' I called Art on the telephone, and he said, 'Can you come out?' I told him I'd take the first plane from Chicago in the morning, and Art said, 'I'll be looking for you,' and he began to cry. I told him not to cry—that I'd be there—and hung up. While I was doing my little packing, I heard the screen door open and shut, and I asked my husband did he hear that? He said yes and went to the door, which was latched, as always. I finished packing, and the phone rang and it was my mother, and she was crying. She told me there was no need for me to go, that Art had passed. My husband and I looked at each other and said it must have been just when that screen door opened and closed."

Wonder Woman

Dorothy Donegan is a virtuoso pianist, an electric performer, and a transcendent clown, and she has been doing what she does for fifty years. She is almost the last of the vaudeville-tinged pianists who came up in the late thirties and early forties, and included Maurice Rocco, Loumel Morgan, Harry the Hipster Gibson, Rose Murphy, and Nellie Lutcher. (There were funny bands then, too, among them the Spirits of Rhythm, Slim and Slam, and Louis Jordan and His Tympani Five.) Rocco and Morgan stood and danced while they played; Gibson wore white gloves and sang mocking songs about marijuana; Murphy chirruped and clicked in a Betty Boop voice; and Lutcher sang and hummed in falsetto, her arms moving like snakes.

Dorothy Donegan is a better musician and actor than any of them. A panoply of emotions, ranging from evil to benign, crosses her face, and she moves like a Balinese dancer. She has thickened in the beam over the years, but she still has an hourglass figure, and she doesn't have any bones; she sways as seamlessly as wheat in the wind. Sometimes she lifts her arms from the keyboard and shapes her hands into little cages so that arms and hands become cherry pickers. She often wears high heels on the stand, and when she gets going she pounds them on the floor like jackhammers. The rest of her clothes tend to be equally flamboyant. During a two-week engagement at the Fortune Garden Pavilion, she wore a black scoop-necked camisole decorated with sequins; a long black sequinned jacket rimmed with black and white checks; black-and white checked sequinned pants; a black silk turban; a long red-and-black scarf; a heavy gold choker; and a black silk garter, fastened low on her left leg. Sometimes she will get up from the keyboard near the end of a number and dance into the audience on her high heels, her knees bent, her head ducking up and down, her fingers snapping then return to the piano and, still standing, finish with booming chords.

She has a strong, pleased, amused face. Her nose is shapeless, and she has a restless upper lip and wide-spaced eyes. While she plays, she will shut her eyes and screw her mouth into a fearful whorl. Or she will open her mouth slightly and look into the middle distance, her eyes half shut, while playing a fast walking bass in her left hand. She will pop her eyes and push out her lower lip, as if she were going to smack someone, or she will wrinkle her nose prettily and lower her head, as if she were accepting compliments. She will make an O-mouth, squinch her eyes, and play drenching tremolos. She will start humming loudly and look satanic— her eyes hard and staring, her eyebrows lifted. But when there are heavy people in the audience she will drop most of this gallimaufry and, demure and girlish, just play, her head tipped forward and her eyes following her racing hands.

One morning in the middle of a run at the Fortune Garden, she talked about herself. She was sitting on the end of her bed in a midtown hotel room, and she had just finished a late, second breakfast of juice, corned-beef hash, and coffee. (She has diabetes, and eats several small meals a day.) She was dressed in navy-blue sweatpants with double white piping down the outside of the legs, a navy sweatshirt with stripes on the sleeves, slippers, and a knitted navy-and-white hat, worn low. She talks in a Southern drawl punctuated with sudden, hurry-up word jams and with statements that turn into questions and end half an octave higher than where they started. She has a wonderful laugh. It descends in long, easy stages, like the levels of a Malaysian rice paddy. She shouts when she answers the telephone, the first syllable of her "hello" a C and the second a D. She spaces her talk with Southern country colloquialisms.

"I live in a big old house in West Los Angeles," she said. "I've got a reverend who stays with me and pays rent. I practice about four hours a day when I'm home, which isn't as often since my name's been getting before the public. I'm now a Steinway artist, and I'd like a nine-foot Steinway grand, but they cost sixty big ones. I was born and grew up in Chicago, and what I like the most about California is the weather. The weather in Chicago and here can be meaner than a Mississippi sheriff. I was born in Cook County Hospital on April 6, 1922, and so I'm an Aries woman, which means I'm hardheaded and stubborn. If somebody tells me 'You ain't goin',' I'm gone. My mother was a sometime domestic, and my father was a chef-cook with the C. B. & Q— the Chicago, Burlington & Quincy Railroad. He loved to play the trumpet, but he was a better cook. He cooked that rice and gravy and fried chicken, and when he did a turkey he used milk and butter and wrapped it in cheesecloth and cooked it into submission. He worked forty years on the railroad, and he died in

1958, a stroke. He was tall and brown-skinned and handsome, but his head was smaller than his body. I think he had Indian blood. He loved cards—bridge and whist—and he'd cuss in a loud voice if he lost. He had come up to Chicago from Huntsville, Alabama, around 1916. That was where Tallulah Bankhead was from, Speaker Bankhead's daughter? His name was Donazell—Donazell Donegan. That's a curious name, but nobody's perfect. My mother was born Ella Day, in Newton, Mississippi, where she taught school. She was tall and pretty and gregarious, and she looked a little like Josephine Baker. Her first husband divorced her for a more experienced woman. She always married railroad men, because they were away from home so much—five days away, five days home. She liked a lot of privacy. We had a great big flat, and she rented out rooms to supplement her income, at forty dollars a month. She told me never to marry a man until he proved he could bring home the money— I wish I'd listened. But she said first you have to love yourself. She married another railroad man after my father died, and she passed in 1972. I had a younger brother, Leon, who was an engineer in the Chicago school system. He died three years ago, mostly of drink.

"My mother had two boarders, sisters named Felicia and Eula Mae, and they told her she should buy a piano, and she did, for fifty dollars. I started taking lessons from Alfred N. Simms when I was eight. He was from the West Indies, and I studied with him about five years. He taught Cleo Brown, who had the most powerful left hand I ever heard when I was growing up. Then I went downtown and studied with Rudolph Ganz, the head of the Chicago Musical College. He taught me Gershwin's 'Preludes.' At DuSable High School, I came under the thumb of Captain Walter Dyett. His ear was so sensitive he could hear a mosquito pee on a bale of cotton. I was already recognized as a child prodigy. In 1943, I gave a concert at Orchestra Hall. In the first half, I played Rachmaninoff and Grieg, and in the second I drug it through the swamp—played jazz. Claudia Cassidy reviewed the concert on the first page of the Chicago *Tribune*. She said I had a terrific technique and I looked like a Toulouse-Lautrec lithograph. I had dyed my hair red for the concert, and I was wearing a white satin gown."

The telephone rang, and Dorothy Donegan let loose a "hello." She talked less than a minute, and fell silent, listening. She moved her head slowly up and down, and rolled her eyes twice. "That was my agent," she said after she hung up. "He likes talkin' better'n listenin'. Around that time in Chicago, the pianist Roselle Gayle brought Art Tatum to my house. Tatum wanted to meet this red-headed girl he'd heard about. He listened to me play, and he took me under his wing. He'd sit at the keyboard, a whiskey at one end and a beer chaser at the other, and show me different things. One was a run on just the black keys with his thumb tucked underneath. But he was a little sly. Sometimes he'd show me two ways to do the same thing to confuse me. He would always tell me to stay light, to use that *leggiero* touch. He'd say about something difficult, 'If it don't fit, don't force it.' He told me I was his favorite woman pianist. 'You never know about that girl,' he'd say. 'You never know what she's going to do. She surprises you.' He was supposed to be blind, but when he played cards he'd hold each card up to his right eye like this. I know he could see women. He kept his money in different pockets the ones here, the fives here, the tens here. But he didn't spend any money. He was as tight as the instep of a chicken. I worshipped Tatum, and, of course, I worshipped Vladimir Horowitz. Tatum was the Horowitz of jazz, and Horowitz was the Tatum of classical music.

"By this time, I was working around the clubs in Chicago, first at Costello's Grill, on North Dearborn. My mother would pick me and my paycheck up, which was a great big thirty-five dollars. Then I was at Elmer's Cocktail Lounge, and after that, for two hundred a week, which was big money, at the Garrick Stage Bar. Red Allen had the band and Alberta Hunter sang. She wore diamond rings, and she'd tell me, 'Life is beautiful if you save your money.' My first manager was Joe Sherman. He was one of Joe Glaser's boys, and he was a pugilist. He'd tell me to lead with my left, and he'd hit me across the back and push me up on the stage. I was at the Garrick eight months. Then I went across the street to the Latin Quarter. There were chorus girls, and dancers like the DeMarcos, and comedians like Jerry Lester and Benny Fields and Lou Holtz. Fifty years later, I still remember one of Holtz's jokes. It was about this man who bought a bird for his wife for a thousand dollars. It was a fantastic bird, and it spoke fifteen languages. One day, when the husband came home from work, he looked around and couldn't find the bird anywhere. He asked his wife, 'Where's the boidie?,' and the wife said' 'In the oven.' The husband couldn't believe his ears. 'That boid cost a thousand dollars, and you put him in the oven!' The wife said, 'If he was so smart, and spoke fifteen languages, why didn't he say something?'

"In 1944, I had an offer to go to Hollywood and appear in a revue called 'Sensations of 1945.' Eleanor Powell was in it, and Sophie Tucker and W. C. Fields and Cab Calloway and Woody Herman. I played in a duo with the pianist Gene Rodgers. They offered me a contract for seven years at seven hundred and fifty a week, but the manager I had then turned them down, and all I got was three thousand a week for the two weeks I worked. The manager's name was Burt Gerbis, and he was known as Corkscrew Gerbis, because he was so crooked. My first job in New York was at the Zanzibar, and later, in the fifties, I worked off and on at the Embers. Jo Jones was kind of the house drummer there, and he would call me one of his 'kiddies,' because he was ten years older and used to give me advice and such. One night, when I started a classical piece he got mad and said, 'Play some music,' and threw a drumstick at me. I picked it up and threw it back and hit him in the head. People thought it was part of the act. At that time, there was still a wartime entertainment tax in night clubs. It was twenty per cent, and they put it on if there was any singing or dancing—any entertainment other than straight music. I was doing a lot of wiggling then, moving my derrière around and snapping my fingers and carrying on, and the I.R.S. decided I was entertainment and put the tax on. That hurt business, so I went to the musicians' union, and the union asked, can she wiggle as long as she's playing? And they said yes, and took the tax off.

"I married my first husband, John McClain, in 1948, and he's still alive. We had a son, who's been managing Janet Jackson. McClain and I had a club for a year in the early fifties in Los Angeles, but he paid me with a mink coat, instead of a regular salary, so I quit. I was temperamental about things like that, and about color. I didn't like working where there were two pay scales, one for whites and one for blacks, but I didn't have a choice. I married two more men after that, and I think I've been married three times too many. Every time there were dry periods in the sixties and seventies and I couldn't find gigs, I'd marry again. Then, when I got work, I'd drift away. I didn't work that much in the sixties—nobody did after rock came in. But I was at Jimmy Weston's a lot in the seventies. A lot of the people you saw in there were hoods and cops. And I played Michael's Pub and George Wein's festivals."

Dorothy Donegan loves interpolation, and she may flavor "The Man I Love," say, with bits and pieces of Chopin, Fats Waller, Rachmaninoff, and Nathaniel Dett. (At one of several tumultuous concerts she gave on a jazz cruise on the S. S. Norway, she mixed "Jitterbug Waltz," "Rhapsody in Blue," "Caravan," "The Flight of the Bumblebee," "Bye Bye Blackbird," and "The Battle Hymn of the Republic" into a dozen or so standards she played.) On fast numbers she swings as hard as any pianist who ever lived, and on slow ballads she is as delicate as a rose. Her technique rivals Art Tatum's. She is completely ambidextrous, her runs plummet; and she can play so fast that the individual beats merge into a kind of rhythmic glissando. She can produce thunder in her low registers and, seconds later, that *leggiero* touch in her high registers. Here is how she describes what she might do with "Tea for Two": "I play the verse first, doing it like Tatum, chromatically. Then I mix in a melody from 'Nola' in the right hand, and keep 'Tea for Two' going in the left. Suddenly, I accelerate into overdrive, which is what I call double time. I modulate, and pass into a difficult passage where I go from a D major to E major to C-sharp to D seventh to B major and to the diminished. I do a cycle of fours, and it comes out chromatically. I put in some fireworks, maybe a fast boogie bass, and relax with the 'Second Hungarian Rhapsody,' playing it in octaves. I throw the melody back and forth between my hands, showing a little Horowitz. Here is where I put in some 'Juba Dance,' by Dett. Near the end of the piece, I do a Chopin polonaise. I close with some beautiful church chords, and play the 'Tea for Two' melody again. After the clapping, I repeat the melody, ending on some high Pope Gregory chords. I first worked this 'Tea for Two' out in 1955, but it changes all the time, and I don't play it too often, because it might get stale on me.

Sometimes you make a mistake when you're improvising, and when you try to correct it you might come up with a new idea, and you develop that. Every night is a developing process. You shake in a little of this and a little of that, like making spaghetti sauce. There are only twelve notes on the piano, so nothing is original, nothing is new. I just dive in. If it comes out right, good. If it doesn't, try again."

Dorothy Donegan's drummer, Ray Mosca, has worked with her off and on for thirty years. She continues to astonish him. "I've played with Earl Hines and Teddy Wilson and Mary Lou Williams and Oscar Peterson and Hazel Scott, but Dorothy has the most power of all of them," Mosca has said. "She has the power of an orchestra. She changes all the time. She may play the same tunes, but they are always different. And every set is different from the last one. She may change things around every eight bars, so you can't take your eyes off her. She's smart like a fox, and in that way she reminds me of Dizzy Gillespie. She goes in and out of focus. She'll come on like she doesn't know what's happening at all, when she does, or she'll pretend she's up on what you're talking about when she doesn't know a thing. She'll come on jiving and kidding, then knock you out with some knowledge. She's not on the same emotional level all the time. She's very high or very low, but when she's got the highs she's full of fire. She has a tremendous memory for people and places. She can run into someone over in Europe she hasn't seen for ten or fifteen years and remember their name, the names of their children, and the name of their dog. Dorothy's been stuck in jazz rooms all her life, and that's been her problem. She comes from a classical background, and she still plays a lot of classical stuff. I heard her play a fifteen-minute piece in Europe, and she tore the place up. She should start concertizing, like she did on the Norway. She gets very tired playing three sets a night in a jazz room."

The Jelly Roll Morton disciple Bob Greene followed Dorothy Donegan at a concert of jazz pianists on the Norway. "I was in the unenviable position of coming after Dorothy," he said afterward. "She played a sedate 'I Can't Get Started,' lulling everyone. Then she tore into a 'Tea for Two' that made everybody stand up and shout. All I could do was play Morton's 'Mamie's Blues' and 'Tiger Rag' and get off as fast as possible. But it worked out, because she learned something from me and I learned something from her. After the concert, she told me, 'I'm going to steal that "Tiger," ' and she did. She played it two nights later, and she got it perfectly, all three parts, and she turned it inside out. And I learned from watching her a new way to play left-hand octaves. Instead of using her wrist, she raises her arm so that it looks like a swan's neck—the wrist arched, the little finger stiff—and lets it fall back to the keys in one graceful swoop." She free-associates when she plays, and it must take great control for her to keep everything from running away. I think she's better than Art Tatum. Tatum's runs and arpeggios often struck me as decoration, as gingerbread, even as filler. Her flash is integrated into the music itself."

Bits of wisdom, philosophy, surrealism, and comedy rise continually in
Dorothy Donegan's conversation. These stay in the mind:
   "I think Adam Clayton Powell tried to pass as colored."
   "If you learn one concerto, you can live off it a year."
   "When I hear a pianist play something I like, I gorilla it—take it over."
   "I heard Beethoven was colored."
   "The saxophonist Teddy Edwards once told me a pork chop ain't got an
enemy in the world."
   "People are dying who never died before. It's getting lonely at the top
of the tree."

You Must Start Well and You Must End Well

Propelled by his brand-new Pulsar watch, which he resolutely kept set
five hours ahead, at London time, Stéphane Grappelli, the formidable
sixty-seven-year-old violinist, did not waste a second when he was in
New York in 1974, and during his ten-day stay he went to West Forty-seventh Street and bought his Pulsar; kept an eye on Nigel Kennedy, a
cherub-faced English prodigy who is a protégé of his friend Yehudi
Menuhin and a Juilliard student ("You must laugh more, Nigel"); walked
a league or two every day; delightedly spent most of an afternoon in
Macy's; averaged four or five hours' sleep; drank an unaccustomed
amount of wine at the opening of Zoot Sims and Dave McKenna at
Michael's Pub and grew quite jolly; attended the beginning of a typically
thunderous Mahavishnu Orchestra concert; visited with his compeers
Jean-Luc Ponty and Martial Solal (piano); gave a gentle and careful concert at Carnegie Hall ("The sound was a bit deesturbed. I couldn't hear
myself, so I was not quite at home. If I can hear me, I'm safe. I didn't
expect that ovation. I am always prepared for the worst"); played fourteen immaculate sets at Buddy's Place during his six days there; and confirmed what a good many people over here have long suspected because
of his recordings—that he has pulled even with Joe Venuti, his American
counterpart and long the best of jazz violinists. Adapting the violin to jazz
at all is a feat, and doing it with the grace and skill and daring of Grappelli
is a signal achievement. Grappelli's new preëminence has finally brought
to a close the long evolution of European jazz musicians from ardent, self-
denigrating copyists to unavoidably attractive professionals. Indeed,
Grappelli, together with the gypsy guitarist Django Reinhardt, initiated
the trek in 1934, when the Quintet of the Hot Club of France, of which he
and Reinhardt were nomnal coleaders, made its first recordings.

Grappelli's style has changed little since then. Its inspirations are diverse and subtle. They include the piano playing of Bix Beiderbecke ("It have a fantastic *psychologique* effect on me"); the buoyant, baroque dance music of the twenties and early thirties; the singing of Louis Armstrong; George Gershwin, both as pianist and as composer; Billie Holiday; Frankie Trumbauer; Art Tatum "He was for a long time the only reason for me to come to this country. Then, when I am ready, he died, and— *incroyable!*— I miss him"); and Django Reinhardt, whose inventions have yet to be entirely absorbed. Grappelli's playing is often called elegant, but there is more to it than that. It has, at its best, a controlled ecstasy. It is fluid yet structured, flamboyant yet tasteful, lyrical yet hardheaded. Grappelli is a superb melodist; that is, he can play a song straight while subtly so altering its melodic line that its strengths double. And he is a tireless improviser. At fast tempos, he often gives the impression that he is carrying on two solos at once. He will start a chorus with a long, molten phrase in the middle register and, without warning, leap into the highest register; there, continuing his chain of thought, he begins solo No. 2 (while his opening middle-register passage still courses through the listener's mind); then, after flashing along almost above hearing, he will, again without pause, drop back to solo No. 1 (while No. 2 still seems to be sailing along), and close the chorus by plummeting into his lowest register for a double-stop. He is fond of rhapsodies, which he plays with a blueslike directness, and he is fond of the blues, which he plays rhapsodically. His tone is clear and measured; it doesn't go thin at fast speeds and it doesn't balloon at slow speeds. For a long time after Reinhardt's death, in 1953, one heard little of Grappelli, even though he worked almost steadily. He began to shine again in the seventies. The reasons were many: Reinhardt was inevitably receding in memory; Grappelli had just spent the better part of five years at the Paris Hilton, and the younger generation, astonished by his joyousness and honesty and musical aplomb, took to him; he began recording prolifically again, often with startling results (collaborations with Menuhin and the vibraphonist Gary Burton); and for the first time he started travelling widely.

Grappelli stayed at the Americana when he was here, and he made his trip to Macy's and back on foot. It was a cold, blowing afternoon when he set off, and he went down Seventh Avenue at a near jog. He had on a sweater and a thin safari jacket, and he said he was cold. His white hair has receded, but it is long at the neck. A block from the hotel, Grappelli pushed the time button on his Pulsar and red numerals appeared: 7:26. "I do not want to lose the London time," he said, in his soft, somewhat high voice. "I love London, and it comforts me to always have it with me. I must be back by five o'clock at the hotel for an appointment, and since I am very nervous I must be on time. Djangoo was always late, and often he forget to appear at all at night, because his only watch was the sun. He was taciturn and childish. He was illiterate, and he spoke French—joost.

He had the intelligence of the *paysan*. He did not have the intelligence of the poet, except when he play. He was not handsome and he often dressed badly, but he have great personality. When he walked down the street, people turned to look at him. Ah! The troubles he gave me! I think now I would rather play with lesser musicians and have a peaceable time than with Djangoo and all his monkey business. One time, Djangoo and I were invited to the Élysée Palace by a high personality. We were invited for dinnair, and after dessert we were expected to perform. Djangoo did not appear. After dinnair, the high personality was very polite, but I can tell he is waiting, so I say I think I know where Djangoo is when I don't know at all. The high personality calls a limousine and I go to Djangoo's flat, in Montmartre. His guitar is in the corner, and I ask his wife where he is. She says maybe at the *académie* playing billiards. He was a very good player of billiards, very *adroit*. He spent his infancy doing that and being in the streets. His living room was the street. *Alors*, I go to the *académie* and when he sees me he turns red, yellow, white. In spite of his almost *double* stature of me, he was a little afraid. In the world of the gypsy, age count, although I am only two years older than him. Also I could read, I was instructed. He have two days' *barbe* on his face and his slippers on, so I push him into the limousine and we go back to his flat to clean him up a little and get his guitar. Djangoo was like a chameleon; *à toute seconde* he could change keys. He was embarrassed about everything, but his *naturel* self came back, and when we arrived at the Élysée and the guard at the gate saluted the limousine, he stick up his chin and say, 'Ah! They recognize me.' He disappeared again when we were playing a posh place in Biarritz named The Four Seasons. We were, for once, living just like customers in a good hotel. Djangoo says he is going fishing and I tell him I will go along to keep him company, even though I do not like to fish. Djangoo loved fishing! He would cut a branch and fasten some incredible string and find a worm and catch a big fish while people with *moderne* stick catch nothing. I go to his room, but he is gone— clothes, everything. I look and look and I finally find him in an abandoned caravan outside the town. I say to him, 'Now what have you done? For once, we have a good lodging. What push you to leave that hotel?' He say, 'Oh, I don't like all that carpet. It hurt my feet.'

"He was always trying to be something he wasn't. The first time we went to England, in 1937, the impresario made up a very good contrac'. We get travel by first class going and coming. When the impresario show the contrac' to Djangoo, Djangoo studied it a long time—he cannot read, remember—and suddenly he banged his finger down on the page and said, 'I don't like that!' I looked where his finger is and it is the business about the first-class travel. I laugh and laugh and tell the impresario never mind, Djangoo is making a big joke, that's the way he always is. *Alors*, that same trip we play a concert at the Cambridge Theatre, and the master of ceremonies introduce me before Djangoo. Djangoo looked around and when the time comes he won't play. The other two guitarists in the group are terrorize of him and they just stare at him. So I started with the bass and finally after two or three choruses Djangoo started to play. I did not speak with him for one week, and always after that there was a little tension from him to me."

Grappelli stopped for a light at Fortieth Street. He looked up and down Broadway, and said rhetorically, "Why is this the only street that run diagonal in New York? Very strange." The light changed and he scuttled across the street, hugging himself to keep warm. The wind plumed his hair and made him squint, and his small, narrow face was fierce and hawklike. "When I first met Djangoo, it was 1931 and I am just coming back to the violin. Three or four years before, I had shut my violin box and *pouf!*—Stéphane Grappelli, pianist. I learn the piano the way I learn the violin and how to cook—from books and from watching others. I like the piano for two reasons: I discover I can play parties by myself in the Sixteenth Arrondissement for Madame This and Madame That and make a lot more money, and I discover I like the *harmonique* aspect of the piano. I am nineteen, and I play the piano in a French band at the Ambassadeurs, in Paris, for two seasons. *Voilà*—one thousand dinnairs every night for five hundred men and five hundred women all covered with diamonds. Two or three maharajas. Clifton Webb singing Cole Porter's 'Looking at You.' Paul Whiteman playing. Bing Crosbee, who was one of the Rhythm Boys, asking me at the bar, 'Hey, man! Where can I get a *chasseur?*' Fred Waring and twenty girl singers going from table to table. Oscar Levant and George Gershwin playing 'Rhapsody in Blue' on one piano with two keyboards. I manage to congratulate Gershwin on his way out, near the kitchen. I grasp his hand and nearly kiss him. He smile and was very polite to me. *Alors*, after that I spend two seasons with Gregor and his Gregorians. Gregor was an Armenian who was picking up about ten languages and who arrive every night at the Palais de la Méditerranée, in Nice, in a Renault with two black chauffeurs. Gregor was a teetotaller, but if we go to a night club after work he sometimes had a little drink, and it would go right to his head. One night, he have a drink and he say, 'Hey, Stéphane, you used to play the violin. Why do you not play it now?' Well, by then I haven't played it in three or four years, but I'm having a little drink myself, so I borrow a violin and play and I play *gauche*. Just three days away from the violin is like sitting in a chair with arthritis too long: it take the feet a while to get going again. But Gregor stay after me and pretty soon I am back with the violin, and I stay with it until this day. After Gregor, I go back to Paris, which was marvellous then. I play violin and saxophone, which I learn in the South of France in a little café where painters like de Kooning come in in bare feet and short pants and where the Prince of Wales sit in on drums with us. And I play accordion, too.

"One night when I finish work, this big, dark, funny-looking man come in and say, 'Hey! I'm looking for a violinist to play hot.' It was Djangoo. But I lose contact with him for two years until I take a job playing for tea between five and seven in a hotel on the Champs-Élysées. There are two bands, and Djangoo is playing rhythm guitar in the other one. One evening, between sets, after I fix a new string on my violin and am testing it, Djangoo starts to play, to accompany me. It go very well. 'Hey, tomorrow we do it again' he say, and 'Yeh! Yeh!,' I say. Soon Djangoo's brother Joseph come in and *he* has a guitar and join us. He play rhythm, and it was the first time I ever heard Djangoo take a solo. Then Louis Vola, who is head of one of the bands and plays the bass, come with us. *Alors*, Pierre Nourry, a young businessman, say, 'Why not do a concert?' He rents a small amphitheatre in an *école de musique*, and we give our first concert. The place was filled up and they would not let us get out. And that was the beginning. A few weeks later, Djangoo bring in still another guitarist, and we decide we need a name. Hugues Panassié, the *critique*, has begun the Hot Club of France, so I suggest we call it the Quintet of the Hot Club of France, and *voilà!*—it stick. We make our first records on Ultraphone, and we do 'Sweet Sue,' 'Tiger Rag,' and 'Lady Be Good.' Djangoo is like a child, he wants so badly to hear how he sounds. The records are a success, and pretty soon we start working together all the time. One of the best jobs we get is at Bricktop's, in Paris, for four months. The Quintet came in from ten until 6 a.m., and during the intervals I play piano for a marvellous singer named Mabel Mercer. Incredible clientele there, due to Bricktop—the English gentry like Lady Mendl, the King of Italy, the King of Belgium, Cole Porter. Every night, I ask Mabel Mercer to sing 'I've Got You Under My Skin.' It drive me mad the way she do it. So the Quintet compose a tune in her honor called 'Mabel.' "

Grappelli charged through the Herald Square doors at Macy's and came to a stop ten feet inside. His head moved in a hundred-and-eighty-degree arc, and he smiled and lifted one hand, palm up, as if he were asking a throng to rise in honor of what he saw. "Iss *magnifique*," he said. "There is *absolument* nothing like this in Paris or London. I wonder, where are the gadgets?" During the next hour, Grappelli ascended gradually by escalator, giving off a rich "Ah" at the top of each flight. He bought steadily but carefully, and by the time he had reached the ninth floor he had acquired half a dozen pairs of fit-any-size socks in white, red, and red-and-black checks; a lined leather jacket, which he put on; an aluminum measuring cup, and two adapter plugs to use on his hot plate in London and Paris; a couple of wild, multicolored shirts and an equally blazing pair of bellbottoms ("These colairs, they are very good for the stage"); and a bottle of pear vinegar from Oregon ("If you brush your teeth with this kind of vinegair constantly, they will get very white"). From the ninth floor, he descended to the basement, where he found a restaurant and had a leisurely cup of coffee. He sat at the counter, and ceaselessly skated a saltcellar back and forth while he talked. He suddenly wondered if he had double-locked his hotel room, for he had left his violin on his bed. "That violin is from 1742," he said. "Nicola Gagliano was the maker. It is not as good as a Strad, but I am used to a smaller car, and to switch to a Rolls now would be difficult. That Gagliano is like a person, and I must be very careful not to let it get too hot or too cold. Coldness change the tone, and too much heat, like those terrible lights at Buddy's Place, make the glue melt, which is why I try and stand in a shadow there when I play. Before you play, you must prepare your way—first your violin and next yourself. If I'm doing a concert, I must have a good diet and I must be in the theatre at least one hour before. I must not be distract by anything—disease, chagrin, or too much sadness, although being sad is sometimes a great help to my playing. Not too long before I play, I take a large whiskey to give me courage. Fifty years ago, Maurice Chevalier told me, 'You must start well and you must end well. What is in the middle is not so important, because no one is listening then.' The alcohol make its effect. It liberate me and I'm free to improvise. Improvisation—it is a mystery, like the pyramids. You can write a book about it, but by the end no one still know what it is. When I improvise and I'm in good form, I'm like somebody half sleeping. I even forget there are people in front of me. Great improvisers are like priests; they are thinking only of their god. Sometimes I get an attack of memory. I have been playing 'Nuages' twenty-five years, and then one night I completely forget it. And once when I'm playing 'Lady Be Good' I think of the letter I just get telling me the water in the bathroom in the house I own at Chartres does not transport itself properly. Mostly, I improvise on the chords of the people playing behind me. The more good the chords, the better I play. I have made progress in the last four years since I stop smoking. My cerebral is clearer.

"The house at Chartres was a farm. I make the living room from the *grange*, the barn, and put a pavement in, and a huge red carpet. I would like to build an atelier, too. But I am almost never there. I have a flat in London, on Beaufort Street, where my grandson live, and I have a flat in Paris, on Rue de Dunkerque, that an ex-drummer of mine take care of. I have a flat in Cannes, where my daughter live. But I love London. I live there during the war, and I think I will get rid of everything and take a place there that has a porter and service. When you get old, you must have protection. My daughter's mother was a very good-looking woman, younger than me, but very *difficile*. I can't retire. What shall I do? I have always work since I am twenty years old, because I must keep away the miseries that happen to me as a child. Also, when I'm not working two weeks, I'm *mélancolique*. The world stop. And I like different scenery. If I am offer a beautiful contrac' in the best place for a year I refuse it. I must fold up my blanket and my cot and move on. When I am at the Paris Hilton so long, I discover it is stupid to stay in one place so much."

Grappelli paid for his coffee, zipped up his jacket, and went out into Herald Square. The wind was blowing hard, and the streets were in shadow. It was four-thirty, and Grappelli headed up Broadway smartly. "This jacket is pairfect," he said. "It will be very good at Chartres. But my head, it is still cold. I must find a hat. The miseries I have as a child start when I was three and I lose my mother. It was 1911. My father was a Latinist and a professor of philosophy, and he was always penniless. He had come from Italy when he was nineteen, and he could never go back because of his politics. Whenever he get a few francs together, he went to the Bibliothèque Nationale to work on his translation of Vergil, which he said would be the best ever made. He was not a gypsy, like Djangoo, but he live like one. He was the first heepie I met in my life. When my mother die, he had no choice, and he put me in a very strict *catholique* orphanage. When I was six and the war of '14 was breaking out, he realize that that pension was not right. We were unique together, my father and I, and he was very unhappy about what would happen to me. He find out that Isadora Duncan was looking for a young subject to personify an angel. I was hired, but I only was there about six months. I was not born to be a dancer. I listen only to the music, which was a revelation to me and which was sometimes a pianist and sometimes a chamber orchestra. Isadora Duncan's school was in trouble anyway, because she had so many Germans in it, so when my father came on *permission* from the Army, he took me out and put me in another orphanage. After Isadora Duncan, it was not a pleasure to go back to a Dickens-type pension. This place was supposed to be under the eye of the government, but the government look elsewhere. We sleep on the floor, and often we are without food. When my father came back from the war, I was in bad condition. Undernutrition. Since then, all my life I have been *lymphatique.* Feeble. Several times I nearly die. My father and I find a room and life starts again.

"My father love music, and he would take me to the top floor of the concert hall to hear the great orchestras. I became habitual to listening to music, and I was getting hungry to play something. My father found a little violin in the shop of a shoe-repair man who was Italian, and finally he bought it. There was no money for lessons, so, as with everything, my father took a book from the Bibliothèque and we learned solfeggio together. It was not very fast, but I learn. I learn, too, from watching the street violinists. When I was fourteen, I went to work in a pit band in a *cinéma*—three hours for the matinée and three hours in the evening. There were two violins and a piano and a cello, and I manage. In fact, I remain there nearly two years, and it was when I learn to play the violin. I also heard my first jazz in a shop nearby that had a Victrola. One record was 'Tea for Two' with a vocal, and the other was 'Stumbling,' by somebody called Mitchell's Jazz Kings, which I never discover any more about. The pianist at the *cinéma* was a little illuminated, a little *fou.* He told me he had invent a way to play Chopin better than Chopin himself. I took him to hear those records. He was still living musically in the middle of the nineteenth century, so the music explode in his head. After that, whenever Charlie Chaplin came on, we play 'Stumbling' and 'Tea for Two.' When I was fifteen, I start dividing my time between the *cinéma* and playing in the streets, which my father never find out about. I work with an old guitarist, and we play in restaurants, too, when they would let us in. So things are getting better. My father and I get a flat with two rooms and a kitchen. By this time, when I was making a little bit, I get more power over my father and we get a piano, and that is when I start to learn it."

Grappelli found a tiny Knox hat shop just off Seventh Avenue in the Forties. He tried on a big white fedora but settled for a narrow-brimmed maroon one. He punched his Pulsar. It was five minutes to ten, London time, and he raced out the door and up Seventh. "Djangoo have a hat like this once," he said. "But, *naturellement,* he lose it. He spend the war in France, and afterward we gave our first big concert ever, at the Salle Pleyel, in Paris. We were together in and out after that. Djangoo took up the electric guitar, but he was playing it with the enormous strength he use on the acoustic guitar, and it was no good. He retire more and more in the late forties, for in the world of the gypsy it is the women who get the money. Then in 1953, someone arrange an American tour for Djangoo and me. I go to Paris to look for him, but he is nowhere. Then, three months later, I hear the news: His brains have burst and he is dead."

A block from the hotel, the wind seized a piece of paper from the sidewalk and shot it into the air. Grappelli was startled, and he stopped and shouted, "Look at that!" He bent over backward and, holding his hat on with one hand, pointed at the paper, which was dancing violently around ten feet above him. "*Merveilleux!*" he shouted again. "What city has so much beautiful commotion!" He righted himself, looked at his Pulsar, and ran the last block.

Demi-Centennial

The pianist and composer Joe Bushkin is the size of a bean pole, but he is highly detailed. He has a handsome, foxy face, a sharp nose, wavy black hair that is turning gray, and Lincoln eyes. His face, worn by the winds of music, is wrinkled. He has a guttural voice and the trace of a stutter. He becomes a dervish when he plays. Grimaces and expressions of exhilaration cross his face. He sways back and forth, as if he were rowing in thick weather, sometimes leaning back so far he disappears. His small feet dance intricately and furiously beneath the piano, and he marks successful arpeggios by shooting his right leg into the air. He is tireless. When he is not rowing, he weaves from side to side, and every few minutes he turns his head to the rear so fast it appears that it may go all the way around. No matter how long or how fast he plays (he cherishes uptempos), he keeps his music on an ecstatic plane.

Bushkin has spent little time in New York since he moved to California, with his wife and children, in the early sixties. He took a short gig at Michael's Pub in 1975, and a year later he accompanied Bing Crosby's troupe during a brief stay at the Uris Theatre. In the fall of 1982, he played three weeks at the Café Carlyle, and he returned the following January. He talked about himself in his midtown hotel suite. He had made the living room an extension of himself. A rented electric piano sat by the door. Three big pieces of poster paper, covered with telephone numbers, addresses, and appointments, were taped to the wall behind a small desk. On the desk were a cassette player, a cassette copier, and two telephones, one installed by him. He moved continuously while he talked—standing loosely in the middle of the room, stretching out for three or four minutes on a sofa, perching a foot on the edge of a chair. He can talk steadily for hours, in a sometimes impenetrable stream of consciousness. Almost constant expletives link his words.

A swatch of Bushkin talk might go like this: "Frank Yerby—you know, the writer—used to come into the Embers every night in the early fifties, and I was embarrassed, because I was playing the same goddam library every night. One time, he said, 'Come over to my house in the South of France and hang out,' and I did. I got a note from Bing saying he was going to Paris. He had a compulsion about dictating notes. If you called and he was out and you left a message, you'd get a precise note telling you why he wasn't there—he was in Canada fishing, he was in New York on business, whatever. He always carried a Dictaphone and answered his mail on it the minute he read it. Leo, his stand-in for thirty-five years, would transcribe the letter and sign Bing's name so that it looked just like Bing's Bing. I was going to go from France to Italy, I wanted to get some of that atmosphere. Yerby took me up some stinking mountain in the French Alps to ski. I had never skied in my life. I don't know why Yerby did this to me, I was a pretty good houseguest, but he took me up there and skied off. I panicked. So I sat down on my skis and went all the way down and up to this snack bar at the bottom of the mountain. Yerby was there, and he said, 'What are you doing here? You're supposed to be on the mountain with the instructor I sent.' Well, I was frozen into the position I was in, and I spent three days in bed that way. When I did loosen up, we went to a flea market in Nice, and there was this old painting. It was some king, and it looked just like Bob Hope. I wanted to give it to Bing as a gag. The dealer was asking five hundred dollars, but it wasn't a five-hundred-dollar gag. Yerby told me that the dealer didn't care about the painting—it was the frame. It was the kind of huge golden frame that if you were a dentist you'd repair it with putty and cotton wads and the glue dentists use. So I bought the picture and Yerby peeled it off the frame and rolled it up. I took it to Paris, and Spencer Tracy was there and he said it was a goddam good painting. Bing arrived and he cracked up. Now, I'm gone, I leave Europe, and I don't see Bing for a year or two, a stretch of time. I say, 'What did you do with the painting of Hope?' Bing said he had Paramount frame it, and he hung it in his dining room and asked Hope for dinner. Hope thought Bing had had it painted, and he refused it when Bing offered it to him. When Bing laid his steely-cold blues on someone, they generally thought it was a put-down, but he was just careful. People were always after him for something."

Bushkin is given to sayings that fall between maxims and one-liners:

> I come from a large, poor family, and I never knew what it was to sleep alone until I got married.
> I don't drop names; names drop on me.
> There is no money in swing music.
> I'm happy ninety-five per cent of the time, and the other five per cent I'm asleep.

This is what Bushkin said of his life: "I was born in New York City on November 7, 1916. We lived on a Hundred and Third Street between Park and Madison, in a tough Jewish-Italian-Irish neighborhood. I have a brother, Arthur, who's two years older. He played violin but ended up a C.P.A. He's retired, and he and his wife, Mildred—she taught at Rutgers—live in Tucson. My father's name was Al, and he came over from Kiev to beat the Army rap—the conscription. My mother lived around the corner in Kiev, but they met in New York. He opened a two-chair barbershop here. He had been a cellist, and he kept his cello and a music stand in the shop, and he'd play between customers. He was very particular, my father. He wouldn't take just anybody off the street, and he never had anyone work for him, because he said if a man was good enough to cut hair in his shop he was good enough to be in business for himself. In order to maintain his family in an apposite style, my father went along with the tide. He always had a Morris Plan loan out. He got income from slot machines that he kept in a room behind the shop, and from alcohol that he had stored in cans. He cut the hair of one of the big gangsters in the guy's apartment. People liked my father. He was a good loser and a good winner. My mother's name was Ruth Hirsch. She was a typical, plain Russian woman who cooked beautifully. She kept the house spotless and herself the same. No matter when any of the rest of us got up, she was up first, nicely dressed and every hair in place. She was totally subservient to my dad. He chose all her clothes, and I never remember her contradicting him. Of course, she knew his temper. Once, he threw a piano stool at me and just missed. My parents were the way they were because they were so damned glad to be in this country and because they wanted to be respected. My dad never lost his love of music. He would take Arthur and me—one one week, one the next—to the Sunday-morning concerts at the Capitol Theatre. Eugene Ormandy was the first violin in the orchestra. And he took us to Carnegie Hall to hear Percy Grainger and Brailowsky and Josef Hofmann. He told me Hofmann would get bigger and bigger as the concert went on, and he was right. Hofmann filled the place with so much music that he seemed huge when he had finished.

"I went to P.S. 171. It was on a Hundred and Third Street between Fifth and Madison, just across the way from the Academy of Medicine. The big joke in school was that they kept an ape in there and that one night he would escape and knock off the principal. I started piano when I was ten. I took lessons from Sarah Brodsky, who was eighteen and beautiful and lived above us, on the third floor. She charged fifty cents, and I studied with her six months. A nicely dressed old man named Kosoff owned our building, and he'd come around to collect the rent. Once, when he was sick, his son came. He was just back from Europe. He told me to go out of the room where our piano was, and he began picking out notes and asking me to identify them. I got them all. Then he did two notes and three, and I got them. I had perfect pitch. He told my father he wished to give me piano lessons. He lived on Riverside Drive, so every week my father shut his shop and took me over and waited—that's the way he was. The lessons were three dollars—about twelve haircuts, or five hours of work for him. Kosoff would tell me that I was not reading the notes—that I was faking—when I played for him. He said that I must learn to write music before I learned to read it. He'd make me copy pieces into a copybook and then play the piece from that. I took lessons from him until I was thirteen. Then I had a bicycle accident. I was doing the no-hands bit on a Hundred and Sixth Street and a truck hit me, and I landed in broken glass. My right hand and the left side of my face were cut up, and I was taken to the hospital at Fifth Avenue and a Hundred and Sixth. When I got home, my father had no idea what had happened, and he was so upset he whacked me on the good side of my face. Later, he came to my room with a tray of food, kissed me on the forehead, and fed me dinner. But he never said a word about hitting me. I couldn't play the piano for a while. I had been crazy about learning the trumpet, so I added that to my musical arsenal. My father bought me one—a dollar a month, and lessons for a quarter. I was in the school band within three months. I loved the trumpet—just one note at a time. It's not like the piano—that hammer is out to land once you hit the key, and you practically have to beg it to come back.

"I went to DeWitt Clinton High, but it was too scholastic. They called my father in, and I ended up in a trade school on Eighteenth Street. I learned to paint signs and do posters and layout. I was very good, and if I weren't a musician I'd be a layout man. I was also doing club dates on the piano at three dollars a night for Benny Goodman's brother Irving, who had a band out on Long Island. Around this time, I went with my father to a cousin who was a dentist. His office was way up on Edgecombe Avenue. We were the last patients, and when we were finished my cousin and my dad decided to have a drink. They walked through a billiard parlor at the end of a hall in his building and into a speakeasy. A black band was playing, and that music hit me like a cosmic fusion: I knew where I wanted to be the rest of my life. I found out later it was one of the bands that Elmer Snowden, the banjo player, had around Harlem. My first real job on piano was in the summer and fall of 1932 with Frank LaMarr at Roseland Ballroom in Brooklyn. Hey, it's not too late to celebrate my demi-centennial! Most of the twelve or so guys in the band were Italian, and they'd bring their own homemade wine. By midnight, there would only be four of us left on the stand. My next job was with Paul Tremaine and His Band from Lonely Acres. They were at a Chinese restaurant in the Forties. You could have lunch for thirty-five cents, music included. Then I got a job at the Prince George Hotel in Hoboken, which turned out to be a whorehouse. It was run by a marvellous woman named Nan. You didn't mess with her. Once, she waited until this drunk who was bugging me put his hand on me, then she knocked him across the room. It was a real 'Melancholy Baby' world. The band consisted of an alto-saxophone player and me, and when we weren't on the stand I accompanied the jukebox on my trumpet. I made forty dollars a night—9 P.M. to 5 A.M. I started buying thirty-dollar suits at Mervin S. Levine. My father couldn't believe I was making all that money, so one evening he pulled a 'Big Sleep' and followed me. When he saw where I was working, he took me out of there, and it broke Nan's heart. My dad still had his arms around me. After that, I heard that Lester Lanin was taking a group to Boca Raton for the winter. Lanin himself played drums at the audition, and he played so loud I didn't take the job. I wound up at the Famous Door—this was in 1935—playing intermission piano. I was home. Bunny Berigan had the band—Eddie Condon on guitar, Mort Stuhlmaker on bass, and George Zack on piano. Sometimes Dave Tough would sit in, along with a good tenor player named Forrest Crawford. One night, George Zack passed out and they asked me to fill in. I played all the bridges wrong, and I guess what made me nervous was the beauty of Berigan's playing and being exposed to the clarity of the guitar and bass. Condon had a marvellous chord sense. I learned from him how to keep chord patterns simple and colorful. In fact, Condon sketched out the chords for the opening and middle sections of Berigan's recording of 'I Can't Get Started.' The Famous Door was in the bottom of a narrow town house. It had a bar and about fourteen tables, and the piano was near a window that looked out on Fifty-second Street. It got its name from a fake door covered with signatures of famous people which was set up on a little stage near the bar. I guess the place had some trouble, because the sheriff shut it in 1936. Berigan used to play behind me when I sang, and he let me do duets with him on trumpet. It was beautiful. I joined Joe Marsala at the Hickory House, farther west on Fifty-second Street. He had Red Allen on trumpet, Artie Shapiro on bass, and Danny Alvin on drums. Marty Marsala, Joe's brother, replaced Red, and Buddy Rich came in. He was a great improvement on Alvin's boom-boom-boom bass drum—until he started playing too loud behind my solos. Also, Joe had hired Adele Girard on harp. Sometimes I felt like I needed an ear treatment at Bellevue after work. So I called Bunny

Berigan, who had his own big band, and asked when I could go back with him."

Bushkin came up when Earl Hines, Teddy Wilson, and Art Tatum were kings, and when Clyde Hart and Billy Kyle were brilliant apprentices. A little of all these pianists is in his playing, but his style—elegant, flashy, swinging—is his own. It is hornlike rather than pianistic. The listener is conscious not of notes being struck so much as of a singing, nonstop single-note melodic line that demolishes bar lines and ends only when it runs out of breath. At high tempos, this melodic line hums and hurries, pushing the air before it. Bushkin's notes fall between the center and the front of each beat. He pushes his time as hard as it will go without racing. His improvisations are fashioned of long, descending arpeggios that whip and curl down the keyboard, and curious sideways ascending figures that have a two-steps-forward, one-step-back effect. Occasionally, he passes his melodic lines through belling octave chords, through tremolos, and through loose Jess Stacy passages. Some of the fervency in his playing falls away when he works in slower tempos, but his light touch and easy sense of dynamics take up the slack. Bushkin talks about his playing this way: "There are a lot of songs that don't lay well on the piano, that don't improvise. 'Melancholy Baby' is one. When I play, I empty my mind, so that I can put something new in it. What the drums and guitar are doing guides me. The bass player, though, has to follow my thoughts. I don't pay any attention to the chords, which are automatic. The melody is my framework. I don't tell my fingers where to go—I try to have the patience not to tell them where to go. But if they mess up I take them back to where they messed up, so that the error becomes a part of the improvisation. I see a kaleidoscope in my mind when I play. I look for holes in it to jump in and out of. But you can't get too carried away—you might jump in one and never get back."

Bushkin rejoined Bunny Berigan in April of 1938. "In the summer of 1939, we played the Panther Room in the Hotel Sherman in Chicago, and Muggsy Spanier had the other group," Bushkin said. "Business matters were beyond Bunny. MCA booked the band, and they were supposed to take fifteen per cent of what he made, but they seemed to be taking everything, because he owed them so much money. We didn't get paid for five weeks. I was sending home for money, and a lot of the guys were borrowing from a saloonkeeper across the street. We finally met in Bunny's hotel room one night. You never saw him without a cigarette burning in the right side of his mouth, and you never saw him without his whiskey and his cool. He was lying on his bed smoking, his glass of whiskey on the bedside table. He said, 'Go see Petrillo at the union and tell him you haven't been paid in five weeks. It's the only way you're going to get any money.' Nobody wanted to go, so we all marched over next morning like an army. We were taken into a big room with a long table, and there was Petrillo—James C. himself—seated like Napoleon at the head of it. 'All right, what's the problem, fellas?' he said. Then he said, 'Boy, Bunny Berigan, he's some trumpet player, that guy.' Petrillo played a little trumpet himself. Each of us had to tell what we were paid, which was embarrassing, because the salaries were so mixed up. The third trombone was getting maybe eight-five a week, while the first was only getting sixty. Petrillo called MCA and told them he'd shut down music in Chicago if our money wasn't there by two o'clock that afternoon. It was, and when we went back to the hotel we each gave Bunny some money, because he was broke, too, and we loved him.

"Bunny's band went bankrupt not long after, and I joined Muggsy Spanier. We worked with Fats Waller in a show that had a singer, a tap dancer, and two guys who danced on roller skates. I'd met Fats three or four years before, and I knew he hated the road. When he saw me, he hugged me and said, 'Boy, I can *smell* that Eastern soil!' The show was supposed to be a battle of music, and we sat back to back on our piano benches. He'd get off a beautiful run and say just loud enough for me to hear, 'It's so easy when you know how.' Then Muggsy's band broke up, and pretty soon I was down to no eating money. I became intermission pianist at Kelly's Stable, in New York. Benny Goodman was at the Waldorf, and the one thing I wanted was to be in the Goodman band. Jess Stacy and Teddy Wilson had left, and he had Fletcher Henderson on piano. Fletcher was a wonderful arranger, but he wasn't much of a piano player. Benny also had Charlie Christian and Dave Tough and Lionel Hampton, and they'd stop by at Kelly's Stable almost every night. Finally, they took me to audition for Goodman. I knew Benny, I knew his book. I knew he kept his overhead low and his music complicated. I auditioned, but I didn't get the job—Johnny Guarnieri did—and it broke my heart. I stayed at the Stable four months. Then Bunny Berigan, who had gone with Tommy Dorsey, told me Tommy was looking for a piano player. I went out to Frank Dailey's Meadowbrook, in New Jersey, and sat in with the band for a set. We played some blues and everything went all right. I didn't hear anything for twelve days. Then I was told to report at the Paramount Theatre for the first show the next morning—no rehearsals, no discussion of salary, no word from Dorsey himself. It was rough, but Berigan was my first-base coach, and Sy Oliver, Tommy's arranger, taught me how to get through the arrangements. I joined in January, 1940, and stayed two years. I wrote "Oh! Look at Me Now," and the band recorded it with Frank Sinatra, and we had a kind of hit. I liked Tommy, because he liked me. He was hard on his technical musicians—his lead men—but if you were an improviser, like me, you could do no wrong, because improvising was the missing link in his own playing.

"What's there to say about the war? I went in in 1942 and got out a master sergeant when it was over. I played in a couple of Army Air Forces bands, I was one of the musical directors of Moss Hart's 'Winged Victory,' which played on Broadway for six months, and I was sent to the South Pacific, where I checked the Armed Forces radio stations to make sure they were playing V-Discs when all they had to play was V-Discs. I was glad when it was over. I came back to New York and hustled for five years. I did studio work for NBC. I studied with Stefan Wolpe. I was with Benny Goodman for a short time, but we didn't see eye to eye. I did radio jingles and made every kind of record you can think of. I wrote a song for Louis Jordan. I toured South America with Bud Freeman. I took the part of a bandleader in Garson Kanin's play 'The Rat Race.' I was still a stutterer, and Garson wanted me to stutter, but on opening night I was so scared I didn't stutter at all. I didn't stop stuttering for another ten years. I went to a great psychiatrist named Morty Hartman, who told me that first I had to get rid of my father, then my mother, then him, and when I'd done all that I'd be Joe Bushkin and stop stuttering, and that's what happened. Until then, I was an introvert outwardly and an extrovert inwardly. I opened at Billy Reed's Little Club on the night that 'The Rat Race' opened, and around two o'clock Georgie Auld came in and whispered in my ear, 'Joey, you better hang on to this gig. I just read the reviews.' I went into the Embers when it opened, in 1951, and I was there off and on many years, generally with Milt Hinton and Buck Clayton and Jo Jones. When I started, Art Tatum was the other attraction, but it didn't bother me. It was like I was a lawyer and he was in medicine—like we were in two different professions. The best thing that happened to me at that time was I married my Fran. Her name is Francice Oliver Netcher, and she's of Dutch and English extraction. She comes from a well-to-do family, and she's a queenly woman. We met in Chicago during the war, and we didn't take to each other at all, but by the time I went overseas we were getting along, and she wrote me every day. One of her faults is that she refuses to lie or have anyone tell her a lie. I can tell her anything as long as it's the truth. It's when I don't that I get in trouble. She was going to the Art Students League when we were married, and she had an apartment in River House, which we still have. We have four great daughters—Nina, Maria, Tippy, and Chrissy. Two are still at home, which is a twenty-four-acre horse farm in Santa Barbara. We raise thoroughbreds. We bought the place in 1971, after living three years in Hawaii. Before that, we lived near San Francisco, and, before that, in Los Angeles. The girls grew up on horses, and they used to compete at Madison Square Garden every year. Chrissy was on the U.S. Junior Olympic Team in France, competing against eleven other countries. And she won the Junior Working Hunter Championship at the Garden when she was twelve. I love the ranch, but I get feeling penned up. Do you know why I'm out playing again? Too many people have come up to me and said, 'Didn't you use to be Joe Bushkin?' "

Super-Drummer

Buddy Rich was staying at the Warwick Hotel, and when he walked out of the elevator on his way to a benefit performance at Rikers Island, he shot out, spraying the lobby with early-morning glances. He was dressed in a hip-length, single-button, black-and-white checked sports coat, pipestem black trousers, black Italian shoes, and a blue shirt open at the neck, and he had a black duffel coat over one arm. He is short and lithe and slightly stooped, and he has monkish pepper-and-salt hair. His somewhat battered nose connects his two most striking features—a generous mouth and Buddha eyes, which are kept at a steady, alert squint. The bags under his eyes suggest Duke Ellington's seignorial pouches, and deep lines run down from the sides of his nose. He looks like a middle-aged man with a boy peering out from inside. He smiled, showing square, very white teeth. "Man, I was up I don't know how late last night at Sol Gubin the drummer's house out in Jersey," he said. "His wife is a magnificent Italian cook and I couldn't eat enough. We were still at it at two in the morning. It was beautiful."

A black man with a brush mustache approached Rich and they shook hands. "Hey, Carl," Rich said. "This is Carl Warwick, or Bama, as we used to call him. He played trumpet in my band in 1946. He's with the city now and he set up this Rikers Island thing. He came in the club the other night and spread out all these papers on the table and began this spiel about the prison and the boys and this and that and I said, 'Hell, Carl, you want me to come out and play for you say so and I'll come out and play. It's as simple as that.' "

Warwick laughed. "O.K., Buddy. We've got a car and a driver outside."

"What kind of cats you got out there, Carl?" Rich asked after they had gotten in.

"Mostly short-term misdemeanors. Anything from a month to three years. Petty thievery and some addicts. If you steal anything worth over ninety-nine dollars, that's a felony. So very few of these cats ever take over ninety-nine dollars' worth. They know the value of everything. We've got about five thousand inmates. Most of them are repeaters. I had a guy who was back an hour after he got out. He was supposed to report to the Parole Board that day and didn't and they picked him up. And a lot of cats come back when it gets cold, when that old malnutrition and Jack Frost set in."

"If one of them gets hit three times, is he finished?" Rich asked.

"Not with misdemeanors—just felonies. You can get nine thousand misdemeanors but only three felonies. Rikers Island is like a big Y.M.C.A. The only rough place is processing, where they try to get the idea across that you're in a prison. We have a pretty good prison band now, but we're short on drummers."

"Don't look at me, Carl. I'm happy in my work." Rich laughed. "You know, I've never been in jail—I mean as a non-visitor. The C.I.A. and the F.B.I. investigated me before I made a State Department tour. Clean. 'The man doesn't even spit on the sidewalk,' the report said."

Rich shook his head in presumed self-admiration and looked out the window. The car was on the Queensboro Bridge, and the river below was furrowed with sunlight.

"My new band is a straight-ahead band. I've never compromised and I'm not about to start now. People come up to me and say, 'How come you don't smile when you're up there playing?' I say, 'Did you come to see my teeth or to hear me play?' I'm no Charlie Glamour. If you like my playing, never mind me. When I was thinking of organizing this band, a man who was interested in backing it came to my house in Las Vegas. He told me, 'You have to forget what you are and who you have been. It's not that important—that you're a great drummer and all. Start fresh and be commercial and you'll be safe and make some bread.' I told him to get the hell out of my house. I'm the same with the guys in the band. I tell them, 'Your life's your own when you're off the stand. But every night I own you for five hours.' I ask no more than I give myself. I kill myself every night, and I expect them to wipe themselves out, too. And everybody's got to be clean. If a new guy comes on the band, he's got to match the personality of the band. No cliques. No headaches. Everybody jells, everybody gets along. If a guy plays consistently well for a couple of weeks, I'll lay ten more on him a week. If a guy cops out on me, I'll buy him a first-class one-way ticket to wherever he wants to go. The great thing about the guys in the band is that they think like me. It makes me feel good. There's a certain resentment when you have to tell people what they have to do. If musicians are unhappy, they won't play well. If they are playing beneath them, they won't play well. I want them to play with *their* emotion. I ask them, 'Who do you want for this arrangement? Who'd sound right?' And we all decide. I'm rejuvenated about what's been going on with my band. I look forward to going to work every night. And I look forward to tomorrow. A lot of draggy things happened in the so-called good old days. Sorry about the Civil War and all that, but *I* don't remember the Civil War."

At the gate to Rikers Island, Rich signed the register and was given an identification badge. The car passed through a flat, treeless expanse, broken here and there by wire fences and low buildings, and stopped in front of one of the buildings. Rich was greeted inside by a portly, rumpled, cigar-smoking black man—Warden James Thomas. Thomas ushered Rich into his office. The walls were covered with enormous paintings done by the inmates. Rich, frail and birdlike in the surroundings, stared at a dark painting of the head of Jesus crowned with thorns. Then he smiled.

"That's amazing. You know who that is? Sammy. Sammy Davis. Look at the nose and the mouth and the chin. Even the eyes. All Sammy's."

The warden, puffing on his cigar, sat down behind his desk. "We get a lot of the stars out here to entertain the inmates," he said. "Dizzy Gillespie was here not long ago, and so was Carmen McRae. The hall only holds fifteen hundred men, so there is a lot of jockeying for seats. But we try and rotate the men."

Warwick poked his head into the office and said the band had just arrived. Thomas led the way through two steel doors and into a long corridor. He pointed out a dining room, a corridor hung with more paintings, and a cell block. "You might want to see where the inmates sleep," he said. "We're overcrowded. This block was designed for three hundred men and there are nearly five hundred in here." There were several tiers of small, dark cells. Each cell had a double bunk, a toilet, and a basin. Rich shook his head. "Can you believe people live here!" he said in a low voice. "Animals have a better deal in the zoo." Clumps of flat-eyed prisoners stood against the walls in the corridor. Rich, walking quickly, his hands clasped under the tail of his duffel coat, looked at them and nodded. One man raised his hand in a half salute and started to smile. Rich said, "Hello. How are things?" Rich entered a gymnasiumlike hall packed with men. A ten-piece prison band, set up below the stage, was pumping unevenly through a Charlie Parker blues. Recognition flickered across the faces of the musicians as Rich went by, and he ducked his head and smiled. He took the steps at stage right two at a time. His band, in tan uniforms, was putting up its music stands in front of a backdrop of Park Avenue on a wet winter night. The words "Welcome Buddy Rich" were pasted across the middle of it. Rich's limousine-size set of drums was already in place, and he sat down behind them. There were two crash cymbals, and between them, at a lower level, a tiny sock cymbal and a giant ride cymbal. His snare drum, a high-hat, and a small tomtom formed a semicircle in front of him, and to his right were two bigger tomtoms. His bass drum was large and old-fashioned. He tunked each drum with a stick, moved his high-hat closer, and looked down at the assembled band. "All set? O.K. Number Thirty-five." The musicians riffled through their music.

All true professionals can step in an instant from the world into their work. A veil of concentration immediately dropped over Rich, and he bent forward and began a soft roll on his snare drum. A half smile masked his face and he kept his head turned to his left. He brought the roll to a quick crescendo, dropped into a pattern of rimshots and heavy bass-drum beats, and shouted. "One, two, three, four!" The band roared into a medium-tempo blues. Rich sat back and looked out at the audience. A broad-toned lyrical tenor saxophonist soloed. Midway, Rich shouted "Hmmmmyeh!" and tossed off a fill-in that shot from his snare to his big tomtoms and ended on the bass drum. He underlined the close of the last ensemble chorus with generous cymbal splashes. Then his pianist jumped up, lifted his right hand and at a nod from Rich brought it down and the piece finished with a resounding thump. The applause was scattered. Rich, ignoring the audience, called out another number and gave the downbeat. It was a fast blues. The applause was again scattered and scattered after Duke Ellington's "In a Mellotone." A good part of the audience, which appeared to be in its late teens and early twenties, didn't know who Buddy Rich was, and Rich suspected it, for the next arrangement was a rock number called "Up Tight." The audience began to tap its feet and sway back and forth. The tenor soloed, and rhythmic handclapping began. The number ended and the audience whistled. Rich smiled and called to his pianist, who started "Green Dolphin Street" at a medium tempo. Rich picked up his wire brushes. The pianist played the first chorus, and for the next two he and Rich exchanged eight- and four-bar breaks. Rich's breaks were delicate and funny. In one, he worked out a soft tap-dancer's pattern on the snare, paused, struck his bass drum twice, then rattled his brushes over the tops of his cymbals. In another, he slipped into double time, racing from his small tomtom to his snare to his big tomtoms in sudden stops and starts. Each break was met by pleased guffaws, and after the last one, in which he whisked lazily between his cymbals and the rim of his snare, the audience shouted and laughed.

He mopped himself with a towel, picked up his sticks, and began a fast swelling-and-subsiding series of rolls, his bass drum in sonorous half time underneath. He machine-gunned his high-hat, moved back to the snare and into a thousand-mile-an-hour tempo, and shouted, "Yeh go-oh!" The band burst into "Clap Hands! Here Comes Charlie!"—one of Chick Webb's great display pieces. There were alto, tenor, and trumpet solos. The band fell silent, and Rich, crouched over his snare drum, his teeth clenched, his elbows flat against his sides, fashioned a steady, whispering series of snare-drum figures. He slowly multiplied the beats, letting his volume build, all the while keeping a beat on the bass drum. The snare-drum figures were flattened into a roll, which presently became stately sea swells. Mouths fell open in the audience and the wings of the stage filled with onlookers. Rich began dropping in rimshots, at irregular intervals, that energized the creamy thunder of the rolling. He abandoned his snare and began flying around his entire set, flicking one crash cymbal again and again. Back to his snare drum and a flurry of rimshots backed by a succession of jammed bass-drum beats—elephants moving in quickstep. The bass drum fell silent and Rich's left hand chattered by itself on the snare while his right hand floated lackadaisically between his crash cymbals and his tomtoms. His volume began to sink, and he loosed ticking, dancing figures on his snare rims, abruptly crashed into a complex roll, and settled on the upper half of his snare, his sticks moving so fast that they astonishingly formed two sets of triangles, their apexes joined. The audience shouted, Rich waded around in his cymbals, the band came in, and the number ended. Warden Thomas appeared, shushing the audience. "We thank Mr. Rich, we thank him with all our hearts. And I would like to tell you that Mr. Rich has told me that he is donating—yes, donating—the very set of drums he has just played on to Rikers Island."

Rich draped a towel around his neck and tucked it into his soaking shirt. "I didn't know I'd get this wet," he said, "or else I would have brought a change of clothes. Whooeee! I'm dripping, man, dripping. Where's my coat? I've got to get back to New York. What time is it?" Warwick said it was three-thirty, and pumped Rich's hands. Rich ran down the stairs into the auditorium. The house band was playing again and the hall was beginning to empty. A guard grabbed one of Rich's hands and shook it. He looked to be about Rich's age. "That was fantastic, Mr. Rich. I came in to see you at the club the other night with the wife. If I'd knew you'd be out here today, I wouldn't have spent all that money. Wonderful, Mr. Rich."

In the car, Rich shivered a little, pulled his duffel coat around him, and leaned into the corner of his seat. He looked tired. "That was weird, wasn't it? I thought for a while we wouldn't get those cats moving. They were sort of lifeless, but what do you expect? The whole penal system is rank. It hangs me up—people in jail. Can you imagine two guys living in one of those cells? There must be some better way. I know a lot of hoods. Maybe I dig more of them than I do straight cats. They're what they are and if you're what you are with them—beautiful. Everything's straight. And when someone pulls a Brink-type job and no one is hurt, that's brilliant, that's groovy. Four stars. He beat you with his brain. He's a swinger. But of course crime is a drag and so's prison, and so what are you going to do?

"I had a beautiful family and I guess that's one of the things that keeps you straight. I was born in Brooklyn. My father and mother were a vaudeville team—Wilson and Rich. My mother was from Brooklyn. She was a singer and a heavy-made woman and very pretty. She died much too young, about fifteen years ago. My father was a soft-shoe dancer and a blackface comedian, which embarrasses me now, but it was accepted then. He was from Albany. He's a little shorter than I am and he lives in Miami. He was a liberal father, a good father, a good man. He was strong and nice-looking and had a great sense of humor. When you stepped out of line you got a shot in the mouth and that straightened you out. He came to see me at the Sands in Vegas a little while ago and he got upset when I wouldn't let him stay up for the four-o'clock show. My mother and father called me Pal and my two sisters—they're older—called me Broth. I have a kid brother who's in television. Until twenty years ago we lived in a great big house near Sheepshead Bay. There was fun going on constantly. It was the kind of house that when I worked at the Astor with Dorsey in the early forties and came home at two o'clock in the morning everybody would be up and we'd all sit down in the kitchen and have

French toast and they'd say, 'All right, what happened tonight? How did it go? Who came in?' Everything's still groovy. No jealousy. I stayed with my sister in L.A. a little while ago and it was a ball. One sister is a fair dancer and one is a fair singer and my brother played tenor for a while. I started as a dancer and a singer and a drummer. By the time I was two I was a permanent part of my parents' act. They'd bring me onstage dressed in a sailor suit or a Buster Brown collar and I'd play 'Stars and Stripes Forever' on a drum. I had long, curly hair. When I was seven I travelled around the world. My part of the act gradually became more powerful and my parents gradually stepped aside. My father travelled with me, and sometimes we took a tutor. I only made it through the sixth grade because we were always on the road. I taught myself mainly to read and write. By the time I was fifteen—that would have been in 1932 or so—I was making a thousand dollars a week. I was the second-highest-paid kid star, after Jackie Coogan.

"I started getting interested in real drumming, jazz drumming, in my early teens. I heard the Casa Loma band at the Colonnades Room at the Essex House and Tony Briglia was on drums. He had the greatest roll I've ever heard. Smooth as milk. I began to study drummers and I listened to O'Neil Spencer for his brushes and to Leo Watson, who was a scat singer and a terrific drummer, and to Lee Young, Lester's brother, and to Chick Webb. Webb was startling. He was a tiny man with a hunchback and this big face and big, stiff shoulders. He sat way up on a kind of throne and used a twenty-eight-inch bass drum which had special pedals for his feet, and he had those old gooseneck cymbal holders. Every beat was like a bell. And I loved to listen to Davey Tough. He tuned his drumheads so loose they flapped. And he hated soloing. But he had that touch. Gene Krupa appealed to me for his showmanship. It overshadowed his playing. And I watched Sid Catlett. He was the best cymbal player I've ever heard. I listened to everybody and decided I wanted to be my own self. I don't think I sound like anyone but myself.

"Around 1937, I started hanging out in a place in Brooklyn called the Crystal Club. It had a small group with Henry Adler on drums and Joe Springer on piano and George Berg on tenor. Henry would invite me to sit in, and Artie Shapiro, the bassist, would sit in, too. Shapiro was with Joe Marsala's group at the Hickory House and he asked me to one of the Sunday-afternoon jam sessions they used to have there. Everybody in New York fell in. I went three Sundays in a row and never got to play. On the fourth Sunday, at about five-forty-five—the session ended at six—Marsala summoned me. I played 'Jazz Me Blues,' or something like that, and then Marsala said,'Let's play something up.' In those days, I lived up. I started out at a tempo like this—taptaptaptaptaptap—on a thing called 'Jim-Jam Stomp.' People were beginning to leave, but they turned around and started coming back in just as if a Hollywood director had given instructions in the finale of some crummy Grade B movie. The number broke the place up, and Marsala invited me back to play that night. I called my dad and he said he guessed it would be O.K. I played two sets and Marsala asked me to join the band. My dad was a dyed-in-the-wool vaudevillian, and when I told him he said,'What are you going to *be*, Pal? A *musician?*' I said, 'Just give me a chance.' I joined the union and went to work for sixty-six dollars a week, which I took home to Dad. He gave me an allowance of ten bucks a week. Marsala told me just to play with woodblocks and a sizzle cymbal and no high-hat and a lot of ricky-tick stuff on the rims. But gradually I brought in other equipment and we moved over to a four-four beat. I didn't know any musicians and I discovered pretty quickly that you have to build up protection, an immunity to feelings. It was Dickie Wells, who was a club owner and a big man in Harlem, who gave me the confidence. One morning the Three Peppers, the intermission group at the Hickory House, took me up to Wells' place for a breakfast dance. A group named the Scotsmen were playing there, and they wore kilts. They had Teddy Bunn on guitar and Leo Watson on vocals and drums. They later became the Spirits of Rhythm. I'd never been to Harlem and I was worried because I knew they really played up there. The Peppers introduced me to Wells and he told me, 'I want you to play and if you don't it'll be your you know what.' He wasn't very encouraging. Well, I played and it was a very exciting thing for me. I came off the stand and Wells hugged me and said, 'You're my hundred-year man.' Beautiful. From that time on it was straight ahead. For some reason, I've always had a great thing going with colored cats. No conflict—just with white cats.

"I stayed with Marsala a little over a year and then I joined Bunny Berigan. His records don't show the enthusiasm of the band. It was a funloving band, with music second. I was on the band six months. We had two one-week location jobs and the rest of the time it was one-nighters. Bunny was one of the great drinkers of our time. We were doing a one-nighter in York, Pennsylvania, and when the curtains opened Berigan came out playing his theme, 'I Can't Get Started.' He walked right off the front of the stage and into the audience and lay there laughing—with a broken foot. But he had the foot set and came back and finished the night. I went with Artie Shaw next. I made my first movie with the Shaw band—'Dancing Co-Ed.' It had Lana Turner and Lee Bowman. And we also did the Old Gold radio show. Bob Benchley was the master of ceremonies. I got to know him very well. He liked me. I used to laugh at the subtle things. He struck me as being a beautiful man. My stay with Shaw ended at the Pennsylvania Hotel here. One night he got fed up and walked off the bandstand and went to Mexico and didn't come back. A conflict grew up as to who would take over the band, so I left and joined Tommy Dorsey. That was in 1939, and I was on the band for most of the next six years. Dorsey was the greatest melodic trombonist in the business, but he was a drag to work for. We never really got along. He was another heavyweight in the juice department. Leaders like to have you play their way, but I knew what I wanted to do and did it. He always resented my talking back to him, but he respected what I played and knew it was good for the band. When I left, he hired Alvin Stoller. Stoller and I hung out together, and I guess Stoller had acquired some of my personality, because he gave T.D. such a rough time that Dorsey finally told him, 'There are three rotten bums in the world—Buddy Rich, you, and Hitler—and I have to have two of them in my band.' "

Rich laughed and rubbed a hand over his face.

"I formed my own big band in 1946. Frank Sinatra backed it with two certified checks, each for twenty-five thousand dollars. I knew what I wanted in music, but it was the beginning of the decline of big bands. People advised me to cut the band down. I had nine brass, five reeds, and four rhythm. But I couldn't see it. I'm a very stubborn guy. I maintained there were enough rooms around the country to supply work. In two years I was flat broke. We'd gone from twenty-five hundred a night to seven hundred. It became a panic band. But it went down swinging and it went down in one piece.

"I worked on and off in the fifties for Norman Granz' Jazz at the Philharmonic with cats like Bird and Sweets and Pres and Oscar Peterson, and most times it was musically satisfying. I organized a small band in 1952 and had it about a year, but I missed that big-band thing. You don't shout with a small band. I got a call from Harry James, but that got to be a bore after a while. I was never really satisfied after having my own band. The perfect big band was always in my mind. Then, in 1959, I learned the hard way that I had to slow down."

The car pulled up in front of the hotel. In his room, Rich took off the towel, which was still drapped around his neck, and his shirt and sports jacket, then put on a bathrobe. He ordered coffee and drummed on a table with his fingers. Then he sat back and put an unlighted cigarette in his mouth.

"I had another small group at the time and we were playing in a bar in New Orleans. I was getting into a solo when my left hand began to go numb. I tried to get the feeling back in my fingers and then I had difficulty breathing. I didn't know what was happening. I had never thought about a heart attack in my life. I played a short solo and then I told John Bunch, who was with me then, that I wasn't feeling so well, and I walked back to the Roosevelt Hotel. I couldn't seem to get air in my lungs. I walked into the lobby and the desk was way down at the end. It looked about a mile away. When I got there, the night clerk said, 'Mr. Rich, somebody better go upstairs with you.' A bellboy came up. I drew a hot tub and sat in it until daylight. Well, I ended up in an oxygen tent. I was there ten days, and then I was in the hospital here for several months. The opinion was that I would never play drums again, and I was told to go home to Miami and stay there for a year. After a month, I'd had it. When you're not doing anything, everything is amplified. I called Joe Glaser and told him I wanted to go back to work, but he wouldn't have any part of it. I'd made several records as a singer, so I took a job here in the Living

Room. I was successful enough, but the audiences kept saying "When will he play? When will he play?' and that forced me back into playing. A couple of things happened since then—once on the thirteenth tee at the Paradise Valley in Vegas. I was playing with B.—Billy Eckstine—and he was driving and I started to wheeze and grabbed my chest. He started running up and down the fairway yelling and shouting like a bunch of Keystone Cops. Then I keeled over. When they got me back to the club-house, all B. said was 'You'll do anything to win a hole.' Beautiful."

The coffee arrived.

"Who knows why? I was told it was twenty years of anxiety, tempera-ment, and unhappiness. And I used to have terrible eating habits—three pounds of spaghetti at four in the morning after work and then go to bed. Put all those things together, and it tears you apart. Well, I'm not a drink-ing man and I'm strong by nature, with good recuperative powers. I use my mental capacity to fight bad things off. I never wanted any part of sympathy. I had only one arm for a while. It was about fifteen years ago and we'd just gotten off the bus in Dayton, Ohio. I never could sleep when we arrived anywhere and so I went and played some handball and I tripped and broke my left arm in three places. It was put in a cast and I had a sling made to match my band uniform, and I played with my right hand and used my foot as a left hand. Solos, too. I never missed a day for the three months the cast stayed on."

Rich refilled his cup and lit a cigarette.

"Of course I'm never supposed to get excited because I have the worst temper in the world. When I lose it, oh baby. Whatever happens to be around—an axe, shoes, a bottle—I'll use it. One night a singer who was splitting the bill with us barged into my dressing room and started curs-ing me up and down and asking me who do I think I am and telling me what a stuck-up son of a bitch I am. Well, it happens this girl bugs me. She's got star eyes about herself. So I just sat there and smiled and looked at her. Joe Morgen, the press agent and an old, old friend, was with me. She started swinging at my head. I can't stand anybody putting their hands on me. I covered my head, and Morgen, who's a little guy, pinned her arms behind her back and said 'Why don't you behave like a lady?' and hustled her out of the dressing room. When the door was shut the top blew off. My mind was red. I picked up a chair and smashed it to pieces against the wall. The only thing that kept me from killing her on the spot was the thought in the back of my head: You do this, idiot, and there goes the band and everything else. It was the only thing that saved that broad. I was a pretty rough guy in the old days, and I made some enemies. Matter of fact, I've had three or four threatening calls since I've been here. One time this voice says, 'O.K., Rich, we're going to break your wrists,' and another time a different one—or maybe the same voice disguised—says, 'You come out of the hotel tonight and we'll break both your legs.' In the old days I would have made a few calls to Brooklyn and gone out and found the bastard. I can't tell you how many beefs I got into in the

Marines, which I enlisted in in 1942. I was 3-A—the sole support of my family—but I was affected by the war propaganda. I became a judo instructor and a combat rifleman, but they never sent me overseas. I was the only Jew in my platoon, and I wasn't used to hearing stuff about the Jews don't know how to fight, the Jews don't do anything but make money, the Jews started the war, and so forth. After the first dozen beefs, I didn't hear any more talk like that."

Rich looked at his watch. It was six-thirty. "Hey, time to get dressed. I like to get to the club around eight-thirty. I'll grab a bite at Mercurio's, which is just around the corner, and then walk over."

Ten minutes later, Rich came out of his bathroom. He looked brand-new. He had on a double-breasted navy silk-and-mohair suit with a hip-length jacket, a blue-and-white striped shirt with a high collar, and a blue tie. He picked up a gray tweed overcoat and slapped all his pockets.

The elevator was empty except for a tall heavyset man with a crew cut. Rich stared at him, leaned over, started to say something, and stopped. In the lobby, he said, "You know who *that* was? That was Johnny Unitas, man."

The headwaiter at Mercurio's greeted Rich effusively. Rich ordered a vodka gimlet, veal piccata, and a large side dish of spaghetti with meat sauce.

"Maybe my technique is greased elbows, and maybe it's because the Man Upstairs talked to my hands and said 'Be fast' and they were. I've never had a lesson in my life and I never practice. I stay away from drums during my daytime adventures. You won't find a pair of sticks or a practice pad or anything connected with drumming in my house or my hotel room. That way each night is an expectation, a new experience for me. All these guys get from practicing is tired wrists. If you have something to play, you hear it in your heart and mind, and then you go and try it out in front of an audience. I read a little drum music, but an arranger can't write for a drummer. Only the drummer knows where the fills and the accents go. When we get a new arrangement, I don't play it. I sit out front and listen. Then I play it once and that's it. I don't see anything in my mind when I solo. I'm trying not to play clichés. I tell myself, 'Make sure you don't play anything you played last night.' Playing a drum solo is like telling a story. It has a beginning, a middle, and a bitch of a punch line. I try and play a drum solo constructed along a line. What comes out is what I feel. I'm telling you about my wife, my daughter, what nice people I was with before I got on the stand. When Johnny Carson comes in I try and play in that light, funny way he has. When Basie comes in, I play with love. Some nights people tell me I've played vicious, and they're right. Maybe I've been thinking about thirty years of one-nighters or maybe about what a drag it was in the Marines. But the next night I'll come to where I'm playing and say, 'Sorry, little drums, I'll be tender tonight.' Drums can be as musical as Heifetz. You don't pick up sticks as if they were hammers. It's a matter of using your hands to apply pressure. You *apply* the power, the beauty. When I think that I can't play the way I want to play, I'll hang up my sticks. That'll be it. There'd be nothing more horrible than to hear some guy say, 'Poor Buddy Rich, he doesn't have it anymore. ' "

Rich took a forkful of spaghetti.

"I'm told I'm not humble, but who is? I remember being interviewed by a college kid once, and he said 'Mr. Rich, who is the greatest drummer in the world?' and I said 'I am.' He laughed and said, 'No, really, Mr. Rich, who do you consider the greatest drummer alive?' I said 'Me. It's a fact.' He couldn't get over it. But why go through that humble bit? Look at Ted Williams—straight ahead, no tipping of his cap when he belted one out of the park. He knew the name of the game: Do your job. That's all I do. I play my drums."

First And Last

Child prodigies do not grow up easily. Sometimes, burdened by their gifts, they become quirky and eccentric, and retire from the world. Sometimes a mysterious stasis sets in, and they sink into melancholy. Sometimes they suffer temporary reversals, usually in midlife, then revive and carry on brilliantly. That is what happened to the virtuoso drummer Louis Bellson. He began playing at three, owned a set of drums at nine, taught percussion at thirteen, joined the musicians' union at fourteen, and, at seventeen, won a nationwide drum contest sponsored by Gene Krupa. During the next dozen years or so, he went on to work with the big bands of Benny Goodman, Tommy Dorsey, Harry James, and Duke Ellington. Then two things happened: he married the singer Pearl Bailey* and became the drummer in her accompanying big band; and he slipped into the ever-expanding shadow cast by Buddy Rich, who is seven years his senior. Bailey and Rich continued to thrive, while Bellson, a gentle, self-effacing man, remained more or less in the wings, despite excellent recordings made in his own name and occasional, widely praised solo appearances (his stint as the drummer in Duke Ellington's first Sacred Concert, given twice in 1965). In the seventies, Pearl Bailey's career began to slow (she went to college and was invited to join the United States Mission to the United Nations), and Bellson came out more frequently as the leader of big and small bands of his own, and as a side-man with all-star groups (the two Swing Reunion concerts, given in 1985 on successive nights at Town Hall, with Benny Carter, Red Norvo, Teddy Wilson, and George Duvivier). In 1987, Buddy Rich died suddenly, and

*Pearl Bailey died in 1990, not long after this chapter was written.

Bellson, the last of the great swing drummers, moved out permanently from the shadows.

The first—and some think still the greatest—swing drummer was Chick Webb. A hunchback, under five feet in height, Webb died in 1939, at the age of thirty. He was an exhilarating, almost overweening performer, who played with a power and precision and depth of timbre that completely belied his handicap. Buddy Rich learned from him (Webb patterns could be heard in Rich's last recorded solos), and remembered seeing him at the Savoy Ballroom in Harlem, where Webb was in residence with his marvellously ungainly big band during most of the thirties. Webb took the ricky-tick quality out of jazz drumming, and he was the first to tune his drums in such a way that each had a rich sound. He was the first expert cymbal player, pitching his cymbals to match the general tenor of his various band sections, and using them to wash and thicken his soloists. His own solos, rarely longer than twelve bars, were highly concentrated. He kept to his snare drum, issuing numbing staccato and double-time figures and filling the air with explosive rimshots. The jazz chronicler Helen Oakley Dance knew Webb well, and she has said of him, "Chick couldn't read music, but after the band had run down a new arrangement he would sing every part. If someone hit a wrong note on the stand, he'd know who it was, and he'd call him on it. If he wasn't getting what he wanted from the band, he'd get angry, and they'd whisper, 'Look out, that hump is breathing!' He had tuberculosis of the spine. Like most black people at the time, he wouldn't go to a hospital because he was convinced they'd let him die there. Sometimes he'd come off the stand and faint, he was in such pain. Or he'd send in a sub like Kaiser Marshall. But he was a fighter. There was such fire in his playing. There was such fire in his drums. Before he started a set, he'd hit his big bass drum twice: Boom! Boom! And everybody in the audience would cheer." Every drummer studied Webb, but none achieved the lift and momentum he gave a big band, with the exception of Sidney Catlett, who carried Webb's flag forward after Webb's death. You can still hear Webb today, in the work of the drummers Panama Francis and Gus Johnson— and, in a subtle, oblique fashion, in Louis Bellson.

Bellson is medium-sized and has the cheerful, even-featured handsomeness that mothers and aunts relish and pretty women are at ease with. His feet are small and his hands are like steel. When he picks up a pair of wire brushes and plays, the effect is of great strength effortlessly used. He smiles a lot, and he talks rapidly, with little hitches that are like snare-drum offbeats. He is an emotional man, in a laughing, guarded way. Here is what he recently wrote about two of his idols, Sid Catlett and Jo Jones (the mixed metaphors compound the emotion in his words): "Big Sid and Papa Jo were the Leonardo and Michelangelo of this century. Their drum sets were perfect canvases and their strokes equalled the flight of huge birds in the sky. They left us beautiful paintings and a rich heritage, *never to be forgotten*."

Bellson is generally in New York when Pearl Bailey is at the U.N., and on one of those visits he spoke about his life and his career: "I was born July 6, 1924, in Rock Falls, Illinois, but my family moved to Moline when I was eleven or twelve. Moline is about 160 miles west of Chicago, over near the Iowa line. I was christened Luigi Paulino Alfredo Francesco Antonio Balassone. The middle names were for uncles and godfathers. My father, who was in the music business, changed the name to Bellson because it was easier to write and pronounce. There were four girls and four boys, all of them still living. The girls came first—Edie, Dee Dee, Josephine, and Mary. Two live in Las Vegas and one in Moline and one in Kewanee, Illinois. I'm the second of the boys, so it was Frank, me, Anthony, and Henry. Tony and Hank are drummers. Tony lives in Chandler, Arizona, and Hank tests drumheads for the Remo drum factory in Los Angeles. My father was born Luigi Balassone, in Naples. He'd been married to my mother's sister. When she died, he married my mother. She was born Carmen Bartelucci, in Rome. She died at the age of ninety-two, a year ago. She was about five feet tall, and, unlike a lot of short Italian women, she kept her weight down. She did all the cleaning and cooking, and she made everything we ate. She was a firebrand. She loved music and dancing. My father died in 1960, at the age of sixty-eight. He was huge—six feet two and two hundred and fifty pounds. He was quiet and peaceful and had great patience. He read the papers, he was up on politics. He made his own wine. We always had wine at meals, and I used to take some to school in a Coke bottle. The teachers never found out. My dad had a store, the Bellson Music Company. He built the showcases and painted the signs—things he had learned in Italy. He told me that he had an Italian professor who said he had to learn everything there was about music. And he did. He played every instrument except the accordion— his fingers were too big. He taught us the brass instruments and the saxophones and the strings. He taught us the great arias, and he made us aware of everyone from Bach to Ravel. He loved jazz, too. He let us in on everything, and I thank him for that. We lived in an apartment in Rock Falls and a house in Moline with two stories and a basement. After school, we went right to the store. We'd clean windows and put up Christmas decorations and sell records and sheet music. When we were around thirteen, we'd help with the music lessons. I became the percussion instructor.

"There was music every night in the store. Monday, there was a fifteen-piece accordion band. Tuesday, a woodwind ensemble with flutes, clarinets, oboes, and all the saxophones. There was a brass ensemble on Wednesday, and a concert band on Thursday. Friday, a string orchestra. We practiced in the store on weekends, when we had access to the studios. I started playing when I was three. I had a parade drum with gut snares. I studied with Roy Knapp for two years, starting at fifteen. I played at a local tavern called the Rendezvous. It had a piano player named Speck Red and a drummer named Percy Walker. They let me sit

in on Tuesday nights. That was where I learned some of the basics of jazz
drumming.

"I also sat in with bands that were passing through. One was Ted Fio
Rito, the Fio Rito who wrote 'When Lights Are Low' and 'I Never Knew.'
He wanted to hire me, but I had three months of high school left. So he
said if I was interested to join him at the Florentine Gardens in
Hollywood after I graduated, and I did. The Mills Brothers were the main
attraction there, and I stayed three months. One night, Freddy Goodman,
Benny's brother, told me Benny was looking for a drummer, and would I
like to audition? I went to the Paramount Studio, where Benny was making a movie, and the costume people put me in a tuxedo, and I played a
quartet number with Benny in the movie. All he said after was that the
band was leaving for New York that Thursday and to be at the station. Of
course, it helped that before I joined Fio Rito I had won a Gene Krupa
drum contest. It was nationwide, and it got a lot of publicity. I worked
with Benny at the New Yorker Hotel. In New York, I got to hear and
know drummers like Big Sid Catlett and Davy Tough and Jo Jones, people I'd only heard on records. How great it would have been if every
aspiring drummer could have listened to Sid play and talk. I played loud
then—bang! crash! real gung ho—and he told me never to hit my cymbals too hard. 'Let them breathe,' he said. He also said, 'Your drums are
your own orchestra. Your snare is the soprano, the small tomtom is the
alto, the big tomtom is the tenor, and the bass drum is the bass.' When Sid
took a solo, it was as if he was weaving, and when he finished, there it
was, with its colors and flowers and patterns—a beautiful carpet. Sid and
Jo Jones could do time steps and the shim-sham-shimmy. I took some tap
dancing. You had to do these things. That kind of dancing worked right
into your drumming. I still think like a tap dancer when I play.

"Uncle Sam got me in 1942. I was stationed in Washington, D.C., at the
Walter Reed Annex, in Silver Spring, Maryland. I was part of a full
orchestra, and out of it came a dance band and chamber groups. A lot of
the musicians had been at the Eastman School of Music. We played for
dances at night, we played concerts almost every day, we played in the
hospitals. When I got out, in 1945, I went back with Ted Fio Rito for several months, then rejoined Benny Goodman for a year. I started using two
bass drums instead of one when I was with Fio Rito the second time. I'd
had the idea in high school. I drew a picture of the set I had in mind—two
bass drums, measuring twenty by twenty inches, five small tomtoms
stretched across them, and two floor toms on the side. I took the drawing
to the Slingerland drum people in 1940, but they weren't interested, and
it wasn't until 1946 that the first set was built—by Gretsch. I joined
Tommy Dorsey in 1947 at the Casino Garden ballroom in Santa Monica,
and when Tommy saw the two bass drums the wheels started going. He
had a great show sense. He could look out at an audience and know
immediately what to play for it—tempo, material, mood. He told me, 'I
want the people out front to realize you're using two bass drums.' I sug-

gested we put the drums on a revolving platform. We had a motor built, and when we opened at the Strand Theatre in New York there I was on this platform in front of the band. Tommy controlled it. When I soloed, he'd stop me when my back was to the audience, and the lights would go out. I had a phosphorescent patch on each drumstick and a phosphorescent headband. All the audience saw was these lights leaping around. It was a great theatrical gimmick. You *worked* with Tommy. Once, we did six straight months of one-nighters, without a single night off. Some days, we'd be on the bus for five hundred miles.

"I was with Dorsey three years, and then I went with Harry James. Juan Tizol, the trombonist who had been with Duke Ellington, was in the band, and so was Willie Smith, the Lunceford alto saxophonist. I was staying in Tizol's house in Los Angeles, and one day he said, 'Would you like to join Duke Ellington?' Well. We approached Harry, and he said, 'Go,' and we joined Duke. It was 1951. I came to think of Duke as my second father. He paid the same attention to everyone, whether he was a newspaper boy or Toscanini. He was no disciplinarian. Sometimes Paul Gonsalves and Ray Nance would go on a binge for four or five days. He never said a word when they showed up. He'd get back at them that night by making them stand out there—and they probably not feeling too good—and take chorus after chorus, telling the audience how much they loved to play for them. He told me, 'If I had to deal with temperaments, I'd be under the ground.' I was interested in arranging. I had studied it as a kid, and I had written arrangements for Harry James and Tommy Dorsey. Tizol persuaded me to bring them in—'Skin Deep' and 'The Hawk Talks'—and Duke recorded them. Anyway, I asked Billy Strayhorn how he had voiced a certain piece of his, and he hemmed and hawed and changed the subject. I was embarrassed at bothering him, and I apologized. But later Duke sat me down beside him at the piano and showed me how he would give this note to Johnny Hodges and this one to Gonsalves, how he'd put Jimmy Hamilton's clarinet on top and Harry Carney's baritone in the middle and Gonsalves' tenor on the bottom. It was that kind of voicing that made his saxophone section sound like it had ten men in it. Duke wrote all the time. Once, on a plane trip, he turned around and asked me if I had any manuscript paper, and I said, 'Sorry, it's packed.' He took off his coat and drew five lines on one sleeve and wrote out the notes he had in his head. Tizol scored the melody when we got to the gig, and we played it that night. Duke and Strayhorn were full of superstitions. Nobody was supposed to wear anything with yellow in it. Nobody was supposed to button a shirt all the way down the front. Nobody was supposed to whistle in the dressing room.

"Ellington's arrangements never had drum parts. But not once did he say, 'This is how Sonny Greer did it.' He said, 'Do it your own way.' He made you create. He used to call me in for special events in later years. In 1965, I played his 'Golden Broom and the Green Apple' with the New York Philharmonic. There I was with twenty minutes of music to play and a hundred musicians sitting behind me, and all he had told me was that the first part was in waltz time. The same year, he asked me to sit in at the Grace Cathedral in San Francisco for his first Sacred Concert. He said, 'I want you to play a drum solo in church. You are the thunder and lightning.' That's what I thought about when I soloed at the end of 'David Danced Before the Lord,' while the band played and a choir chanted and all hell broke loose. Some nights, the band swung so hard I couldn't believe it. Some nights, it was on fire. Duke introduced me to everything I hadn't known before about music—and life."

Bellson uses a huge set of drums. It includes two twenty-four-inch bass drums and five tomtoms, ranging from a six-inch concert tomtom to two sixteen-by-sixteen-inch floor tomtoms. He also uses two roto-toms (shallow, dishlike drums with just one skin) and a five-and-a-half-inch snare drum. His drums are made by Remo. He generally has five Zildjian cymbals. There are two large ride cymbals, two slightly smaller crash cymbals, and a twenty-two-inch Chinese cymbal. His high hat has fourteen-inch cymbals, with an extra-heavy cymbal on the bottom. When his whole set is assembled, its gold and silver colors gleam and wink and shimmer, and it looks, before he sits down and anchors it, as if it might slowly and soundlessly ascend.

Bellson's accompanying is casual and annealing. It forms a light, steady flow of sounds, made up of suggestive but unobtrusive cymbal strokes and endless accents, carried out on his snare, his tomtoms, and his bass drums. He seems to hear every note that is played around him and to have the proper complement for it. He never overpowers, he never underplays. His solos are logical extensions of his accompanying. They are louder, they can be melodramatic, but they have the same grace and motion. He moves constantly from one part of his set to another, not in the speed-of-light way of Buddy Rich, but in the legato, melodic manner of Jo Jones and Sid Catlett. The snare drum is the center of his solos, and he will use staccato strokes, double-time strokes, and quick rolls, all varied by side strokes to his tomtoms and his cymbals. Fast tempos bring out the Lear in him. He goes along for a while, doing his roundelays, spilling hundreds of rimshots, and gradually preparing his listeners for the storm to come. This arrives when he begins what amounts to a single-stroke roll with his feet on his two bass drums. Soon it is a solid, thunderous wall of sound, decorated by snare and tomtom explosions and occasional cymbal crashes. A vein stands out on his forehead, his face reddens, and his feet move faster than feet were ever supposed to move. When the wall of sound becomes unbearable, he abruptly stops, flickers around his set in a Catlett, winding-down manner, and it is over. These theatrics jelly the audience and probably make Bellson's ankles tremble, but the next number begins, and he leads the way lightly, a smile on his face, his Atlas strength intact.

When Pearl Bailey is in New York, she is completely absorbed by her work at the United Nations. But this is what she said one evening about her husband: "We've been married thirty-seven years. We live together and we work together, but we haven't hit each other yet. We are very different. I can stay indoors six weeks and never go out. I have my needlepoint, my books, my cooking. Louis has to move. He loves that telephone: 'Listen, man. I'll take the gig.' 'Listen, man. I'll call you back.' He's an introvert and I'm an extrovert. I do the cooking, he does the dishes. He's neat as a pin. We cross a busy street and he sees a cigarette butt, he picks it up. If one of my pots gets a little dark on the bottom, he goes out and buys a new one. Many people beat a drum; Louis plays it. I see Louis as an awesome artist. If that man looked at me the way he looks at his drums, I'd be delighted. I love my husband. I don't tell him every day. The deed of love is stronger than words. He is loyal. He's family to the hilt. I believe there's nothing he wouldn't do for me. There is a lot of loving among musicians, too. They have a oneness. They hug when they meet, and they hug when they part. If music is their God, they are the holiest of men. He sings in his sleep—out of tune. He doesn't read much, so I'll lay a book I think he'll like by his side of the bed. It may take a while, but he gets into it and he'll read it. I first met Louis outside the Howard Theatre in Washington, D.C. Juan Tizol had told me about him: 'You should meet this wonderful young man. He doesn't go out. He has no girlfriend.' Tizol came out of the theatre with a young man. 'Hi. I'm Louis.' 'Hi. I'm Pearl.' Two weeks later, we were married in London. We have two adopted children. Deedee is twenty-nine, and Tony is thirty-five. I lay the parables on them, Louis soothes them."

Louis on Pearl: "She's the most honest person I've ever met. She's got tremendous ESP. She scares me the way she psyches people out, the way that she can tell you that this person she's just met will be a friend and that this one is disturbed—the way she gets to the crux of a person. Her natural ability overwhelms me. She has perfect pitch. She can start a song cold without a note. She's a great ad-libber. She has a wonderful theatre sense. She's the same onstage as she is offstage. When our kids were growing up, she was the disciplinarian and I was the softie. She took them to the circus and let them know about museums. She has given them whatever values they have. She's a joy to be with. I haven't figured her out, and I never intend to. Sometimes it's tough to go out shopping or to a restaurant. People won't give her any peace. But she doesn't sign autographs. She just says, 'Give me your name and address, and I'll send you a picture.' I come home with my pockets full of names."

Bellson resumed talking about his career: "Pearl and I started going on the road after I left the Duke, in 1953. She had a band with people like George Duvivier on bass, Taft Jordan, Joe Wilder, and Dick Vance on trumpets, Butter Jackson and Jimmy Cleveland on trombones, and Hilton Jefferson and Selden Powell on reeds. We had tap dancers, including Honi Coles and Cholly Atkins and her brother Bill Bailey. We had a choir of twelve or fifteen voices. Don Redman was her arranger and conductor.

I think there were sixty people in the package. We played the Apollo Theatre in Harlem, the Howard in Washington, the Earl in Philadelphia. We did Vegas and the Coconut Grove in Los Angeles. It was costly, but it didn't sink. We toured for a long time. Then she gave it up and took the lead in an all-black *Hello Dolly* on Broadway. Walter Winchell counted seven standing ovations one night. She did the show two years, and we went back on the road. When we were home, we lived in Northridge, California, and before that we had a place in Apple Valley, in the desert, a hundred miles from L.A. Seven years ago, we left Northridge and moved to Lake Havasu City, in Arizona. It has nineteen thousand people and London Bridge. We have a little house on the third tee of a golf course. We were on the road constantly until the late seventies. Now Pearl likes to do only theatres and concerts. She's not happy about hotels anymore. Of course, she's still part of the U.S. Mission to the U.N., and that takes several months of the year. When I'm not working with Pearl, I take my big band or a small group out for short gigs. There don't seem to be any more of the two-, three-, or four-week gigs we used to have. It's just a weekend or five days in and out. I have a pool of musicians on the East Coast I call on and a pool on the West Coast. And I still do drum clinics in schools and colleges. I like the kids to know what came before them, who the great masters were, and what they sounded like.

"Pearl and I got racist letters when we were first married, some of them real raunchy. We had trouble in restaurants and hotels, and the like. But we didn't wait around with chips on our shoulders. We figured we were two human beings in the entertainment field. The N.A.A.C.P. asked us to join in the fifties— for five hundred dollars. Pearl isn't a joiner. Her reply was 'Why should I pay all that money to be part of the world that God has already put me in?'"

Pres

Very little about the tenor saxophonist Lester Young was unoriginal. He had protruding, heavy-lidded eyes, a square, slightly Oriental face, a tiny mustache, and a snaggletoothed smile. His walk was light and pigeon-toed, and his voice was soft. He was something of a dandy. He wore suits, knit ties, and collar pins. He wore ankle-length coats, and pork-pie hats— on the back of his head when he was young, and pulled down low and evenly when he was older. He kept to himself, often speaking only when spoken to. When he played, he held his saxophone in front of him at a forty-five-degree angle, like a canoeist about to plunge his paddle into the water. He had an airy, lissome tone and an elusive, lyrical way of phrasing that had never been heard before. Other saxophonists followed

Coleman Hawkins, but Young's models were two white musicians: the C-melody saxophonist Frank Trumbauer and the alto saxophonist Jimmy Dorsey—neither of them a first-rate jazz player. When Young died, in 1959, he had become the model for countless saxophonists, white and black. He was a gentle, kind man who never disparaged anyone. He spoke a coded language, about which the pianist Jimmy Rowles has said, "You had to break that code to understand him. It was like memorizing a dictionary, and I think it took me about three months." Much of Young's language has vanished, but here is a sampling: "Bing and Bob" were the police. A "hat" was a woman, and a "homburg" and a "Mexican hat" were types of women. An attractive young girl was a "poundcake." A "gray boy" was a white man, and Young himself, who was light-skinned, was an "oxford gray." "I've got bulging eyes" for this or that meant he approved of something, and "Catalina eyes" and "Watts eyes" expressed high admiration. "Left people" were the fingers of a pianist's left hand. "I feel a draft" meant he sensed a bigot nearby. "Have another helping," said to a colleague on the bandstand, meant "Take another chorus," and "one long" or "two long" meant one chorus or two choruses. People "whispering on" or "buzzing on" him were talking behind his back. Getting his "little claps" meant being applauded. A "zoomer" was a sponger, and a "needle dancer" was a heroin addict. "To be bruised" was to fail. A "tribe" was a band, and a "molly trolley" was a rehearsal. "Can Madam burn?" meant "Can your wife cook?" "Those people will be here in December" meant that his second child was due in December. (He drifted in and out of three marriages, and had two children.) "Startled doe, two o'clock" meant that a pretty girl was in the right side of the audience.

Eccentrics flourish in crowded, ordered places, and Young spent his life on buses and trains, in hotel rooms and dressing rooms, in automobiles and on bandstands. He was born in Woodville, Mississippi, in 1909, and his family moved almost immediately to Algiers, just across the river from New Orleans. When he was ten, his father and mother separated, and his father took him and his brother Lee and his sister Irma to Memphis and then to Minneapolis. Young's father, who could play any instrument, had organized a family band, which worked in tent shows in the Midwest and Southwest. Young joined the band as a drummer, and then switched to alto saxophone. An early photograph shows him holding his saxophone in much the same vaudeville way he later held it. Young once said that he was slow to learn to read music: "Then one day my father goes to each one in the band and asked them to play their part and I knew that was my ass, because he knew goddam well that I couldn't read. Well, my little heart was broken, you know; I went in crying and I was thinking, I'll come back and catch them, if that's the way they want it. So I went away all by myself and learned the music." Young quit the family band when he was eighteen and joined Art Bronson's Bostonians. During the next six or seven years, he worked briefly in the family band again, and at the Nest Club, in Minneapolis, for Frank Hines and Eddie Barefield. He also worked with the Original Blue Devils and with Bennie Moten, Clarence Love, King Oliver, and, in 1934, Count Basie's first band. In an interview with Nat Hentoff, Young recalled playing with Oliver, who was well into his fifties and at the end of his career:

> After the Bostonians, I played with King Oliver. He had a very nice band and I worked regularly with him for one or two years, around Kansas and Missouri mostly. He had three brass, three reeds, and four rhythm. He was playing well. He was old then and didn't play all night, but his tone was full when he played. He was the star of the show and played one or two songs each set. The blues? He could play some nice blues. He was a very nice fellow, a gay old fellow. He was crazy about all the boys, and it wasn't a drag playing for him at all.

Soon after going with Basie, Young was asked to replace Coleman Hawkins in Fletcher Henderson's band, and, reluctantly, he went. It was the first of several experiences in his life that he never got over. Hawkins had spent ten years with Henderson, and his oceanic tone and heavy chordal improvisations were the heart of the band. Jazz musicians are usually alert, generous listeners, but Young's alto-like tone (he had shifted to tenor saxophone not long before) and floating, horizontal solos sounded heretical to Henderson's men. They began buzzing on him, and Henderson's wife forced him to listen to Hawkins recordings, in the hope he'd learn to play that way. Young lasted three or four months and went to Kansas City, first asking Henderson for a letter saying that he had not been fired. Two years later, he rejoined Basie, and his career began. The pianist John Lewis knew Young then: "When I was still very young in Alburquerque, I remember hearing about the Young family settling there. They had a band and had come in with a tent show and been stranded. There was a very good local jazz band, called St. Cecilia's, that Lester played in. He also competed with an excellent Spanish tenor player and house-painter named Cherry. I barely remember Lester's playing. He had a fine, thin tone. Then the family moved to Minneapolis, and I didn't see him until around 1934, when he came through on his way to the West Coast to get an alto player for Count Basie named Caughey Roberts. Lester sounded then the way he does on his first recordings, made in 1936. We had a lot of brass beds in that part of the country, and Lester used to hang his tenor saxophone on the foot of his bed so that he could reach it during the night if an idea came to him that he wanted to sound out."

Young's first recordings were made with a small group from Basie's band. The melodic flow suggests Trumbauer and perhaps Dorsey, and an ascending gliss, an upward swoop, that Young used for the next fifteen years suggests Bix Biederbecke. Young had a deep feeling for the blues, and King Oliver's blues must have become a part of him. He had a pale tone, a minimal vibrato, a sense of silence, long-breathed phrasing, and an elastic rhythmic ease. Until his arrival, most soloists tended to pedal up and down on the beat, their phrases short and and perpendicular, their rhythms broken and choppy. Young smoothed out this bouncing attack. He used long phrases and legato rhythms (in the manner of the trumpeter Red Allen, who was in Henderson's band with him), and he often chose notes outside the chords—"odd" notes that italicized his solos. He used silence for emphasis. Young "had a very spacey sound at the end of '33," the bassist Gene Ramey recalls. "He would play a phrase and maybe lay out three beats before he'd come in with another phrase." Coleman Hawkins' solos buttonhole you; Young's seem to turn away. His improvisations move with such logic and smoothness they lull the ear. He was an adept embellisher and a complete improviser. He could make songs like "Willow Weep for Me" and "The Man I Love" unrecognizable. He kept the original melodies in his head, but what came out was his dreams about them. His solos were fantasies—lyrical, soft, liquid—on the tunes he was playing, and probably on his own life as well. The humming quality of his solos was deceptive, for they were made up of quick runs, sudden held notes that slowed the beat, daring shifts in rhythmic emphasis, continuous motion, and often lovely melodies. His slow work was gentle and lullaby-like, and as his tempos rose his tone became rougher. Young was also a singular clarinettist. In the late thirties, he used a metal clarinet (eventually it was stolen, and he simply gave up the instrument), and he got a plaintive, silvery sound.

Young bloomed with Basie. He recorded countless classic solos with the band, giving it a rare lightness and subtlety, and he made his beautiful records accompanying Billie Holiday—their sounds a single voice split in two. Late in 1940, Young decided to go out on his own, as Coleman Hawkins had done years before. He had a small group on Fifty-second Street for a brief time, and went West and put a band together with his brother Lee. The singer Sylvia Syms hung around Young on Fifty-second Street as a teen-ager: "Lester was very light, and he had wonderful hair. He never used that pomade so popular in the forties and fifties. He was a beautiful dresser, and his accent was his porkpie hat worn on the back of his head. He used cologne, and he always smelled divine. Once, I complained to him about audiences who talked and never listened, and he said, 'Lady Syms, if there is one guy in the whole house who is listening and maybe he's in the *bathroom*—you've got an audience.' His conversation, with all its made-up phrases, was hard to follow, but his playing never was. He phrased words in his playing. He has had a great influence on my singing, and through the years a lot of singers have picked up on him."

Jimmy Rowles worked with Young when he went West: "I don't know when Billie Holiday nicknamed him Pres—for 'the President'—but when I first knew him the band called him Uncle Bubba. Of all the people I've met in this business, Lester was unique. He was alone. He was quiet. He was unfailingly polite. He almost never got mad. If he was upset, he'd take a small whisk broom he kept in his top jacket pocket and sweep off his left shoulder. The only way to get to know him was to work with him. Otherwise, he'd just sit there playing cards or sipping, and if he did say something it stopped the traffic. I never saw him out of a suit, and he particularly liked double-breasted pinstripes. He also wore tab collars, small trouser cuffs, pointed shoes, and Cuban heels. In 1941, the older guard among musicians still didn't recognize his worth. They didn't think of him as an equal. He was *there*, but he was still someone new. And here's an odd thing. His father held a saxophone upside down when he played it, in a kind of vaudeville way, so maybe Lester picked up his way of holding his horn from that. Whichever, the more he warmed up during work, the higher his horn got, until it was actually horizontal."

The Young brothers played Café Society Downtown in 1942, and, after stints with Dizzy Gillespie and the tenor saxophonist Al Sears, Young rejoined Count Basie. He was drafted in 1944, and it was the second experience in his life that he never got over. There are conflicting versions of what happened, but what matters is that he collided head on with reality for the first time, and it felled him. He spent about fifteen months in the Army, mainly in a detention barracks, for possession of marijuana and barbiturates and for being an ingenuous black man in the wrong place at the wrong time. He was discharged dishonorably, and from then on his playing and his personal life slowly roughened and worsened. John Lewis worked for Young in 1951: "Jo Jones was generally on drums and Joe Shulman on bass, and either Tony Fruscella or Jesse Drakes on trumpet. We worked at places like Bop City, in New York, and we travelled to Chicago. He would play the same songs in each set on a given night, but he would often repeat the sequence the following week this way: if he had played 'Sometimes I'm Happy' on Tuesday of the preceding week, he would open 'Sometimes I'm Happy' this Tuesday with a variation on the solo he had played on the tune the week before; then he would play variations on the variations the week after, so that his playing formed a kind of gigantic organic whole. While I was with him, I never heard any of the coarseness that people have said began creeping into his playing. I did notice a change in him in his last few years. There was nothing obvious or offensive about it. Just an air of depression about him.

"He was a living, walking poet. He was so quiet that when he talked each sentence came out like a little explosion. I don't think he consciously invented his special language. It was part of a way of talking I heard in Albuquerque from my older cousins, and there were variations of it in Oklahoma City and Kansas City and Chicago in the late twenties and early thirties. These people also dressed well, as Lester did—the porkpie hats and all. So his speech and dress were natural things he picked up. They weren't a disguise—a way of hiding. They were a way to be hip— to express an awareness of everything swinging that was going on. Of course, he never wasted this hipness on duddish people, nor did he waste good playing on bad musicians. If Lester was wronged, the wound never healed. Once, at Bop City, he mentioned how people had always bugged him about the supposed thinness of his tone. We were in his dressing room, and he picked up his tenor and played a solo using this great big butter sound. Not a Coleman Hawkins sound but a thick, smooth, concentrated sound. It was as beautiful as anything I've ever heard."

Young spent much of the rest of his life with Norman Granz's Jazz at the Philharmonic troupe. He had become an alcoholic, and his playing was ghostly and uncertain. He still wore suits and a porkpie hat, but he sat down a lot, and when he appeared on "The Sound of Jazz," in 1957, he was remote and spaced out. He refused to read his parts for the two big-band numbers. (Ben Webster, who had been taught by Young's father, replaced him.) When he took a chorus during Billie Holiday's blues "Fine and Mellow," his tone was intact but the solo limped by. The loving, smiling expression on Billie Holiday's face may have indicated that she was listening not to the Lester beside her but to the Lester long stored away in her head. The tenor saxophonist Buddy Tate drove down with Young from the Newport Jazz Festival the next year: "I first met Lester when he was in Sherman, Texas, playing alto. A little later, I replaced him in the first Basie band when he went to join Fletcher Henderson. He didn't drink then, and he didn't inhale his cigarettes. He was so refined, so sensitive. I was with him in the second Basie band in 1939 and 1940, and he had a little bell he kept on the stand beside him. When someone goofed, he rang it. After the 1958 Newport Festival, I drove back with him to New York, and he was really down. He was unhappy about money, and said he wasn't great. When I told him how great he was, he said, 'If I'm so great, Lady Tate, how come all the other tenor players, the ones who sound like me, are making all the money?' "

The arranger Gil Evans knew Young on the Coast in the forties and in New York at the end of his life: "Solitary people like Lester Young are apt to wear blinders. He concentrated on things from his past that he should have long since set aside as a good or bad essence. The last year of his life, when he had moved into the Alvin Hotel, he brought up the fact that his father had been displeased with him when he was a teen-ager because he had been lazy about learning to read music. But maybe his bringing that up at so late a date was only a vehicle for some other, present anger that he was inarticulate about. Sometimes that inarticulateness made him cry. A long time before, when I happened to be in California, Jimmy Rowles and I went to see Pres, who was living in a three-story house that his father owned. We walked in on a family fight, and Pres was weeping. He asked us to get him out of there, to help move him to his mother's bungalow in West Los Angeles. We had a coupe I'd borrowed, so we did— lock, stock, and barrel. Those tears were never far away. I was with him in the fifties in a restaurant near Fifty-second Street when a man in a fez and robe came in. This man started talking about Jesus Christ, and he called him a prophet. Well, Pres thought he had said something about Jesus and 'profit.' He got up and went out, and when I got to him he was crying. I had to explain what the man had said. I don't know where he got such strong feelings about Jesus. Maybe from going to church when he was young, or maybe it was just his sense of injustice. He couldn't stand injustice of any kind. He had a great big room at the Alvin, and when I'd go up to see him I'd find full plates of food everywhere. They'd been brought by friends, but he wouldn't eat. He just drank wine. One of the reasons his drinking got so out of hand was his teeth. They were in terrible shape, and he was in constant pain. But he was still fussy about things like his hair. He had grown it long at the back, and finally he let my wife, who was a good barber, cut it. At every snip, he'd say, 'Let me see it. Let me see it,' before the hair landed on the floor. It was amazing— a man more or less consciously killing himself, and he was still particular about his hair."

The tenor saxophonist Zoot Sims, who listened hard to Young in the forties, also saw some of this harmless narcissism: "We roomed together on a Birdland tour in 1957, and one day when he was changing and had stripped to his shorts, which were red, he lifted his arms and slowly turned around and said, 'Not bad for an old guy.' And he was right. He had a good body—and a good mind. Lester was a very intelligent man."

Young died at the Alvin Hotel the day after he returned from a gig in Paris. He had given François Postif a long and bitter interview while he was in France, and, perhaps wittingly, he included his epitaph in it: "They want everybody who's a Negro to be an Uncle Tom, or Uncle Remus, or Uncle Sam, and I can't make it. It's the same all over: you fight for your life—until death do you part, and then you got it made."

Bird

Charlie Parker died at the age of thirty-four, in 1955, and he was one of the wonders of twentieth-century music. Like his all but interchangeable spiritual brother, Dylan Thomas, who died a year earlier, Parker was labyrinthine. He was a tragic figure who helplessly consumed himself, and at the same time he was a demon who presided over the wreckage of his life. He was an original and fertile musician who had reached the edge of self-parody. He was an irresistibly attractive man who bit almost every hand that fed him. He lived outside the pale of his own times, yet he indirectly presaged, in his drives and fierce independence, the coming of Malcolm X and Eldridge Cleaver. And he was, albeit succored by a slavish cult, largely unknown during his life.

Parker was born in a Kansas City suburb to a knockabout vaudevillian,

Charles Parker, and a local eighteen-year-old, Addie Boyley (or Bayley). When he was eight or nine, his parents moved to Kansas City proper, and when he was eleven his father, who had become a Pullman chef, disappeared almost completely from his life. Grammar school went well, but after he had spent two years in high school as a freshman he dropped out, and by the time he was sixteen his life had already begun to accelerate dangerously. He had got married, he had become a professional, self-taught alto saxophonist, he was a member of the musicians' union, he was a neophyte figure of the teeming Kansas City night world, and he had begun using drugs. When he was eighteen, he went to Chicago and then to New York, where he became a dishwasher in a Harlem restaurant and fell under the sway of its pianist, Art Tatum. He also played in a couple of taxi-dance-hall bands, and jammed tentatively around Harlem. In 1939, he went home, joined Harlan Leonard's band, then Jay McShann's Kansas City band. John Lewis, then a student at the University of New Mexico, has noted the effect that McShann's radio broadcasts had on him: "The alto solos on those broadcasts opened up a whole new world of music for me. I'd known Jay McShann from the time he used to barnstorm in the Southwest . . . but the alto saxophone was new and years ahead of anybody in jazz. He was into a whole new system of sound and time. The emcee didn't announce his name [and] I didn't learn it was Charlie Parker until after the war." The effect of a McShann broadcast on the black members of Charlie Barnet's band was no less electric. Somebody played ten spectacular choruses of "Cherokee" during a McShann broadcast they heard backstage at the Newark theatre where they were working, and when their show was over they rushed to the Savoy, found out who the soloist was by asking McShann to play the tune again, and took Parker out to dinner. Parker quit McShann in 1942, and, after a period of rootlessness and semi-starvation in Harlem, joined Earl Hines's big band, a crazy, warring group made up almost equally of old-line musicians and young beboppers. He then passed briefly through the brilliant, short-lived avant-garde big band led by Billy Eckstine, and by 1945 had settled down with the many small bands he would lead and/or record with until his death.

He had also settled, irreversibly, into the role of Gargantua. He was divorced and remarried when he was twenty-two, and the new marriage was, as far as anyone knows, the last legal liaison of the four he had. He lived in hotels and boarding houses. He had become a baffling and extraordinary drug addict—one who, unlike most addicts, was also a glutton, an alcoholic, and a man of insatiable sexual needs. He would eat twenty hamburgers in a row, drink sixteen double whiskeys in a couple of hours, and go to bed with two women at once. At times he went berserk, and would throw his saxophone out a hotel window or walk into the ocean in a brand-new suit. His sense of humor was equally askew. Early one morning he took a cab to the trumpeter Kenny Dorham's apartment (Parker spent a good part of his life in cabs, using them as his office, as rendezvous, as places to sleep, as compact, mobile fortresses), got Dorham out of bed, asked for a light, and went on his way. In 1947, he collapsed, and spent six months in a state mental hospital in California. (He had gone to the coast the year before with the first bebop band to travel west of the Mississippi; it also included Dizzy Gillespie, Al Haig, Milt Jackson, and Ray Brown.) During his stay in the state hospital, where his astonishing recuperative powers soon became evident, Parker was cared for by a doctor who was also a fan. Ross Russell, Parker's first biographer, has set down the doctor's thoughts about him: "A man living from moment to moment. A man living for the pleasure principle, music, food, sex, drugs, kicks, his personality arrested at an infantile level. A man with almost no feeling of guilt and only the smallest, most atrophied nub of conscience. Except for his music, a potential member of the army of psychopaths supplying the populations of prisons and mental institutions. But with Charlie Parker it was the music factor that makes all the difference. That's really the only reason we're interested in him. The reason we're willing to stop our own lives and clean up his messes. People like Charlie require somebody like that."

Parker's wild excesses never seemed—at least until the very end of his life—to interfere with his music. It is now agreed among jazz musicians that drugs dislocate and dilute their improvisations; it was just the other way with Parker. The only times he could not function were when he was strung out and needed a fix. His style had matured completely by the time he made his first small-band records, in 1945. Parker's playing did not, as has often been claimed, spring magically from the virgin soil of the Southwest. Other musicians had a hand in its creation. When he was a teenager, Parker bathed night after night in the unique, rocking music of Kansas City. No matter where he went, he heard the blues—the heavy, sad, windblown blues of Lips Page, Pete Johnson, Joe Turner, Herschel Evans, and Buddy Tate, and the light, rolling, new-coin blues of Count Basie and Lester Young. Young became his idol, and when Parker first went on the road he took along all Young's records and committed his solos to memory. Parker also worked in Kansas City with Buster Smith, a saxophonist whose style bears a speaking likeness to Parker's early playing. He picked up technical advice from a well-trained local bandleader, Tommy Douglas, and when he got to New York he studied Art Tatum, who unwittingly showed him how to play at lightning speeds, and how to devise wholly new harmonies. Some of these early wingings into the blue were disastrous. When he was fifteen or sixteen, he brazened his way onto the bandstand during one of the tough, endless Kansas City jam sessions, and, trying some fancy stuff in a roaring "I Got Rhythm," lost his way. The drummer, Jo Jones, stopped playing, grabbed a cymbal, and threw it on the floor at Parker's feet: He had been "gonged off" the stand. From such embarrassing acorns Parkers grow.

Parker had a unique tone; no other saxophonist has achieved as *human* a sound. It could be edgy, and even sharp. (He used the hardest and most technically difficult of the reeds.) It could be smooth and big and sombre. It could be soft and buzzing. Unlike most saxophonists of his time, who took their cue from Coleman Hawkins, he used almost no vibrato; when he did, it was only a flutter, a murmur. The blues lived in every room of his style, and he was one of the most striking and affecting blues improvisers we have had. His slow blues had a preaching, admonitory quality. He would begin a solo with a purposely stuttering four-or-five-note announcement, pause for effect, repeat the phrase, bending its last note into silence, and then turn the phrase around backward and abruptly slip sidewise into double time, zigzag up the scale, circle around quickly at the top, and plummet down, the notes falling somewhere between silence and sound. (Parker was a master of dynamics and of the dramatic use of silence.) Another pause, and he would begin his second chorus with a dreaming, three-note figure, each of the notes running into the next but each held in prolonged, hymnlike fashion. Taken from an unexpected part of the chord, they would slip out in slow motion. He would shatter this brief spell by inserting two or three short arpeggios, disconnected and broken off, then he would float into a backpedaling half-time and shoot into another climbing-and-falling double-time run, in which he would dart in and out of nearby keys. He would pause, then close the chorus with an amen figure resembling his opening announcement.

But there was another, quite different Parker—the Parker who played extraordinary slow ballads, such as "Embraceable You" and "Don't Blame Me" and "White Christmas." Here he went several steps farther than he did with the blues. He literally dismantled a composer's song and put together a structure ten times as complex. New chords and harmonies appeared, along with new melodic lines that moved high above the unsounded original. (He would, though, always inject pieces of the melody as signposts for the listener.) He could do anything he liked with time, and in his ballads he would lag behind the beat, float easily along on it, or leap ahead of it; he would do things with time that no one had yet thought of and that no one has yet surpassed. His ballads were dense visions, glimpses into an unknown musical dimension. Although they were perfectly structured, they seemed to have no beginnings and no endings; each was simply another of the fragmentary visions that stirred and maddened his mind. Thus his 1947 version of "Embraceable You" (first take) , which, so intense, so beautiful, remains one of the sensations of music. Parker's fast thirty-two-bar tunes were meteoric. He used multitudes of notes but never a superfluous one. His runs exploded like light spilling out of an opened doorway. His rhythms had a muscled, chattering density. He crackled and roared.

Parker turned the world of jazz around, and the effects are still felt. One hears him in the work of such saxophonists as Charlie McPherson and Phil Woods and Sonny Stitt and Sonny Criss, and less openly in the playing of Sonny Rollins and John Coltrane and Ornette Coleman. One hears him in almost every guitarist, pianist, trumpeter, bassist, drummer, and trombonist over forty, and he is still audible in the instrumentalists of the present generation, although most of them may not know it. But Parker's legion of admirers have, by and large, missed his main point. He widened the improvisational boundaries of time and harmony and melody, but he did not reject what had come before him, for at bottom he was a conservative, who found new ways of expressing the same things that King Oliver and Louis Armstrong and Sidney Bechet had said earlier. His admirers donned his form and ignored his content. Countless players appeared who used a thousand notes in every chorus, who had hard, smart tones, and who indulged in fancy rhythmic patterns. Yet they sidestepped the emotions that governed all that Parker played. The ironic results were the hard-boppers of the late fifties and the cul-de-sac avant-garde of the early sixties. Fortunately, most of this happened after he was dead, and so he did not suffer the horrors that Lester Young endured during the last decade of his life—the musical claustrophobia of hearing yourself reproduced again and again in the work of almost every young saxophonist and of knowing, at the same time, that your own powers have dwindled to the point where the new men are playing better than you are.

For a time after his release from the hospital in California, Parker cooled it. But the pace of his life quickened again, and by the early fifties it had got completely out of control. He collapsed on the street, he got into fights, he tried to commit suicide. He slept, when he slept at all, on floors or in bathtubs or in the beds of friends. He cadged drinks, and he panhandled. His horn was usually in hock, and he missed gigs. And at last his playing faltered; he began to imitate himself. One reason was physical; he no longer had the stamina to sustain his brilliant flights. The other was more subtle. Like Jackson Pollock, he felt that he had reached the end of his explorations. The blues and the thirty-two-bar song no longer were challenges. He had, he thought, discovered every chord change, every rhythmic turn, every adventurous harmony. He talked of big orchestral works, and he considered studying with the composers Stefan Wolpe and Edgard Varese. But there were exceptions, and one of them was the famous concert given in May of 1953 in Massey Music Hall, in Toronto. On hand with Parker, who arrived without a horn and had to borrow one from a music store, were Dizzy Gillespie, Bud Powell, Charles Mingus, and Max Roach. Parker had long had ambivalent feelings about Gillespie. He admired him as a musician, but he resented Gillespie's fame—the story in *Life* about Gillespie and bebop, in which Parker was not even mentioned; the Profile of Gillespie written for *The New Yorker* by Richard O. Boyer. Gillespie, though, has long had life in sharp focus. Parker was the opposite—a closed, secret, stormy, misshapen figure who continually barricaded himself behind the put-on (using his deepest voice, he announced at the concert that Gillespie's "Salt Peanuts" was by "my worthy constituent,"). Gillespie was a challenge that night, and so was the rhythm section, which played with ferocity and precision. Parker responded, and in "Wee," "Hot House," and "Night in Tunisia" he soloed with a fire and a brilliance that match anything in his earlier work.

Parker's death was an inevitable mixture of camp, irony, and melodrama. He had been befriended by the Baroness Pannonica Koenigswarter, a wealthy, intelligent eccentric who lived in the Stanhope Hotel and drove herself to jazz clubs in a silver Rolls Royce. Her apartment had become a salon for musicians. In March of 1955, Parker secured a gig at George Wein's Storyville, in Boston, and on his way out of New York he stopped at the Stanhope to say hello. The Baroness offered Parker a drink. To her astonishment, he refused, and asked for ice water. His ulcer was acting up, and cold water would, he said, quench its fire. Suddenly he started vomiting blood. The Baroness's doctor examined him and said that he would have to go to a hospital at once. He refused, so he was put to bed and given antibiotics. Several days passed, and he seemed to improve. On a Saturday night, he was allowed to sit in the living room and watch Tommy Dorsey's television show. He was in good spirits. During a juggling act involving bricks, which he remembered having seen in Kansas City as a child, he started laughing, choked, and slumped in his chair. He died a minute or two later. At that instant, according to the Baroness, she heard a single huge clap of thunder. The official cause of death was lobar pneumonia, but Parker had simply worn out.

The tenor-saxophonist Buddy Tate had run into Parker not long before. "I first knew him in Kansas City in the thirties, when I was with Andy Kirk," he has said. "He hadn't gotten himself together yet, but he was admiring Buster Smith, who always played Kansas City style. When he first came to New York, we'd hang out together some. He didn't have any work, and nobody knew who he was yet, but he'd be up at Monroe Clark's Uptown House every night. I'd have him over to the house, and my wife would put on a pot, but he would never eat. I tried at the time to get him into Basie's band, but Basie wouldn't have him, and he never forgot that. But he was always nice and kind and soft around me. I never saw him mad at anybody.

"One morning a week before he died, I was walking down Forty-second Street toward Grand Central. It was about ten o'clock, and I'd been on some sort of big-band record date, just playing clarinet. I saw this man way down the sidewalk, and it was Bird. He was hard to miss, with those out-of-style suits that didn't fit, and those big, old, wide granddaddy suspenders he always wore. When I got close, I saw he was all swollen up. I knew he'd been very sick and in the psychiatric part of Bellevue. He said, 'I'm so glad to see you. How you been?'

"I told him fine, and he said, 'Take me for a taste.'

"We went into a bar, and I thought he'd settle down for a few, but he only had two shots. I'd heard he was so strung out he was sleeping on the stand at Birdland and that they'd had to fire him and that he owed the string section that had been backing him up $2500, which he didn't have.

We talked about an hour. He said he wished people would call him for record dates like the one I'd just been on, and I told him they probably didn't because they'd think he'd want a thousand for a little old forty-two-dollar date, and he said no, he'd do it for free, just to sit in a section again and play with the other guys. Of course, he rarely had his own horn. He'd play anybody's, any old Sears, Roebuck job, so long as it had a mouthpiece and a reed. I told him I was working up at the Savoy, and he said, 'Oh, I been hearing about you, and I'm going up there to listen.' Bird had played with Jay McShann at the Savoy one of the first times he came to New York. But he never did come uptown, and I never saw him again."

Dizzy

In the early evening of June 18, 1978, near the end of a concert on the South Lawn of the White House, Dizzy Gillespie, who had just finished a funny, rambunctious duet with the drummer Max Roach ("I understand where he's going before he does, and he understands the same thing about me"), walked the few feet to where President Carter was standing and listening, and, using a couple of "Your Majesty"s, asked the President if he would sing the bebop tune "Salt Peanuts" with him. Gillespie demonstrated its tricky melody, and he and Carter sang it. Gillespie thanked him, and asked him if he would like to go on the road with his band, and Carter said, "I might have to after tonight."

Gillespie—master trumpeter, marvellous mimic, comic dancer, rocketing scat singer, lyrical composer, and a founder, with Charlie Parker, of bebop—is seventy-two, and he remains irrepressible. His famous trumpet style is still in place. It is at once a streamlining of Roy Eldridge's fireball playing of the late thirties and a deft translation of Parker. His trumpet runs, delivered from his high register to his middle register, are downhill racers. He likes to blare, filling a note to bursting and letting it float smartly away. His breaks, in a number like "A Night in Tunisia," momentarily blind you. He plays with a mute more often than he used to, and he sounds as if he were humming in the next room. His ballad numbers once leaned this way and that but now are steady and majestic. He is unmistakable: the hurrying silver tone, the sly, jumping attack, the epigrammatic melodic fills, the rhythmic bobbing and weaving.

Gillespie was born John Birks Gillespie in Cheraw, South Carolina, the youngest of nine children of James and Lottie (Powe) Gillespie. He was a devilish child, who fought a lot and was whipped a lot. When he was nine, his father, a discontented man, died; when he was twelve, he took up the trombone and the trumpet; and when he was eighteen he was in

Frank Fairfax's Philadelphia band and was nicknamed Dizzy. He went to Europe with Teddy Hill's band in 1937, and two years later he joined Cab Calloway, who fired him after they got into a fracas over a spitball that Calloway mistakenly thought Gillespie had shot at him. He married a dancer named Lorraine Willis in 1940 in Boston ("Dizzy didn't fool around with all that other stuff," she once said. "He just asked me to get married, and I said, 'O.K.' "), and she has long been his guide and his ballast.

He discovered Charlie Parker around the same time, and Parker changed his life. By 1945, he had the first bebop band on Fifty-second Street, had made the first bebop recording (with Coleman Hawkins), and had taken the first bebop band to California. In 1946, he formed a big bebop band, and in 1948 he took it to Europe. It played in Scandinavia, then foundered, and was rescued by the French critic Charles Delaunay. Gillespie, who rarely dwells on dark things, recently remembered this about the trip: "We were in a bus somewhere in Denmark and I looked out the window and saw this guy riding along on an ice scooter. I stopped the bus, and asked him if he'd like to get in, and let me ride his scooter, and we swapped." He gave up his big band in 1950 and, three years later, played in the Toronto concert with Charlie Parker, Bud Powell, Charles Mingus, and Max Roach that turned out to be the crowning bebop event. In 1955, Parker died, and the great bebop revolution was over. Gillespie, lending himself to the establishment for the first time, took a new big band to the Middle East for the State Department in 1956, and he has lived more or less within the establishment ever since, as an eccentric, brilliant musician and a subtle comic figure who wants you to laugh at him because he has been laughing at you all along.

Gillespie has spent most of his life on the road. During his early years, he travelled to make money. But during the past ten or fifteen years travelling has become an obsession. Like Duke Ellington and Louis Armstrong, who never stopped going in their last decades, he is in constant motion. ("I think in terms of degrees of latitude rather than miles," he has said. "I look at being on the road like it's an education.") So far in 1990, he has appeared in Japan, France, Puerto Rico, Cuba, Newfoundland, Namibia, Spain, Holland, Italy, Sweden, Germany, Czechoslovakia, Russia, Greece, Scotland, Denmark, Switzerland, and Israel, and he is scheduled to play in Brazil, Argentina, Chile, England, and the Netherlands. He will also have worked in the United States during this year in New York; Bloomington; Greensboro; Springfield, Illinois; Sarasota; Fort Smith, Arkansas; Salem, Virginia; Fort Lauderdale; Miami; Atlanta; Tuscaloosa; Philadelphia; Los Angeles; Cincinnati; Boston; Hampton, Virginia; Waterville, New Hampshire; Seattle; Washington; Monterey; Dallas; Knoxville; Crawfordsville, Indiana; Cleveland; Chicago; and New Orleans. When American worthies reach seventy, honors and awards begin falling on them like snow. Last year, Gillespie received his fourteenth honorary degree, was made a Commandeur d'Ordre des Arts et Lettres by the French, got a Grammy Lifetime Achievement Award, and was given the National Medal of Arts by President Bush. This December, he will receive a Kennedy Center award.

On a May evening in 1990, Gillespie was scheduled to play a one-night stand with his quintet at the Lone Star Roadhouse, on West Fifty-second Street. His old friends Cynthia and Donald Elwood were taking him to dinner at Tout Va Bien, the venerable bistro on West Fifty-first Street. He had finished a six-day stint at Blues Alley, in Washington, the night before, and, just before *that*, had spent three days in Spain, acting in a film called "Winter in Lisbon." Before that, he had spent three days giving concerts in East Berlin, Moscow, and Prague. Virginia Wicks, who had done publicity for Gillespie in New York in the fifties and had come out of retirement to do his Berlin-Moscow-Prague tour, had been invited to dinner, too, and she got to Tout Va Bien first. She is handsome and calm and white-haired, and she talked about the tour. "I live in Los Angeles now," she said, "and I ran into Dizzy eight or nine months ago at a concert he gave in Santa Monica. I hadn't seen him in a long time, and we hung out backstage. Three or four months later, he called me out of the blue—'Hi, Wicks!'—and asked me if I'd like to do advance work on a benefit concert he was going to give in East Berlin in May. He said he was on his way to Cuba—or Cooba, as he calls it—and he'd get back to me soon. A month after that, he called from Nova Scotia and said there would be two more concerts—one in Moscow, the day after the Berlin concert, and one in Prague, the day after the Moscow concert. The concerts were being sponsored by the Baha'i community, which Dizzy has been deeply involved with for many years. I was out of practice and a little scared of the whole project, but I said yes, I'd do it. The concert in East Berlin was held at the Palast der Republik, and, thank God, it was a huge success. We flew to Moscow the next morning—it's a much longer flight than you'd think—and on the way from the airport Dizzy said he had a sore throat and wanted to find some lemons and garlic to treat it. We stopped at a free market, where there aren't any queues, because everything is so expensive. The lemons were tiny and cost three dollars apiece. I warned Dizzy about the garlic, because we had a press conference before the concert, but, whatever he did, he never smelled. And he never got a cold. The concert was electric. There was a palpable hush of anticipation before each number, and when the audience recognized a tune it screamed its approval. And the applause at the end was astonishing.

"After, we were taken to a restaurant in an old house where there was an immense horseshoe-shaped table covered with long-stemmed roses and bowls of caviar. Then they drove us in this silent black limousine through alleyways and around Red Square. There was a full moon, and it was like a dream. I said something to Dizzy when we got to Red Square, but he was sound asleep.

"Václav Havel and Shirley Temple Black, who is our Ambassador to Czechoslovakia, were both at the Prague concert, which was in the Palác Kultury. The concert was very long, but no one left. Dizzy got a standing ovation that lasted literally ten minutes. It went on and on, but he didn't reappear. That wasn't like him, and I began to worry that something might have happened to him. I sent word, and it turned out that he had gone to his dressing room way downstairs and hadn't heard a thing. He came onstage and played an encore, and everything was all right."

The Elwoods arrived, with Gillespie in tow. They are small and tweedy and full of moxie. They live in Boston, and they first met Gillespie there in the mid-sixties. It was a cool evening, and Gillespie, who is not a clotheshorse, was wearing a Sherlock Holmes hat, a houndstooth jacket, rumpled striped brown pants, a navy-blue T-shirt, and a couple of medallions suspended from a long gold neck chain. He hasn't changed much in the last ten years. He has a medium-length grayish Afro, and he looks grizzly. His huge and celebrated cheeks are broadsides in repose and spinnakers in action, and he has a scimitar smile and a thousand tiny, even teeth. He likes to smile and roll his eyes in mock surprise, but most of the time his eyes are narrowed; they take in much and send out little, and when he puts on his dark-rimmed, two-tone glasses they disappear.

No one talks like Gillespie. His voice is potatoey, burred, edgeless. His consonants and vowels are indistinguishable, a gumbo. His laughter barks. In the seventies, he began taking on a formidable front porch, but he has lost much of it, and he can once more hiphop around the stage between solos, do his funny dances, pop his eyes, stick out his tongue, and make some of his listeners put him down as an Uncle Tom —this wily, powerful, relentless anti-Tom.

Virginia Wicks and Cynthia Elwood sat against the wall, and Donald Elwood and Gillespie sat across from them. Gillespie said he hadn't had anything but a cup of coffee all day, and he was hungry. The waitress, who was French, recognized him, gave a little shriek, and asked him for his autograph. He obliged, and asked her for a menu. Then she asked him if he had a photograph of himself to add to the gallery of notables on the wall. He shook his head and looked at Virginia Wicks, and she said she'd send one to Tout Va Bien. Gillespie bent his head to study the menu, and his trumpeter's bottom lip, heavy as a plate, slid forward. He decided on mushroom soup and frogs' legs. Donald Elwood looked up from his menu and said, "What did the waiter say when he was asked what the soup du jour was? He said, 'I don't know. They change it every day.'" Gillespie barked, and ate a piece of French bread.

Virginia Wicks told the Elwoods that Dizzy had just finished shooting a movie in Spain. "I play an old American musician who gets fed up with America and moves to Copenhagen. I wash cars; then I meet this young French piano player, and he gets me playing again. There's a gangster, and I have an attack and end up in the hospital. I saw the attack later, and, you know, I was surprised—it really looked like an attack. I die at the end of the movie. I fall over, and they catch me before I hit the floor."

Cynthia Elwood asked Gillespie about his house in Englewood, New Jersey. "Lorraine and I have been there twenty-five years!" he said. "I probably enjoy it more by being away so much, and coming back for little visits. We've got a young boy from Texas working for us who did some jobs for my cousin. He's like an overseer. He doesn't overcharge us, and sometimes he works four or five days and won't take any money. He just finished building what we called a porch back home but I guess is what you call a deck up here. It's so nice I'd like to put a bed on it."

Gillespie ate his frogs' legs with his fingers, and the bones, as clean as toothpicks, began to pile up on his butter plate. Like most road-hardened jazz musicians, who often subsist on junk food, Gillespie eats good food with relish and great concentration. He said little until he had finished his frogs' legs and a salad. Then he talked at random, moving from subject to subject as it pleased him.

BIRD

"I haven't seen the movie. I think it would just make me feel sad. I've heard from musicians that it doesn't delve into his music, that it doesn't talk about all his women. And the guy who plays me—he never met me, he doesn't know me, so how could he play me? Bird didn't use drugs in front of me. I saw him shoo guys away when I was around—the people who used to hang around musicians with coke, and all. I'd laugh at that. One time, I ran into him at Basin Street West, and he looked so forlorn. He said, 'Dizzy, save me.' I didn't know what to do, but I told him, 'You've got to do that yourself, Bird.'

"I first heard him in 1940 in Kansas City, when I was on the road with Cab Calloway. A young trumpet player in Jay McShann's band named Buddy Anderson told me, 'I want you to hear this alto player.' Well, I'd played with Don Byas and Chu Berry and Coleman Hawkins and Ben Webster, and I didn't think there was anything else to hear in that line. But I heard him, and we jammed together all day at the Booker T. Washington Hotel. Roy Eldridge had been our cup of tea—all us trumpet players—but Charlie Parker turned everything upside down. He was a great blues player, and all his music was bluesy. I always liked to hear him talk, particularly when he used his cultured-professor accent. We worked together awhile in the early forties in Earl Hines' band, and one time we played a white dance in Pine Bluff, Arkansas. This white guy threw some money up on the bandstand during intermission when I was sitting there by myself at the piano. He said would I play such-and-such, and I ignored him. After the dance, I was coming out of the men's room—the only time we were allowed in there was after the whites had left—and someone came up behind me and hit me on the head with a bottle. It was the same guy. I started to go for him, the blood all over me, and five guys grabbed me. Charlie Parker was one of them, and he looked at the guy and said, 'You took advantage of my friend, you cur.' "

GOING HOME

"Almost everybody is nice to me in Cheraw. They had a Dizzy Gillespie day there a while back and the ex-mayor gave a cocktail party for me, and I asked him if it would be all right for me to bring my cousin. I needed a haircut first, so my cousin and I went uptown to a colored barbershop. Full, and people waiting. We went to the other colored shop in town, and it was the same. I told my cousin to take me to a white barbershop. The owner was alone, sitting in a barber chair and reading the paper. 'What can I do for you?' he said. I said I wanted a haircut, and he said, 'Sorry. We don't cut colored hair.' Then he said, 'I know you,' and he started talking about my family and such, but I walked out. Later, I got a letter from Cheraw asking me if I would mind if they put up a sign on the outskirts saying Dizzy Gillespie was born there. I said I would mind—it would embarrass me if someone I knew came through and wanted a haircut and couldn't get it. But later I relented."

IMPROVISING

"The hardest part of the music is improvising, and it gets harder the older you are. Improvisation is a gathering together of all the evidence you have of how to resolve going from here to here to here. It's similar to painting. You add colors in your mind, you build colors. Bright yellow is generally loud, green is soft. I'm a more melodious player than I used to be, but rhythm is still my business. I see rhythm when I play, I understand rhythm, my best shot is rhythm. Harmony is next. The most difficult thing for me is playing in obtuse keys like A-natural and F-sharp and E. A long time ago, I found out that you've got to learn some piano to do the job as a horn player. You can only play one note at a time on a horn, but there are all the notes in the chord spread out before you on the piano. When Miles Davis first came to New York from St. Louis, he'd be at my house all the time. Lorraine would put a plate out for him. He was very inquisitive. 'Man, where did you get such-and-such a note from?' he'd ask. I'd sit down at the piano and show him.

"The only trumpet lesson I ever took was from that Grupp, used to teach here in New York. I paid him for three lessons, but I never went back after the first one, so he owes me."

BILL WHITHWORTH

"Back in the early sixties, I played Little Rock, and at that time you couldn't stay in a hotel—you stayed at people's houses. I stayed with Bill Whitworth, who used to play some trumpet. He's the editor now up there in Boston at the *Atlantic* magazine. I stayed at Bill's house with him and his mother. She greeted me: 'Come upstairs and let me show you where you're going to sleep.' I saw this sofa bed in the living room all made up, and I said that would be fine, I didn't want to take anybody's bed. But she said, 'Oh, no! I sleep down here all the time!' I got a letter from Bill later telling me, 'You should know that your being a guest in our house was a crowning achievement. I'm so famous I'm thinking of running for public office in North Little Rock. The sheets you slept in haven't been washed, and all the brass players come from miles around to kiss them.' "

RETIREMENT

"I'll never stop playing as long as I can do physically on the trumpet what I want to do. Look at Doc Cheatham. He's eighty-five and playing as good as ever. Cheatham never drank much, never took coke, never used grass. He's a perfect example of what to do for longevity."

At eight-thirty, Gillespie, in company with the Elwoods and Virginia Wicks, walked up Eighth Avenue and turned east onto Fifty-second Street. The Lone Star Roadhouse is just up the block. Virginia Wicks and the Elwoods took a table down front, and Gillespie went backstage to find his musicians. A jump band called Bob's Diner was holding forth at ear-blasting volume and was being filmed by a Japanese television crew. Bob's Diner finished its set with a thunderous riff blues, and Gillespie's quintet came onstage to warm up. But it wasn't easy. Bob's Diner had left behind a loud, steady electronic hum, and no one seemed to know how to get rid of it. Gillespie, not looking upset, was upset, and at first he refused to play. Then, a resilient and kindly man, he decided to turn up his amplifiers and go ahead. He had Ron Holloway on tenor saxophone, Ed Cherry on guitar, John Lee on bass, and Ignacio Berroa on drums. It was bulging, 3-D Gillespie. Everything was exaggerated—the volume, the length of the sidemen's solos (Gillespie has never been a garrulous soloist), the force of the ensemble passages. Gillespie himself was utterly professional. He played with a smooth doggedness, with the patience and care of someone who gives good value, no matter the distractions. He played a long "Manteca," a long, slow blues, and a long "Night in Tunisia." He took a nice muted solo in the first number and in the blues, but he opened up in "Night in Tunisia," making the famous break explode. The crowd, made up mostly of people in their late twenties and early thirties, seemed to know who Gillespie was, and gave him shouts and whistles; he responded with some dancing, a few eye-rollings, and a jowl-shaking.

A week later, Donald Elwood faxed Virginia Wicks a drawing that Gillespie had done on a manila envelope Elwood had on the table at Tout Va Bien. Here it is:

Elwood told Wicks he couldn't remember what Gillespie had said the drawing was of, and wondered if she would mind asking him, since he was playing at the Vine Street Bar & Grill in Los Angeles. Gillespie studied the drawing, and said that he couldn't remember what it was supposed to be, either, but that it looked to him like three seals on a sled. Of course, it isn't. If you look carefully, Gillespie's initials, J. B. G., emerge from the squiggles. So much for asking a busy man a foolish question.

Gillespie died two years later. Virginia Wicks was with him when he became sick, and later she said: "Last January, there was a month-long seventy-fifth-birthday celebration for Dizzy down at the Blue Note—six nights a week, two shows a night. A lot of young musicians came to play with him. He had to push himself hard, but I think he felt he wasn't coming up to where he should be. Anyway, he was very tired when it was over, and he was looking forward to taking a week off. But he rarely checked his schedule—he liked to be surprised about where he was going next—and it turned out that he had to go directly to Washington for a night and do two weeks of one-nighters somewhere out West. He ended up in Emeryville, near Oakland, and I went up from L.A. to be with him. During a long photo session the afternoon of his opening, he told me, 'Wicks, I don't feel so good. I must have eaten something bad.' Well, he was an eater, he loved food. After his first set that night, he sat more heavily in his dressing room than usual, and his color wasn't right. When Whale, his road manager, told him it was time for the second set, he said, 'I can't.' It was the first time in his life."

He was taken to a hospital, and the doctors found that his diabetes had got out of hand. He stayed two nights, then finished the gig. He was scheduled for a week in Seattle, and when everybody told him not to go he said, "Don't tell me what I have to do." ("Not mean, just stubborn," Wicks said.) He went home, to Englewood, after Seattle and had a six-hour operation for an intestinal blockage, and, though he seemed to improve, he never really recovered. "He used to say that he knew everybody and everybody knew him," Wicks went on. "And it was true. He had a little book filled with the names of people he knew all over the world, and when he arrived at such-and-such a place, he'd call—'Hi, this is Dizzy'—and they'd come and hang out with him. He never took advantage of who he was, and he never acted like a star. I don't know how stars get from here to there, but Dizzy walked down the street."

A Difficult Instrument

For a long time, jazz was dominated by clarinettists. The earliest members of this ruling class were from New Orleans, where they flourished between 1890 and the First World War. They included the Lorenzo Tios, father and son, Alphonse Picou, George Baquet, and Big Eye Louis Nelson Delisle. The next generation of clarinettists, also from New Orleans, is more familiar: Johnny Dodds, Yellow Nunez, Larry Shields, Jimmy Noone, Sidney Bechet, George Lewis, Albert Nicholas, Edmond Hall, Omer Simeon, Leon Roppolo, Raymond Burke, Barney Bigard, Louis Cottrell, Jr., Irving Fazola. The New Orleans clarinettists used the Albert-system clarinet, which has exceedingly diffcult fingering and a woody, generous, pleased Edwardian sound. They were, by and large, legato, baroque players, who swooped and soared, who bent notes and loved glissandos. They translated the fretwork around them into sound, and they made the New Orleans ensemble work. They lighted the dark, rough sounds of the trumpet and trombone, and they made the ensembles melodically and harmonically tight. The third generation of clarinettists, often influenced by the New Orleans clarinettists who had gone north after the First World War, were a more disparate group, and they came from everywhere. The New Orleans players Edmond Hall, Barney Bigard, and Irving Fazola moved among them easily, and they were, for lack of a better term, swing clarinettists. Some worked in small bands, but most ended up in or at the head of big bands. Their ensemble function reduced to occasionally floating angelically over the band in the closing chorus, the swing clarinettists became primarily soloists, and few bands in the thirties and early forties lacked their star clarinettist. These included Benny Goodman, Artie Shaw, Jimmy Dorsey, Woody Herman, Joe Marsala, Ernie Caceres, Danny Polo, Jimmy Hamilton, Frank Teschemacher, Pee Wee Russell, Buster Bailey, Johnny Mince, Lester Young, Benny Carter, Prince Robinson, Jerry Blake, Clarence Hutchenrider. Goodman and Shaw governed from opposite poles. Goodman, an arpeggio player, had great facility and passion. Artie Shaw was cooler, narrower, and deeper. He was an even better melodist, and though his tone was smaller than Goodman's, he was more interesting harmonically. Musicians tended to relish Shaw. Some of the clarinettists between Goodman and Shaw, though less skilled, were stunningly original. Lester Young summoned up lemons and small rooms. Irving Fazola, using an Albert-system clarinet, had a portly, brocaded tone, while Edmond Hall, also using the Albert system, had a harsh, reedy, jumpy attack. Pee Wee Russell was staccato, exhilarating, absurd, and beautiful. Benny Carter was oil and ease and elegance. But the big bands, with their four- and five-man reed sections, caused saxophonists to proliferate, and by 1945 they had just about replaced clarinettists as the principal reed soloists. At the same time, bebop, which was simply too difficult rhythmically and harmonically for most clarinettists, arrived, and the clarinet, king for almost fifty years, fell out of jazz. Nonetheless, a fourth and final class of jazz clarinettists appeared, and it contained just two members—Tony Scott and Buddy De Franco. Scott, a restless, volatile, gifted man, moved on the edges of bebop for a time, then went abroad and into avant-garde jazz. De Franco, unbearably challenged by Charlie Parker, attacked bebop head-on and mastered it. He developed such fluency and invention and speed that he was considered the supreme jazz clarinettist. His work has never faltered, and he has kept the instrument alive in jazz simply by playing it so well. In the late sixties and early seventies, he put his clarinet aside in order to lead the perennial Glenn Miller band. The rest seems to have refreshed him. The coolness and near arrogance of his earlier playing has given way to thought and warmth and even passion.

De Franco appears in New York occasionally, and he talked about his life during a visit. He is a tall, handsome, kingly man. He has brown hair, a high dome, a long delicate Roman nose, a serious chin, and blunt clarinettist's fingers. His eyes are large and clear, and he talks quickly and with great assurance. His smile eases his imposing face. He is a constant student of his instrument: "There are several reasons that the clarinet is such a difficult instrument. The oboe, the flute, the saxophone are all octave instruments, but the clarinet's three registers—chalumeau, middle, and altissimo—are built in twelfths. If you press the octave key on a saxophone, you go up or down an octave, but on a clarinet you go twelve tones, from, say, low F to middle C. Saxophones have pads over the air holes. When you press a key, the pad closes the hole and you get a note. Clarinets have seven tone holes and no pads, and you have to close them with the ends of your fingers. So you have to have absolute finger control. If any air escapes, you get a terrible squeak or no note at all. Going from the middle register of the clarinet to the altissimo is very awkward because the fingering changes completely. That's the reason so many clarinettists seem to lose control when they go into the top register, why they tend to shriek. Clarinets are made of granadilla wood, which comes from the south of France and North Africa. It is one of the hardest of woods, almost like a metal, and it has to be seasoned several years after it is cut. Even so, heat and cold affect the wood to an astonishing degree. A night club's heating up during a set will make your instrument sharp, and air-conditioning will do the reverse. Too much expansion and contraction of the wood can ruin the bore. You have to develop an embouchure that is good enough to compensate for this constant fluctuation. If I were a symphony clarinettist, I'd use a closed mouthpiece and a soft reed. But to play jazz, I use a stiff reed and an open mouthpiece. That way, I can get percussive effects and be heard over a loud rhythm section, and even over a big band. Most bassists and some drummers are electrified now, and I have to use a very stiff reed and twice the lung power. It is quite exhausting. What is also exhausting is the amount of time you play on the average night in a club. If you play three one-hour sets, you may play a third of that time, which means one solid hour of clarinet playing. Perhaps that is why there have been so few good clarinettists.

"I was with Tommy Dorsey off and on between 1944 and 1949, and that toughened and strengthened me as a player. Dorsey wrote the book on show-biz types. He was all the good and bad characters in one. He was voluble, generous, prejudiced, dirty-mouthed, impatient, a terrific musician. He'd call in a specialist if you were sick. He'd help you out if you were having financial troubles. He had the highest-paid band in the business, and after he'd bought a yacht from Walter Chrysler he took us all on a cruise through the Florida Keys. For a time, we had our own railroad car. But he could be very rough. He loved the shock. Two old ladies came up to him once during an intermission and one of them said, 'I know your mom's sister,' or some such, and Dorsey said, 'Why don't you talk to her and not bug me?' A kid who had just joined the band told Tommy a bad dirty joke, and Tommy laughed, 'Ha, ha, ha,' and said, 'You're fired.' We had our first falling out over my solo on 'Opus 1,' which was a big hit record in 1945. Wherever we went, he wanted me to play the solo that was on the recording because he said that was what people expected—what they came to hear. I was an itchy kid, so I kept changing the solo, and he got more and more unhappy. Finally, he told me he wasn't interested in my creativity, and he fired me. I settled in New York, and things didn't go so well. A few months later he called: 'You little shit. You got enough wrinkles in your belly yet?' I told him I was doing great when the fact was I had checked into the Piccadilly Hotel and got the first week's tab— three hundred dollars, which would be like fifteen hundred now. I told him I'd want three hundred a week if I rejoined and five hundred right away. He turned away from the phone and said, 'I knew it. The son of a bitch is broke!' He said yes, and I went back. The next uproar, I quit and settled in California, and the strangest thing happened. For six months, I couldn't get work, and I couldn't understand it. Well, I found out later that Tommy, who had a lot of influence and sway, had blackballed me, and to please him nobody would hire me. But I rejoined him again, and we became quite friendly and were close until he died. There was no nonsense on the bandstand. There was a ten-dollar fine if you weren't present a half hour before the show, a twenty-five-dollar fine if you missed the show, and a ten-dollar fine if you smiled on the stand. When you soloed, he'd never take his eyes off you, and if he felt a little malicious, he'd make you go on and on until you were ready to drop." De Franco told the British jazz critic Steve Voce this Dorsey story in *Jazz Journal*: He and the pianist Dodo Marmarosa missed the band train from Louisville to St. Louis and caught up with it by hiring a private plane for three hundred and fifty dollars. Dorsey was in the diner. "He got up from his seat and suddenly he saw us," De Franco told Voce. "It seemed like a full two minutes we watched him, and he went through all the phases of emotion in that time. I grabbed a ketchup bottle, because 'Step outside' was one of his frequent ideas. The veins stood out on his forehead, his face got red, he was flexing his muscles, grunting and groaning, and he came over and glared at us for a long while. Then he suddenly started to laugh. 'You guys are ridiculous,' he said. 'You remind me of when I was a kid. I can't get mad at you. You tried to get there, you hired a plane. Stick around, I'll give you both a raise.' "

De Franco is all business when he plays. He stands straight and motion-less, and points his clarinet at the floor—unlike Benny Goodman and Artie Shaw, who in exultant moments would rear back and point their instruments directly at God. De Franco's playing is constant motion. The clarinettists who preceded him seemed to hang their melodic lines between their notes. De Franco doesn't appear to use notes. His solos are pliable, glistening tubes of sound that move steadily up and down the instrument's three registers. His solos are always disappearing over the next ridge, and it is not easy to keep up with them, no matter what the tempo. He has a sunny, aluminum sound, a Bauhaus clarity and smoothness. His tone, even in the chalumeau register, has none of the plumminess of Irving Fazola or the low-register Pee Wee Russell. He uses almost no vibrato, and he likes avalanches of eighth notes, often repeat-ed two or three times. He uses double-time passages that blur in the ear. He likes little out-of-breath pauses, placed oddly, and he likes to skid from an arpeggio into a glissando, as if he were sliding into base. One of the finest recordings he ever made was with Art Tatum in the mid-fifties, not long before Tatum's death. Both men, masters of the rococo, have jokey tendencies. Tatum mimics De Franco, De Franco races Tatum, Tatum surges up and around De Franco, De Franco floats away, just out of reach, Tatum encircles De Franco with an enormous arpeggio, De Franco ducks away with an equally enormous counter-arpeggio. De Franco recalled the session: "I was sick that day, but it wasn't an occasion I would have missed. It was a game between us of can you top this? He'd play some astonishing figure and laugh, or turn and make a face at me over one shoulder. Or he'd rest his right hand on his knee and play with just his left hand, making it sound like both hands. I think he could have outwitted Charlie Parker.

"I first heard Parker in the mid-forties. It was uptown at some club. He had just come in from upstate—skinny, with a mop of hair. He borrowed a horn and sat in. I was completely turned around. I couldn't sleep for two days. I decided immediately that that was it: I was determined to articulate like that on the clarinet. I changed my reed and opened up my mouthpiece. I've worked toward that articulation ever since. I've also learned a great deal more about the essence of jazz over the years. I think it began in the mid-forties when I was between bands and sat in with

Stuff Smith, the violinist, in Chicago. He had Jimmy Jones on piano and Sid Catlett on drums. My God, the intensity of Catlett's drumming—I got a message, a light went on, I knew what *swinging* was. I feel more, physically and emotionally, than I once did. I used to suffer from stage fright, and that made my playing cautious and mechanical-sounding. You have to show off what you have but control that showing off. Your brain is always miles ahead of your technical facility, and you have to realize that. I see nothing in my head when I improvise, and I'd just as soon forget the chords once I've learned them. But you can sort of see where your solo is going in your mind's eye. You can see your melodic line ahead. When I have a strong piano player, I try and float over his harmonic structure, over the blanket of his sound. We all have our little improvisational patterns, but I try and not put these patterns in at the same time or in the same mix. And you have to keep the melody at hand. It's arrogant to destroy a melody. Listen to Artie Shaw's solo on his recording of 'Star Dust.' It's the greatest clarinet solo of all time.

"My early training was more along the classical than the jazz line. I was born in Camden, New Jersey, on February 17, 1923. My parents moved to Philadelphia when I was three, and I was raised there. My full name is Bonifacio Ferdinando Leonardo De Franco. Bonafacio, which means 'good face,' was my grandfather's name. Leonardo was my father's name and Ferdinando came from an uncle. We were five children. The youngest died at a year. My older brother, Leonard, plays bass and is still active in Philadelphia. I have a married sister in Cherry Hill, New Jersey, and my younger brother, Anthony, who started out as a bassoonist, lives with my Aunt Grace, who has never married. My father's parents and grandparents came from central Italy, where the people have blue eyes and light hair, sometimes blond. My father was tall and heavy—an impressive-looking man and a remarkable man. Most of his life was a thread of tragedy. He lost his sight before I was born—an infection that had been given the wrong treatment. He said that he didn't do a thing for a year after he went blind, except feel sorry for himself. Then he enrolled in the Overbrook School for the blind, and learned how to tune pianos and to cook and type. He didn't catch on right away as a piano tuner, so he tried the candy-vending-machine business, but that didn't work either. Leonard and I would take turns making his route with him, and if we were late, he'd grab his cane and be off by himself. Sometimes we had no money, and had to eat candy bars for dinner. My father was an amateur guitarist, and he joined a band of blind people called the Jovial Night Owls. It was primarily a string band, and they played tunes like 'Sweet Sue.' The thing about my Dad, he always found time to play for us, or to tell us a story. He was born in Philadelphia, like my mother. Her name was Louise Giordano. She was dark and had brown eyes and was frail. She was a high-strung, bright, sensitive woman, who was always correcting our English. She worked as a secretary and in cigar factories to help out, but she finally gave up. There were too many children and not enough money. She attempted suicide, and in the end asked to be put away. Aunt Grace took us in, one by one, after my mother left. She lived in a row house with my grandfather and grandmother Domenica, and with Uncle Anthony and Aunt Lucy. She fed us and clothed us and got us through school. My mother spent the rest of her life in a state institution. Sometimes she knew us when we visited, and sometimes she sat there for hours and didn't say a word. She died in the mid-sixties. My father remarried twice, but only one marriage worked out to any degree of happiness. He died not long after my mother.

"I went to Mastbaum Technical High School, which was almost like a music school. The trumpet players Red Rodney and Joe Wilder were in my class. I started in on mandolin when I was five and switched to clarinet when I was eight or nine. Chap Cottrell was my first teacher, and he also taught me alto saxophone. My next teacher was Wally De Simone. He was in the pit band at the Earl Theatre, and he taught me every Sunday for nothing. He lived nearby, and he'd walk by our house to see if I was practicing. I hate to practice now, but it was fascinating to me then. It was a grand feeling every time you mastered another aspect of the instrument. The first jazz clarinet player who had any effect on me was Johnny Mince, a very underrated player with Tommy Dorsey. Then I heard Benny Goodman, and was enthralled. He had fire and facility. I later became an Artie Shaw fan. He was more linear in his musical thinking than the arpeggiated Chicago players like Goodman. And he was more modern harmonically Those three clarinettists have always been top for me.

"When I was fourteen, I entered a nationwide contest run by Tommy Dorsey to find the best young jazz player. Willy De Simone told me, 'You're going to win, and this is how you're going to do it. You are going to wear shorts, and you're going to play 'Honeysuckle Rose,' and during the last eight bars you're going to hit a high A. While you're punching out that high A, you're going to hold out your left arm to show you are playing the clarinet and holding this fantastic A with just one hand.' I won, and when I met Tommy Dorsey afterward, he said, 'Stick to it, kid, and you'll be in my band.' I sailed through Mastbaum in three years instead of four, and it was the first time I enjoyed school. I had been sluggish before. Around this time, my brother Leonard and I started going to Billy Krechmer's jam sessions in the Downbeat Room. Whoever was in town— Teddy Wilson or Georgie Auld or Charlie Christian—would drop by and play, and we were allowed to sit in with these big-timers. Johnny Scat Davis, a trumpet player and bandleader who had been with Fred Waring, heard me at one of the sessions and offered me a job. I was fifteen. He had to sign special papers so I could travel with him. He paid me sixty dollars a week, and I sent half of it home and lived on the rest. I joined Gene Krupa's band in 1941. He had Charlie Ventura and Roy Eldridge and Anita O'Day. Dodo Marmarosa was on piano. He had been with Scat

Davis. I learned then that I could never be a doper—that I could not alter my consciousness and still play well. I had heard an acetate I'd made when I'd had a few drinks, and it was embarrassing. I was with Gene at the Golden Gate Theatre in San Francisco when he was busted for possession of marijuana, and it was a sad business. Krupa was one of the best people in the business. We had got word backstage that agents were searching our hotel rooms, so Krupa sent his valet back to the hotel to get an envelope that was in a jacket pocket. The valet walked through the hotel lobby with the envelope in his hand and was stopped and that was it. Gene went to jail for three months, and it was headlines all over the country. I went from Krupa to Charlie Barnet. He had Pete Candoli and Neal Hefti and Oscar Pettiford, and Gil Evans was writing arrangements. Barnet was a delightful person. His mother had given him the money to get having a big band out of his system, which of course he never did. Everything was a kind of party. Dodo Marmarosa had joined with me, and he featured us both. I went with Ted Fio Rito for a short time, and on to Tommy Dorsey.

"In 1950, after I had left Tommy Dorsey for good, I joined Count Basie's small band. He had Clark Terry and Wardell Grey and Gus Johnson. He made any group sound like him, and he did it all from the piano. I never heard anyone play so much by doing so little. His philosophy was: Settle down, we'll get there. And: Don't smother people with notes. Every once in a while, he'd take the tempo up. All right, he'd say. Now you can smoke, and we would. Boyd Raeburn had a good band, an experimental band, and I went with him. George Handy and Johnny Richards were doing the arrangements. Then, in 1952, I put together my own big band. I had to be Benny Goodman and Artie Shaw. Willard Alexander, the booker, advised me not to do it, but who do you listen to at that age? Your ego outdistances your brain. I had good people—Jimmy Lyon, Bernie Glow, Lee Konitz, Earl Swope, Gene Quill—but I didn't know anything about leading a big band. The band had no identity, and it was the wrong time—big bands were over. It lasted less than a year, and I lost a lot of money.

"The rest of the fifties, I had a good group for two years with Art Blakey and Kenny Drew. I was hot, and we did good business. I joined Norman Granz's Jazz at the Phil., and made a lot of records for Norman. I had a marvellous but totally unsalable group with Tommy Gumina on accordion, Carl Perkins on piano, Scott La Faro on bass, Pete Jolly on piano, Howard Roberts on guitar, and Billy Higgins on drums. Then 1960 rolled around, and the night clubs went topless or to rock. Concerts dropped off, and nobody would put out a record for you. It was understandable. Kids like to participate when they listen to music—vicariously or as dancers. They couldn't do either with bebop. The music was too complicated to partake in, and you couldn't dance to it. Rock answered their prayers. I did West Coast studio work and school clinics. It was an abyss, and I barely survived. In one year, my income went from six figures to six thousand dollars. Then I ran into Willard Alexander. He said, 'What are you doing?' I said, 'Starving.' He looked at me and said, 'You're going to be the next leader of the Glenn Miller band. I'll get back to you in forty-eight hours.' Willard always said he'd get back to you in forty-eight hours, and mostly that would be the last you heard. But he called the next day and hired me, and I ran the Glenn Miller band for eight years. That band is like a religion. It's booked years in advance all over the world. Our theme song, 'Moonlight Serenade,' made grown men and women cry. We could *hear* the love for Miller's music wherever we went. But I had so much to do running the band that I had to stop playing, and for several years I didn't touch my clarinet.

"In 1975, I decided to start a jazz career again. I also got married. It's taken me three times to find the right wife. Her name is Joyce, and we have a little boy, Chad. I bought some property in Panama City in north-western Florida, and built a house a hundred yards from the beach. It has the best beaches in the country. I only work about thirty weeks a year. When I go abroad, I take Joyce and Chad. She's in real estate at home. She buys little houses and fixes them up and rents them. When I'm there, I help out. I'll hang a door, fix a lock. Then I'll set up a crab trap off the beach and do a little fishing. It's all the life I need."

Chanting with Buster

When Jimmy Rowles at last began his brave invasion of New York City in January of 1973, perhaps a hundred people took note. But this was hardly surprising. Rowles's previous visits to the city, in the forties and fifties, had been brief and in the semi-visible guises of accompanist for Evelyn Knight and Peggy Lee and of big-band pianist for Benny Goodman and Woody Herman. The rest of his career had been spent around Los Angeles, in a variety of equally subaqueous roles that included studio work, fleeting nightclub appearances, countless recordings for other people, and coaching singers and nonsingers, one of whom was Marilyn Monroe. "The studio sent me over to this sumptuous office on the lot where she was supposed to be," he once said, "and when I got there the blinds were drawn and the place looked empty. Then I saw this form asleep on the sofa. I didn't know what to do, so I sat down in a chair and lit a cigarette and dug it all. 'Here I am,' I thought, 'sitting alone in the dark with the most beautiful woman in the world.' Then I got nervous. So I cleared my throat several times and she woke up." Johnny Mercer had brought Rowles with him from Los Angeles as his accompanist for a Town Hall concert, and five months later, Rowles took a two-week gig at Michael's Pub and concurrently appeared in the

Newport Jazz Festival-New York. Perhaps a hundred more people took note, and one of them was Barney Josephson who has installed Rowles in his Cookery for a seven-week engagement that sets one Rowles record and nearly breaks another: It is the longest solo stint he has had outside Los Angeles, and the second-longest he has had anywhere.

One night, a half-hour before his first set, Rowles was sitting by himself at a table near the piano. He does not stand out in crowds. Compact and medium-sized, he is gray-haired and bespectacled and clerkly looking. His face is chipped and worn, and he has a low, gravelly voice. His mod California clothes, instead of accenting him, almost extinguish him. "It was a little strange in here at first," he said. "I felt like I was playing in a cafeteria, what with all the dish sounds and steady talking. And I don't think I ever played in a club without a bandstand, with the piano right down on the floor in the middle of the tables. A bandstand gives you a little defense, a little privilege. But I'm getting used to it, and Buster Williams, the bass player who'll be with me until Tommy Bryant takes over, is a big help. A lot of the tunes I play he doesn't know, but he's got awful ears. He grabs the structure and chords of a new tune after the first chorus, and he doesn't forget it if I play it a couple of nights later. But *my* ears have been giving me trouble. They've been stuffed up ever since I got off the plane, like as if I caught a little cold out there and carried it east with me. I've been thinking more and more lately that its time for me to be doing something like this. I'm fifty-five years old and it won't be that much longer before I get away, like all my friends seem to be doing. This past year, Ben Webster, Don Fagerquist, and Frank Beach all passed. And a couple of weeks ago it was Bobby Timmons, who was only in his thirties. So I figure it's time to play the way I want to play, time to see if I can make a go of it outside the studios and accompanying people." Rowles paused, and waved to a waitress. "Honey, get me a vodka-tonic, please. My wife, Dorothy, was all for the move, and that means everything to me, because she's smart musically and every other way. Lord! The other night, I found myself staring at the back of some woman's legs because they looked exactly like Dorothy's. That's how much I miss her already. We met in '36. She was going to a high school on one side of Spokane, where we were both born, and I was going to one on the other side, and we met at a dance I was playing at her school. When I went down to L.A. the first time, in 1940, I asked her to wait a year, and if it worked out I'd send for her and we'd get married. It did and we did, and it's been thirty-two years. She's been my life's blood. Of course, it wouldn't be right if we didn't fight at least once a week. She's thrown me out of the house as much as two weeks at a time. Once, when I came back, she was gone, and there was a note: 'Try and straighten up. And feed the animals.' She stayed away two weeks, and I didn't find out until later that she was just around the corner.

"We've got three kids, and they're *all* musical. Several years ago, my older daughter—her name is Stacy—saw a trumpet up in the attic which

Frank Beach had given me. Chuck Peterson, the high-note man with Tommy Dorsey, had taught me a little trumpet when we were in Skinnay Ennis's band in the Army. Stacy said 'How do you play it?' and I showed her the scales. And last year, when she was eighteen, she won first prize at a big-band contest, and then she played at the Monterey Festival, and was hugged and kissed by Dizzy Gillespie and Clark Terry. And my younger daughter, Stephanie, who we call Zip, is into the flute. So I asked Arthur Gleghorn, a great English flute player who works in the studios out there, would he come by and play for us. We laid in plenty of vodka, and his old lady brought him over and he sat by our pool and played for hours—Ravel and Debussy—and it was fantastic. My son, Gary, plays organ and guitar. He's thirty-one. He began to break away from me when he was fourteen. I couldn't tell him where the sun rose, he knew so much. But he came around in his early twenties. He's a car genius, and he stops by and gives my arm a squeeze and works on my car, and everything is fine.

"Uh-oh. It's five after eight. Time to work." Rowles took a small blue box out of his pocket. It had the words "Tacky-Finger" on the lid. With careful, ritualistic movements, he dipped the ends of his fingers into the waxlike substance in the box and then massaged them. "I saw a teller in a bank put this stuff on before she counted a pile of bills, and now I can't live without it. It keeps my fingers from slipping off the keys into my lap. Before, I used to rub them under any old table to get them tacky, and later I'd have to wash the keyboard." Rowles went to the piano, picked up the bench, and put it behind the cash register, near the front door. He replaced it with a Cookery chair. In one motion, he sat down, leaned over, poised his fingers a second over the keyboard, and sank into a very slow "Mood Indigo." He moved in a gentle, circular fashion, as if he were leafing through a stamp album, and he punctuated his felicitous phrases by pointing his right toe at the ceiling. It lasted close to ten minutes, and was followed by an equally long and introverted version of "Prelude to a Kiss." Rowles's engine steadied, and the tempo went up in "I Can't Get Started." A light seemed to go on within the tune, and one could see the outline of its pleasant bones. A ruminative "Skylark" came next, and Rowles closed the set with a candent version of Fats Waller's "Jitterbug Waltz."

He remained at the piano half a minute, and, letting his hands hang loose, vibrated them vigorously, like a swimmer loosening his muscles. "I've got to go downstairs and chant with Buster," he said. "I'll be back in ten minutes." Jazz musicians, like poets, are prone to inscrutable remarks; here is what Rowles had told a friend about Thelonious Monk: "I went into this restaurant in Tokyo six or seven years ago, when I was on a tour, and there was Monk standing at the bar. He was wearing one of his funny hats, and the whole time he revolved slowly, his hands raised and fluttering like moths around his head. When he came face to face with the bar, he'd stop, take a drink, then start spinning again. I'd seen him before, of course, but I'd never talked to him, so I introduced myself. I made a couple of attempts at conversation. Silence. Then he said, 'You got any kids?' I told him I had a son who was twenty-four, and I was about to mention Stacy and Zip when he said, 'He's too old. Get rid of him.' And he never said another word." And here is what Rowles said one night at Michael's Pub when he was asked how he was. "Oh, I feel more like I do now than when I first came in."

Rowles's playing demands exactly as much as it offers. Every tune is multi-layered, and, except for those rare times when he tires and repeats certain phrases, it has no soft spots. His singular harmonic sense governs his attack. He uses strange, flatted chords that seem to leave his phrases suspended and unresolved. They are questioning chords. His delicate runs have the same upturned, searching air. They begin in odd places, and while a run is moving buoyantly up the keyboard it suddenly breaks off, there is a pause, and the run resumes, descending through the very notes just played, as if Rowles were trying to knit the two parts. The melody slopes along in the middle distance, and his immaculate time is a further stabilizer. His touch is almost Tatum-light, and even his rushes of hard, no-nonsense single notes in fast numbers have no clamor or urgency. His chords and broken, winding runs suggest a hesitant, puzzled attitude, a continual where-do-I-go-from-here approach. But this is only an illusion, a polite way of not overwhelming the listener.

Rowles reappeared. "I chant with Buster a lot," he said. "He's into the Buddhist thing, and chanting keeps him cool. 'Nam Myoho Renge Kyo' we go, over and over, in unison. I don't know what it means, but it makes you feel like you're doing your rosary. It makes you less conscious of yourself, and I always get in my own way during the first set every night. My playing is a matter of concentration, a matter of intensity. A jumble of things flash constantly through my mind, like people's faces and what I'm going to play in the channel, and all the while the melody is with me subconsciously. I have that, and I have the chords. They're the carpet, and my playing is like dancing on that carpet. I learned how to accompany singers and horn players by listening to the backgrounds that arrangers like Sy Oliver and Duke Ellington and Mary Lou Williams wrote for their soloists. Particularly Mary Lou when she was with Andy Kirk. In fact, I want to meet her while I'm here. It's unbelievable how much I owe that woman. It's unbelievable how much I owe a lot of people. Like Donald Brown, a Blackfoot Indian from Montana, who got me going in the right direction when I was a kid. He played tenor. When I first knew him, I was deep into Guy Lombardo. He was my favorite band, and I loved his piano player Freddy Kreitzer. Brown heard me doing some Lombardo tune at the piano in the gym at Gonzaga University, where I went for a year and a half, and he said, 'Ace, what are you doin' that for? You should be listening to the Benny Goodman Trio.' He took me downtown to a record store, and when I heard Teddy Wilson in the Trio, that was it. It changed my whole life. Brown had absolute pitch and radar ears. If I played a Wilson or Tatum record and asked him about certain chords, he'd tell me to slow the turntable down, which you could do on those old windup Victrolas, and he'd spell out every note. Another person I'll always owe is Ben Webster. I met him late in 1939, in Seattle, where I was studying law—or at least my family thought I was—at the University of Washington. My real father, whose name was Hunter, passed when I was three months old, and I was raised by my mother and a stepfather, who adopted me and gave me his name. My mother had studied guitar, and she played the piano real well by ear, but he was in the rug business and wasn't musical at all, except when he'd come home with some cronies at two in the morning and get me up to play the piano while they sang gems like 'Ace in the Hole.' Anyway, Ben had just joined Duke Ellington, and I knew Ben was *the* man.

When I was twenty-one and legally free, I dumped the law thing for good and took off for L.A. I played with Slim and Slam. Slim was into his crazy vooterini talk then, and he played the piano with the backs of his hands as well as the regular way. Then I played intermission piano for Art Tatum. Man, I was smothered I was so scared. I couldn't believe his hands. They were stubby, but they stretched like cobras when he wanted to reach a tenth or more. And the way they moved, he didn't look like he was playing at all. I'd ask him how he did such-and-such, and he'd show me. But if I mentioned his fantastic touch, all he'd say was 'Oh, I don't know' and start talking about Westerns or baseball. Once, I hung out with him for three days and three nights, and sometimes he'd play seven or eight hours at a stretch. Dorothy and I were married by then, and when I got home she was so mad she Art-Tatumed me right out of the house for a week. I never travel without Art; I have six cassettes of him over in my hotel room. I worked with the Spirits of Rhythm, too. Teddy Bunn was in the group and so was Leo Watson. And I worked with Lee and Lester Young. Lester was the coolest man I ever met. He had his own language. He'd turn to me on the bandstand and say, 'Startled doe. Two o'clock,' which meant if you looked into the audience at where two o'clock was you'd see this pretty chick with big eyes. 'Bob Crosby's in the house' meant a cop had just come in, and 'Bing and Bob' meant the fuzz were all over the place. When I first knew him, he said, 'There's a gray boy at the bar who is looking for you.' 'What's a gray boy?' I said. 'Man, *you're* a gray boy,' he said, smiling with those green teeth he had then, 'and I'm an Oxford gray.'

"And everything that was good was 'bulging.' It was a telescoping of a phrase that had started out 'I've got eyes for that,' which meant 'I like that,' and became 'I've got great big eyes for that,' and then 'I've got bulging eyes for that.' But if he didn't like something or somebody, all he did was puff out his cheeks—no words at all, just balloon cheeks."

It was nine-thirty, and Rowles applied more Tacky-Finger, then went back to the piano. He began an intense study of "Willow Weep for Me," an immovable song that ultimately bowed to his relentless exploration.

He seemed to tunnel right through "The Man I Love," circumventing its singsong, steplike melody. "My Buddy," its melody decked out with embellishments, and properly played as a waltz, followed. It gave way to "Miss Brown to You," which he sang in a pleasant, husky voice. Freddie Hubbard's "Down Under," Billy Strayhorn's "Lush Life," and an ancient tune called "In the Middle of a Kiss" came next, and he closed with a rocking, medium-tempo rendition of Duke Ellington's "Cottontail" which included a paraphrase of Ben Webster's famous solo.

Rowles put a fat, leather-bound loose-leaf book on his table, and went to get a fresh vodka-tonic. "I call that *My Book*," he said when he returned. "It has all the tunes in it I play—maybe a thousand or so." The neatly typed titles were arranged by letter and by category. There were no fewer than seventy waltzes, among them "My Mom," "Dancing with Tears," "Millicent," "Charade," and "Many Happy Returns." The letter "I" began: "It's Like Reaching for the Moon," "I Was Doing All Right," "It Don't Mean a Thing," "It All Depends on You," "I'll See You in My Dreams," "I'll Never Be the Same," and "I'll Remember April." And the letter "S" started out: "Suppertime," "Some Saturday," "Solitaire," "Something," and "Skylark." "I've written some of my own songs and lyrics in the last couple of years. Just off-the-wall stuff. There's one about tennis, a game I love and think of as physical chess. And there's one about Monk, and one about Fred Astaire, and a thing about missionaries called 'Behind the Faith.'" He started to sing softly, "I loved the Matto Grosso/All the wild Indians in it/ Shooting food with spears/ And shrinking heads." And he went on, "Just imagine their reaction/ When a missionary shows up/ And tries to tell them how to live/ As if they didn't know already.

"Ben Webster and I used to play a lot of golf in the fifties, when he lived on the Coast. We'd tee up, and all these fancy types would be waiting their turn, mumbling under their breath about that big black guy who was holding them up. Ben would have one of his little hats on the back of his head, and he'd stand there before the ball, his big front sticking out, and talk to himself: 'Now, Ben, do it just like when you were in the Masters. Keep your head down, and not too many Wheaties.' And he'd take a terrific swing—pouf!—and the ball would dribble ten feet. We only saw each other on the tees and greens, but we laughed our way around the whole course. Then last summer I got a feeling, a notion. I hadn't seen him for years, and something told me it was time to get over to Copenhagen, where he was living. After I worked the Newport Festival here, I went to Europe with Carmen McRae. She gave me a week off, and I got up to Copenhagen and stayed on Ben's couch. He wasn't in good shape. He was drinking a lot and his legs hurt him, and he was enormous. He never wore anything the whole time but his shorts, and he'd sit in a little swivel chair and talk about 'the Judge,' which is what he called Milt Hinton. Ben was a Jekyll-and-Hyde. He was a sensitive cat, and when he wasn't drinking he was soft-spoken and polite and as gentle as cream. But after two drinks, forget it. Benny Carter was the only man he'd listen to when he was like that. If Ben was roaring around and Carter happened to be there, he'd say, 'Cut it out, Ben. Go sit down and behave yourself,' and Ben would. Ben used to say of Carter, 'There's a man who can bake a cake as light as a feather and whip any man.' One night in Copenhagen, we put Ben to bed—there were always people flowing in and out—and went out to see the sights. I got back late, and there was Ben stretched out on the marble floor like a gingerbread man. I still don't know how I got him into bed again. When I had to leave to meet Carmen, Ben hung out the window, still in his shorts, his huge shoulders and chest bare, and waved and waved and kept saying, 'Come back, S.H.,' which is what we called each other. 'Come back and see me soon.' Ten days later, the cable came saying that he had got off."

Like a Family

The Modern Jazz Quartet has had just two personnel changes in its off-and-on thirty-one years of existence. It invented a semi-improvised collective approach that defied the banality of the endless solo and the rigidity of conventional arrangements. It developed the heart-to-heart and head-to-head musical interplay and sensitivity of a string quartet. And it perfected a subtlety that misled the unknowing into regarding it as a cocktail group and the knowing into scoffing at it as staid and stuffy. Because of its instrumentation and its constant interweaving, the group has a tintinnabulous texture. It shimmers, it rings and hums, it sounds like loose change. As in any first-rate mechanism, its parts are as notable as their sum. John Lewis's style is single-noted and highly rhythmic. His simple, seemingly repetitive phrases are generally played just behind the beat, where much of the secret of jazz lies. He is an emotional pianist—in a transcendental way—and he succeeds, where most pianists fail, in transmitting his emotion. Milt Jackson is a consummate foil. He is profuse, ornate, affecting, and original. His solos, inspired by Charlie Parker and Dizzy Gillespie, are open at both ends; that is, they seem to have started before we hear them and to go on after they have stopped. Whereas Lewis has a dry, belling tone, Jackson reverberates and rolls, continually threatening to spill over onto the rest of the group. Percy Heath moves between, through, and under Lewis and Jackson, supporting them with a beautiful tone and an easy exactness. Connie Kay is much the same. He is precise yet driving, and he gets a resilient, perfectly tuned tone on his drums and cymbals that both embellishes and strengthens the total sound.

Heath is tall and thin and patrician. He has a high, receding forehead and a pharaoh's nose. Kay is even taller, with a full, monolithic face that conceals sharp, lively eyes. Jackson is short and bird-boned, and is dominated by a slightly askew owl face. Lewis looks like a Teddy bear, and when he moves he runs, even from room to room; he has handsome, untroubled, intelligent eyes. Lewis speaks softly, allowing his constant smile to carry half the weight of his words. Heath's near-shouting is rounded by continual laughter. Jackson's speech is quiet and slurred and almost subliminal, while Kay sounds like his bass drum.

If the Modern Jazz Quartet ever recorded an autobiographical work, it might sound like this:

I *Masters of the Music*

LEWIS

The original Quartet was made up of Milt and Ray Brown and Kenny Clarke and myself, and we decided to try and become a group after a record date early in the fifties for Dizzy Gillespie's recording label. There were things wrong in the music around us that we all agreed on, and some of them were long, long solos and that formula on a tune of everybody playing the melody in the first chorus, followed by a string of solos, and then the melody again. We didn't work together steadily until 1954. We lost Ray Brown before we really got started, because he married Ella Fitzgerald and we couldn't afford him anyway. Then I went back to school—the Manhattan School of Music—and after I'd graduated Milt didn't know whether he wanted to be just a member of a group or the leader, so while he was deciding I took a job with Ella as her accompanist, during which time the Quartet, or a quartet, with Percy Heath and Horace Silver on piano and Clarke and Milt worked the first Newport Jazz Festival. We made our first record in 1952 and had our first gig late that year, at the old Chantilly, on West Fourth Street. Kenny Clarke left us in 1955. He was sick and we talked about it and he said he knew he'd be better off on his own just then, so he left and Connie Kay came in. Kenny is still one of my favorite drummers. He's profound. You can listen to him all by himself, without anything else. And I think he plays even better now in Europe than he did then.

KAY

I joined the Quartet in February of 1955. Lester Young, who I'd been with, was out of town with Jazz at the Philharmonic, and I was thinking of taking a job with Sonny Stitt, the alto player, until Lester got back, but Monte Kay, the Quartet's manager, called me one morning and said the Quartet had a concert that night in Washington, D.C., and then a two-week gig at Storyville, in Boston, and would I like to go along? I met John at Penn Station and he filled me in on difficult pieces like "Django" going down on the train. I knew Milt real well and I'd met Percy and John. I understood it was a two-week gig, but when it was over nobody said anything and nobody has yet and that was thirty years ago.

JACKSON

The quartet has been like a marriage. It's become a way of life. You get to know each other's habits and mannerisms. At all times, each one knows what the other is going to do. John and I are more active than Percy and Connie musically. In fact, John is more than active, he's reckless the way he runs from place to place. He's been hit a couple of times by cars. He's got to be more careful of himself. John is always coming up with new ideas, and that keeps it from getting monotonous. Of course, there are times when I like to straighten out and just swing, get away from that controlled thing and play that old-time music. I generally take a group out in the summer—maybe Jimmy Heath, Percy's brother, and Cedar Walton and Bob Cranshaw and Mickey Roker. I took a band out several years ago and there was quite a lot of work, but things are slow now, so I've given up on it. I make records on my own, and I've thought of setting up a studio and teaching, just as a means of coming off the road. But as long as the Quartet is going the way it is, I don't have the time. So when I'm not working, I'm home playing pool and learning to swim.

HEATH

I guess I took over the job of handling the Quartet's money because I handled the contract for our first gig at the Chantilly. I'm supposed to give out the checks every week, just as Connie is supposed to make hotel reservations and take care of transportation, but we have an attorney and a road manager and a booker and a travel agency now, and they take care of most of those details. But we used to do it all, and I suppose you have to go through that discipline at first. We probably make as much money as any jazz group. In Europe, they generally pay your travel, and some festivals do here, but most of it is on us. And we spend a good deal of our pocket money on the road just to live right. We consider that we're of such calibre and station that we should stay in the best places and eat the best food. Some years the Quartet has a little money left over, and one year we invested it in a new ski resort in New York State, which was fine until they foreclosed the lift. I understand the enterprise is a great success now. But we've kept aside enough to start a pension plan and we have our own publishing company, but none of us could live on that. Milt and John probably make twice as much as I do. John has his movie scores and royalties, and Milt has royalties and recordings and the separate gigs he takes every summer. But I have no complaints. June, my wife, hasn't had to work since 1949, when we first moved to New York and lived on Sugar Hill, where we had some fish-and-chip days. But the whole thing with the Quartet is that we have made some money, but we have never conformed. We have built up a lot of prestige, and been paid for doing it.

LEWIS

I got out of the Army in 1945, and when I went back to the University of New Mexico they told me I might as well go to music school. I'd met John

Hammond through David Sarvis, who taught in the drama department at the university, so I went to New York and entered the Manhattan School of Music, and John helped me financially and every other way. Before I'd left home, in Albuquerque, I'd heard radio broadcasts from Billy Berg's, in Los Angeles, where Charlie Parker and Dizzy Gillespie were playing with Ray Brown and Milt Jackson, and it was unbelievable. When I got to New York, I played one-nighters while I was waiting out my union card. I worked on Fifty-second Street with Allen Eager and Eddie Davis and with a band that Hot Lips Page and Walter Page had. Joe Keyes, a most remarkable trumpet player, was in it. In the meantime, Kenny Clarke had come back from the service and through him Dizzy hired me as a pianist for my summer-school recess, and then he asked me to come and play with the band. I had to make a decision about the school and Dizzy. I decided I'd learn more from Dizzy, so I joined him in September, 1946. Kenny was in the band, and Ray Brown and James Moody. We went on ninety one-nighters in a row, and it was a very emotional tour—always a lot of fun and a lot of crying. Ray Brown left and we lost two drummers and the pianos were always half a tone out of tune and the audiences weren't too great because they didn't know how to dance to that music. It was really a concert band, which we found out when we went to Europe, in 1948, where we left everybody's mouth hanging open. Dizzy was marvellous to work under. He was never late, and that was when I learned not to be late. You have to get that over with.

I was disgusted with my playing at the time and I told Dizzy he better get someone else. But he talked me into staying. He always looked after me. Once, when I got sick on the road, he brought me all the way back to New York to the hospital. I finally left Dizzy because I wanted to go back to Paris. If you ever go to Paris, you'd leave anything because of it. It's the jewel of jewels. I stayed there for five months, then came back to join Miles Davis' little band, with Gerry Mulligan and Eddie Bert and Max Roach. It was exciting, something new. Then Miles got me a job with Illinois Jacquet, who had his brother Russell and J. J. Johnson and Joe Newman and Jo Jones. I was with the band about eight months and I never saw so much money. Jacquet was making suitcases of money. We had to play "Flying Home" about four times a night, but I always found something in it. Norman Granz wanted me to come with his Jazz at the Philharmonic, but I decided I wanted to go back to the Manhattan School of Music. I got all the way to the airport on the way to meet Granz before I turned around and came back. Norman is a hard man to say no to and we weren't the greatest of friends for five or six years. But I got my Bachelor of Music, and in 1953 my Master of Music.

KAY

Sid Catlett was my man, my idol. The first time I heard him I was working after school and on Saturdays in a Chinese art gallery in the Fifties, and one day I passed Café Society Uptown, which was between

Lexington and Park on Fifty-eighth Street, and the door was open and music was coming out. I stepped in and Teddy Wilson's band, with Big Sid, was rehearsing, and when I heard Sid that was it. I got to meet him a while later, when he was working on Fifty-second Street at the Downbeat Club. He was out on the street after work trying to get a cab to go home and I offered him a ride in a little raggedy 1935 Studebaker I had. "O.K., Bub," he said, which is what he called everybody. I drove him to One Hundred and Fifty-sixth and Amsterdam, where he lived, and after that I'd drive him all over and he'd always tell me to stop by any time—ground floor, right at the back. One night we drove around to a lot of clubs. We went into Nick's and he sat in, we went somewhere else and he sat in with a bebop band, and then he sat in with a swing group. He could play with anybody or anything. He was a happy-go-lucky person. Nothing bothered him. I think the secret of his playing was in his attitude toward things. He wasn't fazed even when he took a job at Billy Rose's Diamond Horseshoe. These showgirls would each bring a part of his drums onto the stage, singing something about him while they did, and then leave him up there all alone, where—bam!—he was supposed to play an unaccompanied solo absolutely cold, the lights on him and on his tuxedo, which was covered with sequins. He taught me little things. He'd stop by where I was working and tell me my left hand was too inactive or my beat on the ride cymbal was too loud, and he'd show me things at his house. But I learned the most from him in his attitude—his quiet, beautiful way toward things, whether it was the world situation or just people.

LEWIS

I was less influenced by piano players than by other instrumentalists, like Lester Young and Coleman Hawkins and Ben Webster, and trumpet players like Roy Eldridge and Harry Edison. I was formed more from hearing horn players. I learned some things from Earl Hines, not too many, and some of Count Basie's things, and of course the greatest pianist was Art Tatum. I'm happy it happened that way. I didn't get trapped into mechanical things, piano things.

When I take a solo, I try not to look at my fingers. It distracts me from the music-making. And after I learn a piece, I stop thinking about the rules—the bars and the harmony and the chords. I think about other things, even other music. If you break through those mere rules, destroy them, that's good, and it can become quite a marvellous experience. It's not just sadness or joy, it's something beyond that, perhaps exhilaration, but that's rare. When you start to play, an idea comes along, and that dictates where you have to go. Sometimes things go wrong, and many times you find a nice way of getting out of a phrase that is better than the original way you were going. But you have to be a musician first and an instrumentalist second. It's more important to be a master of the music than a master of an instrument, which can take you over.

KAY

I don't like to take drum solos at all. Drums are a flat instrument, and besides Catlett is gone and there's only one Buddy Rich. I know how I feel when other drummers solo. It seems like you've heard them all before. There just aren't that many original people around. But when I do solo I think of the tune I'm playing. I try to fit what I'm playing into the composition rather than do just twelve bars of rudiments. The melody goes through your mind and you go along with it, fitting yourself to it. Also, my solos are always short, which I learned from Lester Young. He never took more than two or three choruses and neither did Charlie Parker, but they always managed to say all they had to say.

JACKSON

When I solo I come down from the melodic line and the chords that are being played, or anything else, like a phrase the drummer might play, which can turn what you're doing into something lyrical. And I keep the melody in mind. I always remember the melody and then I have something to fall back on when I get lost, and with the human element I do get lost, but I've always been able to find my way back. Of course, your troubles and pleasures will come out in your music. But you do the best you can to entertain. Jazz is an art, but it's in the form of an entertaining art. I'm most relaxed in the blues or in ballads, which are my criterion. I get the most results from myself then and I reach the audience quicker. My blues come from church music and my ballads from the fact I'm really a frustrated singer. Lionel Hampton was the only influence I've had technically on the instrument. I heard him one night at the Michigan State Fair, in 1941, when he had Dexter Gordon and Howard McGhee, and that night really got to me. In style and ideas, I adapted myself to Charlie Parker and Dizzy. I can get around the mechanical feeling of my instrument by making glisses and grace notes, so that it sounds more like a horn. I still use a prewar Deagan vibraharp, and every two or three years the Deagan people take it apart and put it together again for me.

LEWIS

When I'm working behind Milt, I try and be out of the way and at the same time supply something that might even improve on what he's playing. And I try to supply patterns that are strong rhythmically. It's easy to underestimate rhythm-making. I can never guess what Jackson is going to do next. I'm supporting him but I'm also moving along parallel to him. I learned to play collectively in Dizzy's band. I was trying to find a way to function, to add something, since most of the time I could play anything and no one would hear me anyway, and one night it happened up in Boston behind Dizzy when he played "I Can't Get Started." My discovery was related, too, to the way Kenny Clarke played drums in Dizzy's band. He complemented everything that was going on.

Ideas for compositions pop into my head all the time and I write them down in a notebook. The things you hear and see go back in the brain and eventually something comes out—melodic fragments or an opening for a piece or ideas of how something I've already written could be improved. The music I've heard inspires me, but it works negatively. The music I've heard suggests music I've never heard. It points to something that doesn't exist, that might be a little better, and I try to supply that. A piece can take a few hours or a couple of days to write. My writing and my playing are connected. I can take ideas I have written or maybe not written down yet ideas just floating around back there. I can take those ideas or written things and expand on them each time I improvise, so in that way the pieces I write are never finished, never complete. The reverse—taking an idea or a phrase from a solo of mine and letting it inspire a new composition—is trying to happen to me for the first time, and I don't know whether to let it happen or not.

The group dictates what I write. I think in dramatic terms. Anyone playing the solo part in a concerto is dramatic, and it's the same thing with our little tiny group. In a piece like "Three Little Feelings," the star characters are Percy and Milt and Connie. They are given things to do that focus on them. I have written a lot of pieces based on the commedia dell'arte. I find the idea of the commedia attractive. They had to do the same things as jazz musicians. They never wrote things down. They developed pieces based on the prominent characters or events of the town they were working things which would attract their audience. So they created their jobs, just as jazz musicians do. And, of course, I love the blues. Blues pieces are easier to write. You have a little form to fill out. I try to find blues in all non-blues—just in the way a group of notes goes together in a particular short phrase. I keep feeling those elements in non-blues music—the music in southern Yugoslavia, in Hungary, the music in North Africa and the Middle East, and in flamencan music. I don't believe in too much form. Music should have surprise in it, and too much fugue or any formula like that takes away the pleasure, which is what bothers me about what Gunther Schuller was trying to do with his Third Stream. I'm not interested in that. But I am interested in the classical *orchestra*—particularly the stringed instruments, which still have to be brought successfully into jazz.

II *Beginnings*

HEATH

I was born April 30,1923, in Wilmington, North Carolina, but when I was eight months old we moved to Philadelphia. I have an older sister, Betty, and two younger brothers—Jimmy, the tenor player, and Albert, the drummer. Pop was an automobile mechanic. He was a wild little guy, a great guy, and sharp and handsome. He played clarinet with the Elks. It was part of a weekly cycle. On Mondays he'd pawn the clarinet and get twenty dollars and pay his bills, and on Saturday, when he got paid, he'd get the clarinet out of pawn and play with the Elks on Sunday, and on Monday, back to the pawnshop. I said to him once,"Pop, if you just keep the clarinet out of pawn one week you'll be all right and you won't have to pay that dollar interest." But it was his thing, his habit, and he never kicked it. He had Bessie Smith records, and every once in a while he'd pull out his clarinet and do Ted Lewis or his own Silas Green routine—Silas Green from New Orleans. In the early thirties, he rented space in a garage and had his own shop, and up until then we had money. Then the Depression ran the small businesses out, and he took a W.P.A. job for a couple of years, and went back to being a mechanic for somebody else. My mother was a hairdresser. She was a choir singer, and her mother before her, in the Baptist church, where I spent a lot of time when I was growing up. Those old sisters screaming and falling out in church, you felt something going through you when you watched them. We had a family quartet. My grandmother sang alto and my mother soprano. I used to sing on a sepia kiddie hour on the radio, and the kids who made it on the show got special passes to the Lincoln Theatre, where we would get to go backstage and shake hands with Fats Waller and Louis Armstrong and Duke Ellington.

I went to school in Philly until the last two years of high school. There was an all-colored school across the street from my grade school and the Italian and Jewish kids in our block had to walk three blocks to their school, which we all thought was a joke. From junior high on it was integrated, but six years of separation and the damage was done. Being thrown suddenly together couldn't undo it. I played a little violin in junior high and I had the second chair in the first-violin section at graduation. But it was rough getting home through the streets—you know, a little skinny black guy named Percy carrying a violin. I chopped and hauled wood after school, and hauled coal and ice in the summer. I'd bring home four or five dollars a week, which was all right in those days. My father's mother had a grocery store in Wilmington, and we used to go there for the summers, and so I stayed down there and finished up high school. I came back to Philly when I was seventeen, and went to work with my father and the two of us enrolled in a night school that specialized in mechanics. This lasted a year or so, and when I saw I wasn't getting anywhere at the shop—I'd be upstairs really involved in a carburetor job when they'd call up, "Hey, Percy, come on down and wash this car or do this grease job"—I said, "O.K., Pop, maybe I'm a dummy, but I'm going someplace else." I went to work for the railroad and ended up handling big equipment, moving engines around the yard, and I earned a boiler-washer's rating. I started going out with girls and I had a car. I was making a lot of overtime and I'd get these fat paychecks—eighty dollars and more every two weeks, which beat the twenty bucks I was making with Pop. Then after a year or so I got a bright idea—volunteer for the Air Force and get into aircraft-mechanics school. I took the physical. Underweight. They told me to come back in thirty days. I went home and slept late and ate bananas and went back. Still underweight. My number came up and I was drafted and I realized why I was told I was underweight: They didn't have any colored aircraft-mechanics school.

I made a great score in the mechanical part of the aptitude tests the Army gives you, and one day I was asked, "Do you want to be a pilot or a navigator or a bombardier?" I was amazed. I remembered reading about some guy standing up in Congress when this program was announced and saying, "This is all very well and they've come a long way, but they aren't ready for *flying* yet." I was sent to Keesler Field, in Biloxi, Mississippi, where we lived in tents in a low area way over on the wrong side of the base, separate and unequal. The closest we got to an airplane was at Saturday parades when somebody would look up and say, "Hey, there goes a B-24." Then we were shipped to the Tuskegee Army Air Force Base, at Tuskegee, Alabama. I graduated in January, 1945. Seven hundred of us started out and twenty-eight graduated. I was a lieutenant and had my wings and my boots and everything but a forty-five, which is the last thing they issue before you go overseas. I never got my forty-five. The European war ended and I got out and there I was with all that training and no place to use it. There were umpteen million white pilots with multiple-engine ratings coming back and I was a Negro with a single-engine rating. So I had to find something captivating to me. Having become an officer and a gentleman, I naturally didn't want to go back to all that dirt and grime. I'd heard a record with Coleman Hawkins and Sid Catlett and John Simmons, the bass player, and decided that's for me. I decided to go back to music. I went to the Granoff School of Music in Philly and studied harmony and I took lessons on the bass from a little old guy named Quintelli. I learned the C scale and how to read stock parts and I joined the union. I'd already worked in non-union places in some really funky neighborhoods in Philly. Then my brother Jimmy came home from Nat Towles' band. He'd heard Charlie Parker for the first time, and Johnny Hodges and Cleanhead Vinson just weren't it anymore. So we had continuous practice sessions at home. My mother was a great woman to put up with it. We even wrote out Parker's "Billie's Bounce" for Pop to play on clarinet. He made it sound just like a march. So we learned bop and had gigs. I worked with a Nat Cole-type trio for five or six months and then became part of the house rhythm section at the Philly Down Beat Club, along with Red Garland and Charlie Rice. Everybody played with us—Coleman Hawkins and Eddie Davis and Howard McGhee. I worked in a rhythm-and-blues band led by Joe Morris and joined McGhee in 1947, and I was with Fats Navarro and J. J. Johnson and Bud Powell and Art Blakey and Miles Davis after that, and in 1950 I went with Dizzy.

KAY
My parents lived in New York, but my mother's brother lived in Tuckahoe, and I was born there on the twenty-seventh of April, 1927. I was

the only child. My parents are West Indians who came from an island named Montserrat. Their name is Kirnon and I was born Conrad Henry Kirnon. Originally the name was Kiernan, which was the name of one of my great-great-great-grandfathers, who was Irish. My father had a tailor shop in New York, and when that didn't do too good he got a job as an elevator operator, which he did until he retired. My mother had odd jobs doing housework and down in the garment center. She was musically inclined. She played piano and organ in church and she sang a little. She taught me how to play piano. She insisted I learn, but I didn't like it. My father played a little guitar. My mother used to let me stay up and listen to Cab Calloway broadcasts and I'd take the wooden bars out of coat hangers and shape them into drumsticks and play on the hassock. And a friend of mine had an uncle who kept a snare drum under his bed and we'd sneak it out and play it. So I always loved drums. I had my first gig right around the corner from where we lived in the Bronx, at a place called the Red Rose. All the guys were young and the only seasoned professional was the piano player, Jimmy Evans. He'd grown up in Monk's neighborhood, in the West Sixties, along with Elmo Hope and Tiger Haynes. The drummer at the Red Rose got sick and they had heard me practicing out of the window and asked me if I wanted to go to work. My parents said yes, and I stayed there weekends on and off for a couple of years. After the Red Rose, I was at Minton's, in Harlem, in a trio with Sir Charles Thompson and Miles Davis. We'd play one set and generally that was it. The rest of the evening it would be people sitting in—Charlie Parker and Dizzy Gillespie, Milt Jackson, Georgie Auld, Red Rodney. I remember when Ray Brown first came there. Freddie Webster came in all the time and he showed Miles how to get those big oooh sounds, those big tones Miles uses now. I was with Cat Anderson's band after that and then I toured the South with a rock-and-roll group led by Frank Floorshow Cully. I wanted to see what it was like down there. Cully was a tenor player and he was just like his nickname. He'd jump up and down when he played and stick the saxophone between his legs and do splits. Randy Weston, the pianist, was in that band, and it wasn't a bad band. The bass player hit all the wrong notes, but he had a hell of a beat. You just closed your ears and felt the beat. We travelled in a seven-passenger Chrysler, and we went as far as Lubbock, Texas, and both coasts of Florida and Mobile, Alabama. I wasn't too surprised because I'd heard how things were down there, but it was still a revelation. We worked at a big roadhouse for several weeks that used to feature people like Blue Barron and Horace Heidt—we were the first colored band that had ever played the place—and during intermission we were supposed to go back in the kitchen and stay there. But you'd be offered drinks by customers and you didn't know whether to accept and stay out front or get on back. In those days it didn't pay to be a pioneer. We'd pull up at a restaurant and be told to go around to the kitchen and there you'd find a regular booth with a Formica-top table, and all, which was fine with me because they always piled your plate up. At orange juice stands you'd have to drink your juice off to one side, and if we stopped at a grocery store they'd sell us cold cuts and canned stuff, but we had to eat it in the car. Once we ate in a restaurant owned by a colored cat and I told him if we get together, organize and the like, maybe we can do something about all this crap. Well, he wanted to fight me. He had two restaurants, he said, and everything was all right.

By this time I could get a job with anyone. My main asset was I could keep good time. I had made a whole lot of rock-and-roll records for Atlantic Records. I was with Lester Young off and on for five or six years. Lester and I were like buddies. When I joined him, I already knew him, but he didn't know I was joining him. I met him down in Penn Station and asked him what he was doing, and he said, "I'm waiting for the drummer, Lady Kay," which is what he always called me. "Well, I'm the drummer," I said. "What! You're the drummer?," and he fell out. He was a sweetheart to me. He was very shy. He didn't love crowds or to be around strangers, and he didn't like to eat. All that alcohol. He'd leave home for work with a fifth of Scotch every night and everybody in the band would work on it to keep Lester from getting too drunk. It was terrible I drank so much Johnny Walker. Later, the doctor told him to switch to cognac—a *little* cognac—so it was a whole bottle of cognac every night. A lot of the jive talk you hear now on TV I first heard from Lester, and when he and Basie and Old Man Jo Jones got together they all talked it. He wasn't a forceful person, but he'd get fed up. One time he had a trumpet player who took the same solo on a certain tune every night, and when he'd start Lester would look at me and say, "Damn, Lady Kay, there he goes again," and we'd sing the whole solo note for note right along with the trumpet player. Lester didn't feel he was getting the recognition he deserved and finally he got to the point where he didn't care whether he lived or died. I used to ask him why he didn't play his clarinet once in a while, and he'd always say, "Lady Kay, I'm saving that for my old age."

JACKSON

There were six boys in my family and I was the second. I was born in Detroit on January 1, 1923. My mother was from Georgia and my father from Winston-Salem. She had a very religious background the Church of God in Christ, which we call the Sanctified Church. She was a housewife and she worked in a defense plant during the war. My father was quiet but very lively, always on the go. I guess that's why I stayed so small— always moving so much. Also, it's a trait of Capricorn. My father was a factory worker with Ford and Chevrolet, and he played three or four instruments—piano, guitar, and so forth. I started on guitar when I was seven, and I was completely self-taught. I didn't study anything until I took piano lessons at eleven from a Mr. Holloway. I took them two years. By time I got to high school I was playing five instruments—drums in the marching band, timpani and violin in the symphony, guitar and xylophone in the dance band—and I sang in the glee club and choir. But

I was concentrating on drums. Then the music teacher asked me if I wanted to take lessons on the vibraharp, as something else to do. I'd finished the drum course and was even helping other kids on drums, so I tried vibraharp and got hung up on it immediately. I gave up the drums altogether and concentrated on vibes. By 1939 I had two things going. I travelled all over on weekends with a local gospel quartet, the Evangelist Singers. We broadcast every Sunday over CKLW from Windsor. I got into it through my playing in church. If they needed vibes, I made that; if it called for drums, I made that; if it called for guitar, I made that; if it called for piano, I made that. The other thing was I started playing vibes with Clarence Ringo and the George E. Lee band. Sugar Chile Robinson was in the first group I played with. I had met Dizzy Gillespie in 1942 and through him I had an opportunity to join Earl Hines' big band, which he was with. At least there were about to be negotiations to join the band, but I got drafted and ended up in Special Services in the Air Force. I never went overseas and I got out in 1944, and went back to Detroit, where I organized a little group called the Four Sharps. It had guitar, bass, piano, and me, and we were sponsored by the Cotton Club.

The Four Sharps stayed alive a year, and then Dizzy came through and sat in one night and persuaded me to go to New York, so I went, in October of 1945. He had Ray Brown and Max Roach and Charlie Rouse. We worked the Brown Derby on Connecticut Avenue in Washington, went back to New York, and out to Billy Berg's, in Los Angeles. We had Stan Levey on drums, Al Haig on piano, Ray Brown, Charlie Parker, Lucky Thompson, Diz, and me. We took the train. Man, four and a half days. We left on a Tuesday and got there Saturday. I guess we stayed out there six or eight weeks. Slim Gaillard had the other group at Berg's, and they wound up as the stars. People went for the new jive language he sang, and anyway Slim is a very entertaining man. And Frankie Laine would come in every night for his two numbers. The audiences couldn't understand what we were doing, but it didn't bother me. I'd just turn my back on them and listen to Charlie. That was all I wanted to hear. When we got back to New York, Dizzy organized his big band, and that's where I first met John Lewis. Klook—Kenny Clarke—was responsible for bringing John in. I stayed with Dizzy until 1947 and then worked with Howard McGhee and Jimmy Heath and Percy, and in 1949 and 1951 was with Woody Herman, and then I went back to Dizzy.

John and Ray Brown and Klook and myself had actually played as a group as early as 1947. We'd play and let the rest of the band rest. I guess it was Dizzy's idea. I stayed with Dizzy until 1952, when we tried to get the Quartet going. Ray Brown left, so we hired Percy Heath. John suggested the name of the group.

LEWIS

I was born in La Grange, Illinois, a suburb of Chicago, on May 3, 1920, but by July I was sitting in Albuquerque, where my grandmother and great-grandmother lived. They'd come from Santa Fe and my mother from Las Vegas, New Mexico, which was there long before that other one. My people came down from the Cherokees—the Virginia Cherokees. I don't know much about my father, Aaron Lewis, except that he came from Chicago and was an interior decorator and played good fiddle and piano. He and my mother were divorced not long after I was born, and my mother died of peritonitis when I was four. I remember that. So I was raised by my grandmother, and by my great-grandmother. Except for my mother, they were strong women. My great-grandmother knew Pat Garrett, who shot Billy the Kid, and I think she even knew Billy. And she knew Geronimo, the Apache chief, who was a remarkable man, a very clever, intelligent man. My grandmother was a caterer and my grandfather had a moving-and-storage company. I never knew him. He accidentally shot himself in the foot duckhunting and developed tetanus. And my great-great-grandfather had owned the Exchange Hotel in Santa Fe. I had a good childhood. Albuquerque was a town of just twenty-five thousand in those days and everything was so special—the Spanish culture and the air and the cleanness. We lived right in the middle of town and there were very few Negroes. It was the people of Spanish extraction, or Spanish and Indian extraction, who had the hard times, not the Negroes. I went to the public schools and the atmosphere was very competitive. Once you got on the honor roll, you had to *stay* on it.

Everybody played something in my family, so I started on the piano at five or six. It was drudgery, and I tried to revolt on the grounds the lessons cost so much, but failed. I took lessons forever. When I was ten or so I was in a little band. We were Boy Scouts winning music-achievement badges. Our first gig was in a real night club. We played from nine to twelve and were paid a dollar apiece and all we could eat, and someone came along to watch over us. There were local bands around and a lot of Southwest bands came through town. Eddie Carson had one of the local groups and I had cousins who played in it. Sticks McVea, who was a fantastic drummer, would bring his band in from Denver. Freddie Webster was in it, and he had a wonderful piano player named John Reger. John Hammond wanted Reger to play with Benny Goodman, but Reger's wife wouldn't let him go East. I'd take Reger's place some nights. And the Bostonians would come through, with Jay McShann on piano and Howard McGhee on trumpet. Lester Young sometimes played in town. He knew my whole family. By the time I was fourteen or fifteen, I was working in dance halls and night clubs. I had to learn Spanish music to play the fiestas. When I went to the University of New Mexico, I became the leader of a dance band there, and Eddie Tompkins, the trumpet player who had been with Jimmy Lunceford, would sit in. I took arts and sciences for two years, then became fascinated with anthropology. I devoured everything on the subject, and kept my music going at the same time. Then, six months before graduation, I was drafted. It's the only thing I've ever had against the Japanese people. I was in the Army four years, in Special Services, and the best thing about it was that I met Kenny Clarke in France in 1943 or 1944. At the time, there was a surplus of pianists and drummers, so Kenny and I took up trombone. It was all right. In fact, I can still play it.

III *Room To Live In*

JACKSON

I built my house in Scarsdale in the early seventies. My wife, Sandra, and I moved up there with our daughter, from Hollis, Long Island, where we'd lived for nine years. It's been beautiful. No hostility. The people around us have some money and they're not concerned with whether you're a Negro. We have all kinds—Jews, Italians, Negroes—and they just aren't concerned with it. I've handled the race thing fairly well. I've been pretty outspoken. I don't know whether it helps or hurts, but it gives me a clear outline on life and myself. The first thing a man has to do is take stock of himself. You have all these people who go to school and study and still don't know themselves or what they want in life. I never had that trouble. From the age of seven I knew I would play music. There was never any doubt in my mind. I've always had my feet on the ground, had a good idea of where I was going. Like in high school, I wanted to learn something about my ancestry. I wanted to know where my forefathers came from and what they did. I was regarded as a troublemaker, asking questions like that. And in 1943, during the Detroit race riots, I wanted to organize and go back to Detroit from the Army instead of going to Europe and fighting somebody else.

HEATH

We live in a big old white 1902 house in Springfield Gardens, in south Queens. It's near Farmers Boulevard, where the farmers used to take their stuff up to market. I bet we live on the only block in the city limits that has just four houses on it—ours, an old Colonial house whose owner, a lady, was born in our house, and two others. There aren't even any sidewalks out front and we have fruit trees in the back yard. The neighborhood was a model integrated one when we moved there in 1958, but it's changed. The white families have begun moving out and the area has become one of families where both parents work and the kids have keys to their houses to let themselves in, which is where the trouble starts. We never go out when I'm home. I seldom go in to New York anymore, unless it's to rehearsals or if we have a gig there. It's too much to go and see all those cats standing around, half of them without gigs.

LEWIS

The group is a coöperative and always has been. We don't have any such thing as a leader, in the old-time concept of a leader. I serve as artistic director and musical director. Occasionally, I *have* to make the group do something, and later they generally see it's what we should have done. Sometimes I cut things so fine trying to make everyone happy it frightens me. We've gotten along well or we wouldn't still be together. We're smart enough and clever enough to give each other room to live in, to have respect for each other's personalities. It's not a perfect marriage by any means; it's normal travelling by sea, with stormy periods and all. The time we see of each other outside of our work is reduced even more than it was. We see enough of each other when we're out on the road, where we always have separate rooms. Milt gets up early and I do, too. Percy and Connie don't. Some of us, Connie in particular, like to watch TV and some don't.

I bring in the music and the arrangements and the group starts learning. Every now and then I put something in a piece that they can't play, so there isn't any dullness. They are fair readers. It takes us a long time to learn things, but they're much faster than they used to be. It generally takes us three hours to learn a piece, which is the length of a standard rehearsal. The whole thing on my part is to anticipate this or that musical difficulty, which means spending more time writing and thinking. We have hundreds of numbers in our repertory, and it grows and changes all the time. Sometimes I change certain passages in numbers, and tempos automatically tend to get faster through the years. And the group grows steadily and understands the music better, and that contributes to change. When we haven't played a number for a long time, we have to sit down and start all over with it. Gradually each piece comes to sound as if it is improvised all the way through. Some actually are and some are almost all written. The length of a piece is pretty much dictated by where it is in the concert program, and the program is figured out, balanced out, from the first number to the last, so that it has a design and structure. So the program as a whole comes first, the pieces next, and the solos last. We don't have any prearranged signals, aside from somebody just looking up from his instrument, for letting each other know when one of us is finishing a solo. Jackson almost always takes the same number of choruses and I just seem to know when he is finishing, and it's the same with him when I solo. We abhor long solos. If good things don't happen in the first chorus of any solo, it's generally not going to happen at all.

HEATH

The group didn't take its first vacation for a long time. I guess I pushed hardest for it. My wife and I have three boys—Percy, Jason, and Stuart,— and this business of working all year, it was *nothing*. It was a double existence. If I'm out there on the road worrying about what's going on at home, I might as well not be there. So I had to tell June, "Whatever comes up is on you, Snooky," and she's handled all the cuts and bruises and sicknesses that come along with kids. When I first brought up the vacation idea, it was "Oh my . . . Hmm . . . Well, I don't know, the *Quartet* comes first." Damn! Anyway, we took our first vacation out on Fire

Island, and it was not the vacation we had hoped for. I lugged all this electrical gear out there—hi-fi, tape recorder, toaster—and trundled it down the boardwalk to our house, the people I passed nodding their heads and mumbling about what a great generator we must have, and of course we got there and no electricity. Then I discovered David Amram and some other cats were staying nearby, so I ended up jamming every night. On top of that, fishing—particularly surfcasting—is my thing, but nothing happened. I don't think a fish passed that beach all summer. So the next year we went out to Montauk and we've rented a house there ever since. We drive down the beach and fish and never see anybody for miles. There's a great group of people doing surf-fishing. They're from all walks. Sometimes I go to the Rockaways just south of where I live and once at dawn I was fishing and I noticed this figure way down the beach. We moved toward each other slowly and finally I thought, He looks familiar, and when we got near enough to see each other there was Ed Shaughnessy, the drummer on the "Tonight Show." We fell out—two jazz musicians meeting up at dawn on an empty beach. I don't see how people *don't* fish. To get that close to the fish in Montauk and not get involved—I don't see how people do it. Just to realize that big bass are swimming in between them in the water—unbelievable. I'm looking forward to the time when I can be by the seashore and in the sun chasing fish all year. Then if I take any vacation, it'll just be from fishing. Right now, messing around with all that salt water isn't the best thing for a bass player's hands. It softens them up. But I'm always practicing, and I start rehearsing seriously a week or two before we come back and my hands are generally O.K. by the time we play our first gig.

LEWIS

I met Mirjana, my wife, in Yugoslavia when the Quartet was on tour there. Her sister was going around with a Yugoslavian jazz pianist who worked in a group patterned after ours. I spent a lot of time with him and one night we went to Mirjana's house and I met her. She was going with someone else. I liked Yugoslavia very much. I liked it so much I went back every year to the jazz festival they have in June, and I'd spend most of my time with Mirjana's sister and her boyfriend. Then in the summer of 1962 Mirjana and her sister and the pianist—they were married by now— came to visit me in the South of France, where we were vacationing. They spent two weeks, and two weeks later Mirjana and I were married. You can only get married on Wednesdays and Saturdays in Zagreb, so we got married on a Wednesday, and on Thursday I had to leave for a South American tour, and it took two months to get all the papers so that Mirjana could join me. Both she and her sister are pianists, and their father was a voice teacher. He was a remarkable, great human being. He taught at the New England Conservatory. Her mother was an actress on stage and in films and she worked in the Underground during the war. We have two children—Sacha and Nina.

HEATH

June is one in a million, one in eighteen million. She comes from Philly, and when I met her she was working in a record shop. She had a falling-out with her family over things like having pictures of colored musicians on her walls. But she loved the music and she found the players were pretty human people. She'd stop by when we were practicing at my parents' house after the war, and I wouldn't even know she was there. She'd be sitting in the corner reading a book. It wasn't a matter of my choosing another race. It was a question of finding a good woman. I quit shaving back then—I couldn't stand all that scraping and chopping every day and she didn't mind. She was willing to go to New York with me in 1949 and willing to take a gig as a nurse's aide at thirty dollars a week while I sweated out my union card. I guess what finally drove us out of Philly was one night when we were walking home from a movie or something and this cop pulled up beside us and says, "Are you all right, Miss?" June looked at him and said, "What do you mean?" "Well, I'm just doing my job," the cop says. "Of course I'm all right," June said, and we went on. And you know, that cop was a neighborhood cop and he knew who I was.

KAY

I still love to play, but it's not like when I was younger. I don't seem to see and hear that fire—that musical fire—that was all around us then. I don't seem to hear that kind of music anymore. Generally the people I like to play with just aren't around. They're in the studios or out of town or they have their own groups. But when I get the chance I like to play with Ray Brown and Sonny Rollins and Jimmy Heath and John—John Lewis. To my mind, John plays very underrated piano. I like to play with Dizzy and Miles and I like Oscar Peterson and Clark Terry. I like to play with big bands, too. I don't think it's any harder. I play the same way as with a small group. A lot of drummers make the mistake with big bands of being louder and heavier, but all that does is bog things down. Playing with the Quartet can get a little monotonous. Sometimes you have to play the same numbers over and over to please the people. But no one in the group ever plays the same thing twice. It's always new, always different, and I have just about complete freedom. Sometimes John writes out a drum part to give me an idea of what he wants, but then I can change it around to the way I want it, and I'm absolutely free behind the soloists. I can feel by what they're playing when a solo is coming to an end. I can feel that they've just about run out of what they want to do. And I can feel when someone might want to change the rhythm or double the tempo.

HEATH

A group sound is one thing to work for and individual virtuosity is something else. I don't worry about the virtuosity thing. Most bass solos, particularly if you don't know the tune, sound the same. The bassists figure out certain sounds and patterns and just fit them to whatever it is they're playing. I used to hang around with John Simmons a lot and then with Oscar Pettiford. O.P. and I would play bass-and-cello duets all night. Ray Brown showed me how to hold the bass properly. I always considered Ray the walker, the rhythm man, and Pettiford the soloist. But I'd rather be part of a group. I have to play certain parts as written, but you can hand a group of notes to ten different players and each one will read them differently. It's up to me to make those notes say exactly what they have to say, in a particular spirit. What we have over most groups is simple: We've played together longer. Another advantage is doing exactly what we want to do by creating music and selling musical entertainment. We've taken jazz into the concert halls of the world, even into the Mozarteum, in Salzburg. We've performed with a lot of symphony orchestras, and respect for jazz has grown among symphony players. Some of them have even become jazz players. For a long time, white Americans only understood polkas and fox-trots and waltzes, but through rock they're beginning to understand the jazz feeling, even if it comes from listening to an imitation of Muddy Waters from England. Jazz has always been considered a dirty music, an evil music, a colored music, and the country is still ashamed of it.

Jazz is a funny thing. If you ever let the externals dominate—classical music or Eastern music or Brazilian music—you have something else. But as long as you can incorporate little bits and pieces from the East or Vienna or Brazil and still keep the special feeling of that dotted eighth, that pulse, that afterbeat, then it's fine. It's the same thing with the long solos, the Coltranes. I'd go hear Coltrane and after the set, which might be one long solo, I'd say, "Hey, 'Trane. How are you, man? You sound good," or some such, and I'd beat it out of there, so that I didn't have to say any more. That music was just one facet of existence; all it did was shout Help! But all you had to do was look away from the chaos Coltrane's music was staring at and you'd find the ocean still there, the beauty and peace still there.

The way you play has to do with the way you feel that night. You hear that your kid was punched in the face three thousand miles away or you're lonesome and haven't found anybody to talk to or you're tired of the town and sick of each other—it all comes out in the music. After all, those people up there on the stand or the stage are *human*. You have to know how it feels to be miserable, how it feels to be sad, how it feels to be in the dumps before you can project it. When that slave cried out in the field, he wasn't just making music, he *felt* that way.

Einfühlung

The defenses of Ellis Larkins seem not so much conscious as a hapless reaction to a precocious childhood. Larkins was born in Baltimore in 1923, and at the age of eleven made his début as a classical pianist by playing a movement of Mozart's Coronation Concerto with the Baltimore City Colored Orchestra. The newspapers hailed him as a "prodigy" and a "genius," who would rank with "Chura Cherkassky, the other lad whose career was launched in Baltimore." A newspaper photograph made of Larkins before the concert resembles a tintype. He is dressed in a dark suit with knickers and a Buster Brown collar with a flowing cravat, and he is standing stolidly beside a grand piano, his left arm draped over the treble end of the keyboard. His hands are much as they are today—big, square, and strong—and so is his masklike face, with its downturned mouth, alarmed, myopic eyes, and windmill ears. During the next five or six years, Larkins, in the manner of the tri-motor literati of the period, was often billed as Ellis Lane Larkins, and he gave a series of appearances, one of which was covered in a Baltimore paper in April of 1937:

> Ellis Larkins, a thirteen-year-old Negro, gave a piano recital in the Common Room at 4:30 o'clock on Sunday, the eighteenth. The recital was sponsored by Mr. Privette. Though it was scheduled for four o'clock, it was half an hour late in starting, because the young pianist arrived a few minutes late.
>
> The program started with a Pastorale by Scarlatti in C Major and contained also Mozart's Sonata in C Major; Seven Preludes, A Flat Major Etude, and Fantaisie Impromptu by Chopin; Brahms' Rhapsody; a Moment Musicale by Schubert; Lento by Cyril Scott; and a Prelude in G Minor by Rachmaninoff.
>
> When questioned after the performance, the young aspirant said, "I don't like to practice." His playing, however, plainly showed that he had practiced very much since he started taking lessons at the age of six. During the whole hour, Larkins had no music before him, but sometimes played so fast that his fingers could not be seen.
>
> When Larkins commenced playing, he had a small audience, but more arrived as the recital continued. His playing was continuous, with only two intermissions of two or three minutes each. To the audience it seemed that he played unlike a young boy, but like a great pianist.

The great pianist would change in certain ways and remain unchanged in others. He still cares little for practicing or for rehearsals (an hour and fifteen minutes is about all he can manage), and he still doesn't use music. But he is punctual nowadays; his hands, though fast, are generally visible; and his two- or three-minute intermissions sometimes last upward of an hour, and separate sets just fifteen or twenty minutes long. Larkins came to New York in 1940 to attend Juilliard, and before long he began to retreat into various encircling shadows. To help support himself, he went to work in night clubs, which are eternally dark. (He had learned jazz from recordings and from frequent visits to the Royal Theatre, in Baltimore, where the big bands played.) He tried being a sideman, and even a leader, and then slipped into the near-anonymity of accompanying singers. In the mid-fifties, he vanished into the studios as an accompanist and vocal coach, and except for a short turn with Larry Adler in 1959 he didn't reappear until 1972, when he took a job as a solo pianist at Gregory's. But his mini sets and maxi intermissions made it seem as if he were barely there. He lasted at Gregory's two years, and after that he flitted from The Cookery to Michael's Pub to Tangerine to Hopper's to Larson's to Daly's Daffodil before settling down at the Carnegie Tavern, at Fifty-sixth and Seventh Avenue.

Larkins' style also gives the impression of continually being on the verge of withdrawing, of bowing and backing out. It is uncommonly gentle. His touch is softer than Art Tatum's, and the flow of his melodic line has a rippling, quiet-water quality. Nothing is assertive: his chords, in contrast to the extroverted masses that most pianists use, turn in and muse; his single-note lines shoot quickly to the left or the right and are gone; his statements of the melody at the opening and closing of each number offer silhouettes. But Larkins' serenity is deceptive, for his solos have a strong rhythmic pull. It is clear that he once listened attentively to Earl Hines and Teddy Wilson, and possibly to Jess Stacy. Larkins' short, precise, dashing arpeggios suggest Wilson, and so do the even, surging tenths he uses in his left hand. He attempts a vibrato effect by adding the barest tremolo to the end of certain right-hand phrases, recalling Stacy and the early Hines. His intent is immediate pleasure—for the listener and for himself—and it is also to celebrate the songs he plays. He endows and sustains them, indirectly fulfilling a nice maxim laid down by the drummer Art Blakey. "Music," Blakey said, "should wash away the dust of everyday life." There is probably no better accompanist than Larkins. When a singer accepts accompaniment, he asks the accompanist to take over part of the arduousness of performing, for which he repays the accompanist by excelling. The perfect singer-accompanist relationship is contrapuntal. The singer creates one melodic line and the accompanist another line: they move separately but indivisibly. Larkins provides an aura for the singer—a constant cushion of chords, melodic suggestions, dynamics, and rhythmic pushes and retards. He anticipates and celebrates the singer, guessing unerringly where the singer will take the melody next and applauding apt phrases. He embraces the singer without touching him and leads him without pointing. Accompanying provides Larkins with what he has sought since childhood: to be an indispensable second voice.

The singer Anita Ellis rarely uses any other accompanist. One afternoon, she and Larkins rehearsed for an album they were soon to record. Larkins arrived at Anita Ellis's apartment, on the upper East Side, at one o'clock sharp. He was dressed in a gray Glen plaid suit and a bright-yellow sports shirt—an ensemble that resembled a muffled yell. Larkins talks as little as possible, but when he does talk he issues clumps of words. Some are intelligilble and others he swallows, leaving curves of sound that have more to do with music than with words. But he offers help in the form of hand signals, which he hoists once or twice during almost every utterance. These are the shadows of his words, spoken and unspoken, and they are a pleasure to watch, for they flicker and insinuate and dance. Larkins still has a boyish figure. His stomach protrudes, and his back is concave. His arms and legs are spindly, and he has long, anchoring feet. He wears heavy, protective horn-rimmed glasses, and his only expressions are a smile that passes over his face so quickly that his teeth never show and a flaring of the eyes that he uses when an exclamation point is needed.

Before he sat down at the piano, which he addresses flawlessly—his back straight, his knees just below the keyboard, his elbows clamped to his sides—he cracked all his knuckles and violently shook each hand at the floor, as if he were forestalling cramps. Anita Ellis, got up in a white Castelbajac blouse and white pants, stationed herself behind the piano. She said she had talked that morning with Gil Wiest, the owner of the Carnegie Tavern and of Michael's Pub, where she and Larkins held forth for seven classic weeks in the fall of 1974. "He told me that you're a complete gentleman, Ellis," she said in her lyrical, quickstep way of talking. "And that you pack them in."

Larkins opened his mouth in mock amazement and held up three fingers. "I haven't seen Gil for three months," he said. "He leaves me absolutely alone."

"All right, Ellis," she laughed. "Shall we do Burke and Van Heusen—'But Beautiful'?" She sang, "Love is funny or it's sad, or it's quiet or it's mad," and Larkins began pedalling beside her, supplying coloring chords and anticipatory runs. He took an eight-bar solo, and, as is his wont, mouthed the lyrics as he improvised. She went into a sudden crescendo in the last eight bars, and they finished quietly.

She put the music of Duke Ellington's "Prelude to a Kiss" on the piano, and Larkins played the first eight bars in slow, legato fashion. He stopped, and she said, "You do that so laid back it's marvellous. I want to try it, too. Will that interfere?"

He shook his head and began, and she sang with him. He stopped at the end of four bars. "That's *too* far behind, Anita," he said. He began again, and she followed more closely. His chords moved along with her, and he led her into the bridge with a bright cluster of single notes, and at the close of the bridge he paused and said, "Should I wait for you?"

"You don't have to wait for me, Ellis."

He finished the chorus and said, "You were too far behind."

"I haven't been listening to you. I've just been doing my thing."

They did one more chorus, and at its end she inserted four bars of humming. They were slightly off pitch, as she had been in several places in the song. "The trouble with that song," Larkins said, "is that if one tone goes off, it all seems to go off." She nodded and laughed.

They did a slow, delicate, almost transparent version of Billy Strayhorn's "A Flower Is a Lovesome Thing." The melody, as in most of Strayhorn's pieces, has a misterioso quality, and it moves in long, gradual steps. It is not a singer's song, and when they had finished she said, "We'll go back to that next week. I don't know, I can't seem to find that song. I can't seem to get it in place. Maybe it should be a half tone higher."

Larkins shrugged and, holding one hand horizontally over his head, raised it an inch. "Maybe we can try it in a different key," he said.

They did buoyant versions of "Spring Will Be a Little Late This Year" and Stephen Sondheim's "Anyone Can Whistle." She sang forcefully, and Larkins grew appropriately loud, and on the last eight bars of "Whistle," when she sang "I can slay a dragon" Larkins churned and boiled, leaning on his loud pedal and moving his shoulders up and down.

"Wheeeee," Anita Ellis cried. "Let's take five."

Larkins went to the kitchen to get a drink, and when he got back she said, "Ellis, after this album let's do one with just bar songs, the songs that any old piano player and singer used to sing in any old bar—songs like 'I Don't Want to Cry Any More' and 'You've Changed' and 'You Don't Know What Love Is.' "

Larkins nodded and opened his eyes very wide.

"Speaking of bars," she said, "I saw 'The Joe Louis Story' the other night on television. Do you remember that, Ellis? We were in a bar scene, and I sang 'I'll Be Around.' I think the producer had heard us do it at the Village Vanguard. We were much better than I thought. They filmed it at Grossinger's, and we met Louis."

Larkins nodded and made a single fist in the air.

They did Alec Wilder's "Who Can I Turn To," and just before the bridge, Larkins slipped in a sleek arrangement of double-time chords which had the effect of throwing Anita Ellis's words into graceful slow motion. "I love to do that song," Anita Ellis said. "It's such a collaboration. Let's do 'Summertime,' Ellis."

"Let's wait until next time," he said, a smile flickering across his face.

She ignored him, and began the song a cappella. Larkins joined her with loose chords and a sprinkle of ascending single notes. They created a sense of "quietude," which she had earlier said she wanted in the album. But when she sang "One of these mornings, you're going to rise up singing" she gave a startling shout that Larkins answered with quick, heavy chords. The thunder died away, and she hummed the repeat ending of the song, and the two pure and beautiful voices—voice and piano—crossed and recrossed one another.

A Basie-like "I Hear Music," with a lot of galloping Larkins chords, was followed by a bluesy "Moanin' in the Mornin' " and a studied, careful "Out of This World," which slid in and out of tempo.

Larkins struck a final chord and jumped to his feet. He offered Anita Ellis his delicate handshake and said, "That's it. It won't do any good, but I have to take my beauty nap. I'll be here next week." He was in the elevator before the front door had closed. An hour and twenty-two minutes had elapsed since his arrival.

Anita Ellis crossed her living room and sat by a picture window that looks over Carl Schurz Park and the East River. "The most remarkable thing about Ellis is that he has such *Einfühlung*—such in-feeling, or sympathy. He really feels *with* you. I can change my way of doing a song and not say anything to him, and he will catch it immediately. I *think* all the time when I sing, making up my own stories behind the songs. The song isn't Alec Wilder or Burton Lane any longer. Ellis understands this, and the song becomes just Ellis and me and what's going on in my head. Theatre singers don't generally like Ellis. He's not a pounder. He's too inventive, too corrective. If he finds what he considers a weak chord in a song, he changes it. He listens and invents. He composes all the time. And he doesn't compromise. He plays and you have to sing. Of course, a temperament goes with all his sensitivity. Sometimes his mind is just on other things and he clump-clump-clumps. But that's rare, and I can usually jolly him out of it.

"I first met him at the Blue Angel around 1950. When he played for me, I realized he was *there*, and I became freer than I'd ever been before. He was quiet and gentlemanly, but you knew right away that he was a feelingful and articulate man. He'd call me once in a while, sounding so tentative, and ask me if I'd like to go down to Bon Soir with him and hear Mildred Bailey sing, and he'd tell me how much he liked to accompany her and what a fine musician she was. My opening night at the Blue Angel, I was so frightened that he sent me flowers and said I was the best singer he'd ever heard. He lived in a hotel in the West Forties, and I think he led a very Spartan life. There were always pretty ladies around, but they didn't seem to be *with* him. He was always just Ellis. Although he has been married twice, you don't think of Ellis as having a life outside music. His friends are mostly musicians, and when he isn't playing or with them he's watching television or he's asleep. In the late fifties or early sixties, he had a son. When the child was two or three, Ellis would take him to rehearsals, and I think he was a genius—a miniature Ellis. Once, I had to rehearse a Japanese song, with all these quarter tones, and I was having a time of it, but Ellis's little boy sang the notes just like that. The child became his lifeline. To see Ellis on a piano bench with his son right beside him was a rare oneness. It reminded me of a drummer I'd seen in the jungle in British Guiana on a trip with my husband. The man sat there hitting this great drum with his huge hands, and all the while his little son, who was folded into his lap, kept his hands right on top of his father's. But Ellis's son was suddenly taken away from him by the child's mother, and Ellis didn't know what to do. Finally, he went to the Coast to get away from here, and he worked for Joe Williams. After he came back, in the early seventies, the boy reappeared, and Ellis was beside himself. Then, not so long after, the boy was killed in a motorcycle accident in Montreal. It was a dark, destructive, tragic thing. But Ellis goes on, and he plays as beautifully as ever and looks as elegant as ever. Ellis is never dégagé. He has an air about him that makes certain people feel better about liking jazz. I sometimes think of Ellis's playing as being so of a piece that it comes down to one note—one perfect, hypnotic note."

Larkins arrived at work that night a few minutes before eight. He wore a tuxedo with a ruffled shirt. He ordered a brandy at the bar and sat down with some friends on a banquette opposite the bandstand. At eight-fifteen, Larkins moved to the piano. He cracked his knuckles and shook out his hands, and started a medium "Stormy Weather." He often does medleys, and when "I've Got the World on a String" followed, it was plain he was into Harold Arlen. "I Gotta Right to Sing the Blues" came next, and by the close it was also clear that so far he was only idling, that he was, perhaps, somewhere else and would in all probability not be back until the next set. Everything in his style was in place—the cycling tenths, the shapely chords, the reverence for melody—but it was in soft focus. "Ill Wind" gave way to "Come Rain or Come Shine," and he completed the set, which lasted twenty minutes, with a careful "Blues in the Night."

Larkins sat down at a table near the piano with an admirer from New Zealand who was passing through New York and had spent the four nights of his visit listening to Larkins. The New Zealander asked Larkins why he hadn't made a solo recording in twenty years, and Larkins explained that in 1973 he had recorded enough material for Ernest Anderson, the public-relations man and old-time jazz fan, to fill seven L.P.s, but the editing hadn't even been done. The New Zealand man said he had heard that Larkins had been a child prodigy and asked if he would talk about his childhood.

Larkins let loose a barrage of abstract hand signals, looked quickly over his left shoulder, and stared briefly at the man. Then he shrugged, and said, in approximate translation, "I was the oldest of six children, of whom three boys and one girl are left [*counts off four fingers of his right hand*]. My father was short and stocky and very strict. He did catering and janitoring, and sometimes he'd take me with him. He was also a violinist, and he played with the Baltimore City Colored Orchestra and Chorus, which was formed in 1931 or 1932. He started me on violin when I was two, and he began showing me notes on the piano when I was four. I'd spin one of those piano stools as high as it would go, and perch on top [*rapid spinning motions with his rightforefinger*]. The Baltimore City Colored Orchestra played at various high schools for black audiences, although whites were welcome. I'd go with my father to rehearsals and play cymbals and triangle [*holds an imaginary triangle in the air with his left thumb and forefinger, and makes striking motions with his right hand*], and, when I got old enough, violin and assistant piano. My first piano teacher was Joseph Privette, and I went to him through a Dr. Bloodgood, whom my father worked for. Then I studied with Privette's teacher, Austin Conradi, and eventually with Pasquale Tallarico and Gladys Mayo. I made my début with the Baltimore Orchestra when I was just eleven, and I gave a lot of recitals after that in churches and schools and at friends' houses. My father arranged everything. Both my parents were born in Baltimore. My mother was a quiet, pretty, easygoing person, and she played the piano. One day when I came home from school, she was playing a hymn and I told her it was in the wrong key, and she said, 'That's right, but I just transposed it' [*rolls his eyes and cocks his head*]. So she knew what she was doing. Between 1936 and 1938, when I was in high school, I also studied at the Peabody Conservatory. But I was aware of what was going on on the other side of the fence. I heard a lot of jazz on the radio [*cups one ear, as if listening*]—Fats Waller and Count Basie and Earl Hines and Teddy Wilson—and I caught all the big bands at the Royal Theatre. I graduated from high school in 1940 and came directly to New York to attend Juilliard, where I had a three-year scholarship. This came about through a young divinity student in Baltimore named Godwin who'd heard me play and brought me to Juilliard to audition. I lived on Manhattan Avenue with a woman whose mother was in our congregation in Baltimore, where I'd been an altar boy and all that [*pats the top of his head with one hand*]. When I came to New York, I had every intention of being a classical pianist, but I started working as a jazz pianist simply out of the need for money. The guitarist Billy Moore heard me and told John Hammond, who got me into the union. I joined Moore's trio, and we went to Cleveland. I was still at Juilliard, and my teacher told me he didn't care what I played so long as I didn't lose my approach to the instrument. I didn't hear Art Tatum until I came to New York. The first time was at an after-hours place uptown. All the pianists there played, then Tatum sat down with his beer next to him and washed them all away [*pretends to clear the tabletop with one vigorous sweep of his hands*]. I went into Café Society Uptown with Billy Moore on September 14, 1942, and when he got sick in December I took over with a trio made up of Bill Coleman on trumpet and Al Hall on bass. Teddy Wilson had a sextet there, too, with Emmett Berry and Ed Hall and Benny Morton and Sid Catlett, and we alternated playing for dancing between the floor shows. If Teddy got sick, I'd replace him. I went into the Dubonnet in Newark, and Max Gordon came all the way over to ask me to come into his Blue Angel. I was there with the trio a year. In 1945, I went back to Café Society with Ed Hall, who had taken over the band, and after that I divided my time between the Blue Angel and the Village Vanguard [*makes piano-playing motions in the air to his right, then to his left*]. The Blue Angel closed in the early sixties, and rock came in, and I went into the studios as an accompanist and a vocal coach. It kept me alive through the fifties and sixties, and in 1968, I moved to the Coast and became Joe Williams' accompanist."

The New Zealander asked him how he liked being an accompanist.

Larkins nodded his head quickly up and down once, and looked at his watch. "I first comped for my father when I was five or six, and in high school I played for vocal groups and did a little arranging. I try and keep my ear alert and I try and keep myself aware of the lyric. After a while, you sense where a singer is going and where she isn't. You lead her and you keep out of her way. The two voices—the pianist's and the singer's—should move side by side and contrapuntally, and it becomes a little game between them [*shakes cupped hands, as if they contained dice*]. I can play by myself anytime, but it is a great challenge to play off of someone else. I never lose the melody when I play solo. I give the melody at the beginning of a song and at the end. In between, when I improvise, I make little melodies of my own, and it becomes a way of expressing myself, of improving the original—you hope [*opens his eyes wide*]. Three things go on in my head when I solo: the melody; the lyrics, which I say to myself as I go along; and a kind of imaginary big band, which directs the voicings—the chords I play—so that some will resemble the reed section and some the brass. I also see things impressionistically in my head [*shields his eyes scout-fashion with one hand*], and this is triggered by certain words in the lyrics. The word 'shimmering' in 'autumn in New York' makes me see shimmering leaves and shimmering lights, and the lyrics of 'Bidin' My Time' make me see life just rocking easily along. But some songs you leave alone, some songs you can't improve, and you just play them and get out—songs like 'Willow Weep for Me' and 'Someone to Watch Over Me' and 'The Man I Love.' "

Larkins checked his watch again, and excused himself. He went to the piano and into a Gershwin medley, and it was immediately apparent that he was back. He experimented with time all through the set, playing an exquisite slow "I Got Rhythm" and a rocking "'S Wonderful." He did "The Man I Love" at three different speeds, keeping the melody clear and in the forefront, and he did an ad-lib "Lady Be Good." "Someone to Watch Over Me" was precise and languorous, and he closed with a medium, extended "I've Got a Crush on You," which he made into a love song and a hymn and a lullaby. Then, in one unbroken motion, he stood up, bowed and clapped his hands to the applause, dropped down the bandstand steps, and covered the four feet to the bar, where he held up one tall finger.

Being a Genius

Harold Rosenberg once wrote, "Folk art stands still. It neither aspires upward, like academic painting, nor advances forward, like the inventions of the modernist art movements . . . No one is anyone else's forerunner, and the question of who did it first . . . does not arise. All works of folk art exist simultaneously in the peaceable kingdom of individual imaginings and skill." Rosenberg was writing of the great American primitive painters—and tinsmiths, carpenters, furniture-makers, potters, and wood-carvers—of the eighteenth and nineteenth centuries. But his words also apply to the jazz musicians and jazz singers and tap dancers who, untutored, irrepressible, obsessed, have sprung from every American climate and soil during the past seventy or eighty years. One of the most startling and original members of this primitive army, which includes Duke Ellington and Louis Armstrong and Charlie Parker, was the pianist Erroll Garner.

Garner was born in Pittsburgh, and died in Los Angeles, in 1977, at the age of fifty-three. His sister, Martha Murray, has said of the Garner family: "Mother was born in Staunton, Virginia, and she graduated from Avery College, here in Pittsburgh. She was a quiet person who got a lot out of life. She had patience. She would never speak down on anybody. She had humor. She had that insight into people, and she had profound wisdom. She took an interest in everything we children did. She saw good in everybody, and she lived by 'Do unto others as you would have them do unto you.' She was about five foot five, and she had a round face and a very pleasant smile. She had beautiful eyes, but later in her life she lost her sight. She never complained or was reproachful. She never lost her serenity. In fact, you wouldn't have believed she was blind. When one of us walked down the street with her she moved straight along. She didn't use a cane, and she didn't feel with her feet. She didn't lose her timing. She had a fine contralto voice, and she and Father sang in the church choir. Father had a lovely tenor voice, and he also sang in a quartet. He had wanted to be a concert singer, but he suffered from asthma. He was about the same height as my mother, but he was slight-built. He was outgoing and had a marvelous sense of humor. He liked to dress well at all times, and at Easter he wore a morning coat and striped trousers. He was the essence of perfection when it came to that.

"We lived in a brick row house on North St. Clair, in the East Liberty section of Pittsburgh. It was owned by our church, and we had two floors in the center house. The church sat a block away, on Euclid Avenue. I was the oldest, then there was my brother Linton, and Ruth, who lives in Pasadena, and Berniece, who still lives in Pittsburgh. Erroll was the baby of the family. He started playing the piano between the ages of two and three—with both hands. Father had given Mother a Victrola, which had beautiful mahogany wood, and Mother would play recordings at our bedtime. The next morning, Erroll would pull himself up on the piano stool and play exactly what he had heard the night before. Miss Madge Bowman taught us all piano—Erroll excepted. When she played a new number to show us how it would sound when we learned it, Erroll would play the number right off after she had gone. He kind of took lessons from her for a while, but he never could learn to read. Miss Madge was a graduate of the Pennsylvania College for Women, and she was an accomplished teacher. Finally, she took Erroll to Carnegie Tech and had him play for the professors, and they told her that there was no need for him to read music, that he would play the same whether he learned or not. He was your average rascally boy, but he was friendly with everybody, and, being a genius, he was invited by everybody to play their pianos. Of course, pianos were very fashionable then, and you didn't have a home if you didn't have a piano. Because Erroll's legs were so short, he completely wore out the panel below the keyboard of our piano by keeping time on it with his feet. We came out of a household where we entertained every Sunday—Linton and I washed many a dish behind company. I do remember that a Mr. Duckett—Mr. William Duckett, I believe—was one of the people who would stop by. He lived in Boston, but his parents lived in our neighborhood, and when he visited them he came to our house and played the piano. Everybody sat so quiet you would have thought we were in a concert hall. He played excellent ragtime, and he'd play three or four numbers. It was simple things like that that the whole family got a kick out of—in particular, Erroll. Mother used to say after Erroll had left home that she thought he never had realized when he was young just how much he *did* play. When he did realize what his gift was, he never got to the point where he was too good to speak to his old Pittsburgh friends."

Linton Garner is a professional pianist. He has said, "Our father was named Ernest, and he was from North Carolina. He was in maintenance with the Westinghouse Company. He played saxophone and guitar and mandolin, and he'd had a band. My mother, Estella, was strong and solid and stout. We were poor people. It was rough at times, but we never went through that starvation period. Our parents always had enough for us to eat. We had a good home. The house was full of music and full of friends. Erroll had that kind of lightning mind where he could play anything he heard. When he heard a player piano somewhere, he'd come home and imitate all those old trills and tremolos. We listened to Earl Hines and Art Tatum and Teddy Wilson, and Fats Waller was strong with us, too."

Erroll Garner went to junior and senior high school at Westinghouse High. Carl McVicker was director of instrumental music, and he once said of Garner, "Besides Erroll, I had Billy Strayhorn and Fritzy Jones, who later became Ahmad Jamal. Fritzy didn't like playing for people, and he'd put his head in his hands when he had to. Strayhorn liked to play in public, and so did Erroll. In fact, he was crazy about entertaining. He had a low I.Q., so he was put in an ungraded class run by Mrs. Lyons—naturally, we called it the Lyons Den. She taught her students the basics of math and reading and writing. When Erroll wasn't with Mrs. Lyons, he played the piano by the hour, or played tuba in the band, which he picked up by ear. Erroll was a lovely boy, and he was absolutely no nuisance. He was with us from 1936 until 1940. One time, when I was rehearsing the stage band for the show we gave every spring, we hit a part in the stock arrangement we were using that our pianist just couldn't get the hang of. The kids started saying, 'Let Erroll try! Let Erroll try!' Erroll was sitting in the back listening, and since he couldn't read I didn't see what help he could be, but I told him to come up and try. He sat down and improvised a passage that was three times better than what was written in the score, so we used him."

Garner was short and was shaped like a wedge. He had fullback shoulders and long arms. His hands were rangy and long-fingered and loose. They moved like thieves on the keyboard. He wore his hair patent-leather style, and he had a narrow face and a beaked nose. He looked like a pirate. He had a blue-black beard and a huge brush mustache and heavy-lidded eyes. When he played, his music was refracted through his face and body. His body kept time. He gave ecstatic smiles, popped his eyes, made "O's with his mouth, and peered crazily at his sidemen, his eyes half shut with delight. All the while, he issued a stream of loud basso-profundo rhythmic grunts.

There was little waste in Garner's career. He came to New York in 1944. He worked at the Melody Bar, on Broadway, and at the Rendezvous, and Jimmy's Chicken Shack, uptown. Then he landed at Tondelayo's, on Fifty-second Street, and he was off. The first of three voices from that time belongs to the bassist Slam Stewart: "Around 1944, I had John Collins, the guitarist, and Art Tatum in a trio at the Three Deuces, on Fifty-second Street. Tatum took sick, and I asked Erroll Garner to fill in for him. Erroll was working as a single down the street at Tondelayo's, and he'd play a set there and then come over and play a set with us, and he fell right in wonderfully. They let him leave Tondelayo's, and he worked with us full time. We were together a year and a half or two years, and we had many a good time together. We built a pure friendship, and we were always talking about our music and what we were going to play next."

The next is John Collins': "I heard Erroll in Pittsburgh around 1941. I was with Fletcher Henderson's band, and I heard him in some little club. He was already different, he was already a stylist, and that is surely one mark of greatness. Everybody else was going the bebop way and all, but Erroll went his own route and stuck to it. What I think I admired most about him in Pittsburgh was the way he mopped his face with his handkerchief. He wiped it between measures, and he never missed a beat. I worked with him in Slam Stewart's trio on Fifty-second Street and in

Paris. When we got off the plane, there was a big reception committee, and we thought it was for Coleman Hawkins, who was with us and was coming back to Paris for the first time since 1939. But it was for Erroll. He'd already won some kind of prize, and they were there to honor him. In the seventies, he moved out to the Coast, where I had lived a long time, and he was very strange. I only saw him once, and that was when he sat in at a place where I was playing. He looked fine and he played marvellously. But I never saw him again, or even heard from him, and I think it was because he was already ill and didn't want anybody to know. He never liked to dwell on the dark side of things."

The third voice is Sylvia Syms': "The first time I saw Erroll Garner, he had that patent-leather hair and that smile in his eyes, and he was wearing an old blue overcoat that might have belonged to his father and was too long. Art Tatum had sent him as a courier to bring me a little glass piano with his and my initials on it. When it broke, Tatum replaced it with one from Van Cleef & Arpels, which I finally gave to Erroll, because he pestered me so long about it. Tatum told me that he adored Erroll, and that was strange, because they were so different. Tatum was something of a stuffed shirt, while Erroll was so articulate in his street-smart way. Erroll loved chubby ladies. I ran into him once after I had taken off about forty pounds, and he looked at me with his head on one side and said, 'You shouldn't have ought to have done it, Sylvia.' Later, after I'd gained it back, he said, 'Now, that's how a woman should look.' He was a very generous man. I remember walking to Jilly's with him in the sixties and I don't know how many times he stopped to say, 'Hey, baby,' and reach into his pocket and lay something on whoever it was. But he was already doing that in the forties in the White Rose Bar at Sixth Avenue and Fifty-second Street."

By 1950, his career had been taken over by Martha Glaser, who made Garner famous. During the next twenty-five years, he worked an endless round of concerts (many with symphony orchestras), night clubs, and television appearances. He also made thousands of recordings. Recording studios tend to stymie jazz musicians, but Garner bloomed in them. This is George Avakian's description of a 1953 Columbia recording session:

> Erroll rattled off thirteen numbers, averaging over six minutes each . . . with no rehearsal and no retakes. Even with a half-hour pause for coffee, we were finished twenty-seven minutes ahead of the three hours of normal studio time—but Erroll had recorded over eighty minutes of music instead of the usual ten or twelve, and . . . his performance could not have been improved upon. He asked to hear playbacks on two of the numbers, but only listened to a chorus or so of each before he waved his hand.

The drummer Kelly Martin worked with Garner in the fifties and sixties: "I joined Erroll in Pittsburgh in 1956 and left him in Pittsburgh in

1966. Shadow Wilson had been Erroll's drummer before me, and he told me, 'You got to watch Erroll all the time. You got to listen and watch.' Erroll liked to have his bass player sit on his left, so that the bass player could see his left hand. And he liked to have his drummer sit so he could see the drummer's hands. His way of playing and creating was all in his face, and his way of talking was in the piano. He hardly said anything to the audience, he never even introduced his sidemen. If he was going to take an intermission, he'd make a little series of upward notes at the end of a piece, and we'd know. If he was down or upset, we could hear it in his playing. There were all kinds of secrets. Once, we were having a drink together between sets, and when my glass was empty I started playing on it with the swizzlestick—*chink-de-chink, chink-de-chink*. So Erroll started the first number of the next set in the key that the swizzlestick made on the glass. Erroll didn't like to rush into what he was going to play, and those long, crazy introductions gave him time to settle himself. We almost never knew what he would play, but we got so we could almost think in his vein. He loved people, and he loved to play for them. When we hit a loud crowd, he'd handle them by playing softer and softer until finally his hands were actually just above the keyboard. Then somebody would notice that Erroll wasn't making any sound at all and would shush the racket, and Erroll would lower his hands onto the keys and pick up where he'd left off. We almost always wore tuxedos. Eddie Calhoun, who played bass most of the time I was with Erroll, used to say, 'Man, it's hard to swing in a tuxedo,' and I seconded that. Erroll could make anybody swing, though. We played a concert in this big, beautiful hall in Helsinki, and before we started that audience was so stiff you could hear it breathing. After the first number, there was a sharp lull—then here come the hands.

"Erroll's mother was blind when I met her, but she was a well-adjusted woman. I met Erroll's father at the same time, and we stole away from the crowd to some Class D bar where the bartender knew him and would give him enough whiskey in the glass so he could at least see it. Erroll told me once that he thought he'd rather be blind than deaf, because he played by sound and he didn't have to see out of his ear to hear. Sometimes he'd make up whole new tunes during a performance, and he'd grin at Calhoun and me and growl in that voice, 'Stick with me, stick with me.' "

Garner also "wrote" songs, some of them striking. He told the drummer Art Taylor in "Notes and Tones" how he had written "Misty":

> I wrote "Misty" from a beautiful rainbow I saw when I was flying from San Francisco to Chicago. At that time, they didn't have jets and we had to stop off in Denver. When we were coming down there was a beautiful rainbow. This rainbow was fascinating because it wasn't long but very wide and in every color you can imagine. With the dew drops and the windows being misty, that fine rain, that's how I named it "Misty." I was playing on my knees like I had a piano, with my eyes

shut. There was a little old lady sitting next to me and she thought I was sick because I was humming. She called the hostess, who came over, to find out I was writing "Misty" in my head. By the time I got off the plane, I had it. We were going to make a record date, so I put it right on that date. I always say that wherever she is today that old lady was the first one in on "Misty."

Garner's sound was by turns robust and delicate, rococo and spare, "down" and sentimental, discordant and melodic, driving and lackadaisical. Every number was an adventure. You knew certain stylistic flourishes would appear—the on-the-beat left-hand chords (possibly inspired by his days as a tubist); the right-hand tremolos (echoes, perhaps, of player-piano rolls); the stiff-legged, staccato single-note lines in the right hand; the startling dynamics; the spinning, funny, tantalizing introductions, some of them a dozen or more bars in length and complete iconoclastic compositions in themselves; the octave chords; and the fragments of parody and interpolation—but you never knew when or in what combination. Garner constantly surprised his listeners and himself. You would hear him suddenly drop into several choruses of stride piano (having never heard him play any before), and do it with a rocking, irresistible ease. You'd hear him play a delicate melodic chorus, break off and go into an eighteen- or twenty-bar arhythmic passage, in which each hand spun out a different, almost atonal single-note line, and pick up the melody again. You'd hear him play thunderous chords and drop into a legato right-hand figure that was so soft a cat would walk right by. You'd hear him turn an up-tempo ballad into a wild rhythm machine—the left hand hammering steadily, the right hand high heels on marble. Garner, like all great primitives, was trapped inside his style, but he never allowed it to harden into self-parody. He kept reaching farther and farther into the mysterious area where his uniqueness had come from. Garner does not sound like any other jazz pianist; whatever there once was of Earl Hines or Teddy Wilson or Fats Waller had long been abstracted. But the colors and vividness and originality of Garner's playing have been so encompassing that there are few pianists who don't at one time or another sound like him.

The pianist Jimmy Rowles has spoken of Garner: "I don't think there is a jazz pianist, young or old, who hasn't been influenced by Erroll Garner. He laid down his own little laws, and everyone obeyed. I met him around 1950, when he was playing solo piano at the Haig in Los Angeles. He was just starting that left-hand four-four, *thrum-thrum-thrum-thrum* thing, using his left hand as a full rhythm section. I was working across the street at the Ambassador with the Modernaires or some group like that, and I'd listen to him between sets. He liked to kind of growl when he talked, and I think I learned to growl from him. When Erroll walked into a room, a light went on. He was an imp. He could make poor bass players and poor drummers play like champions. When he played, he'd sit down and drop his hands on the keyboard and start. He didn't care what key he was in or anything. He was a full orchestra, and I used to call him Ork. When he was at the Haig, he'd come over after his set and say, 'What do you think? Do you think I'm right or wrong?' and laugh. And I'd always say, 'You're right, Ork. You're right.' "

The pianist and arranger Sy Johnson has also studied his Garner: "A famous classical pianist once told Erroll that he should record all the time—that he shouldn't wait for recording dates and such but should go into a recording studio whenever he got a chance and capture what his head was always full of. One time, he went into a studio and played for hour after hour. Just by himself—no bass and drums, which he never needed anyway. The tape that came out of it is the most amazing solo jazz piano I have ever heard. *Everything* on it is a tour de force. It is a man taking endless chances. It is tapping a keg and out comes a torrent. He had astonishing hands. He could write—sign autographs—with both hands. His hands used to unfold on the keyboard and keep going, and he is supposed to have been able to reach a thirteenth. What distinguished him from every other jazz piano player, though, was his rich and profound quality of time. He could play a totally different rhythm in each hand and develop equally what he was doing in each hand. He was way down deep in the time thing. He was this magnificent pianistic engine."

Garner was a private man. As far as anyone knows, he never married. He loved to sit in, and he liked to box. He was fond of clothes, and he sampled golf. He had a kind of private language, as he told Art Taylor:

> "Who chi coo" is an expression that Sarah Vaughan and I used all the time, years ago.. . We used to hang out together in Atlantic City. It means magnificent obsession. If I dig what you do, what you're playing, you're a magnificent obsession; if I don't, I say nothing . . . People who don't really know me call me Erroll. But Sarah Vaughan, Peggy Lee, and Carmen McRae all know me as "Who chi coo," and that means they love me as much as I love them.

He also told Taylor:

> I do a lot of walking, I just go around and watch people; that feeds me and gives me ideas . . . I'm not the type to sleep the day away . . . I like to get out in the daytime and see what others are doing, because they're the same people who come to hear you play the concerts. I like being with people. It feeds me and helps to make my day complete.

Bobby Short knew Garner for a time when Garner lived in Carnegie Hall. "He was always a happy, jolly fellow," Short has said. "He had a nice duplex. He'd wear a head rag around the house, which is the privilege of genius, and he enjoyed being domestic and cooking for himself and his dog. I always liked the answer he gave once when someone mentioned his not being able to read music. He said, 'Hell, man, nobody can hear you read.' "

Bob's Your Uncle

George Shearing doesn't like his listeners to get too close. During the first part of his career—in England, where he was born, in 1919—he hid behind the styles of other pianists. He was considered England's Meade Lux Lewis, England's Art Tatum, England's Teddy Wilson. In the second part of his career, which began in the late forties, just after he settled in this country, he disappeared inside his smooth, famous quintet (vibraphone, guitar, piano, bass, and drums), emerging occasionally for a solo chorus but in general restricting himself to sixteen or twenty-four bars. The disguises he has used in the third part of his career, which started in the late seventies, when he gave up his quintet, are his most refined. He now works in a duo with a bassist (the Canadian Neil Swainson) , but he is no more accessible than he ever was. He has long been thought of as a jazz pianist, but he is apt these days to play Kurt Weill's "Mack the Knife" at a very slow tempo, clothing it with thick Bartók chords. Or he will play the "Moonlight" Sonata straight for sixteen or twenty bars (he is an excellent classical pianist), and then, in the same tempo and using Beethoven harmonies, slip seamlessly into Cole Porter's "Night and Day," staying with it a la Beethoven for a chorus or so before easing back into the sonata. He will play Porter's "Do I Love You" in Mozart fashion, and his own "Lullaby of Birdland" as a Bach fugue. Or he will do a sorrowing, almost chanting rendition of Jobim's "How Insensitive," and give Alec Wilder's "While We're Young" a full-scale ballad treatment, filling it with substitute chords and Art Tatum decorations. What is always present is a superlative pianist, who can play Mozart with a feathery correctness, then improvise with swinging abandon. Shearing has a beautiful touch, which falls somewhere between the sparkle of Nat Cole and the buoyancy of Art Tatum. His jazzlike playing is colored by Teddy Wilson and Hank Jones and Erroll Garner and Bud Powell, but he does not have a style in the conventional sense. He has perfected a unique *sound*, a kind of handsome aural presence, made up of his airborne tone; his wit (he has a pleasant, slightly foggy tenor, and he puts words to "I Can't Get Started" which go, "When I first met Benny G., He said, 'Hi, Teddy,' to me"); his extraordinary harmonic sense; and his refusal to use pianistic clichés. Shearing recently talked about his playing in his apartment, which is in the East Eighties:

"When I sit down at the piano, I make sure my stool is in front of middle C," he said. "Then I know I have three Cs on my left and four on my right. I have my seven octaves, and I know just where I am and where I can go. I've heard too many players slog the piano. I feel sorry for an instrument that is brutally treated. I love tone production—connecting my notes so that they sing, instead of coming out clump-clump-clump. When you improvise, in addition to your tone production you must have a musical atmosphere in your head—a musical climate. You must have compounds of scales and arpeggios to fit the chords you improvise on. Sometimes as I improvise I hear a horn in my head, or an alto or a tenor saxophone, or a flugelhorn. On a slow ballad, I hear Hank Jones, who is so good he should be deported. The gift of improvisation is being able to weave from one chord to another. It's a question of immediately getting what's in your mind into your fingers. If you could explain it, which I can't, all the surprise and spontaneity and unexpectedness would disappear.

"I no longer wish to work all the time. My ears get tired. I want to play bridge with my wife, Ellie. I want to work on my VersaBraille computer. I want to build up my compact-disk library. I want to do more disk-jockeying. I want to ride my tandem bike. Eventually, I probably won't play in public anymore, but I'll certainly play here."

Shearing and his bassist have frequently joined forces with the singer-composer-instrumentalist Mel Tormé and his drummer, Donny Osborne, and they have developed an effortless and engaging act. Shearing accompanies Tormé's singing, Tormé plays piano with Shearing, Shearing sings by himself and with Tormé, Tormé plays drums with Shearing. Tormé has said this about Shearing:

"I call George the Master. He is a blissful, constant surprise musically. When we do two performances in an evening of songs like 'Star Dust' and 'Dream Dancing,' each version George plays is a spontaneous and exquisite work of art. He's got a marvelous facility for inventing substitute chords in great songs. A lot of pianists use substitute chords simply to call attention to themselves, but George does it to enhance and embellish the song. Add to that the incredible warehouse in his brain of classical music and of popular songs that no one else has ever heard of. He's a lovely man, and the only time I have seen him irascible is when people around him don't do their job right. The last time we worked together, he played a solo number in which he got softer and softer, creating a hypnotic delicacy and quietude. When he was almost beneath hearing, the sound man suddenly turned up the volume, wrecking everything. George made his feelings plain after the show."

Shearing has also worked often with Marian McPartland, his old friend and compatriot. She said the other day, "I first heard George in 1948 or 1949, at a club called the Silhouette, in Evanston, Illinois. He had his original quintet, with Denzil Best on drums and Marjorie Hyams on vibes and Chuck Wayne on guitar and John Levy on bass. It was, of course, a mixed group, and whenever George was asked about it he'd say, 'I don't know what color they are. I'm blind.' Without question, he's a genius. Every time I hear him or play with him, I rediscover how much music of all kinds he's absorbed. And he writes wonderful music—tunes like

'Lullaby of Birdland' and 'Conception,' which has a bebop melodic line as good as any Charlie Parker wrote. And there's 'Changin' with the Times,' and 'Bop's Your Uncle,' which is a play on the old English expression 'Bob's your uncle,' which means everything is O.K. He loves to joke around and laugh. I've played with him, and he'll put you on the spot by suddenly changing keys or going into a different style. And his puns are famous. It's hard to think of him as blind, because he constantly challenges himself. Sometimes I'm embarrassed to be around him and hear him talk about all the things he's doing outside of music. We've confided in each other at different times. George knows things about me that no one else does, and I probably know secrets about him."

Shearing lives with his wife in a comfortable, modern apartment. It has a sunken living room with yellow walls, an oatmeal wall-to-wall carpet, a fireplace, a Bösendorfer grand piano, an Eames chair, a wall of Braille books, and a marble head of Shearing by Ben Deane. Shearing's workroom, just off the foyer, contains two side-by-side upright pianos, his Braille word processor, all kinds of sound equipment, and a reclining chair that vibrates, massages your back, and plays tapes of birds singing in a ruined English abbey. Ellie Shearing is an excellent cook, and her sit-in kitchen has a six-burner electric stove and a plate warmer built into a wall. Shearing has a portable floor-to-ceiling temperature-controlled wine cellar in one corner, and in it are Chateau Lafite-Rothschild, Acacia Chardonnay, Fetzer Zinfandel, and Beaulieu Vineyard's Georges de Latour Private Reserve. (Shearing still marvels at the time he invited the jazz producer and oenophile George Wein to dinner and gave him, as a test, a decanted bottle of the Georges de Latour, vintage 1970. Wein took two sips and named the vineyard, the wine, and the year.) The apartment also has a stately dining room and a bedroom. Shearing moves around a lot, and when Ellie Shearing rings the lunch bell he travels the fifty feet or so from the living room to the kitchen in about three seconds. He also likes to lie flat in his Eames chair and talk, his hands crossed on his stomach. This is what he said one afternoon:

"Blindness is more of a nuisance than a handicap. People say they forget I'm blind, and that's the best compliment they can pay me. I have no desire to live a single day in an undignified way. I was born blind, and when I was a kid in London I used to go everywhere by myself. I went on the road with my quintet for ten years with guide dogs. It was one of the most enlightening experiences of my life. Maybe I'm a devout coward on the road, but I like my hotel rooms if possible to have the bathroom on the left, two chairs with a table between them, and a closet and bureau on the right. I can distinguish light and dark, and I like the window to be in front of me when I enter. An empty room is full of acoustics. In a full room, like this, sound dies. I have to snap my fingers in a full room that I don't know to find out when I'm approaching a wall or a bookcase. This is called facial vision. The movement of air is important. I can tell where people are around me simply by the way they displace the air. I think of sound as the vibration of air, and I think of color—I really don't know what color looks like—as the vibration of light. I used to travel by myself in New York taxis, but I don't much anymore, because you never know where you will end up. In general, getting around New York is wonderful, because of the grid pattern and the sharp corners. It's harder to lose your sight during your life than to be born blind. If you nurse the impairment, though, you'll be a pathetic blind man rather than a productive one. A sense of humor never hurts. Once, Ellie and I were waiting for a table in a local restaurant. It was very crowded, and a waitress carrying a huge tray of empty dishes tried to squeeze between Ellie and me. I didn't know what was happening, and I had my arm through Ellie's. The waitress said, 'Hey, what's the matter with you? Are you blind?' I said, 'As a matter of fact, I am.' Ellie said she will never forget the expression on the woman's face."

Shearing laughed, and his laughter loosened his imposing looks. He has a beaky nose, a high forehead, and grayish hair. He tilts his head up slightly when he is listening. Shearing stopped talking, sat up, stood, and, turning, went quickly up the living-room steps, across the foyer, and into his workroom. He talked as he went. "I've started writing some memoirs," he said, "and I'd like to read aloud what I've done. I've finished the first chapter, and begun the second." He sat down at his VersaBraille machine and began to read, his fingers moving over a Braille tape. Here is some of what he read:

"It appears that at the age of three I made gallant but improper attempts at producing music. I used to hit the piano with a hammer. The Shillington Street School, where I went, was in Battersea, in southwest London. The area was known as the Latchmere, so called because of a well-known pub, which benefitted from the same handle. This was just one of many pubs dotted around the neighborhood in case the inhabitants got thirsty. And, regrettably, they did. On numerous occasions, children would be heard crying outside pubs while adults inside were doing their level best to get to be the way I was born. It is with sadness that I relate the fact that my mother was a serious contestant. My mother, however, did her very best to keep these miseries at a minimum after I was born. Almost everything was purchased by the Y.P. method (Yours Perhaps). The installment collector was known as the tallyman. He would appear every week to collect his money. More often than not, he would be greeted with a friendly 'I'll see you next week.' This rather unpleasant task was often foisted upon one of us kids. In which case, it would be 'Mum will see you next week.' Purchases would be made far in excess of what would seem necessary, so that we could have collateral to borrow money to buy more, to have collateral to borrow, and so on.

"Dad was a coal man. This meant that his job was to carry as heavy a load as possible from his horse and cart to a private home or a place of business. He would leave home at about 6 a.m. and return about the same hour p.m. He worked for the same firm for three months short of fifty years and received the equivalent of twelve dollars a week. He got to retire on a handsome pension of a dollar a week. Like all working-class Englishmen, he was very proud. In my teens, when I thought of changing jobs, my dad would say, 'Why do you want to do that, son? The boss has been good to you.' I could never understand why paying me my hard-earned salary was being good to me. But through all this seeming consideration of management Dad was a very strong Labour man. He used to take me to the park on Sunday afternoons to hear some guy speaking in favor of Labour and, at times, for or against Communism. When no such oratory was to be found, we would witness part of a cricket match. Of course, we were never late home for afternoon tea, which would consist of watercress sandwiches and wonderful cake made by my mother.

"Were I more adept at putting things in their proper order, I would have saved some of the sweetness of the foregoing lines to lessen the depression of some of those to come. I remember the sound of rats scampering across the linoleum floor and the sound of my dad's boot trying to hit and kill them. I remember women begging their husbands not to get in a fight outside a pub when they had had too much to drink.

"Let's take a brief glimpse at my mother's life. Dad was earning a poverty-line salary. Mother had nine kids to raise, so she took care of the family during the day and cleaned railway trains at night. It's no wonder she tried to abort me—the youngest of the family. And no wonder I became blind in the process. Although she tried drowning her sorrows in drink, I feel that she really had a guilty conscience about my position and did her very best to repent.

"To this day, I am grateful that blind children were required to spend four years in residential school between the ages of twelve and sixteen. Linden Lodge was the name of the school I attended. Although it could not be counted among the twenty most beautiful residences in England, we had wonderful grounds, with a lawn, flowers, tennis courts for the staff, football and cricket fields, and all the things a little boy from Battersea didn't know existed. Cricket and football were played in the open air only by the partly sighted children. We blind kids played handball by using a football with a bell on it. Cricket was played inside by using a fair-sized balloon with a bell on it."

Shearing got up and went back into the living room and sat in his Eames chair. "That's all I've written so far," he said. He crossed his hands on his stomach. "I learned my Bach and Liszt and studied music theory at the Lodge. When I graduated, I went straight to work in a pub. A year or so later, I joined Claude Bampton's All-Blind Band. It was sponsored by the Royal National Institute for the Blind, and had been put together under the aegis of the bandleader Jack Hylton. There were fifteen of us, and we played Jimmie Lunceford and Benny Carter and Duke Ellington. We carried our own rostrum, and six grand pianos for the finale. Our suits were from Hawes & Curtis, on Savile Row. None of the bands of top condition would have dreamed of surrounding themselves with such glamour. Our leader was sighted, and he used a huge baton, which went swish, swish and told us what was what. Our music had been transcribed into Braille. We played all the major theatres in England and Scotland, and the tour lasted almost a year. I had my first contact with jazz in that band. Someone would pick up the new Armstrong or Berigan or Tatum record and say, 'Here's the new sender'—a good musician being known at the time as a solid sender. Through the band, I met Leonard Feather, who lived in London, and he helped me get recording dates and radio broadcasts. In 1941, I married my first wife, Trixie. I'd met her in an air-raid shelter where I used to play four-handed piano with the song plugger I was rooming with. Trixie and I had a daughter, Wendy, who now lives in North Hollywood. I had three or four jobs at once during the war—in theatres, supper clubs, jazz clubs. I had my own little band, and I also worked for the bandleader Ambrose. I toured a lot with Stéphane Grappelli, who spent the war in London. My mother was bombed out three times. We were Cockneys, and Cockneys tell jokes all the time. Here's one: This bloke says to his wife, 'Come on, Liza, the siren just went off.' She says, 'Hold it, Alf. I'm looking for my teeth.' And he says, 'Never mind that. They're dropping bombs, not sandwiches.' Around this time, I heard a recording of me speaking, and that told me I should do something about my Cockney accent. One time, I came home from school and my mother asked me what I had studied and I said, 'Six pieces of suet.' Or that's what she thought I had said. When she saw the teacher next, she asked her why we had been studying suet, and the teacher said the subject was 'Seek peace and pursue it.' Ellie tells me that when we visit London I revert to my old accent, and that if we stayed long enough she wouldn't understand a word I said. And when I see Grappelli I start talking like him: Stéphane, we go eat now.' I saved some money during the war, and in 1946 I visited New York. American musicians like Mel Powell and Glenn Miller had told me in England that I would kill them over here. I wasn't sure. Why would they want England's Teddy Wilson when they had the genuine article? But I liked New York so much I came back for good the next year.

"My first job was at the Onyx Club, on Fifty-second Street. I was the intermission pianist for Sarah Vaughan. I would be announced—'Ladies and gentlemen, from England the new and exciting pianist George Shearing'—and somebody would yell, 'Where's Sarah?' Then I spelled Ella Fitzgerald at the Three Deuces. She had Hank Jones and Ray Brown and Charlie Smith with her. When Hank took a night off, I played for Ella. I began to be asked to sit in on the Street, and Charlie Parker took me for walks between shows. Leonard Feather had moved to New York, and he introduced me to people and arranged gigs for me. In 1948, I played the old Clique Club, at Forty-ninth Street and Broadway, with Buddy De Franco on clarinet and John Levy and Denzil Best on bass and drums. We broke up after the engagement, and Leonard suggested I keep Best and Levy and add Marjorie Hyams on vibraphone and Chuck Wayne on guitar. I did some arrangements. Marjorie did some. We used a unison-octave voicing, like Glenn Miller's reed section. Our first New York gig was at Cafe Society Downtown, for $695 a week. We did the Blue Note in Chicago, and then the Embers and Birdland in New York—and the quintet took off. It lasted twenty-nine years, and a lot of wonderful musicians passed through—Cal Tjader and Gary Burton on vibes, Joe Pass and Toots Thielemans on guitar, Ralph Pena and Al McKibbon on bass, Charli Persip on drums. Toward the end, we traveled in a twenty-six-foot motor home with nine airplane seats and a couch and a refrigerator. On our last big tour, in the seventies, we did fifty-six concerts in sixty-three days, and I think that's what finally did me in."

Ellie Shearing brought in a tea tray and sat down. "Is that tea, Ellie?" Shearing asked. She said yes, and he made appreciative noises and said he would like a sugar and a half and enough milk to color his tea. "When I first came to this country," he said, "I couldn't believe what you got in a restaurant when you ordered tea. A cup of water that had never come to a boil and a tea bag sitting in the saucer. I'd tell the waitress, 'The water was good for my indigestion, now please bring me some tea.' " Shearing drank his tea quickly and excused himself, saying he wanted to get on with the next chapter of his memoirs. Ellie Shearing reminded him that they were supposed to have dinner at the Harvard Club with an old friend. She is trim and pretty and full of laughter. She has a long face, a wide smile, and auburn hair, tightly swept back. Her voice is big and carries easily around the apartment's corners. She is a quick, energetic talker.

"I marvel at the differences between George's and my background—at the fact that we ever came together," she said. "I was born in Harvey, Illinois, on August 22, 1932. My father was a Lutheran minister who had the same church—the first church he was given—for fifty-two years. His name was Rudolf Geffert, and he was born in Reed City, Michigan, the oldest of nine children. His father and his father's father were Lutheran ministers. He was short and dark and quiet, with a dry sense of humor. He did the Chicago *Tribune* crossword puzzle at breakfast, and he liked to translate Hebrew and Greek into English just for fun. I had three older brothers, and my mother did most of the raising of the children. Her name was Meta Hackbarth. She was little and always overweight, and she was a good plain cook. I was grown before I learned that all food wasn't fried and gray. She was well liked by the congregation, even though she had no patience for small-mindedness. She was born in Wausau, Wisconsin, and raised on a farm, and she hated it. To get away, she went to a normal school and became a teacher. After high school, I spent two years at Thornton Junior College and three at DePauw University. I was a piano major and a voice minor. I graduated in 1955, and my first job was writing radio commercials at WSBT, in South Bend. My second job was running a radio talk show in Niles, Michigan. Then I taught choir at a junior high school in East Grand Rapids. The next summer, I got into summer stock in New England through my old high-school speech teacher, Mae Sexauer. My mother was livid when she found out: her only daughter going on the wicked stage. She told me that I would bring shame on the family, that she'd disown me. But she eventually came to see me. After summer stock, I got a little apartment in New York, on Thirteenth Street between Avenues A and B, and I taught music in a high school out in Levittown. I worked one summer in 'Around the World in Eighty Days' at Jones Beach, and I was in 'To Broadway with Love,' a spectacle that ran at the Texas Pavilion during the 1964 World's Fair. I had been doing choral work around town, and I auditioned for Norman Luboff and was his alto soloist for three years. In 1967, Norman told me I should go to Hollywood and work in the studios, and I did that for four years. I kept body and soul together by teaching remedial reading in the Hollywood public schools. One of my students was a ten-year-old who had lived in communes all over the West. He could shoot, skin a deer, and make deerskin clothes, but he couldn't tell an 'A' from a 'B.' Within six months, he was reading at third-grade level. I told him I looked forward to teaching him the next year, and he said, 'I'm sorry, Miss Geffert, but my parents are moving again, and I don't know where I'll be.'

"I met George in 1971, at a Christmas party at his place in San Francisco. He was married, and I was dating someone regularly. We didn't see each other again for two years. By that time, George was divorced from Trixie, and we began housekeeping. We were married in 1984, in my dad's church. One of my brothers, who's a minister, performed the ceremony. When George and I started living together, I had been alone for a long time. I had to learn not to leave doors half open, not to kick my boots off in the middle of the room, not to not put things back after I had used them. George is very independent. He does not expect to be waited on. He's very sensitive, both emotionally and physically. His fingers are so delicate that he can feel dust on a table. Living with George can be difficult—sometimes on the road we're together twenty-four hours a day—but he's my best friend, and he's great fun."

Zoot and Louise

Zoot Sims had a rustic air. His stoop suggested a man who has milked a lot of cows. His face was rough and handsome and wind-carved. Through the years, his thick, wavy, strawberry-blond hair took on a porcupine look. He had a broad, gap-toothed country smile, and he liked to wedge a cigarette between his front teeth and make a hideous bumpkin face. His prehistoric Selmer tenor saxophone, bought secondhand in St. Louis in the late forties, completed the bucolic image. (Sims finally bought a new Selmer, in Paris in the sixties and he also bought another secondhand Selmer, in Boston. But neither saxophone ever replaced the original.) But Sims' exterior was deceptive. It hid a big-city wit who never seemed off balance, and it hid a player of high lyricism. This lyricism resulted in an indelible jazz event. It took place at the jazz party Dick Gibson held in Aspen in September of 1969. It was Gibson's pleasure to invite thirty or so musicians and during the almost non-stop weekend concerts to mix the musicians in endlessly different combinations. Five groups had already gone by on Saturday evening when the violinist Joe Venuti came on with Lou Stein on piano, Milt Hinton on bass, and Morey Feld on drums. Venuti did a fast "I Want to Be Happy" and a blues, and was joined by Zoot Sims. The two men stepped immediately into an up-tempo "I Found a New Baby' " with Venuti handling the melody and Sims playing close, tight variations. It was clear after one chorus that something special was happening. Each man soloed with great heat, then went into a long series of four-bar exchanges, in which Sims parodied Venuti's figures, and Venuti, delighted at the challenge, attempted more and more complex parody-proof figures. Caught in their own momentum, the two closed with a jammed ensemble that swung so hard it was almost unbearable. Their tones and timbres and rhythmic attacks were so similar and so dense, yet so distinct, that they sounded, as this writer put it at the time, "like one instrument split in half and at war with itself." When the number ended, people shouted and leaped into the air. Sims left. Venuti did a cooling violin duet with Lou McGarity, and McGarity left. Venuti looked around and said, "Where's Zootie? Where's my Zootie?" Sims reappeared, and the two nearly duplicated their feat with a ferocious "I Got Rhythm." The audience, though stunned, wasn't surprised. Sims had been swinging hard for twenty-five years.

Sims has long been associated with the legion of white tenor saxophonists who proliferated in Lester Young's shadow in the forties. These included Bill Perkins, Stan Getz, Herbie Steward, Al Cohn, Jimmy Giuffre, Allen Eager, Bob Cooper, and Brew Moore. But Sims began as an admirer of Coleman Hawkins and Ben Webster, and came later to Lester Young. His style involved elements of all three. His tone in the middle register suggested Webster's, and he sometimes used Webster's descending tremolos. Young's pale, old-moon sound came into view in Sims' high register. Hawkins underlay his drive, his heat, his need to take the audience with him. Sims was a consummate melodic improviser. The melody never completely disappeared. You sensed it, no matter how remote or faint; it moved behind the scrim of his sound. His playing was rhythmically ingenious. Billie Holiday's rhythmic derring-do must have sunk in somewhere along the line. He would deliver an on-the-beat or legato phrase, fall silent (letting the beat click by), slip into a double-time variation of what he had just played, fall silent again, let loose an upper register cry, and slide down a glissando to a low-register honk. He stepped forward and stepped back, raced forward and fell back. He developed irresistible momentum. All the while, he constructed winsome melodies—melodies that seemed to have been broken off the original song, heated up, and quickly reshaped in his image. His tone had warmth, but it was not enveloping. Nor did it let light through. Sims was revered for his uptempo excursions, but he was a sensuous ballad player, and his blues were full of melancholy. He had taken to listening to Johnny Hodges' passionate and elegant blues in his last years. He had also taken up the soprano saxophone. He called his horn 'Sidney,' and he played in tune and with great lyricism. Although Sims recorded often, his quicksilver lyricism does not always come through on records. Maybe he had to be seen to be heard. He was what he played; he played what he was.

Sims was not loquacious, but in 1976 he gave this résumé of his beginnings: "I was born in 1925, in Inglewood, California, which is south of Los Angeles, right by the airport. It was all lemon groves and Japanese gardens then. I was the youngest of six boys and one girl. My mother and father were in vaudeville, and they were known as Pete and Kate. He was from Missouri, and she was from Arkansas. My mother never forgot a joke or a lyric, and she performed at the drop of a hat right up until she had a stroke a couple of years ago. My father died in 1950. He spent his last years on the road, scuffling, and he never sent any money home. It was out of sight, out of mind for him. But there was never any falling out among us. When he came for a visit, everybody forgave him, including my mother. I don't know how we made it. The gas and water were always being turned off, and we moved a lot. One move got me off the ground, though, because we had to go to a new school where they were recruiting kids for their band. They gave me a clarinet and my brother Ray a tuba and my brother Bobby drums. I was about ten. I liked the clarinet fine, even though it made my teeth vibrate, which is why I don't play with a biting grip today. Most sax players bite through their mouthpiece; mine hardly has a mark on it. I played clarinet three years, until my mother bought me a Conn tenor on time. I kept it through my Woody Herman days in the late forties, and I finally sold it for twenty-five dollars. I never had any lessons. I learned by listening to Coleman Hawkins and Roy Eldridge and Ben Webster, and later to Lester Young and Don Byas. My mind was elsewhere at school, which I quit after one year of high. When I was fifteen or sixteen, I worked in an L.A. band led by Ken Baker. He put these supposedly funny nicknames on the front of his music stands—Scoot, Voot, Zoot—and I ended up behind the Zoot stand, and it stuck and the John Haley I was born with disappeared. Then, instead of joining Paul Whiteman, who invited me, I went with Bobby Sherwood. It was like a family, and Sherwood was a father image to a lot of us. Sonny Dunham was next, and after him it was Teddy Powell. I spent nine weeks on the Island Queen, a riverboat out of Cincinnati that had a calliope player who knew 'Don't Get Around Much Anymore.' In 1943, I joined Benny Goodman, and he had Jess Stacy and Bill Harris. In 1944, Sid Catlett asked me to take Ben Webster's place in his quartet after Ben got sick, and we played the Streets of Paris, in Hollywood. I got drafted and ended up in the Army Air Forces later that year and fought the Battle of the South. I was stationed in Huntsville, Valdosta, Biloxi, Phoenix, Tucson, and San Antonio, where I played every night in a little black club. I got out in 1946 and rejoined Benny, and then I went with Woody Herman and became one of the Four Brothers, with Herbie Steward and Stan Getz and Serge Chaloff. I loved that band. We were all young and had the same ideas. I'd always worried about what the other guys were thinking in all the bands I'd been in, and in Woody's I found out: they were thinking the same thing I was."

Sims stayed with Herman until 1949, then gigged around New York and rejoined Benny Goodman. He passed through Stan Kenton's band and Gerry Mulligan's sextet, then, in 1956 or 1957, formed a group with Al Cohn. They played together off and on until Sims' death, in the early spring of 1985. When he wasn't with Cohn, he worked as a single or with his own quartet. He was on the road much of his life, and he appeared all over the world. It was a patched-together career, and he scuffled continuously until 1970, when he married a remarkable woman named Louise Ault. (His first marriage ended in divorce.) She was an assistant to Clifton Daniel at the Times, where she had worked since the early fifties, and she gave Sims the first security he had ever known. It was soon apparent. His come-as-you-are clothes were replaced by tweed jackets and gray flannel pants and loafers, and he cut his hair. His playing took on a new fullness and warmth; by the mid-seventies he had become a saxophonist of the first rank.

Musicians idolized Sims, particularly those who worked with him. The guitarist Bucky Pizzarelli: "Zoot and I played as a duet at Soerabaja off and on for two and a half years in the mid-seventies. The owner, Taki, was Greek, and he called Zoot Zeus. Zoot lived at Sixty-ninth and Second, and Soerabaja was at Seventy-fourth and Lexington, and whenever he wasn't on the road he'd fall in and we'd play. He loved the job. When we were finished, I'd drive him home and he'd say, 'I'll give you a dollar a block or a pothole whichever comes first.' We also worked one-nighters with Benny Goodman's sextet, and we went on the road with piano and bass. We'd do school clinics. He'd shy away from them, but the kids loved him. He was a dream to play with. He was always good, he was always charged up, he never pussyfooted. He used to tell me it was concentration—that music was all a matter of concentration. Doing the duet with him was tough at first. He was very demanding. He didn't like different harmonies. He wanted to hear the straight harmony that went with the tune. He'd growl at you on his horn if things weren't going right. Just being around Zoot was special. He seemed to gather everybody together. After a job, he liked to sit and talk and laugh. One night, when we were playing Toronto, musicians started dropping into our hotel room—Charlie Byrd, Rob McConnell, and the like—and we must have played five or six hours. Charlie played unamplified, and Zoot played standing on the bed in his bathrobe. He loved to sit in. He sat in one night at the Hotel Pierre with my trio and broke the place up. He wasn't at all like people thought he was—super-hip, that kind of *down beat* thing. He was the opposite. He was a real country boy."

The composer, pianist, and singer Dave Frishberg: "I worked with Zoot at the old Half Note from the fall of 1963 to 1968 or 1969. I thought of him as the greatest natural jazz musician I'd ever heard. He'd play two notes, and the rhythm section fell immediately into place. I was sitting in a hotel room in Denver just after I had heard he was sick, and I was listening to some of his records, and I felt overwhelmed. I wrote him a letter telling him how much I loved him and admired his playing. I told him that if Al Cohn was the Joe DiMaggio of tenor saxophonists, he was the Ted Williams. I never got to know him terribly well playing with him. He kept himself at a remove. In fact, I saw him as moody. He'd be irascible early in the evening, then later on he'd be soft as a grape."

Jimmy Rowles: "I first met Zoot in 1941 in a night club in southeast Los Angeles called Bourston's. They had Sunday jam sessions. He was only fifteen or sixteen, dressed real tatteredly, and he didn't look like a musician. He already sounded like Ben Webster. I guess he hadn't heard Lester Young yet. He played great, and we thought, Who's this guy? He'd come in weekends, and suddenly he was gone, working with local bands, and later with Woody Herman. I didn't see much of him again until I went to New York in the early seventies. He had been at the Half Note with Al Cohn a long time, and I think he was a little jaded. We put together a quartet, with Michael Moore or Bob Cranshaw or George Mraz on bass, and with Micky Roker or Mousie Alexander on drums, and at first we seemed to play the same thing over and over. He didn't know many songs, so I began to go to his apartment in the afternoon and write out songs in a key that would be good for him—tunes like 'Gypsy Sweetheart' and 'Dream Dancing' and 'In the Middle of a Kiss.' Once he got the hang of songs like that, he loved them. He had a wild sense of humor. If we had a new drummer who couldn't keep time or got the tempo wrong, Zoot would stop everything, and say, 'O.K., this is where we started. I'll give you one more chance.' There was a pianist he had worked with who swayed all the time, and he said he couldn't play with him anymore because he made him seasick."

Al Cohn: "Zoot and I were first together in Woody Herman's band in 1948 and 1949. We formed our own group in the late fifties, and worked together until the end of his life. Playing was both an escape and a serious vocation for him. He used to talk about the ecstasy factor—the times when your playing becomes a kind of ecstasy. Once he sat in somewhere and played 'Sweet Lorraine' for half an hour. He told the piano player, who was really a bassist, the name of another tune, and the pianist said 'Sweet Lorraine' was the only tune he knew, so Zoot said, 'Play it again,' and they played it for another half hour. He didn't look like a sophisticate, but he was a sharp, fun-loving guy. And this quality never left him. Not long before he died, his doctor came in to take a look at him, and Zoot said, 'You're looking better today, Doc.' "

Louise Sims lives in a small white 1937 clapboard house in West Nyack that she and Sims bought in the mid-seventies. It sits on an acre of sloping ground that also contains a garage and a toolhouse. Other houses flank it, but there is an empty woods across the street. Louise Sims sat at her dining-room table and talked about her life and about Sims. She is a trim, graceful woman, with graying shoulder-length hair. She laughs a lot, and she has a pleasant, rich voice. Behind her, a picture window looked out on the back yard, which is terraced, has two windmills (one from Japan and one from Cedar City, Utah), three apple trees, Sims' rose garden, and a flagstone patio. Between the house and the garage is a horseshoe court. Sims is everywhere in the house. Pieces of driftwood that he whittled sit in the living room (one has an owl's head carved in it, and is called Owl Cohn), and model airplanes he made hang near windows. A small den is filled with photographs of musicians and with Sims' recordings and tapes, and downstairs is a carpeted music room, furnished with a piano (picked out by Jimmy Rowles), a full set of drums (compliments of Jake Hanna), and a refrigerator. The acoustics are so good that Sims had decided to record there.

Louise Sims sipped a mug of tea and talked of her early life: "I was born in Honolulu, the youngest of three daughters. My father's name was Mark Choo, and he was one of the first sports promoters on the islands. In the twenties, he translated and interpreted for the migrant workers, who were from China and Japan and the Philippines and Korea. He lived and died sports, so he started setting up boxing matches in the fields on Friday nights. He set up a ring and ropes, and since the workers didn't have much money he'd charge them a few cents. Then he added wrestling, and his career went on from there. His bitterest disappointment was that he never had a son. He tried to teach my oldest sister, Beatrice, to play catch, and that was a disaster. The next sister, Edith, was a tomboy, so he tried to teach her golf, and she turned out to be left-handed. There was no hope in me—I was interested in ballet and tap dancing. But he took us to every sports event on the islands, and the three of us are the most knowledgeable sports women I know. I'm told that I sat on Babe Ruth's lap when the Yankees played an exhibition game, and I remember being stuffed under the ring when a riot broke out after a Filipino boxer lost a match. My father was slight and very gregarious. He was from the southern part of Korea, and my mother was from the northern part. She was Carrie Kim, and she married when she was seventeen and just out of high school. She was a very pretty woman—

feminine, petite, soft. Her husband and her children were her life. She had no servants, and she never knew how many people my father would bring home for dinner. She and Daddy loved music. She had a beautiful voice, and he played for her. He died in 1951, but my mother is still alive. She lives in Manhattan with Beatrice. Bea did public relations for Olin, and took early retirement. My mother visits me and Edie, who lives in New Jersey. She's been married thirty-two years to Irv Polansky, who's a pharmacist. She has two children—Mark, an F-16 pilot, and Phyllis, who's in computers.

"I was about ten when Pearl Harbor happened. It was a Sunday morning just before eight and a friend of Bea's called and said,'Turn on your radio!' We lived on a high hill, and there were sounds way in the distance like excavating, and we could see black smoke. Then the radio went off the air. Later, we were blacked out—one bulb per room—and we were issued gas masks and given tetanus and typhoid shots. I went to high school in Honolulu. We were all A students. Bea and Edie had gone to the University of Hawaii and done brilliantly. The pressure was on me to do the same, and as a result I wanted to go to a college as far away as possible. I got scholarships to Goucher and Bryn Mawr and Sarah Lawrence and Mount Holyoke. But I didn't want to go to college on scholarship, so I went to Beaver College, in Glenside, Pennsylvania. It was small, and just ten miles from Philadelphia and ninety miles from New York. I had four of the best years of my life there, and I'd do exactly the same thing now. I'd given up on ballet and tap, so I majored in English and journalism. I graduated in 1952. I went home first, and then moved to New York. *Mademoiselle* had a training program, which I looked into, and I filled out an application at the *Times*. I went through weeks of interviews there. Finally, the personnel director said I had a nice telephone voice, and he gave me a job as a temporary receptionist-stenographer. Then I became his secretary. I had never had a job before, but I had taken typing and shorthand in high school—thank God. In 1954, I was made third secretary to Arthur Hays Sulzberger, who was the publisher of the Times. One secretary took care of his Columbia University business—Columbia was celebrating its two-hundredth anniversary, and he was running it. Another secretary handled *Times* business. And I was supposed to take care of the overflow. I was so nervous the first week that when Mr. Sulzberger asked me if he had dictated such-and-such a memo to me, I said, 'It wasn't to I. It must have been to one of the other girls,' and he said, 'Well, send she in here.' After one of his secretaries left, I became co-secretary, and stayed with him until 1961, when he died. Over the years, Mrs. Sulzberger has been a kind of fairy godmother to me. She's ninety-three, but her mind still does mental gymnastics. Then I worked for Clifton Daniel. Once Zoot came by to pick me up at the office. At the time, he was with a Dick Gibson group at the Roosevelt Grill. Clifton told Zoot he recalled taking his best girl to the Roosevelt Grill but that the dancing was somewhat different then—and suddenly this sedate, silver-haired man broke into a fantastic Charleston, and Zoot almost fell over. When Clifton was assigned to Washington, I became Max Frankel's assistant. It was 1972. He was head of the Sunday department, which was still a separate operation. When it was put under the news umbrella and Abe Rosenthal, I became Abe's administrative assistant. I never had a boss I didn't like at the *Times*. All of them had integrity, and all had dedication and love for the paper. I learned from each of them.

"Then, on the morning of January 24, 1980, I woke up and noticed that my left eyelid was red. I thought maybe something had bitten me, and I didn't think anything of it. I went to work. Around eleven, I saw that the eyelid was swollen. I suspected that I had a fever, and I didn't feel very well. The medical director of the *Times* said I might have herpes, and that I should see my internist right away. I did, and he agreed. I also saw my eye doctor, and *he* agreed. I remember being in his waiting room and hearing this loud voice and looking around to see who was talking and discovering to my horror that it was me. My internist had said I might experience terrible pain, and had given me some pain killers, and my eye doctor had wanted to give me steroids. By this time I was very rocky. I called the Times and said I wouldn't be back, and I called a Carey limousine to take me home. I had left my car in a commuter's parking area up here, and I was determined to drive it back to the house. I asked the limousine driver to please follow me home for safety, and he did. To this day, I don't know how I made that drive. The swelling was so bad my left eye had disappeared, and my right eye was almost closed. I had to push my right eye open in order to see to use the phone to call my neighbor. She drove me to the Nyack Hospital. She also got hold of Zoot, who was at Bourbon Street, in Toronto. I had a fever of around a hundred and five, and I must have looked horrible. They thought I either had herpes or a bacterial disease called erysipelas. They kept asking me what religion I was and who my next of kin was. Then Dr. Martha MacGuffie, who's head of plastic surgery at Nyack, happened to take a look at me, and something rang a bell. She had worked one summer with a Dr. Meleney, a gangrene specialist. She was convinced that I had gangrene, and an infectious disease specialist from Northern Westchester Hospital concurred. Streptococcus and staphylococcus bacteria had somehow entered the top left of my face. It was suggested later that the bacteria had got there because of improperly sterilized instruments used in a root-canal job I had had done on an upper-left tooth just a few days before. Dr. MacGuffie had to operate four times to remove all the diseased tissue. I have had four more operations since then, involving skin grafting and the like. I have no feeling in the left side of my face, and I cannot close the eye. I use eye ointment and drops, and I have special goggles to wear outside in windy weather. I can't drive, and reading and writing are difficult. The worst thing is not working. I'm not up to commuting. I'd have to move back to New York, and I don't want to do that yet. This house is so full of Zoot I can't bear leaving it."

Louise Sims went into the kitchen to heat up a Stouffer's pizza for lunch. She said that this was about the time of year when Zoot cut back his rosebushes and packed their lower stems with earth. They were at the left of the yard—tall and gangly. The sun was out, and leaves were blowing from right to left. A pair of cardinals flew across the yard in the opposite direction. Louise Sims set her timer, and sat down again. "I met Zoot in a roundabout way," she said. "I guess that's the way you meet all the people who come to mean a great deal to you. I was editor of my college yearbook, and I was sent to a conference of yearbook editors in Chicago, where I met John Orr, who was at the University of Alabama. I ran into him in New York later, and we dated. Through him, I met Dick Gibson, who had also gone to Alabama, and Jim Ault, who became my first husband. We were married in 1956, and Dick was the best man. Jim and I were divorced in 1964. In 1968, Dick asked me to one of his jazz parties, and I met Zoot Sims there. I went again the next year, and saw Zoot again. I had been going out with someone who lived in San Francisco, and we had more or less decided to get married. After the party, I flew to the Coast to house hunt, and when I got back to New York Zoot called and said, 'Hey, where have you been?' We were married a year later by a justice of the peace in Mount Kisco. Mrs. Sulzberger gave us a reception, and it was an amazing conglomeration: old *Times* people; Bert Lahr's widow; jazz musicians; Barry Cullen, a Village restaurateur, whose daughter was Zoot's goddaughter; and my family. None of Zoot's family could make it from California. He moved into my apartment, on East Sixty-ninth Street. I had been the wife with Tiffany crystal and expensive bric-a-brac, and I could see right away that those days were over. What was needed was furniture to put your feet on. Zoot was a passionate Ping-Pong player, and one of the first things he gave me for the living room was a Ping-Pong table. Those were the days when he was playing a great deal at the old Half Note. I'd get home from the office, and we'd eat. He would go to work, and I'd go to bed. When he got home, at four or five in the morning, I'd get up and cook eggs while he and whoever he'd brought home played Ping-Pong. Then I'd take a shower and get dressed and go to work. Zoot had no wardrobe outside of a dark-blue suit and some funny-looking jackets and slacks. He loved clothes, but he had never got around to doing anything about them. I took him to Brooks Brothers and Paul Stuart, and after that he let me pick out all his shirts and ties. By the mid-seventies, I realized that his drinking was getting out of hand. We had bought this house because Zoot wanted to live in the country, and I felt it would be healthier for him up here away from temptation. And it was. He rarely drank here, and sometimes he was home for weeks at a time. We moved here in September of 1976, kept the apartment for two years more, and then let it go.

"He liked to have a purpose each day when he was home, and he'd ask me for a list of things to do. He was good with his hands. He'd work on his Volvo—a 1962 model that he called the Red Devil. He became a whittler. He could draw, and he had a feeling for line and color. He loved doing the Times crossword, even though he was a terrible speller. He once gave me a birthday party at the New York apartment and hung a banner across the living room which read, 'HAPPY BERTHDAY.' In good weather, he worked on his roses and his tomatoes. He was a farmer in his soul. He'd talk to his roses when they were attacked by Japanese beetles. After I got sick, he had the back yard terraced, and he put in some impatiens, which he called shady ladies. He was a fine cook. His meat sauce was famous, and so was his chili. It took a long while to get used to his ways, which were never predictable. If he finished eating first when we had people for dinner, he'd take his plate out, then collect all the unused silver. When we were given jars of tomatoes or jelly and they were empty and had been washed and were ready to be returned, he'd tear off strips of paper and write on each one, 'Please fill this up again,' and put them in the jars. I took him to Hawaii after we were married, and he loved it. He even played golf—in his shorts and sandals. He started out one day with six balls and hit the sixth one into some kiawe bushes, which are like cacti. He went into the bushes and came out fifteen minutes later, his pockets full of golf balls. He didn't like complications, and he didn't complicate things. He had a way of seeing right to the core of a situation. He was kind and gentle. I don't think he took an aversion to more than three people in his life. A friend borrowed his alto saxophone and hocked it, but Zoot never said a word to him. The same thing happened when someone borrowed his car and totalled it.

"In the summer of 1984, Zoot was found to have cancer, but he was in such poor shape the doctors decided they couldn't operate. So he took radiation treatments. He went on a jazz cruise in the Caribbean in the fall, and he enjoyed that. He insisted on going to Finland and Sweden in November for two weeks—against my wishes and his doctor's orders. When he came home, my heart broke, his face was so thin and white. During the winter, he played at Struggles, in Edgewater, and at the Blue Note and the Church of the Heavenly Rest. He played his last gig in Ohio. Then he went into Mount Sinai for the first of three visits. In between, he lay on a sofa in the living room. He felt cold all the time, and he'd wear a sweater and a jacket, and I'd cover him with a blanket and turn the heat way up. He had this marvellous ability to straighten his shoulders and go on. He'd say, 'If it is, it is.' I had long since taken over his booking and contracts and publicity. I wanted him to be the best at what he did, and I was very pleased that he let me help him.

The Key of D
Is Daffodil Yellow

Four scenes from the life of Marian McPartland, the graceful English-born jazz pianist. The first scene takes place early in the spring.

She is seated at a small upright piano in a corner of an elementary-school classroom on Long Island. She has the easy, expectant air that she has when she is about to start a set in a nightclub. Her back is straight, she is smiling, and her hands rest lightly on the keyboard. Her blond hair, shaded by pale grays, is carefully arranged, and she is wearing a faultlessly tailored pants suit. Twenty or so six-year-olds, led into the classroom a few moments before by a pair of teachers, are seated at her feet in a semicircle. She looks at a list of kinds of weather the children have prepared. "All right, dears, what have we here?" she says in a musical English alto. "Did all of you do this?"

There is a gabble of "yes"es.

"Hail, snow, hurricane, cloudy day, rain, twister, fog, wind, the whole lot. Now, I'm going to pick one out and play something, and I want you to tell me what kind of weather I'm playing about." She bends over the keyboard and, dropping her left hand into her lap, constructs floating, gentle, Debussy chords with her right hand. A girl with a budlike face and orange hair shoots a hand directly at her and says, "Rain, gentle rain."

"That's very good. It is rain, and gentle rain, too. Now what's this?" She crooks her arms and pads lazily up and down the keyboard on her forearms. She stops and smiles and gazes around the faces. There is a puzzled silence. A boy with strawlike hair and huge eyes raises a hand, falters, and pulls it down with his other hand. "Fog," says the little girl.

Marian McPartland laughs. "That's very close, dear, but it's not exactly right." She pads around on the keyboard again. "What's like a blanket on the ground, a big blanket that goes as far as you can see?" The large-eyed boy shoots his hand all the way up. "Snow! Snow! Snow!"

"Right! But what have we now?" Dropping her left hand again, she plays a quick, light intricate melody in the upper registers. "Twister!" a pie-faced boy shouts. "No, hurricane," a boy next to him says.

"Could you play it again?" one of the teachers asks.

"Well, I'll try." She plays the melody, but it is not the same. There are more notes this time, and she plays with greater intensity. "I think it's wind," the orange-haired girl says.

"It is wind, and wind is what we get when we have one of these." She launches into loud, stabbing chords that rush up and down the keyboard and are broken by descending glissandos. She ends on a crash. "Twister! Twister!" the pie-faced boy cries again.

She shakes her head. "Now, *listen*, listen more closely." Again she improvises on her invention, and before she is finished there are shouts of "Thunder!" "Lightning! " "Twister!"

"I don't think I'd even know what a twister sounds like," she says, laughing. "But the rest of you are very close. Which is it—thunder or lightning?" She plays two flashing glisses. "Lightning!" a tiny, almond-eyed girl yells.

"Very, very good. Now this one is hard, but it's what we have a lot of in the summer." She plays groups of crystalline chords in a medium tempo. It is sunlight. A cloudy day and a breeze and a hurricane follow, and when the children's attention begins to wane, she starts "Raindrops Keep Fallin' on My Head." The children get up and stand around the piano and sing. Two of them lean against her. She finishes one chorus and starts another, and at her behest the children clap in time. She gradually speeds up the tempo until the clapping is continuous and the children, hopping around as if they were on pogo sticks, are roaring with laughter. She finishes with a loose, ringing tremolo. The teachers thank her and sweep the children out of the room. She takes a lipstick out of an enormous handbag and fixes her mouth. Then, in the empty room, she starts noodling a medium-tempo blues. Soon it is all there: the tight, flowing single-note lines and the rich chords; the flawless time; the far-out, searching harmonies; and the balancing, smoothing taste. She plays three or four minutes, and then, as a group of ten-year-olds comes billowing through the classroom door, she switches to the Beatles' "Hey Jude."

Marian McPartland lives in an apartment on East Eighty-sixth Street. It is on the seventeenth floor, and it faces south. From the windows of her compact living room, the Empire State and the Chrysler Building and New York Hospital are knee-deep in brownstones. There is a small terrace, with chairs and a couple of boxes of geraniums. A grand piano, which faces away from the view, dominates the living room. Paintings hang on two walls, and the third is covered with photographs, most of which she is in. The business end of the piano is covered with sheet music and musical manuscript, and there are careful stacks of records on the floor below the photographs. She is wearing a flowered top and pants and a big leather belt, and she looks mint-fresh. She makes tea and sits down facing the panorama. She is extremely handsome. Her face, with its long, well-shaped nose, high forehead, wide mouth, and full chin, is classically English. She smiles a great deal and keeps her chin pointed several degrees above the horizon. She has the figure of a well-proportioned twenty-year-old. "I've been teaching four or five years," she says, crossing her legs and taking a sip of tea. "Clem De Rosa, a drummer and the musical director of the Cold Spring Harbor High School, got me going. I teach about six weeks out in that area every year. I started out doing assemblies with a quartet and then with a trio, but I didn't think we were getting across to the kids. Last year, I went into the classrooms with just a bass player, and this year I'm doing it by myself. I love to work with the little ones—especially the slower ones. I guess it has to do with listening. I'm trying to make them shed their fidgeting and their fears and make them listen. Very few of us ever learn how. I think I was first made conscious of it when I was in kindergarten in England and we had a teacher who used to take us on long walks in the woods and fields and make us listen to the birds and the wind and the water lapping in brooks. During the summer, I teach and play at college clinics, and it's terrific fun. Musicians like Clark Terry and Billy Taylor and Gary Burton do a lot of it, too, so there are always wonderful people to play with, to say nothing of the kids themselves. I wish there had been clinics and such when I was growing up. Becoming a jazz musician in those days, with my background and my sex, was like pulling teeth. It just 'wasn't done,' as my father used to say. I was born in Slough, near Windsor. But we moved to Woolwich a few months later, and then to Bromley, Kent, when I was about four. Bromley was much nicer than Woolwich, which resembled Astoria, New York. My family was upper-middle-class and conservative. All my mother's side lived around Slough and Eton and Windsor. My great-uncle sang at St. George's Chapel at Windsor Castle, and my grandmother lived in The Cloisters, on the grounds. Queen Elizabeth knighted another great-uncle, and now he's Sir Cyril. He and Aunt Sylvia came over when I was working in New York at the Hickory House in the fifties, and they were shocked and mystified by the whole scene. Uncle Cyril took me aside, between sets at the club, and said, 'Margaret'—I was born Margaret Marian Turner—'Margaret, does your father *know* what you're doing?' My father was a civil engineer who was involved with machine tools. He was an avid gardener, and clever at everything he did. When I was quite little, he made a goldfish pond with all sorts of pretty rocks on the bottom. He let me help him, and it was a great source of pride. I was Daddy's girl, in spite of the fact that I think he would have liked me to be a boy. My mother always used to say to me when she was annoyed, 'You're just like your father, Margaret—pigheaded!' I think they did quite a lot of bickering and carrying on. My mother was rather a critical person, but I suppose it was her upbringing. It was forever 'Do this, do that, pick up behind you, don't be late.' I was harassed by it, and it took me years to grow out of it.

"My schooling was of the times. I started in at a one-room school, where I drew pictures of little houses with snow falling. Then, for less than a year, I went to Avon Cliffe, a private school run by two wellmeaning women. I was a frog in the school play, and I was not pleased by that. There was a nursing home, next to the school, where my grandmother spent her last days, and she'd wave to me out of the window every afternoon when I left. After that, I was sent to a convent school. My sister,

Joyce—there were just the two of us—was always ailing with bronchitis, and I think my mother enjoyed hovering over her. But I was the strong, healthy ox. Even so, I was scared of some of the nuns. I was hopeless in some subjects, and they were always grabbing me by the neck and locking me in the laundry room. My mother said I'd have to go to boarding school if I didn't shape up. I didn't, so they put me in Stratford House, in a neighboring town. It was a nice school for nice girls from nice families. We had a matron with a starched headdress and we were told when it was our turn to take a bath and we were taught how to make a bed with hospital corners. I couldn't stand the school food or the smell of cooking, and I got sick headaches. But there were good things. I think I learned how to string letters and words and sentences together on paper. And I designed the school emblem—three sweet peas, entwined. It was quite beautiful. And I wrote the school song.

"I had started playing the piano when I was three or four. It was at my great-uncle Harry's, and the keyboard was all yellow. And I remember playing, sitting up high on a stool, at kindergarten with children all gathered around. My mother would make me play for her friends, and while I played they all talked. When I finished, she'd say, 'Oh, that was very nice, dear.' I was angry, but I wouldn't have dared pop out with 'You weren't listening!' When I was nine, I asked my mother if I could take piano lessons. She said, 'Margaret, you already play the piano very well. I think you should take up the violin.' We went up to London and bought a violin, and I took lessons, but I never enjoyed the instrument. I played in concerts and competitions, but then my teacher died, and that put an end to it. I was studying elocution with Miss Mackie, at Stratford House, around this time, and I had a crush on her. I used to ask my mother if she'd invite her over for tea or dinner. Mummy was a nervous hostess, but finally Miss Mackie came, and it was she who advised my parents to send me up to the Guildhall School of Music, in London. My parents were always saying, 'You better think of what you're going to do after school; we aren't going to keep you forever,' which made me feel like a bit of aging merchandise. I went up to London and played for Sir Landon Ronald, who was the head of the Guildhall, and I got in. I commuted every day from Bromley, and I really worked. I studied composition and theory and piano, and I won a scholarship in composition. I took up violin again, because we students had to have a second instrument, and I studied singing with Carrie Tubb, a retired opera singer. The other day, I came across six pieces I wrote then. They have titles like 'Pas Seul' and 'Reverie,' and actually they are pretty well put together. But I'd never claim then that anything I'd done was good. The reaction would have been immediate: 'How can you be so immodest, Margaret!' "

The telephone rings, and Marian McPartland talks for a minute. "That was Sam Goody's. They want more of my records. Some women buy fur coats; I have my own record company. It's called Halcyon, and I've put out four albums to date three with myself and rhythm, and some duets with Teddy Wilson, which turned out surprisingly well. Sherman Fairchild helped me get it going. He died two years ago, and he was a great jazz buff and a friend for twenty years. Bill Weilbacher, who has *his* own label, Master Jazz Recordings, gives me advice, and a small packaging firm handles the distribution and such. A printing of five thousand LPs costs around fifteen hundred dollars. Whatever I make I put right back into the next record. The big companies are impossible, and a lot of musicians have their own labels. Stan Kenton has his, George Shearing has his, Clark Terry has his, and Bobby Hackett has started one. I think this do-it-yourself movement is terribly important, particularly in the area of reissues. What with all the mergers among recording companies, I'm afraid of valuable records being lost. Not long ago, I wrote the company that recorded me at the Hickory House in the fifties and asked if they intended reissuing any of the albums. I think they'd have some value now. But I got the vaguest letter back. So they won't reissue the records, nor will they let me. It's not right. I think that musicians should get together catalogues of everything they've recorded and perhaps form some sort of cooperative for reissuing valuable stuff. Anyway . . ." Marian McPartland laughs, and says she is going to make lunch.

She sets a small table and puts out pumpernickel and a fresh fruit salad. "I was listening to everything indiscriminately at the Guildhall, and I was beginning to learn all sorts of tunes. I have fantastic recall, but I don't know where half the music that is stored in my head has come from. I also started listening to jazz—the Hot Club of France, Duke Ellington's 'Blue Goose,' Sidney Bechet, Teddy Wilson, Bob Zurke, Art Tatum, and the wonderful Alec Wilder octets. I was playing a sort of cocktail piano outside of the classroom, and once, when my piano professor at the Guildhall, a solemn little white-haired man named Orlando Morgan, heard me, he said, 'Don't let me catch you playing that rubbish again.' Well, he never got the chance. One day I sneaked over to the West End, where Billy Mayerl had a studio. He played a lot on the BBC, and he was like Frankie Carle or Eddy Duchin. I played 'Where Are You?' for him, and a little later he asked me to join a piano quartet he was putting together—Billy Mayerl and His Claviers. I was twenty, and I was tremendously excited. The family were horrified, but I said I'd go back to the Guildhall when the tour was over. My father charged up to London to see 'this Billy Mayerl.' He didn't want any daughter of his being preyed on, and he wanted to know what I'd be paid—ten pounds a week, it turned out. So my parents agreed. The quartet included Billy and George Myddelton and Dorothy Carless and myself. She and I were outfitted in glamorous gowns, and we played music-hall stuff. We played variety theaters—a week in each town. We lived in rented digs in somebody's house. If it was 'all in,' it included food. Some of the places were great, and they'd even bring you up a cup of tea in the morning. Meanwhile, my family had moved to Eastbourne. The tour with Billy lasted almost a year, and then I joined Carroll Levis's Discoveries, a vaudeville show, and

I was with them until the early years of the war. By this time, my family had given up on me. But my father would catch me on his business trips, and he'd come backstage and wow all the girls in the cast. I was going around with the manager of the show. He was a comedian, and he was also Jewish. My father would take us out to dinner and he would manfully try not to be patronizing. But it was beyond him. He would have liked me to work in a bank or be a teacher, and here I was playing popular music and going around with someone who was not 'top drawer.' I don't think it was real anti-Semitism; you just didn't go around with Jews and tradespeople. When I was five or six, and my mother found out that one of my friends was the daughter of a liquor-store owner, I wasn't allowed to see her anymore."

The phone rings again, and Marian McPartland talks with animation. "That was my dear friend Alec Wilder. He wanted to know if I'd done any writing today. He's incessant, but he's right. For a long time I procrastinated and procrastinated. I'd start things and let them sit around forever before finishing them. Alec gave me a set of notebooks, and I jot ideas down in them in cabs and at the hairdresser. Tony Bennett recorded my 'Twilight World,' which Johnny Mercer wrote the lyrics for, and it's just come out on Tony's new LP. Johnny is another great friend. One evening, he and Ginger, his wife, and his mother came up here, and Johnny sat right over there by the piano and sang about fifteen songs. It was a marvelous experience." Marian McPartland clears the table, and sits down in the living room with a fresh cup of tea.

"In nineteen forty-three, I volunteered for ENSA, which was the English equivalent of the USO. I traveled all over England with the same sort of groups I'd been with, and then I switched to the USO, which paid better and which meant working with the Americans! Boy, the Americans! The fall of nineteen forty-four, we were sent to France. We were given fatigues and helmets and mess kits, and we lived in tents and ate in orchards and jumped into hedgerows when the Germans came over. At first I played accordion because there weren't any pianos around. I met Fred Astaire and Dinah Shore and Edward G. Robinson, and I worked with Astaire in a show that we gave for Eisenhower. We moved up through Caen, which was all rubble, and into Belgium, where I met Jimmy McPartland. A jam session was going on in a big tent, and I was playing, and in walked Jimmy and saw me—a female white English musician—and the my-God, what-could-be-worse expression on his face was clear right across the room. But it was a case of propinquity, and in the weeks to come it was Jimmy on cornet and me and a bass player and whatever drummer we could find. We'd go up near the front and play in tents or outside, and it was cold. He annoyed me at first because he almost always had this silly grin on his face, but I found out that it was because he was drinking a great deal. Somewhere along the line he said, 'Let's get married.' I didn't believe him, so one morning I went over to his place very early, when I knew he'd be hung over and close to reality, and asked him if he really meant it, and he said sure and took a drink of armagnac. I guess I was madly in love with him. We were married in February, in Aachen, and we played at our own wedding.

"When we got to New York, early in nineteen forty-six, we went straight to Eddie Condon's, in the Village. I was so excited I couldn't stand it. Jimmy sat in and so did I, even though my left wrist, which I'd broken in a jeep in Germany, was still in a cast. We stayed for a while with Gene Krupa, then we went to Chicago to stay with Jimmy's family. A colonel with our outfit had given the news of my marriage to my parents when he was on leave in England. My father was stiff-upper-lip, but Mummy told me she cried a whole day. I guess my not telling them first was a rotten thing to do, but we were so isolated. You couldn't just pick up a phone at the front and tell them you were going to get married. But when Jimmy finally met them, he charmed them completely. My mother was really crippled with arthritis by then, and he made her laugh, and Jimmy took my father to the movies. They told me, 'He's not like an American. He's so polite.' In Chicago, I became greatest of friends with Jimmy's daughter, Dorothy, who was very beautiful and just fifteen. Jimmy had been married before, and Dorothy had been their only child. Jimmy had sent a lot of money back from Europe, and the first six months in Chicago were spent hanging out and treating people. All anybody seemed to do was drink, including Jimmy, and eventually it got to be one crisis after another. I left him a couple of times, and once I even booked passage on the Queen Elizabeth. But it was all done without much thought; I seemed such a brainless person then. And I think I must have been quite awful to Jimmy. One of Mummy's dire predictions was 'If you become a musician, Margaret, you'll marry a musician and live in an attic.' And that's exactly what happened; our first place in Chicago was a furnished room in an attic. But there were a lot of nice times, too. Jimmy and I started working together, and Jimmy was always marvelous in that he was proud of me, he wanted to show me off. We worked with Billie Holiday and Sarah Vaughan and Anita O'Day, and I met Duke Ellington and Count Basie. And we'd go fishing up in Wisconsin and sit there by some lake and cook fish and eat them and watch the sun rise. I had learned all the good old Dixieland tunes from Jimmy, but I was also listening to the new sounds—Charlie Ventura and Lennie Tristano and Charlie Parker.

"Jimmy and I had split up, musically, by the early fifties, and my first gig all by myself in America was at the St. Charles Hotel, in St. Charles, Illinois, and not long after that I left for New York. I played solo piano at Condon's and then I went into the Embers, with Eddie Safranski on bass and Don Lamond on drums. Coleman Hawkins and Roy Eldridge were brought in as guest stars, and we backed them. I was so nervous I had to write down what I was supposed to say at the close of each set. I played Storyville, in Boston, and then I went into the Hickory House in nineteen fifty-two, and I was there most of the next eight years. The best trio I had

was Bill Crow on bass and Joe Morello on drums. Sal Salvador introduced me to Joe one night. He was at the bar, a skinny bean pole in a raincoat, and he looked like a studious young chemist. I asked him to sit in,
and I was flabbergasted. I'd never heard anyone play drums like that.
When Mousie Alexander, who was with me then, left, Joe joined us, and
I was so enamored of his playing that I let him play a lot of solos."

Marian McPartland looks up at the ceiling and laughs. "Whenever I
think of Joe, I think of swinging. It was impossible not to swing with him.
And whenever I think of swinging, I think metaphorically. Swinging is
like being on a tightrope or a roller coaster. It's like walking in space. It's
like a soufflé: it rises and rises and rises. The fingers and the mind are
welded together. But it's dangerous. You have to leave spaces in your
playing. You can't go on like a typewriter. Sometimes I do, though, and I
leave no note unplayed. It's hard to say what goes on in your head when
you're swinging, when you're really improvising. I do know I see the different keys in colors—the key of D is daffodil yellow, B major is maroon,
and B flat is blue. Different musicians spark you into different ideas,
which is why I like to play with new people all the time. Especially the
younger musicians. They're fearless. Joe used to play enormously complicated rhythmic patterns once in a while and confuse me, and I'd get
mad. Now I'd just laugh. Playing with lots and lots of different people is
like feeding the computer: what they teach you may not come out right
away, but it will eventually. Unless you have a row with someone just
before you play, your state of mind doesn't affect you. You can feel
gloomy, and it will turn out a marvelous night. Or you can feel beautiful,
and it will be a terrible night. When I started out, I had the wish, the need,
to compete with men. If somebody said I sounded like a man, I was
pleased. But I don't feel that way anymore. I take pride in being a
woman. Of course, I have been a leader most of my career, and that helps.
I don't feel I've ever been discriminated against job-wise. I have always
been paid what I was worth as a musician. So I feel I've been practicing
women's lib for years.

"The Hickory House was a good period for Jimmy and me. He was on
the wagon and we were both working, and we lived on the West Side. For
the first time in my life, I began spending all my waking hours doing
things that had to do with just me, and one of them was a big romance
that went on, or off and on, for years. But I wanted to keep things together with Jimmy, and we bought a little house out in Merrick, Long Island,
and Jimmy's daughter came and lived with us. Joe Morello left in nineteen fifty-six to join Dave Brubeck, and it was terrible, but he had to move
on. In nineteen sixty-three, after the Hickory House gig was over and I'd
worked at the Strollers Club, in the old East Side music hall called The
Establishment, I went with Benny Goodman. I thought I'd be perfect for
Benny, because I had worked so long as a sideman with Jimmy, and of
course Jimmy and Benny played together in Chicago as kids. But I had
the feeling I wasn't fitting in. Bobby Hackett was in the band, and he'd

tell me, 'Marian, don't play such far-out chords behind Benny,' and I'd say, 'Well, why doesn't Benny say something to me?' One night, Benny and I had a couple of drinks, and I told him I knew he wasn't happy with me and to get someone else. All he said was 'Oh really, you don't mind?' and he got John Bunch. So all of a sudden, nothing seemed right—my work, my marriage, my romance. When I got back to New York, I started going to a psychiatrist, and I stayed with him six years. He was tough but very good. He indirectly precipitated a lot of things. The romance finally broke up, and I cried for a week. Jimmy and I got divorced. I didn't really want to do it, and neither did he, but it turned out we were right. Jimmy hasn't had a drink in five years, and I'm twice as productive. We've never lost touch with each other. We still talk on the phone almost every day, and he stops by all the time. In fact, he said he'd come by today."

The doorbell rings, and Marian McPartland jumps up. "Speaking of the devil! That'll be the old man now." Jimmy McPartland comes into the living room at sixty miles an hour, gives her a peck on the cheek, plumps a big attaché case down on the coffee table, takes off his blazer, and sits down. He opens the attaché case. It has a cornet in it, and several hundred photographs. He puts the cornet beside him on the sofa and dumps the pictures on the coffee table. "My God, will you look at these, Marian," he says, in a booming voice. "I found them the other day out at the house, and some of them go back thirty or forty years. There's your father, and there we are, with Sarah Vaughan and Charlie Shavers and Louis Bellson. And here we are on the ship coming over. Look at you in the GI togs and look at me. Thinsville."

She leans over his shoulder and giggles.

"Here we are playing in that pub in Eastbourne when we went to visit your family. And here you are holding a fish we caught in Wisconsin."

"They should be put in a book, Jimmy. They'll just get lost."

McPartland pulls a tape out of the attaché case.

"A guy gave me this on my South African trip, a couple of weeks ago. I'd never heard it before. We made it in England in nineteen forty-nine. You were on piano and you wrote the arrangements. It'll surprise you."

She puts the tape on a machine, and Bix Beiderbecke's "In a Mist" starts. A complex ensemble passage introduces a Jimmy McPartland solo. "Listen to that intro," she says. "How awful."

"It's not, it's not. The clarinet player is out of tune. You know, I don't sound bad. Not bad at all." The tape finishes, and McPartland opens his mouth and points at one of his upper front teeth. "Look at thiff," he says to her through his finger. "The damn toof if moving back. Walking right back into my mouf."

She stares at the tooth, frowns, and straightens up. "You should go to Dr. Whitehorn, Jimmy."

"Jimmy, are we still going out to dinner?"

"Sure, babe. That Brazilian place around the corner you like so much.
"I'll go get dressed."

McPartland shuffles through the photographs. "Marian is amazing. There's no one I'd rather be with as a person, as an all-around human being. I have terrific respect for her as a musician and as a person. She's talent personified. Musically, she has that basic classical training, and she's meshed that and her jazz talent. She's just begun to do it really successfully in the past two or three years. And she's a great accompanist. She flows with horns and singers like a conversation. Marian didn't have good time when I first heard her. Her enthusiasm was overwhelming, and she'd rush the beat. I'd tell her to go along with the rhythm, to take it easy. She sounded like Fats Waller, and, in fact, the first tune I ever heard her play was his 'Honeysuckle Rose.' It was in this tent in Belgium. I go in and there's a girl playing piano and she looks English. I thought, God, this is awful. I wouldn't play with her until I'd had a couple of drinks. I proposed after six or seven weeks. Real offhand. 'If it doesn't work out,' I'd say, 'you can just go back to England.' She tried to act real GI, but I could see she was a fine, well-bred person and not a Chicago juvenile delinquent like me. Visting Marian's parents was like being in an English movie to me. They were mid-Victorian in style. Her mother was in a wheelchair and very well-dressed and very particular. Everything at a certain time, everything regulated. Tea at four, dinner at eight. If I was late coming back from fishing or golf, Marian's mother would say, 'James, you're late. We've started our tea.' Her father, who was a great engineer, used to knock his brains out in his garden, and I'd help him until the pull of golf or fishing got too strong. He was a nice, conservative gent."

Marian McPartland has been standing for some moments in front of the sofa. She is in a Pucci-type dress and white boots, and she has a fur coat over one arm. "Daddy once slapped my hand for saying 'Blast it!' "

McPartland digs a frayed envelope out from under the photographs and pours out a lot of German currency. "We used to go into people's houses over there and rifle them. That's where all this came from. Some of it is inflation money from after the First War. It was a terrible thing to steal like that, but everybody did it."

"You used to appear with bagfuls of old cobwebby wine bottles."

"I was just well-organized. Once, you needed a piano for a special show, and the colonel gave me the name of this collaborator in the town. I got eight guys together and a truck, and we went to his house and there was a beautiful piano. Brand-new. I told him he'd get paid for it, and we brought it back to the theater."

"I was really impressed," she says. "You said you were going out to find me a new piano and you did. It was one of your finest moments."

It is Marian McPartland's opening night at the Café Carlyle. By nine-forty-five, when the first set is scheduled to begin, the room is filled, largely with friends and well-wishers. She sits down at the piano, and she is a handsome sight. The room, with its fey, old-fashioned murals and rather dowdy trappings, is out of the late thirties, and she brings it up to date. In the light, her hair is golden and bouffant, and she is wearing an ensemble that has been thought out to the last fold: a close-fitting cranberry turtleneck, a gold belt, brocaded cranberry and gold palazzo pants, and a gold pocketbook. She looks calm and collected, and, smiling slightly to herself, she goes immediately into a warming-up version of "It's a Wonderful World." (Her accompanists are Rusty Gilder on bass and Joe Corsello on drums.) Despite her outward cool, she sounds jumpy. Her chords blare a little, an arpeggio stumbles, her time is slightly off. In the next number, a long, medium-tempo "Gypsy in My Soul," which she introduces as a carry-over from the days at the Hickory House, she begins to relax. Marian McPartland came of age when pianistic giants roamed the earth, and their footsteps still echo dimly in her work. So does the work of Bill Evans. But in the past five years she has moved beyond adroit adulation into her own realm. It is, in the way of Johnny Hodges and Sidney Bechet and Tatum, an emotional, romantic one. Her slow ballads suggest rain forests. The chords are dark and overhanging, the harmonies thick. And her slow blues are much the same. Her foliage is thinner at faster tempos. There are pauses between the single-note melodic lines, and her chords, which are often played off beat. "Gypsy in My Soul" is sumptuous, and so is the theme from "Summer of '42." But then she moves through medium-fast renditions of "All the Things You Are," part of which is translated into contrapuntal lines, and "Stompin' at the Savoy," which is full of winding arpeggios. A slow blues goes by, and then she pays Alec Wilder tribute with a blending of his three best-known tunes—"I'll Be Around," "While We're Young," and "It's So Peaceful in the Country." They are fresh, mindful versions, and Wilder, who is on hand, looks pleased. She closes the set with "Royal Garden Blues," and after the applause she stops briefly at Wilder's table. He asks her how she feels. "I was flipping at first," she replies. "But then the marvelous vibes from all these dear people got to me, and it began to feel very good. Very, very good, in fact. I think it's going to be a nice date."

Super Chops

Like his friend and great admirer Bobby Hackett, Dave McKenna's life pivots on paradox. He has been a jazz pianist since the late forties, but it is almost impossible to get him to talk about music beyond, for example, the random observation that there is no such thing as the pure improvisation he constantly practices. He moved to Cape Cod in 1967, but he has only been in the ocean once. In a society that deifies the automobile, he does not drive. He is one of the hardest-swinging jazz pianists of all time, but he lives a quiet, unswinging middle-class life made up largely of eating, playing rumbustious Ping-Pong with his sons, Steven and Douglas, and watching sports on television—particularly the Red Sox, who have been with him all his life. He plays the piano with great authority but considers himself a barroom or dance-band pianist. The amplified bass fiddle has become the dominant instrument in jazz during the past decade, but McKenna's left hand is so rhythmically powerful that it brushes the new bassists aside. He is among the best of the post-Tatum pianists, but he stays low: he is rarely in New York, and in order to hear him one must travel to Schenectady, the Cape, Rochester, Boston, Newport.

One night before work at Bradley's he had dinner at Antolotti's, on East Forty-ninth Street. He was dolled up in a three-piece tan corduroy suit, and he ate with his customary relish—a dozen clams on the half shell, two orders of gnocchi with marinara sauce, veal piccata, salad, and cheesecake, all washed down with a couple of Martinis, a white Corvo, a good Barolo, and espresso. He delivered this brief litany between Martinis: "I'm crazy about Italian cooking, and my ambition is to eat at every good Italian restaurant in New York. There must be at least fifty of them. When I was at Bradley's last year, I went to Gino's, on Lexington at Sixtieth, and the Amalfi, which moved a while ago from West Forty-seventh to East Forty-eighth. Tony Bennett hangs out there when he's in town. I go to Patsy's, on Fifty-sixth. Ballato's, down on East Houston, is great, and Joe's, on Macdougal, is a down-home, peasant-type place. I come here a lot, and I guess Elston Howard does, too, because I've seen him twice. I haven't been to Vesuvio, on West Forty-eighth, for years, but it used to be fine. I've been to Romeo Salta, and I go to San Marco, on West Fifty-second. I went recently to San Marino with Zoot and Louise Sims. I tried Il Monello, at Seventy-sixth and Second, and Parioli Romanissimo, where Bill Buckley goes. Some guitarist from Boston told me that Parioli has the best chocolate cake he ever had, which is interesting, because I usually don't go to Italian restaurants for chocolate cake. I'd be willing to take gigs in New Haven just for the white pizza they have there. I guess I'd like to be a Craig Claiborne. That's my idea of putting your heart and your soul into your work."

He arrived replete at Bradley's, and during his first set, in which he built a medium head of steam, he fashioned one of his free-association songfests. He has said that stringing together songs with common themes helps pass the time when he is playing. (He also likes to speed up fast numbers, as if he were trying to get them over with as quickly as possible.) He warmed up with "Darn That Dream," "At Sundown," and "When Day Is Done"—which falsely presaged an essay on songs having to do with evening or night, for he abruptly veered into "Silk Stockings" and "Blue Skies." Then came "My Ship," and he had found his text: "Lost in a Fog" was followed by "Red Sails in the Sunset," "On Moonlight Bay,"

"How Deep Is the Ocean?," "The Devil and the Deep Blue Sea," "Wave," and "I Cover the Waterfront." He closed the set with a beautiful, rocking blues and Zoot Sims' "Red Door."

McKenna sat down at a table near the piano, a fine concert grand left to Bradley Cunningham by the late Paul Desmond. McKenna is a man-mountain. He has a massive eagle's head, a logger's forearms, and hot-dog fingers. He is well over six feet, and, possibly for streamlining, he wears his brown hair flat and straight back. When he is at the Cape, he likes to talk about New York and how much he'd love to live there again, and when he is in New York he likes to talk about the Cape. For a while, he spoke with some heat of why the Red Sox had blown the pennant, and when he was asked how the summer had been at the Cape he said, "Good. I like to be around salt water, but the ocean is overstated. Sand is gritty and the ocean has waves. Last year, I went swimming in a fresh-water pond, and if I lived near one I'd go in three or four times a day— or would have. Since I've gained weight, I'd never go to a public beach. I'd have to have a private pond."

One afternoon a year or so before that, McKenna, who was stretched out on a beach chair in his back yard in South Yarmouth, talked about his house and his early life. The house is a gray-shingled bungalow and the back yard is largely macadam, from which sprout two basketball nets. A stone barbecue and a picnic table at one edge look unused. The sur-rounding landscape is scrub pine and sand. McKenna had on a red-flow-ered sports shirt, worn outside khaki pants, and sneakers. His chair was surrounded by the sports pages of the Boston *Globe* and *Herald American*. "My wife, Frankie, got the house for ten thousand," McKenna said. "And we had to borrow a thousand for the down payment. It only has three small bedrooms. I could use a music room. It's still fresh air here, but the new houses are beginning to hem me in. When we moved, it was all woods. There was nothing next door, and there was nothing behind me. I figured no one would build across the street between me and Route 6, but they did. The beauty of being here was all that land to roam in. I'm used to that from the fields and farms there were around Woonsocket, Rhode Island, where I was born. I was born there in 1930. My mother, Catherine Reilly, came from South Boston. She still plays piano. She stud-ied violin with a member of the Boston Symphony. She played the top tunes of the time, but not too forcefully—'Lazybones' and 'Stormy Weather.' She's got good ears and knows all the chords and can transpose anything, and she reads better than I do. But I don't think she ever could have been a dedicated musician. She's got too much of a sense of humor. My father was from Woonsocket. He drove a parcel-post truck. He was a street drummer—that is, he played snare drum in military bands, like the Sons of Italy—and he also played drums in dance bands. He had a fan-tastic roll. His musical likes included brass bands and the 'William Tell Overture.' But there's nothing wrong with that. Sousa marches are really put together well, and I've always thought 'The Star-Spangled Banner' should never be sung but should be played by a good Sousa or Goldman band. A brass band makes it much more stirring. My father's father and grandfather had been drummers before him—his Grandfather McKenna played drums in the Civil War. I was the first non-drummer in three or four generations. I have a younger brother, Donald, and two sisters, Jean and Pat. Jean teaches school and lives with my parents, in Woonsocket, and she's a pretty good semi-pro singer. She's not a belter and she has good pitch. Pat lives in Barrington, Rhode Island, and is married to a schoolteacher. Woonsocket wasn't a bad place to grow up in. It was a family town, and it was mostly French-Canadian, like all the mill towns in New England. There was semi-professional baseball, and we used to go up to Boston to see the Braves and the Red Sox. I've been a Sox fan since I was seven. I was always more of a fan than a player, although I was in a kind of softball league for a while in New York in the fifties. I played in the outfield, and the team I was with included Zoot Sims and Carl Fontana and Al Cohn, and we played in Central Park. We didn't have a name, and once we beat Jimmy Dorsey's band, which showed up in uniforms. My mother didn't think it was right for her to teach me piano herself, so she sent me to the nuns in parochial school, and they taught me that in-between music with John Thompson music books, and I wasn't interested. But I listened every morning on the radio to 'The 9:20 Club from Boston' and I heard records by Benny Goodman and Nat Cole and the boogie-woogie pianists. When I was twelve or thirteen, I started playing at showers and weddings, and I joined the musicians' union at fifteen. When I was sixteen, I played with Boots Mussulli around Milford, which was just over the border from us in Massachusetts. Milford was eighty per cent Italian and eighty per cent musicians. That's where I learned about Italian food. There were never any bass players, so I had to finagle around a lot with my left hand to make it sound full, which is why I have that guitar effect—that strumming thing in my left hand now.

"I joined Charlie Ventura's band in 1949. Jackie Cain and Roy Kral had just left, but he still had Ed Shaughnessy on drums and Red Mitchell on bass. I went with Woody Herman's band in 1950, and stayed until I was drafted, in 1951. That was the band that had Conte Candoli and Rolf Ericson and Doug Mettome and Don Fagerquist and Al Cohn and Sonny Igoe. I was a disgraceful, drunken kid, and Woody should have fired me. But the Army solved that. After I was drafted, I tried to connect with a service band, but it didn't work. l took basic training with the M.P.s and I did a lot of K.P., and then they sent me overseas—to Japan, where I went to cooking school, and on to Korea. The Koreans were not allowed to touch any of the food, so we had to do all the cooking. I learned how to bake a cake for a hundred men, and how to make pancakes, but my biscuits were like rocks. l remember the *bong* they made when they landed on the mess tray. l was over there a year and a half. We could hear the artillery all the time, and once we were strafed and I was the last guy left in the cook tent. It was a situation where you pressed yourself so close to the ground your belly button made an imprint. That same time, a fat mess sergeant fainted after he discovered that two .50-calibre bullets passed right through the place he always sat in the tent. There was a service band up the road in Korea, and a drummer from Providence who was in it tried to get me in, but the only opening was for accordion. I'd never played one, so this drummer and another guy borrowed one, and they pumped it while I tried to play, but I couldn't get the hang of it, and I didn't make the band.

"When I got home, Boots Mussulli said I sounded the same, even though I'd hardly touched the piano since I'd been away—which is strange, because I've never had that many chops. My mother desperately begged me to use the G.I. Bill and go to college, but I rejoined Charlie Ventura. I spent the rest of the fifties with Ventura and Gene Krupa and with Stan Getz and a group that Zoot Sims and Al Cohn had. I was with Buddy Rich in 1960. I worked a lot in the sixties with Bobby Hackett and at Eddie Condon's place, in the East Fifties. New York was my headquarters, even though I never had an apartment and lived in hotels. Once in a while, I'd go back to Milford just to eat."

Between 1970 and 1977, McKenna's headquarters were at The Columns, in West Dennis. Housed in a handsome mid-nineteenth-century clapboard building to which huge ante-bellum columns had been added, it was owned and operated by a gentle, self-effacing man named Warren Maddows, whose great delight was to join McKenna near closing time for a couple of Tony Bennett-inspired songs. (Maddows died in 1978.) At first, McKenna played on a bandstand in the small bar to the left of the front door. It was cluttered and noisy and cheerful, and musicians like Bobby Hackett and Dick Johnson frequently sat in. (As a duet, Hackett and McKenna came close to equalling Louis Armstrong and Earl Hines. They became inextricable, like light and dark.) During the summer of 1971, Teddi King sang with McKenna for a month. Zoot Sims and Earl Hines and Teddy Wilson and Joe Venuti and Red Norvo spelled McKenna when he took his rare off-Cape jobs. Maddows never made any money from The Columns, but he often kept it open into the winter, and he gradually expanded it. By the summer of 1977, he had added a spacious yellow-and-white tent to the rear of the building, and late that August he hired Teddy Wilson to play duets with McKenna. One set in the middle of the first week went like this:

McKenna, gleaming in a blue shirt, white pants, and white shoes, sat at a low upright and played "Lover, Come Back to Me," "Dixieland One-Step," "Misty," and "That's a Plenty," and retired. Wilson, in a conservative tie and jacket, effortlessly unreeled "Stompin' at the Savoy," "Tea for Two," "Basin Street Blues," "I Can't Get Started," "Moonglow," and an Ellington medley. McKenna, his face impassive and pleasant, listened to Wilson, and, when Wilson finished, talked about music.

McKenna talks rapidly and without preamble. "There was a point in the mid-fifties when I got away from jazz and into listening to songs," he said. "Harold Arlen and Jerome Kern and Alec Wilder. Song-writers are my heroes, and I've always wanted to be one. Take Alec Wilder's 'I'll Be Around.' That's the greatest pop song ever written. I should be learning new songs every day. Instead, I'm playing a lot of the same tunes, and I don't like that. Some pianists can play entire scores, but I can't do that. I don't think I know any of 'My Fair Lady' or any Leonard Bernstein." When McKenna complains, which he does a lot, it means he's feeling fine. He said, "I'd have more fun if I could play just two nights a week. With six nights, you don't have the enthusiasm. It takes the heat off you when you play for dancing, which people are happier doing than just sitting around in their bodies listening. People are always after you to play hot, but I don't have super chops. I don't know if I play jazz. I don't know if I qualify as a bona-fide jazz guy. I play barroom piano. I like to stay close to the melody. When I play, I just tool along, and the only thing I think about is what I'm going to play next. But I like to sound even and professional, to keep everything on an even keel. Very few jazz musicians are complete improvisers. The greatest have little patterns they follow. I have my own patterns, my own licks. Sometimes I play in runs, because people like to hear those things. Also, I'm getting paid to do that, so I have to stick them in once in a while. But I like to deëmphasize them, I like to play more sparingly. I play so many single-note lines because I've listened more to horn players than to piano players. But I loved Nat Cole. He came the closest to bending notes on the piano, except maybe Oscar Peterson. I'd rather listen to Nat Cole than Art Tatum. Tatum makes you sweat too much. I'm more at home playing alone. I appreciate the coloration of a bassist, but I'd rather play alone or with a little band. I'd love to play in a Dixieland band like the one I worked in at Condon's. 'Whiskey-land jazz,' Hacket called it."

A second upright had been placed akimbo to the first, and after the intermission Wilson sat down at the piano that he and McKenna had used and McKenna took the second one. The two pianists faced one another, and McKenna, looking as if he were about to play in his first recital, immediately deferred to Wilson, who selected the tunes and set the tempos. (At the start of the gig, McKenna, in typical knock-himself-down fashion, had expressed fear that he would not be able to keep up with the fast tempos he knew Wilson would set.) The first number, "How High the Moon," was fast, and a pattern was set: Wilson played the first chorus, McKenna soloed for two choruses, Wilson soloed, and the two exchanged four-bar breaks before playing the last chorus together. Neither pianist betrays much emotion when he plays. Wilson, his back straight and his head tipped slightly forward, occasionally shuts his eyes briefly and presses his lips together, and McKenna, bent over the keyboard like a tall person stooping to talk to a child, wrinkles his brow and evinces a slight gathering of cheek muscles below his right ear. In recent years, Wilson, perhaps weary at last of perfecting his exquisite miniaturistic solos, has relied more and more on his patterns, and his playing has taken on an automatic gentility. McKenna, who once resembled a controlled Tatum with dashes of Nat Cole and Wilson, has been going in the opposite direction. His rhythmic power, spelled out by his ingenious left hand—an avalanche of guitar chords, ground figures, sharp offbeats, and pouring single-note melodic lines—has become unfettered. The rock-rock, rock-rock, rock-rock of his time is hypnotic. Nothing remains still before. it. He places his notes so that they jar and sharpen the beat. He likes to emphasize the first note of a phrase and then, unexpectedly, the fifth or sixth. He likes to shake up the listener. He also likes to insert arpeggios and double-time phrases. It is a joyous, foraging style, and by the end of Wilson and McKenna's second number it was clear that McKenna was blowing Wilson out of the water. Wilson would effect a resplendent chorus, and then McKenna, his left hand rolling and rumbling, would roar into his chorus, and all memory of what Wilson had just played would be gone. A fast "Who's Sorry Now?" went by, and the two settled into a long medium blues. Wilson approaches the blues as if he were nibbling grapes, but McKenna shoulders his way in, scattering boogie-woogie basses, stoptime choruses, and low-register explosions in both hands. Wilson remained unperturbed, and the last number, a short, driving "I'll Remember April," was anticlimactic.

The summer after Maddows' death, McKenna went into the Lobster Boat, several miles down Route 28 toward Hyannis. It has a huge white mock ship's prow that points into a parking lot running along the highway. Behind the prow are a lozenge-shaped lounge and a big, boxy dining room. The lounge has a bar and a small bandstand opposite, which holds an upright piano. The wall back of the bandstand is curved and contains a couple of dozen portholes, each of them fitted out with a hanging plant. The piano bench is flanked by carriage lamps fastened to the wall, and there are candlesticks on the piano and a glass chandelier over it. The ceiling is beamed and decorated with signal flags and ship's wheels, and the patrons sit below in a comfortable rummage shop furnished with sofas, director's chairs, captain's chairs, overstuffed chairs, side tables, and standing lamps. It is three New England parlors placed end to end. A color television set behind the bar was showing a Red Sox-Yankees game, and when McKenna arrived, at eight-twenty, he plunked himself at the bar and watched. Frankie McKenna had driven him over, and she sat at a table next to the piano with a good local Billie Holiday singer named Shirley Carroll. At a quarter to nine, McKenna tore himself away from the television and went into his first set. He had had dinner in Yarmouth Port, in an Italian restaurant called La Cipollina, and had put away a small pizza, chicken piccata, linguine with red clam sauce, a salad, half of Frankie McKenna's shrimps with sweet peppers, and a mocha pudding with whipped cream. He was in a benevolent mood. He began with

"Don't Take Your Love from Me," and went on through "The Moon of Manakoora," "Sleepy Lagoon," "Isn't It Romantic," "My Romance," and "My Funny Valentine," ending with a blues, three songs in which Shirley Carroll sat in, and a medium bebop tune. He swung quietly but hard.

He returned immediately to the game, and Frankie McKenna talked about herself and her life with McKenna. She is short and has shingled gray hair and a soft Carolina accent. She is a pretty woman, with a long-suffering face and a smile that closes her eyes. (McKenna has a tempestuous side, and if he doesn't work it out through his playing or in several banging games of Ping-Pong it is apt to spill over on his family.) "I was born an only child and grew up in North and South Carolina," she said in a gentle voice. "My parents were divorced when I was sixteen. My father, Jimmy Wiggins, was a salesman who could charm the bark off a tree. He was medium-sized and dark-haired and well-mannered—a Southern gentleman. His mother was a McQueen, and derived descent from Mary Queen of Scots. He died several years ago. My mother had long since remarried. She's an attractive lady and a champion bridge player. I went to the University of South Carolina two years on scholarship, and, because I was very poor, took practical courses—secretarial courses. Then I went to New York and lived with a group of Carolina girls who had a large apartment on Riverside Drive. I worked first as a secretary to a sales manager of a lingerie company, but come summer I'd take a leave of absence and go home. I liked being Southern in the North and having an accent, and all that. I also worked for a public-relations outfit and as a secretary at ABC Records. I took little night jobs, too—at Downey's Steak House and Basin Street. I met Dave in 1959 in Junior's Bar & Lounge, a musicians' hangout, and we were married three months later. My mother came up on the plane practically carrying the whole wedding—flowers and all—in her arms. I had a two-room apartment across from London Terrace, on Twenty-fourth, and when Steve was born, it was awful. We moved to a fourth-floor walkup at Ninth and Twenty-first, and Douglas was born. I had everything pretty well organized. Summers, I got a portable swimming pool and put it on the roof and filled it from a hose I'd attached to my kitchen sink. Our dog Midge chased a beach ball around the roof and the kids chased her and the people from next door threw pennies in the pool. We came up here the first time in the mid-sixties, and each year we'd buy a junk car and at the end of the summer park it in front of our building and let it die. In the fall of 1966, we decided to move up. It was too much in New York with two small children and Dave's hours and the stairs to walk up. I got to do the moving, because Dave was working, and a man named McCarthy, who lived over us and had offered to help in a weak moment, drove me up in his station wagon. We moved into this house in April of 1967.

"Dave is a complex person. He's honest and he's moral. He doesn't put people down, and he's never squandered money. He's a good father, even though he doesn't take the boys fishing, and all that, and he prefers not to be the disciplinarian. But he's very good in a quiet way when someone gets out of hand. He loves his roots, and he loves house and home. He's the most unmechanical person I've ever seen. I can't stand to watch him when he has a screwdriver in his hand. I have to walk away. But it doesn't matter, because I'm a fixit. That's my therapy. Dave was very, very shy when we were married. His mother told me that he could never accept any kind of compliment when he was growing up. It got him all flustered, and he'd pretend he hadn't heard. But he's getting better, and I think he's beginning to admit to himself that he might be a good piano player."

The Red Sox were leading the Yankees by three runs, and McKenna's second set was effervescent. He played a string of "baby" songs—"Baby Won't You Please Come Home?," "Baby Face," "Melancholy Baby," "Gee, Baby, Ain't I Good to You?," "Oh, Baby," and a very fast "I Found a New Baby." When he finished, he headed back to the bar, commenting first on how hot it was up on the bandstand and how he wished he could go home and watch the rest of the game in peace.

The Westchester Kids

In one form or another—big bands, small bands, trios, solo pianists—jazz was everywhere in this country in the late thirties and early forties. Five or six nights a week, the four radio networks broadcast live music from Chicago, St. Louis, New York, Boston, and points between, and myriad local wires placed in clubs and roadhouses sustained the faithful for fifty miles around. Indeed, jazz of some sort could be heard in countless clubs and roadhouses as well as in hotels and ballrooms and theatres, and, before gas rationing and the wartime thirty-per-cent entertainment tax, it was simple and cheap to drive twenty or more miles to the Glen Island Casino or the Palladium Ballroom or the Bradford Hotel to hear Tommy Dorsey or Red Norvo or Count Basie. Every town of five thousand and over had a record store with at least one listening booth where you could sift the dozen or so new releases that came in every week, and there was no problem, as there is now, in ordering special records, like the Jones-Collins Astoria Hot Eight's "Tip Easy Blues" on Bluebird or Albert Ammons' "Bass Goin' Crazy" on twelve-inch Blue Note. Nor could the neophyte get lost in this lovely new musical landscape, for there were plenty of maps: Ramsey and Smith's "The Jazz Record Book" and "Jazzmen", and Hugues Panassié's "The Real Jazz;" the little magazines of jazz, like *Jazz Information* and *The Jazz Record*; and the more commercial *Metronome* and *down beat*, with their news and gossip, their record reviews, which alternated between the ecstatic and the crabby (off-pitch

third trumpeters beware!), and their lost-and-found columns, which listed temporarily misplaced musicians. ("Where is Freddy Bonso, the fine
solo alto sax man last heard of two years ago with Bob Chester?" To
which an answer would come a couple of months later: "My sister mailed
me your column where who would have guessed it I am mentioned.
Well, I left the music business and am selling insurance here in Topeka.
P.S. The new Bob Chester record of 'Strictly Instrumental' is solid even
without me. Ha. Ha.")

New York was Mecca, and the jazz in the air was dense and crackling.
There were always six or eight jazz clubs on Fifty-second Street between
Fifth and Seventh Avenues, and to the east on Fifty-eighth was Cafe
Society Uptown. In the Village were the Vanguard and Nick's and Cafe
Society Downtown. Harlem had Clark Monroe's Uptown House,
Minton's, Small's Paradise, the Savoy, the Apollo, and a network of after-
hours places. And there were at least half a dozen big bands on view at
any given time in the hotels and movie houses. All this was garnished
with radio shows, occasional concerts (still very much an innovation), and
visits to the Commodore Music Shop, on East Forty-second Street, where
musicians of the Condon persuasion were often on view, weighing their
hangovers and putting the touch on Milt Gabler, who owned the place.

Every art needs its callow celebrants. In the early forties, those surrounding jazz often came from white middle-class families. Jazz loosed
them from the neo-Victorian domestic regimens of their parents. These
celebrants revered the music, and the closer they got to it the better. To sit
ten feet from Art Tatum's right hand at the Three Deuces was sublime.
The careers of these adulators followed a predictable curve. They teethed
on Glenn Miller and Harry James and Tommy Dorsey, and then one day,
in a record shop or at the house of a slightly older acquaintance
renowned for his record collection, they heard a 1926 Jelly Roll Morton or
a Louis Armstrong Hot Five or an early Duke Ellington. The music
sounded harsh and uneven and disturbing. But in six months they were
also digging King Oliver and Fats Waller and James P. Johnson, and a
year later, they were into Ellington and Billie Holiday and Count Basie.
At the same time, to ease their enthusiasm, many of them took up instruments. Self-taught and highly imitative, they found their way into small
Dixieland bands patterned on Muggsy Spanier's Ragtime Band or Bob
Crosby's Bob Cats or Sidney Bechet's New Orleans Feetwarmers. They
played with passion and dedication until they went to college or were
drafted, and then they gave it up. Many of them even disliked being
reminded in later years of the feelings they had once bared. But a
tiny number decided defiantly that they would not be firemen or
policemen but would become jazz musicians. (The parents of most of
them were aghast at their decision.) One of the best and toughest of these
iconoclasts is Bob Wilber, who is a soprano saxophonist, a clarinettist, a
gifted arranger and composer, and an invaluable preserver and enhancer
of jazz tradition.

Wilber has wavy reddish-blond hair and a small pointed face, and wears glasses, and from the tenth row of Carnegie Hall he looks about seventeen or eighteen. Up close, though, his face reveals miniature signs of wear and his hair is misted with gray. He has intelligent, restless eyes. He is a small man, but he stands with his legs planted wide apart when he plays, and he has a deep and precise voice. His manner gives pause to frivolity. Wilber loves Cape Cod, and when he can he visits his father and stepmother in Orleans. He sat in a Boston rocker in the high-ceilinged living room of a renovated barn on his parents' place and talked. The rocker had a good, if faded, townscape painted on its crest rail, and his head moved irregularly across it. "I first got interested in jazz when my father brought home the original Victor recording of Duke Ellington's 'Mood Indigo.' I must have been three. I remember the strange sound of the horns and the steady *bring bring bring* of the banjo. I heard my first live jazz when I was thirteen and my father took me to Café Society Uptown to hear Teddy Wilson's band. I don't recall much about the band, even though it had Emmett Berry and Edmond Hall and Benny Morton and Sid Catlett—most of whom I'd play with one day. But I do remember the beautiful blue drapes behind the bandstand and the musicians' maroon jackets and the elegant atmosphere. We had constant music at home. My father had learned ragtime in college at its very height—he graduated in 1913—and he'd play every night when he came home from work. He also had a love for the musical theatre and bought sheet music all the time. Several years after the Café Society visit, a bunch of us from Scarsdale, where I grew up, started sneaking down to Nick's in the Village when we were supposed to be at the movies in White Plains. There were three upright pianos in a row at Nick's, then a space, and then the bandstand, and we'd sit between the pianos and the stand, and only inches above us would be Pee Wee Russell's or Chelsea Quealey's or Brad Gowans' feet. Inevitably, one night we missed the last train. We sacked out in the waiting room in Grand Central and took the milk train, and there were plenty of 'Good Lord!'s and 'Where have you been?'s. Then we began hanging around Fifty-second Street. It was an incomparable education, and all the clubs seemed to tolerate underage kids. We'd go to Kelly's Stables to hear Coleman Hawkins. We heard Billie Holiday with Al Casey, and Dizzy Gillespie and Charlie Parker and Milt Jackson. Jackson was playing the worst set of vibes I've ever heard; they literally clanked. Every Sunday afternoon, from five until eight, there were jam sessions at Jimmy Ryan's. The most marvellous combination of musicians showed up—Pete Johnson, the boogie-woogie pianist, and Pete Brown, the huge alto player, and sometimes during the 'Bugle Call Rag' finale the trumpets alone included Roy Eldridge and Hot Lips Page and Sidney de Paris and Bobby Hackett. Our other headquarters besides Fifty-second Street was the Commodore Music Shop. It had glassed-in record booths in the back, but best of all was standing around and waiting to see Pee Wee or Hackett come in.

"I was still in the Boy Scouts when I started playing the clarinet. I wanted to be in the marching band at school, because it was glamorous. I went
to the band director, and he gave me a trumpet and told me to try it over
the weekend. I couldn't make a sound. He gave me a clarinet the next
Friday, and by Sunday I was playing 'Row, Row, Row Your Boat.' The
director was Willard Briggs, and he was an excellent clarinettist and my
first teacher. I'd been listening to Benny Goodman and Artie Shaw, and I
started playing jazz right away. A lot of kids in Scarsdale and Larchmont
and even Greenwich were interested in jazz, but it wasn't like kids and
rock today, which is social. We shared a passion for *music*. There was a
nucleus of fifteen or twenty of us, and we were always on the lookout for
somebody's living room to jam in. We also played at U.S.O. dances.
Servicemen would be farmed out to various families for Sunday dinner
and then would be taken to a local country club for a late-afternoon
dance. We'd get the gig because the U.S.O. couldn't afford anything better, and we'd jam the whole time, playing 'After You've Gone' and 'Sweet
Georgia Brown' at way-up tempos, which the poor souls had to dance to.
Dick Wellstood came over from Greenwich with Charlie Traeger, the bass
player, and with this little thin kid with spectacles named Johnny
Windhurst, who was older and sounded like Bix. We'd listen to Jelly
Roll and King Oliver and Louis, and even to Red Norvo's 'Congo
Blues,' which had Dizzy and Bird, along with Teddy Wilson and Slam
Stewart. It was the first bop we'd heard, and we thought it was funny. We
couldn't take it seriously.

"When I graduated from high school, in 1945, I was set on being a
musician. My parents wanted me to follow the Ivy League route, but I
couldn't see it. If you were into jazz then, you were automatically a kind
of loner. It was still a special music. We compromised, and I went to the
Eastman School, in Rochester, that fall. There was very little jazz up there,
and *everything* was happening in New York. Bunk Johnson had just come
up from New Orleans, and Woody Herman was at the Pennsylvania
Hotel with the first Herd, which was *the* band. But there I was in this
chilling, inhospitable place, and at the end of the term I told my parents
I didn't want to go back. I told them I wanted to study jazz, even though
I had—and still have—an interest in legit clarinet. My father asked me
how I proposed studying jazz, and I said by going to New York and hanging out on Fifty-second Street and in the Village. So I did. I'd play in sessions around Westchester and take off for the street or Nick's. Red
McKenzie had a group at Ryan's called the Candy Kids, and he had
Johnny Windhurst and Eddie Hubble on trombone. Hubble had a
Pierce-Arrow convertible with isinglass windows, and after that he and
Windhurst found a Rolls with an open cockpit for the chauffeur. We'd
roar around Westchester in those cars and then down to Ryan's, and pretty soon we got to be called the Westchester Kids. Out of all this came our
first real group, which a trumpet player, Bob Mantler, named the
Wildcats. John Glasel was on trumpet, and we had Hubble and Wellstood

and Traeger. We were the first band in New York, and maybe in the East, to do what Lu Watters and Turk Murphy had been doing on the Coast—playing the music of the Hot Five and the Red Hot Peppers and the Creole Jazz Band. I moved into an apartment in New York with Wellstood in 1946. Eddie Condon's had opened on West Third Street that winter, and Eddie Hubble waited there for a day or so before it opened, so that he'd be the first customer. He was, and he was under-age, too. Milt Gabler gave us a chance to sit in at a Sunday-afternoon session, and he liked us and offered us a job. I already had a day job in the stockroom at Textron, and when *The New Yorker* did a story on the Wildcats, the president of Textron called me in and congratulated me on the fine public-relations job I'd done by mentioning the company. He also said that he understood I was sometimes a little late for work, and that, in view of what I did at night, the company would make allowances. I guess I took him literally, because I came in later and later and pretty soon Textron and I parted ways.

"By this time, I had started studying with Sidney Bechet. Milt Mezzrow had told me that Bechet was opening a school of music and needed students. Bechet lived on Quincy Street in Brooklyn in a house with tall French windows that reminded him of New Orleans. He had boarders upstairs and a girlfriend who took care of him. I was his first student, and we got on from the beginning." (Bechet describes their first lessons in "Treat It Gentle": "This boy, when he first come to me, he thought this old clarinet would blow itself. He said, 'I can't play all that without breathing!' But I gave him a little sherry to build himself up. He was a bit anaemic then, you know. And they said, 'You take it easy—he shouldn't be taking that stuff. You're rushing him too hard.' But I said, 'I got to build him up or he'll never blow.' ")

"At lessons, Bechet would sit at the piano and demonstrate," Wilber said. "He was particular about form: Give the listener the melody first, then play variations on it, then give it to him again. And tell a story in every tune you play. He also told me not to bother with the soprano, which I'd started fooling around with, but to stick to the clarinet. I was living in the Village and was short of bread, so after a couple of lessons I moved in with Bechet and slept on a couch in the parlor. He loved to compose at the piano. He even got hold of an early tape recorder and recorded his piano. His personality came through in his piano playing even more than it did on his horns. It was stark and strong, and he had a beautiful sense of harmony. But he had a beautiful sense of harmony on the soprano and the clarinet, too, and he liked to surprise people with it. He also had a great notion of passing on the traditions of jazz music. He felt that younger people weren't interested in the music's past. Sidney was a very intense man. If he took a dislike to something, he could be savage and dangerous. But generally he was charming and warm, and he had a good sense of humor. Like Louis Armstrong, whose success he had mixed feelings about, he spoke that special New Orleans argot, with its 'der's and 'erl's, and he often got names wrong. Max Kaminsky was Mac Kavinsky, Brad Gowans was Brad Garfield, and Earl Hines was Earl Hine. I lived with Bechet six or eight months, and during part of that time he had a group at Ryan's, and I would sit in and we'd play duets. And we did shots together on Rudi Blesh's radio show with Baby Dodds and Pops Foster and Georg Brunis. Because of the duets, Brunis nicknamed us Bash and Shay, after the way Sidney pronounced his name. My style was naturally close to Bechet's, and when I started to change it, all he said was 'that's all right, that's all right. He's finding his own way.' "

Wilber got up and looked out the window. A tan field, recently cut, sloped toward a black pond—Ice House Pond. On the far right, abutting the road, was a white-shingled 1825 house, and on the left, beyond the field, were pine-woods. The old New Englanders loved small rooms, because small rooms kept the heat, and at the same time they loved doors, which let them escape from room to room. The Wilbers' house is a crowd of tiny rooms which eases through door after door on the ground floor, past the coffin door, or front door, up the steep front stairs and through the second floor, and down the back stairs. It is a handsome house furnished with American country pieces and hooked rugs, which float like islands on the painted, speckled floors. Wilber's father bought the house in 1943, for "a ridiculous figure," and Wilber must have been happy there. He was certainly relaxed. Whenever one of the Wildcats visited, they would take a rowboat out to the middle of Ice House Pond and jam. One day, Mrs. Moore, who was august and in her nineties and lived on the far side of the pond, stood outside her house and listened, and then gesticulated at the boys, and Wilber's heart sank: she was going to give them what-for for all the racket. They rowed over, and Mrs. Moore cried, "You boys sound terrific, but you better come in now and have some milk and cookies."

Wilber sat down and talked again. "In 1948, Hugues Panassié organized a jazz festival in Nice and Sidney was invited, but he had taken a gig at Jazz Ltd. in Chicago and they wouldn't let him go. So he sent me. I was there a week and then took a six-week tour around Europe for the Hot Club of France. The most marvellous part of the trip was working with Baby Dodds. He was, to my way of thinking, possibly the greatest jazz drummer. He was a percussionist more than a drummer. He thought of drums in terms of colors, and how to mix them. He was fanatical about tuning his drums, and he'd be on the stand a half hour before showtime, tightening and tapping, tightening and tapping. His time was superb, and his whole playing was heavy and low. The tonality was down where it didn't get in the way, as so much modern drumming does. He principally used his bass drum and powerful, accented press rolls on his snare drum, and he didn't have a high-hat. But he had a ride cymbal, and he played it in a way that young drummers think they invented—just four beats to the bar: *ting-ting-ting-ting*, his head down low, and his right arm crooked like a dancer's over his head and the cymbal, and his whole body shimmying and shaking in time to the music. It was an unbelievable experience to have Baby behind you. The year before, when I went into the Savoy in Boston opposite a fine jump band led by Tab Smith, I had Baby, and Norman Lester on piano. Then Kaiser Marshall replaced Baby, and Dick Wellstood replaced Lester. We did an excellent business, and the owner said expand, so I hired Henry Goodwin on trumpet, Jimmy Archey on trombone, and Tommy Benford on drums. We played Jelly Roll and Willie the Lion and early Duke and King Oliver, and the band gathered momentum. The Savoy had an all-black clientele, but white college kids began lining up down the block on weekends. It was hard work at the Savoy—seven nights a week, plus a Sunday matinee and a couple of rehearsals. The guys in the band made about a hundred and a quarter a week, and I got two hundred. It seemed like an awful lot of money. We stayed at the Savoy for eight-week stretches and would be spelled by someone like Ed Hall, who'd bring in Ruby Braff and Jimmy Crawford. But I felt we were getting stale, and between sets I'd run out to a record store to listen to Charlie Parker or over to the Hi-Hat to listen to Lester Young. We got an offer from Ryan's, but I turned the band over to Archey, and he stayed at Ryan's on and off for a couple of years.

"I gigged around, spent a summer up here playing in a trio, and in the fall of 1950 took a band into George Wein's first Storyville, in the Copley Square Hotel in Boston. I had Joe Thomas on trumpet and Vic Dickenson on trombone and Big Sid Catlett on drums. Thomas and Vic left, and the de Paris brothers took their places. My playing was in a weird state of flux. You could hear Bird in it, and Buddy De Franco. I learned a lot from Big Sid. He'd take a solo on a medium-slow 'Stompin' at the Savoy'—the kind of loose-elbows tempo most drummers fall apart in if they try and solo—and eventually get up from his drums and go into the audience, playing on the floor and on chairs and tabletops, and everybody would go wild. It was Sid's last gig. When the place shut down for a couple of weeks, he went back to Chicago, where he'd been working at Jazz Ltd., and not long after that he collapsed backstage at the Civic Opera House. But we had a forty-first-birthday party for him at Storyville. Hoagy Carmichael sat in and sang, and Louis Armstrong and Sonny Greer stopped in. That summer, I came up here, and I listened a lot to Lee Konitz and Lennie Tristano. In fact, I studied with Lennie when I got back to New York. He had a concept of developing your intuition to the highest level, of getting your head and body together. He was intrigued with moving bar lines around, with using the higher intervals in chords, and with using two different rhythms at once. Tristano was a brilliant musician who was determined to do something different, but he had no interest in Louis Armstrong or in the past, and after three or four months I left him. The Korean war was on, and I got drafted and ended up on Governors Island, playing solo clarinet in a concert band and feeling that it was time to stop being known as Sidney Bechet's protégé. So I took lessons from the great Leon Russianoff. He said, 'Let's get an open sound,' and he started me from scratch. I studied with him five years. For a time, my jazz playing was destroyed, and it took a while to get back to playing without self-consciousness.

"Russianoff made me understand even more that the clarinet resists being played in a loose way, that it can be pushed only so far. The big temptation on the clarinet is to noodle, to play extraneous notes. Making the instrument sound like an extension of yourself is a hundred per cent more difficult for a clarinettist than for a saxophonist or a brass player. Two of the best clarinettists we've had were Lester Young and Pee Wee Russell, and they were successful partly because they disregarded all the rules. For Lester, the clarinet was simply a different facet of his expression. He probably used a very soft reed to get that soft, wispy sound. And he certainly didn't disregard the microphone. Lester played the clarinet like a first-year student. Pee Wee had a nervous condition, of course, and he was subtle and devious in his thoughts and his playing, but he was a studied musician. He told me once, 'I only listen to three clarinettists— Benny Goodman, you, and me.' My favorite clarinettists are Johnny Dodds and Benny Goodman. Dodds had a surprising technique for his time. He'd weave beautiful melodies through a simple seventh chord, and he had a sublime way with the blues. He was very nearly the greatest blues player we have had. Goodman was perfect in his idiom. The marvellous relaxation he had with a pop tune—with everything, in fact! He could translate whatever came into his head directly onto the clarinet. He breathed and talked on it, and it *was* an extension of him. But he should have given Reginald Kell lessons, instead of the other way around. He started sounding like Kell, which is no drag, but it wasn't as good as Benny Goodman. I've loved other clarinettists. Irving Fazola was terribly simple, but he never made a mistake. Jimmie Noone was remarkable, although he had a sentimental streak in his playing and he had a faulty harmonic ear. Bechet always fought the clarinet, but he could fly on the soprano saxophone. Artie Shaw had a great lyric intensity. They say he worked his solos out beforehand. Certainly they are more like compositions than improvisations. He had a brilliant way of using sequential figures against the rhythm. He was very clever. I don't know why the clarinet has fallen by the wayside. Maybe Goodman set such high standards that he frightened everybody else away. Maybe it's because bop phrasing didn't transfer to the clarinet—because that constant stream of eighth notes didn't fall easily under the fingers. Maybe electronics washed it out. It's strange how fashionable the soprano saxophone has become. I suppose it's because John Coltrane put his blessing on it near the end of his life. Zoot Sims plays it right, and so does Kenny Davern, but most tenor players who have taken it up get a small sound—a bad-oboe sound. To me—a clarinettist, who thinks of his instrument as little—the soprano is big and should have a big sound. It should also be played in tune, but that's just about impossible. Trick fingering is the only way to correct, or come close to correcting, its endless pitch problems."

Wilber talked about improvisation, which he considers as mysterious as speech. "How, after all, do people learn to talk?" he said. "If the musician thinks about improvisation for long, he won't succeed. The less he thinks, the more successful he's going to be. It's like swimming, which is an extraordinary combination of muscle and timing. If you think about each breath, each stroke, your arms and legs get out of sync, your breathing falters, and you sink. Swinging is swimming well, and it has a distinctive rhythmic feel. It's the contrast between a steady pulse and the syncopated figures against it. It's the excitement of simultaneously going with the beat and battling it. The rhythmic element is what releases the intuitive powers in great players. Intense swing sharpens their reflexes and carries them away. They might be thinking melodic lines and chords, but then the intuitive powers take over and it's like going on automatic pilot. The notes are ripping and they're totally free.

"During the past thirty or so years, improvisers have become too involved with harmonic possibilities—the passing chord, the altered chord, the note added to the high part of the chord. Often, melodic beauty has been vanquished. Harmony has dominated melody when it should have been a servant to it. Harmony should decorate the melodic cake. What finally happened, of course, was the harmonic prison of bebop. Bebop was nothing but running the chord changes. The ensembles were not developable; all you had was chords. That's why the arrival in New York of old Bunk Johnson in 1945, at the time when bop was bursting forth, was so refreshing. Bop was vertical and Johnson's New Orleans music was horizontal. There was no playing in thirds; the ensembles were all marvellous counterpoint. But the harmonic prison has been pretty much destroyed. Ornette Coleman revolted against it, and he opened the gates for free jazz, which ignores all the rules, musical and social.

"The resurrection of Bunk Johnson was a prime instance of the curious fact that all the museum work, the musical anthropology, that has been practiced in jazz has been done by middle-class whites. Why? Whites have gone back and exposed the roots of what began as a black music, while black musicians have almost exclusively practiced the cult of the hip. We have been the conservatives and they have been the revolutionaries. I look at the New York Jazz Repertory Company, of which I'm a director, as an educational thing. We hope when we play Ellington or Morton or Beiderbecke or the Savoy Sultans that the audience, black and white, will get excited enough to go out and buy the records and listen some more. But repertory concerts are of great benefit to the musicians who play them, too. It allows them to get a glimpse of the inside of musicians who have come before them. When I give a Tricky Sam Nanton solo that I've transcribed to a trombonist in the Repertory orchestra, I tell him to play it note for note first, so that he can get a feeling for its beams and nails, and *then* play it his own way."

Wilber began to look restless, and said that in fifteen minutes he had to practice. "I was born in New York on March 15, 1928. My mother and father lived on Sullivan Street, in a kind of development of duplex apart-meets built around a courtyard. My mother died of cancer when I was six months old, and my father didn't remarry until I was four or five. Until then, I was raised mostly by a Miss Breed, a wonderful Boston lady. We moved to Gramercy Park, and I went to Friends' Seminary, on Stuyvesant Square, and we settled in Scarsdale when I was seven. My father said that one snowy day he watched my older sister and me trying to slide down the base of Edwin Booth's statue across from The Players club, and decid-ed it was time to move to the country. My father was born in Mount Vernon, Ohio, the son of a minister. He was with Macmillan before the First World War, and when he retired, in 1958, he was a vice-president of Appleton-Century-Crofts in their textbook division. He loves tennis and fishing and sailing and camping, and he's been terrifically civic-minded, as has my stepmother, who is from New Jersey and whose father was in U.S. Steel. I've always made a living playing jazz, but between the mid-fifties, when I got out of the Army, and the late sixties, when the World's Greatest Jazz Band started, I had my share of scuffling. Right after the Army, the nucleus of the old Wildcats got together and we formed a cooperative band called The Six. Our intention was to bridge the schism between modern and traditional music. Our first job was at Childs Paramount on Broadway, but we were too modern for the audiences there. The same thing happened when we went into Ryan's. But when we got a gig at the Cafe Bohemia in the Village, where Cannonball Adderley and Bird played, we were too old-fashioned. Thank God, most of that parochialism has disappeared! The Six lasted a year or two, and then I went into Eddie Condon's. I was studying with Russianoff and was get-ting facility all over the horn, and I guess I tried to make every solo per-fect, because one night Condon, a couple of sheets to the wind, said between numbers, 'Hey, kid! Make a mistake!' But the Condon style of playing had lost its freshness, and in 1957 I joined the superb band Bobby Hackett had at the Henry Hudson Hotel. It had Dick Cary and Ernie Caceres and Buzzy Drootin and Tom Gwaltney, and everyone doubled on about six instruments. Hackett's band was ingenious, but the audiences at the Henry Hudson were only interested in dancing. When Capitol record-ed it, they made Hackett play Dixieland stuff, and the real, adventurous, funny flavor of the band was never caught. I went on to Benny Goodman after that. He had a big band, and in it were Herb Geller and Russ Freeman, from the Coast; the bassist Scott La Faro, who was killed in an auto accident; old Taft Jordan; and Pepper Adams, whom I'd met in Rochester. Benny had commissioned all these up-to-date arrangements by Bill Holman and Shorty Rogers, and we rehearsed them for a month. We opened in Burlington, Vermont, and the audience was dumbfounded. They just sat there behind their faces, New England fashion. Benny was furious. He told us to take those damn things out of the book, and we went back to 'Sing, Sing, Sing' and 'Don't Be That Way.' I played tenor with Benny, and he gave me solos. He really felt like playing then, and it was a treat to hear him night after night. Then I went into the new uptown Condon's with Max Kaminsky, did occasional jingles, worked the band on the Jackie Gleason show, and did a Lester Lanin gig now and then. I was just floating, and what suddenly gave me direction was coming upon a curved soprano saxophone in the window of an instrument store on West Forty-eighth Street. I'd pretty much given up on the soprano in 1953, but I blew just one note on this curved one, and it was beautiful! It sang. I used it more and more when I was with the World's Greatest, and it helped me through the dry times after Carl Fontana left and Lou McGarity died and the band began to play by rote."

Wilber looked at his watch, seized his clarinet case, which was at the ready by the door, and took off for the house. A couple of minutes later, rigorous, piping clarinet scales came across the lawn, and there was no pause.

Easier Than Working

Here is how the pianist Dick Wellstood made his living in the first half of 1978. He is referring to a daybook in which he records all his jobs: "On the third and fourth of January, I had a record date with Marty Grosz for the Aviva label, and on the fifth and sixth a Fats Waller date for Chiaroscuro. I played a private party on the ninth in Toms River, New Jersey. There was a remake of some of the Waller sides on the Twelfth, because one of the participants had been under the weather the first time around. On the thirteenth, I did a party in Fairfield, Connecticut, and the day after that I went to Europe for six weeks, and gave concerts in Holland, Germany, Switzerland, Scotland, and England. I returned March 1st, and on the ninth did a concert at the Downtown Athletic Club. Four days later, I played a dance at the Harbor Island Spa, in West Long Branch, New Jersey, with my old friend Paul Hoffman, who leads a society band and has kept me alive off and on the last ten years. In fact, I had a regular job with Hoffman all during this time, and I would take a night or two off when extra dates came along. On the seventeenth, I had a solo appearance at the Bay Head Yacht Club, in New Jersey, and on the eighteenth a concert in Boston for George Wein. On the nineteenth, I did a duo with Kenny Davern in Morristown. Back to the Bay Head Yacht Club on the twenty-fourth for a solo appearance, and on the thirty-first for a duo. From the fourth to the ninth of April, Kenny Davern and I played the King of France Tavern, in Annapolis, and on the fourteenth and then on the nineteenth I was at the Yacht Club again. On the sixteenth, I took a band I'd had at Michael's Pub into the east branch of the Monmouth

County Library, and on the twenty-second I sat in with a local Dixieland band at the Essex Fells Country Club. I did a two-day jazz party with Lou Stein at the Greenwich Country Club over the last weekend in April, and on May 5th I was back at the Yacht Club. I did a private recital in Toms River on the eighth. On the twelfth, thirteenth, nineteenth, and twenty-sixth, I was at the Yacht Club. On the twenty-eighth, Kenny Davern and I did another duo, at the Marriott Inn in Providence, and on June 2nd I was at the Yacht Club. On the third and fourth, I went with the World's Greatest Jazz Band to Andover, Massachusetts, and to Providence, and I sat in with a pickup group at a party in Summit on the ninth. I had a private party in Westport the eleventh, the Yacht Club on the sixteenth, and a wedding and the Yacht Club on the seventeenth. On the twenty-third, I did a private party in Chicago, and on the twenty-fifth a concert for the Newport Jazz Festival, in Stanhope, New Jersey. The Yacht Club closed June, and a party at Bill Buckley's home in Connecticut opened July. I might add that playing cha-chas with Paul Hoffman was just as much fun as anything I did in Europe. I have a fantastic weakness for workaday music like Hoffman's."

Here is how Wellstood made his living one night a year later. It was an evening in the middle of a long engagement at Eddie Condon's, on West Fifty-fourth Street. Wellstood, however, was not playing with the house band, or even as the intermission pianist. As an experiment, he had been put in the cocktail slot, from five-thirty to eight-thirty, and he felt disoriented. The newspapers had listed him as the intermission pianist, and he suspected that his audience was made up largely of neighborhood people, who talked sports at the bar and gave him dirty looks when he began to play. Wellstood arrived close to five-thirty, and the place—long and narrow and high-ceilinged, with the bar and the bandstand on one side and banquettes and tables on the other—was almost empty. Wellstood looked as if he had just come in from judging an afternoon of racing at the Bay Head Yacht Club. He had on pressed khakis, a white open-collared shirt, and a blue blazer. His hair was tousled, and he wore glasses that were halfway down his nose. He looked a lot better than he had a year and a half before at an engagement at the Carlyle. Then he had worn a tuxedo and a ruffled shirt, which seemed to get between him and the keyboard, and his hair had been forced into a pageboy. Later, he had reported, "Opening night at the Carlyle was one of the worst nights of my life. I couldn't play anything. My hands had turned to lead and so had my head. Worst of all, Alec Wilder had come in with a couple of friends, and I think it was the first time he'd ever heard me live. He left immediately after the first set, looking pained in the brow, and that made me feel terrible." At Condon's, Wellstood's attractive beamish smile was back. He went to the bar and poured himself a Coca-Cola, and sat down at a table. Laminated on the tabletop was an enlarged facsimile of the Okeh label of McKenzie and Condon's "Sugar," recorded in 1927, the year Wellstood was born. He went to work on his hands. He kneaded them, then made vigorous washing motions. He pulled each finger, bent it backward and forward, and pulled it again. He put the tips of his fingers together and pressed them until his hands were palm to palm. He made a fist of one hand and socked the palm of the other, as if he were breaking in a baseball mitt. Then he let both hands hang loosely at his sides and shook them vigorously.

"Last evening wasn't bad at all," he said as he worked on his hands. "I played well, and somewhere around eight a whole bunch of jazz fans came in, so I played for them until after nine. The only trouble was that the hammer of the G above middle C broke, but I doubt whether anybody noticed. Once, the English pianist Harold Bauer gave a concert in San Francisco, and an F-sharp got stuck just after he'd begun his last piece. He struggled with the note, trying to disguise that from the audience, trying to keep it from ruining the piece, trying to get *through*. When he came off stage, his manager said to him, 'Harold, I've listened to you up and down the world for twenty years, and that last piece was the most moving performance I have ever heard.' Which means that audiences are rarely on the same wavelength as performers. In fact, two very different things are going on at once. The musician is wondering how to get from the second eight bars into the bridge, and the audience is in pursuit of emotional energy. The musician is struggling, and the audience is making up dreamlike opinions about the music that may have nothing at all to do with what the musician is thinking or doing musically. If audiences knew what humdrum, daylight things most musicians think when they play, they'd probably never come."

He settled himself at the piano, a Baldwin grand that faces the door, and made mock pounding motions on the broken G. The bandstand at Condon's is roughly the size and shape of a longboat and contains a jumble of stools, chairs, tulip-shaped floor ashtrays, microphones, wires, and drums. The piano forms the cabin, and under it that evening was a large cardboard box of pretzels. Next to the pretzels were several tiers of shelves on which were salt and pepper, sugar, A.1., ketchup, cruets, and mugs, and beyond the piano's foreleg was a pail, and in it, for sweeping the deck, a broom. Wellstood went into a rollicking medium-tempo "There's a Small Hotel." He kept the lid of the piano shut. He had said that the piano, which he and the pianist John Bunch had been asked to choose, had a "glassy" sound. "Hotel" gave way to "Ain't Misbehavin'," which he has probably played eight thousand times, and into which he folded two more Wallers—"Squeeze Me" and "Blue Turning Gray Over You." Wellstood has been through and come out the other side of the music and styles of Scott Joplin, Joe Lamb, James P. Johnson, Willie the Lion Smith, Fats Waller, Zez Confrey, Earl Hines, Joe Sullivan, Count Basie, Cedar Walton, Ray Charles, Bill Evans, and Thelonious Monk. He has peered into their musical minds and savored the contents. He can play James P.'s "Carolina Shout" as Johnson played it, but you'd never mistake his version for Johnson's. Wellstood's touch is heavier, and he

plays with more force. His rhythms and dynamic sense are more pronounced. He has removed the gingerbread from Johnson's playing, the
airborne laciness, and replaced it with a sleek muscularity. In many ways,
his Waller is better than Waller himself: he doesn't loaf the way Waller
did, and he uses harmonic colorations Waller never thought of.
Wellstood's blues are big, leisurely houses, full of tremolos, stark bass
chords, and the sly humor of interpolation and retards. He has described
stride piano this way: "Technically, stride piano is late Eastern ragtime.
It's the way black pianists played in Harlem in the teens and twenties. It
has an oompah bass—that is, your left hand makes a seesawing motion
between a single bass note, struck at the bottom of the keyboard, and a
chord struck some two and a half octaves farther north. The ragtime players only stretched an octave or an octave and a half, but the wider span
gives you a fuller sound. The syncopated figures in the right hand
include thirds and sixths, chromatic runs, and tremolo octaves. The left
hand is the timekeeper—the keeper of momentum—and the right hand
must never get too strong or it will make the left hand wag, and all the
tension will go out of your playing. To me, James P. Johnson was the
greatest stride pianist, and he was king until Art Tatum arrived in New
York in the early thirties. James P. never forgave the pianist Joe Turner for
first bringing Tatum here."

Wellstood slipped into a slow ballad—a form he more or less ignored
until 1974, when he became a full-time solo pianist—and converted it into
chordal layers, each rising slightly above the last, each filling the melodic confines. He moved on to Kurt Weill's "Bilbao Song," and then to an
Ellington medley, into which he fed bits of "Lush Life," "Sophisticated
Lady," "Perdido," and "Caravan." His glasses make a nose-length slide
every number, and every eight bars or so he gasps slightly. When he tries
something he's not sure of, he purses his lips. If he blows it, he rattles his
head and balloons his cheeks. Michel Legrand's "What Are You Doing
the Rest of Your Life?" came next, and Wellstood went into a medium
"How About You." Before that was done, he had applied James P.
Johnson offbeat chords in the right hand, doubled the tempo for a nine-
ty-mile-an-hour Art Tatum stride passage, let loose a few
turn-around-and-jump Thelonious Monk runs, and demonstrated that it
is a song he cares about. He closed the set with quiet readings of "She's
Funny That Way," "I Concentrate on You," and "I Would Do Most
Anything for You."

Wellstood got another Coca-Cola and sat down facing the door.
Musicians spend most of their time in night clubs looking at the front
door, for through it all blessings flow—audiences, money, girls, liquor,
bookers, writers, and rich people looking for talent for their parties. Two
men who had just come in and were standing at the bar approached, and
one had a violin case. A Lord-this-cat-wants-to-sit-in look flickered across
Wellstood's face, and his shoulders tightened. The man with the case said

he'd come to fix the broken G, and he opened the case and took out his tools. Wellstood's shoulders relaxed, and he got up to show the tuner the damaged note.

Wellstood returned to his chair, and said, "I've been playing solo piano long enough to find out it can be very dangerous. Of course, it's wonderful in that you can do anything. You can play in any key, change keys when you want, halve the tempo, double it, triple it, play out of time, drop beats and pick them up later, accelerate or decelerate, finish a tune before the chorus ends. But you have to be damned sure that your time, which you play such hob with, doesn't go to hell and you find yourself speeding up or slowing down without premeditation. That's happened to some very good solo piano players. I'm one of those players who rely on the vessel of divine spirit—on what some call inspiration. When it comes by itself, you don't have to worry. You go into a trancelike state. But when it doesn't come you have to fall back on all kinds of patterns and figures. After all, when you're paid to play you *have* to play, and you can't go below a certain professional level. When I improvise, I think in terms of sounds, not of chords or melody. Some of my things may not have conventional harmonic continuity, but if they *sound* right and have rhythmic coherence, I'll do them. I learned to play the piano in public, and I've recently begun to try and relate my playing more to that public, even though it rarely grasps all that you're trying to do. At one time, I related my playing to the critics or to such eternal matters as the year that I first used an augmented ninth, or the year that I first played with Coleman Hawkins, or the like. For a long time, I had most of my playing mapped out. I liked the idea that once you got a solo worked up on a tune, you could use it over and over. After all, there are very few geniuses in jazz who create new things night after night. Most of us are lucky to have a couple of good, sparking nights a month. I think of myself as a contemporary musician who uses tools that are out of fashion. But lately I've been trying to get away from stride into more modern things, and when I do, I sound like Monk, which isn't so strange when you consider that Monk came directly out of the stride tradition. I like doing ballads and wandering around through a lot of new chords. I'm getting better as I get older, I think. My brain used to shortcircuit a lot, but that's stopped. Actually, I've become quite excellent, and I often wonder why I don't work constantly."

The tuner told Wellstood that he had glued the hammer and that it should be perfect by the time the house band started that night. Wellstood tilted back slightly in his chair and clasped his hands behind his head. He removed one hand, pushed his glasses up his nose, and clasped his hands again. He looked as if he were sitting in his East Side apartment, which is small and is lined with Smollett, Aldous Huxley, Robert Musil, Samuel Johnson, Nabokov, Meredith, Hazlitt, Gibbon, Chesterton, F. R. Leavis, and Thomas Love Peacock.

"Whenever I ask myself why I stay in this business, the answer is always the same: it's easier than working. I've tried writing. I can make a sentence, but my paragraphing is terrible. Anyway, if I had it for writing, I'd have written something important. I did try the law in the fifties. I read the Holmes-Laski correspondence, which I loved. It made me think, Why not go to law school? I did three years of prelaw at N.Y.U. in two years, and three years of law school at the New York Law School in two more years, and I passed my New York State bar exams. I was finishing work at three-thirty in the morning and getting up at eight for four years. I applied to about two hundred firms, and the closest I got to success was with a partner in a fancy place who knew something about jazz. That cheered me so much I told him a couple of ribald musician stories and that was that. When I was at N.Y.U., I studied a lot of Latin, which I really like. Now I'm about to start German so I can read Nietzsche, who makes me laugh.

"I joined Roy Eldridge about the time that I began prelaw. I was with Conrad Janis for seven years after Roy, and everybody passed through his band—Herman Autrey and Johnny Windhurst, Eddie Barefield, Art Trappier, Lawrence Brown, Dicky Wells. I worked on and off at the Metropole, at Seventh Avenue and Forty-eighth, from 1957 to 1965. All the musicians groused about it at the time, but, as John Bunch said the other day, 'that was it, that is where it was at.' I loved the energy and vulgarity of the place. It had a big marquee, and there were always winos dancing under it. The room was long and narrow, with mirrors going down both walls. A bar ran along almost the whole north wall, and the musicians were obliged to stand in a row on a platform above it. You couldn't hear yourself or anyone else, and you played together by watching each other in the mirrors. There was also a room upstairs for the posh acts. Sometimes I'd be there all afternoon with a trio and all night with someone like Red Allen. Between sets, everybody went to the Copper Rail, across Seventh Avenue. It was just a plain bar, but hundreds of musicians passed through every week. Honi Coles and the other tapdancers hung out and danced every night. Red Allen would come over and bait Roy Eldridge, who always seemed to be there, and Roy would get mad and take out his horn and start demonstrating some musical point. The place became a Mecca for European jazz fans, who'd stand around and gawk at Roy and Ben Webster and Coleman Hawkins and Charlie Shavers. At the time, I lived at Ninetieth and Lexington, and I'd pedal to work on my bike every afternoon. I'd carry the bike up to the third floor to a little room where I changed. After the afternoon session, I'd go back up and put on a tux, and when I'd finished for the night, I'd put on my street clothes and lug the bike down to the street, saying 'pardon, pardon, pardon' to all the swells waiting on the stairs to get in to see Chico Hamilton. I also spent time at Nick's and Bourbon Street, and I was with Gene Krupa's quartet for three years. Charlie Ventura was the horn player, and it was a no-ego assignment. He was there to fill in between drum solos. Sometimes Krupa would let him go on for chorus after chorus and sometimes he'd give him just one. I liked Gene. He was a man who liked baseball and church, and he got a good sound out of his drums. But with that heavy bass drum and that on-the-beat playing, his head was always back in the Chicago of 1928. I moved to Brielle, New Jersey, in 1966, and by 1970 things were rough. Rock had taken hold, and sometimes I didn't get a call for three or four months at a time. It was then that I began working with Paul Hoffman. I had to play floor shows as well as cha-chas, and I loved it. It was the first time I ever felt useful in the music business."

Wellstood smiled, looked at his watch, and returned to the piano. He went immediately into Jelly Roll Morton's mournful "Sweet Substitute." James P. Johnson's "Mule Walk" was followed by his "Caprice Rag," and Wellstood settled into a long "Everything I Have Is Yours." His public prose efforts have been limited largely to liner notes—generally written for his own albums, but not always. Here are two paragraphs from a set done for an Earl Hines album, in which Wellstood first knocks the Master down and then graciously picks him up and sends him on his way:

> Democratic Transcendent, his twitchy, spitting style uses every cheesy trick in the piano-bar catalog to create moving cathedrals, masterpieces of change, great trains of tension and relaxation, multidimensional solos that often seem to be *about* themselves or about other solos—"See, *here* I might have played some boogie-woogie, or put this accent *there*, or this run here, that chord there . . . or maybe a little stride for you beautiful people in the audience. . . ." Earl Hines, Your Musical Host, serving up the hot sauce.
>
> Hines is not a "stride" pianist. His rhythm is too straight four-four, too free. He does not possess the magisterial dignity of James P. Johnson, the aristocratic detachment of Art Tatum, the patience of Donald Lambert, the phlegmatic unflappability necessary to maintain the momentum of stride. Hines needs silence in the bass, room to let the flowers grow, space to unroll his showers of broken runs containing (miraculously) the melody within, his grace-noted octaves . . . and his wandering, Irish endings.

His prose often has a fine straight-from-the-shoulder turn. This is how he ends a long, complex description of stride piano playing, done as part of the liner notes to a Donald Lambert album:

> If all this sounds rather difficult and complicated, you may be sure that it is. In a world full of pianists who can rattle off fast oom-pahs or Chick Corea solo transcriptions or the Elliott Carter Sonata, there are perhaps only a dozen who can play stride convincingly at any length and with the proper energy.

"Everything I Have Is Yours" gave way to a cathedral of his own—a pondering, exultant "St. James Infirmary Blues," full of low-register turnings, broken tremolos, descending thirds, and ringing upper-register chords. Its flags moved in slow motion, and its final bass notes boomed. A snappy "If Dreams Come True," with a double-timed Art Tatum stride passage, went by, and then came a dreaming "Lullaby of Birdland," in which Wellstood kept turning the melody inward. He closed the set with Wayne Shorter's "Lester Left Town."

Wellstood went over to Seventh Avenue and had a hamburger, and when he got back he said, "Well, one more quick set should do it, considering how long I played last night. But first I'll rest a little. You need more rest at fifty than at forty, I've discovered. When people hear that I was born in Greenwich, they automatically think Hotchkiss, Yale, white shoes, and all the rest, but I was born in clam-digging Greenwich, not backcountry Greenwich. I was an only child. My father was in real estate, but he died when I was three. My mother made sixty dollars a month as a church organist, and we ate meat once a week. She also rented the other half of our house and gave two-dollar piano lessons. When things got too tight, she boarded me out in Maine, where she had friends. She was a short, determined lady, who was born in 1887. She graduated from Juilliard in 1911, before it was Juilliard, and she learned a lot of heavy Brahms there. I was born late in her life, so I grew up with people who were often a lot older, and that must be why I've spent so much time playing older music with older musicians. In many ways, I had a Victorian upbringing. My mother and I didn't get on too well, and I've figured out since her death that I probably *was* right about a lot of things we fought about. Anyway, I've completed the Victorian Age and am moving into the Edwardian. I went to public schools in Greenwich and in Maine, and for five years I went on scholarship to the Wooster School, in Danbury. I graduated in 1945. I wasn't an athletic star, and I found that people would pay attention to me if I played boogie-woogie after lunch at school, and it's all grown from that. By 1944, I was playing in a teen-age canteen in the cellar of the Greenwich Y. Charlie Traeger, who had taken up bass, heard me and invited me to a jam session at his house in Cos Cob. By the next year, I was jamming once a week in somebody's living room with Eddie Phyfe and Eddie Hubble and Johnny Glasel and Bob Wilber. I heard James P. Johnson and Willie the Lion Smith at the Pied Piper, on Barrow Street, in the summer of 1944, and they made a tremendous impression. I also heard a stride pianist named Johnny Williams, who played at the old Rye Hotel with a drummer who used temple blocks and had a picture painted on the front of his bass drum. Around then, we started going to the Hollywood Café, at a Hundred and Thirty-third and Seventh Avenue. It was owned by Tom Tillingham, but everyone called it Tom Tillum's. It was a regular nothing bar where the locals drank beer and yelled, but it had a back room with a red piano in it, and on Monday nights all the piano players gathered there—Art Tatum and Marlowe Morris and Willie Gant and the Beetle and Donald Lambert and Gimpy Irvis. Gimpy would take off his shoe and play the bass note with his left foot. In those days, musicians weren't as polite as they are now—'Hey, Dick, you sounded great!' 'Hey, Dick, you were really cooking!'—and they told each other how awful they thought they were. This was particularly true when they had cutting contests. One Monday, Donald Lambert sat down and played this fantastic stride piano. His left hand was a streak, his right hand a flea. Tatum was there with Marlowe Morris, who was one of the most interesting of the new pianists. Tatum didn't move after Lambert finished, and when the room quieted down, he leaned over to Morris and said, 'Take him, Marlowe,' and he did. I even sat in one night—right after Tatum. It was part gall and part stupidity. I was under the sway of moldy-fig writers who said that Tatum wasn't all that much, that James P. was still king. Anyway, we stopped going to Tillum's when singers started coming in eighteen in a row and doing 'Prisoner of Love' like Billy Eckstine. I saw a lot of James P. and Willie the Lion. James P. never said anything, and I was so in awe I never spoke to him. But I got to know Willie a little. Willie always said he was at least part Jewish—I heard him sing 'Alexander's Ragtime Band' in Yiddish, or what he claimed was Yiddish. He taught me his 'Zig-Zag,' which I made the mistake of learning by rote and consequently forgot completely.

"In 1946, Wilber and I moved into an apartment at Broadway and a Hundred and Eleventh. We'd do the Sunday-afternoon jam sessions at Jimmy Ryan's, and every now and then we'd go a couple of days without eating. I worked with Wilber and the old drummer Kaiser Marshall at the Savoy in Boston, and in 1948 Sidney Bechet sent for me to come and play at Jazz Limited in Chicago. I took it as the same sort of imperial summons as the one issued in 1922 by Joe Oliver from Chicago to Louis Armstrong in New Orleans. I went back to Boston with Wilber, and when Jimmy Archey took over the band, I stayed on. They had a businesslike attitude toward their work. They went to work on time, and they wore blue suits and white shirts and red ties, and they all knew how to read and were proud of it. They were cheerful and accomplished, and it was a job like any job, only it was night work instead of day work. Also, when they got a solo down on a certain tune, they played that solo, or something close to it, every time they did the tune. As a matter of fact, most jazz musicians repeat themselves all their lives, and have a good time doing it. It made me realize that maybe 'jazz' was largely the invention of a bunch of European-oriented intellectuals in the thirties—guys who thought they had found in 'jazz' a European-type art music."

During his final set, Wellstood played James P. Johnson, Gershwin, Zez Confrey, Cole Porter, Fats Waller, a rag, Maceo Pinkard, Eubie Blake, the Beatles, and Thelonious Monk. When he finished, an attractive blondhaired woman about Wellstood's age got up from a table near the door, and he said hello. He took her arm, and they went out, turning right instead of left, which would have taken them into the sunset.

Aesthetic Vitamins

First-rate jazz trumpeters tend to be diminutive. Consider Louis Armstrong, Bix Beiderbecke, Roy Eldridge, Charlie Shavers, Bobby Hackett, Billy Butterfield, Ray Nance, Ruby Braff, and Miles Davis. The larger the lyrical soul, it would seem, the smaller its house. This is certainly true of Braff, an eloquent five-foot-four-inch featherweight. In addition to being wispy and poetical, Braff is also an anachronism. He came to the fore in the mid-fifties, as part of a tradition (Armstrong, Eldridge, Buck Clayton) that had been declared dead, or at least obsolescent. Young trumpet players no longer idolized Armstrong; instead they followed the mercurial, multi-noted ways of Dizzy Gillespie and Fats Navarro. When Braff appeared, the florid, brilliant Clifford Brown, created largely by Navarro and killed at twenty-five in an automobile accident, was the new, young, champion trumpet player. Braff, by contrast, was a throwback, a return to an unfashionable way of playing that was devoted to melody, lyricism, and grace. But none of this matters anymore. Gillespie's academy grew old and gave way to the avant-garde of the sixties, while Braff, perfecting his anachronistic form and battling the whims of fashion and economics, has become a tradition unto himself.

Braff is, in the best way, a rococo performer who uses a lot of notes, sagacious flourishes, and a scarlet tone. He favors the middle and lower registers; daring and frequent intervals; fast, short runs; mix-'em-up rhythmic tricks (legato/on-the-beat/double time/legato); and melody. He achieves an expansive cave of sound in the lower registers. "I love the bass and the cello," he explains. "I love the low register of the clarinet. I love Harry Carney. I have a great need for those sounds. I change my embouchure when I move down there, and I move into another room, another world." Braff is, as well, an extraordinarily precise horn player, whose exactness once caused Alec Wilder to observe that "every note he plays is the *center* of that note." Braff loves melody, and he plays it in a way that lies between embellishment and full-scale improvisation. He does not, in the manner of many improvisers, impose himself on the tunes he plays; rather he heats them up so that their colors and curves and textures gleam and shine. He points up their treasures, but he leaves them intact. He will start a slow ballad by playing the notes as they are written, but he will celebrate them by moving along just behind the beat. Then he will descend, suddenly and softly, into his lowest register, roam there almost inaudibly, and rise swiftly to the start of the second eight bars of the tune, which he will play on the beat but which he will alter by skipping certain notes and by adding others, in the form of miniature calligraphic flourishes. He will be more adventurous on the bridge, and, raising his volume (as the years have gone by, he has taken to playing softer and softer, without setting aside his mastery of dynamics), bob up and down through several big intervals, duck downstairs again, and then start the final eight bars a beat or two late. He will restate the melody, again gently subtracting and adding notes, and go out with a series of low tones, the last one terminated by a barely wavering vibrato.

The house that shelters these graceful sounds is oddly built. Braff is cylindrical, and he has substantial feet, small hands, and long arms. His head, with receding brownish hair, is round and affirmative. He has a trumpet player's mouth, wide and rather flat, and he has heavy-lidded hazel eyes. These eyes, continually at half-mast, move like lighthouse beacons, and they dominate his face. His voice, anchoring all, is heavy and sonorous. When he plays, he stands motionless, his legs slightly apart, his horn pointed just above the horizon. The only parts of him which move are his lips and his fingers. He keeps his eyes mostly closed, occasionally opening them halfway and rolling them back when he takes a breath and is ready to start a salutary phrase. He radiates the stone-stillness of absolute concentration.

Braff is obsessed by two things: talking and playing. So he recently spent a perfect day, talking out the afternoon in a midtown luncheonette and playing out the evening in a recording studio, where he rehearsed rigorously with the group he leads with the guitarist George Barnes.

Braff at the coffee shop: "Louis Armstrong's playing was a fat, warm, glowing thing," Braff said. "It gave me butterflies. When I got to know him, I knew I was dealing with a musical genius. He was deadly serious about music, and he had a fantastic degree of concentration and energy. Think of playing improvised music for fifty-five years! But there was no end to the amount of steam that he could turn up, even at the end. He told me once that when you play there are always two bands— the one you hire, and yourself. When the hired one is good, you turn them up mentally and dig them. But when they're not, you turn them off and *you* become the band. "If you spend your life depending on other musicians,' he'd say, 'it's too bad for you.' Louis laughed a lot at life, like when he had that all-star group in the forties, with Sid Catlett and Jack Teagarden and Earl Hines and Barney Bigard, and he told me, 'Man, that band! Pretty soon I'm going to surprise them and let all those leaders go.' He was a very joyous host. He took real pride in making you comfortable, even in his dressing room, with fifty people standing around. He had total recall, and he loved telling stories. He'd act out every part, and I'd always think, What a pity he'll never have the chance to do straight acting roles. There was no phase of the entertainment business he didn't understand, and I *know* he could have been a great hard-core actor. He also remembered every smell and taste and feeling he'd had. He once described how as a kid he'd seen this circus trumpeter with his uniform and shining buttons and shining trumpet, and how good it made him feel, and suddenly *you* felt the way *he* did when he saw that circus cat. He also carried every bit of music he'd ever heard in his head. He was intelligent and he was tough, in that he did what he felt he had to do in this world. Louis was no cream puff. And that sense of time he had! He even laughed in time and told his stories in time. When one of his sidemen was doing his feature onstage at a concert, he'd step into the wings and tell me a story, and the last word always came the split second before he was supposed to be back onstage to play. He could play four quarter notes a certain way, and you could stand beside him and play the same notes in the same way, but your time would not be as good as his.

"Louis knew that emotion without skill is no good, and I think I've finally reached the point where the two are working together. I never used to practice at all, but several years ago I became aware that there was something wrong with my embouchure. It was very rubbery, and I had to fake certain things, like getting quickly from upstairs to downstairs on my horn. I started going to Joe Shepley's house. He's a studio trumpeter, and studio musicians don't fail when they play. I watched him practice for hours, and got inspired and started taking lessons from another trumpeter, Bernie Privin. He got me going enough so that I can practice now from the exercise books. It's hard, heavy labor—those exercises. But I play better now than I ever have. I also studied a couple of years with Sanford Gold, the piano teacher. He showed me how to take chords apart, and he showed me I could write my own things. And Louis taught me another way of practicing. 'Make up a two-bar phrase or a four-bar phrase,' he'd say, 'and keep working at it until that two-bar phrase or four-bar phrase is a complete and perfect thing, a small jewel.' It sounds easy, but it's unbelievably difficult. All this new knowledge gives me the freedom to excel, to use to the fullest what I have.

"A performer is a person who needs immediate communication and an immediate reward. Of course, you're naked when you perform. So you must always know how good or how bad you are. The only way to do that is to carry a yardstick in your head—a yardstick made up of a great Armstrong solo or of a good solo of your own—and measure yourself constantly against it. A jazz musician doesn't have time to wait around for inspiration. You create it yourself, and the way you do it is to recall something that made you happy and inspired before, like Louis's remembering that shining circus trumpeter. That way you summon up feelings of warmth and joy. And you have to keep a backlog of music in your head; you have to constantly replenish your musical supply by listening to records or the radio. This is all part of the flow of excellence, which has to be checked every day. You have to put your aesthetic vitamins in the pot every morning and stir and pour.

"Improvisation is adoration of the melody. It's imagination coupled with a strong sense of composition. The best improvisations I've heard came out of melodic thinking. When I play 'I Got Rhythm,' I play it because I love the melody, and I keep that melody singing along somewhere in my head. Running its chords doesn't interest me. What does is trying to superimpose a new melody on the original, to build in layers, like Louis did. When I play one of his records, I'm mesmerized at first with what he put on top, with the *surface*. When I play it again, I hear the second layer, and then the third. Every time I play it, I hear something I didn't know was there before. But a great solo is also this: it surprises you each time you hear it, even though you know every note by heart.

"I feel very formal about music, and that includes the way you dress onstage and the way you talk into a microphone. I used to be a wise-ass on microphone, cracking bad jokes and such, but I know now I was trying to make it with the musicians because I was insecure. There's a star system, and it shouldn't be destroyed, like the young musicians are doing now. Fred Astaire is a star. But if he'd worked in sleazy places in disreputable clothes, his talent would have suffered, and he wouldn't have star status. Look at Ellington. I get goose bumps every time that man walks out on a stage. And Goodman—the epitome of professionalism and care and tone. It's based on the understanding that you're an entertainer, and you can't be an entertainer until you play well enough to communicate with your audience. And it has to do with the American dream: if you're good enough, you'll make it because somebody's going to pick up on you. But if you destroy the star system, what is there to shoot for? It was never the artist's job to play ugly, to parade his ugly dreams in public."

When Braff drives downtown in his Toyota sports car from Riverdale, where he lives, he parks in a municipal garage at Eighth Avenue and Fifty-third Street, which he uses as his "midtown office." At eight-thirty in the evening, he left the coffee shop, got his car, and picked up George Barnes, who lives around the corner. They arrived at nine at the loft building where they were to rehearse. Hank O'Neal, who has a desk job with the CIA during the day and makes records for his own label, Chiaroscuro, at night, rents a couple of floors in the building, and they contain an apartment and three huge workrooms, one of them a recording studio: He is a tall, thin, gentle Southerner, and he greeted Braff and Barnes warmly. The guitarist Wayne Wright and the bassist John Giuffrida round out the quartet and they were already there. The studio had the usual jungle of cables and microphones, but there were also a sofa and comfortable chairs. A couple of thronelike leather chairs were side by side in the center of the room, and Braff and Barnes headed for them. Braff had a new cornet, and he shook it and flexed its valves. "Every new horn needs a mouthpiece made for it, and not one from another horn," he said. He chuckled and lifted his eyebrows. "And what do you know—I ain't got one. So it's going to be a bitch getting used to this tonight." Wright and Giuffrida, stationed to the rear of Braff and Barnes, were look-alikes in mod spectacles, monkish hairdos, and work clothes. They smiled whenever Braff or Barnes said anything. (Neither Braff nor Barnes is noted for equanimity.) Barnes got up and walked

around. He is the same height as Braff, but he is ovoid. He has a round
head, a small, crinkly face, and short arms. He wears his pants high, and
they carry him like a vessel. He lit a giant cigar and sat down again,
picked up his guitar, and rested his right foot on a brick he carries to
every job. He and Braff glanced at one another. Braff leaned back in his
chair and closed his eyes, and suddenly they were into a fast blues. Braff
soloed first, then Barnes. He has spent much of his career in studios, and
he has a curious singsong way of playing. His notes vibrate like Django
Reinhardt's, and he has an extraordinary sense of dynamics. Some of his
notes whisper, and some ring like a clarinet's upper register. The two men
exchanged four-bar breaks and winged through the closing ensemble.
One second of silence, then Braff cackled and said, "You see what happens when you lay off three whole weeks. Man! Let's try something else."
It is Braff's own "With Time to Love." He played softly, and there were
several deep-register phrases. Barnes was even softer, and the room filled
with gentle, stirring sounds. The number ended with a sighing Barnes
note, and he and Braff looked at each other. "Hey!" Braff said. "That's
togetherness!"

Earlier at the coffee shop, which was almost empty: Braff took a sip of coffee, and lit a cigarette. "I was born in 1927 in Roxbury, a suburb of Boston.
There were four children—an older brother, who was killed in World War
Two; my oldest sister, who died a few years ago; and my next oldest sister, who lives in Randolph, Mass. My parents were both thrown on boats
and sent over here from Russia when they were young. It was the time of
the pogroms, and Jews were being slaughtered. But imagine the guts of
coming to this country and not knowing the language and going to work
in a factory! My mother was somewhere in her teens, and she had a sister in Boston, where my parents met. My father was the same age when
he came over, I think, but he was already a carpenter and a cabinetmak-
er. He had a very inventive head. He once made a window where you
pressed a button and it opened into the room so that you could wash it
without hanging outside and breaking your neck. And when the office-
furniture outfit he was working for bought a new truck, before he'd drive
it he parked it in an alley and took it entirely apart, and then put it back
together so that he'd know exactly how it worked. My parents live in
Brighton now, and I jump up to Boston every six months or so to see
them. All their records in Russia are gone, but they estimate they're about
ninety, or close to it. They still have things amazingly together, far more
than most of the musicians I run into at Jim and Andy's bar. About fifteen
years ago, my mother decided to learn English, so she could write to me.
My father long ago picked up on English because he was out in the
world, but my mother has always been at home. So she started studying
the newspapers, and now she writes and I can understand her. Words
come out funny. She'll say 'Good lucky' at the end of a letter, and when
she really gets up against it she clips out the word she wants from the

newspaper and pastes it on the page. It's a Yiddish household, and I still speak it fluently.

"I knew from the time I walked I wanted to play music. But there were many, many fights about it at home. My father's father had been a clarinettist, and most musicians, outside of the symphony, were regarded as *klezmer*, a Yiddish word for a sleazy person. I wanted a tenor saxophone, and I screamed at them for years. Saxophones looked comfortable and shiny, and they had these pearly buttons. There was a strap you put on, and there was the business of choosing the right reed and wetting it and putting it into the mouthpiece. It was a sharp ritual. When I was seven, my sisters went to the Conn instrument company and looked at saxophones, but all they probably saw were baritones and such, which would have been ridiculous with my size. So they bought a trumpet. It looked silly, this puny thing with three valves and a little mouthpiece, and I felt terrible about it. But I took lessons from an old man who had been a circus trumpeter, and then he died. So I played with the radio endlessly, and that way I learned all the tunes. I never practiced from the exercise books when my family was around, because it irritated them, particularly my father when he came home from work. To this day, I use a mute in my apartment, and I can't stand anyone hearing me practice. But maybe this secretiveness helped me get so many quiet tones on the instrument—that and the fact I would *still* like to sound like a saxophone. The trumpet probably saved me. I felt literally imprisoned in school. I never listened to the teachers, and anyway three-quarters of them were not crazy about kids at all. So I continually got poor marks, and of course I'm sorry now. I can write music faster than I can read the papers. Recently, I've been picking up on Alec Wilder's book about American songs, but I have to stop every minute or two because of the big words he uses. When I finish a chapter, I make out an alphabetical list of the tough words and look them up and write down their meanings. Then I take the list and go back and read the chapter again.

"I didn't get into listening to jazz until I was fourteen or fifteen. I knew the Dorseys and Artie Shaw and Ziggy Elman and Glenn Miller, but I didn't know Louis Armstrong or Bix Beiderbecke. I started listening to the poolhall hustlers down the street. They'd go to the Ray-Mor Ballroom all the time, and they were far better critics than the real ones. They'd say: 'Oh, man, I went to see Goodman last night, and you know he had Harry James playing lead on "King Porter Stomp," and that's not right. And that tempo he chose for "Stompin' at the Savoy" was way off.' They were participating, they were deep into it, they knew everything. I began going to people's houses who had collections of Basie and Billie Holiday and Ellington and Armstrong. One was Mayo Duca. He was a marvelous trumpet player and a fanatical Armstrong collector. I think he had every record Louis ever made. In fact, Louis would stay with him when he was working in Boston, and sit at a typewriter and write his letters and listen to his records. When you went to Mayo's house, he had a coffeepot in every room, and he'd run from room to room, drinking coffee and explaining every note on every record before he put it on, so it took all night to hear about three records.

"Around this time, I took some more lessons from a cat named Bob Gordon who came to the house every Saturday afternoon. He was a club-date trumpeter. The things he gave me I learned by ear when he thought I was reading them. I also started playing professionally at places like the Silver Dollar Bar—sometimes in the afternoon, sometimes in the evening, when I had the cab fare to get home. My parents weren't too happy about it; in fact, it wasn't until I was twenty-two that they finally gave in on my becoming a musician. In Boston, there were no steady gigs, unless you played badly. So I'd work here and there a couple of weeks at a time, and the first big-time date I had was at the Savoy, with Edmond Hall. Vic Dickenson was in the band, and Ken Kersey and that beautiful, smiling cat Jimmy Crawford. This was the late forties. I'd already been down to New York and back a couple of times, but I wasn't ready yet, and those were lean times. On one New York trip, I stayed at the Saint James Hotel, in midtown, and tried to get a day job, things were so bad. An agency sent me to a place where they made transformers. They put me in an apron, and I was supposed to wind wire around sharp, nickelplated things, and right away I cut my fingers to ribbons. By ten-twenty, I'd had it. The next day, the agency sent me to a sweatshop where they drilled holes in pieces of wood to put Christmas trees in, and I lasted until ten-twenty-five. 'You just weren't cut out for work,' the agency said. The only gig I had during this time was a one-nighter in Allentown, Pennsylvania, with Somebody and His Smiling Irishmen. We stood all the way on the bus, and when we got there the leader told us, '*Every*body in this orches-tra smiles when *I* smile, and frowns when *I* frown, and that goes whether you have a horn in your mouth or not.' Man, I thought, what have you gotten yourself into? The gig was in a ballroom, and during the first inter-mission I conned my pay of fifteen bucks from the guy on some pretext and ran outside and asked a cabbie what he'd charge to take me to New York. Fifteen dollars. I was back at the Saint James in two hours.

"After the Savoy date in Boston, I worked with Sid Catlett at George Wein's first Storyville there, and it was Sid who brought me to New York for good. He was something—that great big man with those little balls of drums arranged so tightly around him. He'd say, 'I can swing seventeen men with one wire brush and a phone book,' and he was right. He always had a room with a family, and he'd ask me to come to these rent parties where he lived. Two or three bucks and all the whiskey and sandwiches you could handle. I finally found out that the parties were for *him*. He loved to gamble, and he always needed bread. Before we came to New York, he took me by his place one night, and he showed me how to pack. He had two suitcases and all these camel's hair coats and twenty pairs of shoes and all, and he rolled everything into tight, perfect sausages. When we got to New York, he opened the suitcases and took everything out, and not a wrinkle! Fantastic! I've tried many times to pack that way, but my clothes come out like an unmade bed. Sid took me around town, introducing me to people, and when he played down at Bob Malz's Central Plaza, he made Malz hire me. Then, in 1953, I got a break. I was invited to play at an arts festival at Brandeis University, and John Hammond heard me the first time. After I'd played 'Sleepy Time Down South,' he grabbed the mike and said, 'That's *marvellous!*' John and his way of talking all the time with words like 'marvellous' and 'wonderful' and 'great.' I've had telephone conversations with him that go like this:

'Hello, Ruby. This is John. How are you?'

'Well, I'm in bed with pneumonia and I feel awful.'

'Wonderful, Ruby. Now what I called about . . .'

"Just after Brandeis, John started making his Vanguard recordings with Buck Clayton and Edmond Hall and Mel Powell, and he used me. Those records got a lot of notice, and for the first time I was on the map. I also recorded with Ellis Larkins, just the two of us, and John took it to Richard Rodgers, who was putting together *Pipe Dreams* for Broadway, and I was hired. It wasn't a speaking part. I was supposed to be an idiot wetback, but I did play a couple of times during the show. *Pipe Dream*s was based on John Steinbeck's *Sweet Thursday*, and he was at most of the rehearsals. He even got to be my coffee runner. He also told me all these wild stories. Or lies, which I guess is a writer's right. It's hard to believe that I talked with Richard Rodgers every day and watched him work. If they needed sixteen bars, he'd sit at the piano and write out those sixteen bars just like that, note for note. Then Oscar Hammerstein would fit the words to the music right away. How pleasurable it must have been for those two to work together! After *Pipe Dreams*, which lasted seven months, I worked and recorded with Benny Goodman. People say Benny is a strange cat, and I guess he is, but I got along with him. We were rehearsing at Nola Studios, and they had unhinged a big door to move an organ or something, and the door fell over on me and cut my lip so badly the doctor Benny sent me to said I'd never play again. I lost all feeling in my lips for six months, but Benny *made* me play with him every weekend at Basin Street in that little band he had with Urbie Green and Paul Quinichette. It was terrible, but it probably rescued my career."

At the recording studio, the quartet moved into a medium-tempo version of "Looking at You," notable for the four-bar exchanges at the end, in which Barnes mimicked Braff's passages so well he made Braff laugh. A fast "Liza" followed, and then a lullaby reading of the Beatles' "Here, There, and Everywhere." "This horn is much lighter than my old one," Braff said. "My old one, I might as well have been playing a baritone, it was so heavy. You have to be young and stupid to play one like that." The group settled down for a yearning version of Louis Armstrong's "No One Else but You." It recalled an equally eloquent rendition that Braff and Pee Wee Russell had played one night at the Newport Jazz Festival. In the next number, there were several starts and stops. Wright was having trouble with a tricky two-bar fill phrase. He tried it three times, to no avail, and Braff chuckled and said, "Don't worry, Wayne. There are at least a dozen out-of-work guitarists up at Jim and Andy's this very minute." Wright maneuvered the phrase and they finished the number. Braff sat down at the piano and played a pretty tune. "Duke heard me play this once," he said. "Hey, Ruby, You're going to lay that fine little tune on me, aren't you?' Isn't that something? Duke Ellington wanting a song I wrote!"

The coffee shop was filling up with the early-dinner, Salisbury-steak crowd. Braff ordered his third cup of coffee. "The group was one of those great accidents," he said. "A couple of years back, when Bucky Pizzarrelli and George Barnes had their duo at the Upstairs at the Downstairs, I sat in with them. George knocked me out. He had a way of phrasing with me almost as if we had the same timbre, as if we were the same instrument. I kept thinking about this phenomenon, and one morning not long ago I was driving home and I stopped at Jim and Andy's on the chance George would be there. It was three-thirty, but I knew he was an insomniac. By God, he was, and we talked for a while and I said, 'Let's consolidate forces,' and he said, 'Right!' At eleven the same morning we met at his house and played for hours and had a ball. We wanted a kind of Freddie Green-Walter Page guitar and bass combination behind us, and we got Wayne Wright and John Giuffrida, and we started rehearsing like crazy. We made our first public appearance at the Newport Festival, and every notice was good. We recorded what we'd played right after, and since then we've made a record with Tony Bennett, and we're also going to do a documentary film with him, and then go into the Rainbow Grill. I've spent all my life knocking on doors, but now they're knocking on ours. So it's the right combination of souls.

"I've lived up in Riverdale for eighteen or nineteen years. I lived in Pee Wee Russell's building down on King Street before. You'd think my joint was an insane asylum to see it. I never thought it would be permanent, so I've never really furnished it. I thought I'd wait until I had an apartment in New York and one in London and one in Paris and maids and chauffeurs and then buy some decent furniture. I cook everything in a frying pan, and I cook and eat and wash up in twenty minutes. I don't think food should be too important. When I was on tour in Europe with George Wein, we'd go to a fancy restaurant in Paris and spend about three hours, and then George would say he knew another place that had fantastic desserts, and we'd go there for another hour, and then somewhere else for coffee. It sent me up the wall. I've come close to getting married a couple of times, but I married music a long time ago, and a wife would have to understand that. Anyway, there's only room for one nut in a household, and I have first claim on that.

"I don't feel right if I'm not playing, but there have been times when I haven't had a gig in six months. What I'd do, if I couldn't call a session, was go through an entire concert in my mind—an invented concert, note for note, right down to the lights and the applause. If it went well, I'd sometimes make actual notes about it: that's something to remember, something to use. But how to keep your spirits up when you're not working is another kind of discipline. One thing, I stay away from the negatives; they can bring you down and tear you apart. Another is a one-night gig. It can wipe out months of difficulty. Otherwise, it's just get through the week and then everything will be cool. But you can't abuse your music at such times by going and making a rock-and-roll record or something. I'm an optimist. I've always felt that things would be all right, that I'd be rewarded. I know I'm good and I know I'm unique. If I had to go out and hire someone just like me, it would be impossible, because he doesn't exist."

A Day with the Duke

A day spent in New York with Duke Ellington, then seventy-one, in the spring of 1970. It began at three-thirty in the afternoon at the National Recording Studios at Fifty-sixth and Fifth, where he was to record part of the music for a ballet commissioned by the American Ballet Theatre. The ballet was called "The River," and would be given its premiere at the New York State Theatre at Lincoln Center. He greeted a friend with his French two-kisses-on-each-cheek and said, "What time did I call you last night?"

"Around twelve-thirty," the friend replied.

"I didn't get to bed until ten this morning, what with working on the ballet. I'm tired, babe, tired."

But he looked extremely well, and even his working clothes—an old blue sweater, rumpled gray slacks, and blue suède shoes—looked good. He went immediately into the recording booth, which, like most of the places Ellington went, was crowded with relatives, friends, and hangers-on. Present were Stanley Dance; Michael James, Ellington's nephew and an aide; Joe Morgen, his press agent; an admirer of thirty-five years, standing named Edmund Anderson; and a couple of women. Ellington examined some sheet music and went out into the studio. He spoke to several members of the band and got loud laughs in response and, standing in the center of the studio, said, just before the first take, "We're going to get lucky on this one. Derum, derum, derum! One, two, three, four!" Rufus Jones started a rapid machine-gun beat on his snare drum, which was echoed on a glockenspiel and on timpani. The band came in, and the piece, called "The Falls," turned out to be unlike anything Ellington had done before. But then nothing new of his is quite like anything he has done before. The section passages of "The Falls" were brief but dense and booting, there were solo parts by Paul Gonsalves, and there were extraordinary dissonant full-band chords. And all this was done against the *rat-tat-tat-tat* of the snare, the glockenspiel, and the timpani. It was tight crescendo music, and it was reminiscent of early Stravinsky, except that it was unmistakably a jazz composition. Ellington conducted (Wild Bill Davis sat in on piano), using the traditional upside-down-T-square motions in a slow, wooden way. All the while he chewed on something and rocked his head from side to side.

While the piece was played back, he sat in the recording booth with his head bowed, his eyes closed, and a hand on each knee. He looked up when it was over. "A waterfall—you can always see the top and you can always hear the bottom," he said. "So you've got the top and the bottom, and you can put anything you want in between."

He returned to the studio, and Anderson said, "Last November, I shot some film of the band in Paris. Afterward I told Johnny Hodges [he had died a short time before], who in all the thirty-five years I knew him never said more than two words, 'I got some great footage of you tonight.' He shouted at me, 'Not tonight! Not tonight! My eyes looked so bad!' which was all the more amazing when you consider that on the stand Hodges kept his eyes closed most of the time."

Ellington led the band through six or seven more takes until he got the right one, and after a break he went to work on a part of the ballet called "The Mother." It was slow and ruminative, and included a lovely flute solo by Norris Turney. Again, there were several takes, and the session ended at six-thirty. Ellington made some phone calls, kissed several women hello and goodbye, and, surrounded by Morgen, Dance, and a friend who was driving for Ellington, a broad-shouldered Greek named Chris Stamatiou, left the studios for the City Center to talk with Alvin Ailey, who is choreographing "The River."

Down on Fifth Avenue, Ellington asked Stamatiou where his car was, and Stamatiou said in a garage around the corner. Ellington asked him how far it was to the City Center, and he said a block or so—an easy walk. "You mean you want me to *walk* a block? Well, I might as well, but it'll be the longest walk I've had in years," Ellington said. He started west on Fifty-sixth Street, moving in the determined, stiff way of older men with tired feet. He got a lot of double takes, and whenever he passed a garage or a restaurant with its complement of New York early-evening sidewalk loungers, he was greeted with, "Hey Duke!" or "Mr. *Ellington!*" Each time, he looked interested and said "How you been?" or "How's everything?" and shook hands as if he were greeting friends he hadn't seen in twenty-five years. He went in at the back door of the City Center and up to the sixth floor, where he sat down abruptly with Ailey at a small table by the elevator door. They talked for twenty minutes, and then went down to wait for Stamatiou and the car. They continued talking, but the car didn't come, and after fifteen minutes Dance called the garage and found out that the car had broken down. Ellington kissed Ailey goodbye, and got into a cab and headed downtown. Dance and Morgen were with him. It was about seven-thirty.

"We're going to the Half Note," Dance said. "Hugues Panassié's son Louis is in the country making some sort of film on jazz, and he asked Duke if he would mind coming down to the Half Note to be in a short sequence."

Ellington, who sat next to the taxi-driver, a young, bearded man, pulled a bright scarf out of his pocket and knotted it around his head turban-fashion. The driver, peering at Ellington out of the corner of his eye, missed a crucial right-hand turn at Dominick Street, and the Holland Tunnel appeared. Ellington asked Morgen if he knew where the hell they were going, and Morgen said he had seen the Dominick Street turn just after we passed it. The driver made a hundred-and-eighty-degree swing in front of the Tunnel and stopped a moment later at the Half Note. Ellington took off his scarf and got out.

Inside, Ellington gave Panassié, an engaging man in his thirties, the de-rigueur greeting and asked him what to do. Panassie said he would like him to sit at the bar for a few minutes and answer a couple of questions. Mike Canterino, one of the owners of the Half Note, gave Ellington a Coke, and, bathed in blinding light, he sat down on a bar stool. "You know, I'm not really dressed for this sort of thing, but let me light a cigarette, so I'll look sophisticated," he said. He knocked over the Coke and said, "Oh, my! I'm the only nuisance I know who *knows* he's a nuisance!" The cameras rolled, and Ellington, looking as if he were in his living room with a few friends, spoke intimately about Panassié's father ("He serves the same muse I do"), and went on, "I don't think any music should be called jazz. I don't believe in categories. Years ago, uptown, I tried to get the cats to call it American Negro music or Afro-American music, because jazz just isn't right. Louis Armstrong plays Louis Armstrong music, Art Tatum plays Art Tatum music, Dizzy Gillespie plays Dizzy Gillespie music, and if it sounds good, that's all you need."

At about eight o'clock the klieg lights went off, and Panassié thanked Ellington. The three men walked to Sixth Avenue to find a cab, and on the way Ellington kept hitching up his trousers, which were secured by an old belt buckled at one side. "When I got that degree in Indianapolis last week, I had this same problem," he told Dance. "I was wearing a gown and all, and when I went out on the stage my pants started slipping, and I had to pull them up right through the gown. I don't know whether it's this stomach I've got that's causing the trouble or whether it's just that my bottom is getting smaller."

At Sixth Avenue a young black policeman greeted Ellington: "Hey, Duke. You waiting for the A train?" Ellington said he was waiting for a cab, but asked if there was an A train somewhere around to get back uptown in. A cab arrived, and Ellington gave the driver his sister Ruth's address on Central Park South.

Miss Ellington's apartment, which looked out over the Park, was mostly off-white, and the windows were hung with heavy glass-bead curtains. There were a couple of big glass-topped tables, and in the corner was a small bar. She greeted her brother warmly, and he slumped into a chair, stretched his legs out straight, and threw his head back on a cushion. He closed his eyes. Miss Ellington, who wore a big blond wig, a yellow blouse, and purple slacks, asked him if he wanted some Chinese food. He said no, he was just going home to bed. Stamatiou appeared, and, leaning over Ellington, apologized about the car. Ellington grunted and waved one hand. A man in a white coat brought him a Coke, putting it down carefully on a paper coaster that showed a bass drum with a caricature of Ellington's head on it and the word "Duke" beneath. Dance asked Ellington about the ballet.

He opened his eyes halfway, took a sip of Coke, and lit a cigarette. His eyes closed again. "I'd been thinking about it for a while, and a year or so ago I was lying on a hotel bed in Vancouver and Alvin Ailey was with me and the story just came out," he said. "The river starts out like a spring and he's like a newborn baby, tumbling and spitting, and one day, attracted by a puddle, he starts to run. He scurries and scampers and wants to get to the marsh, and, after being followed by a big bubble, he does, and at the end of the run he goes into the meander. Then he skips and dances and runs until he's exhausted, and he lies down by the lake—all horizontal lines, ripples, reflections, God-made and untouched. Then he goes over the falls and down into the whirlpool, the vortex of violence, and out of the whirlpool into the main track of the river. He widens, becomes broader, loses his adolescence, and down at the delta, passes between two cities. Like all cities on the opposite sides of deltas, you can find certain things in one and not in the other, and vice versa, so we call the cities the Neo-Hip-Hot-Cool Kiddies' Community and the Village of the Virgins. The river passes between them and romps into the mother— Her Majesty the Sea—and, of course, is no longer a river. But this is the climax, the heavenly anticipation of rebirth, for the sea will be drawn up into the sky for rain and down into wells and into springs and become the river again. So we call the river an optimist. We'll be able to play the ballet in any church or temple, because the optimist is a believer."

Then Dance, at Ellington's behest, read the eulogy he had written for Johnny Hodges. It began, "Never the world's greatest, most highly animated showman or stage personality . . . but a tone so beautiful it sometimes brought tears to the eyes. This was Johnny Hodges. This is Johnny Hodges. Because of this great loss, our band will never sound the same." It ended, "I am glad and thankful that I had the privilege of presenting Johnny Hodges for forty years, night after night. I imagine that I have been much envied, but thanks to God, and may God bless this beautiful giant in his own identity. God bless Johnny Hodges."

Joe Morgen said, "Hey, Duke, you're on television now, with Orson Welles on the David Frost show."

Ellington opened his eyes, heaved himself to his feet, and moved rapidly out of the room, saying, "Oh, he's one of my favorite people—Orson Welles. I've got to see him."

Mingus at Peace

Charles Mingus, the incomparable forty-nine-year-old bassist, composer, bandleader, autobiographer, and iconoclast, has spent much of his life attempting to rearrange the world according to an almost Johnsonian set of principles that abhor, among other things, cant, racism, inhibition, managerial greed, sloppy music, Uncle Tomism, and conformity. His methods have ranged from penny-dreadful broadsides to punches on the nose. The results have been mixed. They have also been costly, and have landed Mingus on the psychiatric couch and in Bellevue (self-committed), lost him jobs, and made him periodically fat. ("I eat out of nerves.") At the same time, Mingus' experiences have been steadily distilled into a body of compositions that for sheer melodic and rhythmic and structural originality may equal Monk and Ellington. (Their content has been equally fresh, for they have included, in the Ellington manner, everything from love songs to social satire.) These experiences have, as well, been reflected in his playing, which long ago elevated him to virtuosic rank. But now Mingus has taken another step. He has written a book about himself— "Beneath the Underdog: His World as Composed by Mingus" (Knopf).

The book is impressionistic and disembodied (it has almost no dates), and has a taste of all the Minguses. It is brutal and dirty and bitter. It is sentimental and self-pitying. It is rude and, in places, unfair (the curt handling of the great Red Norvo). It is facetious and funny. It is awkward and unerringly right, and it is the latter when Mingus' fine ear is receiving full tilt. Duke Ellington's verbal arabesques have never been captured better:

> [Juan] Tizol [an Ellington trombonist] wants you to play a solo he's written where bowing is required. You raise the solo an octave, where the bass isn't too muddy. He doesn't like that and he comes to the room under the stage where you're practicing at intermission and comments that you're like the rest of the niggers in the band, you can't read. You ask Juan how he's different from the other niggers and he states that one of the ways he's different is that HE IS WHITE. So you run his ass upstairs. You leave the rehearsal room, proceed toward the stage with your bass and take your place and at the moment Duke brings down the baton for "A-Train" and the curtain of the Apollo Theatre goes up, a yelling, whooping Tizol rushes out and lunges at you with a bolo knife.

The rest you remember mostly from Duke's own words in his dressing room as he changes after the show.

"Now, Charles," he says, looking amused, putting Cartier links into the cuffs of his beautiful handmade shirt, "you could have forewarned me—you left me out of the act entirely! At least you could have let me cue in a few chords as you ran through that Nijinsky routine. I congratulate you on your performance, but why didn't you and Juan inform me about the adagio you planned so that we could score it? I must say I never saw a large man so agile—I never saw *anybody* make such tremendous leaps! The gambado over the piano carrying your bass was colossal. When you exited after that I thought, 'That man's really afraid of Juan's knife and at the speed he's going he's probably home in bed by now.' But no, back you came through the same door with your bass still intact. For a moment I was hopeful you'd decided to sit down and play but instead you slashed Juan's chair in two with a fire axe! Really, Charles, that's destructive. Everybody knows Juan has a knife but nobody ever took it seriously—he likes to pull it out and show it to people, you understand. So I'm afraid, Charles—I've never fired anybody —you'll have to quit my band. I don't need any new problems. Juan's an old problem, I can cope with that, but you seem to have a whole bag of new tricks. I must ask you to be kind enough to give me your notice, Charles."

The charming way he says it, it's like he's paying you a compliment. Feeling honored, you shake hands and resign.

Mingus' relationship with jazz critics has been generally amiable, and the lumps landed on them in the book are pretty funny. A party is given for Mingus when he first arrives in New York from the West Coast around 1950. No matter that the critics named were never in the same room at the same time in their lives, or that at least two of them were still in college and unpublished. Mingus is talking to Dizzy Gillespie:

> "Man, that's a lot of talent, don't you dig it? I see Leonard Feather, he's a piano player. There's Bill Coss and Gene Lees—they sing, I heard. Barry Ulanov must play drums or something, dig, with that *Metronome* beat. Martin Williams can play everything. I can tell by the way he writes. Put Marshall Stearns on bass and let Whitney Balliett score and John Wilson conduct. Let all them other young up-and-coming critics dance. How would you like to review that schitt for the *Amsterdam News*?"

But the best parts of the book deal with Fats Navarro, a brilliant, concise trumpeter who died at the age of twenty-six in 1950. He tells a young and ingenuous Mingus what it is really like to be a jazz musician:

> "Mingus, you a nice guy from California, I don't want to disillusion you. But I been through all that schitt and I had to learn to do some other things to get along. I learned better than to try to make it just with my music out on these dirty gang-mob streets, cause I still love playing bet-

ter than money. Jazz ain't supposed to make nobody no millions but that's where it's at. Them that shouldn't is raking it in but the purest are out in the street with me and Bird and it rains all over us, man. I was better off when nobody knew my name except musicians. You can bet it ain't jazz no more when the underworld moves in and runs it strictly for geetz and even close out the colored agents. They shut you up and cheat you on the count of your record sales and if you go along they tell the world you a real genius. But if you don't play they put out the word you're a troublemaker, like they did me. Then if some honest club owner tries to get hold of you to book you, they tell him you're not available or you don't draw or you'll tear up the joint like you was a gorilla. And you won't hear nothin' about it except by accident. But if you behave, boy, you'll get booked—except for less than the white cats that copy your playing and likely either the agent or owner'll pocket the difference."

On a Sunday night a week or so before his book was published, Mingus was sitting at the bar of a restaurant on West Tenth Street. He was dressed in a conservative dark suit and tie, and he was in his middle state. That is, he was neither thin nor huge. A Charlie Chan beard was arranged carefully around his mouth, and he looked wonderful. A year before, his face had been gray and puffy; he had not played a note for two years, and he was very fat and had a listless, buried air. Now he was sitting at the bar sampling a tall white drink. "Ramos gin fizz," he blurted out. "Milk or cream, white of an egg, orange flower water, lemon juice, gin, and soda water. I used to drink ten at a sitting in San Francisco." Mingus talks in leaping slurs. The words come out crouched and running, and sometimes they move so fast whole sentences are unintelligible. He finished his Ramos fizz and ordered a half bottle of Pouilly-Fuissé and some cheese. He pronounced the name of the wine at a run, and it came out "Poolly-Foos." "We went down to the peace demonstration in Washington this weekend to play, and it was a drag," he said. "They've never had any jazz at these things, and it seemed like a good idea, but we never did play. My piano player didn't show, and my alto sax couldn't make it, so we only had four pieces, and it wouldn't have made any sense going on like that. I went to bed right after I got back this morning. I hadn't been to bed in two nights. I can't sleep at night anyway, but I do all right with a sleeping pill in the day. I even had a wonderful dream just before I got up. I had everything under control. I was on a diet and losing weight all over the place, and I felt so good. But a dream like that is worse than a nightmare. You wake up and the real nightmare starts."

Mingus asked the bartender if he could get some lobster and was told that the kitchen had closed. "Maybe they got some across the street in that steak house," Mingus said. He told the bartender to keep the rest of the wine—that he'd be back right after he'd eaten. He crossed the street and went down some steps into a dark, low, empty room. Mingus moved lightly but gingerly and, squeezing himself into a booth, ordered lobster tails, hearts of lettuce, and another half bottle of Poolly-Foos.

"My book was written for black people to tell them how to get through life," he said. "I was trying to upset the white man in it—the right kind or the wrong kind, depending on what color and persuasion you are. I started it twenty-five years ago, and at first I was doing it for myself, to help understand certain situations. I talked some of it into tape recorders, and that girl in the white Cadillac in the book, she helped me type it up. But I wrote most of it in longhand in the dark backstage or on buses on huge sheets of score paper. The original manuscript was between eight hundred and a thousand pages. It went up and down, what with parts of it getting lost. I started looking for a publisher more than ten years ago. Things hadn't loosened up yet, and a lot of them looked at it and it scared them. It was too dirty, it was too hard on whitey, they said. McGraw-Hill finally bought it, but they put it on the shelf for a long time. Then Knopf got interested and bought it from McGraw-Hill."

Mingus asked the waitress for a glass of water. She was young and blond. "Say, you my same waitress? It's so dark in here you look like you keep changing." Mingus leaned back and smiled his beautiful smile.

"I'm your waitress," she said, putting a hand lightly on his left arm. "Are you Jaki Byard?"

"Jaki Byard? Jaki Byard? He's my piano player. He's a super-star now. I'm glad you my same waitress. Now, bring me that glass of water, please. Then I got hold of Nel King, who wrote a movie I was in, and she put the book in shape. It took her a year and a half. A whole lot of stuff has been left out—stuff about blacks wearing Afros because they're afraid not to, and skin-lighteners, and my wife, Celia. There was a lot about her in there, but she didn't want to be in the book, so I left her out. I wrote it abcdefgh at first, but then I mixed up the chronology and some of the locations. Like that party when I first came to New York in the late forties. It didn't take place at any apartment in the East Seventies but over at the old Bandbox, next to Birdland. The critics were there, and they didn't stop talking once. They kept right on even when Art Tatum and Charlie Parker sat in together for maybe the only time in their lives. It was the most fantastic music I ever heard. Tatum didn't let up in either hand for a second—*whoosh-hum, whoosh-hum* in the left, and *aaaaaaaaarrrrrrrrrhhhhhhheeeeee* in the right— and neither did Parker, and to this day I don't know what they were doing. The passages on Fats Navarro are the best part of the book. I loved Fats and I could hear his voice in my head the whole time I was writing him down. But that's just my first book. It's not an autobiography. It's just me, Mingus. My next book will be my life in music."

Mingus finished his lobster tails and wine and went back across the street. He telephoned his manager, Sue Ungaro, and arranged to meet her in ten minutes at a Japanese restaurant at Twelfth Street and Second Avenue. It was almost one o'clock. Mingus emptied his bottle of wine and took a cab across town. The restaurant was shut, and Mrs. Ungaro was nowhere in sight.

"I better walk over to her place, maybe meet her on the way," Mingus said. The street was deserted, but he reached into a coat pocket and took out a big East Indian knife and, removing its scabbard, held it at the ready in his left hand. "This is the way I walk the streets at night around here. I live down on Fifth Street, and we got so much crime I'm scared to be out at night." He passed St. Mark's in the Bowerie and headed west.

Mrs. Ungaro was putting some trash in a garbage can in front of her building. She is a pretty, slender strawberry blonde, and she was wearing bluejeans, clogs, and a short, beat-up raccoon coat.

"They closed," Mingus said, pocketing his knife. Mrs. Ungaro said she'd still like something to eat. They took a cab to the Blue Sea on Third Avenue and Twenty-fourth Street. It was closed. Mingus told the driver to make a U-turn, and go down to a small bar-and-grill on Tenth and Third. He and Sue Ungaro sat in a semicircular booth under a jukebox loudspeaker. She ordered a hamburger and salad and Mingus asked the waitress, who was wearing false eyelashes and a black knitted see-through pants suit, for a dish of black olives and some Poolly-Foos.

"Poorly what?" she said, moving her lashes up and down like a semaphore. "I don't know. I'm just helping out tonight, because I've known these people a long time."

The manager, a short man in shirtsleeves with gleaming glasses and a big paunch, said they had Soave Bolla. A half bottle in a straw basket was put in an ice bucket on the table. Mingus scrunched it down in the bucket and piled ice cubes carefully around its neck.

He looked at Sue Ungaro and smiled. "It's been five years, baby. You know that?" She nodded and took a bite of hamburger. "Sue wrote in for the Guggenheim I just got. I want to write a ballet with the money—an operatic ballet. I've had it in my head for years, like I had the book in my head. It'll have to do with Watts, where I was born and raised, and I want Katherine Dunham to choreograph it. I know her very well, and we've talked about it a long time. But getting the Guggenheim wasn't as easy as filling out forms. I had to carry about fifty pounds of music over for them to see. If I don't finish the ballet this year, I'll apply again."

"Charles wants to put together a seventeen-piece band," Sue Ungaro said. "And he wants to use some of the Guggenheim money, but they won't allow it. It's only for composition."

"If I do finish the ballet, I'll apply anyway so that I can write some chamber music. That's what I started out doing years and years ago, and I want to go back to it. I've been teaching all winter, one day a week, at the state university at Buffalo. The Slee Chair of Music. They invited me, and I've been teaching composition to about ten kids. They're bright, and they get their work done on time. I used some of my own pieces, showing them how to work with a melody and no chords or sets of chords, and no melody or just a pedal point, to give them a sense of freedom. But I feel sorry about jazz. The truth has been lost in the music. All the different styles and factions went to war with each other, and it hasn't done any good. Take Ornette Coleman." Mingus sang half a chorus of "Body and Soul" in a loud, off-key voice, drowning out the jukebox. It was an uncanny imitation. "That's all he does. Just pushing the melody out of line here and there. Trouble is, he can't play it straight. At that little festival Max Roach and I gave in Newport in 1960, Kenny Dorham and I tried to get Ornette to play 'All the Things You Are' straight, and he couldn't do it."

Mingus took a sip of wine and made a face. "I don't know, this doesn't taste right."

"Maybe it isn't cold enough," Sue Ungaro said.

Mingus fished out his knife, deftly cut the straw basket off the bottle, and put the bottle back in the ice. The waitress appeared and said: "Everything fine, honey?"

"The wine doesn't taste right. It's not cold enough."

The waitress took three ice cubes out of the bucket and plopped them in our glasses and splashed some wine over them.

"Hey, that'll make it all water," Mingus said, seizing the bottle and jamming it back in the bucket.

"I'm just helping out, sir, like I said."

"She'll make the reputation of this place," Mingus mumbled.

"The Black Panthers have been to see Charles," Sue Ungaro said, "but he won't go along with them."

"I don't need to. I'm a single movement. Anyway, I don't like to see the blacks destroying this country. It's a waste of time. The militants have nothing to sell. And that's what this country does best—sells. Makes and sells thing to the world. But the militants don't sell *nothing*. All the black pimps and black gangsters know this, because they *have* something to sell, like the king-pimp Billy Bones in my book. Man, he made millions of dollars around the world. The black people don't like themselves to begin with. You've got all these variations of color and dialect. You've got terrific economic differences. You never hear anything from the wealthy blacks, but they don't like the militants. Some of them been working at their money seventy-five years, in real estate or whatever, and they not about to let the militants come and take it away for something called freedom. Hell, what's freedom? Nobody's free, black or white. What's going to happen is there will be one hell of a revolution and it'll be between black and black. Like the big trouble in Watts, when the blacks were ready to shoot the blacks. It all started when a truckload of militants arrived and started throwing bombs into the black stores and such. Well, man, the shop owners—and I grew up with a lot of them got upset and came charging out with guns, and by this time the truck had moved on and the white cops had arrived and saw all these blacks standing around with guns and started shooting them, and that was it."

Mingus leaned back, out of breath. The manager passed the table and Mingus asked him if he had any fresh fish. The manager went into the kitchen and came back with a handful of cherrystones. Mingus looked surprised. He ordered half a dozen on the half shell, and some vintage champagne.

"No vintage," the manager replied. "I got a bunch of vintage in last week and it was dead and I sent the whole mess back. I'll give you regular. Piper Heidsieck."

The clams arrived and Mingus coated each one with lemon juice and cocktail sauce and about a teaspoonful of Tabasco. "Hell, a while back, I took my daughter to Columbia to hear What's-His-Name, Eldridge Cleaver, and right away all I heard him saying was mother this and mother that. Well, I didn't want my daughter hearing that. That's vulgarity no matter if the man is right or wrong. I left. I took my daughter and left right away."

Mingus looked relaxed and content. In fact, he looked as if he had finally got the world straightened around to his liking. The talk wandered easily along between jukebox selections, and Mingus and Sue Ungaro discussed astrology (Mingus: "My birth date is four/two-two/two-two. The astrologists have never been able to get over that"), weight problems (Mingus: "Man, I get to this size and it's painful. My arms hurt all the time up here from banging against the rest of me"), the effects on the stomach of too much vitamin C, the sorrows of drug addiction, and the fact that Mingus suddenly has more "visible, taxable" money than ever before in his life.

The lights started to go out. It was almost four o'clock. Mingus went to the men's room, and Sue Ungaro said: "I don't really like Charles' book, and I've told him. I think the sexual parts are too savage, and I think that Charles himself doesn't come through. It's the superficial Mingus, the flashy one, not the real one." Mingus reappeared and the waitress let us out the door. "Night, now," she said with a couple of semaphores. "It's been a real pleasure serving you."

Two nights later Mingus opened at the Village Vanguard with a sextet for a week's stand. It included Lonnie Hillyer on trumpet, Charlie McPherson on alto saxophone, Bobby Jones on tenor saxophone, John Foster on piano, Mingus, and Virgil Day on drums. Mingus the musician is a tonic to watch. He becomes a massive receiver-transmitter, absorbing every note played around him and then sending out through his bass corrective or appreciative notes. The result is a two-way flow which lights up his musicians who, in turn, light up his music.

Whenever he has felt out of sorts in recent years, Mingus has taken to offering lacklustre medleys of bebop numbers or Ellington tunes, completely ignoring his own storehouse of compositions. But at the Vanguard he brought out refurbished versions of such numbers as "Celia" and "Diane." They were full of his trademarks—long, roving melodies, complex, multipart forms, breaks, constantly changing rhythms, howling ensembles, and the against-the-grain quality he brands each of his performances with. Most of them were also done in Mingus' customary workshop manner. When a number would start hesitantly, he would rumble, "No, No, No," and stop the music. Then the group would start again.

Sometimes there were three or four false starts. In all, there were half a dozen long numbers in the first set, and they were exceptional. Mingus soloed briefly just once, on a blues, but everything was there. Dressed in a short-sleeved shirt and tie, he sat on a tall stool and played, and he looked as serene as he had on Sunday.

At the beginning of the following week, Knopf gave a publication party for "Beneath the Underdog," with music. It was held in a couple of box-like, orange-carpeted rooms in the Random House building on East Fiftieth Street. It was jammed, and Mingus' sextet, with a ringer on bass, was playing "Celia" at close to the one-hundred decibel level. There were more blacks than whites, and Mingus, again dressed in a dark suit and tie, was talking with a lady of his proportions. It was like seeing Sidney Greenstreet and Eugene Pallette porch to porch. Ornette Coleman, dressed in a glistening black silk mandarin suit, said he had just completed a piece for eighty musicians that sounded just like his playing. Nel King said that Mingus' book had been a lot of work and that perhaps her being a woman was a help in managing his tempestuous moods. Max Gordon, a Mingus supporter from the early days, was standing with Mingus and Sue Ungaro and a tall, slender youth in a beard, straw hat, and cowboy boots. Sue was still in her bluejeans and clogs. "Meet my son, Charles, Jr.," Mingus said. He poked Charles, Jr. in the stomach. "*He* doesn't have any weight problem. And look at his beard! I can't grow any more than what I have on my face." Mingus asked his son if he had read his book.

"Listen, I haven't even seen it yet," Charles, Jr., replied. "Besides, I've been working on my play."

A man who had joined the group said that one of the minor but unavoidable axioms of the literary life was that children never read their parents' books. Mingus grunted. Nel King approached and told him she wanted him to meet someone. She asked Mingus before she towed him away how he liked the party.

"It's strange, man," he said.

A Trombone Mouth

Where around New York can you hear the elusive master trombonist Jimmy Knepper? In the late eighties and early nineties, he appeared in most of the half-dozen concerts given by the American Jazz Orchestra at Cooper Union, but at each one he only took five or six choruses, some of them reshapings of transcribed solos by such earlier masters as Duke Ellington's Tricky Sam Nanton and Count Basie's Dicky Wells; he spent four nights at the West End Gate in a quintet put together by his friend and admirer the pianist Dick Katz; he led a trio for one night at Bradley's; he led the repertory group Mingus Dynasty for two six-night stints at the Village Vanguard; he turned up for several nights with Buck Clayton's swing band at Fat Tuesday's; and, for his own pleasure and to keep his lip and arm limber, he played occasional one-night stands at the Dock of the Bay, on Staten Island, not far from where he lives. The tenor saxophonist and pianist Loren Schoenberg played with him there, and he has said of Knepper, "Jimmy is the most flexible of all the trombonists. He has built his own phraseology out of Charlie Parker's vocabulary. He's not trombonistic, and his style is self-effacing. The dazzling way he gets around the instrument, you couldn't play what he plays on any other instrument. He never loses coherence, and he never relies on devices. In fact, he has an abhorrence of clichés. Whenever the American Jazz Orchestra plays a warhorse, Jimmy goes at recreating whoever's old solo in eight different ways before he gets it right. He's always willing to let his music take full responsibility for itself. There is something calming about his playing, a repose. What he plays and what he is as a person form a whole, and that's very rare among musicians. Jimmy functions best in surroundings someone else creates. He's a better sideman—horrible word—than leader. You make a frame for him, and he'll make a beautiful picture to go in it. Jimmy is also a consummate musical copyist. His musical manuscripts are functional, neat, inspired, like his playing. He is also a crossword-puzzle maven. When I go on the road, I like to take a crossword puzzle to bed at night. It relaxes me and keeps me company. Once, when Jimmy and I were on the road together, our puzzles got mixed up, and when I got into bed and picked up my puzzle, which I had been struggling with, I discovered I had Jimmy's. It was completely filled out, and I was devastated and couldn't get to sleep for a long time."

Dick Katz talked about Knepper before they worked together at the West End Gate: "Jimmy has a vocal way of playing that is matched to bebop lines. His intervals sound impossible, but he makes them. He lays way back rhythmically. He rarely plays on the beat, or in the pocket, as musicians say. He places his notes in the cracks—here, there, everywhere. He's a meticulous musician. He gets to every job early, and warms up with long tones. And he's a first-rate composer—very Ellingtonian. When he puts a group together for a gig, he has a hands-off policy; he lets things happen. He's an easygoing man, but he's not easy to know."

Knepper looks like what grocery clerks looked like when there were grocery clerks. He's tall and polelike and bespectacled, and when he starts to sit down he bends in the middle as if he were hinged. Every time he appears somewhere, he seems to be thinner. "I lose a pound a year, and if I live long enough I'll just disappear," he once said. He has a high forehead and Clark Gable ears, set low on his head, like stabilizers. His hair is puzzling: sometimes it looks fluffy, and sometimes it looks thin and pasted on. He wears heavy horn-rims that tend to slip down his nose, hiding his eyes. Smiles occasionally start at the edges of his face, then withdraw, but most of the time his face is expressionless. It's a mask that is not really a mask, though, because Knepper hides little when he talks. He talks easily and steadily and slowly, and he punctuates what he says by pufffing on short cigarettes that he rolls as he speaks. They keep going out, and that makes them last a long time. He talked about his life one day, and here is some of what he said:

"I've been involved in landlordism in recent years. My wife, Maxine, and I live on Ward's Hill, in northern Staten Island. You can walk to the ferry in twenty minutes. We have a view of the city, of Brooklyn Bridge, even of the George Washington Bridge. We stumbled on the house in 1961, and buying it was one of the best moves we ever made. We own another house, with a five-room apartment in it and a ten-room apartment, and we rent both of them out. That house only cost nine thousand five hundred dollars, if you can believe it. Some years, it makes more money than I do. We also own a house with two apartments in Port Richmond, and we rent that out, too. And I inherited a house in Los Angeles from an aunt, and that's just started renting. All this real estate has kept me in the music business without me panicking and having to look for some other kind of work. In fact, the mortgages are all paid and we own everything outright, and that makes my declining years more relaxed.

"We moved to Staten Island from a cold-water flat on East Twenty-fifth Street in 1959. One day, when our two kids were little and Maxine was sick, I took the real-estate section of the paper and a map and went to Staten Island. I figured Staten Island would have some trees and some room. I found a little house on the road to the Verrazano Bridge. Then we moved to the house we're in. We have a boy and a girl. Robin is thirty-six, and she lives in Matamoras, Pennsylvania. She has three little boys, and she's a social worker. Our son is Timothy Jay—both children were named after birds—and he lives in the house in Los Angeles. I sent him out there three years ago to fix it up, but nothing happened, and we had to go out and light a fire under him. He's thirty-four and he used to drive a cab in New York at night, carrying a knife and a crowbar for self-protection. I didn't think much of that, so I sent him to Los Angeles to stir up his life and give him some responsibility.

"Los Angeles is where I was born—on November 22, 1927. I have a brother, Robert, who's a year and a half older. He's a librarian in L.A. He's a family person, and he keeps sending me copies of death certificates of people vaguely related to us. My mother was a nurse and my father a cop. She divorced him when I wasn't even two, because he'd got in the habit of knocking her down. I only saw him three or four times. My brother looked up my father's career later on, and found out that he may or may not have accidentally killed his third wife, and that he was an alcoholic. My mother, who was just a little over five feet, spent her whole life nursing. When I was four, she put my brother and me in Page's Military Academy, on Cochran Avenue. We boarded, and went home on weekends. When I was seven, the bandmaster gave me an alto horn to play, then a baritone. When I was nine, he gave me a trombone. He said I had a trombone mouth. We also went to a Catholic military school, even though we were non-Catholic, and I finally graduated from a public high school in 1944."

Jazz musicians were nomads when Knepper came up. Most of them were in big bands, which still travelled up and down the country to play at theatres and in ballrooms and hotels and night clubs. But the big bands, beset by economic problems, were dwindling, and Knepper was one of the last graduates. (The on-the-job training they offered has never been replaced.) After teen-age stints on the West Coast with the bands of Frank Morehead and Chuck Cascales, he went on the road with Tommy Reynolds, quit, and returned to Los Angeles to work with his friend Dean Benedetti. In 1948, Knepper joined Freddie Slack's band at the Sherman Hotel, in Chicago. ("I started taking goofballs and was fired. A youthful indiscretion.") Later that year, Knepper hitched across the country with Benedetti and helped him to record Charlie Parker on Fifty-second Street. (These legendary on-the-spot recordings have been issued in full by Mosaic.) Between 1950 and 1951, he was with Charlie Spivak and Charlie Barnet. He also worked for a stunning week with Charlie Parker at the Showboat in Philadelphia, with Al Haig on piano, Tommy Potter on bass, and Roy Haynes on drums. "The first night, Parker kept lurching to his right, and I thought he had some sort of tic," Knepper said. "But the spring on his concert F-sharp key was broken, and he had to lean sharply to the right to make it open. Parker was astonishing. I could hear every kind of music in his solos—bits of Wagner, a Rudy Wiedoeft phrase, Stravinsky, Bartók. Musicians are technique-minded now and they can play a thousand notes a chorus, but I have never known anyone who played more cleanly. He articulated each note. Parker must have done his woodshedding"—practicing—"when he was very young, because he didn't practice. Someone like John Coltrane never stopped. He'd practice in his dressing room, on the bus, and at home. Drinking didn't seem to affect Parker's playing. He'd accept drink after drink during intermission and put away maybe a pint of whiskey. They'd lean him against the wall when he got back on the stand, and off he'd go. Parker gave the impression he knew everything. Architects thought he must have had architectural training, poets thought he was a poet, painters thought he was a painter. You could never catch Bird out."

Knepper married Maxine Fields in 1954, in Tucson. She had played trumpet with the International Sweethearts of Rhythm and with Ina Ray Hutton. She was born in Elkhart, Indiana, and her father had been a trombone player. Knepper's nomadism continued. In 1956, he got a job with Ralph Marterie in Chicago, and Maxine joined him, their year-old daughter in tow. Knepper had converted Maxine into a drummer, and while they were in Chicago she sometimes worked with a pianist in Sault Sainte

Marie. They "milled around" Chicago, living in a hotel that had a Murphy bed in the kitchen. They bought a car, and Knepper quit Marterie and they drove to New York, arriving on Halloween in a terrible rainstorm. Knepper soon ran into the alto saxophonist Gene Quill, and Quill got him a job with Claude Thornhill. They toured Air Force bases in North Africa, Germany, and France. Knepper had started writing arrangements, and he did two Elvis Presley tunes for Thornhill. When he got back to New York, the trombonist Willie Dennis told Knepper that he was leaving Charlie Mingus's band, and Mingus, remembering Knepper from a one-night gig in Los Angeles ten years before, called him.

The epochal part of Knepper's life began. Mingus, who died in 1979, was a brilliant bassist, an unruly if highly original composer, and an eccentric, tyrannical bandleader, who fired musicians on the stand and lectured his audiences. Working for Mingus either made you or broke you: whatever happened, it was an ineradicable experience. Knepper lasted, off and on, for four years.

"The first Mingus rehearsal I went to was in his apartment, on Fifty-third Street," Knepper said. "I discovered he had a prejudice against writing his pieces down. Instead, he'd hum a few bars and say, 'All right. You got that?' Then he'd hum another few bars. It took hours and hours to learn anything, but there was an advantage to Mingus's method. When you see a bunch of triplets and dotted eighths and sixteenths on paper, you tend to read them mechanically, without getting the right emphasis and smoothness. Mingus gave you all that in his hums. I made my first record date with him, and I think we did 'The Clown,' then 'Reincarnation of a Love Bird' and the 'Haitian Fight Song.' We worked at the Vanguard and the Half Note, but jobs were spotty. We also recorded for Atlantic and Columbia. In 1960, Mingus got work in San Francisco, and we made a nightmare trip to the Coast. Roland Kirk and Doug Watkins and Dannie Richmond were in the band, and we went in three cars—a Buick convertible that Mingus wanted to sell on the Coast, because he thought he'd get more money for it out there; a Cadillac limo; and a Peugeot. Dannie Richmond drove by himself in the Buick, Mingus and I were in the Cadillac, and the rest in the Peugeot. When we got to the Holland Tunnel, Mingus asked the guy in the toll booth, 'How do you get to San Francisco?' The tollman said, 'Take the New Jersey Turnpike until it ends, the Pennsylvania Turnpike until it ends, the Ohio Turnpike until it ends, and the Indiana Turnpike until it ends. Then ask someone how to go from there.' When we got outside the city, Mingus said, 'Jim, you drive. I don't have a license,' and I drove most of the rest of the way. Right off, we lost touch with the other cars, and Mingus, accusing me of losing them on purpose, started saying things like, 'It probably makes you nervous driving in a caravan with a bunch of niggers.' But it went in one ear and out the other. If there is one thing I've never been hung up about, it's color. The trip took four days, and we only had three proper meals. The rest of the time we ate fried chicken and candy bars. We did two weeks in San Francisco and a week in L.A., and I quit.

"Except for a record date in 1961, I didn't see Mingus again until 1962, just before the disastrous concert he gave in Town Hall with that huge, thirty-piece band. He called me and said he needed help—would I copy some music for him? After I started, he said he also wanted me to write background figures, but I told him it was his music and he should do it, it should be his composition, and suddenly he called me a white faggot and punched me. I thought I'd better fall down in case he decided to hit me again, and I did. There was no blood, or anything, but he broke off a capped tooth in front and exposed a nerve, and of course I couldn't play. People told me I should do something, so I got hold of a musicians' lawyer, Max Cohen, and sued Mingus, and he was found guilty of criminal assault and put on probation. My teeth problems are still going on. For a long time, I had a removable steel bridge that hooked on to four top teeth. Now I have dentures on top and a fixed bridge on the bottom. I can push notes out, but I have trouble with slurs. And it's hard to play with a plunger mute, which puts pressure right up in your face. I didn't play with Mingus again until the late seventies, when he put together a group for the Newport Festival. I saw him for the last time not long before he died. He was confined to a wheelchair, and I learned later that he had told someone that I had more understanding of his music than anyone who had ever worked with him.

"Mingus talked a lot of nonsense about whites, but he married three white women, and he had great respect for white musicians like John LaPorta and Gil Evans and Lennie Tristano. People who knew Mingus for forty years said he was no good, but I liked him. He had trouble with black and white, and he was childish and all the rest, but he had exuberance and warmth. I have mixed feelings about Mingus's music. Some of the pieces, like 'Goodbye Pork Pie Hat,' are good, but a lot of the others are bullshit. He told me once that all he wrote was ditties. He said that Duke Ellington wrote compositions but he wrote ditties, and I think that—and his inability to complete many of the things he wrote—bothered him most of his life."

Two more musicians talk about Knepper. The first is the alto saxophonist Lee Konitz, who came up just after Charlie Parker: "Jimmy is still searching for ways to do better what he does. He was in my nine-piece band in the seventies, but I've had occasion to play with him one to one with just a rhythm section, and he was ready to mix it up and play counterpoint, or whatever. He was very adventurous. We rode together on the subway after the memorial service for Mel Lewis, and he wanted to know how to play free, without any underlying structure. He thought I had found a way to do that. I told him he was a moldy fig, and he laughed."

The second is John Lewis, who, in addition to being the leader of the Modern Jazz Quartet, is the musical director of the American Jazz

Orchestra: "Jimmy is one of the most meticulous musical people I know. His range of expression is wide, wide, wide. The wonderful notes he plays are not necessarily picked out of the chords. Chords are secondary to his musical ideas. We do a lot of repertory work in the orchestra, and when I give him a transcribed solo from an Ellington or Lunceford record he takes that solo and absorbs it and turns it into something new and beautiful."

The slide trombone is a bully, because of both its wayward tone and the constant challenge of finding the right notes with the slide, and it has dominated many of its players. Fighting back, they have cracked frenzied jokes on the instrument, making rude noises and elephantine slurs. Or they have attempted to tame it by making it sound limpid and honeylike (Tommy Dorsey, Lawrence Brown, Bobby Byrne). But Knepper, using little vibrato and no funny noises, sings on his instrument. He has an endless, uncontainable melodic river in his head, and it pours out through his trombone. He likes long phrases, some of them more than eight bars and made up of an intricate mixture of triplets and eighth notes, generally arranged comfortably behind the beat. These phrases often start in odd places and end in odd places, and this oddness is hypnotic. The notes he chooses are almost always surprising; they may be outside the chords of a tune or beyond its melody. Knepper's solos are delivered whole and at one volume and seemingly in one breath. He has never played a melodramatic solo in his life.

Knepper talks about his playing the way he talks about everything—laconically and as a matter of fact. "I have never been ambitious or goal-oriented," he said. "I've never beaten my own drum, or gone at the business of being rich and famous, or even just famous. I tend to work when I get called. Actually, the longest jobs I have had have been outside of jazz, in Broadway shows. I did about thirteen hundred performances of 'Funny Girl,' or three years and three months, and I did a year and three months in the revival of 'On Your Toes.' Getting that check every week was a pleasure.

"Improvisation is a great mystery. You play something, and you play an answer to it. Then you play something to wrap it up. Nothing is going through your mind; you're not thinking of anything. Every now and then, you surprise yourself. Where did that come from? So many musicians have told me that they learn the lyrics of the tunes they play, and the lyrics go through their minds when they improvise. I can't understand that. Lyrics would just get in my way. And I try not to think about the chords. I learn them, then I forget them. When I was coming up, I listened to Ray Nance and Sweets Edison and Buck Clayton. And to Lester Young and Charlie Parker, and to that monster technician Lawrence Brown. I used to transcribe Bird's solos and try and play them on my trombone. Lately, I've been working on a system of alternative positions on my slide. I play a harmonic-overtone series. Every note on the trombone is available in two or three places on the slide. If you're moving your slide out, it makes sense to keep going instead of pulling the slide back, then going out and in, out and in. Your playing is much smoother using the alternative positions. Of course, this system is chancy. Some of the notes in the alternative positions are slightly out of place, and there is always the possibility you will miss one. I'm a pretty good teacher, but I don't like doing it. Anyway, I can tell somebody everything I know in fifteen minutes.

"Musicians of my generation either are keeling over or have lost the spark. But I'll never retire. Last year, I appeared in public maybe forty days out of three hundred and sixty-five. You could say I'm in semi-retirement, but I'm a musician, so actually I've been semi-retired for the last forty years."

Joe Wilder

If you know what the beautiful, elusive sixty-three-year-old trumpeter Joe Wilder looks like—he is short, dapper, and dark, and he has a heavy, round head, with lamplike eyes and a wide smile—you might catch a glimpse of him in the pit band of "42nd Street." Or you might find him in the band that does the " Miss America Pageant" every year in Atlantic City. Or you might see him in one of Peter Duchin's bands, or in Dick Hyman's quintet. Or—this is rare—you might find him in a jazz concert or accompanying a singer in a night club or at a festival. Failing all that, you could at least hear him by buying, on the Concord label, "Benny Carter: A Gentleman and His Music" and "Hangin' Out: Joe Newman & Joe Wilder"—the first jazz recordings he has been featured on since the late fifties. Wilder was one of the earliest musicians to move easily between the world of straight music and the world of jazz, and he was certainly the first black musician to do so. He paved the way for Wynton Marsalis before Marsalis was born. He settled in New York late in 1947, and here is how he has divided his time since then:

"I joined Lucky Millinder at the Savoy Ballroom, then worked with Dizzy Gillespie for a short time. I went with Noble Sissle at the Diamond Horseshoe, and I got a call to do my first Broadway show. This was early in 1950. They were just beginning to use blacks in pit bands, and the show was 'Alive and Kicking,' with Jack Gilford and Carl Reiner. It ran six weeks, and I went back to Sissle and into 'Guys and Dolls.' Billy Kyle was on piano and Benny Morton on trombone. During the day, I attended the Manhattan School of Music, where I got a B.A. in 1953. I studied advanced technique with Joseph Alessi, who was the first trumpet of the NBC Symphony, and I studied orchestral repertoire with Bill Vacchiano, who was first trumpet with the Philharmonic. I played the First Brandenburg Concerto under Jonel Perlea, who had conducted at La Scala and was with the Met for a while. Later, I was first trumpet with the Manhattan Brass Quintet, and I soloed with the ABC Symphony. My great ambition was to be with the New York Philharmonic, but although I played with the orchestra several times, I never made it. In the early fifties, I'd done a couple of record dates with Billy Butterfield, who was working at ABC, and I guess he liked my playing, because he said he'd try and throw some studio work my way. He called in a couple of months, and I subbed for him on a radio show—this must have been in 1952—and Frank Vagnoni, who hired the musicians at ABC, told me he'd like to have me on call. In 1954, I went with Count Basie for four or five months, but it wasn't much of a challenge—mostly blues in different tempos. Then I did Cole Porter's 'Silk Stockings.' They checked with Porter to see if he minded having a black musician in the band, and he told them if I could play his music properly it was fine with him. I did 'The Most Happy Fella,' and meantime I was working as a sub at ABC. In 1957, I became a full-time staffer. l was with ABC until all the staff bands were cut out, in 1974. I was doing 'The Dick Cavett Show' with Bobby Rosengarden at the time. I kept studying. Since the studios have closed, I have done 'Lorelei,' with Carol Channing, and 'Shenandoah,' and I've been in '42nd Street' since 1981. I'm playing fourth trumpet, and that pleases me. I'm not as strong as I used to be. I can't endure that much steady blowing. I also made a lot of records during the ABC years. I recorded with Basie and Leonard Feather and the pianist Hank Jones. I did an all-star trumpet record on Savoy, and an old ten-inch L.P. on Bethlehem with the alto saxophonist Pete Brown. And I made my own records for Savoy and Columbia. I recorded with Benny Goodman, too, during a State Department tour of Russia with his band in 1962. In the late sixties, I recorded Alec Wilder's 'Sonata for Trumpet and Piano,' which he wrote for me in 1963."

Joe Wilder's jazz improvisations clearly reflect his classical training. He has a huge tone. It seems to spread as a solo unfolds, and it is equally generous in all registers. Jazz trumpeters often pay little attention to tone; their ideas, their emotions, and their stylistic leanings determine how they sound. But there are exceptions—among them Billy Butterfield, Bobby Hackett, and Charlie Shavers—and Wilder has learned from them. His solos move on a series of single-note planes that are divided by multinoted climbs or dives, by intervals, and by silences. There is a staccato feel to the way he phrases—a meticulous pushing of notes before him. He does not share the fashion among contemporary jazz players for the arpeggio and the fifty-note phrase. He is highly selective about his notes, and he gives them equal attention. He likes to play slow ballads, and he makes them into tonal excursions. His vibrato, generally smooth and tight, loosens, and he issues a river of sound guided languidly by the notes of the melody and by discreet bends and turns of his own. He makes the song gleam. His blues are sumptuous, too. He uses a lot of repeated riff-like phrases, and he applies a fretwork of half-valved notes, tremolos, trills, and growls. He often takes up a plunger mute on slow blues, and where Cootie Williams got an abrasive urgency with his plunger mute, Wilder gets a stately, oracular sound. When he plays up-tempo standards, his spacious, carefully weighed style sometimes stiffens: stateliness has its own pace. But his enfolding tone never falters.

Wilder is a gracious man who talks quickly, in a deep, hog-calling voice, and he laughs every other sentence or so. He talked of his playing and of his early days:

"Playing concert music demands great discipline. You can't be sloppy. You know what the repertoire will be for such-and-such a program, and you practice, then rehearse, and when the performance arrives you're ready. The emotional satisfaction comes from playing what is written as beautifully as possible. You tell the composer's story. When you improvise, you tell your own story. That is the great difference between the two forms. My jazz style stems largely from my concert background. Knowing something about composition helps, because you're composing when you're improvising. The melodic material determines to a great degree what I do. If it is simple material, I try and make it more ornate. If it is ornate, I try and simplify it. You try not to trample on a nice melody. You alter it here and there. Mistakes can swing you off into a wholly new direction, and often it is better than the one you were going in. I like to have the first two or three bars of a solo thought out, and sometimes what the soloist before me is doing determines that.

"My father worked both sides of the musical fence, too, and it was he who got me into music. I was born in Colwyn, Pennsylvania, which is on the outskirts of Philadelphia. We were one of six or seven black families in Colwyn, which had a lot of Pennsylvania Dutch. The biggest things in the town were the Fels-Naptha soap company and the Woolford Wood Tank Manufacturing Company. The air was generally full of the smell of the resin they used in the soap. My dad drove a truck for a stucco company, and when we moved to Paschall, next door to Colwyn, he drove a truck for a coal company. He also did odd jobs during the Depression. We generally ate, but he wasn't always successful. He had started as a cornet player. Then he took up the tuba and, finally, the bass violin. He played with the Cornucopia Masonic band and with the Philadelphia Rapid Transit band. There were two Transit bands—black and white. I remember the white band marching down Broad Street, at New Year's, with a full line of giant sousaphones coming at you like elephants. In the late thirties, he gave up truck driving and became a full-time musician. He worked in Philadelphia with Billy Kyle's little band, with Mme. Keene's band, and with Gertie Monk's band. She was a piano player and a cousin to Thelonious Monk, whose uncle, incidentally, was the first black policeman in Philly. My dad was in Mercer Ellington's first band in New York, in the forties, and somewhere along the line Duke Ellington wanted him. My dad was born Curtis Wilder, in North Carolina, in 1900, and he came to Colwyn when he was twelve. He pushed his age up and got into the Navy in the First War, and he was on the ship that brought James Reese Europe's band back from France. And he was in the Second War for two and a half years. He's taller than I am—about five-ten—and he weighs a hundred and seventy-five. He still lives in Philadelphia, and he's eighty-five but he looks sixty-five. He was somewhat stern as a father, and I can remember some of the talks he had with me. I must have got a swelled head once, because he said, 'You know, Joseph, there are many boys who play the trumpet as well as you do, and there will always be people who will play as well. You will never be one hundred per cent perfect.' And he was a stickler for promptness: 'Joseph, if you work at all you must be on time. It is better to be an hour early than a minute late.' He also told me that I didn't need drinking or drugs to play well—that, in fact, they had the opposite effect. He was right, of course, but as a result I kept away from the users and missed getting to know people like Charlie Parker well, which I regret now.

"My mother died in 1975, just before her seventy-third birthday. She was born in Philadelphia. Augustine Olive Brown. She was short and stout. She was a very good, natural person, and very gregarious. She loved to sing, and she encouraged my elder brother and me in music. She'd pull us back and keep us from straying off the path, and if she had to she'd come down on us physically. We lived in a row house in an integrated area in Paschall. We were all poor, and we got along very well. The Willahans, who were Irish, were behind us, and the Andersons, who were Scandinavian, were next door. The Carusos and the Casertas, who were Italian, were nearby, and so were the Kocherspergers. Mr. Kochersperger was an engineer on the B. & O. When he was going to bring a train through on the tracks that crossed the foot of our street, he'd tell us to be there with our buckets and he'd throw coal off for us, which helped with the coal bills. Whenever I hear any sort of racial ranting, I think back to those people, and they calm me down. My youngest brother, Edward, was in the Korean War, and he wrote me and told me what a hard time the Southern whites were giving him. I wrote back and told him to think about the Willahans and the Andersons and the Casertas. It must have helped. When he was wounded, a Southern white went up on the hill where he was shot and brought him down. There were four sons in our family. Curtis, Jr., was the oldest. He was a bass player, and he was charismatic, like my mother. He died of cancer, in 1963, and he was my best buddy. Calvin came after me. He was in the European Theatre in the Second War, under General Mark Clark, and he's a rigger in the Navy Yard in Philadelphia.

"My father started me on the trumpet when I was eleven. I studied with him first, then with Fred D. Griffin, who had also taught my father. Griffin was a black cornettist on the same level as such famous white classical cornettists of the time as Del Staigers and Walter Smith. Griffin played in marching bands, and he played solos with piano accompaniment on WCAU when they had ten or fifteen minutes of empty air time. The lessons I had with him were mainly physical. I'd play a wrong note and he'd whack me hard on the knee and yell, 'That's a D, not a C!' I studied with him two or three years at fifty cents, then a dollar a throw, which was a lot during the Depression. I also picked up things from Walter Freese, a classical trombonist who was a friend of our neighbors the Elliots. He'd hear me practicing and tell me to come over. I went to Tilden Junior High School, and the musical director was Alberta Lewis. She exposed us to light classical music and to marches, and we played in churches as well as at school. There was a children's hour sponsored by Horn & Hardart on the radio every Sunday morning, but all the kids on it were white. A couple of Philadelphia businessmen named Sam Kessler and Eddie Lieberman, who owned the Parisian Tailors, started a Sunday-morning program featuring black kids, called 'The Parisian Tailors Kiddies' Hour.' I was a regular on it, and I'd play a solo on a popular song. I didn't know a thing about improvisation, so I played absolutely straight. My father would go over the number with me the week before. The programs were broadcast from the Lincoln Theatre, where all the big bands played. Part of their contract was to accompany us on the program, since it was Sunday and they had no shows. When Louis Armstrong brought in his big band, he gave me a pass, and said, 'Kid, you're going to be a good trumpet player. You come and listen to me every day this week.' Well, I went once, and that was it. Louis didn't sound like Del Staigers or Walter Smith, so I wasn't interested. When the Mills Blue Rhythm Band came through, a member of the reed section saw how tarnished my brass cornet was, and he polished it until it gleamed. His name was Crawford Wethington, and I've been looking for him ever since to thank him. I hear of him once in a while, but we always miss.

"Alberta Lewis was responsible for getting me into the Mastbaum Technical High School, which was practically a music school. I studied with Meyer Levine and Ross Wyre, and they made me aware of all music. Ross Wyre made me listen to movie music. There was a beautiful trumpet solo on the soundtrack of a Glenn Ford movie, and it turned out to be by Manny Klein, one of the great trumpet players of all time. And Wyre taught me that you are never discourteous to a fellow-musician, no matter what blunder he commits. I listened to the bands on the radio—particularly to Gus Arnheim, who was my father's favorite, and to the Mexican bands on the shortwave. My father would tell me to study Arnheim's trumpets and the way the trumpets in the Mexican bands were double- and triple-tonguing. He would ask me what key Arnheim was playing this or that number in, and I got the answer right so many times we discovered I had perfect pitch. Around this time, my father would take me to hear a local dance band whose first trumpet was a friend of his. He wanted me to learn to read dance-band arrangements. He told me to sit by the second trumpet and listen to what he and the first were doing and, if I felt comfortable, to play along in the third-trumpet part. I can remember arriving one night and overhearing his friend say to the second trumpet, 'Here comes Wilder with that blamed kid again.' I started listening to jazz, too, and I worked in small bands around Philadelphia. I heard Dizzy Gillespie, who was in Frank Fairfax's band, and I heard Charlie Shavers with John Kirby. I'd hear little things that Shavers did, and I'd say to myself , 'Now, can I do that?' And I'd work and work until I had it. Charlie Shavers was one of the great trumpet players. There are players who have a certain spark, a first-class, never-fail ignition system, and Charlie was one. Dizzy Gillespie is another, and so is Clark Terry, and so was Fats Navarro. And Doc Severinsen and Freddie Hubbard and Clifford Brown, who died so young, and Bill Coleman, who was so lyrical and right. On the classical side, the never-fail players are Johnny Ware, with the New York Philharmonic, Raymond Crisara, who's a professor of music at the University of Texas, and Adolph Herseth, the first trumpet of the Chicago Symphony. And now there's Wynton Marsalis, who is phenomenal.

"While I was still in high school, I joined a local band called the Harlem Dictators, and on summer vacation we played in a hotel in Annapolis. We imitated everybody. The John Kirby band would come in, and I first met Charlie Parker. It was 1939, and we called him Indian, because he was sort of round and stiff, like a cigar-store Indian. He was very serious and was always studying music. After I graduated from Mastbaum, I got a call to take over the first-trumpet chair in Les Hite's band. He was on the road, in Lansing, Michigan. I was nineteen and reluctant to go. My mother came to the bus station to see me off, and I almost died. I was in my seat in the bus with the window open, and she was on the platform talking in a loud voice—'Now, you behave yourself out there, Joseph. Don't get into any foolishness, don't do anything to embarrass your family,' and on and on—with everybody leaning over and listening. I had a rough time in the Hite band at first, because I could sight-read real well and there was some jealousy. I had taught myself on the train going back and forth between Mastbaum and my home, which was about an hour's ride. But we soon got along. Dizzy Gillespie had had his famous run-in with Cab Calloway, and he joined the band. Dizzy and Walter Williams were the other trumpet players, and all they did was tell jokes, and sometimes I got laughing so hard I couldn't play. Dizzy replaced a trumpeter named Forrest Powell. He could play growl trumpet almost as well as Cootie Williams, but there always seemed to be something wrong with his chops. If we had a gig by the water, he'd say he couldn't play because he had by-the-water chops. At morning rehearsals, he'd have early-morning chops. Late at night, he'd get late-in-the-evening chops. After a year or so, I went with Lionel Hampton's band. It had Dexter Gordon and Joe Newman and Ernie Royal and Illinois Jacquet and Milt Buckner, but I was disappointed. I was still naive enough to expect a bandleader to lead. I got called up by my draft board in 1943, and I joined the Marines and went to Camp Lejeune. I was in Special Weapons for a while and then got into the post band. The singer Bobby Troup—Captain Troup—was the band officer, and I became the assistant bandmaster. I came out in April of 1946, a technical sergeant.

"I went back with Hampton, but I left after three months, when I had a chance to go with Jimmie Lunceford. He was intelligent and a fine musician and somebody to admire. He kept the band deportment at a high level. Anybody who drank on the bandstand forfeited the night's pay, and the money went into a fund that paid for a party at the end of the month. Lunceford died on the road, of a heart attack, at the age of forty-five, and they tried to keep the band going, but it didn't work. I left in New York, and joined Sam Donahue, in Washington, D.C. I replaced Doc Severinsen, and I was the only black. It was the happiest band I was in, and when there were racial incidents I felt sorrier for the rest of the guys than I did for myself. Some of the incidents were ludicrous. Once, in a night club down South, one of the trumpet players asked the girl photographer in the club to take a picture of the trumpet section. She refused, because of me. Well, they finally persuaded her, but the prints were all out of focus. I stayed with Donahue several months, and went on the road with Herbie Fields. Then I came back to New York for good, and joined Lucky Millinder. He was named Lucius, but he was called Lucky because he gambled all the time. When he lost, we didn't get paid.

"I have been married twice. I met my second wife, Solveig Andersson, when I was with Count Basie, and we were married in the late fifties. She is Swedish, and a lovely person. We have three girls. Elin is with a radio station in New York. Solveig is at college in the city. And Inga-Kerstin works on Wall Street. We moved into our apartment, up on Riverside Drive, when we were married, and I was the third black person there. But the building has gone down, and I might have to move out to Long Island. It's not what I want to do at all. It would be starting over again, and I'm very fond of New York City."

The Answer Is Yes

Jane Hall, the wife of the guitarist Jim Hall, is a slender, gentle, intelligent woman in her thirties. When she talks about her husband, she reveals a mixture of devotion and objectivity, and when she talks about herself it is as if she were telling a fairy tale. "I was born an only child in New York and grew up in Harrison," she says. "My father was in textiles, and he was a self-made man, who never graduated from high school. He loved golf and business and piano players like Fats Waller and Erroll Garner, although he came to appreciate the subtler sounds, too. He had a good sense of humor and was sort of a ham, and all my friends always wished he was their father. He was very different from Jim. Dad always wanted him to have more—more records, more fame, more money. But he realized Jim didn't have that kind of push. Just before Dad died, he said he wished Jim would be nicer to himself. It meant a lot to me—his appreciation of Jim's kindness and gentleness. My mother complemented my father. She was from a large family and was more reserved. She designed children's clothes before she married and gave up her career. But my father always relied on her taste. They were a striking couple together, particularly when they were dancing, which they loved.

"I met Jim in 1960. At the time, I was going out with Dick Katz, and one night when we were going to have dinner he brought Jim along. The only Hall I knew of in jazz was Edmond. I didn't see Jim again until the following winter. I was taking a night course at the New School, and I asked Dick if he'd babysit for Debbie, who's my daughter from a previous marriage. He brought Jim along again, and when I got home I discovered that Jim had somehow coaxed Debbie's dog out from under the bed, where she'd barricaded herself all day. We all sat around and talked for hours, and I fell in love. I'd never met anyone who *listened* like Jim. We started going out, but it was five years before we were married. Jim was very much against marriage. I went back to college in 1967 and graduated, and then I went to social-work school. I'm a psychotherapist at Greenwich House, and I have my own practice, too. Jim has been nothing but supportive and positive through it all. And that extends to my music. I write a couple of songs a year, and I sing. Jim accompanies me, and he's even recorded some of my tunes. He's helped bring out my musicality. He's done the same with Debbie. She plays piano, and Jim works with her. He's been a father to her, which is what she never had.

"One of the things that impress me about jazz musicians is their camaraderie. There's a complete lack of narcissism, of competitive feeling. I don't think the same warmth exists even in sports. Jim has a great kinship for his fellow-musicians. The first time he took me to the old Half Note to hear Zoot Sims and Al Cohn, he said, 'You have to listen. You can't talk while they play.' After the first set, Al told me that not only could he see me listening, he could *feel* me listening. I've thought a lot about the pressures on jazz musicians, too. Jim was scared to death at his first job after he'd quit drinking. But since then his playing has grown and grown. He surprises me every time I hear him. I used to listen to him with my eyes closed, but now I don't. Just watching him concentrating and so in tune with his instrument and with his listeners is an experience."

Hall, though, doesn't look capable of creating a stir of any sort. He is slim and of medium height, and a lot of his hair is gone. The features of his long, pale face are chastely proportioned, and are accented by a recently cultivated R.A.F. mustache. He wears old-style gold-rimmed spectacles, and he has three principal expressions: a wide smile, a child's frown, and a calm, pleased playing mask—eyes closed, chin slightly lifted, and mouth ajar. He could easily be the affable son of the stony-faced farmer in "American Gothic." His hands and feet are small, and he doesn't have any hips, so his clothes, which are generally casual, tend to hang on him as if they were still in the closet. When he plays, he sits on a stool, his back an arc, his feet propped on a high rung, and his knees akimbo. He holds his guitar at port arms. For many years, Hall's playing matched his private, nebulous appearance. When he came up, in the mid-fifties, with Chico Hamilton's vaguely avant-garde quintet (it had a cello and no piano), and then appeared on a famous pickup recording, "Two Degrees East, Three Degrees West," that was led by John Lewis and involved Bill Perkins, Percy Heath, and Hamilton, he sounded stiff and academic. His solos were pleasantly designed, but they didn't always swing. But as he moved through groups led by Jimmy Giuffre, Ben Webster, Sonny Rollins, and Art Farmer, his deliberateness softened and the right notes began landing in the right places. Then he married Jane, and his playing developed an inventiveness and lyricism that make him preeminent among contemporary jazz guitarists and put him within touching distance of the two grand masters Charlie Christian and Django Reinhardt. Listening to Hall now is like turning onionskin pages: one lapse of your attention and his solo is rent. Each phrase evolves from its predecessor, his rhythms are balanced, and his harmonic and melodic ideas are full of parentheses and asides. His tone is equally demanding. He plays both electric and acoustic guitars. On the former, he sounds like an acoustic guitarist, for he has an angelic touch and he keeps his amplifier down; on the latter, a new instrument specially designed and built for him, he has an even more gossamer sound. Hall is exceptional in another way. In the thirties and forties, Christian and Reinhardt put forward certain ideals for their instrument—spareness, the use of silence, and the legato approach to swinging—and for a while every jazz guitarist studied them. Then the careering melodic flow of Charlie Parker took hold, and jazz guitarists became arpeggio-ridden. But Hall, sidestepping this aspect of Parker, has gone directly to Christian and Reinhardt, and, plumping out their skills with the harmonic advances that have since been made, has perfected an attack that is fleet but tight, passionate but oblique. And he is singular for still another reason. Guitarists are inclined to be an ingrown society, but Hall listens constantly to other instrumentalists, especially tenor saxophonists (Ben Webster, Coleman Hawkins, Lester Young, Sonny Rollins) and pianists (Count Basie, John Lewis, Bill Evans, Keith Jarrett), and he attempts to adapt to the guitar their phrasing and tonal qualities. In his solos he asserts nothing but says a good deal. He loves Duke Ellington's slow ballads, and he will start one with an ad-lib chorus in which he glides softly over the melody, working just behind the beat, dropping certain notes and adding others, but steadfastly celebrating its melodic beauties. He clicks into tempo at the beginning of the second chorus, and, after pausing for several beats, plays a gentle, ascending six-note figure that ends with a curious, ringing off-note. He pauses again, and, taking the close of the same phrase, he elaborates on it in an ascending-descending double-time run, and then skids into several behind-the-beat chords, which give way to a single-note line that moves up and down and concludes on another off-note. He raises his volume at the beginning of the bridge and floats through it with softly ringing chords; then, slipping into the final eight bars, he fashions a precise, almost declamatory run, pauses a second at its top, and works his way down with two glancing arpeggios. He next sinks to a whisper, and finishes with a bold fragment of melody that dissolves into a flatted chord, upon which the next soloist gratefully builds his opening statement.

When the Halls were married, he moved into her apartment, on West Twelfth Street. It faces south and is at eye level with chimney pots and the tops of ailanthus trees. The off-white walls are hung with a lively assortment of lithographs, oils, and drawings. A tall cabinet, which contains hundreds of L.P.s, is flanked by full bookshelves. A sofa, a hassock, a fat floor pillow, a couple of canvas Japanese chairs, and a coffee table ring the window end of the room. An upright piano sits by the front door, and Hall's electric guitar rests on a stand by the kitchen door. Hall generally gets himself together around noon. He will sit down on the sofa with his back to the window and sip a mug of tea. Like many shy people, he is a born listener and a self-taught talker. He weighs his words as he weighs his notes. He speaks softly and has a mild Midwestern drawl. He had, he said, been pondering improvisation. "Somebody asked me once, 'Why do you improvise, why do you want to take a good song and change it?—and that stumped me. Maybe jazz musicians *are* egomaniacs, as Alec Wilder claims. Maybe they feel they're above the songs they play and that they have to improve them. I've always been of the notion—though most of my musician friends disagree with me—that 'Body and Soul, would never have been anything special if Coleman Hawkins hadn't made his record of it. Yet I believe I treat the tunes I play with respect, and I know I always follow the gist of their lyrics. Improvisation is just a form of self-expression, and it's very gratifying to improvise in front of people. I feel I'm including them in what I'm doing, taking them someplace they might like to go and haven't been to before. I like to draw them in, and if you can get an audience on your side, then you can finish a set with something abstract or different and they'll come right along. I like my solos to have a beginning and a middle and an end. I like them to have a quality that Sonny Rollins has—of turning and turning a tune until eventually you show all its possible faces. Sometimes I'll take a motif that I might have stumbled on while I'm practicing, and develop it throughout a solo. It's a compositional approach, and it helps you get control over your playing. But if a solo is going well, is developing, I let it go on its own. Then I've reached that place where I've gotten out of my own way, and it's as if I'm standing back and watching the solo play itself.

"When I do the melody of a tune, I try to make it come out mine. I also try sometimes to get the melody to sound as it would on a wind instrument, as though I've got the airstream of a saxophone or trumpet to hang on to. I think of the way Ben Webster played 'Chelsea Bridge,' with his fantastic sense of space and the way he'd let a note slide from sound to the breathing just below sound, and I'll go after that effect. I'm like Marian McPartland, I guess, in that I think of the keys in colors. A flat is reddish orange, G major seems green, E flat is yellow. I try never to bring distractions onto the bandstand, but if I do I know I always have a sort of floor to rely on. I know I won't ever really be terrible. Being tired doesn't seem to matter. I've seen guys on the road who were wiped out get up and play sensationally. Being tired seems to cut the fat and allow the musicality to come out.

"I've been playing a lot in duos with just bassists, and it involves a terrific amount of listening. I play off of the bass notes and try to make it always sound like a duet and not just guitar solos with accompaniment. All the accompanying I've done is a help, because accompanying is hearing the whole texture from top to bottom of the music around you and then fitting yourself in the proper place. When I was with Sonny Rollins, I found out right away he didn't like to be led, so I'd lay back a fraction of a second and let him show me where he was going and hope I could follow. When I was with Art Farmer, it was totally different. He liked the background laid down first, so he could play over it. And the whole timing was different, too. When I play behind Paul Desmond, it becomes a question-and-answer thing between us. But all you're trying to do is swing, and swinging is a question of camaraderie. You could be playing stiffly, but if everybody is playing that way the group will swing. But if one person is out of sync, is dragging, it feels like somebody is hanging on to your coattails."

Hall went into the kitchen to get another mug of tea, and when he came back a big gray-black cat appeared from the bedroom. It gave Hall three thunderous meows, sat down at his feet, and stared intently at him. It meowed three more times. Hall laughed and took a sip of tea. "O.K., Pablo. Cut it out. We didn't get him until he was a year old, and I think he was raised with dogs, because he's more like a dog than a cat. He greets me at the door when I come in and says goodbye when I go out, and he follows me around all day here. I was speaking of Ben Webster. After I finally left the Jimmy Giuffre Trio, in 1959, I went back to the Coast, and I was in a band Ben had with Jimmy Rowles and Red Mitchell and Frank Butler. We worked for a while in a club on the Strip called the Renaissance, and at first I didn't get paid. Then I think everybody in the band chipped something in. Anyway, Ben and I hung out a lot. He didn't have a car, and he lived with his mother and grandmother way over on the other side of L.A., but he'd never ask me to pick him up. What he'd do is call me whenever we had a gig and say, 'We'll meet at my house first.' I think his mother had been a schoolteacher. One evening when I went to get him, he was stretched out on the sofa snoring—the whole works. He must have been up all night, and we couldn't budge him. He had a reputation of taking a sock at whoever tried to wake him. So his mother and grandmother would lean over him and say, 'Ben, Mr. Hall is here and it's time to go to work,' and then jump back about two feet. I finally suggested that I get a wet towel or something, and they looked at me with their mouths open, and said, 'Oh no, he don't like *any* surprises.' Ben was very melodramatic, and he talked in that big voice just the way he played. Another time I went to get him he had a washcloth on top of his head and he was shaving. Some Art Tatum records were on and he kept running out of the bathroom and mimicking fantastic Tatum figures. Then he started telling me what Tatum was like—he loved to talk about the great ones he knew who were gone—and the next thing I knew he was crying. I never saw any of the meanness he was famous for, except once he fell asleep in the front seat of my car and when I woke him he cursed me. But the next minute he apologized.

"I had gotten to know John Lewis, and he called me about this time— it was the early sixties—and told me I had to come back to New York, that that's where it was at, and that I could stay in his apartment because he was away on the road so much. Well, I did for two or three months, and John loaned me money and everything. Then I sublet Dick Katz's apartment, and not much was happening. I felt I had a reputation by then, and I was too proud to call people about jobs. I did work in a duo with Lee Konitz opposite Miles Davis at the Village Vanguard when he had Cannonball and Philly Joe Jones and Bill Evans, and the audience would listen to Miles as if they were in church, and then talk all the way through our set, which was about the way everything seemed to be going for me then. Suddenly, I began getting notes from Sonny Rollins. He didn't have a phone and I never answered mine, so he'd stuff them in the mailbox, and I think the first one said, 'Let's talk about music.' He was coming out of a two-year retirement and was putting a group together, and he wanted me, in addition to Walter Perkins and Bob Cranshaw. We rehearsed afternoons at the old Five Spot, and at first it was a little mysterious. Sonny would let me in the front door with one hand and continue playing with the other, and then disappear, still playing, into a back room and stay there maybe a half hour. We opened at the Jazz Gallery, and it was a great success. But I had to put *everything* into it. I was with him off and on for over a year, and wherever we went he brought the house down. There was something about the way he got himself across to an audience, as if he were right out there playing into its collective ear. It was a great experience, a turning point for me. Then, in effect, he fired me. There were two reasons. One was musical. He wanted to experiment with Ornette Coleman's trumpet player, Don Cherry, and that was beyond me. The other had to do with a cover of *down beat*. It was a guitar issue, and they had me in the front of the picture with Rollins set behind, and the talk began. 'Why does he need a white boy in the group?' and the like, and Sonny would tell me in various ways that people were putting pressure on him to get rid of me, and that was it. Then I ran into him one night a while ago at a club, and when he was leaving he leaned over and said, 'Sometimes I lose touch with myself,' and that made amends. I've always felt that the music started out as black but that it's as much mine now as anyone else's. I haven't stolen the music from anybody—I just bring something different to it. After that, I joined a nice little group Art Farmer had, with Steve Swallow on bass and Pete La Roca on drums. But I was having trouble keeping things together. I had to concentrate on my work and I had to keep my drinking under control, which wasn't working too well. So finally, in 1965, I decided I had to get off the road after ten years and get things squared around. I came back to New York, started going to A.A., and Jane and I got married. I didn't want to go into night clubs again right away because of the atmosphere and the drinking, but I had to work, so I got a job in the band on the Merv Griffin Show. That was a shock. I'd felt, in my way, that I'd been doing something important all those years on the road, but suddenly I was like a stagehand. You're there in the studio but you're not there. It was very rare for any of Griffin's guests to acknowledge anyone in the band, and you'd think some of them would have known Bob Brookmeyer or Jake Hanna. I began to lose my identity. If I don't play what I want to play, improvise and all, I sink down. I forget I've ever done anything good musically at all. All the while, I was thinking about finally being a leader, and when I'd been with Griffin about three and a half years I got my courage up to go into clubs again, and I organized my own group. Clubs don't bother me too much now, but I only like to work two-week gigs and then regroup myself. I don't know why, but when I work it takes a lot out of me. I play every day here, I write some, and I have some students. With Jane working, we get along fine. Even so, I occasionally get in a panic. I wake up at night and think, What am I doing, what kind of a life is this? I've thought of giving it up and going into something else, but I know that would be crazy the minute I pick my guitar up again. So when I ask myself, Am I going to want to go into saloons and play guitar when I'm fifty or sixty or seventy, the answer is yes."

The telephone buzzed. "That was Jimmy D'Aquisto, out in Huntington," Hall said when he hung up. "He's a great guitar-maker, and he's made me my acoustic guitar, which is the first new guitar I've had since I was a kid. I got my old Gibson, over by the kitchen door, second-hand from Howard Roberts, on the Coast, in 1955. Jimmy has done some experimenting. The body, or box, of the guitar is a little thinner than usual, and, to compensate, the front and back of the box are arched a little more than usual and the f holes on either side of the tailpiece are bigger. He's strung it with lightweight steel strings, but I'm still experimenting with different weights. And he has kept the bridge low, which makes the strings more responsive. Most important, he hasn't put any electrical stuff on it. I've used it twice in public—at concerts at Yale and the New School. The Yale thing was a kind of shakedown cruise because the acoustics where I played—it was a church—were so strange. But I felt good about it at the New School. In that auditorium the sound creeps along the walls and gets everywhere, and even though I didn't use a mike, I think they heard me in the back. It's such a beautiful instrument. Unlike most guitars, it just doesn't have any bad spots. It's still strange to me. The dimensions are different enough so that it takes me a while to warm into it."

The telephone buzzed again, and Hall went into the kitchen, after he finished talking, to make a drink of one part grape juice and two parts 7Up. The sun was pell-melling in the window, and he lowered the venetian blind. "Jack Six just called. He played bass with Dave Brubeck three or four years, but we've been doing duets recently. We've got a gig coming up at Sweet Basil, so I thought it would be a good idea to practice some. He's on his way from Jersey right now.

"My mother gave me my first guitar for Christmas when I was ten. I was living with her and my brother in Cleveland. I was born in 1930, in Buffalo, but we only stayed there a few months and then came to New York for a while and moved out to Geneva, Ohio, where my Uncle Russell had a farm. He was one of my mother's brothers, and he had taught himself electronics. Her other brother, Ed, taught himself guitar and how to make blueprints. He'd play things like 'Wabash Cannon Ball.' I spent a year on Uncle Russ's farm. I was about seven or eight, and I remember the whole time as being dark. There was no electricity in the house, and one of my chores was to take the cinders out. I got some in my eyes once and for two weeks I couldn't see. Then I knocked over a kerosene lamp, which scared the hell out of me, but luckily it snuffed out when it hit the floor. Uncle Russ was married to a strange woman then, and it was the old story of the wife upsetting the husband, who then takes it out on the kids. By this time, my mother and father had split up, and she and I and my brother moved to Cleveland. We lived in rooming houses and my mother supported us. She worked as a secretary at a tool company. It's funny how your perspective changes when you get older. It seems amazing to me now to be in your twenties—which she was then—and to be raising two boys by yourself. I don't remember much about my father, except that he played tennis and managed a grocery store for a time and was a travelling salesman in stainless steel. I never see him, but I think he's alive. My mother lives in Los Angeles. She's active and vivacious, a short, blond lady, kind of sparkly and with a lot of guts. Around 1940, we moved into a brand-new W.P.A. housing project in Cleveland, and we stayed there until I went to music school. It was the first place we'd lived in that no one had lived in before. It had an upstairs and a downstairs, and I think the rent was twenty-four dollars a month.

"It took a year to pay for my guitar, but I lucked up with a good teacher, Jack DuPerow, right away. He had me do scales and guitar arrangements of poptunes. My favorite was 'Music, Maestro, Please!' The accordion was big in Cleveland. In fact, the first group I worked in had accordion, clarinet, and drums, and we played dances on weekends. The clarinet player was into Benny Goodman, and he played Goodman's recording of 'Solo Flight' for me, with Charlie Christian featured, and I thought, What is *that*? It was instant addiction. I bought a 78-r.p.m. album of Goodman Sextet numbers even before I had anything to play them on. By this time, I was studying with Fred Sharp. He had played in New York with Adrian Rollini and Red Norvo, and he introduced me to records by Carl Kress and Dick McDonough and Django Reinhardt. Taking Charlie Christian and Django together, I've hardly heard anything better since, if you want to know the truth. But a lot of my listening was not to guitarists but to tenor saxophonists and pianists. I had Coleman Hawkins' 'The Man I Love' and 'Sweet Lorraine,' with Shelly Manne and Oscar Pettiford, and I had the Art Tatum Trio. I'd listen to them in the morning after my mother had gone to work, because she wasn't too much on jazz then, and I'd think about what I'd heard on the mile walk to school. George Barnes had an octet with a woodwind feeling that broadcast regularly, and all the bands played the Palace Theatre there—Duke Ellington and Artie Shaw, when Shaw had Roy Eldridge and Barney Kessel. I began hanging out with older local musicians when I was fifteen or sixteen—Tony DiNardo, a tenor player who sounded like Lucky Thompson and who got me listening to Lester Young, and Billy DiNasco, a piano player who loved Mel Powell and Teddy Wilson and who worked out a way of his own that was like Lennie Tristano. We had our own group, and we called it the Spectacles, because we all wore glasses. We sang four-part vocals, and they were my first arrangements.

"I did well in high school, and when I graduated I decided to go to the Cleveland Institute of Music. I thought learning more craft would help. I went for four and a half years, and I majored in music theory. I wrote a string quartet for my thesis. I played guitar on weekends, but I wasn't all that involved in jazz. I thought I was going to go into classical composing and teach on the side. Then in the mid-fifties, halfway through my first semester toward my master's, I began thinking two things: I was with people who did nothing but go to school and would probably do nothing else, and I knew I had to try being a guitarist or else it would trouble me the rest of my life. My decision was made for me. Ray Graziano, a good local alto player, was driving a Cadillac—a lavender Cadillac—out to the Coast for somebody, and he asked me if I wanted to go along. I had no money, but I knew Joe Dolny, a Cleveland trumpet player, out on the Coast, and I also knew I could stay with my great-aunt. She was in her nineties, and had lived in Hollywood from the time it was clapboard houses and fields planted with peas. So I quit school, and there we were, driving through all these little towns in that lavender Cadillac, with me in the back seat playing and playing. I moved in with my aunt and got a job in a used-sheet-music store, and I studied classical guitar for a while with Vicente Gomez. Joe Dolny had a rehearsal band at the union hall, and I met a lot of people there like John Graas, the French-horn player. I'd go to his house, out in the Valley, and he recommended me to Chico Hamilton for his first quintet, which had Buddy Collette on reeds, Freddie Katz on cello, Carson Smith on bass, and Chico and me. I got ninety dollars a week, which was a fortune then. I was with Chico for a year and a half, and a lot of good things happened, even though that bass drum of his began getting in my dreams. I met Red Mitchell and Herb Geller and Bill Perkins and John Lewis. When Chico's group went East for gigs at the Newport Festival and in New York, we worked opposite Max Roach's group at Basin Street, where I met Sonny Rollins. That was some experience—being up on the stand and looking out and seeing all your idols staring at you. Then we drove back to the Coast, and it was a weird trip. Chico was the only black man in the car, and he never got out of it. He stayed curled up like an animal in the back seat, and we'd bring him his food. What with one thing and another, but mostly Chico's bass drum, I left and went with Jimmy Giuffre's new trio.

"I was with this group for two different periods, the first starting in 1957. In between came a low point that matched my time with Merv Griffin. I went on the road with Yves Montand. What saved me was that Edmond Hall and Al Hall were both in the tour, too, and I had the chance to listen to them reminisce and to ask Edmond about Charlie Christian, because he had recorded with him. In fact, they were the only records Christian made on acoustic guitar. Before I went back with Giuffre, I toured with Ella Fitzgerald all over South America. I finally jumped ship in Buenos Aires, where I stayed six weeks. The bossa nova was coming up, and one night I went to this big room filled with guitar players. They sat in a circle and passed a guitar around like a peace pipe, and everybody played. I didn't know what to do, so I played a plain old blues. One of the good things about being on the road in other countries is you're not just a tourist, you're something a lot better, something special, and I've made friends all over the world."

The doorbell buzzed, and Jack Six came in, carrying his bass and towing an amplifier on wheels. Six is a big man with a Southern accent, and he and his equipment filled one end of the living room. After Six unpacked, hooked up, and plugged in, Hall whacked one thigh with a tuning fork and rested its handle on the body of his old Gibson. Six tuned up to its silver hum. Hall spread sheet music on the dining-room table, and the two men bent over it in silence. They looked as if they were examining illuminated manuscripts at the Morgan.

"Let's play Janie's tune 'Something Tells Me,'" Hall suggested. "But we'll do it as she wrote it. She's got a couple of modulations in it which make it difficult to sing, so she sort of leaves them out when she's singing it around the house. Who would you say she sounds like, Jack?"

"A cross between Astrud Gilberto and Julie London."

Hall laughed, and sat down on a red kitchen stool. He played quiet, open chords as he went into the graceful, succinct melody. Six came in behind with offbeat notes. The music immediately transformed the room, filling it with motion and purpose. Hall improvised a chorus replete with silences, retards, and quick sotto-voce runs. Six soloed, grunting softly, and the two went out with some lilting counterpoint. A "Chelsea Bridge" reverberating with Ben Webster came next, and was followed by a fast, tricky Jim Hall blues, "Two's Blues." It has a complex, backing-and-filling melodic line, and the first run-through had many bugs.

"Anyway, that's the general idea of it," Hall said, laughing.

"My, those notes certainly go by fast,', Six replied. "It's like Jake Hanna said to the new man on the band after he'd messed up at his first rehearsal: 'I didn't know you couldn't read.'"

After three more tries, the blues fell into shape, and they played another Hall blues—a slow one, called "Careful." Hall said he had written it a long time ago as a "Monk thing." It has an ostinato bass, which the two musicians handed easily back and forth. They had just started "Emily" when the front door opened and Jane Hall came in. She was dressed in a blue pants suit, and she was carrying a bag of groceries, which she set down on the music. There was a round of pecks. She asked how everything was going, and Hall said good and that maybe it was time for a breather. He went into the kitchen to make some grapejuice-and-7-Ups. He set the drinks on the coffee table, put his arm around Jane's shoulder, and gave it a squeeze. Then he sat down next to Six on the sofa. He smiled up at Jane as she passed the drinks and said, "So, did you save any souls today?"

An Insouciant Sound

The pianist Marian McPartland likes to do a little writing on the side, and in 1987 she gathered thirteen of her appreciations and published them in a book called "All in Good Time." One of the best chapters, written in 1960, is about the alto saxophonist Paul Desmond. It was a pioneering, restorative essay. Desmond, a member of the immensely popular Dave Brubeck Quartet since 1951 and a steady winner of the *down beat* readers' poll since 1955, had been temporarily eclipsed by a Charlie Parker soundalike, Cannonball Adderley, and by the avant-gardist Ornette Coleman, and no one had yet written about Desmond with any perception. McPartland made it clear that he was a writer manqué who had become a jazz musician almost by accident, that he was the only major alto saxophonist of his generation who had not modelled himself on Parker, and that he was witty, original, and elusive. The little there is on

Desmond's early life in her chapter is about as much as he ever gave out. He was born Paul Emil Breitenfeld on November 25, 1924, in San Francisco (and died of cancer in 1977 in New York). He took his nom de saxophone from the telephone book. (He said Breitenfeld sounded "too Irish.") His father was German and played the organ in movie theatres, and his mother was Irish and had a literary bent. He loved his father and tolerated his mother. When he was five, his mother became ill, and he was sent to relatives in New Rochelle. He played a solo on chimes at a school assembly, and, instead of following the notes in front of him, he improvised. "It was the first thing I'd enjoyed doing," he told Marian McPartland. "I was kind of a walking vegetable as a kid. Amiable but unfocussed. I didn't realize until about fifteen years later that you could make a living doing this." He returned to San Francisco in 1936 and took up the clarinet and, several years later, the alto saxophone. He spent three years in an Army band in San Francisco during the war, and studied writing briefly at San Francisco State College. He and Dave Brubeck first played together in 1943, and Desmond claimed that this colloquy took place:

Desmond, after hearing Brubeck, who tended to play way out: "Man, like Wigsville! You really grooved me with those nutty changes."

Brubeck: "White man speak with forked tongue."

Desmond and Brubeck met again after the war, in the Geary Cellar in San Francisco, and Desmond described their second encounter this way: "The musical rapport was very evident and kind of scary. A lot of the things we've done since, we did then, *immediately*—a lot of the counter-point things, and it really impressed me. If you think Dave plays far out now, you should have heard him then. He made Cecil Taylor sound like Lester Lanin." Brubeck worked briefly for Desmond (who concluded that he was not cut out to be a leader), Desmond worked briefly for Brubeck, and in 1951 they started the Quartet. They made three live recordings on a small label—"Jazz at Storyville," "Jazz at Oberlin," and "Jazz at the College of the Pacific"—and they caught fire. Columbia Records signed the Quartet in 1954, and it became the most commercially successful jazz group in history. (George Avakian, the jazz scholar and A. & R. man, was working for Columbia at the time, and in July of that year, during a bus ride from New York to the first Newport Jazz Festival, he said that Columbia was trying to decide whether to sign the Brubeck Quartet or the equally new, though not yet successful, Modern Jazz Quartet. The golden remains of the Brubeck group were long ago cast upon the shores of jazz—it disbanded in 1967—while the M.J.Q., going on forty, continues on its subtle, classic, imperturbable way.)

In its final form—Brubeck, Desmond, Gene Wright on bass, and Joe Morello on drums—the Dave Brubeck Quartet was one of the curiosities of jazz. Brubeck and Desmond were opposites. Desmond had a light, ethereal tone, and his solos were lyrical and singing and beautifully con-structed. Brubeck, who had studied with Darius Milhaud and had dreamed of fusing jazz and classical music, was a heavy, erratic, passionate player who depended on repetition and difficult harmony for his effects. He could build a frightening rhythmic momentum with figures of almost no musical interest. Desmond was a blue summer day; Brubeck was thunder and lightning. Yet each man insisted that he would never have got anywhere without the other. Brubeck said Desmond was the best saxophone player in the world, and Desmond said, "I still feel more kinship musically with Dave than with anyone else." The critics loved to jump up and down on Brubeck, and, assuming guilt by association, they tended to dismiss Desmond, too, or take him for granted. (He only won a *down beat* critics' poll once, though he won the readers' poll eleven times—a rare intance of the public's having better ears than the professionals.) Although Desmond managed on occasion to free imself of Brubeck's rhythmic weight, his best recordings were made in duets with the guitarist Jim Hall or with the baritone saxophonist Gerry Mulligan.

Many of Desmond's closest friendships were made after the Brubeck group broke up and he settled in New York. (He had a one-bedroom penthouse on the northeast corner of Fifty-fifth Street and Sixth Avenue.) At the age of forty-three, he more or less retired. He made some festival appearances, went to a Brubeck reunion, and took sporadic jobs with Jim Hall in New York and with the guitarist Ed Bickert in Toronto. He was intelligent and social, and much of his time was spent, Scotch in hand, at Elaine's or Bradley's, talking and listening, and living a fine eighteenth-century life.

Jim Hall has said of Desmond: "I met Paul in the fifties in Cleveland when I was still a student and he came through with Dave Brubeck. But I feel like I've known him all my life. When he was around so much in the sixties and seventies, he'd come over nearly every week to play Scrabble with my wife, Jane. They were so good I just watched. He also played chess, and the piano in his apartment was covered with chessboards. He liked longstanding comical situations. Every time he ate at the French Shack, around the corner from his apartment, he and one of the waiters would get into a thing about the pronunciation of 'vichyssoise.' He loved a paperback book called 'Tops in Pops.' It had stuff on Fabian and Chubby Checker and Elvis and Anita Bryant, and the writing was awful. He'd buy a dozen copies and give them to his friends, and he'd call up— 'Hi, it's me, Desmond'—at all hours and read passages from the book and laugh. And, of course, he'd walk a mile for a pun, like the one he'd invented about all those models who eventually marry rich guys: 'This is the way the world ends,' he'd say. 'Not with a whim but a banker.' And he loved to josh people. He made several records with George Avakian, who tended to do a lot of telephoning in the control booth. Once, he and I finished a take and looked up at the booth to see what Avakian's reaction was. He was on the telephone, so when he hung up Desmond went out in the hall and called him from a public telephone. 'Hi, George, it's Paul,' he said. 'How was the last take?' He always seemed to be around lively people—bright, sparkly people. He was a no-fooling good musician, who could improvise the most gorgeous melodies—some were better than the originals. He also played the piano, and he was pretty good. After he got sick, he had a roadie who came in and did some cooking and let people in and out. One afternoon, when he was sleeping off a chemotherapy session, Charlie Mingus came to see him. Mingus was big then, and he was wearing a black cloak and a big black hat, and he sat down in a chair in Paul's bedroom and waited for him to wake up. When he did, Paul said he looked over and saw this huge black form sitting there and thought, 'Oh, God. This is it. They've come for me.' He's heavily missed. The trouble is, he would have made a great older person."

Desmond became a regular at Elaine's, at Eighty-eighth Street and Second Avenue. He and the writer Jack Richardson were good friends. "I met Paul around 1968," Richardson has said. "We had dinner together a couple of times a week, generally at Elaine's or Bradley's or Casey's. He was a wonderful person to spend time with in a saloon. He loved language, and he got off great one-liners. His social life was spent more with writers and such than with musicians. You'd find him at Elaine's with Bruce Friedman or Frank Conroy or Gay Talese. Elaine's is a strange place. There can be a kind of superficiality there in the talk about writing and art. But everyone always agreed that Paul was one of the few true artists who hung out there. He was a magical presence. Paul implied that he had led a rather puritanical life with the Brubeck Quartet, and that he was going to make up time by indulging in every sort of depravity. He was a good drinker, but he sometimes drank too much and had to be helped home. And he used to dabble in cocaine, which he had come to late in life. He had countless women friends, but he never had a steady girl. I think women had a quasi-custodial relationship with him, nursing him through illnesses and bad hangovers. I felt he was very lonely, that he had a great deal of sadness in him.

"He didn't like to talk music with non-musicians. I passed, because I played a little guitar. In fact, he was so distressed after he heard me play he sent me to Jim Hall for lessons. Paul knew his virtues and his limitations. He had never followed in Charlie Parker's footsteps, but I remember once when we looked at a transcription of some fantastic Parker solo, Paul said, 'My God! That's not human!' I asked him once why he had stayed with Brubeck so long, and he gave two reasons: that he had no head for money and Dave handled all the financial things, all the headaches about leading a group and carrying it around the world; and, second, that Brubeck, being so different, set him off, gave him a frame to stand out against. He felt that when he and Jim Hall played together they were so similar, so simpatico, they were in danger of evaporating. His cancer was diagnosed about a year before he died, and his main concern seemed to be that his illness not cause any embarrassment or dislocation among his friends. And it never did. He handled his affliction with grace and delicacy and unselfishness to the very end."

Desmond's humor was slightly arch, self-deprecating (always the sign of a true sense of humor), punning, and full of hyperbole. Here are some samples:

When he was once asked about his delicate, dry tone, he replied, "Well, I had it in mind that I wanted to sound like a dry Martini."

He liked to call himself "the J. P. Marquand of the saxophone" and, because he detested fast tempos, "the world's slowest alto player."

When he played with unsympathetic musicians, he said, he tended to "shrivel up like a lemoned clam."

On his own reputation: "I was unfashionable before anyone knew who I was."

On Ornette Coleman, who arrived in New York in 1959 and turned the jazz world on its ear: listening to Coleman, whom he admired, was "like living in a house where everything's painted red."

After he settled in the city: "Somemes I get the feeling that there are orgies going on all over New York, and somebody says, 'Let's call Desmond,' and somebody else says, 'Why bother? He's probably home reading the Encyclopedia Britannica.' "

On why he never became a writer: "I could only write at the beach, and I kept getting sand in my typewriter."

But Desmond *could* write, as is clear in some of the liner notes he set down for his own albums and in the only chapter he completed of a book he planned to write about his life with the Brubeck Quartet. The book was to be called "How Many of You Are There in the Quartet?" and the chapter appeared in Punch. It deals with two concerts the group gave in one day at a state fair in Middletown, New Jersey, and it closes with these four paragraphs:

> The main events of the fair have clearly been planned for months: a flaming auto wreck, followed by a flaming plane wreck, each to be dealt with instantly and efficiently by the Middletown Fire Dept. At one end of the oval is a precariously balanced car; at the other end, a truly impressive skeletal mockup of a single-engine plane, tail up. Midway, at ground zero, is the Middletown Fire Truck, bristling with ladders and hoses and overflowing with volunteers.
>
> A hush falls over the stands. At a signal given by the fire chief, the car is ignited. The truck reaches it in two or three seconds, by which time the fire is roughly equivalent to that created by dropping a cigarette on the back seat for two or three seconds. It is extinguished by many men with several hoses.
>
> A murmur falls over the stands. The fire chief, painfully aware that his moment of the year is at hand, signals for the plane to be ignited, also instructing the truck to take it easy, so that the fire should be blazing briskly when it arrives. The truck starts, at about the pace of a cab looking for a fare. The plane goes WHOOSH!, like a flashbulb, and by the time the leisurely truck arrives, has shrunk to a lovely camp-fire' just large enough for roasting marshmallows.
>
> Later, four pasty-faced, grim-eyed men pile into a station wagon and drive away. It may not be a bank-robbery, but it's a living.

Desmond was tall and thin. He had a narrow face and receding dark hair, and he wore black-framed glasses with heavy temples. When he played, he stood motionless, his saxophone held straight up and down, as if he were carrying a flagpole. When he had finished a solo, he would (in his Brubeck days) lean against the crook of the piano, his hands folded over his saxophone (still held close to his chest), his expression bemused and pleasant. The A. & R. man John Snyder recorded Desmond, and he has said, "Paul had a slow way of talking, an almost singsong way. He had a low-pitched voice, and he talked like he'd always had a drink, like he had a smoking jacket on. Everything he said was insightful. He laughed a lot—a bark, a smile, then the laugh. His playing was similar. He had a kind of languid way of playing. There's a slowness in the tone, in the notes themselves. It's an insouciant sound, and it has a timeless golden color. He staked out a lyrical territory that was all his own. And he was a master of interpolation. He'd add bits and pieces of the countless songs he knew to his solos, piecing them together in such a way that they commented on his surroundings or on an experience he had just had. And he did it in a cool way. He was never a showoff."

Despite his placidity, Desmond had a temper. The great drummer Joe Morello has recalled his own early days with the Quartet: "I joined the Quartet in October of 1956 and stayed until it broke up. I had been in Marian McPartland's trio at the Hickory House, on Fifty-second Street, and Dave and Paul would come in to hear me. I'd also been to hear them, and I had trouble with their rhythm section. Then I got a call from Brubeck asking me if I'd like to join the Quartet, and would I meet him at the Park Sheraton to talk about it? I told him that I didn't play the way his drummer played, that I didn't know if I'd enjoy the group or they would enjoy me, that I might not last a week. But we agreed I'd try it, and we opened at the Blue Note, in Chicago. Before we went on, Dave told me he'd be glad to feature me. I did a little drum solo in the second set, and there was a big ovation, and Paul stamped off the stand. Afterward, he said, 'Morello goes or I go.' Dave calmed him down, but, what with the ovations I kept getting, Paul and I didn't talk much for the first year or so. We never came to blows, as the press said we did, but there were times when I think we felt like it. Paul would tell me that if I kept my left hand at my side and just played quarter notes with my right hand everything would be O.K. Or he'd tell Dave after a set, 'My last solo would have been perfect if Joe hadn't put that accent in the last bar.' Or he'd tell me that if I didn't stop setting such fast tempos he'd take a full-page ad in *down beat* saying 'Paul Desmond does not play fast tempos.' Then the discomfort ended, and we practically became a clique. I think it all changed after Paul wrote his big hit 'Take Five' and realized that the tune itself, not my drum solo, was getting the ovations.

"Of course, Paul would get upset with Dave, too. Sometimes Dave would get too busy behind Paul's solos, and Paul would ask him to lay out, and if he didn't Paul would walk off the stage. He always had books with him, and he was a speed-reader. He liked to dramatize things. We were on a plane once to someplace like Afghanistan, and a dove got out of a crate and started flying around the plane. The next day, when he told the story, Paul had birds flying all over and goats running up and down the aisle. After work, we'd go to the nearest lounge or bar to have a drink and relax. But sometimes I went by myself, and the waiter would come to my table and say, 'The gentleman over there would like to buy you a Martini.' It would be Paul. I'd send him a Scotch in return, and we'd wave."

The critic and editor James T. Maher had dinner one night at Bradley's with Alec Wilder and Desmond. "The talk turned to improvisation," Maher said later. "There were two Alec Wilders when it came to improvisation .One was in complete awe of it, and the other got upset if a singer changed as much as a note of one of his songs. So Desmond said, 'Well, you know, the best chorus is the song itself.' That was a real shot in the arm for Alec. When I first heard Desmond, I said to myself, 'I wish that guy would play with more feeling.' Years later, I said to myself again, 'What did you mean by "feeling"?' He kept the song singing. He was a born singer. And it was all in those absolutely pure melodic lines."

When Desmond was coming up, he listened to such alto saxophonists as the huge, jumping Pete Brown; Willie Smith, of the Jimmie Lunceford and Harry James bands; and Duke Ellington's Johnny Hodges. Most true originals absorb their models so thoroughly they can flawlessly reproduce them, or even parody them. During the seventieth birthday party the White House threw for Duke Ellington, in 1969, Desmond, a member of the all-star group that performed in the East Room, reproduced Johnny Hodges so perfectly during one of his solos that he startled the usually unflappable Ellington. Desmond's line about wanting to sound like a dry Martini was funny but inaccurate. A dry Martini has a sharp, edgy taste, and if it had a sound it would be hard and metallic. Desmond's tone was off-white, gentle—almost transparent and almost weightless. It had a brand-new, untouched sound. He used very little vibrato, and he tended to stay in the upper half of his range. There was nothing vocal in his playing, as there was in Charlie Parker's and Ben Webster's. He did not preach, or moan, or shout. Desmond's solos *thought*; they had logic and clarity. He improvised melodies that were straightforward but intricate; his phrases, never breathless, would sometimes go on for sixteen or more bars. The quietness of Desmond's attack was deceptive, and gave a conventional, even timid, air to what he played. But he always moved along the outer edges of the chords he was improvising on, atonality in sight. His rhythmic attack was equally deceptive. He gave the impression of sailing along endlessly in an easy four-four, but he continually altered his time. He played behind the beat, on the beat, and ahead of the beat. He halved the tempo and doubled it, or he floated, using no tempo at all. Like his friend Jim Hall, Desmond was one of the handful of jazz improvisers who demand total concentration. If the listener falters, he is lost; if he remains rapt, he is blessed.

Noel Silverman was Desmond's lawyer and business protector during the last two years of his life. "It took a while to get to know Paul and realize how complicated he was," Silverman has said. "Paul had no paranoia, like so many musicians do. He regarded the music business as the way of the world, not something organized against him. He could be immensely personable when he wanted. He was not shy. He simply didn't go out of his way to get involved in social situations he wasn't sure of. He liked sociable people, and he liked his Dewar's. By and large, he was an excellent drinker. Liquor didn't often defeat him. It was a lubricant, a way to camaraderie. He never lacked for smart female company. I think he had been married once, when he was very young, but he never talked about it.

"I suggested to him three or four months before he died that he make a will. He had no parents, no brothers or sisters, no aunts or uncles. He did have some Breitenfeld cousins that he liked and saw once in a while. I asked him if he wanted to leave something to the Brubecks, and he laughed and said they should leave something to him. But he did leave his saxophone to Michael Brubeck, one of Dave's sons. I asked him if he wanted to establish a scholarship fund for musicians, and he said no, there were already enough bad saxophone players. I asked him what he wanted to do with his piano. It's a nine-foot Baldwin. He and Dave Brubeck had each bought one years before. He said, 'Would it be possible for Bradley Cunningham to have it for his saloon?' Paul and Bradley had closed Bradley's on many, many nights, and Paul felt that the old upright Bradley had had there for years was demeaning to all the great pianists who had to play it. So there Paul's piano sits, in all its much appreciated grandeur. Then I asked him about the rest of his estate, the income from records and from songs like 'Take Five,' and he said, 'Give it to the Red Cross, they're a good outfit.' I don't have the exact figures before me, but I think the Red Cross has received over a million dollars since 1977. I'm beginning to think it's time, in fact, for it to make some sort of public recognition of Paul's generosity, instead of writing me little thank-you notes. Paul wasn't rich, but he was comfortable. I remember when he was in Mt. Sinai I took him a whole bunch of checks and we laid them out on his bed. We added them up, and they came to around a hudred thousand dollars. He laughed and said, 'Well, I don't have any financial problems.' "

When Marian McPartland finished her 1960 piece on Desmond, she showed it to him, and he said he liked it. "But, Marian, do you think it might be better to start it this way? Do you think we could take that story about Brubeck out, and put in this one?" And on, until it had become a kind of McPartland-Desmond piece. But they were always friends. "I used to ask Paul to sit in with me when I was playing in the Bemelmans Bar, in the Carlyle," she has said. "He promised that he would, but he never did. He'd just hang out and have a few drinks. The last time I saw him, he stopped by when he was quite far along with his chemo treatments. I was very pleased to see him about, but shocked at how thin he was. He had a drink, and after I had finished we went over to Elaine's. She had a piano way in the back, and I sat down and played all kinds of tunes that Paul loved. He was determined to keep his life as usual, and he just sat there serenely. He died alone in his apartment on the Memorial Day weekend of 1977. It seemed to me that he didn't want to upset his friends, and so he waited until they had all left town for the holiday weekend. His cleaning woman found him Monday morning."

Here and Abroad

The lucent and eloquent flugelhornist Art Farmer settled in Vienna in 1968, and is one of hundreds of American jazz musicians who have lived abroad during the past sixty or so years. This emigration began in April, 1919, when the Original Dixieland Jazz Band, a stiff ragtimey group from New Orleans, landed in London. Two months later, Will Marion Cook arrived there with his large and impeccable Southern Syncopated Orchestra, which was notable mainly for its single hot soloist—the great clarinettist and soprano saxophonist Sidney Bechet. Between 1925 and 1931, Sam Wooding toured Russia, most of Europe, and parts of South America. He took with him, at various times, the reedmen Gene Sedric, Jerry Blake, and Garvin Bushell, the trumpeters Doc Cheatham and Tommy Ladnier, the trombonist Herb Flemming, and the pianist Freddy Johnson, who in the early thirties taught some of the secrets of jazz to French musicians and to the critics Hugues Panassié and Charles Delaunay. Some of the other jazz musicians who had visited Europe before the twenties were out were the trumpeters Arthur Briggs, Muggsy Spanier, Johnny Dunn, and Henry Goodwin, the clarinettist Buster Bailey, the saxophonists Bud Freeman and Adrian Rollini, and the drummer Dave Tough. (In 1926, the legendary pianist Teddy Weatherford sailed west instead of east, travelling from Chicago to China and eventually ending up in Calcutta, where he died, in 1945.) Brighter and brighter American stars travelled to Europe in the thirties. Louis Armstrong played London in 1932 and 1933, then lolled around Paris, resting his lip. Fats Waller recorded in London. Duke Ellington, and Coleman Hawkins and Benny Carter arrived not long after. Lucky Millinder took his big band over in 1933, and it included the trumpeter Bill Coleman, who spent most of the next fifty years in France. In 1937, the trombonist Dicky Wells arrived in Paris, with Teddy Hill's band, and recorded a dozen numbers, using Coleman and Django Reinhardt. Some of the other American jazz musicians who travelled in Europe during the thirties were the pianists Herman Chittison, Ram Ramirez, and Joe Turner, the violinist Eddie

South, the trumpeters Valaida Snow, Bill Dillard, Bunny Berigan, and Shad Collins, and the drummers Tommy Benford and Kaiser Marshall. Since the Second World War, Europe has been flooded with American musicians. Among those who have stayed there for varying periods are Sidney Bechet, Don Byas, Mary Lou Williams, James Moody, Kenny Clarke, Albert Nicholas, Peanuts Holland, Kansas Fields, Mezz Mezzrow, Bud Powell, Horace Parlan, Keg Johnson, Ed Thigpen, Oscar Pettiford, Dexter Gordon, Art Taylor, Chet Baker, Stan Getz, Ben Webster, Joe Newman, Johnny Griffin, Slide Hampton, Patti Bown, Idrees Sulieman, Benny Bailey, Ted Curson, Mal Waldron, Tony Scott, Red Mitchell, Kenny Drew, Roswell Rudd, Ernie Wilkins, Richard Boone, Joe Albany, Steve Lacy, Thad Jones, and Art Farmer.

Farmer passes through New York about three times a year, and one afternoon, in a friend's apartment, he talked about his life here and abroad. He recalled New York as it was when he first settled here: "I left Lionel Hampton's band in 1953 and moved into the Maryland Hotel, on West Forty-ninth Street. New York was incredible then—your whole waking life was music. I worked Monday nights at Birdland, and I worked for Lester Young. He called me Pres, which was his nickname, and he called other people Lady, which was short for Lady Day, his nickname for Billie Holiday. He was a very quiet, soft guy. I was late a few times, and he said, 'Pres, the man is getting on me. I don't want to hear any strife. I want everything nice. You dig, Pres?' He even wore soft shoes, and when he finished his solo and moved away from the microphone he moved sideways, and then stayed in one spot bouncing up and down in time. One night, he leaned over and said, 'Pres, there are two ladies out there shooting me down. They don't realize that I just want to go home after work.' Of course, he had his own language. 'Take another lung' meant take another chorus, and 'the George Washington' was the bridge of the tune. He was still playing beautifully. Every note meant something, and when I followed him I felt like a fool if I didn't make sense. He made me tighten up and tell a 'story' in each solo. He always said a soloist should tell a story. When I wasn't working, Miles Davis would rent my horn for ten dollars a night. His was pawned, I guess. I'd go wherever the gig was—Hackensack or Brooklyn, or wherever—to make sure he didn't pawn mine. Sometimes he'd come around when I *was* working and give me a hard time: 'Man, you're supposed to rent me that horn.' 'Miles, I'm working.' 'Man, you always rent me that horn for ten dollars.' 'Miles, I have a gig.' And on and on. In 1956, I joined Horace Silver's first quintet, and stayed for a year or two. Then I went with Gerry Mulligan's quartet, which was a shock. Silver is a strong piano player whose accompanying pushes you this way and that, and to suddenly find yourself in a pianoless group was like walking down the street naked. There was nothing between you and the ground except the bass line and Mulligan's occasional backup riffs. I did a lot of avant-garde stuff on the side during this period—with Teddy Charles and Teo Macero and

George Russell. I got the reputation of being able to play anything, so when the music was on the verge of being abstract they'd call me. I recorded for Blue Note and Savoy and Columbia and Prestige and ABC-Paramount. I worked with Thelonious Monk, and I worked with Coleman Hawkins. I recorded for Jackie Gleason. In 1959, Benny Golson and I put together our Jazztet, with Curtis Fuller on trombone and McCoy Tyner on piano. We never got to a very successful point commercially, but the group stayed together off and on about three years. In the early sixties, Jim Hall and I had a quartet, with Steve Swallow on bass and Pete La Roca on drums. Jim is amazing. I could go in and out of the chords, up and down the chords, and he instantly knew what to do. Whatever I played, he was there. By the middle sixties, rock was beginning to be felt, and the bottom was falling out of jazz in New York. The only place someone like me could get work was at Slugs', in the East Village, or the Five Spot, on Third Avenue, or maybe out in Brooklyn. There were also a few places in Boston and Baltimore and Chicago. But that was it. Eddie Bert, the trombonist, told me about the pit bands, and I ended up in Elliot Lawrence's band in 'The Apple Tree,' on Broadway. I had gone to Europe several times in the early sixties, and in 1965 Friedrich Gulda, the Viennese pianist, asked me to be one of the judges of an international competition of young jazz musicians. It took place in Vienna, and while I was there I heard about a radio jazz orchestra that was being formed. They needed a trumpet soloist, and the job was for ten days a month nine months of the year. Considering the way things were here and that my whole life had been lived for the possibility of playing jazz music, I decided to give it a try for a year. It worked pretty well, and in 1968 I gave up my apartment on Twentieth Street and moved to Vienna."

Farmer's face is big and square, and he has large, wide-set eyes and a long, rectangular mustache. His narrow shoulders fly out at right angles from his neck and form one of the narrow sides of the rectangle that is the rest of him. He has beautiful large hands with long, squarish fingers, and his deep, hidden voice sounds as if it were coming from a cave. He is a careful speaker, and his words pass in review as they are released. He is in very good shape. A year or two ago, he took off thirty pounds, and a couple of years before that he quit smoking and drinking. He used to think he couldn't play without drinking; now he couldn't play and drink. It took him a long time to become a first-rate jazz musician. This, he said, is how he began:

"I was born August 21, 1928, in Council Bluffs, Iowa. There were three of us—my sister, Mauvolene, who is two years younger, and my twin brother, Addison, who was born an hour after me. Addison became a bass player, and he died in New York very suddenly of an aneurism in 1963. I still dream of him. We're sitting together and talking, and everything is the way it was. It seems there's a part of him I haven't fully gotten over. My father was James Arthur Farmer, but I have very little memory of him. He and my mother were divorced when I was four, and he died not long after in a steel-mill accident. Around this time, we moved with my grandparents to Phoenix. We moved there because my grandmother suffered from asthma. My grandfather was a minister in the African Methodist Episcopal Church—the A.M.E.—and we lived in the parsonage. He died when I was eight. I recall that he was very lively and agile. He could hold a broomstick parallel to the floor and jump over it. My grandmother was the first black woman to graduate from an institute of higher learning in Iowa, and she started a night school in Phoenix for blacks. She was part Blackfoot Indian—her mother, who had supposedly escaped a massacre, was all Blackfoot. My mother's name was Hazel Stewart, and she was born in Cincinnati. She was short and a little darker than me, and she was very strong. She was also kind and even. She was quite solid in form, but got thinner and smaller as she got older. She played the piano and sang gospel in church. I'd go to the church with her when she practiced, and when she was finished I'd get on the stool and play. My family was full of doctors and lawyers and teachers and ministers, and most of them played music for a hobby. One was a professional—Kenneth Stewart, a cousin of my mother's, who played trombone in Chicago in the thirties with Earl Hines and Sammy Stewart. A cousin born the same day I was took up the horn, but he got the call and gave it up.

"I went through grammar school and the first three years of high school in Phoenix. I started the piano in grammar school and, a little later, took up violin. A tenant we had gave me a violin he had in his trunk. He said to hold the neck of the violin just as if you were picking a pear from a tree. I got so I could play 'Humoresque' and 'Minuet in G.' Then I joined a marching band run by a Catholic priest named Emmett McLoughlin. I had played some bugle for flag ceremonies at school, so they gave me a sousaphone—it surprised me, because it had a mouthpiece as big as a coffee cup. I played that for a year; then they switched me to cornet. I had the mistaken idea that the cornet would be as easy as the tuba, but then I thought I had already mastered the piano and the violin and the tuba. So my ego wouldn't let me put it down. The school system in Phoenix was segregated, and there was no one in our environment who could give me lessons. All the lady in charge of music in our high school ever said to me was 'You play more wrong notes than anyone I ever heard.' I did teach myself to read music pretty well, and when I was about fifteen I joined a high-school dance band led by a tenor-saxophone player named Wesley Dotson. We used stock arrangements taken from Basie and Ellington and Lunceford, with the solos written in. We heard the big bands that came through on one-nighters—Tiny Bradshaw, Erskine Hawkins, Lunceford, Harlan Leonard, Artie Shaw. Shaw arrived for his gig a day ahead and he had Barney Kessel and Roy Eldridge with him. We were playing in some little joint, and Roy sat in on drums. Later, he played trumpet with us. I was too ignorant to appreciate how great he was. The trumpeters I listened to were Harry James and Dud Bascomb, who was with Erskine Hawkins. We also heard the 364th Infantry Regiment dance band at the Papago Park army base, near Phoenix. George Kelly, the tenor player with the Savoy Sultans, was in it, and he'd come by our rehearsals. Once, he wrote out an arrangement of Duke Ellington's 'Azure' for us. He was a kind man. But I have never yet heard an older musician tell a younger musician who asked for help, 'Go away. You're bothering me.' Our average age in the band was sixteen or seventeen but we had ambitions to go on the road, and when Jimmy Lunceford came through we managed to meet him and he gave us the name of a booking agent in Los Angeles. We wrote him, but he never answered. By this time, I knew I had to be in jazz. Two things decided me—the sound of a trumpet section in a big band and hearing a jam session. I had to be a part of those two things, and nothing else in life was that attractive.

"The summer after the third year of high school, Addison and I went to Los Angeles to look around, and we got involved in so many things we decided to stay. We met Hampton Hawes and Sonny Criss and Eric Dolphy. Our mother said, 'All right, but I want you to finish high school.' We got a room and enrolled in Thomas Jefferson High. The big bands were still going, but a lot of the best players were in the service, so we were able to get jobs we ordinarily couldn't have gotten. We went with Horace Henderson and Floyd Ray and Jimmy Mundy. Between times, we worked in a cold-storage warehouse, stacking crates of Idaho potatoes. Sometimes there was no work of any kind, but it was 'If we don't eat today, what the hell—we'll eat tomorrow.' We met Charlie Parker. I can't remember a bad experience with him. He always paid Addison back when he borrowed money. He'd stay here, there, everywhere. He slept on our couch for a while. He and Addison and I would walk up Central Avenue and wangle our way into movies that were half over, and one time we stopped at an after-hours place called Lovejoy's, and Bird sat in with this real poor piano player. I told him later that I was surprised he had done that, and he said, 'You take every opportunity you can.' I made my first trip to New York with the drummer Johnny Otis, who had a big band at the Club Alabam in Los Angeles. We were on the same bill at the Apollo Theatre with Louis Jordan and His Tympany Five. Jordan was very big then, and we were doing seven or eight shows a day. I had developed bad musical habits. I was using the strong-arm method, jamming my horn into my lip to get high notes, and I was making a terrible hole in my lip. I was playing fourth trumpet, and at the end of the first week I could no longer get a sound out of the horn, and Otis had to let me go. Everybody hung out on a corner of a Hundred and Twenty-sixth Street and Eighth Avenue, and the trumpet player Freddy Webster told me I should take some lessons from a teacher named Maurice Grupp. I took one, and told him I had to go home, because I didn't have any money. He said it was essential for me to stay and continue lessons. I got a job as a night janitor at the Alhambra Theatre. I made twenty-four dollars a week.

The lessons were eight dollars, and my room, at a Hundred and Twenty-ninth between Seventh and Lenox, was six. Grupp's studio was on Seventh Avenue in the Forties, and after I'd been to him I'd hang out in the jazz clubs on Fifty-second Street. I met Dizzy Gillespie, and he said he was looking for a trumpet player who could play a real singing lead in his big band, and was I interested? He had John Lewis and Ray Brown and Milt Jackson, and I sat in for three or four nights. Dizzy told me after the last night that he was sorry but the guys in the band thought I was not quite ready. A job opened up with Jay McShann, and we toured all over the South and the Southwest before ending up in Los Angeles.

"Young black musicians caught hell in Los Angeles in the late forties and early fifties. White musicians had the work at the few clubs sewed up, and it wasn't easy getting into the studios, even if you were good enough, which I wasn't. I was scuffling, real hard. I was a hotel janitor and a file clerk at County General Hospital. But I still managed to play with all sorts of people—Benny Carter and Gerald Wilson and Dexter Gordon and Wardell Gray. Wardell, who'd been with people like Benny Goodman, was a big brother to me. Then Lionel Hampton came through, and I was offered a job, even though he already had five trumpet players. Wardell told me I'd be making a mistake if I took it—that they didn't play anything but 'Flyin' Home' and 'Hamp's Boogie-Woogie.' But Lionel was a gift to young musicians, and I learned things in that band I couldn't have learned anywhere else. Also, night after night Hampton played things himself that really got to me. Clifford Brown was in the band, and Quincy Jones and Gigi Gryce and Alan Dawson. There was a brotherly spirit, and we laughed a lot at the crazy things Hampton did. At the Band Box in New York, he had us dressed in shorts, and part of our act was to march out to the street, playing. One night, he tried to march us into Birdland, which was next door, but the doorman wouldn't let us in. We went to Europe in the summer of 1953, and when Hampton found out that a bunch of us had made some records on a Swedish label he blew up and told us that we'd get thrown out of the union and that he'd take our passports and our tickets home—all of which was nonsense. Another time, he got mad about something and he walked up and down the aisle of our bus for at least half an hour cursing each of us out. Then suddenly he said, 'Good night, Gates,' sat down, and went to sleep."

Farmer's style is spare, lyrical, logical. It is descended from Fats Navarro and Miles Davis, and perhaps it has been tinted by such older trumpeters as Emmett Berry and Shorty Baker. It is built on silence. The silences may occur three or four times in a solo and will last from one to three beats. They gather what has come before, and prepare us for what is to come. They let Farmer's improvisations breathe, and they let us breathe. His style is also built on his tone, which has always been rich, even impenetrable. It has been even richer since he switched from the trumpet to the flugelhorn, in the early sixties. The flugelhorn resembles a large cornet and sounds like a deep, soft trumpet. Some flugelhornists seem to sink into their own sound, but Farmer has lost none of his agility and sharpness of attack. Indeed, he is more agile than he was twenty years ago, and so has run counter to the usual jazz brass player's progress from youthful floridity to middle-aged compression. He has no vibrato, and his notes emerge measured and almost clipped. He likes intervals and will easily jump or fall an octave. He likes to repeat phrases, changing a note or two each time, and he likes to enliven things with quick, slanting interior runs and occasional upper-register blasts. He is a gentle, highly melodic player whose solos, with their steplike phrasing and sotto-voce passages (he has a sharp sense of dynamics), suggest sunlight on water: the blue light from the sky is the original melody, the reflected light his improvisation.

Farmer talked about his playing "You have to learn how to use your strength properly if you are a brass player. You have to get your energy into the horn. It is not a question of the size of the player or his air capacity. You have to use your stomach muscles so that all the air gets squeezed into that tiny hole in the mouthpiece, and none of it leaks out the side. That's the most important thing about playing a brass instrument, and once you solve it you can go on to the nuances. Good tone is based in part on the size of the mouthpiece. A lot of young trumpeters use a shallow mouthpiece, which gives them a penetrating sound and makes it easier to hit high notes. A deep mouthpiece gives you a broad, warm sound, but you have to build up the muscles around your mouth to get the high notes. I switched to the flugelhorn to get the right sound. Before, I was hung up all the time trying to get that sound out of my trumpet, and ignoring everything else. Of course, you can go a little crazy on the subject of tone. I have a friend who collects trumpets and flugelhorns, and sometimes I go to his place and try different mouthpieces with different horns, and pretty soon I don't know how anything sounds. So many things go into good tone—the amount of air you put into the horn, the mouthpiece, the condition of your embouchure, the way you feel, and certainly the place you're playing in. A good room or good hall can be an extension of the horn. A bad room or hall can wipe everything out.

"When I was learning to improvise, I'd take solos by Dizzy Gillespie or Fats Navarro off records and place them against the chords to see what they were doing. Now you can go into a music store and buy books of transcribed solos, and your work is done for you. My goal is not to think about the chords of a tune at all—have them second nature, have them stored in my bones. But this gets more and more difficult, because chords seem to have more and more notes. Also, the tunes that people write now come in all kinds of weird shapes—forty bars or fifty or ninety-six, and the bar lengths may be uneven. I rarely know what I'm going to do in a solo more than a measure or two ahead, and what I do may be inspired by a note the bassist plays or by some figure the drummer gets off. You can never force what you're doing. The harder you try, the less happens.

At the best times, it's as if you had been taken over by some other power. This power plays you, and you become the instrument. There are dangers everywhere in improvisation—cracked notes, forgetting a chord, having the bassist or drummer play something you don't like, hearing a loud conversation. All these things can be like a slap in the face. Of course, totally pure improvisation is very rare. Most solos are made up of old elements newly arranged. This is true of even the masters. I worked opposite Louis Armstrong once, and after the first few nights I discovered he played almost the same solo on the same songs night after night. But he somehow made the solo sound new each time. When I'm home, I practice four or five hours a day. I start with exercises aimed at the problems of range, endurance, sound. Then I do intervals and scales. Then I play songs, sometimes by myself, sometimes with tapes. I warm up for an hour before a gig. Your horn has to be warmed up, your body has to be warmed up, your lips have to be vibrating a certain way. If the horn has that proper singing sound, it leads to good things, to good improvisation. It opens your mind to creativity.

"I have a special soundproof room in my house in Vienna to practice in. I live with my wife, Mechtilde Lawgger, and our thirteen-year-old son, Georg. We live in a kind of row house that we built. It's in the city proper, in one of the green belts near the beginning of the Vienna Woods. It is very green, very desirable. If someone asks me where I live and I say the Eighteenth District, they say, 'Oh, *ja, ja.* Good air, good air.' The schools in Vienna are excellent, and I would never move Georg here, because of that. He doesn't get home until five or six every night, and then he has a couple of hours of homework. My wife helps him, or else he would never be able to keep up. Vienna has an element of stability that I think has improved me as a musician. I lead a very quiet life there. I'm an introvert and kind of reclusive, and I'm perfectly content to stay at home. I play in three or four different clubs in Vienna. I work with local rhythm sections in England and Brussels and Holland and Paris and Switzerland. The pay has improved, and is just about equal to what you get here. The people who go to jazz clubs in Europe tend to be more informed than they are in America. They come to hear you only if they like you, and they listen. The only drunk I can remember was in a Swedish club. They removed him once, twice, and the third time they took him and his chair outside. That did it, because the place was packed and there wasn't an extra chair in the house. I'm in Vienna about a third of the year, and the rest of the time I'm on the road—in Europe, in the United States, in Japan. Vienna is full of chauvinism. There is a common feeling that if something doesn't happen in Vienna it's not worth happening at all. There are more songs about the glories of Vienna than about any other city in the world. And everybody has a title, a rank. If you have two doctorates, you are called Doktor Doktor. These titles are put right on the mailboxes. I have no title, but I am very well known, and I feel I have the respect of the people.

"I have not had a single bad racial experience since I have been in

Europe. No one has been rude, no one has ignored me, as people will do here if they don't want to serve you or sell you a ticket, or whatever. There has never been the slightest trouble with hotels or restaurants, although there is now a slight surliness in the air in London. Sometimes people stare at you in remote Austrian towns, but they stare at you the same way they would stare at a car they had never seen before. It is always something of a shock to come back here, because nothing has changed much. The same hangups are there. A person who plays jazz can go anywhere else in the world and never feel like a stranger. There are always people who know who you are even if they have never heard you. There are always people who want you to feel at home, who want to do things for you. I can play the tiniest European town and be recognized. In an American town of the same size, or even in a good-sized American town, I would be unknown."

Herr Professor

The Arkansas pianist Walter Norris passes through New York once or twice a year. He has lived in West Berlin since 1977, and since 1984 has been a guest professor at the Hochschule der Künste, where he teaches piano improvisation. Before that, he was the pianist for the Sender Freies Berlin, a radio studio orchestra. "My friend Rolf Ericson, the Swedish trumpeter, told me about the job with the S.F.B.," he said once when he was here. "I wanted to go back to Europe, where I had been just twice. I knew it would change me and my playing. I knew the job would include improvising as well as playing everything that was put in front of me. I knew the pay was good. I also knew I would have a first-rate concert grand to work on and one of the world's best piano technicians to take care of it. A bad instrument confuses and disorients you. A sensitive instrument brings the music out differently—you can do almost anything. What I didn't know was that I would also have at my disposal a two-metre Bösendorfer and a private, locked room to use it in. Nor did I know that the first year there would be only seventy-nine days of work, leaving the rest of the time for practicing. The work varied constantly. One day, it would be with the full orchestra, and the next with a smaller group with French horns, and the next with the orchestra and a choir. The marvellous thing was that you were physically surrounded by all that music—a luxury that overdubbing has just about eliminated. At the end of 1980, they discontinued the orchestra, and I free-lanced around Europe. Then I was asked to teach at the Hochschule, which is a conservatory for the arts. I had forty-two students this year. I gave most of them a private one-hour lesson each week. Then I met with everybody for two

two-hour classes, in which the students play for each other and I comment. I was going around the clock. The work almost killed me, but I
loved it. I've always tried to work myself to death, just as my mother did
before me. I live in the center of town, on the same street as the
Hochschule. Berlin is a pleasant place. Everything is new. Everything
works. The streets are safe. I was first married in the fifties, and I have
remarried. My wife is French and has a Dutch name—Marie-Rose van
Deinse-Norris. She's a violinist in the Theater des Westens orchestra. She
has two sons, who are both very talented jazz players. It's mostly all work
for us, but I play with the two of them when we have time. I used to do
my bookings in New York, but it's difficult when you're on the other side
of the ocean. A couple of years ago, a man named Bob Schillin called
when I was here and asked me if he could be president of the Walter
Norris fan club, which he was starting, and I told him he was elected.
Eventually, he began to do some booking for me. He lives in New Jersey
and doesn't have many contacts with New York clubs, but he perseveres,
and things work out."

On this visit, Schillin got Norris into a club on the upper East Side, into
a club in Greenwich Village, and into a club in SoHo. The first and last
engagements worked out well, but the Greenwich Village job was difficult—although Norris never let on in his playing or his demeanor. The
piano was out of tune, particularly in the higher registers, and Norris's
bassist had his amplifier turned up. Norris has a delicate, spidery touch,
and, caught between the piano and the bass, he sounded like a remote
and almost inaudible radio broadcast. But enough of his playing came
through. He admires Art Tatum and Bud Powell and Charlie Parker, and
he also admires Dinu Lipatti and Vladimir Ashkenazy. His style is light
and electric. He likes fast tempos, Art Tatum runs, and staccato, half-time
Billie Holiday ritards. He likes to take his left hand off the keyboard and
play long, winding, intricate single-note lines with his right hand, sometimes a cappella and sometimes in counterpoint with the bassist. Then
he'll drop his right hand into his lap and let his left hand loose. The
bassist Red Mitchell, who first heard Norris in California in the
mid-fifties, spoke of him the other day. "He is obsessed by music,"
Mitchell said, "and playing a good instrument is part of that. Your
instrument is an extension of your arms and legs. Walter practices with a
metronome. He's after perfection. You have to have flawless time when
you play with him. There aren't many bassists who at some point don't
rush the tempo or slow it down. But if you meet Walter on his level it can
be great fun. You don't have to think about one, two, three, four. The time
just sits there and never changes. But Walter is not a machine. He is a
super, gentle person, a lifetime friend. I was taken with his soulful touch
when I first heard him."

Norris talked about himself before his first set at the Greenwich Village
club. He is an imposing figure. Thin and slightly over six feet, he has a
large, professorial head. His hair is grayish and receding, and his face is

composed of square, flat sure faces, like a late Cézanne landscape. He keeps his eyes narrowed, and he speaks quickly, leaving nice pauses. His voice is high and slatey, and still has its Arkansas edge. "I teach my students the musical rules," he said, "but I do it as we go along, almost indirectly. For assignments, I might ask them to work on a harmonic sequence—say, a ii-V-I progression—and be able to sing all its parts. Or do a Bach two-part invention by playing the right hand and singing the left, then reversing the procedure. Or I might give them rhythmic exercises to be played against a metronome. Or I might ask them to learn a piece in all the keys. I want them to be able to play any interval in a chord and be secure, and I want them to be able to play in any rhythm or at any speed and be secure. Finally, I want them to develop a sense of coloring and dynamics—important refinements that many jazz pianists ignore. Then, after all this, I tell them not to think. I ask them when they are improvising to concentrate on their breathing—in-out, in-out—and not on what they are playing. So much improvisation is intuitive. I learned that by listening to street-corner singers in Little Rock when I was a kid. They would scat-sing or cup their hands in front of their mouths and pretend they were trumpets or trombones. They were very good, and they didn't know an A from a C. Maybe they only used three or four notes, but they realized that when they hit a wrong note all they had to do was move up or down a half tone to be in the right place. I tell my students to compare the cave paintings with modern art. The cave painter had the same talent as the modern painter. And there's every chance that there were musicians and singers in the cave painters' tribe who were just as good as the painters.

"Of course, jazz improvisation is not unique. Improvisation of some sort keeps resurfacing. We know that Bach improvised, and apparently Beethoven was a way-out improviser, a kind of charter Parker-Coltrane. Mendelssohn improvised, and so did Czerny and Chopin. And Rachmaninoff and Prokofiev. And Art Tatum worked things the other way around. The drummer Billy Exiner told me that he heard Tatum get a Chopin étude down letter-perfect in one hour. When I improvise, I let the harmonic vibrations pull me into the harmonic center of each number. I do not think ahead. It's an unnecessary distraction. I have to use my thinking energy for each instant, for what is coming out. It's my belief that every note we have ever played is programmed in our subconscious, and that when we play the subconscious clicks on and notes come out in combinations that we may have used before or that may be close to those combinations. Our task is to alter those patterns and make something new in the instant they hit the ear—or even before. We must play the way Picasso painted—in one continuous improvisatory motion. But eventually improvising has to be regarded as spiritual, as beyond ordinary secular knowledge. I am skeptical about any musician over forty who is not spiritual."

Norris settled into his first set with two rich ballads, "The Best Thing for You" and "Never Let Me Go." Both began a cappella and ad lib, then went into tempo. Norris's a-cappella chords were loose and spacious; they seemed to rain on the melody. He did a fast "I Get a Kick Out of You," a digging, sombre "Lover Man," and a fast number of his own, "Spacemaker." He hums a rough melodic counterpoint to what he is playing, and he moves constantly. Sometimes his hand shoots into the air at the end of an arpeggio, and when he goes into a fast tempo he jiggles and shakes and looks as if he might fly apart. He wears heavy aviator glasses, but midway in the set he took them off. He also removed his jacket and loosened his tie, folding the jacket and putting it on the piano next to the music rack—an echo of the way the old stride pianists used to fold their coats inside out, so that their sensational custom-made linings would knock their listeners' eyes out. When the set was over, he put his jacket on and straightened his tie. He cleaned his glasses, and ordered a cup of coffee. "Once, in Los Angeles, I went to hear Art Tatum at a club not far from where I was working," he said. "The piano he was playing sounded wonderful. The day after, at a jam session at the same club, I played that piano, and it was horrible. It was out of tune, and the action was unbelievable. I went back that night to hear Tatum, and the piano sounded perfect again. He transcended any piano. His mind went into it and made it sound wonderful. Playing this piano reminds me of what a perfectionist my mother was. She'd stand behind me, and when I made a mistake—*whack*! across my shoulders with a switch. I did progress rapidly, but I already had music in me, and I think I would have progressed anyway.

"I was born in Little Rock on December 27, 1931. On a Sunday. I was an only child who always wished he had brothers and sisters to make up a rhythm section or horn section to play with. My father came from a village in northeast Arkansas called Poughkeepsie. He worked for the Federal Reserve System. He was mild-mannered, and he had a natural understanding of other people's situations. He could always see clearly both sides of a problem. He was not an intellectual, but I think he would have liked to be one. When I was five years old, he began to teach me not to be prejudiced. Little Rock was integrated in the sense that there were white sections and black sections side by side. My father told me that the black people wanted to eat and have a place to live in and raise their children in, just as we did. He said that if black people got hurt the pain was the same as the pain we felt. He said that if something bad happened to a black child the parents felt the same sadness that he and my mother would feel if something bad happened to me. This made great sense to me, and I accepted it. He was always stretching my horizons. When I was older, he'd take me out to lunch at a Greek restaurant or an Italian restaurant or a German restaurant. It gave me a very open feeling about people from other countries. My mother's name was Mary Metcalf. She came from Evening Shade, Arkansas. She was highly energetic: Do more, push,

push, push. She was like a racehorse. She played the piano, and started me in at four and a half. I was bad in school. I thought only of music. When I was eight, I heard a boogie-woogie piano player on the radio. I couldn't believe it. I sat down and taught myself boogie-woogie that day. I had thirteen years of classical training. My teacher, John Summers, was a church organist and choirmaster in Little Rock who improvised in the manner of church music. When I was ten, I was asked to join a band. It eventually grew to nineteen pieces. We'd rent an auditorium and give a dance after a football game, and have a packed hall. We even rented the municipal auditorium in Little Rock, and sometimes we traveled two hundred miles to play after a game. The money we made went into subscriptions to *down beat* and *Metronome* and to the purchase of the newest 78s. We had Charlie Parkers and Dizzy Gillespies two or three months after they were released. The band was integrated, and we never had any problem.

"Three months after I graduated from high school, in 1950, I was drafted for the police action in Korea. I ended up in the Air Force sixteen miles behind the lines, where suicide planes sometime exploded. I tried for two years to get into the service band, but, because of red tape, I never made it. When I got out, I worked in Houston for a great tenor player named Jimmy Ford. In 1953, I went to Los Angeles. It was a golden age in L.A. Before I settled in, though, I heard about a job in Las Vegas. It didn't sound like much, but I went, and it was nine months of paradise. It was in a black club called the El Morocco, which was on an unpaved street on the wrong side of the tracks. I worked in a trio, first as a sideman, then as the leader. The owner of the club was a black man named Oscar Crozier, and he was a marvel. He told us not to honor requests—he'd say to the audience, 'Man, don't bother my musicians.' And when I had to discuss business with him the give-and-take was first-class. The black entertainers on the Strip would come in after work, and so would visiting musicians, and we would play into the next morning. When I got back to Los Angeles, I couldn't believe the amount of music there was—the number of jam sessions. We'd play all Friday night and all Saturday and Saturday night and sometimes through Sunday. We'd go from club to club to club. I'd fall asleep at the keyboard and wake up and wonder what I was playing. This happened every weekend. I was never without work in Los Angeles—the Tiffany, the Haig, the Lighthouse, Zardi's. Two-week engagements in each. And the musicians who were around! Teddy Edwards, Sonny Criss, Lawrence Marable, Leroy Vinnegar, Joe Gordon, Zoot Sims, Herb Geller, Joe Maini, Frank Butler, Jimmy Rowles, Art Tatum, Frank Morgan, Ornette Coleman. I was on Ornette's first recording, 'Something Else!' It was done for Contemporary Records early in 1958. We rehearsed five months, and every time we played Ornette changed his music. When we got to the studio—Don Cherry was on trumpet, Don Payne on bass, and Billy Higgins on drums—Ornette changed everything again, but by this time we were used to it. The session had that good pressure where the music was pulled out of your bones. I'm still happy with that date. The sad side of those years was that so few musicians stayed straight. I had a junkie trio once, and the trouble just to get them started every night! Anyway, I got married in Los Angeles, and we had two children. Then we moved to New York. It was 1960. Very few musicians who come to New York from out of town stay. It's too difficult. They'll stay awhile and go home, come back and go home again, and maybe, if they're good enough and tough enough, come back for good. But I was lucky. I found work right away, and I gigged around until 1963, when I went into the Playboy Club. Kai Winding was the musical director, then Sam Donahue, then me. I worked there eight years, in every sort of musical situation, and I also went to the Manhattan School of Music, where I studied with the great Heida Hermanns. I played so much I developed a muscle spasm in my right forearm. The forearm became as hard as a tabletop, and I couldn't play. I treated it in a whirlpool, and it finally eased. I learned about muscles and playing. I can tell now when it's starting up again. I taught privately after I left the Playboy Club, and in 1974 I joined the Thad Jones-Mel Lewis band. I would rather have worked in that band than in any other band in the world. Thad had written many of the arrangements around his brother Hank, but Hank was generally too busy to show up on Mondays when the band played, so I would take all those solo spots. In 1976, I got the chance to tour Scandinavia as a soloist, but the tour collapsed, and I was stranded in Stockholm. Red Mitchell was living there, and he saved me. It took me seven months to get back to New York. Charlie Mingus hired me. He had Dannie Richmond on drums and Jack Walrath on trumpet. I knew about Mingus's reputation for physical violence, but I thought he was an angel. We had long talks. He was very pleased that I liked the solo piano album he made. He had been stepped on and scarred most of his life. He wanted to be warm, but instead he'd be violent. I think generally played beautifully with Mingus, because it was so dangerous. I had heard that he had slammed the keyboard cover on Jaki Byard's fingers. When it came time for my solo, Mingus would say, in that guttural mutter, 'Blow, Norris!' And I *would*. Then Rolf Ericson told me about the S.F.B. job in Berlin."

It was time for Norris's second set. He pushed his coffee cup aside and rubbed his fingers together. "Jazz improvisation is do-it-yourself music," he said. "You create it with your two hands. It's the free American spirit. In classical music, it's do-as-you're-told. And that's generally the European way. New York, in particular, wakes up the musical vibrations in the jazz animal. New York has more energy than any other city I've ever been in. You feel it in the street. You feel it at night. You'd feel it if half the buildings were torn down. I remember that about New York when I'm not here, and it helps sustain me. I would like to establish the jazz program at the Hochschule firmly, then move on to another city, set up a similar nucleus of playing musicians, and move on again. Maybe every four or five years, like a Johnny Appleseed. Jazz should be far more widely accepted in the world than it is. Do you know how many Europeans learn English just so they can take up jazz?"

Poet

A procession of lyrical, horn-like single-note pianists have come down from Earl Hines. They are, in Count Basie's words, "the poets of the piano."' Mary Lou Williams may have been the first. After she had absorbed Jelly Roll Morton and Fats Waller and Hines and Art Tatum, she became a kind of bebop pianist, and a bebop teacher as well, who showered pianistics on young revolutionaries like Thelonious Monk and Bud Powell. Teddy Wilson was next. (Tatum came a few years earlier, but he was an orchestral pianist.) Wilson's calm, invincible, almost mathematical right-hand patterns transfixed a generation of pianists, among them Billy Kyle, Nat Cole, Hank Jones, Jimmy Rowles, and Lennie Tristano. Kyle's right-hand figures dashed, and he had an electric way of accenting the first note of crucial phrases. By the early forties, Nat Cole had become the most beautiful pianist in jazz. Everything he did sparkled—his touch, his tight, surprising, effortless lines, his deft lyricism. Jones had a crystalline touch, too, and he softened and updated Wilson's right-hand figures. Rowles mixed Wilson and Tatum with his own witty, acerbic harmonic vision, developing single-note lines that suggested Lewis Carroll and Edward Lear. Tristano, working different sides of Wilson and Tatum, spun unbroken melodic lines that never breathed and that had a demonic urgency. John Lewis and Erroll Garner were the last and most eccentric of the Hines-Wilson generation. Lewis was a pointillist and Garner a primitive. Pianists had discovered that they could find almost anything in the abundant Hines. In the mid-forties, Bud Powell, who came out of Kyle and Tatum, hypnotized a new generation of pianists. His single-note figures were nervous, hard, driven. They had, particularly at up-tempo, a coarse quick-wittedness. His admirers came in two groups: the early bebop pianists Dodo Marmarosa, Al Haig, Duke Jordan, Joe Albany, and George Wallington; and the younger and far more original Horace Silver, Tommy Flanagan, Barry Harris, and Bill Evans. (Two exceptional single note pianists who arrived in the fifties but did not follow Powell were Dave McKenna and Eddie Costa. McKenna admired Tatum and Nat Cole, and Costa liked Tristano.) Evans combined Silver and Tristano and Nat Cole with his own special introversions, and, in due course, became the most influential pianist since Bud Powell. Few pianists who have appeared since the mid-sixties have escaped him. Then two totally unrelated things happened: in 1978, Tommy Flanagan quit Ella Fitzgerald, whom he had accompanied for ten years, and in 1980 Evans died. Flanagan went out as a solo pianist (sometimes with bass and drums, or just bass), inching into the sun, and, the most diffident of men, has become Evans' successor.

Jimmy Rowles, the dean of single-note players, has said this about Flanagan "Tommy is a magnificent pianist. I can't think of anything but accolades—as an accompanist and a soloist. We used to hang out a lot at Bradley's. We'd go through songs, talk shop. You'd be surprised at his repertoire. How many pianists around today know 'Down by the Sycamore Tree'? Tommy can be distant at times—loath to open up. But he's a funny man. Whenever I first see him, I always ask him how he is, and he'll say, 'Doing the best I can with the tools I have.' " And Bradley Cunningham himself has said: "Tommy is debonair and witty. I like his company. And I love the way he plays. I hired him about ten years ago, during one of the Newport festivals, when he had a little time off from Ella. I hired him with George Mraz. Nobody came the first night—none of my people. Being in the business, I know that these things happen, and all you can do is throw your hands in the air. Tommy and George kept looking around, then looking at one another. But they were together musically, and after the place closed that night they played some of the most inventive, swinging music I've ever heard. Piano players are supposed to make you laugh, then break your heart, and that's what Tommy does."

Flanagan is of medium height and heft, and he has a bald head with a skirt of grayish hair, and a thick balancing mustache. He wears glasses and has shy eyes. When he talks, he bends his head to the right and examines the left side of the room, or bends his head to the left and examines the right side of the room. He has a soft handshake and a soft voice—his words duck out. But much of this is disguise. He has a handsome, dimpled smile, and he laughs a lot. Flanagan lives with his wife, Diana, on the upper West Side. The living room of their apartment faces south and holds sun much of the day. There are lace curtains at the windows, and two royal-blue velvet sofas. Diana Flanagan's books line one wall, and include Malraux, June Jordan, Alec Wilder, Paul Robeson, James Agee, Duke Ellington, and May Sarton. Flanagan sat in his living room one afternoon and talked about himself. He does so tentatively, as if he had just met the person he is talking about. Flanagan was born in 1930 in Conant Gardens, the oldest intact black community in Detroit. An extraordinary musical eruption took place in Detroit in the forties and fifties—an oblique compensation for the vicious racial conditions in the city at the time.

Flanagan had this effulgence on his mind: "There were older Detroit guys like Milt Jackson and Hank Jones and Lucky Thompson, who left early and came back to play gigs," he said. "And there were local guys like Willie Anderson, who never left. He had long, beautiful fingers, and he was self-taught and could also play bass, saxophone, and trumpet.

Benny Goodman tried to hire him, but he never would go—maybe he was embarrassed at not being able to read. And there was a whole bunch of us—some younger, some older—who didn't get away so fast: Roland Hanna, who went to school with me; Paul Chambers; Doug Watkins; Donald Byrd; Kenny Burrell (he loved Oscar Moore, and we put together a Nat Cole-type trio); Sonny Red Kyner; Barry Harris; Pepper Adams, who came from Rochester and played clarinet when I first knew him; Curtis Fuller; Billy Mitchell; Yusef Lateef; Tate Houston; Frank Gant; Frank Rosolino; Parky Groat; Thad Jones and Elvin Jones, who are Hank Jones' brothers and came from Pontiac, a little way out; Art Mardigan; Oliver Jackson; Doug Mettome; Frank Foster, who's from Cincinnati; Joe Henderson; J. R. Monterose; Roy Brooks; Louis Hayes; Julius Watkins; Terry Pollard; Bess Bonnier; Alice Coltrane; and the singers Betty Carter and Sheila Jordan. We gave weekly concerts at a musicians' collective— the World Stage Theatre. We worked at clubs like the Blue Bird and Klein's Showbar and the Crystal and the Twenty Grand. We played in the Rouge Lounge, and at El Sino, where Charlie Parker worked. As teenagers, we'd stand outside the screen door by the band-stand, looking in at Bird. All this lasted into the mid-fifties. Then people began to leave— Billy Mitchell ended up with Dizzy Gillespie, Thad Jones with Count Basie, Paul Chambers with Paul Quinichette, Doug Watkins with Art Blakey, Louis Hayes with Horace Silver. I stayed around until 1956, when Kenny Burrell and I left for New York.

"They still had jam sessions uptown then—Monday at the 125 Club, Tuesday at Count Basie's, Wednesday at Small's—and they were the best place to get exposure. Of course, if you were new in town you had to wait a long time to sit in. Sometimes I didn't get on the stand until three-thirty or four in the morning. But I made my first record after I'd been here only a few weeks. It was for Blue Note, and it was called 'Detroit—New York Junction,' and Thad Jones and Billy Mitchell were on it, and so were Kenny Burrell and Oscar Pettiford and Shadow Wilson. Not long after that, I did a date with Miles Davis and Sonny Rollins. I met Coleman Hawkins through Miles, and I did a date with him. I had my first nightclub gig at Birdland, when they asked me to fill in for Bud Powell. I first appeared with Ella Fitzgerald that July at the Newport Festival. Then I joined J. J. Johnson, and I was with him a year, and we travelled all over Europe. I stayed in New York after that, working around and recording. I married my first wife, Ann, in 1960. We were divorced in the early seventies. We had three children—Tommy, Jr., who lives in Arizona, and Rachel and Jennifer, who both have babies and live together in California. Ann was killed in an auto accident in 1980.

"I started the first of two long gigs with Ella in 1962, and I stayed with her until 1965. Then I spent a year with Tony Bennett. By this time, I had moved to the Coast. I did mostly casuals, which is what they call club dates. Things were sewed up out there—it was very cliquish. Ella was living in California, too, and in 1968 I got another call from her, and I stayed ten years as her musical director. She was great to work for after you got to know her, but it was rough in the beginning. I was insecure anyway, and when I'd make a mistake she would say something like 'If it's going to be like this, I'm getting out of the business.' So I'd say to myself, 'I've got to tighten up my act. After all, I'm the musical director, and I don't want to be responsible for her quitting.' But she never forgot our birthdays—things like that. Working for Ella was different from working for a lot of singers, because she had such high standards. Her intonation was perfect. Jim Hall once said that he could tune up to her voice. I finally left Ella because the travelling got to be too much for me and because in 1978 I had a heart attack."

The doorbell rang, and Flanagan let in his wife, who was loaded to the gunwales with groceries. "I'm sorry, Tommy," she said. "I couldn't get at my keys with all this stuff. I got some grapes and some cookies. I'll bring them out after I get things unpacked." She is a handsome, dark-haired woman. Her hair sets off her face, which is very pale and has an almost Victorian transparency. Her voice is louder than Flanagan's, and she moves twice as fast. Flanagan sat down again, and said, "My heart attack kept me in the hospital seventeen days, even though they kept telling me it was a mild one. I quit smoking and cut down on drinking and started getting some exercise, which is mostly walking. I walk all over the city. I work up to a good pace. Maybe I take after my father, who was a postman. My brothers and I figured out once that he walked at least ten miles on his mail route. Before he carried mail, he worked for the Packard motorcar company, but the government was a lot safer during the Depression. He was born in 1891, near Marietta, Georgia. He served in the Army during the First World War, and after the war he came North. Before that, he had floated around in Florida and Tennessee. He was about the same height as me, and we looked alike—we both lost our hair early. He loved music, and sang with a quartet, which dressed in spats and all. I saw a picture of him once holding a guitar, but I never heard him play one. I was the youngest of six children, five of them boys. What with so many boys, he laid down the law. He kept us in check. He had a way of sending us to the basement, of taking privileges away. But he showed us all the things of how to be a good person. He had the kind of sense of humor where he'd start telling a joke and laugh so hard he never got to the punch line. My mother, Ida Mae, was short and small and beautiful. She was from Wrens, Georgia. She was born in 1895, and she came North about the same time as my father. She had some Indian blood. They were married just before the twenties. She did a lot of church work—in fact, my parents started a church near where we lived. She loved music even more than my father did. She knew who people like Art Tatum and Teddy Wilson were, and when I'd put on one of their records she'd say 'Is that Art Tatum?' or 'Is that Teddy Wilson?' and that made me feel good. She taught herself to read music. She was shy and easygoing, and very resourceful about things like cooking and sewing. She made a lot of our clothes, and she made beautiful patchwork quilts. It was rough going in the thirties, but she smoothed everything over and always made it seem like we had enough. She died in 1959, and my father died in 1977, at the age of eighty-six. My oldest brother, Johnson Alexander, Jr., moved into my father's house to take care of him before he passed, and my brother and his wife still live there. My sister, Ida, worked for a doctor, but she's retired. She had seven children, the last two twins. My brother James Harvey passed a little while ago, and Douglas works in the Detroit school system. Luther lives in Lansing, and is with a community-service agency. My father's house has a front porch and a back porch, now enclosed, and four bedrooms, two up and two down. There's a milk door in the kitchen, where we used to put the empties for the milkman. When I was little, it still looked very country where we were. The streets were dirt and had deep gullies on both sides. They weren't paved until the late thirties. I walked a mile to my first school, and took two buses to high school, which was not in our area, and which my sister and brothers went to, too. The schools were mixed, but there was a lot of racism everywhere in Detroit. The result, of course, was the race riots of 1943.

"We always had a piano in our house, and I was fooling with it as soon as I could crawl up on the bench. On my sixth Christmas, we were all given musical instruments. I got a clarinet, and the others got a violin and drums and saxophones, and the like. Eventually, we had a little band, and we played some strange music. I didn't like the clarinet too much, because it was so hard to get a sound out of. But I did learn to read music on it. I sent away for a fingering chart to a Dr. Matty, who had a radio program, and I learned through listening to him and because they used the same chart in school. I could play some by the time I got to intermediate school, and in high school I could blend in with the band without sounding too terrible. I started piano lessons when I was ten or eleven, and built up to Bach and Chopin. I studied with Gladys Dillard. Her classes got so big that she opened her own school and had a staff of seven or eight teachers. I saw her recently in Detroit when I gave a solo concert, and she looked real good. All this time, I had been listening to Fats Waller and Teddy Wilson and Art Tatum and to all the big bands. In high school, Bud Powell took hold, and so did Nat Cole. Nat Cole had that same thing as Teddy—a nice, clean technique, a bright attack. He could swing, he made his notes bounce.

"I didn't escape the Korean War. I got drafted near the end, and I spent two years in the Army. I did my basic training at Fort Leonard Wood, in Missouri, which was on the same latitude as South Korea, and even had a similar terrain. So the minute basic was finished they cut my orders to send me overseas. It was nightmare time. Then I discovered that they were holding auditions for a camp show. One of the skits had a pianist in it, and I tried out and got the part and stayed in Missouri. But I went over a year or so later. I had been trained as a motion-picture-projector operator, and I was sent to the port city of Kunsan. The war was still going. Late at night or very early in the morning, this North Korean plane would come over, flying under our radar, and drop a couple of bombs. We called him Bed-Check Charlie. The one good thing about my Army career was that I kept running into Pepper Adams."

Diana Flanagan brought in a plate of grapes and a plate of ginger cookies. Flanagan took two cookies and thanked her, and she went back to the kitchen. Flanagan finished his cookies and ate some grapes. He was silent for a while. Then he said, "The other night at the Vanguard, somebody asked me for the umpteenth time what pianists influenced me. The fact is, I try to play like a horn player, like I'm blowing into the piano. The sound of a piece—its over-all tonality—is what concerns me. If it's a blues in C, you play the whole thing like a circle. You have the sound of C in your head, your mind is clouded with the sound. The chords of a tune are not that important, and neither is the melody. But they are both there if you get lost. Hardly any of my material is new, although it may be new to me. When you add new songs, it gives your playing a lift. I particularly like Kern and Arlen and Gershwin. I also love Ellington and Strayhorn and Tadd Dameron. No matter what you play, though, it's hard work. After I do a week's gig, I like to rest, I like to heal."

Flanagan demands close listening. His single-note melodic lines move up and down, but, since he is also a percussive player, who likes to accent unlikely notes, his phrases tend to move constantly toward and away from the listener. The resulting dynamics are subtle and attractive. These horizontal-vertical melodic lines give the impression of being two lines, each of which Flanagan would like attention paid to. There are also interior movements within these lines: double-time runs; clusters of flatted notes, like pretend stumbles; backward-leaning half-time passages; dancing runs; and rests, which are both pauses and chambers for the preceding phrase to echo in. Flanagan is never less than first-rate. But once in a while—when the weather is calm, the audience attentive, the piano good, the vibes right—he becomes impassioned. Then he will play throughout the evening with inspiration and great heat, turning out stunning solo after stunning solo, making the listeners feel they have been at a godly event.

Diana Flanagan came into the living room. Flanagan stood up and stretched and said it was time for his walk—that today he was going down toward Lincoln Center and back up through Central Park. He put on a tan cap and left. Diana Flanagan took a cookie and sat on the sofa. She said that the two best things she had ever done were to come to New York and to marry Flanagan. "I had come from Ames, Iowa, where my father finally settled," she said. "He was born in Russellville, Kentucky, and when I was growing up we lived in Clarksville, Tennessee, and Hopkinsville, Kentucky, and Goldsboro, North Carolina. My father sold insurance. He sold men's clothes. He worked for Frigidaire. He worked

for National Cash Register. He was a quiet, subtle, sweet person, a courtly person. His name was William Kershner, and he was of Scottish, Irish,
and German descent. Tommy, whose father spent time in Tennessee, and
my father, who spent time there, too, used some of the same colloquialisms—like 'slipperspoon' for 'shoehorn.' My father died in 1971. My
mother is almost ninety, and lives in a nursing home now. She was born
in Philadelphia. Ruth Stetson. Her father was English, and her mother
was French and Irish. She has always been interested in music and books.
She's very witty, very emotional. I had a scholarship and studied music
for two years at the University of Iowa. Then I came to New York. It was
1949. I had always thought New York was my destination. I had been
brought to the World's Fair in 1939, when I was nine or ten, and I never
got over it. I went to Columbia, and took courses in drama. I had been a
violinist, and I was also a singer. I used the professional name of Diana
Hunter, which is pretty embarrassing. I sang around New York, and went
on the road with Elliot Lawrence and Claude Thornhill. Thornhill was
very kind to me. He still played beautifully—those dreaming single-note
things, like 'Snowfall.' In 1956, I married a tenor saxophonist named
Eddie Wasserman. He'd been to Juilliard, and he had worked for Chico
O'Farrill and Charlie Barnet. And he was in the Gene Krupa quartet a
long time. I stopped singing professionally in 1962, and Eddie and I were
divorced in 1965. I went to City College and graduated with a degree in
English literature. Then I studied education at Bank Street. I taught
music, English, and black studies for ten years—first in Bedford-
Stuyvesant and then in the South Bronx. I quit just before Tommy and I
were married, in 1976.

"We read to each other quite a bit. He's interested in everything I am,
and I'm interested in everything he is—except sports. His gentleness and
quietness are deceptive. He is a strong man, and he has a lot of spirit and
funniness. He's lovely to live with. Everything he says has a kind of double meaning—an edge to it. We have a lot of play like that between us. We
laugh all the time. He dances—little tap steps, little side shuffles—around
here, but he won't do it in public. Once, when we went to hear Duke
Ellington at the Rainbow Grill, he took me out on the dance floor and just
stood in one spot, swaying from side to side. I still sing sometimes late at
night, and he plays for me. We know a thousand songs nobody else
knows anymore."

A Walk to the Park

Elvin Jones' ferocity and originality and subtlety on his instrument changed the nature of jazz drumming. For a time in the late sixties, he lived in a first-floor room at the Chelsea Hotel. The room was long and narrow and dark, and it was clearly a bachelor's nest. The bed hadn't been made, and on a small dining-room table were a box of cornflakes and a used cereal bowl with a spoon in it. The bed was flanked by night tables, on one of which was a Welch's Grape Juice jar of water and on the other an overflowing ashtray and a copy of "The Voyage of the Space Beagle." The bureau was littered with aspirin and Band-Aids and a travelling clock, which had stopped. Wedged between a bass drum and a snare drum in a window alcove were a pair of shoes and a bow tie.

Jones rummaged around in a bureau drawer and pulled out what appeared to be a thick sheaf of hotel bills. "I'm the world's worst bookkeeper," he said, in a sturdy, rasping voice. "'I've been living here for several months, and, man, the seventy-some dollars a week I pay is expensive for me. And Pookie's Pub, where I'm at now, is not the highest paying club in town. I make about scale, or about a hundred and fifty a week. This morning I got a letter from my wife, who lives near the Haight-Asbury district in San Francisco—she's no hippie—and my kid is sick again, which means more doctor bills. Everybody wants that bread all at once." He got down on his knees, pulled a box from under the bureau, and took out a copy of his newest album. He wrote something on the back of it and picked up one of the hotel bills. "Let me just lay this album on the man downstairs. Maybe it'll keep him quiet for two or three days." He opened the door and collided with a chambermaid.

"'How's your towels?" she asked. "There's always a 'No Disturb' sign on the door, so's I never can get in here."

"I know it," Jones said, "but I forget it, and I'm not here that much to remember and take it off."

When he returned, the maid handed him some fresh towels. He put them on the table, then went into the kitchenette, got a bottle of Lowenbrau, and sat down on the bed. He picked up a package of French cigarettes and lit one. He was wearing a striped sports shirt, rumpled pipestem khaki pants, and unshined Italian shoes. His head is large and his face is winged by his cheekbones. He has a generous mouth, a firm chin, and a broad smile which is heightened by a missing canine tooth. His eyes flash. He is six feet tall and has wide shoulders and a Scarlett O'Hara waist. His hands are big, with long, thick fingers.

Jones puffed up a couple of pillows and stretched out on the bed. "There. The hecticism of the day is dying down. I've been uptown and back already. I don't get to bed until about four-thirty, but I wake up like a firecracker at ten-thirty, I guess that's what happens to you when you turn forty. But I take a nap around four or five in the afternoon and then I'm all right." Jones waved his cigarette around. "I've been smoking these things since Duke Ellington, who was on a Norman Granz tour in Europe, sent for me. It was about a year and a half ago. I joined him in Frankfurt, and my stay with him lasted just a week and a half, through Nuremberg and Paris and Italy and Switzerland. I was new. It was difficult for the band to adapt to my style and I had to do everything in a big hurry, trying to adapt to them. Then the bass player started playing games with me by lowering and raising the tempos to make it look like I was unsteady, and finally I had to speak to him and he stopped. Hodges and Cat Anderson and Gonsalves and Mercer Ellington knew what was going on, but Duke didn't. And I guess I didn't connect with the anchormen, because they complained about my playing to Duke. I don't know whether Cootie, who kept giving me the fisheye, wanted me to call him Mr. Williams and shine his shoes or what. Also, Duke had a second drummer in the band and he was an egomaniac. So Duke and I talked at Orly Airport and I told him to send a telegram to Sam Woodyard and tell him to get himself over there, because he knew the whole book. I saw Duke later, after he'd found out what had been going on, and everything was fine—no sweat. He told me I could come back with the band any time I wanted. He's such a great man. Given more time under different circumstances—being left alone and all—it might have been a beautiful thing for me. After I left the band, I holed up in a hotel room and slept for three days. I didn't want the terrible headaches I'd had out on the Coast in my last days with Coltrane."

Jones swung his legs over the side of the bed. His eyelids suddenly drooped, giving him a secret, almost drunken expression, and his voice became low and husky. "I joined John Coltrane in 1960. Of all the bands and all the people I've worked with, the six years with him were the most rewarding. It seemed that all my life was a preparation for that period. Right from the beginning to the last time we played together it was something pure. The most impressive thing was a feeling of steady, collective learning. Every night when we hit the bandstand—no matter if we'd come five hundred or a thousand miles—the weariness dropped from us. It was one of the most beautiful things a man can experience. If there is anything like perfect harmony in human relationships, that band was as close as you can come. You felt so close nobody ever wanted anything destructive to happen to anyone else. Coltrane was humble in the finest sense of that word. He was a man of deep thought. He would never say anything trivial. He was honest with people and with himself. He was religious. I think his grandfather was a Baptist minister. I'm a Baptist myself, but I quit going to church years ago. I figure yourself is the church.

"During my time with Coltrane, I could investigate my quest of how to play with other instruments. He left me absolutely alone. He must have felt the way I played, understood the validity of it. There was never any rhythmic or melodic or harmonic conflicts. At least I never felt any, and you can spot those things a mile away. I was never conscious of the length of Coltrane's solos, which sometimes lasted forty minutes. I was in the position of being able to follow his melodic line through all the modes he would weave in and out of, through all the patterns and the endless variations on variations. It was like listening to a concerto. The only thing that mattered was the completion of the cycle that he was in. I'd get so excited listening to him that I had all I could do to contain myself. There was a basic life-force in Coltrane's solos, and when he came out of them you suddenly discovered you had learned a great deal. I didn't want to leave Coltrane, but the personnel had changed. He added another drummer, and I couldn't hear what I was doing any longer. There was too much going on, and it was ridiculous as far as I was concerned. I was getting into a whole area of frustration, and what I had to offer I felt I just couldn't contribute. I think Coltrane was upset, and I know in those last weeks I had a constant migraine headache."

Jones lifted his head and opened his eyes and cleared his throat. "When I heard about him being dead, I didn't believe it. Billy Greene, my piano player, called me early in the morning and told me. Later on, I called Bob Thiele, who recorded Coltrane, and he confirmed it. You know how you react when someone close and dear passes away—that bad feeling comes on you.

"But I've been very fortunate in the variety and number of great musicians I've worked with. When I started out in Detroit, in 1949, there were a lot of clubs and a lot of musicians working—Barry Harris, Billy Mitchell, Paul Chambers, Kenny Burrell, Tommy Flanagan, Milt Jackson, and Doug Watkins. It was a revelation to me, because Pontiac, my home, was like out in the country. I got my first professional gig through Art Mardigan, the drummer, with a five-piece group in a bar on Grand River Street, and everything was fine until Christmas Eve, when it was time to get paid, and I looked out the window and it was snowing like hell and there was the piano player, who was also the leader, running down the street with all the money. So I went back to Pontiac and took a job in a little roadhouse that had a floor show with a Sophie Tucker-type singer. She didn't have *any* music in her, but she was the owner's sweetheart, and when she told him I didn't have any music in me I got fired. Then Billy Mitchell called me from Detroit and wanted me to come into the Blue Bird with him. It was a small place owned by three sisters and a brother, and it had delicious food. I stayed about three years. Tommy Flanagan came in on piano, and Thad, my brother, who'd been on the road or in the Army since 1939, came in on trumpet. Pepper Adams, the baritone saxophonist, sat in, and so did Sonny Stitt and Miles Davis and Wardell Gray. Then Thad went with Count Basie, and six months later I went into the Rouge Lounge. I also played a lot of concerts and all the after-hours places where you could jam. I don't know any other city like Detroit was then. It got behind its musicians and supported them. At the Rouge Lounge, I was working with Kenny Burrell backing Carmen McRae, and one afternoon Ed Sarkesian, who ran the place, got a call from New York from Benny Goodman, who was putting together a big band and wanted me to come and audition. Sarkesian was a great Goodman fan, and when I came to work that night he was ecstatic. His face was lit up like a Christmas tree. He told me about Goodman and then he asked me did I need any money, did I need any clothes, did I need anything at all, and I took off for New York the next day—right in the middle of the week. The audition was at the old Nola Studios on Broadway and Fifty-second Street, and I walked in and the whole band was there. The only person I knew was my brother Hank, on piano. Budd Johnson was in the band, and I think Buck Clayton, but I didn't know them then. Benny wasn't there. They got out the music for 'Sing, Sing, Sing,' and if there's one number I've *never* liked that's it, and anyway they wanted all this heavy four-four time on the bass drum. We started, and I just didn't belong in it. Nothing came out right. Then, in the middle of the next number, the bass player had to leave, and I began noticing the guys in the band looking at their watches. When the audition ended, the manager gave me a nice pep talk and Benny called me later and thanked me for coming and gave me a lot of encouragement. But I didn't get the job. I did get a gig, though, in a quartet with Charlie Mingus and Teddy Charles and J. R. Monterose, the tenor player. There was never a dull moment with Mingus. Eccentric as he seems, it's mostly a put-on. He's really an almost shy man and he tries to be boisterous to cover it up. Half the time he's frightened of one thing or another, like a little boy. But when he stops talking and starts playing, the virtuoso, the genius, comes shining out. That's a different Mingus. We made a short tour to Newport and Toronto and Washington, but Mingus and Teddy Charles argued all the time, and so Mingus had one of his crazy ideas: I'll fire you, he told me, and then I'll quit, and we'll go to Cleveland and play with Bud Powell. We did. When Mingus left the group, Tommy Potter joined, and we stayed with Bud for a year and a half."

Jones sat up and said, "'I'm hungry. Let me order a sandwich and some more beer." He telephoned and then got up and walked around the room.

"Bud was very shaky, very sick," he went on. "He was almost completely withdrawn, but we got along fine. It ended up that I became the leader and was consulted about setting up and various routines. And during the day I'd visit with him and take him to the movies or on long walks. He would open up and be very rational. His thing by then was alcoholism, and all he needed was a couple of drinks and he'd go berserk. I rationed him to two bottles of beer a day and he was all right. But every once in a while he'd get away from me—like once, when some people poured some wine into him and he was found the next morning in an alley in his underwear with even his shirt and tie stolen. Then one night at Birdland during an intermission he took off and I didn't see him again for two years. Before he died, a couple of years ago, he came by an apartment I had on Sixteenth Street on my birthday and brought me an autographed picture of himself as a present. He was the most mistreated man I ever knew—by managers and bookers and club owners and police. Somebody told me that Cootie Williams believes Powell's troubles started when he was in Cootie's band in the forties and they were playing a gig in Philadelphia. Powell got drunk or something and was picked up by the police, and they beat him up so badly—mostly around the head, probably causing brain damage—that his mother had to come down from New York to get him. And he couldn't have been more than nineteen. Man, he never had a chance.

"After that I worked with Tyree Glenn, and then with Sweets Edison. Sweets is a real cat, in the true meaning of the word. As slick as grease. Hip. And what a trumpet player, what a beautiful tone—a tone as pure as mountain water. There's no trumpet player living can play a ballad like Harry Edison. It was funny travelling with him. We had a contract to play a jazz festival in this resort at French Lick, Indiana, in I think it was October of 1959, and so all five of us—Jimmy Forrest, Tommy Potter, and Tommy Flanagan were also in the group—squeezed into this station wagon, and because there wasn't any room inside I tied my drums on top and we drove eight hundred miles non-stop through rain and hail—the drums out in it all—and when we get there we get the greeting 'Where have you been? You were supposed to play *yesterday*.' "

Jones laughed in a loose, swinging way. The sandwich and beer arrived, and he spread his sandwich out beside him on the bed and put his beer on the floor.

"I've had my turn with drugs," he said softly, and took a swallow of beer. "I guess it got started in 1949, after I came out of the Army and began going to Detroit. I developed a secret desire to see what everybody was enjoying so much. I wanted to be one of the crowd, to be hip, down, part of that image. Also, there are times when you just don't want to think of certain things. You want to escape from being a liberal or a conservative or a Democrat or a Republican or a Negro or anything else. You just want to live. And later I'd get in trouble when I wasn't working. I'd suffer from despondency and boredom and general depression. Slowly, you learn the delusions about what you think you are under drugs and what you really are. Whenever I was under the influence it would make me play terrible. It would make me sluggish and slow me down. It destroyed what could have been great performances. I've been drastically embarrassed by being high on the job. It was embarrassing to me and my associates. It seemed that I had let myself and my friends down—the people who depended on me. Oh, I wouldn't be hostile, but I'd sit there and go to sleep in people's faces when they talked to me or walk around in a kind of part oblivion. When drugs really get hold of you, you move into a whole different world—an area where you associate with nobody but other users. You're taking drugs and they're taking drugs and that's your relationship, and you begin to think of them as friends, until you find out they're boosters or thieves or pimps or whatever. You suddenly discover you're involved in criminal activity, that you're about to get involved with the legal branch of the government, which happened to me in Detroit and happened to me again in New York in 1959. I'd been walking around the city all day and I had this little bag of heroin in my watch pocket. I'd been sniffing on it off and on. I'm all dressed up and I go to a hotel on Forty-ninth Street to visit a friend who'd played with Lionel Hampton, and I forget all about that little bag in my pocket. I get in the lobby and this guy sticks a gun in my back and tells me to come upstairs. It was a cop. When I get to my friend's room, there are other cops, and they've got him stripped and up against the wall and they're going over his clothes like a vacuum cleaner. I think they found some benzies—nothing worse than that. Then they started patting me down and they find the bag, and that's it. Man, I felt queer—like I was suspended in the air in that room, watching all this happening down below to two cats I never saw before."

Jones crumpled his sandwich wrapper and put it in the ashtray on one of the bedside tables. "They sent me to Rikers Island for six months. That was depressing, being locked up, and particularly being locked up with all those repeaters. Those guys have worked out this life where they go out in the streets for six months or so and hustle or push and then they get busted and are sent back to Rikers Island, probably to the same job they had before, and after they've eaten three meals a day and gotten their health back and their terms are up they go back to the streets until they get busted again. But what was worst about it was the rats. I have a great fear of rodents. These guys would take food and candy and stuff into their cells, and at night—there wasn't much light—the rats would come and I'd stay up half the night watching and trying to keep them away from me. So that was the last time for me. I've been clean ever since, and I intend to stay that way. I'm not going to abuse myself, I'm not going to get in that groove. I was never on the stuff more than six or seven months altogether in all those years, and in a way I'm glad it happened. I learned from it. I also learned that I could never get a cabaret card to work clubs in New York. I filled out all the forms I don't know how many times and nothing, no card. So what I finally did was go down there and apply under the name of Ray Jones—Ray is my middle name—and I got one. Of course, now they've wiped out the cabaret-card law, which is the best news I've heard in years."

Around eight that evening, Jones took a cab down to Sayat Nova, an Armenian restaurant on Charles Street. He looked refreshed. He had changed into dark pipestem pants, a clean tan button-down shirt without a tie and a vestlike cardigan sweater. "I was never lonely when I was a kid," he said. "I was the youngest of ten children, and I was a twin, an identical twin. But when my brother and me were eight or nine months old we got the whooping cough, and he died. His name was Elvin *Roy*. I can remember the little wooden box sitting on a table in the parlor. I have been challenged on this but have proved it by pointing out the exact spot where the coffin was, so it wasn't just that I was told about it later. My oldest sister and the oldest of all the children, Olivvia, drowned when she was twelve. There was a lake down at the end of our street and she was skating and fell through the ice. The kids she was with got frightened and ran home and nobody told my mother until late that night, and they went and found her under the ice. She was very talented. She was already composing music and, even at her age, giving piano lessons. My brother Hank was born next, and there was Melinda and Anna Mae and Thad. Right above me was Edith and Paul and Tom. Edith still has our house in Pontiac, and she has four children. It's a big old place with three stories and eighteen rooms.

"My father came from Vicksburg, Mississippi, and he died in 1949. He was about six feet four and very lean. He was a lumber inspector for General Motors and a deacon of the Baptist church, as well as a bass in the choir. I'm told I resemble him more than any of the other boys in the family. To me he was a very fine man. His example was in his living. The way he lived—he was as straight as could be—made you want to be like him. He loved to bake. He was up at four every morning and he'd go down to the kitchen and start our breakfast and sometimes pack our lunches. He'd pour coffee into his enormous cup, and when I came down he'd let me drink the spilled coffee in the saucer. Twice a week he'd make a big three-layer cake and put some of my mother's jelly—mulberry or blackberry or strawberry—between the layers. And he'd bake bread and gingerbread. My brother Tom and I would take a piece of gingerbread and make it into a hard ball and I'd put it in my pocket and when we went out we'd pretend it was chewing tobacco. I'd break off a piece and ask Tom, 'Here, you want a plug?' or 'You want a chew?' He'd stick it in his cheek and bulge it out and we'd break up. My mother was a big warm woman and the greatest lady in the world. She gave me every kind of encouragement. She'd tell you to make up your mind at what you wanted to do and then just *do* it. When I finally decided I wanted to be a musician, that was it to her. But she tried to make you into a man before anything else, so that you learned how to take care of yourself, you learned how to survive. That was especially valuable to me in the beginning as a musician. She died of a heart attack in 1951. She had a weak heart but she never let on and she'd never go to doctors."

At Sayat Nova, Jones ordered a beer and egg-lemon soup and shish kebab. "I never learned any prejudices at home," he said. "In fact, I never knew anything about that until the Army. Our schools were unsegregated, and my father and mother taught us you met people as individuals, that you judge a man as a man. They both came from Mississippi, so they must have had good reason to think differently, but they didn't pass any of it down to us. I grew up in the Depression, and I guess we were lucky, because my father always worked. There was plenty of food even though I never saw any *money*. We weren't allowed to go to the movies, because it cost ten cents. And instead of toys from a store I'd go into the woods near our house and make a slingshot or a bow and arrow.

"'I quit school after the tenth grade and went to work at General Motors in the truck-and-coach division, unloading boxcars and stacking assembled motors. I already knew how to do everything in the dry-cleaning line. I had gone to work in my uncle's dry-cleaning shop when I was six or seven. School didn't give me what I wanted. The only interests I had there were music and recreation—sports. I was on the track team, and I set records that still stand. I could high-jump six feet, and I ran the four-forty and could do the hundred-yard dash in nine-five. It would take me nine *minutes* now.

"I started playing drums in junior high. I got a practice pad and sticks and a Paul Yoder method book. When I first looked at those notes it seemed so complicated. I didn't have the least idea of note evaluation. I asked a kid I went to school with about it. He took private lessons for fifty cents and I thought he must be rich. He taught me about whole notes and half notes and quarter notes, and suddenly it dawned on me. I walked around all the time counting—a-one, a-two, a-three, a-four. I went through the whole book and I learned all twenty-six rudiments. I learned that book upside down and back and forth. I was moved from the junior-high marching band up to the high-school band, and in a week I was in the first chair. If anybody really influenced me on drums it was the band director, Fred N. Weist. He made me to realize that the drum is not something to bang on, that it is not a round disc to be pounded. He told me you can hear incoherent sounds in a traffic jam and that music should go far beyond the reproduction of traffic jams. We had quite a collection of records at home, and I'd try and play along with them. It was very unsatisfactory, but I learned how valuable it is to keep time, that that is the drummer's primary function. I listened to all the drummers I could, on records and in person. I'd hear Buddy Rich, say, do something on a record and I'd wonder if he was doing that snare-drum pattern with one hand or two, and finally I'd get a chance to *see* him, with Tommy Dorsey, and I discovered he was using two hands. I saw Jo Jones with Basie, and on records I heard Chick Webb. He takes a little solo at the beginning of 'Liza,' which was made, I believe, around 1938, and it's so melodic and clean and modern it's unbelievable. It could have been recorded last week. I heard Sid Catlett on 'Salt Peanuts' with Dizzy Gillespie and Charlie Parker, and he was flowing and flawless. And I listened to Dave Tough and Max Roach and Kenny Clarke and Tiny Kahn. I began to develop my theories on drums. I figured that a lot of things drummers were doing with two hands could be done with one—like accents with just the left hand on the snare, so you wouldn't have to take your right hand off the ride cymbal. And it didn't seem to me that the four-four beat on the bass drum was necessary. What was needed was a *flow* of rhythm all over the set. I never learned any tricks, anything flashy—like juggling sticks or throwing them in the air. That kind of thing stops me inside. After all, Artur Rubinstein doesn't play runs on the piano with his chin.

"Of course, I learned from my brothers Hank and Thad. When Hank came home in the forties from being on the road with Jazz at the Philharmonic, I'd ask him a lot of questions. He'd tell me different things to listen for in a performance, or he'd tell me to get my wire brushes and play along with him. You don't realize how much you are learning at times like that until much later, when it hits you like post-hypnotic suggestion. I didn't see much of Thad until he joined our band in Detroit. We don't see each other that much, but we're close, particularly in times of crisis, when there seems to be a kind of telepathy between us. To me, Thad and Hank are perfect. I don't know anything bad about them. Hank is the greatest pianist in the world and Thad is the greatest trumpet player. Hank has stubby fingers and hands, but they spread out like wings when he plays. He doesn't feel right if he doesn't practice three or four hours a day. I can understand that. He wants to have that response when he needs it.

"Around 1946, when I was nineteen, I took off for Boston with my brother Tom and a friend. I worked in a dry cleaner's there, and then I went down to Newark, New Jersey, by myself and enlisted in the Army. They sent me to eight weeks of music school at Fort Lee, Virginia, after basic training, and then I was sent to Columbus, Ohio. Part of the time I travelled all over the country with a Special Services show called 'Operation Happiness,' but I was a stagehand rather than a drummer. I went along just to watch. And I began to play at dances on the post and I gained confidence. I never got that many compliments and I never got that much criticism. The men I played with liked me enough not to repudiate my shortcomings. They wouldn't do anything deliberately to hurt me. You give kindness to human beings, you allow them to grow."

Jones took a sip of Armenian coffee, and looked at his watch. It was going on ten. "I'd better get down to Pookie's," he said. "The owner is nervous, and he gets upset if I'm not on the stand by ten. Maybe he's nervous because he just got married." He laughed and went up the stairs from the restaurant two at a time. He found a cab on Charles Street.

"My drums are my life," Jones said, resting his head against the back of the seat. "Sometimes what happens to you during the day affects your ability and shows up in your work. But once you get to your set, you can obliterate all the troubles, which seem to fall off your shoulders. If you aren't happy before, you are when you play. Playing is a matter of spontaneity *and* thought, of constant control. Take a solo. When I start, I keep the structure and melody and content of the tune in my mind and work up abstractions or obbligatos on it. I count the choruses as I go along, and sometimes I'm able to decide in advance what the pattern of a whole chorus will be, but more often five or six patterns will flash simultaneously across my mind, which gives me a choice, especially if I get hung up, and I've had some granddaddies of hangups. If you don't panic, you can switch to another pattern. I can see forms and shapes in my mind when I solo, just as a painter can see forms and shapes when he starts a painting. And I can see different colors. My cymbals will be one color and my snare another color and my tomtoms each a different color. I mix these colors up, making constant movement. Drums suggest movement, a conscious, constant shifting of sounds and levels of sound. My drumming can shade from a whisper to a thunder. I'm not conscious of the length of my solos, which I've been told have run up to half an hour. When you develop a certain pattern, you stay with it until it's finished. It's just like you start out in the evening to walk to Central Park and back. Well, there are a lot of directions you can take—one set of streets going up, then in a certain entrance and out another entrance and back on a different set of streets. You come back and maybe take a hot bath and have some dinner and read and go to bed. You haven't been somewhere to lose yourself, but to go and come back and finish your walk."

Pookie's Pub was on the northeast corner of Hudson and Dominick Streets, a block north of the Holland Tunnel.

Jones groaned as he got out of the cab—the owner of Pookie's Pub was striding back and forth in front of it. He buttonholed Jones and talked intensely into his ear. I could hear the words "time" and "late" and "people inside." Jones said softly, "Now, man, cool it. Don't bug me. When I get here, I *work*." The owner charged through the door, and Jones raised his eyebrows and laughed. He followed the owner in.

Pookie's was narrow and dusty-looking. A bar was on the left and banquettes on the right, with closely packed tables between. At the rear, between the end of the bar and the men's room, was a tiny jerry-built bandstand two feet above the floor. Jones headed for the stand, and the rest of his quartet—Billy Greene, Joe Farrell (tenor saxophone), and Wilbur Ware (bass)—got up from a table and followed.

Jones' drums looked strictly functional. They included an eighteen-inch bass drum, two tomtoms, a snare drum, two ride cymbals, and a high-hat. He hung his sweater on a hook by the upright piano, sat down, and tapped his way around the set with his fingers. He tightened his snares and his bass drumhead and picked up a pair of sticks. Then he looked at Farrell, said something, counted off, and the group went into a medium-tempo blues.

The center of Jones' beat shifts continually. Sometimes it is in his constantly changing ride-cymbal strokes and sometimes he softens these and bears down heavily on his high-hat on the afterbeat. Sometimes swift, wholly unpredictable bass-drum accents come to the fore and sometimes the emphasis shifts to left-hand accents on the snare, which range from clear single strokes to loose rolls. Jones' hands and feet seem to have their own minds, yet the total effect is of an unbroken flow that both supports and weaves itself around the soloists.

Farrell started quietly on the blues and Jones set up light *tic-tic-tic-tic-tic tic tic-i-tic tic-tic* strokes on a ride cymbal, while his left hand played five behind-the-beat strokes on the snare, followed by softer irregular strokes and a shaking roll. The high-hat jiggled unevenly up and down and the bass drum was quiet. Farrell grew more heated, and Jones began throwing in cymbal splashes, bass-drum accents, and complex left-hand figures. His volume rose steadily, though it never eclipsed Farrell, and Jones' quadruple-jointed rhythmic engine was in high gear. Pookie's was rocking. At the end of Farrell's solo, Jones abruptly dropped his volume to some sliding cymbal strokes which shimmered below the opening of the piano solo. Jones scuttled and rattled behind the piano. His snare-drum accents were light and loose, and the center of his efforts fell on the ride cymbal, on which he would run ahead of the beat, fall behind, then catch up and ride the beat before shooting ahead again. During Ware's solo, Jones whispered along on the high-hat, dropped occasional bass-drum beats, and made Ware's tone sound fat and assured. Farrell returned, exchanged some four-bar breaks with Jones, and the number ended with a shuddering rimshot.

Jones' face was as elusive as his motions—a boxer's assortment of jabs and feints and duckings, supported by steadily dancing feet. At first his face looked tight and secret; his eyes were shut and a dead cigarette was clamped in his mouth. Then he opened his eyes, which appeared sight-less, and nodded at Farrell and Ware. Smiling widely, he closed his eyes in a pained way and turned his face toward the wall. A slow version of "On the Trail," from Ferde Grofé's "Grand Canyon Suite," came next, and it was converted into a marching blues. The set closed with a delicate reading of "Autumn Leaves." Jones put on his sweater and jumped down from the bandstand, ordered a beer, talked to a couple of admirers, and sat down at a table. He was mopping his head with a limp handkerchief, and his shirt was so wet it was transparent. "Wait a minute," he said. "Big Jim's at the bar and I just want to check in with him. I don't know what he does, but he's always got plenty of bread and he supports the musi-cians, follows them around to all the clubs. He makes you feel good." At the bar he pounded the back of a chunky, well-dressed man sitting with a platinum blonde. The man jumped off his stool and started shadow-boxing. Jones put up his hands and the two men weaved and bobbed down the bar and out onto the sidewalk, boxing back and forth in front of the door for several minutes, then slapped each other and laughed. A jukebox went on and Billie Holiday started singing. The owner said in an intense way, "Do you know who that is? Do you know what that is? That's Billie Holiday singing 'My Yiddishe Mama.' Tony Scott, the clar-inettist, taped it at a party not long before she died and put it on a record and gave it to me. You won't find that selection on any other jukebox in the world." He darted away, and Jones sat down at the table. "Oh, my. I dig Big Jim." He took a long swallow of beer. "I think this will be one of those rare nights that seems like they're over before they begin, with everybody in the group listening, everybody in the group hearing. I want to build my group into topnotch quality. I want it to make a significant contribution. I'm not interested in flash-in-the-pan activity, and I think the men I have with me feel the same. It takes a lot of the agony out of things. Occupying your time for yea amount of dollars just doesn't work. Jazz is infectious. There's no way to avoid it. If you're going to play music any kind of music—you can't avoid it. It just naturally takes over.This is my first group and I like being a leader, but then I guess I've been sort of a leader in most of the groups I've worked in. A drummer should conduct."

The owner appeared and touched Jones' shoulder, and he made a face. "All right, man, all right," he said. "Man wants some music, we'll oblige him."

The first number, built around Jones' wire brushes, was a fast version of "Softly, as in a Morning Sunrise." Farrell soloed on flute and Greene and Ware followed. Jones handles brushes the way a chef handles a wire whisk, with fast, circular, loose-wristed motions. He began almost inaudibly, with polishing, sliding, ticking sounds on the snare, broken by cymbal strokes. Slowly he broke this gentle flow with bass-drum beats and with jagged, irregular wire-brush strokes on the snare and the big tomtom. These were multiplied and intensified until it sounded as though he were using sticks, and the solo ended. It was a short, perfectly designed warmup. The group went into "Night in Tunisia." It started in a high, intense fashion, and by the time Farrell had finished a ten-minute solo Jones had switched to sticks and Pookie's was ballooning with sound. Then Jones took off. He began with heavy rimshots on the snare, which split notes and split them again, then broke into swaying, grandiose strokes on his ride cymbals, accompanied by lightning triplets and off-beat single notes on the bass drum. Switching patterns, he moved his right hand between his big and small tomtoms in a faster and faster arc while his left hand roared through geometrical snare-drum figures and his high-hat rattled and shivered. He switched patterns again and settled down on his snare with sharp, flat strokes, spaced regularly and then irregularly. He varied this scheme incessantly, gradually bringing in bass-drum beats and tomtom booms. Cymbals exploded like flushed birds. Jones had passed beyond a mere drum solo. He was playing with earsplitting loudness, and what he was doing had become an enormous ball of abstract sound, divorced from music, from reality, from flesh and bone. Jones waded through his cymbals again and went into a deliberate, alternately running and limping fusillade between his snare and tom- toms that rose an inch or two higher in volume. Suddenly he finished. Farrell played the theme and Jones slid into a long, downhill coda that was a variation on the close of his solo, paused, and came down with a crash on his cymbals and bass drum. Jones was back from the Park.

Bright Unison Clarinets

The harder the pianist and arranger Claude Thornhill tried to make a commercial success of his big band, the more musical and original it became. The band flourished just before and just after the Second World War, and Thornhill thought of it as a "ballad" band; that is, it played a lot of slow tunes, many of them with vocals. But Thornhill's ballads, with their unique ensemble voicings (three or four clarinets, a saxophone or two, two French horns, a tuba, and various intermarriages between these instruments and the trumpets and trombones), were more like tone poems than like dance-band arrangements. Somewhere along the line, Thornhill decided he wanted his sections to play without vibrato; the blocks of sound they produced were smooth, rectangular, and weightless. These sounds glided along above the rhythm section, which was always discreet, and they suggested Debussy, and even Berlioz. They spoke of deep velvet, of Matisse reds, of melancholy without tears. It was always October in Thornhill's slow numbers. In the late forties, his ballads tended to get slower and slower, until, as the Thornhill arranger Bill Borden has pointed out, they got "so slow you couldn't even walk to them— unless you were in a funeral procession." At the same time, Thornhill went along with the jazz fashion of the postwar period—bebop. The arranger Gil Evans, who joined Borden in the band in 1941 (and who died, at the age of seventy-five, in 1988), began writing tight, leaping, arcane bop arrangements in 1946, and they were no more danceable than the ballad numbers. But they were brilliant works—the first fresh big-band inventions to come along since the great Ellington concertos of 1939–42. The best of Thornhill fed, directly and indirectly, the entire non-hot side of jazz— Miles Davis and Gerry Mulligan and the Modern Jazz Quartet. The Thornhill band, an ensemble band, was as maneuverable as a chamber group, and it used improvisation largely to offset its late-Victorian sounds. It owed much to Duke Ellington, yet it also showed how Ellington, had he wished to, could have moved into the bebop era.

Thornhill's career meandered for a long time. An only child, he was born in 1909 in Terre Haute, Indiana. His mother had German blood, and his father, whom he disliked, had English blood. Artie Shaw, who for a time was Thornhill's closest friend, has described the Thornhills as "American Gothic," and not the sort of people you dropped in on. Thornhill's mother said at his funeral, "I miss my Claudie. He brung us fame." Thornhill started playing piano around the age of ten, and he ran away from home when he was fourteen. He got a job on a riverboat, in a band led by Heavy Elder. Then he turned up in a Midwest group called the Kentucky Colonels. He and Shaw met briefly at that time, and in the late twenties Shaw got him a job with Austin Wylie's band in Cleveland. The two men had moved to New York by the early thirties. Thornhill worked for Hal Kemp, Don Voorhees, Freddy Martin, Jacques Renard, and Paul Whiteman. In 1934, he passed through Benny Goodman's first big band, and in 1935 he was in the all-star group that Ray Noble took into the brand-new Rainbow Room. He went from Noble to André Kostelanetz's radio show, and in 1938 he gave up New York for Hollywood. (Thornhill apparently learned a good deal about tonal color from the way Kostelanetz used strings and horns.)

Artie Shaw has said this about Thornhill's early days: "Austin Wylie already had a piano player when I brought Claude into the band, but I had persuaded Wylie that he needed two pianists. We played at the Golden Pheasant, next to the old Hotel Winton, where Claude and I roomed. He had a great musical ear but not much time—in a jazz sense. He practiced things like 'Danse Négre' for hours. He had studied for a while at the Cincinnati Conservatory. He was also listening to stride piano. I'd take him to Harlem, after we moved to New York, to hear Willie the Lion Smith, and he loved that. We both did some arranging with Wylie. One day, we started to run down a new arrangement Claude had brought in. We played the intro and the first chorus—probably sweet saxophones and muted trumpets—and then nothing seemed to happen. The rhythm section was still playing, but there wasn't any other sound. Then we realized that Claude was over there at the piano *singing*. He had written in a vocal for himself, even though he wasn't much of a singer. He was a funny-looking gent, with that potato nose and round Germanic face, and we all broke up. It wasn't easy for him to express himself. He was like Basie in that respect. He hid inside himself. But he was more guileful than he appeared, because he generally got what he wanted. This was particularly true when he joined my Navy band, in 1942. I was a C.P.O., and I was responsible for band discipline, but Claude and I couldn't arrive at a modus vivendi. After all, we had been close a long time, and it wasn't easy being thrust into what amounted to a master-servant relationship. He would miss muster or bed check or rehearsals, and resentment began to build on both sides. He was already a heavy drinker, and that didn't help. He made it known that he wanted his own band, so I talked to Admiral Calhoun, and they gave him one before we left Hawaii for the Pacific Islands. Our relationship was never quite the same, and I didn't see much of Claude after that."

There was a second side to Thornhill's New York career in the thirties. He recorded with every sort of jazz group. Perhaps it was just larking for him, or perhaps he really wanted to be a good jazz pianist. He recorded a dozen numbers in 1934 with the rambunctious trumpeter and singer Louis Prima, and he was on the first sides that Benny Goodman made with his new big band. The following year, he showed up on Glenn Miller's first big-band recordings and on a session organized by the Casa

Loma Band arranger Gene Gifford. He recorded with a pickup group that included Bud Freeman, Bunny Berigan, and Cozy Cole. In 1937, he arranged, and played on, the singer Maxine Sullivan's famous recording of "Loch Lomond." Before he went West, he did two dates with Billie Holiday. He even takes a fine sixteen-bar single-note solo on her version of "Forget If You Can."

Not long before he died, Gil Evans recalled how Thornhill happened to move to the Coast: "In the late thirties, Skinnay Ennis, the drummer and a very popular vocalist with Hal Kemp, decided to go out on his own. He took over the band I had at the Rendezvous Room in Balboa, and I stayed on as an arranger. He asked me who the best vocal arranger was, and I said Claude Thornhill. Claude came out and rented a house in West Los Angeles, and we both wrote arrangements for Skinnay's band. Claude was already a fine arranger. Very quick. He had done a lot of arranging in New York. Then, one day, he said that he was going to cash in an insurance policy and that he couldn't decide whether to take the proceeds and go to Tahiti or go back to New York and organize his own band. He went to New York. He brought his band out to the Rendezvous in 1939, and Bill Borden was the arranger. I have a fixed image in mind from this time of Claude with his cigarette holder and his eternal cup of coffee. They were his badges. So were his Adler Elevator shoes. While he was at the Rendezvous, he took his band out to Catalina Island to hear Benny Goodman and Eddie Sauter, who had just joined Goodman. He rented an open fishing boat, and the water was very rough. Everybody was, like, whoof. Except for Claude, who sat there smoking his cigarette and drinking his coffee."

The trumpeter and arranger Rusty Dedrick joined Thornhill the same year as Evans. "I went with the band just before it opened at the Glen Island Casino, and I left early in 1942," he has said. "I rejoined in 1946 and stayed until 1947. There was never much money; we did it for love of the music. Claude was an enigma. He was extremely shy, and it was difficult for him to be a front man. He had had some psychiatric therapy after the war—possibly even electric-shock treatments, which tend to affect the memory. He knew the book by heart, but he would forget names. He'd announce a singer's first name but not her last, unless one of us shouted it to him. He was a funny man, but his humor was off the wall. He had written a silly poem about one of the islands in the Pacific, and he'd recite it to audiences apropos of nothing. The band was so of a piece that musicians visiting Glen Island would say, 'Hey, I love this band, but I wouldn't want to be on it. You must rehearse all the time.' But we didn't. We had those certain sounds—the bright unison clarinets and the low French-horn/tuba sounds—and we had them down perfectly. Sometimes we played new arrangements the first time on the stand."

Gil Evans again: "I drove across the country from California, and I arrived at the casino in the evening, just before the band hit. I was told that Claude was sick and I would have to take his place. Well, he wasn't.

It was one of his practical jokes. When he was with Freddy Martin in the thirties, he arranged to have a series of insulting telegrams sent to Martin from various parts of the country—one every couple of nights. They all said in different ways how awful Martin's band was, and Claude would watch Martin read these things and get mad as hell, and Claude would laugh and laugh—later. But he wasn't much at taking jokes. Once, I set an alarm clock to go off on the bandstand just as he was playing his tinkly piano on 'Autumn Nocturne.' He didn't think it was very funny. He rented a house in Pelham when we were at the casino, and I stayed with him. He'd practice classical exercises on the piano every night until four or five in the morning. His time was something, and so was his touch. I've never heard anyone get a better sound on a piano than he did. And his ear was infallible. When someone in one of the sections went out of tune, Claude would lead the musician through his part and play the correct notes to get him back on pitch. He'd achieve the no-vibrato effect he wanted in the sections by telling the musicians to play with a vibrato; then he'd make them take it down until there was no vibrato. He wasn't really a jazz piano player. He had heard Bix Beiderbecke when he was young, and the two of them had spent an evening together drinking gin. Afterward, Claude put brackets on the wall in his room and hung the empty gin bottle there. What he wanted in his band was that ballad style with the clarinet lead, then alto saxophone and two tenors, and finally the French horns—all pitched an octave below Glenn Miller's reed section. When the band started to run through my arrangement of Charlie Parker's 'Anthropology,' I saw Claude up in the balcony making faces. He was a night owl, and he finally came to my room at three or four one morning and told me he didn't want to play bebop anymore. Claude wasn't really mysterious. He just liked people to think he was. He had one habit, though, that I never understood. He loved to buy clothes. He had closets of new clothes in his house in Pelham, and he had a basement room full of new clothes in a building on West Fifty-fifth Street that he had an apartment in. But he almost never wore them."

In October of 1947, the Thornhill band recorded Gil Evans's arrangement of "Robbins Nest," written by Sir Charles Thompson and Illinois Jacquet for the disk jockey Freddy Robbins. The recording immediately catches you. A sustained, vibratoless single note, played by a combination of saxophones and horns, is held over a medium tempo for two measures, dips a tone, rises quickly against a soft, offbeat brass burst, falls again, and gives way to Thornhill playing the melody with spare, legato Basie-like single notes. This daring, complex introduction lasts just six measures, and is a classic instance of how the Thornhill band almost completely circumvented the big-band clichés of riffs, call-and-response patterns, and empty counterpoint. It made originality sound comfortable and complexity sound simple. A little reed figure binds the end of Thornhill's first eight bars, and at the end of his second eight the reeds appear again and slip into organ chords, which carry Thornhill, still noodling the melody, through the bridge of the tune. Then the reeds and horns assume the melody for the final eight bars of the first chorus. The clarinettist Danny Polo plays a variation of the melody for sixteen bars, and during the second eight is backed by oh-so-soft counterpoint between the reeds and the brass. A tenor saxophonist, playing melody, takes over on the bridge and is echoed by Polo. Then the whole band spins through what sounds like a transcribed bebop solo. There is a brief Thornhill piano interlude, and the band returns for eight bars of melody and a kind of variation of the opening six measures, and it is over. There is a lot of fast and subtle rhythmic footwork on the recording, and Thornhill's use of dynamics is exhilarating. Yet everything is *quiet*.

Musicians loved the Thornhill band. The French-horn player Sandy Sigelstein has said, "I met Gil Evans in the service, and I ran into him in Los Angeles in 1946, when I was with Martha Graham. I was strictly a legitimate player. Gil said they needed a horn, so I joined. Then I discovered I couldn't play four-four time, and I was humiliated. But the challenge was on, and eventually I learned. The camaraderie in that band through music was out of this world. Claude was always good to me, but he was mysterious. He would never call out the next number. Instead, he would noodle around, giving little hints, until we figured out what he had in mind. He knew how to underplay on the piano and at the same time lead with it. That band was like a concert. Several horn players from the Cleveland Orchestra came one night, and so did all the dance-band people. Being in the Thornhill band was an experience that has been with me all my life."

There was never any extra money. The tubist Bill Barber has said "I had been in classical work before I went with the Thornhill band, in 1947. I was only with them ten months. The big-band business had begun to crumble, and the last to be hired were the first to be fired, which meant me. I don't think the band wanted me to leave, because they loved that soft tuba carpet underneath. Claude was a fine musician, but he was a little tight with money. I had a friend who left Benny Goodman because he was so excited about playing with Thornhill, and he estimated that during the year he stayed with Thornhill he lost two or three thousand dollars."

The arranger Bill Borden said this about Thornhill: "I don't know whether Claude was shy or diffident. He was often indecisive. If you asked him to made a decision, he would do the equivalent of shuffling his feet—unless it was something he felt strongly about or something that had to do with music. He was also decisive if someone did something behind his back that he didn't care for. He wasn't above jokes. He'd do this shtick of pretending not to understand. Or he'd break into ragtime piano if a new arrangement had a section that seemed too square. Mostly, he let our arrangements alone, although he'd cut things he didn't like. When I joined the band, in December of 1939, it hadn't settled into a groove. Sometimes it sounded like Jimmie Lunceford, sometimes like Bob Crosby. Claude said he had started out with sixty arrangements, but I suspect it was fewer than that. I suggested he get Gil Evans, who wasn't happy with Skinnay Ennis. The band became a kind of lab for Gil. He super-imposed bebop arrangements on the band in the late forties. Claude never mastered bop on the piano. He sounded a little like he was playing eighteenth-century drawing-room music when he tried. He was a forceful pianist, but he did those tinkling things on 'Snowfall' and 'Autumn Nocturne' because he felt that was what people liked. I never felt that the second band was as good as the first. It could cut the arrangements, but Louis Mucci was never the lead trumpeter that Conrad Gozzo was, and Danny Polo couldn't match Irving Fazola, who had the most beautiful sound I've ever heard on a clarinet. For what it's worth, Claude used to say that his favorite band was Guy Lombardo's. Toward the end of his life, he limped along with a kind of society band, but he had been rehearsing a new big band when he died. In fact, he was supposed to open in Atlantic City the next night."

During the fifties and early sixties, Thornhill took small bands on the road, playing either society-band music or stripped-down versions of his old book. The trombonist and writer Mike Zwerin worked for Thornhill in 1958. He writes in his autobiography, *Close Enough for Jazz*:

> Arrangements written for full sections were being played by only one trombone, two trumpets, four saxophones, a now guitarless rhythm section plus the essential French horn. We worked country clubs, American Legion halls and high-school gymnasiums in provincial towns where Claude Thornhill was still a name. Referring to more successful "ghost bands"—Sam Donahue and the Tommy Dorsey Orchestra, Ray McKinley and the Glenn Miller Orchestra—Claude once said to me after a particularly grungy affair: "I guess you have to be dead to make it these days."
>
> But he kept his dignity as his audience dwindled. His hair was always combed, his suits pressed, his face shaven, his bow-tie straight. I marvel at how much control that must have involved, considering the skid he was on. He knew he had been something special. It had taken imagination, taste, talent and courage to play Charlie Parker's "Anthropology" at fancy hotels and supper clubs when people had paid to hear a band that had won two *Billboard* magazine polls in the "sweet band" category.

A few years earlier, when Thornhill was between bands, he worked for Tony Bennett. "Claude was with me as musical director and pianist for eight weeks in Vegas in the mid-fifties," Bennett said. "My drummer, Billy Exiner, who had been in Claude's second band, suggested him. Claude's attitude was that it was all a vacation, that we shouldn't worry about anything. We were kids and he was the veteran, and he'd teach us what he knew. He was a sweet man. But he didn't care for pretension. A big old-time movie star was on the bill with us. She was a prima donna, and she'd carry on and yell at her chorus girls during rehearsals. She did only one number, and it was called 'Dungaree Doll.' Claude couldn't get over her behavior, and whenever I ran into him backstage or coming around a corner he'd sing 'Dungaree Doll,' and laugh."

By the sixties, Thornhill and his wife were living in New Jersey, and Artie Shaw had an apartment in New York. "The night Claude died, in the summer of 1965," Shaw once said, "I got a phone call at three in the morning from Claude's wife. I hadn't talked to him in a long while, but she said Claude had told her I was his best friend, and then she said that he had just had a heart attack and died. She said he had spent the day in his garden and had told her it had been one of the best days he had ever had. Later, I found out that Claude had been paying frequent visits to my mother, who lived in New York. He had made her promise never to tell me about the visits, and, of course, he never did, either."

Ten Levels

All bebop players were influenced by Charlie Parker, but the alto saxophonist Lee Konitz absorbed his Parker in careful doses. In the beginning, he listened to Benny Carter and Johnny Hodges and Pete Brown, and after that to Lester Young. His first recorded solo, on Gil Evans' arrangement of Parker's "Anthropology," done by Claude Thornhill's big band in 1947, is a sliding, angular blend of Carter and Young, with Carter's peculiar step phrasing and Young's aluminum tone. Young took over increasingly in the early fifties (the late Paul Desmond listened to Konitz in this period); then streaks of Parker began to show. "I started listening to Charlie Parker records in the late forties," Konitz has said, "but he was too strong for me. It took me at least a year to hear him. People said then that Lee Konitz was the only young alto player around who didn't sound like Charlie Parker. Well, later Lee Konitz did sound like Charlie Parker. I often tell my students to learn this or that Charlie Parker solo. He created our études, and to learn a Charlie Parker solo can change your life."

Lester Young's sound and his horizontal attack and Parker's fluidity and bite can still be heard at the back of Konitz' playing. At one time, he and Paul Desmond sounded almost identical. Desmond never changed: his tone remained perfumed and ivory. Konitz' sound has taken on weight and authority and individuality. He has always been free of clichés. He surprises you no matter how many times you hear him play "All the Things You Are" and "You Go to My Head" and "These Foolish Things." His attack is a shrewd mixture of short phrases, often compounded of repeated notes, and long horizontal utterances capped by his barely perceptible vibrato. His solos are full of secrets. Clear, boldface passages are followed by shadowy turns, made up of half a dozen ascending notes or of quick bent notes or of skidding Charlie Parker runs. Konitz likes silence, and sometimes at the start of a set he will play a short phrase, repeat it, and fall silent for two or three measures. He may start a new idea, discard it, and fall silent again. He is an excellent slow-ballad player, who savors the melody, lingering over a note here, eliminating a note there, but never getting in the composer's way. He has in recent years taken up the soprano saxophone, and he plays it with a bright sound but without the rotund Bechet authority. Konitz played the tenor saxophone before the alto, and once in a while he goes back to it. He even recorded on it with Jimmy Rowles and Michael Moore. His playing sounded slow and muffled, as if the tone of the instrument were simply too heavy for a nimble alto saxophonist to move around. Konitz will try anything. He has recorded with traditional bebop groups, with his own nine-piece band, in a jam-session setting, in duos, with free-jazz groups, and, stepping onto Olympus, all by himself.

Between 1947 and 1953, Konitz recorded with four groups that were among the most eccentric and/or modern outposts in jazz: Claude Thornhill, the Miles Davis nonet, Lennie Tristano, and Stan Kenton. He had a rare talent for being in the odd place at the right time. Thornhill was a pianist and arranger who had done studio work, led his own groups, and recorded with Bunny Berigan, Benny Goodman, and Billie Holiday. This Thornhill band, put together in 1946, lasted about three years, and there was no other dance band like it. Gil Evans did many of its arrangements, and his scores called for an instrumentation of three trumpets, two trombones, two horns, tuba, clarinet, alto saxophone, two tenor saxophones, baritone saxophone, and piano, guitar, bass, and drums. Evans had already found his sound. Poised somewhere between Debussy and Duke Ellington, it converted a dance band into a Turner sunset. "I joined Thornhill in Chicago, and I stayed with him ten months," Konitz has said. "'It was my first big-time situation. I was nervous and impetuous, and I had wise-guy tendencies, like wearing brown suède shoes and yellow socks with a tuxedo. A lot of the musicians—like Billy Exiner, the drummer, and Danny Polo, the clarinettist, and Barry Galbraith, the guitarist—were older, so I thought I was hipper, when actually they were hipper than I was. Danny Polo was a great influence. He cooled me off, and I had to learn. I gave up pot a while ago, but I had started smoking in that band. I guess it was a tranquillizing factor. So much so that one night when I walked out to the microphone to solo I simply stood there and dug Exiner and Galbraith and the bassist Joe Shulman, who were cooking like the Basie rhythm section. I stood there and listened for a chorus and then walked back to my seat without playing a note. It was a ballad band with a luxurious instrumentation, and Gil Evans gave it an extraordinary tonal palette. He also taught the band how to phrase bebop. It's a very specific discipline, and I'm still working at it. A lot of musicians avoided its difficulties and went on tangents. I believe

Ornette Coleman was one. I don't believe he ever quite learned his Charlie Parker before he took off on his own. Thornhill himself was a shy man, and all our contacts were good-natured. I suspect the music was a little ahead of him. Gil Evans and I keep in touch, and we have even worked as a duo. In the late seventies, we went to Italy and played concerts. One was in Potenza, in the south. I think it was the first time they'd heard a jazz concert, or maybe even jazz. They were polite, but they couldn't quite sit still. So I walked out into the audience and played, and I could feel Gil back at the piano opening one eye to see where the hell I'd gone. But it worked and they loved it. It was hard, just the two of us. Gil went out bloody every night, but he always felt like doing it again the next night."

Konitz' next recording adventures involved the famous Miles Davis "Birth of the Cool" sessions for Capitol Records, in 1949 and 1950, and Konitz' first sessions with the blind pianist and teacher Lennie Tristano, in 1949. The Davis records grew directly out of Evans' Thornhill arrangements. They also grew out of the commingling in Evans' West Fifty-fifth Street basement salon of Konitz and other Thornhill alumni and such young movers and shakers as John Carisi, Gerry Mulligan, John Lewis, Max Roach, and Davis. The nonet was made up of trumpet, trombone, horn, tuba, alto saxophone, baritone saxophone, piano, bass, and drums. It had one or two brief gigs in New York, recorded twelve numbers, and disbanded. Evans arranged two numbers ("Boplicity" "Moon Dreams"), Mulligan five ("Godchild," "Venus de Milo," "Rocker," "Jeru," "Darn That Dream"), Carisi one ("Israel"), Lewis three ("Move," "Budo," "Rouge"), and Davis one ("Deception"). Davis, Mulligan, Konitz, and Thornhill's tubist, Bill Barber, were on all the numbers; Roach and Kenny Clarke, Lewis and Al Haig, and J. J. Johnson and Kai Winding alternated. The Capitol nonet is the Thornhill band in miniature. Harmony and indirect melody are paramount. Sounds die away, and reënter by the side door. No voice is raised, and the soloists are less important than the ensembles. It is a begloved music, and the principal effect it had on jazz was the West Coast movement of the fifties—a pale, swinging white small-band jazz that eventually faded away when its main players went into the studios. Konitz' part in the nonet was largely decorative, although he had several brief solos. He once told Ira Gitler, "'As much as I enjoyed sitting there and playing with the band and as lucky as I was to get a couple of good licks on the records, I felt I wasn't as completely involved as I would like to have been. If it existed again, I would enjoy it that much more because I would know what a musical potential there was."

In 1980, Konitz was given another chance, and he recently explained how it happened: "Martin Williams, at the Smithsonian, asked if the nine-piece group I had had in the seventies could re-create the old Miles Davis 'Cool' records, and I said we could. He wanted us to play the material at a couple of concerts in Washington. I didn't know where the arrangements were, so I called Miles. I hadn't had any communication with him in years, and he wasn't interested. He didn't want to hear about it. I told Martin we might have to transcribe the recordings. I started listening, but there were lots of passages in the ensembles I simply couldn't decipher. Like in 'Godchild,' which was written by George Wallington and arranged by Gerry Mulligan, who had been the aggressive force behind the Capitol dates. I called up Gerry and went out to his house in Connecticut. We played the record, and he couldn't hear it, either. So he rewrote 'Godchild'—in four hours. It was just wonderful to see him work. And he rewrote 'Jeru' and 'Rocker,' too. Beautiful-looking scores, with delicate, spidery notation sprouting on the paper. Johnny Carisi had his score of 'Israel,' and John Lewis helped me sketch out 'Move,' although he wasn't as interested as Mulligan. When I'd taken all the arrangements to the copyist, I called Miles, because I was on my way to Pittsburgh to do a school clinic on cool jazz and I wanted to know if he had any words for the kiddies. He had a quick response: 'I don't give a shit what you tell them,' in that guttural way he has of talking. So I said, 'Miles, remember my asking you for the arrangements to the "Cool" sessions? Well, we've transcribed them and rewritten them and put them together again.' He said, 'Man, you should have asked me. Those motherfuckers are all in my basement.' I told Gil Evans about the conversation, and he said, 'Miles wouldn't have told you he had everything in the basement if you hadn't first told him you'd gone to the trouble to transcribe the records.' Miles is a bonafide eccentric."

Konitz had met Lennie Tristano in Chicago in the early forties, and he was not to be free of him for twenty years. Tristano died in 1978, at the age of fifty-nine. He was a mysterious, autocratic semi-recluse who attracted disciples and cultivated his own messianic tendencies. He rarely played in public, and he made relatively few records. His energy went into teaching—in a studio on East Thirty-second Street and in a house in Queens. He was an exceptional Art Tatum pianist who liked to experiment with tricky time signatures (5/4 or 3/8 against a steady 4/4), with shifting keys, and with free improvisation. His 1949 recordings "Intuition" and "Digression" preceded the first official free-jazz efforts by at least a dozen years. His restless single-note melodic lines can be heard sometimes in Dave McKenna and in the work of Bill Evans and Eddie Costa, but his influence has never been wide. "I first heard Lennie Tristano in Chicago when I was fifteen or sixteen," Konitz once said. "I was with Emil Flint, and I heard Tristano playing with a Mexican rumba band. I could hear all these fantastic locked-hands chords over the music. I sat in, and he didn't say anything. Years later, in an interview, he said I had sounded rotten. Anyway, I asked him if we could get together, and I started studying with him. We eventually worked together in some of the Chicago cocktail lounges. You can trace Lennie Tristano through Roy Eldridge and Lester Young and Charlie Parker and Art Tatum and Earl Hines and Nat Cole and also through Paul Hindemith and Bartók and

Bach. He was already doing what he became famous for—the long, long melodic lines, the counterpoint, the continually changing time signatures. It was fast company for me, and I always felt in way over my head. In fact, I still don't feel I've mastered Tristano's discipline. His dedication to his music was infectious, and he changed everyone who came in contact with him. He was at his best when he was teaching and playing. Otherwise, he got stranger and stranger. He generally refused to play in public after the fifties, and he took to staying in his pajamas all day. Once you were a part of Tristano's school, you were regarded as a traitor if you left, as I was when I joined Stan Kenton in 1952, even though I needed the work. I left Tristano for good in 1964, and we never communicated again. He had a big old house in Queens in the late fifties, and I lived there two years. I remember sitting on a glassed-in porch and reading 'War and Peace' and feeling like some kind of landowner, while everything around me was actually like a loony bin.

"'I studied with Lennie four or five years in all. It's hard to say exactly what I learned. I mean, you learn the major scales, the minor scales, the triads, but beyond that it's the things you talk about when you're not playing or studying. I once asked him about a large concern of mine, which was to eliminate what was making me play mechanically at the time. 'The hippest thing you can do is not play at all,' he said. 'Just listen.' Since then, I have been very concerned about not playing unless it means something. 'Are you contributing?' I keep asking myself. 'Are you a vital part of the situation?'"

Konitz has little to say of his time in Stan Kenton's huge Art Deco band. "Conte Candoli and Richie Kamuca and Sal Salvador and Frank Rosolino and Bill Russo were in that band," Konitz has said. "It had ten brass, and the reeds served mainly as padding. Every once in a while, one of the sax-ophonists would remove the reed, take the neck off his horn, and look deep into the bell to see if he could find a way to make more noise, to be heard better. But Kenton—that great giant of a man—was always very pleasant to work for. I left the band in 1954. I had married in 1947, and I had five kids. I moved out to Long Island and worked as a single and taught and tried to raise my family, and things were rough for me."

Konitz is a short, rounded man with scholarly hands and small feet. He has a helmet of curly hair, he affects aviator glasses, and his face is longer than it looks. His close-set eyes resemble headlights on a small car. He likes to talk in bursts, which he punctuates with whistles, *phews*, and polite Bronx cheers. An autobiographical paragraph might sound like this:

"I was born in Chicago October 13, 1927. I grew up on the North Side, in the Rogers Park area. I had two brothers, who were six and nine years older. My father, Abe, was in the dry-cleaning business, and he was good-natured, and I think of myself as being like that. I have a recollection of him working *all* the time [whistles]. We never starved, but it was hard going, and sometimes we lived in rooms behind the shop. My father was born in Poland, and my mother in Russia. She was five feet tall, but she was the strong one [*phew*]. I was the outsider in the family. I was light, and everyone else was dark. I was musical, and they weren't. I was, as the joke went, the milkman's son. I became a sort of prima donna early, and they went along with it. When I wanted a clarinet, which I took up at eleven, they got me one. I studied four years, mostly with Lou Honig, who's still teaching [*phhht*]. I've often thought I'd like to take all those lessons over again, because there were so many things that I misunderstood, like proper breathing. I thought for years that I had air going directly into my stomach [whistles]. I played with a little band in grammar school, and I played Ravel's 'Boléro' in a recital—just with a drummer. I played with a dance band in high school, and I sang Tex Beneke vocals and things like "Round the Clock Blues'—this little Jewish kid with horn-rims singing black blues [*phew*]. When I was seventeen, I replaced Charlie Ventura in Teddy Powell's band. Then I went with Jerry Wald, and took up alto saxophone, but Wald never let me take any solos, which was just as well because improvisation was still a mystery to me [whistles]."

Konitz talked about his playing: "Joe Dixon, the clarinettist and teacher, told me once, 'You sound like you're not thinking when you're soloing,' and he's right. He has a scientific attitude, and he puts these melodies together he's worked out. But I don't have a surefire musical vocabulary. I'm riveted to where I am when I play—to the people around me. I hear everything the piano and bass and drums are doing, and I lay the right notes on them, and each of those notes has to affect the following one. It's a lovely experience when it works out with a rhythm section. It's reaching out and touching one another. It's a nice place to be, and you can go anywhere from there.

"I think of improvisation as coming in ten levels, each one more intense than the one before. On the first level, you play the melody, and you should sound as if you were playing it for the very first time. Freshly. If it doesn't sound that way, you're not ready to go to the second level. Playing the melody properly gives you the license to vary it, to embellish it, which is what you do on the second level. The melody is still foremost, but you add little things to it on the third level. Variation—displacing certain notes in the melody—comes in around the fourth level, and by the time you get to five, six, and seven you are more than halfway to creating a new song. Eight, nine, and ten are just that—the creation of wholly new melodies. Moving through these ten levels can take place during a set or over the course of an evening. Sometimes, though, you never get past three or four or five, but that's O.K., because no one level is more important than any other.

"When things got bad in the sixties, I still had little gigs and I always practiced, so I never felt I was falling behind. In the seventies, I married my second wife, Tavia. I worked a lot at Stryker's, which was just down

the street from where I live, on West Eighty-sixth. And I worked a lot at
Gregory's, on the East Side. Then a man from Italy asked me if I would
put together nine bodies for a group. The idea appealed to me, and I got
advice and some arrangements, and we played off and on at Stryker's
and in Europe. We also play at the Village Vanguard a couple of times a
year. I'm middle-aged, but I'm still tooting on my tooter, and I see no end
to it. It's still a severe challenge—never a cup of tea. It's some sort of gift
to me, and I feel very fortunate to be able to earn my bread doing it. I
have plans of really getting active. I'm learning to play the piano. The last
few years, I've had some degree of solvency. It begins to seem possible to
rent a studio. As I see it, I'll play as long as I feel good and then become
an artist-in-residence. You get to the point where you have to start listening to younger players, and that's difficult. I took a couple of piano
lessons from Harold Danko, who has worked for me, so am I going to be
afraid he'll talk around—'Hey, Lee Konitz studied with *me*'? You have to
keep playing with younger people. I hate to deny being moved by something new."

A True Improviser

A short history of jazz improvisation, the heart and soul of the music,
might go like this. It began in the rural South in the nineteenth century as
random gestures of black protest: a bones solo acompanying a buck-and-
wing; the field hollers, which formed a secret, constantly evolving code;
the endlessly invented and often satiric blues lyrics, and the guitar or
banjo variations that decorated them. In short, it began as any kind of
Afro-American music that did not go by the white man's book. When
Reconstruction faltered and racism closed down again, in the eighties
and nineties, black improvisational music had taken clearer shape. It was
played mainly by rough small bands, which in time used cornet or trumpet, a reed instrument, trombone, piano (not always), guitar or banjo,
bass or tuba, and drums. These groups, generally made up of day labor-
ers, were offshoots of the New Orleans marching bands, and their improvisations—embellishments, really—were largely collective. It was an
ensemble music that parted for occasional solos. In his autobiography,
"Treat It Gentle," Sidney Bechet tried to describe what happened in the
early improvisation: "It has to be put inside you and you have to be ready
to have it put there. All that happens to you makes a feeling out of your
life and you play that feeling. But there's more than that. There's the feeling inside the music too. And the final thing, it's the way those two feelings come together." By 1924, two years before Jelly Roll Morton unwittingly memorialized this New Orleans music with his Hot Pepper sides,

Louis Armstrong and King Oliver, also recording in Chicago, and Armstrong and Sidney Bechet, recording in New York, had demonstrated that they were the first jazz soloists—the first true melodic jazz improvisers. During the next fifteen years or so, jazz became a music of soloists, and among the greatest were Armstrong and Bechet, Earl Hines, Bix Beiderbecke, Coleman Hawkins, Red Allen, Jack Teagarden, Benny Goodman, Django Reinhardt, Red Norvo, Lester Young, Art Tatum, and Roy Eldridge. Their predecessors had worked mostly with the blues and with ragtimelike materials built on two or three strains. Armstrong and his followers began using as their stepping-off points the new theatre and movie songs of Jerome Kern and Irving Berlin and George Gershwin and Harold Arlen. They reinvented melody. They would take a Kern or Gershwin tune and improvise a parallel song that both freshened and shadowed the original. By the early forties, they had amassed a body of recordings that were melodically and rhythmically unique and had a spontaneity that had not been heard in Western music since Bach. But jazz has little patience, and by the mid-forties a new kind of improvisation had appeared, shepherded by Charlie Parker, Bud Powell, and Dizzy Gillespie. These three had studied Art Tatum's harmonic edifices, and, borrowing from him, they widened the harmonic base of jazz improvisation by improvising on the chords of a song instead of on the melody. They cast out melody and entered a wilderness of chords, altered chords, expanded chords. Or thought they were casting out melody—their improvisations were in fact highly melodic, but in ways that were undanceable and largely unsingable. Called bebop, it was an engulfing, baroque music through which no silence was allowed to show. Late in 1959, Ornette Coleman, the Texas alto saxophonist, dropped from the skies, and a third kind of improvisation was born. Its adherents threw everything out—melody, chords, keys, choruses, and steady rhythms. They improvised on themselves, on their moods, on the air around them. They made any kind of noise on their instruments which entered their heads—barnyard sounds, jungle sounds, traffic sounds. This was called "free jazz," and for a long time it has laid a disquieting hand on the music.

But there is a savior on the horizon—a fifty-seven-year-old tenor saxophonist named Warne Marsh. He is not well known. For a long time, he worked within the Lennie Tristano enclave. During much of that time, he shuttled between California and New York. He took day jobs, he taught, he played with Tristano students and with a neo-bebop West Coast group called Supersax. In the late seventies, he settled for a time in New York, where he continued to teach, and where he played on an irregular basis at the West End Café and the Village Vanguard. Then he went back to the Coast. During his most recent stay in New York, two things became clear about Marsh: he is one of the most original jazz improvisers alive, and he is perfecting a kind of improvisation that draws on all jazz. It is highly melodic, it uses the long, undulating lines of bebop, and it has a freedom of form and of rhythm and harmony which is akin to free jazz. His old friend the West Coast reedman Gary Foster has said of him, "I first met Warne in 1966 or 1967, and one way or another I have played hundreds of hours with him. He is a complex man, dedicated to one purpose—to be a true improviser. He's quiet to the point of being distracting. Some people take him as aloof. But everything reaches Warne, and what he has cared to absorb comes out distilled a day or two later. I sometimes have the feeling that the jazz world has passed him by. He is never aggressive. His nature is to let people seek him out. But if they do, and the situation is congenial to him, he becomes totally committed. He has the whole tradition of jazz at the tips of his fingers. I hear Louis Armstrong in his work, and Lester Young and Charlie Parker and Lennie Tristano. People who heard Warne when he was a kid have said he was under the sway of Tex Beneke and Ben Webster. His performing is astonishingly consistent. He can always play, and he's never far from his best. It's not in Warne to entertain. If his playing has any entertainment value, it is in its very subtlety. Warne erases the bar line, but he doesn't do it so that it sounds like a musical exercise. He throws his phrases across the bar line the way Lester Young did, but, of course, in a much more complicated way. His sound on the tenor is completely untenorlike, just as Jimmy Knepper's sound on the trombone is completely untrombonelike. Both men seem to use their instruments simply as vessels to contain their notes. They could be playing any instrument. In all the years I've played with Warne—even just the two of us with a metronome—he's always touched me. It's a power I don't hear in a lot of musicians. Most of us don't get to the center of our playing. Warne holds the faith: he can do it all the time."

Marsh is of medium size, and he has small, beautiful hands and a majestic head. His eyes slope at their outer corners, and he keeps them at a ruminative half-mast. He has an aristocratic nose—bold, declarative, shapely—and thinning iron-gray hair. He is an indifferent dresser, whose clothes simply surround him. Shadows of smiles flicker constantly behind his eyes. While he was in New York, he lived in a one-room studio apartment in the Hotel Bretton Hall, a kind of upper-Broadway outpost of the Chelsea Hotel which is filled with musicians and singers and dancers. His studio had a nineteenth-century-atelier quality. The ceiling was high and patchy, and the grayish-white paint looked morose. In one corner were a stove, a sink, and a refrigerator, and elsewhere were a piano, a bed, and several nondescript chairs, one of them generally holding an ongoing chess match. The south wall was covered with quilts, presumably to keep Marsh's sounds in and the trumpet player's next door out. More quilts were suspended over a bay window that looked out onto Broadway. Marsh has no small talk; what he does say is articulate and rounded. He is more high-strung than he lets on. When he talks about himself or about his music, he moves almost constantly, taking short, abrupt steps, his stomach slightly stuck out, his chin raised. On the bandstand, he knuckles his left cheek alarmingly with his left hand while he decides what to play next. Using his words like bricks, he carefully constructed his life one afternoon, and this is what he said:

"I was born in Los Angeles on October 26, 1927. My parents were both motion-picture people. My mother was a classically trained violinist, and she was in an all-female quartet—two violins, cello, piano—that played mood music on silent-movie sets. The idea was to inspire the actors between shots. She was born in Philadelphia, where she studied, and her parents were Russian Jews. Her father, Louis Marionofsky, had played trumpet in the Imperial Army. He deserted and came over in the nineties, settling in Philadelphia and changing his name to Marion, which is my middle name. He ran five-and-dime stores in Philly, and he moved to Los Angeles when my mother was in her late teens. My father, Oliver T. Marsh, was a cinematographer. He did the Nelson Eddy–Jeanette MacDonald films as well as good stuff like 'David Copperfield' and 'A Tale of Two Cities.' He was born in Lawrence, Kansas, and his father was an accountant with the Santa Fe Railroad—before he deserted his family. My father's mother was a tenth-generation Brewster, of the Pilgrim Brewsters. My father started out selling and servicing typewriters. Then Mae Marsh, who was a star in silent films and was one of his sisters and who I'm named after—she was Mary Warne Marsh—got him a job as a second cameraman in Hollywood. He taught himself how to take a motion-picture camera apart and put it back together, and once, on location, when the only camera the company had broke, he fixed it and was promoted to first cameraman. He was socially retiring, and he had no interest whatever in music. He never took a drink until he was thirty-five, and then he never stopped. But it doesn't seem to have got in the way of his work. He died in 1941, at the age of forty-nine. I have a younger sister, Gloria, and a younger brother, Owen. Gloria is a housewife and a painter and manages an art store, and my brother is a cinematographer. They both live in the San Fernando Valley, near my mother, who has moved into a new house and out of the one she and my father bought there in 1933. It was Spanish-style, with the red tile roof and the archways, and it was built in 1926 by a producer. It originally had three acres and a swimming pool and tennis court and track, but the flood of 1939 messed all that up, and after my father died my mother sold everything but an acre or so. She never changed the inside of the house, and it was always a time piece to me, an anachronism. Mother hasn't remarried, and she kept us together after my father's death. She was a generous mother, and she still helps me if I need it. She's had trouble with my career, though—with improvising. What turned her on musically was Gilbert and Sullivan, light opera—that kind of thing. I have to ask myself what jazz means in her mind. Maybe it's the association with New York, which she doesn't like. I don't know.

"My parents first lived in the Hollywood Hills, and I went to a private school there, and public school when they moved to the Valley. I always got between an A and a B average. My father enrolled me in Caltech when I was born—it was a custom of the day—and I planned an academic career. I took up piano and accordion when I was ten, and I picked up on the Magdalena Bach books. By the time I was thirteen, I was able to read music. I asked for an alto saxophone, and I studied with Earl Immel. I learned 'Scatterbrain,' which was a big hit in 1939. The director of my high-school band told me I didn't sound so good on alto and maybe I should get a tenor, so I switched when I was fifteen. I played E-flat tuba, sax, and bass clarinet in high school, and when I was sixteen I started studying classical saxophone with Mickey Gillette. The first musician I was entranced by was Corky Corcoran, who played tenor with Harry James and sounded like Ben Webster. I even tried a couple of lessons with him. I was also listening to jazz in the Central Avenue joints. By 1942, I was in a band called the Hollywood Canteen Kids, playing the U.S.O. and for Ken Murray's 'Blackouts,' which were high-burlesque revues. I also worked with a group called the Teenagers on a once-a-week radio show built around Hoagy Carmichael. When I was seventeen, I began sitting in with Dexter Gordon and Wardell Gray and Lawrence Marable. I graduated from high school and entered the music program at the University of Southern California. Then, in 1946, I was drafted into the Army for eighteen months. I spent nine months at Fort Lee, in Virginia, and the rest of the time at Fort Monmouth, in New Jersey. At Monmouth, I was in the band that marched the troops to and from Signal Corps school. By this time, I had heard Charlie Parker and Lester Young. I spent every spare minute in New York, listening to Parker and studying with Lennie Tristano, whom I'd heard about at Fort Lee from a trumpet player named Don Ferrara. When I got out of the Army, I went back to college, but my head was not in California. The pull of jazz in New York was too strong, and within a year I was back here. Almost immediately, though, I went out on a three-month cross-country road trip with Buddy Rich's first big band— the one with Terry Gibbs and Johnny Mandel and Hal McKusick and Doug Mettome. There was always friction when I soloed, and gradually Rich parcelled out my solos among the other saxophones. Also, I sat right in front of his boom-boom-boom bass drum, which was the size of a small house. I ran into him ten years later, and I was amazed he remembered me.

"When I first studied with Lennie Tristano, he had the ground floor of a brownstone on the upper East Side. Then he moved to the famous studio on East Thirty-second Street, and eventually to Flushing. He had an aggressive, logical mind, and he was enthralling to work with. I had finally met someone who could define music for me. His understanding of it was already at high twentieth-century levels, both in classical music and in jazz, which he had been playing for fifteen years. He made me realize that I could train myself to do anything I wanted, that it is possible to be a better improviser—which was a new concept at the time. What Tristano was trying to show with the so-called free-jazz records he made for Capitol in 1949 with Lee Konitz and Billy Bauer and me was that, properly trained, musicians could now improvise melody and harmony and rhythm and form, putting harmony on harmony, metre on metre, and letting the form go where it would. I don't think he would have agreed with the modal experiments of George Russell, which have an intellectual hook, or with those of Miles Davis. After all, the modal system was set aside three hundred years ago for the twelve keys. You can't modulate in the modal system. You just go from chord to chord.

"I studied and played with Tristano until about 1955, when I went back to Los Angeles. I played there with other Tristano students—the tenor saxophonist Ted Brown, the pianist Ronnie Ball, and the drummer Jeff Morton. I came back to New York in 1958. I took day jobs, mostly clerical—the longest about six months. It was a rough time. I returned to Los Angeles in 1962, and met my wife, and we were married in 1964. Even though I was almost forty, I wasn't ready to get married, to support a wife and children and maintain this crazy kind of life. She is a good woman, and we have two wonderful children. We separated a couple of years ago, and they live in Santa Cruz. Anyway, we came back to New York in 1964 and lived in Lennie's house out in Queens. In 1966, we returned to L.A., and we stayed there until 1978. I started teaching in a studio over a music store in Pasadena—children and jazz students—and I loved it. I worked with Clare Fischer's big band, and in 1972 I started in with Supersax, which was founded by the bass player Buddy Clark and the saxophonist Med Flory. It had five saxophones and a rhythm section, and it played arrangements of old Charlie Parker solos and ensemble figures, with spaces for our solos. Later, the trumpeter Conte Candoli and the trombonist Carl Fontana were added, and some of the other people were Jack Nimitz, Joe Lopes, Bill Perkins, Lou Levy, and Jake Hanna. I quit in 1977, and my wife and children and I moved to Ridgefield, Connecticut, where I taught."

Marsh makes his listeners work. His long, multiplying melodic lines seem to flee, disappearing around corner after corner, moving at a constant speed—all the while drawing us on hypnotically. In the early days of jazz improvisation, the listener could hang on to the bar lines; they fenced the soloist in and preserved the shape of the melody. Marsh ignores such frameworks, allowing his melodic lines to pour until he runs out of either ideas (rarely) or breath. Marsh's tone does not make him any easier to listen to. It is makeshift, and even abrupt; it surrounds his notes, as his clothes surround him. When Marsh and Lee Konitz played with Lennie Tristano, it was sometimes difficult to tell the saxophonists apart. Marsh would rise into the alto range, and Konitz would sink into the tenor range. Since then, Marsh's sound has deepened—or, at least, thickened. Marsh's solos move in a snakelike fashion—shooting forward and up, down and to one side, up and to the other side, precipitously down, then straight up. He also doubles back on himself, tumbles through double-time passages, restrains the time. He likes to move the beat back and forth and just off center. He plays hob with harmony. He moves along just at the edge of the key he is working in, and sometimes he steps outside it. These rhythmic and harmonic liberties give his melodic flow a great spaciousness. The saxophone is a hard instrument not to be emotional on. Marsh's emotions are filtered through his mind. What is moving about him is the logic and order of his phrasing, his little almost sighing connective notes, the sheen and flow of his ideas, his density and prolificacy and urgency.

At his studio, he said, "I became convinced in the bebop days that jazz is a fine art, not a folk music for second-class Americans. I think of it as the most significant music since the Baroque period. It has reëstablished self-expression in music—the individual voice—which ceased in the mid-nineteenth century. It has also reestablished melody. The nineteenth-century composers made it with harmony. Their melodies were often childishly simple, and it was the harmony they wrapped around those melodies that gave their symphonies and concertos weight and grandeur. The interplay of fresh and original melodies was extremely rare until Bartók. I find that I trust myself more and more as a musician. You are, of course, doing two things on the bandstand—performing and improvising. It's very demanding to improvise in front of an audience. When I improvise, there is nothing visual in my head. In the back of my mind, I have a sketch of the song I'm playing, and I also hold on to its mood and feeling. And I listen constantly to what is going on around me. My mind works ahead a bar or two, although I don't think in terms of bars. From the first, Tristano taught us to go around the bar lines and to impose other metres on the four-four time. To a certain extent, the length of a phrase is controlled by instinctive knowledge. So when I begin a phrase I don't have the least notion where it will end. The more I improvise, the closer it comes to singing. I try to play as if I were singing. Lennie said he could sing every note he had ever played. I have no wish to be a virtuoso saxophone player. I want to get away from bebop music, and what I mean is the really stifling form of starting a number by playing a melody, then going into a string of long solos, then restating the melody. I want to structure everything in terms of polyphony and poly-rhythms—the kind of counterpoint that we did with Lennie Tristano thirty years ago and that has been done all too rarely since. Audiences enjoyed it then, and I suspect they'd enjoy it even more now. What I need is the places to play it in—small college halls, maybe—and the musicians to make it work.'"

Good, Careful Melody

The bassist Michael Moore balances the over-amplification and show-off tendencies of most contemporary bassists by ignoring them. He concentrates on perfecting his tone, which is rich and even and affecting. He avoids singsong effects and keeps his volume at a gentlemanly level. Most important, he is carrying to new heights the flag of lyricism and melodic beauty borne by all great jazz musicians since the arrival of Louis Armstrong, and he is doing it with a low-pitched stringed instrument that is prone to all manner of tonal difficulties and has a bare three registers. Marian McPartland has said of Moore, "I first heard him soon after he came to New York from Cincinnati, his home town. In fact, I *hired* him then. He astonished me. He played perfect time, he had pure sound, he chose his notes with great care, and he was quick to learn. He was the best bass soloist I'd ever heard. Most bass solos don't have much content, but his have logic and structure and wholeness. They have such lyricism, such melodic glow, that you don't think of them as bass solos. They are closer to guitar solos, but in the end they're entities unto themselves."

Like all jazz bassists, Michael Moore comes in three parts: the accompanist, the soloist, and the arco player. Bassists and drummers often talk of hitting the "back" or the "front" of their notes, but Moore the accompanist hits his in the exact center. He chooses them according to the situation he finds himself in. He frequently uses the low notes in the chords of a song, but in a duo with Gene Bertoncini he will construct countermelodies. When he plays with Teddy Wilson, he duplicates many of Wilson's left-hand bass notes. Marian McPartland often piques him, and he wages exhilarating contrapuntal warfare. But he shies away from playing with Dave McKenna, feeling that McKenna's left hand is so strong that he would add little to it. Moore's solos are models of melodic beauty, of sheer improvisational exuberance. They surpass the instrument they are played on. He will start a solo with a rapid descending phrase that begins in eighth notes and expands into quarter notes. He will pause, play a triplet, pause again, and repeat the triplet, altering the final note to introduce a falling-and-rising arpeggio delivered with great speed and perfect articulation. He will pause once more, issue five commanding staccato notes and go into a series of rapid ascending notes that keep breaking off. Then still another pause, and he will shoot into his high register and construct an eight-bar melody that turns out to be a jubilant new song. After a flurry of on-the-beat notes, he will close the solo with an unresolved note, which leaves us with a polite question—"Was it all right?"—and the promise of more to come. Moore's arco work is regal and delicate and exact. Most jazz arco playing has a stiff, mahogany sound, and most of it is off pitch, but Moore stays in tune and has a soft and buoyant tone.

Moore lives with his second wife, the singer Anita Gravine, in an old slope-shouldered building on Thompson Street, in SoHo. The apartment has a kitchen, dominated by a photograph of Louis Armstrong and a reproduction of Edward Hopper's "Nighthawks." An adjoining bed-sitting-room looks out on an airshaft. Off the bed-sitting-room is a narrow room with a window at the end, and leaning against one wall are five basses. The bed-sitting-room has a Victorian rocker, a double bed, a Morris chair, and an upright piano. Moore has half a dozen or so students, each of whom averages a visit a month. A session usually lasts an hour and a half, and is intense and difficult. Moore fills his students until they spill over, for he talks as fast as he can play. He stands most of the time, even when he isn't demonstrating passages on one of his basses. He recently gave a young Canadian bassist, Rick Kilburn (who has worked with Mose Allison and Dave Brubeck), the first lesson he'd had in a few years. Before Kilburn arrived, Moore, pacing the bed-sitting-room, talked about music. He is compact, about six feet tall, and has brown hair, and round Irish-burgher features.

"My main problem with the bass has always been sound," he said, sitting briefly in the rocker and pitching rapidly back and forth. "I have a proper bass sound in my head, but it has taken me years to get near it on my instrument. You should be able to carry that sound from room to room, from tune to tune, without losing it. Jack Teagarden always said, 'Don't let the drummer or anybody else wreck your sound,' and he never did. But trying to perfect that sound first is another matter. I use a Xavier Jacquet bass. It's about a hundred and forty years old. If you had a bass made, it would cost at least six thousand dollars, and it might not be as good, because of the new wood. Old wood is looser and transmits vibrations better. Playing an amplified bass (or raising your strings higher from the board—which most bassists used to do) helps. You don't have to pull the strings so hard just to be heard. At the same time, your sound is apt to become distorted, particularly when you record. Trying to get a natural sound on records—a sound that sounds something like *me*—is driving me crazy, because the young engineers, raised on rock and Fender basses, don't know what a natural bass sound *is*. They feed a wire right into their control panel from my pickup, which would ordinarily be connected to my amplifier. And they put a microphone on my strings, and fiddle with their knobs, and you come out sounding like a tree creaking on a winter night.

"It's easy to forget that the bass player plays just about every beat. A whole band can be ruined by a bad bass player. I've decided that the combination of players in a rhythm section is terribly important. There can be a conflict between two players which will make a rhythm section go. When Miles Davis had Ron Carter and Tony Williams on bass and drums,

Carter was the anchor, and Williams tended to rush the beat. That created tension, and tension creates excitement. In John Coltrane's rhythm section, Jimmy Garrison had to be the anchor, too, but for a different reason. Elvin Jones was the drummer, and he has always liked to play off the bass player's time. Elvin has the ability to sound like he's playing on the beat when he's playing both the back of the beat and the front of the beat. Bass players who work with him have to be very strong. Slam Stewart, who was marvellous thirty-five years ago and is marvellous now, is that strong. He plays right in the center of the beat, and he has the nerves of a thief when he plays way up. Listen to the recording of 'I Got Rhythm' that he and Don Byas did impromptu at a Town Hall concert in the mid-forties. Slam makes himself almost invisible, but the notes are all in the right place. That reminds me of what my father, who's a guitarist, once told me: 'You know the right notes, now learn the best notes.' Bass players should be invisible, instead of sounding as if they were all leaders, which is the way it is now. You have to be unselfish. You have to let the other players take most of the shots. Accompanying different instruments raises different problems. Horn players sound one note at a time, but guitarists might hit four, only one of which will be right for me to play. When I played in a trio with Jim Hall a couple of years ago, I discovered that he goes in strange harmonic directions, and that even if I chose the correct note it might *sound* wrong, or it might set the tonality going in the wrong direction. Pianists are all different. Teddy Wilson uses all the bass notes in his left hand, so you have to play a lot of the same notes he plays. Modern pianists leave out the bass notes, and that gives you latitude. More and more modern musicians want the sound of the bass right out front, and I hate that. It's an ugly sound. I just got a new amplifier—a Walter Woods. It's made on the Coast, and it's small and very clear and quiet. If I had my way, I'd play without an amplifier. But it isn't possible anymore. Drummers are louder and louder, and, to compensate, the horn players increase their volume and then yell at the bass player to turn up, turn up. If you don't turn up, you can't hear yourself, and it's like going into battle with just a hammer."

Moore, who had been doing figure eights between the kitchen and the bed-sitting-room, sat down on the piano bench. "When I play a good solo, I feel that I've just been sitting by and listening. I think, Where did that come from? But if I play badly it's my fault. I've always been attracted to melodic players; nothing else moves me. You have to study a song if you want to improvise on it well. I learn the melody and every note in the chords and the best harmonic way through the tune. Then I'll play the melody straight a couple of times, and sometimes before I perform I'll take a drink to dull the old conscious brain and let the subconscious out. All of which means that you discipline yourself first—because that's what music is: discipline—and then throw the discipline out the window. When I solo, I have a brand-new melody in my head. That's why I leave so many spaces in my solos, why I force myself to wait—so that the melody has the time to get itself organized before it comes out. It's nerve-racking. It's like a ballplayer waiting to swing at the last possible second. But it creates tension in the listener, and then release, and that's what improvising is. You have to keep your intuition open, even if you play a wrong note. Gary Burton told me once that there is no note that can't be fixed, and he's right. A good improviser should study good songs. They fill his head with melody, and eventually all that melody will come out in a new form. I see the bass in a strange way. The tone is the same as melody: they get mixed up together. They become indivisible. Of course, I hear things in my head that I can't play—that are perhaps impossible to play on any instrument. But complexity has nothing to do with beauty. You don't have to sound like Coltrane on the bass, which is what most of the young players are trying to do. The bass by nature is closer to the spaced-out playing of Miles Davis and Lester Young. It is also a lower-register instrument, and many bassists forget that. They forget that people don't hear notes down there as easily as they do the higher notes. Pure technique will go right by the listener's ear, whereas good, careful melody will rest in it."

Kilburn turned out to be thin, dark-haired, and relaxed. Moore gave him a bass and stationed him near the kitchen door. He put a book of bass exercises on a music stand. The exercises were by Ludwig Streicher, the Austrian master bassist, whose new methods of fingering and bowing have become a passion for Moore. The Streicher bowing method involves rotating the bow from one side of the hair to the other when crossing strings, to make a smooth, connected sound. The thumb lies lightly over the top of the bow shaft and the little finger on the bottom of the frog. The little finger becomes the bow's rudder. Streicher suggests dropping the left elbow from a horizontal position, so that it points more toward the floor. This eliminates the pain in the arms and sides that bassists often experience after a half hour of playing. He also suggests that bassists stop draping themselves over their instrument. Keeping the left foot cocked against the bottom of the bass's sound box helps in pulling back on the instrument, provided the peg that the bass rests on isn't too long. Moore taught Streicher's methods by demonstration, and Kilburn slowly bent himself to the new ways. Moore told him to go through Streicher's book several times—the new methods would soon fall into place, and he'd have trouble remembering the old ones. Then Moore abruptly sat down at the piano and played a medium-tempo version of "What Is This Thing Called Love?" He played chords hooked together by spindly runs, and Kilburn accompanied him pizzicato, Kilburn soloed, and when they had finished Moore gave him an extended reading, on harmony and scales, which became increasingly abstruse but began this way:

"What are you thinking about in the first part of that tune? What harmonic decisions can you make?"

"A C-sharp diminished scale?" Kilburn said.

"That's one you can use. But there are other possibilities: the C whole-tone scale or the D-flat melodic minor scale."

On the piano, Moore played some of the scales he recommended, and he played some on the bass, his fingers moving like hummingbirds up and down the strings.

Kilburn watched intently. When Moore's lecture on harmony was almost over, Kilburn asked, "How do you think of all these things when you're playing? Do you know them well enough to do them without thinking about them?"

"Yes," Moore said. "Unless the song is new. Then I woodshed first."

"When I have to play a new tune, I learn the chords, but I depend more on my intuition, and what I do often sounds wrong to me."

Moore nodded. "The intellect has to train your ear. You have to feed new information into the computer, and practice that information intellectually. Then, when that information becomes intuitional to your ear, the melody will flow out."

"I'm an ear player, but eighty per cent of the time I can sound like I'm not."

"Most bass players are boring, because they think from the bottom of their instrument to the top rather than from the top down. Streicher's methods make it easier to think from the top. Anyway, you should learn to be a good team player first, like Ron Carter, and worry about soloing last of all. The bass is especially difficult, because the notes aren't right there in front of you. Half of playing the instrument is finding the notes, and half is making them come out clearly and well—particularly the low ones, which tend to run together."

"I've got to clarify all this, and it will take time," Kilburn said.

"That's right. It will. But nothing to worry about."

Kilburn's lesson lasted a couple of hours. When he had left, Moore sat down again in the rocker and drank a beer. He talked for a while of how promising he thought Kilburn was. Then, reminded of beginnings, he talked of his own.

"I started on accordion in third grade in Cincinnati. I took lessons with a friend of my father's for three years, and he never knew I couldn't read music. I won ten dollars in a talent show for playing 'After You've Gone,' in block chords that my father had taught me, and I won simply because I kept going. Then I was out of school a year with nephritis, and that was the end of the accordion. In junior high school, I was told to pick an instrument for the school band that the school would buy, and I chose the tuba. I hated it. I went to Withrow High School, and they needed a bass player for the school jazz band, so I switched then and there. My father bought me a Kay plywood bass, and I studied with Dave Horine. He'd played with my father, and he had a bass shop. I was easily discouraged. When I tried to use a bow the first time, it sounded so bad to me I didn't play at all for months. I studied with Harold Roberts, who was a symphonic bassist. And I became a part of the Withrow Minstrels, a high-calibre musical organization run by George Smith, who was the musical director and something of a legend in Cincinnati. Smith would hire professionals when he needed them for his shows, which were practically Paul Whiteman productions. In fact, he used my father in his very first one.

"I graduated from high school in 1963, and played at the Playboy Club in Cincinnati with a pianist named Woody Evans, then with the guitarist Cal Collins. He was a natural player, but he wasn't much help when you asked him what such-and-such a chord was. He'd say, 'Oh, that's kind of an E chord.' The Cincinnati College Conservatory of Music took me on scholarship for a year. Then Dee Felice, a local drummer, recommended me to Nat Pierce, who was Woody Herman's pianist, and I joined Woody the day after Christmas in 1966. That was the band that had Marvin Stamm and Ronnie Zito and Bill Chase and Frank Vicari and Sal Nistico and Carl Fontana. They'd had a bunch of bass players with bad beats. I couldn't read well, but I knew how to keep time, so I worked out. But I worked out in spite of myself. I was a pretty testy kid. I hadn't been in the band two weeks when I had my first scene with Woody. He's an old-time bandleader who not only knows how to handle a band but knows how to handle audiences as well. He's tough and he's savvy. Scott La Faro was my big influence, and I had all these notions that I was going to free the bass, so during a performance I started accompanying just the saxophones, ignoring the rest of the band. Of course, it was crazy, because the bass player is supposed to anchor the whole band. Then I took a girl on the bus without saying anything to anybody, and *that* bugged Woody. I didn't understand the hierarchy in a big band—that if Stamm or Chase wanted to take a girl on the bus, O.K. They had long since proved themselves. But if a new player like me wanted to, he had to introduce the girl to Woody, just as if he were bringing her home to his family. We had another blowup in Morocco. 'Satin Doll' was the bass feature, and during it Woody would hold the mike on the bass. But halfway through my solo he leaned over and said, 'Watch your intonation, pal.' That did it. Afterward, I picked him up and swung him around and told him he better get another bass player, and left the band. But later I went back and subbed with the band. After all the scenes, you become part of the family.

"I studied two more years in Cincinnati, with Frank Proto, and came to New York in 1968. I worked right off with Marian McPartland. She's always open to new players and new tunes, and she plays better and better and better. You can use confidence when you first come to this town, and she built it up. I was with Marian a year, and with Freddie Hubbard for a while, and then with Jimmy Raney. Then I moved back to Cincinnati. I was married and we had a mongoloid child, and things weren't working out well with him in New York. In Cincinnati, I spent a lot of time with older retarded kids, just to see how they functioned, what they were like. They were often slow and lazy, but my son wasn't. We found that he was educable, and now he talks a mile a minute, and he reads. He's sharp and he's got all the human qualities, and sometimes they get in the way. I wish I could see more of him and be closer to him.

My wife and I were divorced, and I only see him twice a year. After nine months in Cincinnati, I missed New York so bad I came back, and joined the Ruby Braff-George Barnes Quartet. It was tightly structured and had an immediately identifiable sound. None of the solos were long, and we communicated with audiences on both a traditional and a modern level. Barnes was a great guitarist in his older, chunky way. He was totally ordered and never wasted a note. I'd be amazed at the sounds he'd get off sometimes. It was too bad, but a venom developed between the two men after a time. Ruby is the most honest guy I have ever known. He just doesn't know how to smile and say O.K. He *has* to say what he thinks, no matter the grief. But he's a super player and we're good friends. I go up to his place in Riverdale, and he plays me all sorts of Louis Armstrong tapes and tells me wild Sid Catlett stories."

Moore stood up and stretched, and sat down on a stool that Kilburn had used in his lesson. "I was born in a suburb of Cincinnati—Glen Este—in 1945. I'm an only child. My father's sixty-one now, and he has white hair and a white beard. He's not too tall, and he has a great sense of humor. He's a kind of Cincinnati Ruby Braff who always says the wrong thing. He's a really fine guitarist, Charlie Christian style. For years, in the forties and early fifties, he had a Nat Cole-type trio with a piano player named Teddy Raeckel. They were busy until the bottom dropped out in the mid-fifties. My father went into the insurance business, and he was very unhappy. But now he's retired and back in music. He practices several hours a day and works three or four nights a week. He used to dress Brooks Brothers style, but now he's looser, with his beard and all. He sat in with Marian McPartland one night, and she tried to hire him, but he wouldn't do it. My mother's an elegant, white-haired, tall lady who's very composed, very self-contained. She knows herself and is comfortable with what she knows. She came from Ripley, Ohio, and her maiden name was Jeannette Gardner. She has an autobiography written by my great-great-great-grandfather, who was a circuit preacher. He published church music and travelled by flatboat down the Ohio River in 1810. And he cleared the land and fought bears and mountain lions. *His* father fought in the Revolution. There have been a lot of musicians in my family. One of my grandfathers had a country band, and an uncle played bass. My mother taught piano fourteen years. She plays very well, and although she never could have been a performer, I think she sold herself short. She used to try to teach my Dad to read music, but he was scared to death of it. I inherited the feeling. I can read, but it makes me nervous. A couple of years ago, I sent my parents to Europe on a tour. They'd hardly ever been out of Ohio. At first, my father was Mr. World-wise—'I don't want to travel with a bunch of tourists,' and all that. But he bought the Eiffel Tower and everything else he saw in Paris and Rome and Venice and London. When they got back, they looked more alive and happy than I'd ever seen them. They'd bailed me out a number of times, and I figured it was my turn."

A Decent Life

The duet has come into wide use in jazz. Long regarded as a novelty, a diversion, an afterthought, duets were nonetheless recorded (or reported) in the twenties, thirties, and forties by Jelly Roll Morton and King Oliver, by Joe Venuti and Eddie Lang, by Louis Armstrong and Earl Hines, by Lang and Lonnie Johnson, by Armstrong and Django Reinhardt, by Bill Coleman and Reinhardt, and by Duke Ellington and Jimmy Blanton. The most difficult instrumental combination in jazz, the duet has nothing in common with the soloist, on one side, or the trio, on the other. The soloist is a narcissist who sets his own boundaries, goals, and speeds, who makes his own weather. The trio is a crowd, a small band. A duet is like a railroad car: it is indivisible and runs on parallel tracks. Its members must be altruists, teachers, friends, and instigators. Each must match but never outmatch the other. A duet should be as seamless as an egg and as intricate as a snowflake. Duets began to be fashionable in the mid-sixties, partly because they didn't cost much and partly because young jazz musicians, full of technique and invention, were looking for new challenges. At first, these duets were made up of guitar and bass or two guitars, and most of them were born at the Guitar, which flourished in the early seventies at Tenth Avenue and Fifty-first Street. Then came piano and bass (now the most prevalent duet), guitar and trombone, two pianos, guitar and tenor saxophone, piano and guitar, and piano and tenor saxophone. Several years ago, an entire concert of duets was given at the Kool Jazz Festival in New York. With few exceptions, the duets that have appeared have been transitional—brought together for recording dates or night-club engagements. The chief exception is that of Gene Bertoncini and Michael Moore, who have been together, work permitting, since the mid-seventies.

The Bertoncini-Moore duet moves on the same swinging, uncluttered plane as the John Kirby sextet, the Red Norvo trio, and the Modern Jazz Quartet. It favors brevity, gracefulness, and subtlety. It has no show business; it celebrates music. It is harmonically up-to-date and acoustically old-fashioned. (Neither man uses much amplification—and Bertoncini often plays an unamplified classical guitar—yet the two achieve a full sound.) Its arrangements, done by Bertoncini, are direct and unfussy; they frame and underline the solos, and they point up the melodic beauties of its repertory. This repertory includes some seventy-five numbers, many of which have a classical bias. Unlike the Kirby band and the Modern Jazz Quartet, both of which also had a classical bias, the Bertoncini-Moore duet eliminates the line between classical and jazz. Each kind of music reaches over and borrows from the other. Bertoncini joins Ravel's "Pavane pour une Infante Défunte" to Mitchell Parish's "The Lamp Is Low," which is based on the Ravel. He turns George Gershwin's "Prelude No. 2" into a blues with gospel overtones. He combines "Greensleeves" with Jerome Kern's "Yesterdays" and a Chopin prelude with "How Insensitive." He makes a samba out of Rachmaninoff's "Vocalise" and a waltz out of Bach's "Siciliano." Here is how the Ravel-Parish goes: Bertoncini plays the Ravel melody a cappella and ad lib. Then he and Moore do "The Lamp Is Low" in bossa-nova time. There is a loose, winding interlude for both men, a pause, and Bertoncini starts a snapping, medium-tempo improvisation on "The Lamp Is Low." He takes two choruses, and gives way to Moore, who takes one. They exchange eight-bar solos and close with an ad-lib eight-bar rumination on "The Lamp Is Low." Rachmaninoff's "Vocalise" is very different. It is largely an opportunity to hear Moore stretch out on two arco solos. Bertoncini decorates the first solo with chords, then plays the melody by himself. He slips into a samba rhythm and solos with Moore playing pizzicato behind him. Moore returns with his bow, and Bertoncini sends up sprays of chords. Bertoncini and Moore also play standards, and they have a particular affection for Duke Ellington and Billy Strayhorn. They do "Mood Indigo" and "Sophisticated Lady" and "Caravan" and "Don't Get Around Much Anymore," and they make a serenade out of combining Strayhorn's "Lush Life" and "Isfahan."

Although the Bertoncini-Moore duet is a musical democracy, it is, to all intents and purposes, Bertoncini's group. He founded it, he writes its arrangements, and he does the booking and generally keeps the group on the track. He is an affecting, highly original guitarist, who moves easily back and forth between classical and jazz guitar. Moore speaks of Bertoncini with near-reverence. "Gene is one of the few people I totally trust," he has said. "He's a *good* person, and he's a gentleman. He goes beyond being likable. He gets across to people. With a few words, they are charmed and in his camp. Club owners treat him better than they do most other musicians. Gene has a soft way about him, and he doesn't seem like a go-getter, but he's very businesslike and he works constantly for the duo. We first met in Salt Lake City. I was doing a clinic with Marian McPartland, and he had a duo with the bassist Linc Milliman. Later, in New York, I subbed for Milliman, and it went so well that Gene and I did a few duo jobs. We've been together ten years, and it's been an ongoing, developing thing. I wish we could find more work—maybe for three good months of the year. The duo is Gene's main thing, and it's become much closer to the center of my musical life than it was. With all my bread-and-butter gigs, I used to keep one foot out the door, but that's changing. We've talked about how being in a duo is like being married. We've had arguments and scenes. I've gone through periods when I was angry about everything, when I was impossible. But Gene worried about me rather than about himself or the music. I've matured, and we're much closer now. Gene has always had a great conception of what a duo like

ours should be. He never chooses a song unless it moves him, so he chooses unusual things. I wouldn't pick some of them, but I find myself going
along easily. I always hated combining classical music and jazz, but Gene
has made me like it. He can take Ravel's 'Pavane' or Gershwin's 'Prelude
No. 2,' and not disturb it but make it flow together with jazz. It's the same
with Bach and Chopin and Rachmaninoff. Gene's arrangements are flexible, and they're also nets. If you're having a bad evening, that net is there
and you know the music will never fall below a certain level.

"Gene is a unique guitarist. He didn't grow up as a jazz player. He had
classical music in his background, and he used to do a lot of club dates—
dances, parties, bar mitzvahs. He never plays for himself, the way most
guitarists do. He wants people to like his music, but without our having in
any way to sell out. He's not fettered by what's hip. He hasn't listened
widely in jazz. Sometimes when he solos, I don't hear any influences. It's
all him. He has a great ear and perfect pitch and he can read anything. He
does harmonic things I've never heard any other guitarist do.
Improvisation used to be a means for him, but it has slowly become an end.
What he's after is beautiful melody. He's a melodic improviser. He's moved
by all good melody—that strain is in everything he does. He can be very
insecure about his playing. It's the Christian thing: I'm not worthy, and all
that. And playing in front of people is very hard for him. It's one thing to
go out there and do 'I Got Rhythm' and another to do a Bach lute Suite. His
life, his experiences, his feelings—all of them center on his guitar."

Bertoncini feels as intensely about Moore. "You can really hear the music
in a duo," he has said. "It's not covered up, it's not limited. The two instruments can breathe together. The more we play an arrangement, the more
Michael comes up with and the fresher it sounds. There is nothing about
him as a player that I don't admire. Years ago, when I worked in the
Philharmonic Café after concerts, Michael used to sit in and play the arco
parts. I was bowled over by the warmth of his sound, and I still prefer him
to any classical bassist. He is also a great pizzicato accompanist, and a brilliant improviser. I don't know anyone on any instrument who takes you on
a melodic trip like Michael. I love to watch people responding to his solos.
I consider him one of the great living jazz musicians. We've always thought
of the music as being bigger than either of us. I've seen a dark side to
Michael on occasion, but he cares about my feelings and I care about his.
We've certainly never mistreated each other. Sometimes the response to one
of our pieces is such that we will play a tune off the top of our heads. But
I've never believed in jamming in front of people. It's nice to offer your
audience a way in and a way out."

Bertoncini has a cautious, guitarist's handshake and a guitarist's stoop.
His eyes, brown and wide apart, are set back under gray eyebrows. These
announce a tangle of gray hair. He speaks in a soft, withdrawing voice.
You have to lean in to hear him, you have to get on his lee side. His frequent smiles and easy laugh give his words an amiable, self-effacing edge,

and so does the way he moves his head up and down when he talks. He lives in a third-floor walkup in the East Sixties, and his apartment is a nest. The main room is divided between a tiny bedroom, which has a desk and a television, and a slightly larger living room, which has a sofa, assorted chairs, and a fireplace. The fireplace tools include a putter, and a golf ball sits in an ashtray on the floor. There is a chair, a music stand, and a guitarist's footrest between the fireplace and a big south window. A classical guitar rests on the chair. A large needlepoint of Picasso's "Three Musicians" hangs over the sofa. A kitchen, bathroom, and foyer complete the arrangement. The light that pours in the window seems to make the place even more compact. Bertoncini talked about himself one morning.

"It's not easy to be spontaneous on the guitar," he said. "The fingerboard itself is a maze. You never know it completely. There are four positions for every note. A pianist, after all, can *see* his voicings. The way I think of it, you have to do a lot of work before you can play jazz on the guitar. You have to have a thorough harmonic grounding, you have to know about intervallic relationships, you have to practice the scales—major, minor, altered—on every string, and use every fret. You have to know the harmonic windage of the instruments you play with. You have to listen to the improvisers who move you—and only a handful have that special magic. Then, after you have done all that, you have to forget everything you have learned and just play. When I first improvised, at the age of sixteen, music poured out. Of course, I didn't really know what I was doing. The instrument was playing me, and there are still times when it does. I work constantly at my improvising. It's the old business of telling a story. I try to sing a nice song on my guitar over the structure of the tune. I stay aware of the melody and the harmony. I push the intuitive and the intellectual together, even though one sometimes clouds the other up. I touch every note I play. One of the mysteries of improvising is fitting the right feelings to the song—finding the right inflection instead of just stringing eighth notes together. The more you know a song, the easier improvising is apt to be. That's why jazz musicians play certain songs again and again. I'm very close to 'All the Things You Are.' I never lose my place in it. I don't have to think about where it's going. When I improvise on it, it feeds me. I practice four or five hours a day. I like to keep my guitar at hand all the time, and the only time I'm without it is when life tells me I have to be. Then I worry that overnight I might lose everything I have dug out of it.

"I was born in the Bronx, near Mount Vernon, on April 6, 1937. My father and mother were both Italian. His name was Mario, and hers was—is—Anita. I have one brother—Renate, or Renny. He's three years older, and he used to play jazz accordion. My father played guitar and harmonica. He was from Piacenza, in northern Italy, and my mother was from Parma. They lived in nearby villages, but they met here. My father was born in 1901, and he came over in 1917. My mother was born in 1906 and came over when she was five. My father was a handsome, sweet man, a giving person. He was very positive. He set in motion my appreciation of beautiful things. He was always pointing out the beautiful sky and the beautiful air and the beautiful trees. He was a man of the earth who could do anything with his hands. I remember a pear tree he had done some grafting on. One kind of pear grew on one branch and another kind on another branch. When I was little, he bought a house that was a wreck, and within a year he had made it into a palace. Ten years later, he bought another wreck, and this time my brother and I helped rebuild it. What a lot of love there was between us! My dad had worked as a waiter in the Bronx. In the late forties, he went into partnership in a restaurant—Joe's, on Third Avenue between Sixtieth and Sixty-first. He was involved in it twenty-five years. Then he retired and moved up to East Durham, in the Catskills. Joe's was simple and inexpensive, with good food—the kind of place that is just about gone in Manhattan. My father taught me to judge a place by the freshness and originality of its salads and by its Parmesan cheese. He always had escarole in his salad, and his Parmesan cheese was freshly grated and came either from Italy or from Argentina, which makes fine Parmesan. I moved into this apartment twenty-five years ago, and I used to eat dinner with my father every night. He died in 1978. My mother lives near my brother in Dobbs Ferry, and I'm very proud of her. She is not without the pains of age, but she still has her own apartment and drives a car and has her spirit of life. She nurtured my sensitivities, and she never stood in my brother's or my way when we did things that were hard for her to watch. The greatest thing parents can do is give a child its head, and that's what my parents did.

"I had always liked to draw, and a high-school teacher suggested I go to Notre Dame and study architecture. My father wanted me to go to college, even though it was a big sacrifice, so I went. I was the first person in my family with a college degree. I took up the guitar when I was seven, and my first teacher was in Mount Vernon. My brother and I played on the Horn & Hardart 'Children's Hour' on Sunday mornings on NBC television. We were always being called on to play at parties and give little concerts here and there. It was at the 'Children's Hour' that I met the guitarist Johnny Smith, who was on the staff of NBC. He gave me some lessons in between his assignments, and eventually he'd see me about once a month. He never took a penny. I became a kind of protégé, and he was a major influence on me as a guitarist and as a person. I had started playing professionally when I was sixteen, in places in the Bronx, with a bunch of musicians from Mount Vernon. So music was in my bones when I went to Notre Dame. I played in the college dance band and with the concert band, and I even tried to switch to a music major in my junior year, but it didn't work out. Instead, I designed a new Music Department building as my graduating project. My architectural career lasted two weeks. I went to work for a Westchester architect who had been a student of Frank Lloyd Wright. Then I had a weekend gig with Richard Maltby's band, and messed up my part. That upset me so much I told the architect that I had to get back to my music. A couple of nights later, I was at the Capri in the Bronx playing guitar. When my father heard what had happened, he came in right away to listen, and told me that whatever I did he was behind me a hundred per cent. He generally made me feel that I was doing right—almost as if he looked up to me. Later, he would ask my advice about things—whether to buy land in the Catskills, or whatever. Anyway, I designed the house my parents built upstate, and I helped design my brother's house in Dobbs Ferry.

"I worked with the vibraphonist Mike Mainieri in the Bronx. Then a musician named Vince Mauro introduced me to Merv Griffin, who needed a guitarist on his game show, 'Play Your Hunch.' They had musical acts, and Sonny Igoe, the drummer, and George Shaw, the bassist, and I were the accompanists. I got a job at Birdland with Buddy Rich's quintet. He had Mike Mainieri, Wyatt Ruther on bass, and Sam Most on flute. I was always tense with Rich. When he decided we had rehearsed enough, he'd suddenly throw his sticks in the air and say, 'Rehearsal's over!' He had a drill instructor inside him. After work every night, we had to meet in his dressing room, and he'd tell each of us what we had done wrong. But he seemed to like me, and whenever I run into him he gives me a hug. I got into more and more studio work—with Griffin and with the 'Tonight Show,' when it was here and Skitch Henderson was the leader. And I studied with the guitarist Chuck Wayne. It was Wayne who told me to listen to the great classical guitarist Julian Bream, and he has been another essential influence on me. So has Segovia. One of the most enjoyable evenings of my life was spent at a Segovia concert, after which I went down to the old Half Note to hear Wes Montgomery. Montgomery was an intuitive player, and he got off these fantastic, burning, cooking chordal solos that night—the kind of thing I have never heard any other guitarist do. Eventually, I put together my own trio and went into places like the Embers, because I knew I had to cut that studio cord and start expressing myself on the guitar. Too much band work is not good for a guitarist. I also built a reputation accompanying singers. I did college concerts with Paul Winter, and had the experience for the first time of trying to hold a large audience. I recorded with Tony Bennett and Burt Bacharach, and I worked with Benny Goodman and Lena Horne. I knew my time with Benny was drawing to an end when he started asking me questions like 'Say, Gene, are you playing the right changes?' Then Michael Moore and I began hooking up, and it worked so well I turned down two weeks at the Palladium in London with Lena Horne just so we could do a seventy-five-dollar gig together.

"I first went to the Eastman School of Music twelve years ago. Now I go every June and stay into August, and Michael comes, too. It's a situation that has a special magic for me. There are some of the finest students in the country, and they look up to you to be an artist who has everything. And there are exceptional teachers—like the pianist Bill Dobbins. He has analyzed all the great recorded jazz solos, and he can play them note for note. Yet he has his own style. Every melodic line that he starts he fulfills melodically and harmonically. Mike and I always give a concert, and it's one of the most moving experiences of the year."

Bertoncini's style is unlike that of any other jazz guitarist. He has not listened much to Charlie Parker, nor has he fallen under the sway of Parker's descendants. And he has not followed Charlie Christian. He is concerned with sound and with melody. He plays a classical guitar much of the time, and he only uses an amplifier if he is in a noisy musical situation. Even with a pickup, he gets a soft, pure tone. He fashions a lot of single-note patterns in his improvisations, and they are thoughtful and easy. Most Charlie Parker-Charlie Christian guitarists play clouds of eighth and sixteenth notes, obscuring their songs and addling their listeners. They use their wizardry as a boast rather than as lyrical persuasion. Bertoncini fills his solos with rests, and his phrases tend to be short and manageable. You can see both ends of them. Michael Moore points out that Bertoncini is the opposite of the guitarist Jim Hall, whom Bertoncini admires. Moore thinks of Hall as an intuitive player and of Bertoncini as a planner. Bertoncini's solos are highly melodic. They have few arpeggios, few treading-water chordal passages. Their many pauses are handles for listeners, which help them follow the new songs he carefully fashions in each solo.

Bertoncini made two telephone calls, and sat down again on the edge of the sofa. "I feel like I'm living in the center of the world in New York," he said. "It's as if my apartment were a dormitory room and the city the campus. Sometimes on winter days, I walk down Second Avenue into the sun to the Village—and, if I feel good, I go all the way to the Trade Center. In warm weather, I walk through Central Park and run around the Reservoir—just to see all those colors and nationalities at peace. All the reality you could want is just outside your door in New York, and it keeps you honest. It keeps the fat out of your playing and out of your thinking. I've never been a big dater. I have a terrible gift for seeing where a relationship is going, and I always hope I'll have the strength to get out of it, because the pain lasts so much longer than the pleasure. I have this fantasy of someday walking to the Edwardian Room in the Plaza in the snow and of eating there and watching the snow falling outside, but I know when I finally do it I'll probably be married to the person I take with me. My spiritual life is very important to me. It has to do with the Italian-Christian tradition of commitment I was raised in. If you want to play well, you have to live a decent life. You improvise on that life, you play from it. It's important to keep your life clear, materialistically and otherwise. You can't absorb too many things. Sometimes after I play a bad chorus or have a bad night, I feel I don't know anything about the guitar, or even about music. I have to remember that I've discovered that I have something to say, a special expression on the guitar. To do any less than constantly pursue that gift would be wrong."

Ornette

Few twentieth-century innovators have got in their own way as often as Ornette Coleman, the composer, saxophonist, trumpeter, and violinist. When Coleman opened with his quartet—Don Cherry on pocket trumpet, Coleman on plastic alto saxophone, Charlie Haden on bass, Billy Higgins on drums—at the original Five Spot, on Cooper Square, in the fall of 1959, he became an immediate sensation, and he split the hip New York musical community in two. His detractors (John Hammond, Miles Davis, Charles Mingus) said he was a charlatan and a bore, and his admirers (Gunther Schuller, Martin Williams, Leonard Bernstein) said he was a genius who would forever alter improvisatory music. But by 1962 Coleman, who had come from almost complete obscurity in California, had dropped out of sight, and he has reappeared only rarely. He has worked about ten times in New York night clubs since then, and he has given roughly the same number of concerts. His recording career has been equally fitful. He issued nothing between 1961 and 1965, and very little between 1969 and 1975; only a handful of records have appeared since. He is a stubborn and brilliant visionary and a man of great integrity, and these attributes have hobbled him. He quickly decided that many New York club owners and recording executives were greedy, shortsighted, racist, and tin-eared, and that they were not willing to pay him what he had been led to believe he was worth. (He once said, "Being poor is not because money doesn't exist and being rich doesn't mean you know everything. But in America art has more to do with the reproductions and selling than with the art itself. That's one reason why musicians are crazy and painters are crazy when it comes to what they think they're worth.") Coleman countered this seeming mean-mindedness by asking for phenomenal sums for night-club dates and recording sessions, and when he was turned down he shrugged and went underground. Coleman talks and writes the way he plays. He uses straightforward English words, but he arranges them in sometimes incomprehensible ways. He has invented his own language, and it is abstract, aphoristic, poetic, philosophical, comic, and nonsensical. Coleman once gave an interview to the jazz critic Leonard Feather, and in it he said:

> In America you can know exactly who you would like to pattern yourself after and what you'd like to do, but the moment you find something you can do that outdates that—or even to make it better, so to speak—it's no longer the same idea anymore, it's a different thing. And every person that challenges the heart of modern expression is going to come up with that problem. I guess it must be a healthy problem. It could be even more healthy if a solution could be made where every person could

express his consciousness to its fullest without outdating the particular information he's gotten to do that—or to enhance it. The world would be ten times more productive.

He wrote these liner notes for his "Body Meta" album:

What you should never know is to never find out you shouldn't.
If you can read or write and you don't write or read why?
What face would you like for a race other than your own we all don't
    care if its on money when their is no food home job and
     no one cares.
Systems are number by system to provide us a chance to change them
    during one's own life time.
Death wealth knowledge poverty are all you got to change not the
    people. No army wears a different uniform.
A woman loves from within and without news, heard, printed, she is
    called mother.
The most emotional separation is done by the mating of the genders.
Fear of fears in the ears eyes lies dead in the head from unknown
    strangers.
Their are endless ways to take but their is only one way to give and that
    is in person.
The pop. of the earth will never be at the same place at the same time so
    what do we mean when say the end of the world?
Body Meta.

Coleman talks about his life more clearly than he talks about his philosophy or his music. (He has written an unpublished book of musical theory, of which his friend John Snyder, who is a lawyer, record producer, and former trumpet player, has said, "I've worked on the manuscript for hours, for days, with Ornette, but it just doesn't read. The pages won't follow.") He doesn't like to dwell on his early days. He was raised in poverty, and his iconoclasm, which crystallized in his teens, brought him abuse and pain. He has said of those days, "I was born March 9, 1930, in Fort Worth, Texas. I grew up with my mother, Rosa, who died in 1976, and my sister Truvenza, who lives in Fort Worth and is a singer. My other sister was killed in an automobile accident when she was seventeen. My father's name was Randolph. He died when I was seven. I remember sitting on his lap. He was tall and very dark. I've heard since that he could sing and that he played baseball. Also that he was a construction worker and a cook. My father and mother were both born on December 25th, and I think they were from Hearne, Texas. My mother was tall and dark and very strict. She was religious-like, and she didn't smoke or drink or go to night clubs or movies. She only heard me play once—in a concert in 1966—and whenever I went home there would be the records of mine I had sent her, unopened. She'd say, 'Your records are here.' I think she did something like selling Avon products, because I recall my sister taking me to a black woman's house in the ghetto. She had a school in her house, and I played with blocks. I was about two, and it cost twenty-five cents a day. But often we didn't have any money, and I'd go without food.

"I went to two different schools—both black, and both very good and strict. A teacher spanked me once because I told her she was wrong. But I was right, and I believe that to this day. I learned quickly in school that all you had to know was the answers. I also learned that once you found out what you should know you didn't have to be there every day. I had to walk about three miles over a lot of train tracks to my first school, and I'd get tired, and some days I'd never make it. When my mother found out, she near beat me to death. I used to dream of being an adult. I'd see myself as an adult, but I could never see *what* I would be. In high school, I played football, and I liked running. I got my collarbone broke playing football, and it took a long time to heal. When I was in the eleventh grade, my mother bought me an alto saxophone with money I had saved. I taught myself to read, and joined a church band of twenty or twenty-five people. We went to different churches in Texas, and played for conventions. It was a marching band, an 'Onward, Christian Soldiers' band. The only other music I knew about was rhythm and blues. So I was amazed when I heard Lester Young at a jam session in Fort Worth. They were playing show tunes, and they all had this 'bridge' in the middle, which the blues didn't have. So I set out to learn popular songs. But to make a living you had to play rhythm and blues. I got a tenor saxophone and played R. & B., doing all that leaning backward and jumping on table-tops, and that sort of showmanship. I had my own band when I was seventeen. I copied things off the radio, off records. I learned the white repertory, the Mexican repertory, the black repertory. White people liked 'Star Dust,' black people liked 'Flyin' Home.' I would buy sheet music and teach songs to the band. We learned things like Pete Johnson's recording of '627 Stomp.' The alto solo on that first made me want to play the saxophone. One of the people in my band was an alto player named Ben Martin. I liked him better than Charlie Parker. He could play very, very beautiful. He made me cry like a baby, he was so beautiful. He was a cross between Jimmy Dorsey and Charlie Parker.

"I graduated from high school in the late forties, and I got offers for scholarships to black colleges. I went to one meeting at Samuel Houston College, in Austin, but they were too snobby for me, even though I'd heard they had a very good band. I was already supporting my mother and sister, making a hundred dollars a week. Then a minstrel show, 'Silas Green from New Orleans,' came through Fort Worth, and I auditioned and got a job. I told my mother I was going to Dallas. We ended up in Natchez, where I got fired. Then I went to New Orleans and on to Baton Rouge. I guess I looked like a Christ-saves person. I was a vegetarian and religious, and I had a beard and long hair. By this time, I was with a rhythm-and-blues band, and when we finished a dance in Baton Rouge a man told me someone wanted to see me outside. I went out, and there were all these guys. I guess they didn't like my clothes or my hair. One kicked me in the stomach and one in the back. They kicked me and beat me, and took my tenor and threw it as far as they could. I blacked out, and when I came to I went to the police, and the policeman said "Nigger, if you don't get outa here, we're going to finish you off.' I went back to New Orleans, where my friend Melvin Lastie loaned me an alto saxophone that belonged to his brother, and I went home and started playing the alto again."

When he was nineteen, Coleman went to Los Angeles with Pee Wee Crayton's rhythm-and-blues band, and he stayed for most of the next ten years. His style, already formed, alienated club owners and other musicians, and he found little work. He even had trouble sitting in. The tenor saxophonist Dexter Gordon ordered him off the bandstand, and when he attempted to play with the Clifford Brown-Max Roach band the rhythm section packed up. (He never got a chance to play with Charlie Parker, but he heard him at the Tiffany Club in Los Angeles, and decided that he sounded better on records than in the flesh.) Eventually, Coleman found musicians who could hear what he was doing, and many of them are still part of his life—Don Cherry, Charlie Haden, Billy Higgins, the trumpeter Bobby Bradford, and the drummer Ed Blackwell. In 1958, the late Lester Koenig, who owned Contemporary Records, recorded Coleman, and not long after that John Lewis, the leader of the Modern Jazz Quartet, heard Coleman play in San Francisco. Lewis was enormously impressed, and told Nesuhi Ertegun, of Atlantic Records, about him. Ertegun recorded Coleman in California, and was largely responsible for Coleman's début at the Five Spot. But weak glue held all this together. Coleman kept himself alive in Los Angeles by working as a babysitter, a porter, an elevator operator, and a stock clerk. He gave blood at four dollars a pint, and sometimes he survived on canned goods sent by his mother. Other times, he roamed the streets and had nothing to eat. He wore his hair in a croquignole, and he dressed in homemade clothes. He told Leonard Feather, "I'd go out to the San Fernando Valley and sit in with, say, Gerry Mulligan. I was staying in Watts then, and I'd have to hitchhike home. And, every time, the cops would stop me, make me assemble my horn and play it to prove it was mine. Only because I'd be coming out of territory where they wouldn't expect a black person to be." Coleman was married in 1954 and had a son, Denardo, who is a drummer. He is also, Coleman says, the best thing that happened to him in California.

Coleman is a compact man with a gentle, handsome face. His smile is lopsided and boyish. He wears his hair in a short Afro, and various beards and mustaches periodically advance and retreat. He has the even, enclosed air of someone at peace with himself and with the world, whether he can control it or not. His voice is quiet and in the middle range, and he talks in a muffled, hesitant way. His friend John Snyder has studied him closely. "Ornette has a total range of face," he has said. "Sometimes the wrinkles fall off, and his face becomes tight, like a kid's. Sometimes he's all wrinkles, and he makes you feel beat, he makes you feel the worst you've ever felt. He's a magnificent dresser. When he performs, he wears specially made silk suits, but he doesn't like people looking at him. If I were to tell him that one reason people do look at him is his clothes, he'd start wearing black. Ornette is sharp in other ways. A lot of people are marble-eyed—they don't see anything. Ornette looks right inside your head. He has told me things about myself that I simply could not buy but that later turned out to be absolutely true. He is also the most generous person I've ever met. He may not say sorry or thank you, but he'll give you anything. He'll pick up a derelict, take him home, clean him up, and feed him—and not get upset when the guy walks off with something. His generosity makes you generous. If he called today and asked would I peddle his new tape for half a million dollars, I'd do it. And he inspires you. I've sat down and written poems after being with Ornette. You can hear Ornette's goodness in his music, and he is unfailingly kind the way he goes about it. I was a trumpeter for many years, and once he wrote out a little melodic line for me that I just couldn't get. So he played it and told me to play it with him, and I did, and it was like he was literally pulling that line out of me. His group, Prime Time, is made up of a Buddhist, a Muslim, a punk-rocker, and his son, Denardo. He has lived with them, spent years teaching them. He's had trouble with all of them, but he's stuck by them, and now they can do anything he wants.

"Ornette's music, which is supposed to be so free, is closely organized, but his personal life, which should be organized, is chaotic. He doesn't sleep much—maybe four or five hours at a time—and his hours are anything that comes. He doesn't seem to mind where he lives. He's had coldwater flats all over the Bowery. He lived in the Century Paramount Hotel, in midtown, for half a year. He lived in a room in my office a year. I had told him he needed a place to conduct business in, and I put shelves and a desk in a back room, and next I knew he was living there. I'd take him to look at apartments, but he was never interested. He wanted a building. He had two floors that he bought in the late sixties in a loft building on Prince Street, but the rest of the tenants finally forced him out. He had turned the bottom floor into a combination night club, recording studio, rehearsal hall, and meeting place for sympathetic musicians. Some pretty loud music was played there at all hours, and Ornette simply did not understand when his neighbors got sore. To this day, he blames their evicting him on racism.

"There is a myth about how Ornette has never made any money—that he starves. Well, sometimes he *doesn't* have any money and is hungry, but he's made considerable sums, usually from recording contracts. He always asks top dollar. He figures that when he plays he gives a hundred per cent and the record company should give a hundred per cent, and he's absolutely right. Once, in Paris, he was invited to accompany a French ballad singer on a recording, and he said, 'O.K., but you'll have to pay me.' They asked how much. 'Ten thousand dollars,' Ornette said.

Well, they paid him, by God! Sometimes the sums he asks for enrage people. When I was handling his affairs, we dickered with one of the major labels. Ornette wanted three hundred thousand dollars. His reasoning was that there were at least a hundred countries in the world and each one would buy three thousand records—as easy as that. This gent from the record company called me up after we had given them the price, and he said some pretty horrible things. Of course, the joke is that Ornette has given away most of the money he's made."

Coleman's music involves the melodies he writes, the instrumentation he sets them in, and his own playing. His melodies are in odd lengths and shapes, and are distinguished for their lyrical beauty, which is often dirgelike, and for their graceful irregularity. Clear in all he writes is the influence of Thelonious Monk, who admired Duke Ellington. Coleman generally works with a group made up of trumpet, bass, drums, and his alto saxophone. Sometimes he substitutes a tenor saxophone for the trumpet, and sometimes he plays with just bass and drums. He has also worked with (and written for) a string quartet, a woodwind quintet, and a symphony orchestra. In the mid-seventies, he began experimenting with Prime Time, a totally original fusion group made up of two guitarists, a Fender bassist, and one or two drummers. Coleman's playing springs from Charlie Parker. (He has taught himself to play creditable trumpet and somewhat jarring left-handed violin.) His light, voicelike tone and timbre are similar to Parker's, and so are his runs and rhythmic stops and starts. But Coleman uses almost no vibrato, and his melodic concept is far freer than Parker's. He has cast aside chords and keys and harmony and conventional tonality. His solos slide from key to key, and he uses nontempered notes. "The tempered sounds are going to join together someday," he has said, "and it's going to be beautiful." His time changes continually—from a four-four beat to double time to an irregular legato to a floating, disembodied time. At first hearing, Coleman's music sounds obscure and perverse, as if he were deliberately playing flat, in the wrong key, and out of time. But after a while the listener enters his world and dons his logic. Coleman does not improvise on a theme or a set of chords. Instead, he will start from a series of notes, a scale, a rhythmic cluster, an area of pitch, a mood. Coleman's solos at their best are multilayered and hypnotic. They move melodically with such freedom and originality and surprise that they form an independent music. It is also close to a vocal music, for he tries—with a variety of instrumental cries and mutters and moans and whispers—to approximate the human voice.

Coleman talks about his music in coherent bursts or in quasi aphorisms that keep spilling over into philosophy. When he first came to New York, he said this about his playing: "My melodic approach is based on phrasing, and my phrasing is an extension of how I hear the intervals and pitch of the tunes I play. There is no end to pitch. You can play flat in tune and sharp in tune. It's a question of vibration. My phrasing is spontaneous, not a style. A style happens when your phrasing hardens. Jazz music is the only music in which the same note can be played night after night but differently each time. It's the hidden things, the subconscious that lies in the body and lets you know: you feel this, you play this." He has also said, "'Improvising' is an outdated word. I try and play a musical idea that is not being influenced by any previous thing I have played before. You don't have to learn to spell to talk. The theme you play at the start of a number is the territory, and what comes after, which may have very little to do with it, is the adventure. What goes on in my head when I improvise is like human auras. Ideas flow through me the way a child grows. I play the same logic fast or slow. I don't think about feeling, seeing, or thinking. I try to have the player and the listener have the same sound experience. I'm not thinking about mood or emotion. Emotion should come into you instead of going out. All those things are built into your human fibre. When I first picked up the alto saxophone, I played it the way I thought adults must play it. What I played was not something anybody had heard before, yet it was valid. I'm still doing that. Only, I've had to package it."

John Snyder has said of Coleman's playing, "Ornette would rather compose than perform. He doesn't like performing, but when he does perform he is deadly serious. He doesn't want to just make motions. He doesn't want distractions. He doesn't cover himself with a shell. He's like a sponge. He's quick to pick up the feelings of the musicians around him and to use what he is offered. He talks a lot about 'unisons.' He doesn't mean the unison of two musicians playing the same note at the same time. His unison is any group of notes that suddenly come together and have a purity of sound—a clarity, almost a ringing. He also uses the word 'harmolodic,' which he coined and which is a contraction of the words 'harmony,' 'movement,' and 'melodic.' It's his theory of music, and it has nothing to do with what they teach you in music school. I studied theory, and Ornette's is the opposite of everything they teach you. It's the sound in the instrument. It's the structure he's built around his feelings. You cannot play anything you want with Ornette. It takes the same work—more work, if anything—as playing bebop. You cannot hide in Ornette's music. You have to know his structure. It can be a scale or three notes or a little movement. It can be a tonality, a melody, a feeling, a rhythm. This structure will allow you to play, to reveal yourself on your instrument. I've come to think that about the only way to learn how to play Ornette's music is to study with him every day for seven years. Once learned, his music would free a lot of people. It lets a musician take what he is and make music with it. You go where the improvisation is. It's already there, and you explore it. The prime motivation in Ornette's music is to reach people—even though everything in it seems to indicate the opposite."

Cecil

The searing, visionary pianist Cecil Taylor has been rattling American audiences for twenty-five years. He did it at the Great South Bay Jazz Festival in 1958, and he did it at the Kool Jazz Festival in 1984. At the Kool Jazz Festival, in an evening concert at Carnegie Hall, Taylor followed Oscar Peterson, who played nine gleaming numbers and was greeted with Dionysian applause. Taylor did one hour-long number, and before twenty minutes had gone by several hundred people had fled. Taylor and Ornette Coleman are the nominal heads of the jazz avant-garde, but they are very different. Coleman refuses to record or play in public unless he is paid handsomely. Taylor until recent years often played for pennies—when he was asked to play at all. Coleman's music is accessible, but he is loath to share it; Taylor's music is difficult, and he is delighted to share it. Where it should be shared is a problem. He does not always fill American concert halls, and the shape and size of his music—his selections are rarely shorter than an hour—do not fit easily into night clubs. He overruns the standard length of a set; he transfixes his listeners, making them forget to order drinks; and his attack does things to pianos that make night-club owners weep. For all this, Taylor has become something of a star in Europe, and he is at least a cult here. He no longer scuffles, as he frequently did in the fifties and sixties, but, he said not long ago, "It's still living on the edge."

The American aesthetic landscape is littered with idiosyncratic marvels—Walt Whitman, Charles Ives, D. W. Griffith, Duke Ellington, Jackson Pollock—and Taylor belongs with them. He is largely indescribable, and his playing has provoked a flood of similes and metaphors. He has been said to resemble Niagara Falls, a volcano, a great river, thunderheads, a high wind, a cannonade, a stampede. Comparing a difficult music with other musics sometimes gives the listener a handle. Taylor has been linked with Bartók, Debussy, Stravinsky, Prokofiev, and Ives, as well as Duke Ellington and Thelonious Monk. He has certainly listened to Bartók and the rest, but he idolizes Ellington and Monk. He has also admired, at one time or another, Dave Brubeck, Lennie Tristano, Erroll Garner, Billie Holiday, Bud Powell, Horace Silver, Walter Bishop, Miles Davis, and John Coltrane. A Taylor solo is indivisible and has a great variety of pianistic textures. It shifts from key to key to key (it is close to atonal), and has no conventional sounded beat. The rhythms, when they are discernible at all, change constantly. Taylor bases his improvisations on scales or patches of melody. His thematic material dictates his form, which is as elusive as his rhythms. It is possible to listen to Taylor impressionistically—to regard a solo as a bristling, ceaselessly revolving collection of moods, which range from anger to serenity to agitation to passivity to exultation to sarcasm to bemusement. His pianistic vocabulary is complex, and makes that of most jazz pianists seem amateurish. He uses enormous chords; tone clusters; single-note arpeggios of such speed that they are almost indistinguishable from glissandos; runs played simultaneously by three fingers on each hand, the fingers held at an eighty-degree angle to the keyboard; runs and massed notes struck with a fist or elbow. Occasional breathing spaces temper the encyclopedic nature of his solos. And his dynamics are wild: a crashing six-fingered arpeggio may be replaced by a passive sea of middle-register chords, which may give way to room-shaking low-register booms. (Taylor sometimes hits the piano so hard it's surprising the keyboard doesn't buckle.) Listening to Taylor takes patience and courage. He wants you to feel what he feels, to move at his speed, to look where he looks (always inward). His music asks more than other music, but it gives more than it asks. His keyboard strength and endurance are astonishing. That improvised piano can be played for a solid hour or more with such clarity and precision and passion is nearly unbelievable. Taylor is an ecstatic, almost demonic performer. He will pound the lowest register with both hands, his elbows out flat, his head inches from the keyboard. He will play a two-handed run so fast his hands blur. He will linger briefly around high C, his fingers jumping like sparks. He dances his music; his motions make it visible.

Taylor likes to talk about music. Here are things he has said during the past twenty years. The first was to A. B. Spellman, who wrote a valuable discourse on Taylor in "Four Lives in the Bebop Business": "Music is the creation of a language out of symbols, of sounds, sounds that cannot be spoken and therefore create a kind of personal isolation. If there are problems that music cannot answer wholly, you either have to have friends whom you can trust not to destroy you with whatever you give them of yourself, or you have to go to a neutral source."

He said this to the jazz critic Gary Giddins, in "Riding on a Blue Note": "To feel is perhaps the most terrifying thing in this society. This is one of the reasons I'm not too interested in electronic music: it divorces itself from human energy, it substitutes another kind of force as the determinant agent for its continuance . . . The determinant agent of [my] music has to do with ancestor worship, it has to do with a lot of areas that are magical rather than logical."

And this, on the matter of his style, is to the critic Joe Goldberg, in "Jazz Masters of the Fifties": "It began on a very small basis, based on scales. At the time it began, it was based on one single scale which soon became many scales, scales made up of different intervalic constructions, then chords, then diads, and then just combinations of tones, and then just intervals spaced differently, not scales at all, just groups of notes."

Taylor does not make friends easily. One friend is Judy Sneed, a lover of avant-garde jazz and a sometime agent and booker for Taylor. "Cecil has a vile reputation among some of the people he has worked for," she has said, "and there's a good reason for it. He has very high standards. In fact, he's a perfectionist, and when he isn't told certain things about working conditions and such, and they turn out to be not to his liking, he feels cornered, he goes out, he loses his temper. What is really offensive to him is the difference in the way classical musicians and jazz musicians are treated. It's black and white, in all senses. When something goes wrong in his life—like the illness of Jimmy Lyons, his alto saxophonist of twenty-five years—he goes to the piano and he stays there for hours. When he is preparing for a concert, he practices six to ten hours a day. So he doesn't have much of a social life. His career has been painful. His heart hurts a lot. But he doesn't hibernate. He has great interest in all the arts—particularly in dance and theatre and in hearing singers. He's a voracious reader. Cecil is a gentleman, a loving person, a responsible person."

Nat Hentoff first knew Taylor in the early fifties in Boston, and he once said of him: "I used to see Cecil at this tiny fashionable jazz-record store in the Symphony Hall building. He was a student at the New England Conservatory. We'd go to classical concerts, and he was very lucid, very shrewd about what we heard. He'd say, 'Did you hear that? Did you hear that?' And tell me exactly what had just gone wrong in the brass section or the violin section. He didn't have any of the elliptical quality he has now. He was buoyant and fresh. He hadn't been out in the arena much. He talked a lot about Duke Ellington. When he did come out, he had some terrible times. I remember running into him in the sixties, and he told me he hadn't worked in six or eight months. He said he held imaginary club sessions in his room, to keep himself from forgetting what it was like to play in public. I saw him a little while ago in Bradley's, and he told me that when he was coming up there were certain expectations. You paid your dues and went through certain conditions, then you made it among your peers. He feels that no longer exists—that much of the ambience of the music has changed. But he isn't bitter. I think he has too much of a sense of himself for that."

Taylor lives in a brownstone in Brooklyn, not far from the Academy of Music. He bought the house in 1983 ("Europe provided most of the down payment for this house"), and he lives on the bottom two floors. He sleeps in a long, narrow book-lined room on the ground floor, and on the floor above are a music room, facing the street, and a living room and Pullman kitchen, facing a back yard. Both rooms have French windows. There are no rugs on the floors, and the furniture is sparse, but there are red draperies in the music room. Most of the music room is taken up by a grand piano, its prow to the street. Taylor has a Napoleonic mien. He is short, his legs are slightly bowed, and he has broad, intense shoulders. His hair is set in finger-length ringlets, which are grounded by a thick mustache. His head is round, and his nose is sharp. (He wears close-fitting hats onstage, and sometimes he pulls them so low only his nose is visible.) He moves constantly when he talks, and he talks explosively. He uses a lot of "you knows"s, pronounced "knaow." He laughs abruptly, he breaks into bits of solfège. His talk randomly reflects his playing. He spoke one afternoon of himself and his music, and he must have walked a mile between his kitchen and his living room:

"I was born in Long Island City on March 25, 1929. I was an only child, except for my foster brother, Raymond, whom I still see. Raymond lived with us for a couple of years, then went back to his mother. We had a two-family brick house on a Hundred and Eleventh Street in Corona, Queens. My father was Percy Clinton Taylor. He was the head chef at the Rivercrest Sanitarium in Astoria. Two of his younger brothers worked under him. He had come from a little town in North Carolina, and his father was a full-fledged Indian, a Kiowa. My father's face was the color of the back of my hand, but his body was the color of my palm. He had thin lips and a straight nose. He cooked seventeen hours a day during the week, and he cooked at home on Sundays. He was a deeply religious man, and he sang hymns and things like 'Wade in the Water' around the house. But he also loved Louis Armstrong and Bessie Smith and Ella Fitzgerald—and Bing Crosby and Judy Garland. He was not easy to understand. He always spoke softly. Sometimes he'd be silent and just look at you and smile. My mother also had Indian blood. She was my father's second wife, and she was a fireball. We had a chow named Bing, and one night it bit me and she almost went through the ceiling. She was five feet tall and weighed nine-ty pounds. She had black hair and black eyes. Her favorite color was red, and she wore big hats. She was thought of as being very beautiful. She was born in Long Branch, New Jersey, the oldest of six children. I remember going just once to the house where she was born, near some railroad tracks. Her family was great friends with Sonny Greer's family. Her name was Almeida Ragland, and she was called Maitie. She played the piano and danced, and she spoke German and French—I don't know how. She had done some acting in black silent films. She took me to the Apollo Theatre and the Museum of Natural History and to hear Benny Goodman. She was into Basie and Ellington. She gave me a book by Schopenhauer when I was ten. She told me that I was going to be a dentist or a lawyer or a doctor—that piano playing would be an avocation. Then, when I was in my early teens, she died. I moved in here on the fortieth anniversary of her death. My father would not tell me what she died of, but it was cancer, and she was in great pain the last years of her life. After her death, I lived with my father and my Uncle Bill, who played piano and violin and drums. My father never married again, and he died in 1961. I went to P.S. 143, Junior High 16, and Flushing High School. I had always gotten A's and B's, but after my mother's death my grades slipped some. I started piano lessons at five. My teacher was a Mrs. Jessey, and she was married to an NBC percussionist who lived across the street. Then I went to Violet Hamilton, who was a beautiful black woman. I also studied at the New York School of Music, and then with Charlotte Levy. Her brother was Melville Herskovits, the anthropologist. She was the most important teacher I had until I got to the Conservatory. A teacher there showed me how to use my back, to apply pressure with my shoulders. Classical pianists are taught to develop their arms and hands, but I was taught to involve my whole body. Anyway, playing is not a question of energy. It's spiritual transfiguration. If playing were merely physicality, I'd be a basketball player or a miler. Somewhere in this time, I read that Duke Ellington believed that the next generation of jazz musicians would have to have conservatory training. My father had cousins who lived in a mansion in West Medford, outside of Boston, and it was decided that I should go to the New England Conservatory of Music. I was there four years, and I graduated in 1953."

Taylor told A. B. Spellman, in "Four Lives in the Bebop Business," "I learned more music from Ellington than I ever learned from the New England Conservatory. Like learning an orchestral approach to the piano . . . I learned more either outside of school or from the nonacademic aspect of school than I did in the classes." But at the Conservatory he learned the geography of modern classical music, and he polished his technique and began investigating various improvisational approaches. He became involved in the Boston jazz community, which included the saxophonists Andrew McGhee, Gigi Gryce, Charlie Mariano, Sam Rivers, and Serge Chaloff; the trumpeters Herb Pomeroy and Joe Gordon; and the pianists Jaki Byard and Dick Twardzik. He heard Charlie Parker and Bud Powell and Sarah Vaughan in the flesh for the first time, and Stan Getz and Walter Bishop and Art Tatum. He liked Fats Waller better than Tatum. ("I loved the depth of his single notes.") And he began listening to Dave Brubeck and Monk and Horace Silver and Lennie Tristano and Erroll Garner. ("I used to think that he could make whole pieces out of his fantastic introductions.") After graduation, he lived with his father in Queens. "Sometimes", he says, "I'd only find one or two musical jobs a year." These included a week with Johnny Hodges' small band, which had Emmett Berry, Lawrence Brown, and a young John Coltrane; scattered jobs in Harlem, one of them with a rhythm-and-blues tenor saxophonist who played on his back on the floor; thirteen weeks in a coffeehouse across from the Village Gate, on Bleecker Street, where he was sometimes paid less than a dollar a night; a gig at the Art Students League; West Indian dances; a black resort upstate. In between, he took day jobs. Then, in December of 1955, he went to Boston with the bassist Buell Neidlinger, the drummer Dennis Charles, and the soprano saxophonist Steve Lacy and recorded an L.P. for a small Cambridge company called Transition. Like all good revolutionary works, which are eventually rubbed smooth by familiarity, the record was more startling when it came out, in 1957, than it is now. Most of the seven numbers have regular sounded rhythm, and four of the numbers are by other people. (Taylor usually plays his own things.) Taylor had got perhaps halfway to the plateau he has been on for the past twenty years. Monk and Ellington surface again and again, but all through the record there are strong intimations of where he was heading. Late in 1956, he was hired by the old

Five Spot as part of a rhythm section meant to back a multi-instrumen-
talist from Boston named Dick Wetmore. Wetmore appears to have vanished soon afterward, and Taylor brought in Steve Lacy, and they stayed
on for six weeks. In the summer of 1957, he played at an afternoon concert at the Newport Jazz Festival, and the following summer he did the
Great South Bay Festival. He gave a concert at the Circle in the Square in
1959. In the fall of 1960, he took a quartet into the Living Theatre as an
interim replacement for the onstage band in Jack Gelber's "The
Connection." He told Joe Goldberg about it in "Jazz Masters of the
Fifties": "The first night we played, one of the actors said, 'What the hell
is going on up here?' Gelber told me that I was changing the meaning of
his play. I was destroying the meaning in his play by the music I was
playing. Mr. Gelber wished music that was in what he considered, I imagine, the Charlie Parker idiom, the Bud Powell idiom. I, of course, knew
that I was going to do music that was for a theatre piece, which meant
that it would be music that I would create because of the situation presented. For the first time in that play, the actors were not mere props, they
were integrated with what was going on. They called it improvised theatre, but the only improvising that was going on, we were doing it, most
of the time. It was a marvellous experience. It's like life, it was both hell
and beautiful." According to Gelber, it was plain hell for everyone else.
Taylor, going his unbridled improvisational way, doubled the customary
two-hour performance time, and he regularly "destroyed" the piano.
When Gelber attempted to rein him in, Taylor, Gelber has said, "gazed
upon me with uncomprehending beneficence. I was an alien creature
who by chance happened to be blocking his view."

Work was scarce until 1962, when Taylor first went to Europe. He
played in Scandinavia, and his audiences mostly "stood around looking
grumpy." But he went back to Europe regularly in the late sixties, and he
has gone back almost every year since. He tried the academic world without great success in the early seventies, and had rapid residencies at the
University of Wisconsin, Antioch, and Glassboro State College. In the
seventies, he moved forward again. He got a Guggenheim fellowship. He
had two S.R.O. outings at the new Five Spot. He gave a puzzling oil-and-
water concert with Mary Lou Williams at Carnegie Hall. (It was her idea.)
He played with succinctness and great effect at the jazz concert presented by President Jimmy Carter at the White House in 1978. He has given
a joint concert with Max Roach at Columbia, and has played for
Baryshnikov in Los Angeles, Chicago, and Philadelphia.

Music is never far from Taylor's mind. "Sometimes I will work on my
material for two years before I play it," he went on to say. "I get rid of
some pieces right away, because they aren't very good. I put some away
for a year, then go back to them to see how they sound. I am relaxed with
the idea that not every piece I write is perfect. You improve in the smallest steps. At the end of a year, maybe you've developed an inch. I use

what I write as blocks or grids—these are the bases of my improvisations. I don't improvise on the melodies I write. I improvise on their intervals. I'm in a state of trance when I play. I think of groups of sounds. I think of groups of rhythmic ideas. I think of quality of speed and quality of sound. A student asked me once where the pulse is in my music. I asked him how many different rates of breathing there are. I told him that what I'm interested in in my music is the variety of pulses that exist in a given moment. I'm very conscious of body movement when I play. I apply it to the piano in ways never seen before. I sing inside me, and I sing out loud. I write poems and I recite them in the middle of my pieces."

Here is one, from 1983:

> white walls
>   fumes
> ovah polish'd
>   pine
>
> from dream
> pellucid water
>   blued
>   green
> reflect open face
>   moon
>
> separate leaf
> binding oil
>   scent
> rises 'tween
>   motionless
>   creases
>
> wakening
>   the wave wall
>   eye taketh
>   breath come

"They used to snicker at Monk when he got up and danced during his numbers, but what he was doing was simply a natural extension of his music," Taylor said. "My motions are the same. It's rare to find musicians who are loyal and protect you and give you space to be yourself. You learn to value them highly and to give them the same space they give you. Each musician has to play his world in the framework you design for him. Improvisation is the blood that makes the music go. It's also a way to prepare oneself to talk responsibly with others in a musical community. When I first played in public, I couldn't speak for an hour afterward. I was scared to death of audiences. Now I know it is simply people you are playing for. All you can ask is that they listen.

"I am totally antimechanical. I don't answer my phone. I have to be reminded that I have an answering service. But I like to meet other human beings. I'm lucky to be alive. The time has gone very fast."